T0366109

Everything
Including the
Kitchen Sink!
COOKBOOK

Anne Komorowski

Trafford rev. 06/04/2014

 www.trafford.com

North America & international
toll-free: 1 888 232 4444 (USA & Canada)
fax: 812 355 4082

Dedication

I am dedicating this cookbook to my late husband Joseph A. Komorowski, who I had shared 39 years of marriage with, and to my three sons, Scott, Michael, Frank and their wives, Lucinda and Alice. Besides my immediate family, I dedicate this book to my sister, Frances and to my niece, Linda and last to my late long-time friend, Beverly, who passed away this July.

Anne Komorowski

Table of Contents

Chapter 1

APPETIZERS, BEVERAGES
CANDY AND SNACKS

WHERE THERE IS FAITH
THERE IS LOVE.
WHERE THERE IS LOVE,
THERE IS PEACE.
WHERE THERE IS PEACE,
THERE IS GOD,
WHERE THERE IS GOD,
THERE IS <u>NO NEED</u>!

INSTANT COCOA

1 package (16 ozs.) dry instant
  milk
1 cup granulated sugar
¾ cup unsweetened cocoa
¼ teaspoon salt

Sift the above ingredients
3 times; place in covered
container. Store in a cool place.
Yield about 30 servings.

TO USE INSTANT COCOA:

Combine 1/3 cup instant
cocoa with 1 cup hot water
OR combine 1-1/3 cup instant
cocoa with 1 quart hot water.

HOW MUCH TEA?

Allow 1 to 1½ teaspoons of tea
for each cup of hot water.

TO MAKE ICE TEA!
Make double the strength
when brewing tea., then place
over ice cubes, if desired add
sugar and lemon to taste.

CLASSIC EGG NOG

6 large eggs
¼ cup granulated sugar
¼ teaspoon salt
1 quart milk, divided
1 teaspoon vanilla extract

In a large saucepan, beat
together, eggs, sugar, and salt.
stir in 2 cups of milk. Cook over
low heat, stirring constantly;
until mixture thickens. Remove
from heat, stir in remaining 2
cups milk and vanilla. Before
serving, cover and refrigerate
until thoroughly chilled. Yield 12
(1/2 cup) servings.

WHITE LIGHTNING

2 pounds wheat
2 pounds raisins
6 pounds granulated sugar
4 large potatoes
2 gallons water
1 cake of yeast

Place wheat into a large crock;
add raisins, sugar, slices of
potatoes and water. Crush cake
of yeast into mixture; mix well.
Cover and let stand for 3 weeks.
Strain mixture and bottle.

NOTE: You can make the
above recipe for personal
use, however you can not
sell alcohol beverages it is
against the law. It is known as
bootlegging.

APPLE WINE RECIPE NO. I

2½ gallons apple juice
2 pounds granulated sugar
2 pkgs. dry yeast

In a large saucepan, combine together, juice and sugar; cook until sugar is dissolved, stirring constantly. Remove from heat; cool to lukewarm; add yeast; mix well. Pour mixture into a crock; allow to ferment for 2 to 3 weeks, skimming foam every day. When bubbling stops, strain mixture into clean crock; let rest for 2 more weeks. Bottle and cork loosely; check in a week or two, to make sure all bubbling has stopped. When it has, cork tightly; lay bottle down and age for 1 year.

APPLE WINE RECIPE NO. II

16 pounds apple, chopped, cores included
2 gallons boiling water
4 pounds granulated sugar
2 pkgs. dry yeast

Place apples in a crock, pour boiling water over apples. Add sugar; stir to dissolve. Let stand 3 to 4 days, stirring occasionally, then strain. Return juice to crock; add yeast; let ferment for 2 to 3 weeks. Proceed as recipe No. I directs.

GRAPE WINE

Put 20 pounds of fresh-picked, ripe grapes, into a crock; pour 6 quarts of boiling water over grapes. Cool, then squeeze grapes by hand or with a mallet to break skins; mix well. Cover the crock with a cloth; let stand for 3 days. Strain off juice, discard pomades; clean crock. Return juice to crock; add 10 pounds of granulated sugar; let stand for 1 week, covered, in a warm place. Then skim strain and bottle. Cork bottles loosely with cotton; stand upright on a shelf with a temperature of 70 degrees. When fermenting has stopped, pour the clear liquid into clean bottles, discarding the sediment in the bottom of the bottles. Cap or tightly cork the bottles; lay on their sides in a cool place of 40 to 50 degrees.

PURPLE COW DRINK

1 cup milk
2 scoops vanilla ice cream
3 tablespoons grape juice concentrate

Combine all ingredients in a blender; mix until frothy. Yield 2 servings.

STRAWBERRY DAIQUIRI

2 cups milk
2 cups frozen strawberries,
    slightly thawed
1 teaspoon granulated sugar
5 ice cubes

Combine all ingredients in a blender, mix until frothy. Yield 3 servings.

IRISH COFFEE

12 ounces Irish Whiskey
12 cups hot, strong coffee
Whipped cream
Ground Cinnamon
Cinnamon Sticks (optional)

Pour 1 ounce whiskey in cup or mug; pour coffee in; stir. Garnish with dollops of whipped cream; sprinkle with cinnamon. If desired add cinnamon sticks for stirrers.

COCOA MIX

2½ cups instant dry milk
1 cup unsweetened cocoa
1 cup granulated sugar
½ cup nondairy powder
    creamer
¼ teaspoon salt
1 cup miniature marshmallows
    (optional)

In a large mixing bowl, combine together, all the above ingredients; mix well.

Store in an airtight container and in a cool dry place. Use within 6 months. Yield 5 cups

ONE SERVING: Stir 3 tablespoons of mix into 8 ounces of hot water.

BLUEBERRY-ADE

2 cups fresh blueberries
1½ cups granulated sugar (or to
    taste)
Juice of 2 lemons
Juice of 2 oranges
1 cup crushed pineapple

In a blender or food processor, liquefy first 5 ingredients. Taste as you add sugar, you may like less. Serve with ice and a sprig of mint. Yield 3 servings.

SPICED TEA

1 large jar of orange powdered
    drink mix
1½ cups granulated sugar
2 teaspoons cinnamon
½ cup lemon drink mixture
1 cup instant tea
1 teaspoon ground cloves

In a glass jar, combine together, all ingredients; mix well. TO SERVE For 1 cup add boiling water and 2 teaspoons of tea mix.

ORANGE JULIUS

1 cup milk
1 cup water
½ of large can undiluted
    orange juice
½ cup granulated sugar
1 teaspoon vanilla extract
12 to 14 ice cubes

Combine all ingredients in
a blender; process until ice
is finely chopped. Serve
immediately.

BLOODY MARY

12 ozs. OR 1½ cups tomato juice
4 ozs. vodka
4 tablespoons fresh lime juice
Dash celery powder
½ teaspoon Worcestershire
    Sauce
Dash tabasco sauce
½ cup ice crushed

In a blender or food processor,
blend together, all ingredients,
on high, for about 1 minute.
Yield 4 servings.

WHISKEY SOUR

2 tablespoons fresh lemon juice
1 teaspoon granulated sugar
4 ozs. whiskey
1 cup crushed ice

Combine all ingredients; mix to
blend well, for 15 seconds. Yield
2 servings.

HOMEMADE MARSHMALLOWS

½ cup powder sugar
3 tablespoons cornstarch
2 cups granulated sugar
3 envelopes unflavored gelatin
¼ teaspoon salt
1 cup cold water
1 teaspoon clear vanilla extract

Butter a 9x9 inch baking pan.
In a small bowl, combine
together, powder sugar and
cornstarch; mix well. Coat pan
with 1/3 mixture; shake pan
so mixture sticks to bottom
and sides of pan. In medium
saucepan, combine together,
granulated sugar, gelatin
and salt. Add cold water; mix
well; let set for 5 minutes, until
gelatin softens. Cook over
low heat until sugar dissolves,
stirring constantly. Remove
from heat; let cool. Add clear
vanilla. Transfer mixture to
large bowl; beat with electric
mixer on high, until soft peaks
form, about 10 minutes. Pour
mixture into prepared pan;
top with another 1/3 of the
powder sugar mixture. Let
stand overnight, at room
temperature. Next day, cut
into squares; coat each square
with remaining powder sugar
mixture. Store covered at room
temperature. Yield about 50
squares.

CARMEL-NUT COATED MARSHMALLOWS

28 Kraft caramels
2 tablespoons water
16 large marshmallows
1 cup nuts, finely chopped

Melt caramels with water in the top of a double boiler or in a saucepan over low heat. Stir occasionally until smooth. Remove from heat; drop marshmallows, one at a time, into hot caramel sauce; turn with fork until covered. Then immediately roll each in finely chopped nuts. Yield 16 candies.

SOYBEAN COFFEE

Brown soybeans lightly, in oven stir often for they burn easily. It is recommended to heat the oven 350 degrees, then turn it off. When beans are a light brown, remove from oven and grind beans in a food chopper, such as a blender or food processor. Prepare ground soybeans as you would regular coffee, however, you must experiment with the amount for the strength you would like to drink.

OLD FASHION LEMONADE

Juice of 6 lemons (1 cup)
¾ cup granulated sugar
4 cups cold water
Ice cubes

In a large pitcher, combine together, lemon juice and sugar; stir to dissolve sugar. Add cold water; mix well. Add ice cubes. Yield 6 eight ounce servings.

PEPPERMINT PATTIES

1 pound powder sugar
3 tablespoons butter OR
    margarine, softened
2 to 3 teaspoons peppermint
    extract
½ teaspoon vanilla extract
¼ cup evaporated milk
2 cups (12 ozs.) semisweet
    chocolate chips
2 tablespoons shortening

In a large mixing bowl, combine together, first 4 ingredients, then add milk; mix well. Roll into 1-inch balls; place on a waxed paper-lined cookie sheet. Chill for 20 minutes, then flatten with a glass to ¼ inch; chill again, for 30 minutes. Melt chocolate chips and shortening, in a double boiler or in a microwave-safe bowl. Dip patties in chocolate mixture; place on waxed paper to harden. Yield about 5 dozen patties.

BLACK WALNUT FUDGE

2 cups light brown sugar,
packed
1 cup heavy cream
1 tablespoon butter OR
margarine
2 tablespoons light corn syrup
1 cup black walnuts, chopped
1 teaspoon vanilla extract
Pinch of salt

In a 3-quart saucepan,
combine together, brown
sugar, cream, butter and corn
syrup; mix well. Cook over
medium heat without stirring
to 234 degrees on a candy
thermo meter, about 10 to 15
minutes. Remove from heat;
let cool for 15 minutes. Do
not mix. When cooled to 160
degrees, add walnuts, vanilla
and salt. Beat mixture until it is
smooth and creamy. Pour into
a buttered 8-inch square and
creamy. Pour into a buttered
8-inch square.

RECIPES FOR A CROWD

HOT COFFEE (Instant)

Empty 1 jar (2 ounces) instant coffee into a large saucepan. Add 7 quarts boiling water; keep hot. Yield 42 cups.

HOT COFFEE (Regular)

In a large kettle, measure 2¾ cups of regular grind coffee or ½ pound into 7½ quarts of water; put coffee in a double. thickness of cheecloth, tie bag allowing space to coffee to swell. Bring water to a boil; then drop in the bag of coffee, cover. Reduce heat to simmer, for 10 to 12 minutes. Do not boil. Remove from heat and remove coffee bag; serve. Yield 20 cups.

HOT COCOA

In a large kettle, mix together, 1¾ cups cocoa, 1 cup granulated sugar & pinch of salt. Gradually add 2 cups cold water; bring to a boil; stirring constantly. Cook for 3 minutes or until thickened. Add 4½ quarts hot milk; mix well. Remove from heat, just before serving; mix well. Yield 4½ quarts.

HOT TEA FOR A CROWD

In a large kettle, bring 7½ quarts of water to a boil. Meanwhile, place 1¼ cups (3 ozs.) tea, loosely in a homemade bag made out of cheesecloth; tie together. Drop into boiling water, then turn off heat, cover and steep, for 5 minutes; remove bag. If tea is too strong for someone, have hot plain hot nearby to dilute, as desired. Yield 40 cups.

PEANUT BRITTLE

2 cups granulated sugar
1 cup light corn syrup
½ cup water
1 cup butter OR margarine
2 cups unsalted peanuts
1 teaspoon baking soda

Butter 2 cookie sheets. In a saucepan, combine together, sugar, corn syrup and water, over low heat, simmer, stirring constantly until sugar dissolves. Add butter, continue to simmer, stirring constantly, until hard-crack stage, or about 305 degrees on candy thermometer. Remove from heat; stir in peanuts & baking soda. Spread thin on prepared cookie sheets. When brittle has hardened, break into pieces. Yield about 2 pounds.

GRANOLA BARS

3½ cups oatmeal
1 cup raisins
1 cup nuts, chopped
2/3 cup butter OR margarine,
    melted
½ cup brown sugar, packed
1/3 cup honey
1 large egg, beaten
½ teaspoon vanilla extract
½ teaspoon salt

In a large mixing bowl, combine together, all ingredients; mix thoroughly. Press firmly into a well-greased jelly roll pan. bake at 350 degrees for about 20 minutes. Remove from oven; cool slightly, then cut into bars. Store in a tightly-covered container, in refrigerator or a cool, dry place. Yield 15 (1/2" x1/2") bars.

CORN CHIPS

2 cups cornmeal
1 cup whole wheat flour
Water
Salt

In a mixing bowl, thoroughly combine together, cornmeal and flour. Add water gradually, stirring until mixture is the right consistency to roll. On a lightly floured surface, roll out dough cut into 1½ squares. In a deep fryer, heat about a quart of vegetable oil to 350 degrees.

Drop squares, a few at a time into hot oil and fry until golden brown. Remove from oil; drain on paper towels. If desired sprinkle with a little salt.

ORANGE SLUSH

2 cups unsweetened orange
    juice
½ cup instant nonfat dry milk
8 ice cubes
¼ teaspoon vanilla extract

Combine together, all ingredients; place in blender, process until mixture is mixed and frothy; serve immediately.

OLD-TIME POPCORN BALLS

Butter OR margarine
2 cups granulated sugar
1 ½ cups water
½ teaspoon salt
½ cup light corn syrup
1 teaspoon white vinegar
1 teaspoon vanilla extract
5 quarts popped corn

Butter sides of saucepan, then combine sugar, water, salt, syrup and vinegar. Over medium heat, cook to hard ball stage (250 degrees on candy thermometer). Add vanilla; mix well. Slowly pour over popped corn, stirring just to mix well. Butter hands lightly; shape into balls. Yield 15 to 20 popcorn balls.

BUTTERSCOTCH TOFFEE FUDGE

1 pound light brown sugar
1½ cups Marshmallow Crème
¾ cup light cream
¼ cup butter OR margarine
1 cup Butterscotch-Flavored
   Chips
5 (1.25 ozs.) Chocolate-covered
   Toffee
Candy Bars, coarsely chopped

Grease 9-inch square pan. In
a large saucepan, combine
together, sugar, Marshmallow
Creme, cream and butter; mix
well. Over medium heat, bring
the mixture to a full boil. Cook
for 5 minutes, stirring constantly.
Remove from heat, add chips,
stir until melted, then add
toffee bars. Toffee Bars pieces
may not melt completely. Pour,
as it is, into prepared pan; chill
until firm. With a sharp knife,
cut into ¼ inch squares. Store in
airtight container; refrigerate.

BLACK TOP POTATO FUDGE

¼ cup hot, mashed potatoes
1 teaspoon butter OR
   margarine
2½ cups powder sugar
1 teaspoon vanilla extract
Pinch of salt
1-1/3 cups shredded coconut
2 squares unsweetened
   chocolate, melted

In a medium size mixing bowl,
combine together, potatoes
and butter; add sugar,
gradually, beating until well-
blended. Add vanilla, salt and
coconut; mix well. Put mixture
in a greased 8x4 inch loaf pan;
spread melted chocolate
evenly, over top. Chill until firm,
then cut in squares.

CHOCOLATE EGGNOG

1 cup prepared eggnog
1/3 cup chocolate syrup
1 cup whipping cream
2 tablespoons granulated sugar
2 tablespoons unsweetened
cocoa

In a bowl, combine together,
eggnog and chocolate syrup;
set aside. In another bowl whip
cream with sugar and cocoa.
Fold into eggnog mixture;
blend well.

NOTE: This recipe may be
doubled.

TAFFY (old recipe)

3 cups granulated sugar
1 cup water, mixed with
½ teaspoon white vinegar
1 tablespoon butter OR
    margarine
1 teaspoon vanilla extract
1 teaspoon orange juice

In a medium saucepan, combine together sugar, water and vinegar; mix well. Over medium-high heat, bring to a boil. Then add butter, vanilla and orange juice; mix well. Boil until a hard ball forms, test by putting a drop in a glass of cold water. When mixture reaches hard ball stage, then pour it in a baking pan; let cool. When cool, butter your hands, stretch taffy and cut in pieces as you desire. Wrap each piece in paper; store in tightly closed container.

HARD TACK (old recipe)

2½ cups granulated sugar
1 cup light corn syrup
1 cup water
1 teaspoon vanilla extract
Food coloring (optional)

In a saucepan, combine together, all ingredients; mix well. Over medium heat, cook mixture until it reaches 300 degrees on a candy thermometer. Pour mixture into a buttered 8" square pan; let cool and set, then break into pieces.

MILK SHAKES & VARIETIES

FOR 1 SERVING: 1 cup cold milk, shake or beat together, scoop ice cream and other flavoring along with choice of fruit (see below).

BANANA—Use ½ banana, mashed.
STRAWBERRY—Use ¼ cup sweetened berries.
MAPLE—Use 2 tablespoons maple syrup.
CHOCOLATE—Use 1½ to tablespoons of chocolate syrup.
CHOCOLATE MALTED MILK—
Beat 1 tablespoon of malted milk powder into chocolate milk shake.

CHOCOLATE NUT CLUSTERS

1 cup chocolate chips
1 teaspoon butter OR
    margarine
Cashews, peanuts, pecans or
    walnut halves
Miniature marshmallows
    (optional)

In the top of a double boiler, over hot water, not boiling. Add ½ cup of nuts at a time, stirring nuts in chocolate; add a few marsh mallows, if desired. Remove nuts with a fork; place in piles on a cookie sheet, covered waxed paper or foil. Refrigerate until set. Yield about 2 dozen clusters.

CARAMELS

1 cup butter OR margarine
2¼ cups brown sugar, packed
Dash of salt
1 cup light corn syrup
1 can (15 ozs.) sweetened
  condensed milk
1 teaspoon vanilla extract

In a large saucepan, melt butter, over low heat. Add sugar & salt; mix thoroughly. Add corn syrup; mix well. Add condensed milk, stirring constantly. Cook over medium heat to firm ball stage (245 degrees on candy thermometer), for 12 to 15 minutes. Remove from heat, add vanilla. Pour into buttered 9x9x2-inch pan; cool; cut into squares. Yield 2½ Pounds.

CHOCOLATE CARAMELS—
Add 2 squares (1 oz. each) of unsweetened chocolate, with sweetened condensed milk.

PEANUT BUTTER FUDGE
(Microwave Method)

¾ cup butter OR margarine
3 cups granulated sugar
1 can (5 ozs.) evaporated milk
1 pkg. (12 ozs.) peanut butter
  chips
¼ cup peanut butter
1 jar (7 ozs.) Marshmallow Crème
1 cup peanuts, chopped
1 teaspoon vanilla extract

Microwave butter on high, for 2 minutes or until melted.

Add sugar and evaporated or until melted. Add sugar and evaporated minutes or until mixture begins to boil. Mix after 3 minutes, scraping the bowl. Add peanut butter chips, peanut butter and marshmallow crème; mix well. Microwave mixture until melted, for about 3 minutes. Add peanuts and vanilla; mix well. Pour into a greased square 9-inch pan. Let cool; cut into squares.

EASY COFFEE FUDGE

1 small pkg. vanilla pudding
  (not instant)
1 tablespoon instant coffee
¼ cup milk
2 tablespoons butter OR
  margarine
2 cups powder sugar
1 teaspoon vanilla extract
  (optional)
¼ cup nuts, chopped (optional)

Line an 8x4-inch loaf pan with wax paper. In a medium saucepan, combine together, pudding mix, instant coffee and milk; mix pudding mix, instant coffee and milk; mix medium heat, stirring constantly. Cook for 1 minute, then remove from heat. Add sugar and vanilla, beat until smooth; fold in nuts. Pour quickly into pan; spread with additional nuts, if desired. Chill until firm, about 30 minutes. Cut into pieces, cover; store in refrigerator. Yield about 1 pound.

PUMPKIN FUDGE

2 cups granulated sugar
¼ cup cooked pumpkin
¼ teaspoon cornstarch
1/3 teaspoon pumpkin pie spice
½ cup milk, evaporated milk
    OR cream
½ teaspoon vanilla extract

In a medium saucepan, combine together, the first 3 ingredients. Place over low heat; cook, stirring until mixture, when a small amount of mixture is dropped into a glass of cold water to see if it forms a ball. When it does, remove from heat; cool slightly. Add vanilla; beat mixture until smooth. Place in desired container and when cooled cut in to desired pieces.

EASTER EGGS (Chocolate Covered Candies)

3 cups granulated sugar
½ cup light corn syrup
¾ cup water
1 teaspoon vanilla extract
½ teaspoon salt
¼ cup egg whites
¾ cup nuts and/or candied fruit
Chocolate to cover eggs

In a medium saucepan, combine together, sugar, syrup and water; mix well. Over low heat, cook until sugar is dissolved, stirring constantly. When sugar is dissolved, increase heat; bring mixture to a boil; cover; cook for 3

minutes. Uncover; cook to hard ball stage; remove from heat. Add vanilla and salt; mix well; set aside In a small mixing bowl, beat egg whites until stiff, but not dry. Pour sugar mixture slowly into egg whites. Beat mixture until it begins to hold a shape; drop in fruit and/or nuts. With hand, form into eggs of desired size. cool; cover with melted chocolate.

TO MELT CHOCOLATE—cook over low heat; add about 1 tablespoon butter or margarine. Dip formed egg into melted chocolate; allow excess to drip off; set on waxed paper lined pan; refrigerate until eggs hardened; about 1 hour.

GRAPENUTS (cereal)

1 to 1½ cups brown sugar,
    packed
2 cups buttermilk
2 teaspoons baking soda
½ teaspoon salt
3½ cups graham flour

In a medium bowl, combine together, all ingredients; mix well. Bake at 300 degrees ingredients; mix well. Bake at 300 degrees for about 25 to 30 minutes; remove from oven. Crumble and return to oven again, to brown, for about 20 more minutes. Remove from oven; let cool. Then put through a food chopper. Store in an air-tight container

PUPPY CHOW (Snack)

1 pkg. (12 ozs.) semi-sweet
   chocolate chips
2 sticks butter OR margarine
1 cup peanut butter
1 box (12.3 ozs.) Crispix cereal
2 cups powder sugar (optional)

In a medium saucepan, combine together chocolate chips, butter and peanut butter. Over low heat, cook, stirring until smooth. Meanwhile place cereal in a large mixing bowl. Pour melted mixture evenly, over cereal; toss gently to coat well. When coating is set, if desired, toss cereal with powder sugar, shaking off excess. Yield 18 cups.

PERSIMMON FUDGE

1 cup persimmon pulp
6 cups granulated sugar
2½ cups milk
½ cup light corn syrup
¼ cup butter OR margarine
1 cup walnuts, chopped
   (optional)

Peel persimmon, remove seeds, cut in pieces. Place food processor or blender to puree'. In a saucepan, combine together, pulp, sugar milk and syrup; mix well. Over low heat, cook slowly for 1½ to 2 hours, until mixture reaches soft ball stage or 230 degrees in a candy thermometer. Remove from heat; let cool to lukewarm; stir often. Add butter; mix thoroughly. When mixture begins to thicken, fold in 1 cup walnuts, chopped. Spread in buttered baking pan. Cut in squares.

CRANBERRY JUICE

3 cups fresh cranberries,
   washed & picked over
2 cups water
½ cup honey (more or less to
   taste)
½ cup orange juice

In a medium-size saucepan, cook cranberries in water until skins pop open, about 5 minutes, over medium-high heat. Remove from heat; strain. Bring juice to a boil again; add honey; cook for 1 minute. Remove from heat; cool; add orange juice; serve well-chilled. Yield 2½ cups.

CHOCOLATE PRETZELS

1 pkg. (12 ozs.) semisweet
   chocolate chips
36 unbroken pretzels

In a double boiler, melt chocolate, over hot water; mix until smooth. Dip pretzels into chocolate, coating both sides (use tongs or a fork). Remove from chocolate; place on wax paper-lined tray. Refrigerate for 1 hour or until set. Yield about 3 dozen pretzels.

CHOCOLATE SYRUP

5 squares (5 ozs.) baking
    chocolate
2 cups boiling water
1¾ cups granulated sugar
¼ cup light corn syrup
½ teaspoon salt

In a double boiler, with hot
water, melt chocolate; then
add boiling water, remove
pan from double boiler, place
on direct low heat and cook,
stirring until smooth and thick,
for about 2 minutes. Add sugar,
corn syrup and salt, then cook
briskly for 3 to 4 minutes, stirring
occasionally; remove from
heat; set aside to cool. Store in
refrigerator.

TO USE: Allow 1 tablespoon, (or
to taste) chocolate syrup to 1
cup milk. If used as a sauce on
ice cream stir ¼ cup butter OR
margarine, while syrup is hot.

CHEESE CRACKERS

1 jar (5 ozs.) sharp American
    Cheese Spread
¼ cup margarine, softened
2/3 cup flour

In a small mixing bowl, combine
all the ingredients together;
mix well. Knead dough, on a
lightly floured surface for about
30 seconds. Then surface for
about 30 seconds. Then with
foil or plastic wrap; refrigerate
overnight. Next day, preheat

oven to 375 degrees F. Cut
dough into ¼ inch slices. Place
on ungreased cookie sheet.
Bake 10 to 12 minutes, or until
tested done. Yield about 5
dozen.

POTATO CHIPS

3 large potatoes
Vegetable oil for frying
Salt to taste

Peel potatoes; slice thin as
possible. In a large skillet, place
enough oil to fill the skillet
half full. Over medium heat,
warm oil until hot enough to fry
potatoes until lightly browned,
about 2 minutes. With a slotted
spoon transfer fried potato
chips to a paper towel-lined
bowl. If desired, sprinkle with
salt. Yield about 2 servings.

CHOCOLATE CREAM CANDY

1 pkg. (8 squares) semi-sweet
    chocolate
1 cup powder sugar, sifted
1 large egg, well beaten
1 tablespoon milk
*Assorted decorations

Melt chocolate over hot water
in a double boiler, or on low
heat, stirring constantly. Remove
from heat; add sugar, egg
and milk, beat until smooth.
Refrigerate until firm enough
to handle, about 30 minutes.
Shape into ½ inch balls, ovals or
logs. Decorate as desired.

*ASSORTED DECORATIONS

Use ½ cup flaked coconut, ¼ cup chocolate or colored sprinkles, 1/3 cup almonds, finely chopped or pecan halves to be pressed onto the tops. Yield about 5 dozen candies.

HOMEMADE TOFFEE CANDY

1½ cups pecans, finely
  chopped
2 cups granulated sugar
1 cup butter, softened
½ cup light cream
¼ cup light corn syrup
½ teaspoon salt
2 teaspoons vanilla extract
1 pkg. (6 ozs.) semisweet
  chocolate chips, melted

Butter a 13x9-inch baking pan. Sprinkle ½ cup pecans, chopped, over the bottom of pan; set aside. In a large saucepan, combine together, sugar, butter, cream, syrup and salt; mix well. Over medium heat, bring to a gentle boil, reduce heat to simmer. Cook, stirring frequently, until mixture reaches the hard-crack stage (300 degrees on candy thermometer). Remove from heat; mix in vanilla. Pour into prepared pan; cool until firm. Remove from pan; spread melted chocolate over toffee; sprinkle with remain pecans over top. Press into chocolate; cool, then break into bite-size pieces. Yield about 30 to 40 pieces.

TACO CHIPS

1 cup whole kernel OR
  creamed corn
1 cup sharp cheddar cheese,
  grated
½ cup red OR green peppers,
  diced
1 tablespoon onions, chopped
Pinch of cayenne pepper
¼ teaspoon chili powder

In a blender or food processor, place all ingredients; blend at high speed. Spread thinly on a cookie sheet. Dry at 130 degrees, for about 10 hours or until dry on one side. Lift entire corn mixture off the cookie sheet, then turn over. Dry for 2 more hours or until crisp; then break in pieces.

JEZEBEL SAUCE

1 jar (18 ozs.) pineapple
  preserves
1 jar (18 ozs.) apple jelly
1 jar (6 ozs.) prepared
  horseradish
6 tablespoons prepared horse
  radish mustard

In a food processor or blender, combine together, all ingredients; mix until well-blended. Cover; store in refrigerator. Serve with meat, cream cheese and crackers. Yield about 4 cups.

TOMATO JUICE

10 to 12 ripe tomatoes,
    chopped
1 slice onion
1 celery stalk, chopped
¼ bay leaf, crumbled
3 sprigs parsley
Salt
¼ teaspoon brown sugar

In a large saucepan, combine together, tomatoes, onions, celery, parsley and bay leaf. Cook over medium-high heat; covered, until tomatoes are tender, stir ring occasionally. Remove from heat; cool slightly; put through sieve; add salt to taste and brown sugar; mix well. Refrigerate before serving. Yield 4 to 6 servings.

QUICK-MADE ROOT BEER

2 cups granulated sugar
1 gallon lukewarm water
4 teaspoons root beer extract
1 teaspoon dry yeast

Combine together; mix to dissolve sugar. Put in jars with lids; set in the sun for 4 hours. Chill before serving; ready to serve next day. No need to bottle.

ENTERTAINING APPETIZERS

ROAD KILL DIP

1 can (4.5 ozs.) olives, chopped
1 pkg. (8 ozs.) cream cheese,
  softened
1 jar (2.25 ozs.) dried beef,
  chopped
Green Onions to taste

Drain liquid from olives, chop,
then combine with other
ingredients; mix thoroughly.
Refrigerate 1 hour before
serving. Spread on crackers.
Yield about 4 servings.

HOT ARTICHOKE DIP

1 can (15 ozs.) artichoke hearts,
  drained & chopped
1 cup salad dressing, i.e.
  Miracle Whip
1 cup Parmesan Cheese,
  grated
1 clove garlic, minced
Green onions, sliced &
  tomatoes, chopped

Preheat oven to 350 degrees.
Combine together all
ingredients; mix well. Spoon
into 9-inch pie plate. Bake for
20 to 25 minutes or until lightly
browned. Remove from oven;
if desired, sprinkle with green
onions and tomatoes. Serve
with tortilla chips or crackers.
Yield 2 cups dip.

SPINACH DIP

1 pkg. (10 ozs.) frozen spinach,
  unthawed, chopped &
  drained
1½ cups mayonnaise
1 cup sour cream
1 pkg. Knorr vegetable soup
  mix
1 can (8 ozs) water chestnuts,
  finely chopped
¼ medium onion, finely
  chopped

After draining spinach,
squeeze dry (must be dry). Add
remaining ingredients; mix well;
refrigerate before serving.

CHOCOLATE POPCORN

6 cups plain popped corn
1 pkg. (12 ozs.) chocolate chips

Microwave chocolate in a
quart container, on high power
for 3 minutes, stirring after each
minute, until smooth. Pour
over popcorn, stirring gently.
Drop small clusters onto lightly
buttered cookie sheet. Let cool
before serving.

SWEET POTATO CHIPS

3 large sweet potatoes
Vegetable oil for frying
Salt

Peel sweet potatoes; slice thin
as possible in a large skillet,
place enough oil to fill the skillet
half full. Over medium heat,
warm oil until hot enough to fry
sweet potatoes golden orange.
With a slotted spoon transfer
fried sweet potato chips to
a paper towel-lined bowl.
Sprinkle with salt.

HORSERADISH DIP

1 pkg. (8ozs.) cream cheese
2 tablespoons milk
2 tablespoons horseradish,
    cream style
¼ teaspoon Worcestershire
    Sauce
Pinch of salt

In a small mixing bowl,
combine together, cream
cheese and milk, blending
until smooth. Add remaining
ingredients; mix well. Serve
with assorted vegetables or
crackers.

PEANUT BUTTER FUDGE

2 cups peanut butter
1½ sticks butter
1 teaspoon vanilla extract
4 cups powder sugar

In large mixing bowl, cream
together peanut butter and
butter until smooth and
creamy. Add vanilla and
gradually add powder sugar;
mixing well after each addition.
Pour into square baking dish; let
stand until set; cut into squares.
Refrigerate leftovers.

CHOCOLATE COVERED CHERRIES

60 Maraschino cherries with stems
2 cups powder sugar
3 tablespoons light corn syrup
¼ teaspoon salt
2 cups (12 ozs.) semisweet chocolate chips
2 tablespoons shortening

Pat cherries dry with paper towels; set aside. In a small mixing bowl, combine together, sugar, butter, corn syrup and salt; mix well until smooth. Cover; refrigerate for 1 hour. Roll into ½ inch balls, then flatten each ball into 2-inch circle. Wrap each circle around a cherry, lightly roll in hands to seal. Place cherries with stems up, on waxed paper-lined baking sheets, over loosely; refrigerate for 1 hour. Meanwhile, melt chocolate chips, along with shortening in a saucepan, over low heat or in the microwave, mix until smooth and chocolate is melted. Hold cherry, by stem; dip each cherry into chocolate; set on waxed paper. Refrigerate until chocolate hardens; store in a covered container Refrigerate for 1 week before serving. Yield 5 dozen cherries.

CHEESE STICKS SNACKS

1 stick pie crust mix
½ cup Cheddar Cheese, shredded
Pinch of dry mustard
1 teaspoon paprika

Prepare pie crust mix according to package directions; include cheese, mustard & paprika; mix together thoroughly until mixture forms a ball. Roll dough on a lightly floured surface to a 12x8 inch rectangle. With a pastry wheel or knife, cut dough into ½ inch wide and 4 inches long. Place on an ungreased cookie sheet. Bake at 400 degrees for 12 minutes or until golden brown. Yield about 4 dozen sticks.

ROASTED PECANS

1 cup pecan halves
4 tablespoons butter
Salt, if desired

Preheat oven to 300 degrees. Melt butter in saucepan; pour melted butter on a cookie sheet. Add pecan halves; stir pecan halves in butter, coating them on both sides. Bake on one side, for about 10 minutes, lightly salt to taste; turn the halves over, if desired, add more salt. Bake 10 minutes more.

CHOCOLATE-COVERED PRUNES

48 dried prunes, pitted (about
  1 lb.)
48 almonds, whole OR walnut
  halves
2 cups semisweet chocolate
  chips
2 tablespoon creamy peanut
  butter

Stuff each prune with an
almond or walnut half. Melt
chocolate chips in a double
boiler or microwave safe
bowl. Add peanut butter; mix
well. Dip prunes in melted
chocolate; place on waxed
paper to harden. Store in
refrigerator. Yield 4 dozen
prunes.

HONEY-GLAZED PECANS

1 cup granulated sugar
2 tablespoons honey
½ cup milk
¾ teaspoon vanilla extract
Salt to taste (optional)
2 cups *pecan halves

*You can use pecan pieces, if
desired With pieces, you can
make clusters. In a medium
bowl, combine together, all
ingredients, except pecans.
Cook in medium saucepan,
to 240 degrees on a candy
thermometer. Add pecans;
stir to coat nuts. Cook over
medium heat, for 1 minute.
Pour nuts on to a waxed

paper-lined cookie sheet.
Separate pecans with a fork
into single nuts or into desired
clusters. Cool before serving.

COOKIE SNACKS

1 pkg. (10½ ozs.) corn chips
1 cup light corn syrup
1 cup granulated sugar
1 cup creamy peanut butter

Spread corn chips in a greased
15x10x1 inches baking pan. In a
saucepan, over medium heat,
bring corn syrup and sugar to
a boil. Remove from heat; stir
in peanut butter until smooth.
Pour over corn chips; cool.
Break into pieces. Yield about 3
dozen pieces.

HONEY FRUIT DIP

1 carton (6 ozs.) lemon-custard
  yogurt
1 pkg. (3 ozs.) cream cheese,
  softened
1 tablespoon honey
2 medium apples, peeled,
  cored & sliced
2 medium pears, peeled, cored
  & sliced

In a food processor, or blender,
combine together, yogurt,
cream cheese and honey;
cover; process until smooth.
Serve with apples and pears.
Store in refrigerator. Yield about
1 cup dip.

CRACKER JACK POPCORN

½ pound butter OR margarine
2 cups granulated sugar
¾ cup unsulphured molasses
¼ cup dark corn syrup
½ teaspoon salt
1 cup peanuts
6 quarts corn, popped

In a medium saucepan, combine together, the first 5 ingredients; cook over low heat until dissolved. Bring to a rolling boil; remove from heat; pour over popcorn; mix thoroughly, but gently; add peanuts. Put in desired container.

APRICOT CANDY BALLS

1 package (8 ozs.) dried
   apricots, finely cut
2½ cups coconut, flaked
¾ cup sweetened condensed
   milk
2/3 cup nuts, finely chopped

In a large mixing bowl, combine together, apricots, coconut and milk; mix well. Shape into 1-inch balls, roll each ball in nuts. Place on wax paper; let stand until firm, about 2 hours. Yield about 4 dozen candies.

DEVILED EGGS

6 hard-cooked eggs
¼ cup mayonnaise OR salad
   dressing
1 teaspoon vinegar
1 teaspoon prepared mustard
Salt and pepper to taste

Cut, peeled eggs lengthwise into halves, remove yolks, place into a mixing bowl, along with remaining ingredients. Mash with fork; mix well. Fill egg whites with yolk mixture. Arrange eggs on a serving plate. Cover; refrigerate no longer than 24 hours. Yield 6 servings.

*DIVINITY

2½ cups granulated sugar
½ cup light corn syrup
½ cup water
2 large egg whites
1 teaspoon vanilla extract
½ cup nuts, chopped (optional)

In a medium-size saucepan, combine together; sugar, corn syrup and water. Over low heat, cook, stirring constantly, until sugar is dissolved. Cook until on a candy thermometer, temperature reaches 260 degrees, or a small amount of mixture dropped into cold water forms a hard ball. Remove from heat; set aside. Beat egg whites until stiff peaks form, continue beating while pouring hot syrup in a thin stream into egg whites. Add vanilla, beating until mixture holds its shape. Fold in nuts; then drop from a buttered spoon onto wax paper. Yield about 4 dozen candies.

*It is suggested not to make Divinity on humid days.

FOUR CHEESE PATE'

3 pkgs. (8 ozs. each) cream
    cheese, softened & divided
2 tablespoons milk
2 tablespoons sour cream
¾ cup pecans, chopped
4 ounces Brie OR Camembert
    (rind removed & softened)
1 cup (4 ozs.) blue cheese,
    crumbled
½ cup pecan halves
Red and green apple slices OR
    crackers

In a large mixing bowl,
combine together, 1 package
of cream cheese with milk
and sour cream; beat until
smooth. Spread into a 9-inch
pie plate, lined with plastic
wrap, Sprinkle with chopped
pecans. In a mixing bowl, beat
Brie, Swiss, Blue cheese and
remaining cream cheese, until
thoroughly combined. Gently
spread evenly over chopped
pecans, smoothing the top
to form a flat surface; cover.
Refrigerate overnight or up to 3
to 4 days. Before serving, invert
onto a serving tray; remove
plastic wrap. Arrange pecan
halves on top. Serve with apple
slices or crackers. Yield 10 to 20
servings.

PEANUT BUTTER DIP

2 cups brown sugar, packed
1 cups boiling water
2 ozs. light corn syrup
1 teaspoon maple flavoring
2½ cups peanut butter

In a saucepan, combine
together, brown sugar, boiling
water, corn syrup and maple
flavoring; bring to a boil.
Remove from heat. Set aside
and let cool. Meanwhile,
In a large mixing bowl,
combine peanut butter and
marshmallow creme; mix well.
Fold sugar mixture into peanut
butter mixture; mix thoroughly.

CHICKEN SPREAD

1 pkg. (8 ozs.) cream cheese,
    softened
½ cup mayonnaise
2 teaspoons Honey Dijon
    Mustard
1 clove garlic, minced
1 cup chicken breast, cooked
    & finely chopped
¼ cup almonds, chopped
2 green onions, sliced

In a mixing bowl, combine
together, the first 3 ingredients
until well-blended. Add
remaining ingredients; mix
thoroughly; cover. Refrigerate
for 1 to 2 hours, to blend flavors.
Serve with sliced French Bread
or as you desire. Yield about 2
cups.

FLAVORED POPCORN

PARMESAN—Melt 1/3 cup butter OR margarine in a saucepan; add ¼ Parmesan Cheese and ½ teaspoon salt. Pour over 1½ to 2 quarts of freshly popped corn. Toss to mix.

CHEDDAR—Melt ¼ cup butter OR margarine in a saucepan over low heat. Add ½ cup Cheddar Cheese and ½ teaspoon salt. Pour over 1½ quarts of hot freshly popped corn. Toss to mix.

GARLIC—Melt ¼ cup butter OR margarine in a saucepan, over low heat. Add ½ teaspoon garlic salt; mix well. Pour over 1½ quarts of hot, freshly popped corn Toss to mix.

CHILI—Melt ¼ cup butter OR margarine in a saucepan, over low heat. Add ½ teaspoon chili powder and ½ teaspoon salt. Pour over 1½ quarts of hot, freshly popped corn. Toss to mix.

SAUERKRAUT BALLS

½ pound ham cooked
½ pound raw pork
½ pound canned corned beef
1 large onion
1 can (16 ozs.) sauerkraut, well
    drained
2 cups all-purpose flour
2 cups milk
1 teaspoon dry mustard
1 teaspoon parsley, chopped
1 large egg
Bread Crumbs

Put meats and onion through meat grinder or food processor. In a large skillet, cook until mixture is browned. Grind sauerkraut, then set aside. Add flour and milk gradually into meat mixture; mix well. Then add mustard and parsley; mix thoroughly. Continue to cook, stirring until fluffy. Remove from heat; set aside to cool. Then add sauerkraut; mix thoroughly. Roll into balls, about the size of a walnut, then roll in flour. Dip in egg beaten with a little water. Roll in bread crumbs; deep-fry or fry in hot shortening until golden brown. Yield about 4 dozen balls.

PARTY CHEESE BALL

1½ cups walnuts, chopped
3 pkgs. Blue OR Roquefort
    Cheese
1 pkg. (8 ozs.) cream cheese
¼ teaspoon garlic salt
1 tablespoon pimiento, chopped
1 tablespoon green pepper,
    chopped

Spread chopped nuts in a shallow pan; toast at 350 degrees, for 8 to 10 minutes, stirring occasionally, until golden. Blend together cheeses, in a medium mixing bowl; add remaining ingredients; mix bowl; add remaining ingredients; mix until firm. Shape into a ball; roll in nuts; chill, again, covered, until serving time. If desired, serve with small round of rye bread or crackers.

MANHATTAN CLAM DIP

1 container (8 ozs.) sour cream
¼ cup chili sauce OR ketchup
1 can (6½ ozs.) clams, drained
   & minced
¼ cup salad dressing
1 tablespoon green onions,
   finely chopped
1 teaspoon lemon juice
Potato chips

In a small bowl, combine
together, all ingredients,
EXCEPT potato chips; blend
well. Chill before serving; serve
with potato chips. Yield 1-2/3
cups.

NACHOES FOR ONE

2 cups Nacho-Cheese-flavored
   Tortilla Chips
2 to 3 tablespoons canned
   refried beans
3 tablespoons Cheddar
   Cheese, shredded
1 TABLESPOON EACH
ripe olives, sliced
green chilies, chopped
green onions, chopped
TOPPINGS (optional)
Sour cream, fresh tomatoes,
   chopped or guacamole'.

Spread tortilla chips on a 10-
inch microwave safe plate;
top center with refried beans.
Sprinkle cheese over chips &
beans, scatter olives, chilies
and onions on top. Microwave

uncovered, on high 1 to 1½
minutes, rotating plate ¼ turn
once, until cheese melts. Serve
with toppings, as you like. Yield
1 serving.

CAJUN PARTY MIX

½ cup butter OR margarine (1
   stick)
1 tablespoon parsley flakes
1 teaspoon celery salt
1 teaspoon garlic powder
½ teaspoon cayenne pepper
4 to 8 drops hot pepper sauce
   (optional)
2-2/3 cups Wheat Chex cereal
2-2/3 cups Corn Chex cereal
2-2/3 cups Rice Chex cereal
1 can (2.8 ozs.) French Fried
   Onions

Preheat oven to 350 degrees. In
a 15x10 inches baking dish, melt
butter. Stir in parsley, celery salt,
garlic powder, cayenne and
hot pepper sauce. Gradually
add cereal, stirring until all
pieces are evenly coated.
Bake for 20 to 25 minutes,
stirring every 10 minutes. Add
onions, mixing well. Spread on
absorbent paper to cool. Store
in airtight containers. Yield 9
cups of mix.

HORSERADISH DIP

1 pkg. (8 ozs.) cream cheese, softened
3 tablespoons prepared horseradish
1 tablespoon milk
½ cup sour cream
1 tablespoon Worcestershire Sauce

In a mixing bowl, combine together, all ingredients; mix well. Serve with desired vegetables or chips.

STUFFED MUSHROOMS

Prepare 1 box Chicken-Flavored Stuffing. Mix according to package directions; set aside. Meanwhile clean 1 pound of mushrooms, then remove stems. Cut stems in pieces; add to stuffing mix. Arrange mush room caps, open side up, on a baking pan. Fill caps with stuffing; broil at 400 degrees, for a few minutes or until lightly browned.

STUFFED MUSHROOMS

1 pound mushrooms, washed & stemmed
½ cup butter OR margarine, melted
¾ cup Italian-style bread crumbs
¼ cup Parmesan Cheese, grated
4 ounces mozzarella cheese, grated

In a mixing bowl, combine together, butter, bread crumbs, Parmesan cheese mix well with a fork. Stuff each mushroom cap with bread crumb mixture until caps are filled. Top each cap with mozzarella cheese. Arrange caps on a lightly greased baking pan; bake at 375 degrees, until cheese has melted and is golden. Serve hot.

MUSHROOM PUFFS

4 ounces cream cheese, cubed
1 can (4 ozs.) mushroom stems & pieces, drained
1 tablespoon onions, chopped
Pinch of hot pepper sauce (optional)
1 tube (8 ozs.) Crescent Roll Dough

In a blender or food processor, combine together, cream cheese, mushrooms, onions and hot pepper sauce. Cover and process until ingredients are blended. Unroll Crescent dough; separate into 4 rectangles. Press perforations to seal. Spread mushroom mixture, evenly over Spread mushroom mixture, evenly over starting with the long side. Cut each roll into 5 slices; place on an ungreased baking pan. Bake at 425 degrees, for 8 to 10 minutes or until puffed and golden brown. Yield 20 appetizers.

GUACAMOLE'

2 ripe medium-size avocados,
    peeled & pitted
2 tablespoons wine vinegar
1 tablespoon vegetable oil
1 teaspoon garlic, minced
¼ cup onions, finely diced
1 medium-size tomato,
    chopped
Salt to taste

In a large mixing bowl, mash
avocado completely (use
potato masher). Combine with
vinegar, oil, garlic and salt;
mix well. Fold in remaining
ingredients. To prevent from
darkening, cover with plastic
wrap; chill for 3 hours. Serve
with taco chips or tortillas.

MICROWAVE FUDGE

3½ cups powder sugar
½ cup unsweetened cocoa
¼ cup milk
½ cup butter OR margarine
1 tablespoon vanilla extract
½ cup pecans, chopped
    (optional)

Blend together sugar and
cocoa in a 3-quart microwave
bowl. Add milk and butter. DO
NOT STIR. Microwave at 100
percent power, for 2 minutes,
then mix well. Add vanilla and
nuts; mix until well-blended.
Pour into a buttered 8x8-inch
square baking pan. Refrigerate
until set; then cut in squares.

CARAMEL APPLES

1 pound (about 56) vanilla
    caramels
2 tablespoons water
6 medium-size apples
Walnuts, chopped

In a double boiler, combine
together, caramels and water;
stir until melted and smooth.
Stick a wooden skewer into the
blossom-end of each apple.
Dip apple in melted caramel,
turn until completely coated.
(If caramel be comes too
stiff, add a few more drops
of water). After coating each
apple, immediately roll bottom
half of each apple in chopped
nuts. Place apple on a cookie
sheet, covered with wax paper.
Refrigerate until coating is firm.

HOW TO MAKE COCONUT MILK

1 cup fresh coconut, coarsely
    chopped
1 cup hot water

Place coconut and water in
a blender or food processor.
Puree' until a thick fibrous
liquid forms. Line a sieve
with a double thickness of
cheesecloth. Let drain several
hours; discard pulp. Use
accordingly; then refrigerate.

LEMONADE

1 cup granulated sugar
1 cup water

Rind of 2 lemons, cut into pieces. In a saucepan, combine together, all ingredients. Over low heat, stirring until sugar is dissolved. Bring to a boil; cook for 1 minute. Strain; discard rind; add 1 cup fresh or frozen lemon juice (5 to 6 lemons) & 4 cups ice water. Pour over ice in pitcher. Yield 6 to 8 servings.

SALT WATER TAFFY

2 cups granulated sugar
1 cup light corn syrup
½ teaspoon salt
1 cup water
2 tablespoons butter OR
   margarine
¼ teaspoon oil of peppermint
7 drops of green food coloring

In a large saucepan, combine together, sugar, syrup, salt and water. Over low heat, cook slowly, stirring constantly, until sugar dissolves. Cook to hard ball stage (265 degrees on candy thermometer), without stirring. Remove from heat; stir in remaining ingredients. Pour into buttered 15½x10½x1-inch pan. Cool until comfortable to handle. Butter hands; gather taffy into a ball and pull. When candy is light in color and gets hard to pull, cut in fourths; pull each piece into long strand about ½ inch thick. With buttered scissors, quickly snip in bite size pieces. Wrap each piece of taffy in waxed paper. Yield about 1¼ pounds.

NOUGAT CANDY

Grease lightly, a 9x5x3-inch baking pan; set aside, then dust with cornstarch. In a large saucepan, combine 1½ cups granulated sugar and 1 tablespoon cornstarch. Add 1 cup light corn syrup and ½ cup water; cook over medium heat; stirring until sugar dissolves. Continue cooking to soft crack stage (286 degrees on candy thermometer), stirring occasionally to prevent sticking. Meanwhile, beat 2 egg whites to stiff peaks. Then slowly pour syrup mixture over egg whites, beating constantly, using an electric mixer. Beat until mixture becomes stiff; fold in 2/3 cup of candied cherries, chopped. Pack candy into a loaf pan. To serve, cut in 1-inch squares.

RASPBERRY SHRUB (An old-time favorite)

3 pints fresh *raspberries,
   washed & hulled
1½ cups granulated sugar
2 cups water

In a large saucepan, combine together, all ingredients; mix well. Bring to a boil, over medium heat; stirring until sugar dissolves. Remove from heat; strain and cool, then add 1 cup fresh or frozen lemon juice and 2 quarts of water. Serve with ice, if desired.

*NOTE: If a (5 to 10 ozs.) pkg. frozen raspberries, thawed, is used, omit sugar and water.

Chapter 2

BREAD BAKERY, PLUS FLAVORED BUTTERS

WHY IS A COOKBOOK EXCITING?
BECAUSE IT HAS MANY STIRRING EVENTS!

HOMEMADE QUICK BREADS AND FLAVORED BUTTERS

Everyone loves a quick bread. They are easy to make and there are many varieties to make. Also they are versatile in the way that you can make muffins using a quick bread recipe. Quick breads freeze well and can be frozen for up to 6 months. They make nice gifts for someone that is elderly or that lives alone. At Christmas they make gift giving easy. Who doesn't like homemade bakery!

PUMPKIN WAFFLES

2 cups all-purpose flour
2 tablespoons baking powder
¼ teaspoons cinnamon
¼ teaspoon ginger
¼ teaspoon nutmeg
½ teaspoon salt
3 large eggs
1¾ cups milk
¾ cup pumpkin
½ cup vegetable oil
½ cup nuts, chopped (optional)

In a medium mixing bowl, combine dry ingredients; add eggs, milk, oil and pumpkin. Stir in nuts. Bake in hot waffle iron. Yield 4 servings.

COUNTRY ZUCCHINI QUICK BREAD

2 cups all-purpose flour
2 teaspoons baking powder
½ teaspoon baking soda
½ teaspoon salt
2 large eggs
¾ cup sour cream
¼ cup honey
2 tablespoons margarine, melted
1 cup zucchini, grated

In a medium mixing bowl, combine together by sifting, flour, baking powder, baking soda and salt. In a separate bowl, beat eggs with electric mixer, until light and fluffy. Add sour cream, honey and margarine; beat for 1 minute. On low speed of mixer, gradually add dry ingredients, until well-blended. Fold in zucchini spoon into greased and floured 9x5x3 inch loaf pan. Bake at 350 degrees F., for about minutes or until tested done. Yield 1 loaf or 8 to 10 slices.

RHUBARB QUICK BREAD

1½ cups brown sugar, packed
1 large egg
2/3 cup vegetable oil
1 teaspoon vanilla extract
1 teaspoon baking soda
½ teaspoon baking powder
2½ cups all-purpose flour
1 cup buttermilk
½ cup nuts, chopped

In a large mixing bowl, beat together, sugar, egg and oil; mix well. In another bowl, sift dry ingredients together, then add dry ingredients alternately with buttermilk; add vanilla, nuts and rhubarb; mix thoroughly. Put batter into greased loaf pans; bake at 350 degrees, for 50 minutes, or until tested done. Yield

DATE NUT QUICK BREAD

2 teaspoons baking soda
1 pound dates, pitted, cut in
   small pieces
2 cups boiling water
2 cups granulated sugar
.½ cup shortening
2 large eggs, beaten
2 teaspoons vanilla extract
1 teaspoon salt
4 cups all-purpose flour
1¼ cups walnuts, chopped

Put cut-up dates in a small bowl; sprinkle with baking soda. Add boiling water; mix thoroughly; set aside. In another bowl, cream together, sugar and shortening. Add eggs, vanilla and salt; mix well. Add flour alternately with date mixture; mix thoroughly; fold in nuts. Grease and flour loaf pans Bake at 325 degrees, for 50 to 60 minutes, or until tested done. Yild 2 loaves

EGGPLANT FRITTERS

2 tablespoons all-purpose flour
1 large egg
3 cups eggplant, cooked &
   mashed
½ teaspoon salt
Black pepper to taste
Dash cayenne
Vegetable oil for frying

In a medium mixing bowl. Combine together, flour, egg and eggplant; beat until light and fluffy. Add seasoning, drop by spoonfuls into hot oil (375 degrees), fry until browned. Yield 6 to 8 servings.

PUMPKIN SWIRL QUICK BREAD
SWIRL MIXTURE

1 pkg. (8 ozs.) cream cheese, softened
¼ cup granulated sugar
1 large egg

In a small mixing bowl, combine cream cheese, sugar and egg, beat until thoroughly blended; set aside.

BREAD

1¾ cup all purpose flour
1½ cups granulated sugar
1 teaspoon baking soda
½ teaspoon salt
1 teaspoon ground cinnamon
¼ teaspoon ground nutmeg
1 cup cooked pumpkin
½ cup butter OR margarine, melted
1 large egg
1/3 cup water

Sift flour, sugar, baking soda, salt and spices together; set aside. In a large mixing bowl, combine pumpkin, melted butter, egg and water; mix together. Gradually add flour mixture to pumpkin mixture, mixing ingredients thoroughly. Reserve 2 cups of batter Place remaining batter in a loaf pan; then add cream cheese mixture on top, spreading gently. Place remaining batter on top of cream cheese mixture. Insert a butter knife in batter and swirl gently from one end to the other of batter. Bake at 350 degrees F., for 1 hour or until tested done. Yield about 8 to 10 slices.

PINEAPPLE QUICK BREAD

½ cup butter OR margarine, softened
1-1/3 cups granulated sugar
3 large eggs
2¼ cups all-purpose flour
1 teaspoon vanilla extract
½ teaspoon salt
1 cup heavy cream (ie. Half & Half)
½ cup milk
1 cup nuts, chopped (optional)
½ cup crushed pineapple, drained

In a medium mixing bowl, cream butter and sugar together until smooth and creamy. Add eggs, one at a time, beating after each addition. Add flour, baking powder and salt; mixing thoroughly. Add cream, milk, nuts and crushed pineapple mix thoroughly. Grease a 9x5x3 loaf pan, bake at 350 degrees F., for 55 to 60 minutes, or until tested done. Yield 1 loaf or 8 to 10 slices.

COTTAGE CHEESE QUICK BREAD

1 cup cottage cheese
2 large eggs
1 cup granulated sugar
¾ cup milk
2½ teaspoons baking powder
½ cup walnuts (optional)
½ cup raisins
½ cup Maraschino cherries, cut
   in half
2¾ cups all-purpose flour

Combine together thoroughly, cottage cheese, eggs, sugar, milk and vanilla; add flour, baking powder; mix until well-blended, then fold in walnuts, raisins and cherries. Grease and flour a loaf pan; bake at 375 degrees, for about 1 hour, or until tested done. Yield 1 loaf.

POTATO CHIP QUICK BREAD

2 cups all-purpose flour
2½ teaspoons baking powder
½ teaspoon salt
2 tablespoons butter OR
   margarine
½ cup granulated sugar
1 large egg
1 cup milk
1 cup potato chips, crushed

In a medium mixing bowl, sift together flour, baking powder and salt; set aside. In another bowl, cream butter and sugar until light and fluffy. Add egg; mix well. Add flour mixture alternately with milk, mixing thoroughly after each addition. Fold in crushed potato chips. Bake in a lightly greased loaf pan, at 350 degrees F., for about 1 hour, or until tested done. Remove from pan and cool completely on rack, then wrap in plastic wrap and store overnight. Bread slices better the second day. Yield 1 loaf.

SHORTCUT QUICK BREAD

3 cups Bisquick
½ cup granulated sugar
1/3 cup all-purpose flour
1 large egg beaten
1 cup milk
1½ cups nuts, chopped

In a large mixing bowl, combine together, all ingredients; mix thoroughly. Grease a 9x5x3 inch loaf pan; bake at 350 degrees F., for 55 to 60 minutes, or until tested done. Yield 1 loaf or 8 to 10 slices.

ZUCCHINI QUICK BREAD
(with ground ginger)

1½ cups all-purpose flour
1 cup granulated sugar
2 teaspoons baking powder
½ teaspoon baking soda
¼ teaspoon salt
¼ teaspoon ground ginger
2 large eggs, beaten
½ cup vegetable oil
1½ cups zucchini, grated

In a medium mixing bowl, combine together all dry ingredients. Add beaten eggs and oil; mix thoroughly. Fold in grated zucchini. Grease and flour a loaf pan; bake at 350 degrees F. for 50 minutes, or until tested done. Yield 1 loaf.

ZUCCHINI QUICK BREAD
(with ground cinnamon)

1½ cups all-purpose flour
1 cup granulated sugar
2 teaspoons baking powder
½ teaspoon baking soda
¼ teaspoon salt
1½ teaspoon ground cinnamon
2 large eggs, beaten
½ cup vegetable oil
1½ cups zucchini, grated

In a medium mixing bowl, combine together, all dry ingredients. Add beaten eggs and oil; mix thoroughly. Fold in grated zucchini; grease and flour loaf pan. Bake at 350 degrees F., for 50 minutes, or until tested done. Yield 1 loaf.

ZUCCHINI-PINEAPPLE QUICK BREAD

3 large eggs, beaten
2 cups granulated sugar
1½ teaspoons vanilla extract
1 cup vegetable oil
2 cups zucchini, grated
3 cups all-purpose flour
1 teaspoon baking powder
1 teaspoon baking soda
1 teaspoon salt
1 tablespoon cinnamon
1 cup crushed pineapple, drained
½ cup raisins (optional)
½ cup walnuts, chopped (optional)

In a medium mixing bowl, beat eggs, add sugar, vanilla, oil and zucchini; mix well. In a separate bowl, sift together, flour, baking powder, baking soda, salt and cinnamon. Add to egg mixture, a little at a time, mixing well, after each addition. Fold in crushed pineapple, raisins and nuts. grease and flour a loaf pan; bake at 350 degrees F., for about 50 minutes, or until tested done. Yield 1 large loaf.

POPPY SEED QUICK BREAD

¼ cup butter OR margarine, softened
1 cup granulated sugar
2 large eggs
1 teaspoon orange peel, grated
2 cups all-purpose flour
2½ teaspoons baking powder
½ teaspoon salt
¼ teaspoon nutmeg
1 cup milk
1/3 cup poppy seeds
½ cup nuts, chopped (optional)
½ cup golden raisins (optional)

In a medium mixing bowl, beat butter and sugar until smooth and creamy. Add eggs, one at a time, beating well after each addition; mix in orange peel. In separate bowl, sift together, flour, baking powder, salt and nutmeg. Add dry ingredients to butter mixture, alternately with milk, mixing well after each addition. Fold in poppy seeds, nuts and raisins. Prepare a well-greased, flour dusted, 9x5x3 loaf pan. and cool completely on rack. Yield 1 loaf minutes, or until tested done. Cool in pan for 10 minutes, then remove bread from pan. Bake at 350 degrees F., for 1 hour and 10 minutes, or until tested done. Cool in pan for 10 minutes, then remove bread from pan and cool completely on rack. Yield 1 loaf.

PRUNE QUICK BREAD

2¼ cups all-purpose flour
1 cup granulated sugar
½ teaspoon salt
1 teaspoon baking powder
1 teaspoon baking soda
1 tablespoon orange rind, grated
1 large egg, beaten
1 cup *sour milk
½ cup prune juice from cooked prunes
2 tablespoons butter OR margarine
1/3 cup prunes, cooked & chopped
¾ cup walnuts, chopped (optional *Sour milk is made by adding 1 teaspoon v vinegar or lemon juice to 1 cup milk.)

In a large bowl, combine ingredients together; beat at low speed with electric mixer, for 1 minute. Prepare a well greased, flour dusted, 9x5x3 inch loaf pan. Bake at 350 degrees F., for 55 to 60 minutes, or until tested done. Remove from loaf pan, cool on rack and when cool, wrap with foil and store in cool place for 2 days before slicing. (It will slice better.) Yield 1 loaf or about 8 to 10 sliceas.

STRAWBERRY QUICK BREAD
(with nuts)

3 cups all-purpose flour
1 teaspoon baking soda
1 teaspoon salt
1 tablespoon cinnamon
2 cups granulated sugar
4 large eggs, beaten
1¼ cups vegetable oil
2 cups fresh strawberries, sliced
    OR frozen berries, thawed &
    drained 1¼ cups nuts, walnuts
    OR pecans, chopped

In a large mixing bowl,
combine together, by sifting dry
ingredients. Add eggs, oil and
nuts; mix until moistened, then
fold in strawberries; mix gently.
Put in 2 greased loaf pans. Bake
at 350 degrees F., for 60 to 70
minutes, or until tested done.
Remove from pan and cool
rack. This bread freezes well.
Yield 2 loaves, 8 to 10 slices per
loaf. If desired, serve with cream
cheese.

CARROT QUICK BREAD

¾ cup vegetable oil
1 cup granulated sugar
2 large eggs
½ teaspoon cinnamon
1 teaspoon baking powder
1 teaspoon baking soda
1¼ cups all-purpose flour
1 cup carrots, finely grated
½ cup nuts, chopped (optional)

In a medium mixing bowl,
combine oil and sugar; mix well.
Add eggs, 1 at a time, beating
well after each addition. Stir in
dry ingredients; mix thoroughly.
Add carrots and nuts. Spoon
into greased, floured 9x5x3 loaf
pan; let stand 10 minutes before
putting in the oven. Bake at 350
degrees F., for 45 to 50 minutes,
or until tested done. Yield 1 loaf
or 8 to 10 slices.

CARROT-PINEAPPLE QUICK BREAD

Add ½ cup crushed pineapple
to the batter of the above
Carrot Bread recipe.

BUTTERNUT SQUASH QUICK BREAD

3½ cups all-purpose flour
2 teaspoons baking soda
1 cup raisins
1 cup vegetable oil
1 cup water
1½ teaspoons ground cinnamon
1 teaspoon salt
1 teaspoon mace
1½ cups butternut squash, cooked
½ cup honey
4 large eggs
1½ teaspoons nutmeg
2 cups granulated sugar

In a large mixing bowl, combine
flour, baking soda, raisins; set
aside. In a separate bowl, mix
sugar, oil and eggs; beating
thoroughly. Stir in squash, honey
water, spices and salt. Proceed
to add flour mixture to sugar
mixture, stir until just moistened.
Pour batter into 3-9x5x3 inch loaf
pans. Bake at 350 degrees F., for
60 minutes or until tested done.
Remove from pans; cool before
slicing. Yield 3 loaves or 24 to 30
slices.

CHOCOLATE QUICK BREAD (W/ CHOCOLATE HONEY BUTTER)

1 cup granulated sugar
½ cup butter OR margarine, softened
2 large eggs
1 cup *buttermilk
1¾ cups all-purpose flour
½ cup unsweetened cocoa
½ teaspoon EACH baking powder baking soda and salt
1/3 cup nuts, chopped (optional)

TIP—to substitute buttermilk, use 1 teaspoon vinegar OR lemon juice, in 1 cup milk.

In a medium bowl, combine sugar and butter, cream thoroughly. Add eggs, one at a time, mixing well after each addition. Stir in buttermilk. Add flour, cocoa, baking powder, baking soda and salt. Stir just until ingredients are moistened. Fold in nuts; spoon into 9x5x3 inch loaf pan, that has been greased lightly on the bottom only. Bake at 350 degrees F., for 55 to 60 minutes, or until tested done. Cool in pan for 15 minutes; remove from pan; cool completely, before slicing. Yield 1 loaf or 8 to 10 slices. Serve with Chocolate Honey Butter.

CHOCOLATE HONEY BUTTER

½ cup butter, softened
2 tablespoons chocolate-flavored syrup
2 tablespoons honey

In a small bowl, combine together, above ingredients, beat until light and fluffy. Yield 1 cup.

BEER QUICK BREAD

1 can (12 ozs.) beer, flat, room temperature
3 cups self-rising flour
¼ cup granulated sugar

Butter OR margarine, melted. In a medium bowl, mix together, all the ingredients thoroughly. Batter will be thin Pour batter into a greased loaf pan, dusted lightly with cornmeal. Bake at 325 degrees F, for 1 hour 10 minutes; the last 10 minutes brush top with butter. Yield 1 loaf or 8 to 10 slices.

BANANA QUICK BREAD

2 cups all-purpose flour
1 teaspoon baking soda
¼ teaspoon salt
½ cup butter OR margarine
1 cup granulated sugar
2 large eggs
1 teaspoon vanilla extract
3 or 4 small bananas, mashed
1 cup nuts, chopped (optional)

Sift together, flour, baking soda and salt; set aside. In a medium mixing bowl, cream butter with sugar until smooth and creamy. Add eggs and vanilla; mix thoroughly. Fold in flour mixture; add bananas and nuts; mix gently. Spoon into a well-greased loaf pan; bake at 350 degrees F., for about 60 minutes, or until tested done. Yield 1 loaf or 8 to 10 slices.

TOMATO QUICK BREAD

2½ cups all-purpose flour
1 tablespoon baking powder
1 teaspoon salt
1 teaspoon garlic powder
1 teaspoon oregano, crushed
1 tablespoon sugar
½ cup Mozzarella cheese
¼ cup Parmesan cheese
1/3 to 2/3 cup milk
2 large eggs
¼ cup vegetable oil
2 large tomatoes, chopped

In a large mixing bowl, combine together, flour, baking powder, salt garlic powder, oregano, sugar and cheeses. Peel and chop tomatoes; drain off the liquid into a measuring cup, then add enough milk to measure 2/3 cup of liquid. Blend liquid with eggs and oil; add liquid and chopped tomatoes into flour mixture; mix until thoroughly moistened. Pour batter into a greased 9x5x3 inch loaf pan. Bake at 350 degrees F., for 65 to 75 minutes, or until tested done. Cool 10 minutes in pan, then turn out on wire rack to cool.

CHUTNEY QUICK BREAD

2½ cups all-purpose flour
½ cup granulated sugar
½ cup brown sugar, packed
1 teaspoon baking powder
1 teaspoon salt
1¼ cup milk
¼ cup vegetable oil
1 large egg
1 tablespoon orange peel, grated
1 cup nuts, chopped

In a large mixing bowl, combine together, flour, sugars, baking powder, salt, oil, milk, egg and orange peel; mix just to moisten ingredients. Do not over mix. Fold in chutney and nuts; spoon into greased 9x5x3 inch loaf pan. Bake at 350 degrees F., for 55 to 60 minutes, or until tested done. This is a moist bread. Yield 1 loaf.

APRICOT NUT QUICK BREAD

1 cup dried apricots, chopped
2 cups warm water
1 cup granulated sugar
2 tablespoons butter OR
   margarine, softened
1 large egg
¾ cup orange juice
2 cups all-purpose flour
2 teaspoons baking powder
¼ teaspoon baking soda
1 teaspoon salt
¾ cup nuts, chopped
   (Optional)

Soak apricots in warm water for 30 minutes. Meanwhile, in a medium mixing bowl, blend butter, sugar and egg together; mix well; add orange juice. In a separate bowl, sift flour, baking powder, baking soda and salt. Add dry ingredients into creamed mixture; stir just until moistened. Drain apricots; add to batter; add nuts. Pour into a greased 9x5x3 inch loaf pan. Bake at 350 degrees F., for 55 to 60 minutes, or until tested done. Cool 10 minutes in pan before removing bread to a wire rack to cool completely. Yield 1 loaf or 8 to 10 slices.

QUICK BREAD BAKING TIPS

When working with baking powder and baking soda, it is important not to beat the batter; mix batter just enough, to moisten the dry ingredients. The more you mix the batter, the more it causes the flour's gluten to develop and that will result in a tough quick bread, instead of a moist, soft bread.

Glass bakeware retains heat better than metal bakeware, therefore, you need to reduce the oven temperature by 25 degrees.

Lumpy dough is okay; the lumps will disappear, when the bread bakes.

It is best, if you bake the quick bread in the center of the oven and if the bread browns on top too quickly, cover loosely with a piece of aluminum foil.

Cool quick breads in the loaf pan, for 10 minutes, then remove from pan; let cool completely before slicing. Some quick breads slice better the next day. Quick breads freeze well, when properly wrapped. The breads can be kept for a month, and longer, they become dry. To thaw, heat in oven, at 400 degrees, for a few minutes, before serving. And, of course, there is the microwave.

GERMAN APPLE QUICK BREAD

1 cup granulated sugar
1 stick margarine, softened
2 large eggs
2 cups all-purpose flour
½ teaspoon salt
¼ teaspoon baking soda
2 cups apples, diced

TOPPING

2 tablespoons all-purpose flour
2 tablespoons brown sugar
1 teaspoon cinnamon

In a medium mixing bowl. cream together, sugar and margarine. Add eggs; beat well. Add flour, salt and baking soda; beat until well mixed. Fold in apples; pour batter into a greased 9x5" loaf pan; set aside. In a small bowl, combie together, the topping ingredients; mix well. Sprinkle over the top of bread; bake at 350 degrees, for 50 to 60 minutes, or until tested done. Remove from oven and let cool 10 minutes. before removing from loaf pan. Cool completely before slicing. Yield 8 to 10 slices.

BLUEBERRY QUICK BREAD

1¾ cups all-purpose
2/3 cup granulated sugar
½ teaspoon baking soda
1½ teaspoons baking powder
½ teaspoon salt
1 cup pecans, chopped
    (optional)
1 large egg, beaten
1 orange, juice & peel, grated
2 tablespoons butter OR
    margarine
Boiling water
1 cup blueberries
¼ cup all-purpose flour

In a large mixing bowl, sift together, flour, sugar, baking soda, baking powder and salt; add orange peel; set aside. In a measuring cup, combine orange juice and butter; add enough boiling water to make ¾ cup liquid. Add to dry ingredients with the egg. In a separate bowl, combine together, blueberries, nuts and flour; mix until berries and nuts are coated with flour; fold mixture gently into batter. Pour batter into greased 9x5x3 inch loaf pan; bake at 350 degrees, for 50 minutes, or until tested done. Yield 1 loaf or about 8 slices.

SPOON BREAD

1½ cups boiling water
1 cup cornmeal
1 tablespoon butter OR
  margarine
3 large eggs, separated
1 cup buttermilk
½ teaspoon salt
1 teaspoon granulated sugar
1 teaspoon baking powder
¼ teaspoon baking soda
Butter OR margarine

Preheat oven to 375 degrees. In a mixing bowl, place cornmeal. add boiling water stirring until mixture is lukewarm. Blend in 1 tablespoon butter and egg yolks. Add buttermilk, salt, sugar, baking powder and soda; mix well; set aside. Beat egg whites just until soft peaks form; fold into batter. Pour into greased 2-quart casserole. Bake for 45 to 50 minutes or until tested done. Serve with butter.

ORANGE NUT QUICK BREAD

4½ cups all-purpose flour
1¾ cups granulated sugar
4 teaspoons baking powder
1 teaspoon baking soda
1½ teaspoons salt
1½ cups walnuts, chopped
  (optional)
2 tablespoons orange peel,
  grated
2 large eggs
1 cup milk
1 cup orange juice
¼ cup butter OR margarine,
  melted

In a large mixing bowl, sift together, flour, sugar, baking powder, baking soda and salt. Add nuts and grated orange peel; mix well. In a small bowl, beat eggs milk, orange juice and melted butter until smooth. Add egg mixture into flour mixture; mix just until ingredients are moistened. Pour batter into 2 greased loaf pans; bake at 350 degrees for 50 to 60 minutes, or until tested done. Cool in pan for 10 minutes, then remove bread and place on wire racks to cool completely. Yield 2 loaves or 16 to 20 slices.

PEAR QUICK BREAD

½ cup butter OR margarine,
  softened
1 cup granulated sugar
2 large eggs
1½ cups all-purpose flour
½ teaspoon salt
½ teaspoon baking soda
1 teaspoon vanilla extract
½ cup milk
1 cup pears, peeled, cored &
  chopped
½ cup wheat germ
½ cup nuts, chopped (optional)
1 teaspoon baking powder

In a medium mixing bowl, cream butter with sugar until smooth and creamy. Add eggs, one at a time, beating well after each addition. Combine together, dry ingredients, by sifting. Add to butter mixture, alternating with butter milk; mix well. Fold in pears, wheat germ, nuts and vanilla; mix thoroughly. Place batter into a greased loaf pan; bake at 350 degrees, for 1 hour, or until tested done. Yield 1 loaf or about 8 slices.

APPLE NUT QUICK BREAD

2 ½ cups all-purpose flour
1 cup oatmeal. uncooked
½ cup nuts, chopped
1 tablespoon baking powder
1½ teaspoon cinnamon
½ teaspoon salt
¼ teaspoon nutmeg
1¼ cups brown sugar, packed
3 large eggs
2/3 cup vegetable oil
1 teaspoon vanilla extract
2 cups apples, chopped (about
  3 large)

Preheat oven to 325 degrees. Grease bottom only of 9x5" loaf pan. In medium bowl. combine together, flour, oatmeal, nuts, baking powder, cinnamon, salt and nutmeg. In a large bowl, combine together sugar, eggs, oil and vanilla; mix until smooth. Fold in apples; add flour mixture to sugar mixture; mix just until dry ingredients are moistened. Pour batter loaf pan; bake about 1 hour 10 minutes, until tested done. Remove from oven; let cool 10 minutes, then remove from pan; let cool completely before slicing. Yield about 18 slices.

PIZZA QUICK BREAD

3 cups all-purpose flour
1 tablespoon baking powder
1 teaspoon oregano
1 tablespoon granulated sugar
½ cup Mozzarella Cheese, grated
1 teaspoon garlic powder
1 can (16 ozs.) tomatoes, diced
¼ cup milk, more or less, as needed
1 large egg
¼ cup vegetable oil
¼ cup Parmesan Cheese, grated

In a large mixing bowl, sift together, all dry ingredients; set aside. Drain tomatoes, reserve liquid; add milk to liquid to measure 2/3 cup. Add to dry ingredients, along with Mozzarella Cheese, Parmesan Cheese, diced tomatoes, egg and oil. Mix just until dry ingredients are moistened. Pour batter into a greased 9x5x3 inch loaf pan; bake at 350 degrees, for 60 to 80 minutes, or until tested done. Remove from pan to cool.

GLAZED LEMON QUICK BREAD

1/3 cup butter OR margarine, softened
1 cup granulated sugar
2 large eggs
¼ teaspoon almond extract
1½ cups all-purpose flour
1 teaspoon salt
1 teaspoon baking powder
½ cup milk
1 tablespoon lemon peel, grated
½ cup nuts, chopped (optional)

In a medium mixing bowl, cream together, butter and sugar until fluffy. Add eggs, one at a time, beating well after each addition; add almond extract. In a separate bowl, combine together, dry ingredients; gradually add to egg mixture, alternately with milk. Mix just until ingredients are blended. Fold in lemon peel and nuts. Spoon batter into a greased 9x5-inch loaf pan; bake at 350 degrees, for about 60 minutes, or until tested done. Yield 1 loaf or 8 to 10 slices.

GLAZE
Mix ¼ cup granulated sugar with 3 tablespoons fresh lemon juice. Spoon over bread immediately, as bread is removed from the oven.

RHUBARB QUICK BREAD
(with Crumb Topping)

1½ cups brown sugar, packed
1 cup buttermilk
1 large egg
2/3 cup vegetable oil
1 teaspoon vanilla extract
1½ cups fresh *rhubarb,
    chopped
1 teaspoon baking powder
½ teaspoon salt
2½ cups all-purpose flour

*Remember use only the stalks.
In a large mixing bowl, blend
together, the first 5 ingredients;
set aside. In a separate bowl,
sift together, flour, baking soda
and salt. Mix dry ingredients
with brown sugar mixture; mix
well. Fold in rhubarb and nuts.
Spoon in a greased 9x5x3
inch loaf pan; spread crumb
topping evenly on top, Bake
at 350 degrees, for about 45
minutes, or until tested done.
Yield 1 loaf.

CRUMB TOPPING

In a small mixing bowl,
combine together, ½ cup
brown sugar, ½ teaspoon
cinnamon, 1 tablespoon butter
Or margarine; and ½ cup nuts;
chopped; mix well.

APPLESAUCE QUICK BREAD

2 cups all-purpose flour
1//2 teaspoon salt
2 teaspoons baking powder
½ cup butter OR margarine,
    softened
1 cup walnuts, chopped
    (optional)
¾ cup granulated sugar
½ cup brown sugar, packed
2 large eggs
1¼ cups applesauce
1 teaspoon cinnamon

In a medium mixing bowl, sift
together, flour, salt, baking
powder and cinnamon; set
aside. In a separate bowl,
cream butter, with both sugars
until light and fluffy. Add eggs,
one at a time, beating well
after each addition. Add
applesauce to egg mixture;
mix well. Add dry ingredients
gradually, to butter mixture;
mix thoroughly. Fold in nuts;
pour into a well-greased loaf
pan. Bake at 350 degrees,
for about 60 minutes, or until
tested done. Cool in pan for
10 minutes, remove from pan,
cool completely on wire rack.
It is best not to slice bread until
completely cooled. Yield 8 to
10 slices.

LATKES (Crisp Pancakes)

1 medium onion, grated
2 or 3 large baking potatoes
   (1lb.)
Vegetable Oil for frying
1 large egg
½ teaspoon salt
1 teaspoon pepper
3 tablespoons all-purpose flour

Peel onion and potatoes, then grate them. Combine together, in a mixing bowl, add egg, flour, salt and pepper; mix well. Heat about ¼ inch of oil in a large skillet. Drop 2 tablespoons of batter for each pancake, into hot oil. Cook until golden brown, about 4 to 5 minutes, on each side. Drain on paper towels. Latkes are tradionally are accompanied with sour cream or applesauce. You can serve these crisp pancakes as a side dish. Yield 4 servings.

*MAPLE SYRUP QUICK BREAD

2 cups all-purpose flour
2 teaspoons baking powdeer
1cup maple syrup
¼ teaspoon baking soda
2 teaspoons ground ginger
1 teaspoon cinnamon
1/3 cup butter OR margarine,
   melted
½ teaspoon salt
* If desired, you can substitute
   molasses for maple syrup.

In a medium-size bowl, combine, by sifting together, all the dry ingredients. Add melted butter and syrup; mix well. Place batter into a greased loaf pan; bake at 350 degrees, for about 1 hour or until tested done. Yield about 8 to 12 servings.

SWEET POTATO WAFFLES

¾ cup all-purpose flour, sifted
2 teaspoons baking powder
¼ teaspoon salt
4 tablespoons vegetable oil
1 teaspoon nutmeg
1 large egg, separated
1 cup milk
1 cup sweet potatoes, cooked
   & mashed
1 tablespoon granulated sugar

In a mixing bowl, combine together, by sifting dry ingredients. Add egg yolk and milk; beat until smooth. Add sweet potato and oil; continue beating. Fold in stiffly beaten egg white. Bake in heated waffle iron until brown. If desired, sprinkle with sugar and cinnamon. Yield 4 servings. Serving suggestion—Serve with roast, turkey or pork.

GLAZED CRANBERRY QUICK BREAD

¼ cup vegetable oil
½ cup sour cream
¼ cup milk
3 large eggs
2 ½ cups Bisquick baking mix
½ cup nuts, chopped (optional)
2 tablespoons orange peel, grated
¾ cup fresh OR frozen cranberries, chopped
¾ cup granulated sugar

Preheat oven to 375 degrees F. Grease bottom of 9x5x3 inch loaf pan; set aside. In a large mixing bowl, combine together, all ingredients, EXCEPT cranberries and nuts. Beat thoroughly for 1 minute, or until ingredients are completely moistened. Fold in cranberries and nuts. If using frozen cranberries, drain before using. Spoon into loaf pan; bake for 50 to 55 minutes, or until tested done. Remove from oven, cool in pan for 10 minutes, remove from pan and drizzle with glaze (recipe following) evenly over top of bread. Yield 1 loaf or 8 to 10 slices.

GLAZE: Beat ½ cup powder sugar and 2 to 3 teaspoons of orange juice until smooth and desired consistency.

BASIC QUICK BREAD (with variations)

2 cups all-purpose flour
2 teaspoons baking powder
1/3 cup granulated sugar
½ teaspoon salt
1 tablespoon flour
1 large egg
1 cup milk
¾ cup raisins OR nuts, chopped (optional)
3 tablespoons butter OR margarine, melted

Preheat oven to 350 degrees F. Grease a 9x5x3 inch loaf pan. In a large mixing bowl, sift together, flour, baking powder, sugar and salt; set aside. In a separate bowl, beat together, butter, egg and milk, with electric mixer, on medium-high speed, until smooth and creamy; set aside. In another small bowl, combine raisins and nuts with 1 tablespoon flour; mix until coated with flour. Pour egg mixture into flour mixture; mix just until flour mixture is moistened. Fold in raisins and nuts. Spoon into greased loaf pan; bake for 35 to 40 minutes, or until tested done. Remove from oven; cool in pan for 10 minutes. Remove from pan and let cool completely before slicing. Yield 8 to 10 slices.

VARIATIONS OF BASIC QUICK BREAD

CHOCOLATE CHIP—Instead of raisins and nuts, you can add ¾ cup chocolate chips.

POPPY SEED QUICK BREAD— Add 1 tablespoon of poppy seeds to batter.

CITRUS QUICK BREAD—Add 2 teaspoons grated orange peel OR lemon peel to batter for a tart taste.

VARIOUS FRUITS QUICK BREAD— Add ¾ cup apples, peeled, cored and chopped, to the batter, OR any other fruit of your choice.

MARBLE QUICK BREAD—Leave out the raisins of the Basic Quick Bread, put ¼ cup of the batter into a small mixing bowl. Add 2 tablespoons of hot chocolate mix; stir until mixture is thoroughly mixed. Spoon the white batter in the greased loaf pan, then pour the chocolate batter across the top, using a knife, swirl batter gently to obtain a marbled effect.

NOTE: These quick breads are so rich, they can be used for dessert. It can be also toasted and served with butter or cream cheese.

CANDIED FRUIT QUICK BREAD

1 cup butter OR margarine, softened
¾ cup granulated sugar
6 large eggs
1 teaspoon baking powder
2 cups all-purpose flour, divided
1 cup candied fruit, chopped

In a medium mixing bowl, cream together, butter and sugar until light and fluffy. Add eggs, one at a time, beating well after each addition. Sift remaining dry ingredients, retaining ¼ cup flour to be mixed with candied fruit. Fold dry ingredients into creamed mixture; mix well. Add floured candied fruit; mix gently. Pour batter into greased loaf pan; bake at 350 degrees, for 50 minutes, or until tested done. Yield 1 loaf or 8 to 10 slices.

NOTE: If desired, reduce candied fruit to ½ cup, then add ½ cup nuts, chopped.

SWEET POTATO QUICK BREAD

2 cups all-purpose flour
2 cups cornmeal
½ cup granulated sugar
1 teaspoon salt
4 large eggs, beaten
¾ cup milk
1/3 cup vegetable oil
2-2/3 cups sweet potatoes,
    cooked & mashed

In a large mixing bowl, combine together, flour, cornmeal, sugar, baking powder and salt; set aside. In a another bowl, combine, milk, oil and sweet potatoes; mix well. Add egg mixture to the dry ingredients; mix only until just moistened. Pour into a greased 13x9x2 inch baking pan. Bake at 425 degrees, for 30 to 35 minutes or until tested done. Cut into squares;. serve warm, if desired. Yield 12 to 16 slices.

GUM DROP QUICK BREAD

2½ cups all-purpose flour
1¼ cups buttermilk
½ cup granulated sugar
½ cup brown sugar, packed
¼ cup shortening
2 large eggs
3 teaspoons baking powder
1 teaspoon salt
12 cup nuts, chopped
    (optional)
½ teaspoon baking soda
1 cup small gumdrops, cut in
    half
1 teaspoon vanilla extract

In a large mixing bowl, beat all ingredients, except gumdrops and nuts, with electric mixer, at medium speed, about 1 minute or until well-mixed and smooth. Fold in gumdrops and nuts. Pour batter into 9x5x3 inch loaf pan, grease only the bottom of the pan. Bake at 350 degrees, for 55 to 65 minutes, or until tested done. Remove from oven and let cool for 10 minutes; remove bread from pan and cool completely. The bread slices better the next day. Yield 1 loaf or 8 to 10 slices.

CHERRY NUT QUICK BREAD

2 cups all-purpose flour
½ teaspoon salt
1 teaspoon baking soda
¾ cup granulated sugar
½ cup butter OR margarine,
    softened
2 large eggs
1 teaspoon vanilla extract
1 cup buttermilk
1 cup pecans, chopped
1 jar (10 ozs.) Maraschino
    Cherries drained & chopped

Preheat oven to 350 degrees F.; lightly grease a 9x5x3 inch loaf pan; set aside. In a small mixing bowl, sift together flour, salt and baking soda; set aside. In a large mixing bowl, cream together, sugar and butter; add eggs, one at a time, beating well after each addition. Add vanilla, continue beating until light and fluffy. Add flour mixture, alternately with buttermilk. Fold in nuts and cherries gently, but thoroughly. Pour batter into prepared loaf pan; bake for 1 hour, or until tested done. Remove from oven and allow to cool completely before slicing. Yield about 10 servings.

SAUERKAUT QUICK BREAD

2/3 cup shortening
2-2/3 cups granulated sugar
4 large eggs, beaten
1 can (14 ozs.) sauerkraut,
    drained
2/3 cup water
2/3 cup nuts, chopped
    (optional)
3½ cups all-purpose flour
2 tablespoons baking soda
½ teaspoon baking powder
1 teaspoon ground cinnamon
1 teaspoon ground cloves
2/3 cup raisins (optional)

In a large bowl, cream together, shortening and sugar; add eggs, sauerkraut and water. Blend in flour, baking soda, baking powder. Fold in nuts and raisins. Place batter into 2 greased loaf pans; bake at 350 degrees, for about 1 hour, or until tested done. Remove from the oven; cool before slicing. Yield 2 loaves or 12 to 16 slices.

PUMPKIN QUICK BREAD (without eggs)

2½ ll purpose flour
¼ teaspoon salt
½ teaspoon ground cloves
2 cups pumpkin, canned Or
    fresh cooked
2 teaspoons baking soda
1 teaspoon baking powder
2 cups granulated sugar
½ cup raisins (optional)
½ cup nuts (optional)
½ cup vegetable oil

In a medium mixing bowl, sift together, dry ingredients; set aside. In another bowl, combine sugar, oil and pumpkin; mix thoroughly. Add dry ingredients gradually; mixing until well-blended. Fold in nuts and raisins; mix well. Place batter in 2 lightly greased small loaf pans or 1 large loaf pan. Bake at 350 degrees, for 45 to 50 minutes, or until tested done. Yield about 16 slices.

EGGNOG PANCAKES

2 cups all-purpose flour
4 teaspoon baking powder
½ teaspoon salt
¼ teaspoon nutmeg (optional)
2 large eggs, lightly beaten
1½ cups commercial eggnog
2 tablespoons butter OR
    margarine, melted

In a large mixing bowl, combine together, by sifting, flour, baking powder, salt and nutmeg; set aside. In a small bowl, beat eggs, eggnog and butter; add to dry ingredients; mix just until moistened. Pour ¼ cup batter into a lightly greased hot skillet. Turn over when bubbles form on top; then cook until golden brown. Yield 1 dozen.

CHOCOLATE ZUCCHINI QUICK BREAD

3 cups all purpose flour
3 cups granulated sugar
½ cup unsweetened cocoa
    powder
1½ teaspoons baking powder
1½ teaspoons baking soda
1 teaspoon salt
¼ teaspoon ground cinnamon
4 large eggs
1½ cups vegetable oil
2 tablespoons butter OR
    margarine, melted
½ cup raisins (optional)
1½ teaspoons almond extract
3 cups zucchini, peeled & grated
1 cup pecans, chopped (optional)
1½ teaspoons vanilla extract

In a large mixing bowl, Combine together, the first seven ingredients; set aside. In a medium sized bowl, combine eggs, oil, butter and extracts; mix well. Stir into dry ingredients, just until moistened. Fold in zucchini, nuts and raisins. Pour into three greased and floured loaf pans. Bake at 350 degrees, for 55 to 60 minutes, or until tested done. Remove from oven let cool for 10 minutes, then remove from pan to wire rack. Yield 3 loaves, or about 24 to 30 slices.

PEACH COBBLER QUICK BREAD

1/3 cup butter or margarine,
  softened
1 cup granulated sugar
2 large eggs
1/3 cup water
1 teaspoon vanilla extract
1/8 teaspoon almond extract
1 cup fresh OR frozen peaches,
  peeled & diced
1-2/3 cups all purpose flour
1 teaspoon baking soda
½ teaspoon salt
¼ teaspoon baking powder
½ cup pecans, chopped
  (optional)

TOPPING

2 tablespoons pecans, finely
  chopped
2 tablespoons brown sugar

In a large mixing bowl, cream
butter with sugar, until light
and fluffy. Add eggs, one
at time, beating well after
each addition. Add water
and extracts; mix well. Stir in
peaches. In a separate bowl,
combine flour, baking soda, salt
and baking powder; gradually
add to the creamed mixture.
Fold in pecans. Pour batter into
a greased 9x5x3 inch loaf pan.
Combine topping ingredients'
sprinkle evenly over batter.
Bake at 350 degrees, for 50 to
55 minutes, or until tested done.
Remove from oven let cool for
10 minutes, then remove from
pan to wire rack. Yield 3 loaves,
or about 24 to 30 slices.

GREEN TOMATO QUICK BREAD

8 to 10 medium green tomatoes
2/3 cup raisins
2/3 cup water
2/3 cup shortening
2-2/3 cup granulated sugar
4 large eggs
3-1/3 cups all-purpose flour
2 teaspoons baking soda
½ teaspoon baking powder
1 teaspoon ground cinnamon
1 teaspoon ground cloves
2/3 cup pecans OR walnuts,
  chopped

To prepare tomatoes, wash,
peel, core and cut in pieces,
discard seeds. Put through
blender or food processor
until smooth. You should have
2 cups pulp. In a large mixing
bowl, cream shortening with
sugar until fluffy. Add eggs,
one at a time, mixing well after
each addition. Add 2 cups
green tomato pulp, raisins and
water; beat well. In another
bowl, combine together, flour,
soda, salt, baking powder,
spices and nuts. Add 1 cup
of flour mixture at a time to
tomato mixture, stirring well
after each addition. Divide
batter between two 9x5"
greased loaf pans. Bake at 350
degrees for about 1 hour or
until tested done. Yield 2 loaves
or about 16 slices.

CINNAMON SWIRL QUICK BREAD

½ cup shortening
1 cup granulated sugar
2 large eggs
1 teaspoon vanilla extract
1 cup sour cream
¼ cup milk
1½ teaspoons orange peel
2 cups all-purpose flour
1½ teaspoons baking powder
1 teaspoon baking soda
½ teaspoon salt
¼ cup granulated sugar
2 teaspoons ground cinnamon

In a medium mixing bowl, cream shortening and 1 cup sugar, until light and fluffy. Beat in eggs, one at a time, mixing well after each addition. Add vanilla; blend in sour cream and milk. Combine together, flour, baking powder, baking soda and salt; add to creamed mixture; mix thoroughly. Spread half of the batter in a greased loaf pan. Combine remaining ¼ cup sugar, cinnamon and orange peel. Sprinkle all but 1 tablespoon over batter in loaf pan. Top with remaining batter. Cut through batter gently with knife to make a swirling effect with cinnamon. Top with remaining sugar mixture. Bake at 350 degrees for 45 to 50 minutes. Bake at 350 degrees for 45 to 50 minutes.

COCONUT QUICK BREAD

2 cups coconut, shredded
1¾ cups milk
2½ cups all-purpose flour
1 teaspoon ground cinnamon
¼ teaspoon ground cloves
2½ teaspoons baking powder
½ teaspoon salt
1-1/3 cup granulated sugar

In a medium mixing bowl, combine coconut and milk. Let stand at room temperature for 30 minutes. Sift flour, baking powder, spices and salt into a large mixing bowl; stir in sugar. Make a well in center of dry ingredients. Pour in coconut mixture, stir only until ingredients are moistened. Place batter into greased loaf pan; bake at 350 degrees for 1 hour or until tested done. Remove from pan, cool completely before slicing. Yield 1 loaf or about 8 to 10 slices.

CORNMEAL QUICK BREAD

1 cup cornmeal
¼ teaspoon baking soda
1 large egg, beaten
1 cup buttermilk
1 teaspoon baking powder
½ teaspoon salt
1 tablespoon shortening,
    melted

In a medium mixing bowl, combine together all ingredients. Place batter in an greased 8x8 baking pan; bake at 425 degrees, for 15 to 20 minutes, or until tested done. Cool 10 minutes before serving. Yield about 9 squares.

FRUIT COCKTAIL QUICK BREAD

1 pkg. (8 ozs.) cream cheese,
    softened
1 cup butter OR margarine,
    softened
1½ cups granulated sugar
1½ teaspoons vanilla extract
4 large eggs
2¼ cups all-purpose flour
1½ teaspoons baking powder
1 cup fruit cocktail, drained

In a medium mixing bowl, with an electric mixer, on medium-high speed beat together, cream cheese, butter, sugar, eggs and vanilla until light and fluffy. Add flour baking powder; fold in fruit cocktail; mix well. Place batter in 2 greased loaf

pans. Bake at 325 degrees, for 1 hour or until tested done. Cool for 10 minutes, then remove from pans and cool completely before slicing. Yield 2 loaves, or 16 to 20 slices.

HONEY-NUT QUICK BREAD

¼ cup butter OR margarine,
    softened
1 large egg
1 teaspoons baking powder
½ teaspoon salt
1 cup nuts (almonds, walnuts or
    pecans) finely chopped
¼ cup brown sugar, packed
1½ cups all-purpose flour
2 teaspoons ground cinnamon
½ cup milk
1 cup honey, warmed

In a medium mixing bowl, beat butter, egg & brown sugar, about 5 minutes, or until light and fluffy. In a separate bowl, sift flour, baking powder, cinnamon and salt together; add flour mixture to butter mixture, alternately add flour mixture to butter mixture, alternately with milk. Stir until well combined; fold in chopped nuts. Pour batter into greased loaf pan; bake at 350 degrees, for about 1 hour, or until tested done. Cool for 10 minutes; remove from loaf pan; Yield 1 loaf or 8 to 10 slices.

GINGERBREAD QUICK BREAD

1 large egg
½ cup granulated sugar
1 cup sour cream
½ cup molasses
2 cups all-purpose flour
½ teaspoon salt
¾ teaspoon baking soda
1 teaspoon baking powder
¾ teaspoon ground ginger
¾ teaspoon nutmeg
½ teaspoon ground cinnamon
3 tablespoons butter OR
    margarine, melted

In a medium mixing bowl, combine together, egg, sugar, sour cream and molasses; set aside. In another bowl, sift together, flour, salt, baking soda, baking powder, and spices. Add to egg mixture gradually; mix well. Add melted butter, mix thoroughly. Place into a greased loaf pan; bake at 350 degrees, for about 50 minutes, or until tested done. If desired, garnish with whipped topping. Yield 1 loaf or 8 to 10 slices.

GRAPE NUTS QUICK BREAD

2 cups buttermilk
1 cup Grapenuts cereal
3 cups all-purpose flour
1 teaspoon baking soda
4 teaspoons baking powder
½ teaspoon salt
1 teaspoon ground cinnamon
1 cup granulated sugar
1 teaspoon vanilla extract
1 large egg, slightly beaten

1 cup crushed pineapple, drained
1 cup raisins (optional)

Mix buttermilk and cereal; let stand for 10 minutes. Meanwhile, sift together, flour, baking soda, baking powder, salt and cinnamon; set aside. Add to buttermilk mixture, sugar, vanilla and egg; mix well. Add pineapple and raisins, next combine milk mixture with flour mixture; dough will be stiff. Divide dough in 2 parts; place batter in 2 greased loaf pans. Bake at 350 degrees, for about 50 to 60 minutes, or until tested done. Let bread stand for 24 hours before slicing. Yield 2 loaves or about 16 to 20 slices.

IRISH SODA QUICK BREAD

4 cups all-purpose flour
1 teaspoon baking soda
4 tablespoons caraway seeds
½ teaspoon salt
2 cups raisins
2 cups buttermilk

In a large mixing bowl, combine together, all ingredients and caraway seeds; add buttermilk; mix just until all ingredients are moistened. Fold in raisins; place dough in greased loaf pan. Bake at 400 degrees for about 45 minutes, or until tested done. If loaf is browning too fast, place sheet of aluminum foil on top. This bread has a hard crust but a moist inside. Yield 1 loaf or about 8 slices.

MOLASSES QUICK BREAD

1 large egg, beaten
¼ cup granulated sugar
½ cup molasses
¼ cup shortening, melted
2½ cups all-purpose flour
1 teaspoon baking soda
2 teaspoons baking powder
2/3 cup buttermilk

Beat egg until light and fluffy; add sugar, molasses and shortening (cooled slightly). Mix until well-blended. Sift together, the dry ingredients, then mix into egg mixture alternately with buttermilk; mix thoroughly. Place batter into greased loaf pan; bake at 350 degrees, for about 1 hour, or until tested done. Yield 1 loaf or about 8 slices.

MANGO QUICK BREAD

1 cup butter OR margarine
1½ cups granulated sugar
4 large eggs
½ teaspoon salt
2 teaspoons baking soda
4 cups all-purpose flour
1½ cups mangos, diced
2 tablespoons lemon juice
1 cup nuts, chopped (optional)

In a large mixing bowl, cream together, butter and sugar; add eggs, one at a time, beating well after each addition. Add salt, baking soda and flour; mix well. Fold in mangos and lemon juice. Pour into 2-8" loaf pans; bake at 350 degrees, for 1 hour or until tested done. Cool in pan 10 minutes, then remove from pans; cool thoroughly before slicing. Yield 2 loaves or 16 to 20 slices.

PEANUT BUTTER QUICK BREAD

¾ cup granulated sugar
½ cup peanut butter
1 teaspoon vanilla extract
1¾ cups milk
2 teaspoons baking powder
½ teaspoon salt
2¼ cups all-purpose flour

In a medium mixing bowl, cream together, sugar, peanut butter and vanilla; add milk mix thoroughly. In another bowl, sift together, flour, baking powder and salt. Add dry ingredients to creamed mixture; beat well. Place in a greased loaf pan; bake at 350 degrees, for 45 to 50 minutes, or until golden brown. Allow to cool 10 minutes before removing from pan. This is a moist bread. Yield 1 loaf or 8 to 10 slices.

APRICOT PRESERVE QUICK BREAD

2¼ cups all-purpose flour
½ cup brown sugar, packed
1 tablespoon baking powder
½ cup butter OR margarine,
    softened
½ cup milk
1 large egg, beaten
1 cup apricot preserves
1 cup pecans, chopped
    (optional)

In a medium mixing bowl, combine together, the dry ingredients; cut in butter. In another bowl, mix together milk, beaten egg and apricot preserves, just until batter is moistened. Fold in nuts. Pour batter into 2 greased loaf pans. Bake at 350 degrees, for about 1 hour, or until tested done. Yield 2 loaves. This is a moist bread.

BLACK WALNUT QUICK BREAD

2½ cups all-purpose flour
¾ cup brown sugar, packed
2 teaspoons baking powder
½ teaspoon baking soda
¼ teaspoon salt
¼ cup butter OR margarine,
    softened
1¼ cups buttermilk
2 large eggs
1 cup red or green candied
    cherries, chopped
½ cup black walnuts, chopped

Preheat oven at 350 degrees. In a medium mixing bowl, combine together, flour, sugar, baking powder, baking soda and salt. Add butter, buttermilk and eggs; beat at low speed of electric mixer, until ingredients are well-blended. Then beat medium speed for 1 minute. Fold in cherries and black walnuts. Pour batter into greased 9x5x3-inch loaf pan; bake for 1 hour, or until tested done. When done, immediately remove from pan to cool on wire rack. Yield 1 loaf or 8 to 10 slices.

EGGNOG QUICK BREAD

¼ cup butter OR margarine,
    melted
¾ cup granulated sugar
2 large eggs, beaten
2¼ cups all-purpose flour
2 teaspoons baking powder
½ teaspoon salt
1 cup eggnog
½ cup pecans, chopped
    (Optional)
½ cup raisins (Optional)
½ cup candied cherries,
    chopped

In a large mixing Bowl, combine together butter, sugar and beaten eggs; mix thoroughly. In another bowl, combine flour, baking powder and salt. Stir into butter mixture, alternating with eggnog; mix only until dry ingredients are moistened. Fold in pecans, raisins and cherries. Spoon into a greased loaf pan; bake at 350 degrees, for 1 hour, or until tested done. Yield about 8 servings.

CRANBERRY QUICK BREAD

½ cup butter OR margarine,
  softened
¾ cup granulated sugar
2 large eggs
1 teaspoon vanilla extract
3 cups all-purpose flour
3 teaspoons baking powder
1 teaspoon salt
1 teaspoon baking soda
½ teaspoon cinnamon
¼ teaspoon nutmeg
1/3 cup orange juice
1 pkg. (10 ozs.) frozen
  cranberry-orange relish
1 teaspoon orange peel,
  grated
1 cup pecans, chopped
  (optional)

Preheat oven at 350 degrees.
In a large mixing bowl, cream
together, butter, sugar and
eggs until light and fluffy;
add vanilla. In another bowl,
combine together all dry
ingredients; mix well. Add dry
ingredients, alternately with
orange juice to creamed
mixture. Fold in relish, orange
peel and pecans. Spoon batter
into well-greased 9x5x3 inch
loaf pan. Bake for about 60
minutes or until tested done.
Remove from oven; cool in pan
for 15 minutes, then put on wire
rack. When cool, wrap in foil or
plastic wrap. Bread best served
next day. Yield 1 loaf or 8 to 10
servings.

APRICOT HONEY QUICK BREAD

3 cups whole wheat flour
3 teaspoons baking powder
1 teaspoon ground cinnamon
¼ teaspoon ground nutmeg
½ teaspoon salt
1¼ cups milk
1 cup honey
1 large egg, slightly beaten
2 tablespoons vegetable oil
1 cup dried apricots, chopped
½ cup raisins (optional)
½ cup walnuts OR almonds
  (optional)

Combine together, above dry
ingredients. Then combine
milk, honey, egg and oil. Pour
over dry ingredients; stir just
until moistened. Gently fold in
apricots, raisins and nuts. Pour
into greased loaf pan. Bake
at 350 degrees, for 55 to 60
minutes or until tested done.
Cool completely before slicing,
Yield 1 loaf or about 10 slices.

BANANA COCONUT QUICK BREAD

3 large eggs
½ teaspoon lemon extract
¼ cu sour cream
1½ cups bananas, mashed
2 cups all-purpose flour
teaspoons baking soda
½ teaspoon salt
1 cup granulated sugar
1 cup nuts, finely chopped

In a large mixing bowl, sift together, flour, baking soda and salt; set aside. In another bowl, combine together, eggs, lemon extract sour cream and sugar; stir until well blended. Pour egg mixture into dry ingredients; stirring thoroughly. Fold in bananas, coconut and nuts. Pour batter into 2 lightly greased loaf pans. Bake at 350 degrees, for 45 to 50 minutes or until tested done. Yield 2 loaves.

FIG QUICK BREAD

1 cup dried figs
3½ cups all-purpose flour
¾ cup granulated sugar
½ teaspoon salt
4 teaspoons baking powder
3 tablespoons shortening
1 teaspoon orange peel, grated
1 large egg, beaten
1 cup milk

Pour boiling water over figs, cover and let stand 10 minutes. Drain; dry on paper towels. Cut into thin slices; set aside. In a mixing bowl, sift together, flour, sugar, salt and baking powder. Cut shortening into flour mixture with pastry blender or with a fork. Combine orange peel, egg and milk; add to dry ingredients; mix thoroughly. Pour batter into greased loaf pans. Bake at 350 degrees, for 1½ hours or until tested done. Yield 2 loaves or about 8 slices each loaf.

NUT QUICK BREAD

1 cup pecans, walnuts or
    hickory
nuts, chopped
2 cups all-purpose flour
3 teaspoons baking powder
½ teaspoon salt
½ cup brown sugar, packed
1 cup milk
1 large egg, beaten
2 tablespoons shortening, melted

Place chopped nuts in boiling water for 2 or 3 minutes; drain; set aside. In a medium mixing bowl, sift together, dry ingredients; set aside. In another bowl, combine together, milk, egg, shortening and nuts. Add to dry ingredients; mix well. Pour batter into greased loaf pan; bake at 350 degrees, for 1 hour or until lightly browned. Yield 1 loaf.

APPLE QUICK BREAD with topping

¾ cup shortening
1½ cups granulated sugar
3 large eggs
1 ½ teaspoons baking soda
3 tablespoons *sour milk
3 cups all-purpose flour
½ teaspoon salt
1½ teaspoons vanilla extract
3 cups apples, chopped

*SOUR MILK—Mix 1 teaspoon of vine gar OR lemon juice into 1 cup of milk. In a mixing bowl, cream together shortening and sugar. Add baking soda that has been dissolved in sour milk; mix well. Add flour, salt and vanilla; fold in apples. Pour batter into 2 greased and lightly floured loaf pans; set aside.

TOPPING

Combine 4 tablespoons brown sugar, 4 tablespoons all-purpose flour, 4 tablespoons butter and 1½ teaspoons cinnamon. Sprinkle topping evenly over top of batter. Bake at 325 degrees, for 1 hour or until tested done. Yield 2 loaves.

GLAZED PEACH QUICK BREAD

2 cups all-purpose flour
2/3 cup granulated sugar
2 teaspoons baking powder
½ teaspoon baking soda
½ teaspoon salt
½ teaspoon ground cloves
2 tablespoons butter OR
  margarine, melted
2 large eggs
1 can (16 ozs.) peaches,
  chopped & drain &
reserve juice
½ cup reserved peach juice

Preheat oven to 350 degrees; grease and flour 9x5 loaf pan. In a large mixing bowl, beat together all ingredients, for 2 minutes, at medium speed. Pour batter into loaf pan, bake for about 60 minutes or until tested done. Remove from pan; cool completely, then drizzle glaze evenly over bread.

GLAZE

½ cup powder sugar 3 to 4 teaspoons reserved peach juice In a small saucepan, combine powder sugar and juice; over medium heat, bring to a boil. Remove from heat and pour evenly over bread.

PUMPKIN QUICK BREAD (with eggs)

½ cup vegetable oil
2 large eggs, beaten
1/3 cup water
1 cup pumpkin. cooked
1½ cups granulated sugar
1¾ cups all-purpose flour
¾ teaspoon salt
1 teaspoon baking soda
½ teaspoon nutmeg
½ teaspoon ground cinnamon
¼ teaspoon ground cloves
½ cup raisins (optional)
½ cup nuts, chopped (optional)

In a medium mixing bowl, combine together, oil, eggs, water and pumpkin; blend well; set aside. Sift the remaining dry ingredients, then gradually add to oil mixing well after each addition. Fold in raisins and nuts, if desired. Pour batter into a greased and floured loaf pan. Bake at 350 degrees, for about 50 minutes, or until tested done. Yield 1 loaf.

FIG NEWTONS

(Fig Filling recipe below)
1 cup honey
1 cup shortening
1 cup granulated sugar
2 large eggs
Juice & peel of ½ lemon
6½ cups all-purpose flour
2 teaspoons baking powder
1 teaspoon baking soda
½ teaspoon salt

In a large mixing bowl. cream together, honey, shortening and sugar. Add eggs, one at a time, beating well after each addition. Add lemon juice and peel; set aside. In another bowl, combine flour, baking powder, baking soda and salt, by sifting together. Add flour mixture to honey mixture; mix until dough forms. Roll dough out thin on a lightly floured surface. Spread filling over half of dough; cover with remaining half of dough. Cut in oblong slices; bake at 400 degrees, for 12 to 15 minutes, or until tested done.

FIG FILLING

2 pounds dried figs, chopped
1 cup honey
¼ cup water

In a saucepan, place all ingredients; over medium heat, cook for 15 minutes, stirring constantly; cool slightly before placing on the dough.

LIME QUICK BREAD (with glaze)

½ lb. butter OR margarine,
  softened
2 cups granulated sugar
2 tablespoons lime peel, grated
3 cups all-purpose flour
2 teaspoons baking powder
1 teaspoon salt
4 large eggs
1 cup milk

In a medium bowl, cream together, butter, sugar and lime peel. In another bowl, combine together, by sifting flour baking powder and salt. Add to creamed mixture alternately with eggs mixed with eggs; mix well. Place batter in 2 greased loaf pans; prepare glaze, baste over the top; bake at 350 degrees, for 55 minutes, or until tested done.

GLAZE

½ cup granulated sugar
3 tablespoons lime juice
1 teaspoon lime peel, shredded

In a small bowl, combine together, all Glaze ingredients; blend well.

PERSIMMON QUICK BREAD

4 persimmons
½ cup brown sugar, packed
½ cup granulated sugar
2½ cups all-purpose flour
2½ teaspoons baking powder
1 teaspoon baking soda
1 teaspoon cinnamon
1 large egg
1/3 cup milk

4 tablespoons vegetable oil
1 cup walnuts (optional)

Cut tops off of persimmons; discard. Slice persimmon open; scoop out pulp. Discard stems and seeds. Puree' in blender; measure 1 cup puree', then add 1 teaspoon baking soda to puree'. In a bowl, combine together, sugars, flour, cinnamon and baking powder; set aside. Meanwhile, in a large bowl, combine together egg, milk, oil and persimmon puree'; mix well. Add flour mixture; blend thoroughly. Fold in nuts. Put batter into a greased loaf pan; bake at 350 degrees, for 75 minutes, or until tested done. Remove from oven; let cool 15 minutes before removing from loaf pan. Yield 1 loaf or 8 to 10 servings.

ZUCCHINI PANCAKES

1 medium-sized zucchini, grated
  & drained
1 large egg
1 tablespoon vegetable oil
1 cup pancake mix
¾ cup milk
2 tablespoons Parmesan
  Cheese, grated

In a medium mixing bowl, combine all ingredients; mix lightly. Let batter rest for 10 minutes. Add more milk for a thinner pancake. Cook on a lightly greased hot griddle. Yield 2 to 3 pancakes, depending on the size.

FRENCH TOAST

1 large egg, beaten
½ cup milk
2 tablespoons molasses
Dash salt (optional)
4 to 5 slices bread

In a medium bowl, combine beaten egg, milk, molasses and salt; mix well. Dip each slice of bread in mixture. Fry in a little shortening, on both sides, until golden brown. If desired, serve with butter and syrup.

PARSNIP FRITTERS

2 large eggs
2 cups parsnips, cooked & mashed
½ teaspoon salt
1 tablespoon butter OR margarine, melted
¾ cup milk
2 tablespoons all-purpose flour
Vegetable oil for frying

In a medium mixing bowl, beat eggs until light and fluffy. Add mashed parsnips, beat until well-mixed. Stir in salt, butter, milk and flour; mix thoroughly. Fry in a small amount of oil, turning to brown both sides. Yield about 6 to 8 servings.

BELGIAN WAFFLES

2 large eggs
1 cup milk
2-1/3 cups Bisquick Baking Mix
2 tablespoons granulated sugar
¼ cup vegetable oil
1 cup whipped cream
¼ cup powder sugar
2 cups strawberries, sliced OR
    1 pkg frozen strawberries, thawed & drained
Powder Sugar

In a medium mixing bowl, beat eggs for 5 minutes or until thickened. Stir in milk, Bisquick, sugar and oil; mix thoroughly. Bake in waffle iron. Meanwhile, in another bowl, beat whipped cream and powder sugar until stiff; fold in strawberries. Put in between waffles. Yield 6 servings.

ZUCCHINI SQUARES

4 cups zucchini, thinly sliced
1 cup Bisquick Baking Mix
½ cup onion, chopped
½ cup Parmesan cheese, grated
2 tablespoons parsley, chopped
½ teaspoon oregano
½ teaspoon garlic powder
½ teaspoon salt
½ cup vegetable oil
4 large eggs, slightly beaten

Preheat oven to 350 degrees. Grease a 9x13x2 inch baking pan. Mix all ingredients thoroughly. Spread evenly in pan; bake 30 to 45 minutes or until golden brown. Cut in squares, as desired. Yield about 16 squares.

BUTTERMILK BISCUITS

2 cups all-purpose flour
1 teaspoon salt
½ teaspoon baking soda
7 tablespoons butter, divided
1 cup buttermilk

Sift together, flour salt and baking soda into a medium mixing bowl. Add 4 table spoons butter, work into flour mixture by hand until well-blended. Add buttermilk; mix until dough forms. On a floured surface. roll dough to ½-inch thickness. Cut into 2-inch round cookie cutter; place on a greased cookie sheet, touching one another. Melt remaining butter and brush over biscuits; bake at 425 degrees F., for 10 to 15 minutes. Yield about 12 biscuits.

AVOCADO QUICK BREAD

1 large egg
½ cup avocado, mashed (1
   small)
½ cup buttermilk
½ cup vegetable oil
2 cups all-purpose flour
¾ cup granulated sugar
½ teaspoon baking soda
½ teaspoon baking powder
¼ teaspoon salt
¾ cup pecans, chopped
Butter at room temperature

Preheat oven at 350 degrees. Grease a 9x5 inch loaf pan;

set aside. In a blender or food processor, combine egg, avocado, buttermilk and oil, mix until well-blended. Then add flour, sugar, baking soda, baking powder, and salt; mix only until blended; do not over mix. Fold in nuts. Pour into loaf pan; bake for 55 to 60 minutes, or until tested done. Remove from oven; let cool for 10 minutes. Yield 1 loaf or about 8 slices.

NOTE: You can make Avocado Muffins with this recipe, by putting batter into greased muffin pan, fill ½ full. Bake in preheated oven for 25 to 30 minutes. Yield 12 muffi8n.

JALAPENO BREAD

1 pkg. active dry yeast
1 tablespoon granulated sugar
1 teaspoon salt
2 cups warm water
5¾ cups all-purpose flour
¼ cup *jalapeno peppers,
   chopped
¼ cup butter OR margarine,
   melted

In a large bowl, dissolve yeast, sugar and salt in the warm water. Add flour, peppers and butter; mix until dough forms. Knead dough for 5 minutes, put dough in large bowl; cover. Let rise in warm place for 1 hour.

Divide dough into 4 portions; place shaped loaf on lightly greased cookie sheets, about 3 inches apart. Let rise 30 minutes or until double in size. Bake at 350 degrees, for about 25 to 30 minutes or until lightly browned. Yield 4 loaves.

*NOTE: Caution wear gloves when chopping jalapeno peppers; avoid eye contact.

FLAVORED BUTTERS

Flavored butters make foods more tasty and they are easy to make. They will keep for 2 to 3 weeks, in the refrigerator, in a container with a lid. Most flavored butters can be frozen for up to two months. Margarine can be substituted for butter.

For example, lemon flavored butter is great on seafood, poultry, green vegetables and white potatoes. If you like butter with some zing to it, then there is Chili Butter, which you can use on toasty French bread, corn or popcorn. The Horseradish Butter is good to serve with roast beef or corned beef sandwiches.

Mustard Butter would be great when serving ham, roast beef sandwiches or spinach, and the Honey Orange Butter is nice when serving sweet potatoes or yams, acorn squash, carrots or raisin bread.

Following there are many flavored butters to choose from and for you to enjoy. Also at the holidays flavored butters put in a pretty container, along with a quick bread would make a great homemade food gift for a shut-in.

CHOCOLATE HONEY BUTTER

½ cup butter OR margarine, softened
2 tablespoons chocolate-flavored syrup
2 tablespoons honey

In small bowl, combine above ingredients; beat at highest speed with electric mixer until light and fluffy. Yield 1 cup.

COFFEE BUTTER

2 teaspoons instant coffee
½ teaspoon water
½ cup butter OR margarine, softened
2 tablespoons maple syrup

Dissolve instant coffee in water; set aside. Cream butter in small bowl until soft and fluffy. Combine maple syrup and coffee; gradually add to butter, blending thoroughly. Use as a spread for toast, pancakes, or as you desire. Yield about 2/3 cup.

RASPBERRY BUTTER

2 cups (4 sticks) butter, softened
1½ cups raspberry syrup
½ teaspoon ground nutmeg

Combine together, in a medium bowl the above ingredients; mix well. Store in refrigerator until ready to use. Will keep up to 3 weeks. Yield about 2 cups.

CRANBERRY BUTTER

2 cups cranberries, fresh OR frozen
1 cup granulated sugar
½ cup water
¼ cup brown sugar, packed
¼ cup butter

Combine cranberries, sugar and water in saucepan. Heat to boiling stirring until sugar dissolves and berries pop, about 5 minutes. Add brown sugar and butter; heat just until butter and brown sugar are dissolved. Serve hot. Yield about 2½ cups.

HONEY-ORANGE BUTTER

½ cup butter OR margarine, softened
2 tablespoons honey
1½ teaspoons orange peel, grated
½ teaspoon orange juice
¼ teaspoon ground cardamom

In a small bowl combine above ingredients together; mix until well-blended Store in covered container in refrigerator until ready to use. Yield about ½ cup.

LEMON BUTTER

½ cup butter OR margarine, softened
1 tablespoon lemon juice
¼ teaspoon lemon peel, grated

In a small bowl combine above ingredients together; mix until well-blended. Store in covered container in refrigerator until ready to use. Yield about ½ cup.

CHILI BUTTER

½ cup butter OR margarine, softened
1 teaspoon chili powder
¼ teaspoon garlic salt
Pinch ground cumin

In a small bowl combine above ingredients together; mix until well-blended. Store in covered container in refrigerator until ready to use. Yield about ½ cup.

HORSERADISH BUTTER

½ cup butter OR margarine, softened
3 tablespoons prepared horseradish
1 teaspoon lemon juice

In a small bowl combine above ingredients together; mix until well-blended. Store in covered container in refrigerator until ready to use.
Yield about ½ cup.

CHIVE BUTTER

½ cup butter
¼ cup chives, chopped
4 drops Worcestershire Sauce

In a small bowl combine above ingredients together; mix until well-blended. Store in covered container in refrigerator until ready to use. Yield about ½ cup.

MUSTARD BUTTER

½ cup butter OR margarine, softened
2 tablespoons prepared Dijon mustard

In a small bowl combine above ingredients together; mix until well-blended. Store in covered container in refrigerator until ready to use. Yield about ½ cup.

PARSLEY BUTTER

½ cup butter OR margarine, softened
3 tablespoons fresh parsley, finely minced
Dash Tabasco Sauce
1 teaspoon lemon juice

In a small bowl combine above ingredients together; mix until well-blended. Store in covered container in refrigerator until ready to use. Yield about ½ cup.

HONEY PECAN BUTTER

½ cup butter, softened
¼ cup honey
1/3 cup pecans, finely chopped

In a small bowl, beat butter and honey until mixed; add pecans; mix. thoroughly. Yield about 1 cup. Keep refrigerated

ROQUEFORT CHEESE BUTTER

Combine together in a small bowl, ½ cup butter, softened with ½ cup Roquefort cheese, crumbled, and 1 teaspoon Worcestershire.

Blend ingredients thoroughly; refrigerate until ready to use. Allow butter to soften slightly before using. Yield 1 cup. Use on baked potato or French bread, or as you choose.

STEAK BUTTER

½ cup butter OR margarine,
   softened
½ teaspoon dry mustard
½ teaspoon dried dill weed
2 cups sharp Cheddar cheese,
   shredded
½ cup green onions, sliced

Combine butter, mustard and
dill weed, in a small bowl, using
an electric mixer, at medium
speed, beat ingredients until
light and fluffy. Reduce speed
to low; add cheese and onions,
beating until well blended.
Put in covered container and
refrigerate at least 2 hours before
serving. Keep in refrigerator up
to 2 weeks. Yield about 2 cups.

BRANDY BUTTER

½ cup butter OR margarine,
   softened
¾ cup powdered sugar
1 lemon, juice and rind, grated
3 to 4 tablespoons brandy

In a small mixing bowl, beat
butter until light and fluffy.
Gradually add sugar a little
at a time, beating well after
each addition. Add lemon
juice, rind and brandy; mix
well. Refrigerate in covered
container until ready to serve.
Use on your favorite breads.
Refrigerate any leftover butter.
Yield 6 servings

RUM BUTTER

½ cup butter OR margarine,
   softened
¾ cup powdered sugar
1 orange, juice and rind, grated
3 to 4 tablespoons rum

In a small mixing bowl, beat
butter until light and fluffy.
Gradually add sugar a little
at a time, beating well after
each addition. Add lemon
juice, rind and brandy; mix
well. Refrigerate in covered
container until ready serve.
Use on your favorite breads.
Refrigerate any leftover butter.
Yield 6 servings.

ORANGE BUTTER

In a small mixing bowl, beat
together, ½ cup butter and ¼
cup powder sugar, until light
and fluffy. Add 2 tablespoons
frozen orange concentrate
juice, that has been thawed;
mix until well-blended. Yield 2/3
cup butter.

ITALIAN BUTTER

½ cup butter, softened
2 teaspoons dried *oregano, crushed
2 cloves **garlic, minced
¼ teaspoon pepper

Place ½ cup butter, softened, in a small bowl along with the above ingredients. Cream together until well-blended. Place in covered container; refrigerate. Use within a few days or freeze. Use with seafood, steak, chicken, pasta, steamed vegetables or heated Italian bread. Yield ½ cup. *You can substitute 2 tablespoons fresh oregano for dried.

** You can substitute ¼ to 1/2 teaspoon garlic powder.

TARRAGON BUTTER

1 ½ teaspoons dried tarragon leaves,

In a small mixing bowl, place ½ cup butter, softened, cream with crushed tarragon leaves until well-blended. Store in a covered container; refrigerate. Use within a few days or freeze until ready to use. Delicious on seafood, chicken, green beans, baked potatoes or rice.

GARLIC BUTTER

½ cup butter, softened
¼ cup Parmesan Cheese, grated
¼ teaspoon garlic powder

Pinch of basil leaves, crushed (optional) In a small bowl, combine together, all ingredients; mix well. Yield ½ cup.

MAPLE BUTTER

1 stick unsalted butter, softened
½ cup *maple syrup

Whip butter in a food processor or with electric mixer, until soft and smooth. Drizzle syrup into butter; mix well. Store in a covered container, in the refrigerator. *You can substitute honey, if desired.

GRAHAM CRACKERS

2 cups whole wheat flour
1 cup all-purpose flour
1 teaspoon baking powder
½ teaspoon baking soda
¼ teaspoon salt
½ cup shortening
¾ cup light brown sugar
1 teaspoon vanilla extract
¼ cup milk

In a large mixing bowl, combine together, flours, baking powder, baking soda and salt; set aside. In another bowl, cream shortening with sugar until fluffy; add vanilla, mix well. Add flour mixture alternately with milk, mixing thoroughly after each addition. Chill dough for several hours, or overnight. Divide dough into thirds; roll out each portion on floured surface to rectangle, 1/8 inch thick. Trim dough to 5x15-inch rectangle; then cut into six 2½x5-inch rectangle. Make a line down center of dough with back edge of knife. Place on greased baking sheet; Prick each square with a fork. Bake at 350 degrees 10 to 12 minutes. Remove from baking sheets immediately.

BASIC CREPES

3 large eggs
¾ cup all-purpose flour
¼ teaspoon salt
1 cup milk, divided
2 tablespoons butter OR
    margarine, melted

In a medium-sized bowl, combine together, eggs, flour, salt and ¼ cup milk beat until smooth. Add melted butter and remaining milk; mix well. Refrigerate, covered, at least 1 hour. In a skillet, place a little butter or margarine, when heated, drop about ¼ cup batter, spread evenly. Cook until brown on both sides. Serve with fruit, jam or as desired.

PUMPKIN WAFFLES'

2 cups all-purpose flour
2 tablespoons baking powder
¼ teaspoons cinnamon
¼ teaspoon ginger
¼ teaspoon nutmeg
½ teaspoon salt
3 large eggs
1¾ cups milk
¾ cup pumpkin
½ cup vegetable oil
½ cup nuts, chopped (optional)

In a medium mixing bowl, combine dry ingredients; add eggs, milk, oil and pumpkin; stir in nuts. Bake in hot waffle iron. Yield 4 servings.

PIZZA

1¼ cups warm water (105 to 115 degrees)
1 envelope active dry yeast
1 teaspoon granulated sugar
1 tablespoon vegetable oil
½ teaspoon salt
2½ cups all-purpose flour
2 teaspoons cornmeal
1 cup pizza sauce

Assorted toppings, such as pepperoni, sausage, peppers and mushrooms, 2 cups mozzarella cheese, shredded. In a large bowl, place ¼ cup warm water; sprinkle yeast over water; stir in sugar; let stand for 5 minutes. Add remaining water, oil and salt. Mix in flour until dough pulls away from side of bowl. Turn dough onto a lightly floured surface; knead until smooth, about 10 minutes. Coat large mixing bowl, with cooking spray; place dough in bowl, turn to grease top. Cover loosely with plastic wrap; let rise in warm place until almost double in size, about 1 hour. Preheat oven to 450 degrees; punch down dough. Coat two 12" pizza pans with cooking spray; sprinkle pans with cornmeal. Divide dough in half; roll dough to fit pans; press dough against edge to form rim. Bake crust for 10 minutes. Remove crust from oven; top with pizza sauce. Add the toppings; sprinkle with cheese. Bake until cheese is melted, about 15 to 20 minutes longer. Yield 12 to 16 servings.

POTATO CHIP DONUTS

3½ cups all-purpose flour
4 teaspoons baking powder
½ teaspoon salt
2 tablespoons butter OR margarine
¾ cup granulated sugar
2 large eggs
¼ teaspoon nutmeg
¾ cup light cream
¾ cups potato chips, crushed

In a medium mixing bowl, sift together, flour, baking powder and salt. In another bowl, cream butter and sugar until light and fluffy. Add eggs, 1 at a time, beating well after each addition; add nutmeg; mix well. Add flour mixture alternately with cream; mix thoroughly. Fold in potato chips, then chill dough for ½ hour. On a lightly floured surface, roll dough out to about ¼ inch thick. Cut dough with a 2½ donut cutter, dough will be soft. Allow donuts to rest for 15 minutes before frying. (By doing this, donuts will absorb less grease when frying). Fry in 2" or more of vegetable oil, at 375 degrees, for 1½ minutes on each side. Drain on paper towels; if desired, roll cooled donuts in powder sugar. Yield about 3 dozen donuts.

CORN PANCAKES

2 cups fresh, frozen or canned corn, drained
¼ cup onions, finely chopped
1 cup cornmeal
½ cup all-purpose flour
1 teaspoon baking powder
½ teaspoon salt
4 large eggs
1 cup buttermilk
4 tablespoons butter OR margarine

Place corn in blender or food processor, to break up kernels coarsely. Place corn in a mixing bowl; add onion, cornmeal, flour, baking powder and salt; mix well. Add eggs and buttermilk; mix thoroughly. In a large skillet, melt butter. Place large spoonful of batter into hot skillet; cook until bubbles form, then flip pancake over; continue to cook for about 2 minutes or until golden brown. Yield 14 to 16 pancakes.

PECAN ROLLS

1 pkg. active dry yeast
¼ cup warm water
¼ cup shortening
¼ cup granulated
1 large egg
½ teaspoon salt
½ cup scalded milk
2 tablespoons orange juice
3¼ cups all-purpose flour
2/3 cup pineapple OR apricot jam

¼ cup butter OR margarine, melted

In a large mixing bowl, combine together, yeast and water. Add shortening, sugar, egg, salt and milk; blend well. Add juice and 2 cups of the flour; mix thoroughly. Add remaining flour; knead for 10 minutes; set aside, cover and let rise until double, about45 minutes. Punch down and let rest 10 minutes. Roll dough into 10x18-inch rectangle. Brush with melted butter; an d place on top of glaze (recipe follows next page).

GLAZE:

¼ cup butter OR margarine
1 cup brown sugar, packed
1 tablespoon water
1 teaspoon orange extract
1 cup pecans, chopped fine

In a skillet, place first 4 ingredients; heat slowly to boiling. Then boil gently for 1 minute, without stirring Remove. glaze from heat and put into a 8x8x2-inch baking pan. Spread nuts evenly over glaze. Put slices side by side over nuts and glaze. Bake at 375 degrees, for 335 to 40 minutes, or until tested done. Remove from oven and let cool slightly, then remove with spatula. Flip rolls onto plate so glaze and nuts are on top. Yield 10 to 12 rolls.

PITA OR POCKET BREAD

Begin 3 hours ahead
3½ cups all-purpose flour
1 teaspoon salt
1 pkg. active dry yeast
¼ teaspoon granulated sugar
1-1/3 cups water
1 tablespoon vegetable oil
Cornmeal

In a large bowl, combine together, 1½ cups flour, salt, yeast and sugar. In a. 1-quart saucepan, place water and oil; ¼ cup pecans OR walnuts, chopped Cook over medium heat until very warm (about 120 to 130 degrees), but do not boil. Remove from heat, then with electric mixer, on low speed, beat oil mixture into dry ingredients, only long enough for ingredients are mixed. Increase speed to medium, beat 2 more minutes, occasionally scraping bowl. Stir in enough additional flour (about 2 cups) to make a soft dough. On a floured surface, knead dough until smooth and elastic, about 5 minutes, adding more flour as needed, careful to keep dough soft. Shape into a ball; place in a greased bowl, turning over to grease top. Cover, let dough rise in warm place, until doubled, about 1 hour.

Punch down dough, then turn onto a lightly floured surface. Cut dough into 6 pieces, cover and let rise for 30 minutes Meanwhile, lightly sprinkle 3 ungreased cookie sheets with cornmeal. On a lightly floured surface, roll each piece of dough into a 7-inch circle. Place 2 circles on each cookie sheet. cover with towel, let rise in warm place, for about 45 minutes, or until doubled in height. Preheat oven to 475 degrees. Bake 8 to 10 minutes, or until pitas are puffed up. and golden brown. Serve pitas immediately with tour favorite filling. To serve later—Cool 5 minutes, then place warm bread in plastic bags to keep moist and pliable. TO REHEAT PITAS—Preheat oven to 375 degrees. Wrap pitas in foil; heat for 10 minutes or until hot. Yield 6 pitas.

SWEET POTATO MUFFINS

2/3 cup sweet potatoes,
    canned or fresh,
cooked & well drained
4 tablespoons butter OR
    margarine
½ cup granulated sugar
1 large egg
¾ cup all-purpose flour
2 teaspoons baking powder
½ teaspoon salt
½ teaspoon cinnamon
¼ teaspoon nutmeg
½ cup milk
½ cup raisins

Preheat oven to 400 degrees;
grease muffin pans. In a
blender or food processor,
puree' sweet potatoes. In a
medium mixing bowl, cream
together, butter and sugar.
Add egg along with pureed
sweet potatoes; mix thoroughly;
set aside. In another bowl,
sift together, flour, baking
powder, salt, cinnamon and
nutmeg. Add dry ingredients
alternately with milk; mix well.
Fold in nuts and raisins, mix just
until blended. Do not over mix.
Spoon into muffin pan, ¾ full.
Bake for 25 minutes, or until
tested done. Yield about 2½
dozen muffins.

CINNAMON ROLLS (made with cake mix)

2 tablespoons active dry yeast
2½ cups warm water
1 pkg. yellow cake mix
4½ cups all-purpose flour
Butter OR margarine, melted
Cinnamon
Granulated sugar

Dissolve yeast in warm water. In
a large mixing bowl, combine
together, cake mix and flour,
then add yeast in water; mix
thoroughly; set aside and let
rise until double. Turn out on a
lightly floured surface; roll to ½
inch thick. Brush with melted
butter; sprinkle with cinnamon
and sugar. Roll dough up; cut
into 3/4-inch slices; set aside.
Let raise until doubled, about 1
hour. Pour on greased cookie
sheet; bake at 400 degrees, for
about 15 to 18 minutes, or until
tested done.

PEACH MUFFINS

4 cups all-purpose flour
2/3 cup brown sugar, packed
2 tablespoons baking powder
½ teaspoons baking soda
¼ teaspoon allspice
½ teaspoon salt
2 large eggs
2 cups sour cream
½ cup vegetable oil
1 cup peaches, chopped

In a large mixing bowl, combine together, flour, sugar, baking powder, salt, soda and allspice; mix well. In another bowl, combine eggs, sour cream and oil; mix thoroughly. Mix in peaches. Add egg mixture to flour mixture; mix just until ingredients are moisten. Batter will be lumpy; spoon batter into greased muffin pans. Bake at 400 degrees, for 20 to 25 minutes, or until tested done. Yield about 2 dozen muffins.

BASIC FRITTER BATTER

2 cups all-purpose flour
1½ teaspoons baking powder
½ teaspoon salt
2 large eggs
1/3 cup milk

Sift together, flour, baking powder and salt; set aside. In a bowl, beat eggs with milk, then stir into flour mixture; beat until smooth and well-blended. Yield 1 cup batter.

PUMPKIN BISCUITS

2 cups all-purpose flour
1/3 cup nonfat dry milk
¼ cup granulated sugar
2 teaspoons baking powder
¾ teaspoon pumpkin pie spice
¼ teaspoon salt
½ cup shortening
¾ cup prepared pumpkin
1 tablespoon water

In a medium bowl, combine together, by sifting, the first 6 ingredients. Cut in shortening, with a pastry blender, or a fork. Blend in pumpkin and water just until all ingredients are moistened. Knead 15 to 20 minutes on a lightly floured surface. Using a 3" cookie cutter, cut about 9 biscuits. Place biscuits on a ungreased cookie sheet 2" apart. Bake at 400 degrees, for 12 to 15 minutes or until golden brown. Yield about 9 biscuits.

CRISP CRACKER BREAD

¼ ounce package active dry
   yeast
1 cup warm water (105 to 115
   degrees)
2 teaspoons granulated sugar
1 teaspoon salt
3 tablespoons butter OR
   margarine
2½ to 3 cups all-purpose flour
1 large egg, slightly beaten
Salt and pepper to taste
Sesame seeds

Preheat oven at 400 degrees.
In a large mixing bowl, dissolve
yeast in warm water. add
sugar, 1 teaspoon salt and
butter. Gradually add flour, 1
cup at a time, using enough
flour to make dough easy to
handle. Turn dough on to a
lightly floured surface; knead
until smooth (5 minutes). Divide
dough into 4 equal parts,
shape in to balls; let rest 10
minutes. Then roll each ball
into a 12-inch circle. Place on
greased cookie sheets. Brush
with beaten egg, sprinkle with
salt and pepper OR sesame
seeds. Bake for 10 to 15 minutes
or until lightly browned. Cool
completely. To serve, break into
pieces. Yield 4 cracker breads.

PUMPKIN FRITTERS

3 large eggs, separated
½ teaspoon salt
Dash of pepper
2 tablespoons all-purpose flour
1cup pumpkin, cooked and
   mashed
Oil; for frying

In a medium mixing bowl, beat
egg yolks, together with salt,
pepper, flour and pumpkin;
set aside. In another mixing
bowl, beat egg whites until stiff.
Fold egg whites into egg yolk
mixture. Drop by tablespoons
into skillet, with hot oil, about
1-inch high. Fry until lightly
browned; turn and fry other
side. Drain on paper towels.
Serve immediately.

TACO PIZZA (with beer crust)

1 tablespoon cornmeal
1 to 1½ cups all-purpose flour
1 cup whole wheat flour
1 can (8 ozs.) tomato sauce
2 teaspoons baking powder
½ teaspoon salt
¾ cup *beer, room temperature
¼ cup vegetable oil

In a large bowl, combine 1/3
cup of all-purpose flour, whole
wheat flour, baking powder,
salt, beer and oil; mix well.
Stir in ¼ to ½ cup all-purpose
flour to form a stiff dough. On
floured surface, roll dough to

14-inch circle. Grease pizza pan, sprinkle with 1 tablespoon cornmeal. Place dough in pan and press dough to fit pan.

NO FUSS DINNER ROLLS

1 pkg. active dry yeast
1½ cups warm milk (about 110 degrees
1 large egg
2 tablespoons butter OR margarine, softened
2 tablespoons granulated sugar
½ teaspoon salt
4 cups all-purpose flour
Butter OR margarine, melted

In a mixing bowl, dissolve yeast in warm milk; add egg, butter, sugar, salt and 2 cups flour. Beat on low speed of electric mixer, for 30 seconds, then beat on high for 3 minutes. Stir in remaining flour, (batter will be thick). Do not knead. Cover; let rest for 15 minutes. Then fill greased muffin pans ¾ full, then again, let rise in warm place until double, about 30 minutes. Bake at 400 degrees, for 12 to 15 minutes or until golden brown. Remove from oven; brush with melted butter. Cool for 1 minute before removing from pan. Yield about 15 rolls.

WHOLE WHEAT BREAD

2 pkgs. active dry yeast
¼ cup warm water (105 to 115 degrees)
½ cup brown sugar, packed
2 teaspoons salt
2½ cups hot water
¼ cup butter OR margarine
4½ cups whole wheat flour
2¾ to 3¾ cups bread flour

Grease 2 loaf pans; set aside. In a small bowl, dissolve yeast in ¼ cup warm water; set aside. In a large bowl, combine together, brown sugar, salt, hot water and margarine; cool slightly. Then add 3 cups whole wheat flour, mix at low speed of electric mixer until moistened; beat 3 minutes at medium speed. Add remaining whole wheat flour and dissolved yeast; mix well. Add 2¾ cups bread flour, mix until dough pulls cleanly away from sides of bowl. On a floured surface, knead ½ to 1 cup bread flour until dough is smooth and elastic, about 10 minutes to 15 minutes. Place dough in a greased bowl, cover loosely with plastic wrap and clean towel. Let rise in warm place (70 to 75 degrees) until doubled in size, about 1 hour. Punch down dough several times to remove all air bubbles. Divide dough in half; shape; all to rest, covered, for 10 minutes. Shape into

2 loaves; place into prepared pans; cover. Let rise in warm place, until doubled in size, about 30 to 45 minutes. Bake at 375 degrees for 30 minutes; reduce heat to 350 degrees. Continue baking additional 10 to 15 minutes, or until loaves sound hollow when lightly tapped. Remove from pans immediately. Yield 2 loaves.

RYE BREAD

2 pkgs. active dry yeast
1 cup warm water
1 cup warm milk
½ cup molasses
¼ cup shortening, melted
1 teaspoon salt
3 to 3½ cups bread flour
3 cups medium rye flour
1 tablespoon water
1 egg yolk

Grease 2 cookie sheets. In a small bowl, dissolve yeast in warm water, (105 to 115 degrees); set aside. In a large mixing bowl, combine together, warm milk, molasses, shortening and salt; blend well. Add dissolved yeast; add 2 cups bread flour, mix well on low speed of electric mixer, until moistened. Then beat at medium speed, for 3 minutes. Add 3 cups of rye flour and an additional ¾ to 1 cup bread flour, mix until dough pulls cleanly away from sides of bowl. On a lightly floured surface knead into dough ¼ to ½ cup bread flour until dough is smooth and elastic, about 10 minutes.

Place dough in a greased bowl, cover loosely with plastic wrap and clean towel. Let rise in warm place (70 to 75 degrees) until doubled in size, about 1 hour. Punch down dough several times to remove all air bubbles. Divide dough in half; allow to rest covered for 15 minutes. Shape dough into 2-12 inch oblong loaves. Place on cookie sheets; with a sharp knife make 4-¼ inch deep diagonal slashes, on the top of each loaf. Cover; let rise in warm place until doubled in size, for about 35 to 45 minutes. Preheat oven to 350 degrees, meanwhile combine 1 tablespoon water and 1 egg yolk. Brush mixture on each loaf; bake for 35 to 45 minutes, or until tested done. Remove from oven and immediately remove from cookie sheets; cool on rack.

PUMPERNICKEL BREAD

2¾ cups rye flour
3 pkgs. active dry yeast
1 to 2 tablespoons caraway
   seeds
1½ cups water
½ cup dark molasses
2 tablespoons shortening
1 teaspoon salt
2 to 2½ cups all-purpose flour
1 to 2 tablespoons cornmeal

In a large mixing bowl, combine together, rye flour, yeast and caraway seeds. In a saucepan, over medium heat, cook water, molasses, shortening and sauce just until mixture is warm; stir occasionally to melt shortening. Add to dry ingredients; beat at low speed of electric mixer. for ½ minute; scrape sides of bowl. Then beat, at high speed for 3 minutes. By hand stir in enough flour to make a stiff dough. Turn out on a lightly floured surface; knead until smooth. Place in a greased bowl; turn once to grease surface; cover. Let rise until double in size; about 1½ hours. Punch down, then divide dough in half; cover and let rest for 10 minutes. Round each half dough into a smooth ball. Place on cookie sheet, sprinkled with cornmeal; cover. Let rise until doubled, for about 30 minutes. Bake at 375 degrees, for 30 to 35 minutes, or until well-browned. For a chewy crust, brush tops of loaves with warm water several times during baking and only after the first 2o minutes. Yield 2 loaves.

WHITE BREAD

4 cups boiling water
¼ cup shortening
¼ cup granulated sugar
2 teaspoon salt
13 cups all-purpose flour
2 pkgs. active dry yeast
½ cup warm water

In a large mixing bowl, pour boiling water over shortening, sugar and salt; mix well. Cool to lukewarm; stir in 2 cups flour; set aside. Add yeast to ½ cup warm water to dissolve. Then add to shortening mixture; add 4 cups of flour; mix well. Add 7 more cups of flour; mix thoroughly. Turn out on a lightly floured surface; knead 8 to 10 minutes, or until smooth and elastic. If necessary, add more flour. Place in a greased bowl; let rise until doubled, in a warm place, for about 2 hours. Punch down, let rise again about 1 hour. Divide dough into 4 loaves. Roll out each piece with rolling pin, then roll toward you like a jelly roll; seal end of loaf by pressing firmly on each end and tucking under. Place in greased loaf pans; let rise until double, about 1½ hours, bake at 375 degrees, for 45 minutes. Yield 4 loaves.

ITALIAN BREAD

16 cups all-purpose flour, sifted
1 tablespoon salt
¼ cup shortening
1 ounce active cake yeast
5 cups lukewarm water
Butter OR margarine

In a large mixing bowl, combine flour and salt; cut in shortening; mix thoroughly. Dissolve yeast in 1 cup lukewarm water; add to flour mixture. Gradually add remaining 4 cups water; mix well. Turn out onto a lightly floured surface; knead until smooth and elastic, for 10 to 15 minutes. Let stand 10 minutes, uncovered. In a large, greased bowl; place dough, grease top, cover and let rise until doubled, in a warm place. Then turn out on a floured surface; knead lightly, then shape into 5 loaves. Place in greased loaf pan. Let rise again, covered. Bake at 400 degrees, for 45 minutes, or until tested done. Remove from oven; turn on rack; brush top with butter. Yield 5 loaves.

CARROT PANCAKES(with cream cheese spread)

1¼ cups all-purpose flour
2 tablespoons pecan, finely chopped
2 teaspoons baking powder
1 teaspoon cinnamon
¼ teaspoon salt
¼ teaspoon ginger
1 large egg, slightly beaten
1/3 cup brown sugar, pavked
1 cup milk
1 cup carrots, grated
1 teaspoon vanilla extract

CREAM CHEESE SPREAD

4 ounces cream cheese, softened
¼ cup powder sugar
2 tablespoons milk
½ teaspoon vanilla extract
Dash of cinnamon (optional)

In a medium-size bowl, combine together, the first 6 ingredients; set aside. In another bowl, combine together, egg, brown sugar, milk, carrots and vanilla, mix well. Then stir egg mixture into the dry mixture, mix only just until moistened. Pour ¼ cup of batter onto a hot greased skillet. Turn pancake when bubbles form on top, turn over, cook until golden brown. In the meanwhile, prepare Spread, by combining ingredients; mixing thoroughly, until smooth and creamy, if desired, sprinkle with cinnamon. Serve with pancakes. Yield 4 servings.

BAGELS (MINI-SIZE)

1½ cups all-purpose flour
2 pkgs. active dry yeast
1½ cups warm water (115
    degrees)
3 tablespoons granulated sugar
1 tablespoon salt
2¾ to 3 cups all-purpose flour

In a large bowl, combine together, the flour with dry yeast; set aside. In a small bowl, combine warm water, sugar and salt; add to flour mixture. Beat at low speed of electric mixer, for ½ minute, scraping sides of bowl. Then beat at high speed for 3 minutes. By hand, stir in as much of 2¼ to 3 cups of flour, to make a moderate stiff dough. On a lightly floured surface, knead dough until smooth and elastic, for 8 to 10 minutes. Cover dough; let rest 15 minutes. Then shape Mini-Bagels by dividing dough in thirds; cut each third into 16 parts. Shape each part into a small ball, carefully poke thumb through the center; let rest again, for 20 minutes. Meanwhile bring 1 gallon of water to boil; add 1 tablespoon sugar to water. As the water boils, add about 6 bagels into the water; boil for 1 minutes; turn over once; repeat with remaining bagels. Before baking, brush tops with 1 egg yolk & 1 tablespoon water, combined together. Bake at 400 degrees for 20 minutes or until browned. Yield about 4 dozen mini-bagels.

BANANA BREAD STICKS

¼ cup brown sugar, packed
½ cup vegetable oil
2 large eggs
1 cup banana, mashed
1¾ cups whole wheat flour
2 teaspoons baking powder
½ teaspoon baking soda

In a medium mixing bowl, combine together, all ingredients; mix only until smooth. Pour into greased loaf pan. Bake at 350 degrees, for about 1 hour, or until tested done. Cool, then remove from pan; cut into sticks. Spread evenly on a cookie sheet; bake at 150 degrees, for 1 hour or longer until sticks are hard and crunchy. When cool, store in tightly covered container.

RAISIN BREAD

1 cup milk
4 tablespoons shortening
4 tablespoons granulated sugar
1 teaspoon salt
1 pkg. active dry yeast
¼ cup warm water
3½ to 4 cups all-purpose flour
1 cup seedless raisins

Scald milk; in a large mixing bowl, pour over shortening, sugar and salt; mix well. Cool to lukewarm; set aside. Dissolve yeast in warm water, then add to shortening mixture; gradually add flour, then add raisins. mix thoroughly. Turn dough onto floured surface; knead until smooth and elastic. If necessary, work in more flour. Place dough in a greased bowl; cover; let rise until double in bulk. Turn onto a floured surface, roll smooth, then punch down ends and fold under. Place in a greased loaf pan; cover; let rise until doubled, about 1 hour. Bake at 350 degrees, for 50 minutes. Remove from pan and cool on rack.

JERUSALEM ARTICHOKES PANCAKES

1 medium carrot, peeled & grated
1 shallot, peeled & minced
1 teaspoon fresh parsley, minced
Dash of Tabasco (optional)
2 tablespoons all-purpose flour
2 large eggs
½ teaspoon salt
Pinch of pepper (optional)
½ pound Jerusalem artichokes
    (sunchokes), scrubbed well
6 tablespoons vegetable oil,
    divided

In a bowl, combine together, all ingredients, except artichokes; mix well. Just before you are ready to cook, grate artichokes; add to carrot mixture; mix thoroughly. Measure 2 tablespoons of oil in a large skillet. Cook over medium heat; place mound of batter in skillet, flattening slightly. Fry for 3 to 4 minutes on each side, until pancakes are crisp & brown, but soft inside. Keep warm; serve immediately. Yield 12 pancakes or 4 to 6 servings.

TOMATO PANCAKES

Combine 2 cups tomatoes, cooked and mashed, with 1 cup hot water, 1 teaspoon baking soda, salt and pepper to taste. Stir in enough all-purpose flour to make a soft batter. In a large skillet, with a little shortening, put about ½ cup of batter in a hot skillet. Fry each side 2 or 3 minutes, or until pancakes are crisp and browned. Repeat with remaining batter. Serve immediately.

ZUCCHINI WAFFLES

3 cups zucchini, grated
2 large eggs
1½ cups Bisquick Baking Mix
1 cup Cheddar Cheese,
   shredded
1 small onion, diced

In a large mixing bowl,
combine together, all
ingredients; mix well. Bake on
preheated, greased waffle
iron. Serve with meat in place
of potatoes or with mushroom
gravy. Yield 3-9" waffles.

PECAN WAFFLES

1¾ cups all-purpose flour
1 tablespoon baking powder
½ teaspoon salt
2 large eggs, separated
1¾ cups milk
½ cup vegetable oil
1 cup pecans, chopped
Maple syrup

In a mixing bowl, combine
together, flour, baking powder
and salt. In a separate bowl,
combine egg yolks, milk
and oil; mix well. Add egg
mixture to dry ingredients; mix
thoroughly. Meanwhile, beat
egg whites until stiff; fold into
batter. Sprinkle hot waffle iron
with 2 tablespoons pecans.
Pour ¼ to 1/3 cup of batter over
pecans; bake according to
manufacturer's directions, until

golden brown. Repeat with
remaining pecans and batte.
Serve with syrup. Yield 8 to 10
waffles (4½ inches).

PLUM NUT QUICK BREAD

2 cups plums, diced in ½ inch
   pieces
1 cup butter OR margarine
2 cups granulated sugar
1 teaspoon vanilla extract
4 large eggs
3 cups all-purpose flour
½ teaspoon salt
1 teaspoon cream of tartar
½ teaspoon baking soda
¾ cup plain yogurt
1 teaspoon lemon peel, grated
1 cup walnuts, chopped

In a mixing bowl, cream
together, butter sugar and
vanilla, until light and fluffy. Add
eggs, one at a time, beating
well after each addition.; set
aside. In another bowl. sift
together, flour, salt, cream of
tartar and baking soda. Blend
yogurt and lemon peel; add to
creamed mixture alternately
with dry ingredients; mix well.
Fold in chopped plums and
nuts. Grease and flour two
9x5-inch loaf pans. Bake at 350
degrees, for 50 to 55 minutes or
until tested done. Yield loaves
or about 16 servings.

GARDEN TOAST
(Microwave recipe)

2 scallions OR green onions,
    sliced
2 mushrooms, sliced thin
1 tablespoon butter OR
    margarine
1 tablespoon sour cream
Salt and pepper to taste

Combine together, in a microwave dish; vegetables and
butter: cover. Microwave on
high, for 2 minutes or until
vegetables are limp. Add sour
cream and salt and pepper;
mix gently; serve immediately
over toast.

FLAXSEED MUFFINS

1¼ cups all-purpose flour
3 cups flaxseed, ground
1 tablespoon baking powder
½ cup light mo;asses
¾ cup milk
2 tablespoons vegetable oil
½ cup egg substitute

Preheat oven to 350
degrees. Combine together,
flour, flaxseed and baking
powder; mix well. In another
bowl, combine remaining
ingredients; add flour mixture;
mix just until moistened. Pour
batter into greased muffin pan;
bake for about 18 minutes or
until tested done. Yield 12
muffins.

CHEESE CRACKERS

2 cups Cheddar Cheese,
    shredded
½ cup Parmesan cheese,
    grated
½ cup butter OR margarine,
    softened
3 tablespoons water
1 cup all-purpose flour
¼ teaspoon salt
1 cup oatmeal, Quick OR Old
    Fashion Uncooked

In a mixing bowl, beat together,
cheeses, butter and water until
well-blended. Add flour and
salt; mix well. Add oatmeal; mix
thoroughly. Shape dough to
form a 12-inch long roll; wrap
securely with plastic wrap or
foil; refrigerate for about 4
hours. Cut ¼ inch thick slices;
flatten slightly. Bake on a lightly
greased cookie sheet, at 400
degrees, for 8 to 10 minutes or
until edges are a light golden
brown. Immediately remove
from cookie sheet; cool on a
wire rack. When cool, store in a
covered container.

CORN BREAD

1½ cups cornmeal
1½ cups all-purpose flour
1 teaspoon baking powder
1 teaspoon baking soda
½ teaspoon salt
2 large eggs
1-1/3 cups buttermilk
½ cup margarine, melted
½ granulated sugar

In a medium mixing bowl, combine together, by sifting, all dry ingredients. Add eggs, buttermilk and melted margarine. Grease lightly, a baking pan, 9x13". Bake at 350 degrees, for about 30 minutes or until tested done. Yield about 12 servings.

RHUBARB MUFFINS
(with Streusel topping)

1¼ cups brown sugar, packed
½ cup vegetable oil
1 cup buttermilk
2½ cups all-purpose flour
1½ teaspoons baking soda
½ teaspoon baking powder
½ teaspoon salt
1 large egg
2 teaspoons vanilla extract
1½ cups rhubarb, diced
½ cup walnuts (optional)

In a large mixing bowl, combine together, sugar, oil, buttermilk, egg and vanilla; mix well. In another bowl, combine dry ingredients, then add to sugar mixture; mix thoroughly. Fold in rhubarb and nuts. Fill greased muffin tin ¾ full; bake at 400 degrees, for 15 to 20 minutes, or until tested done.

TOPPING

1 teaspoon margarine, melted
1/3 cup granulated sugar
1 teaspoon cinnamon

Combine together, all ingredients, then sprinkle evenly over top of batter.

Chapter 3

FOOD PRESERVATION, INCLUDES CANNING, FREEZING & DRYING FOODS

WORRY IS LIKE A ROCKING CHAIR-IT WILL GIVE YOU
SOMETHING TO DO, BUT IT WON'T GET YOU ANYWHERE!

GETTING READY TO CAN FRUITS AND VEGETABLES!

The **secret** to successful canning is starting with fresh, firm and fully ripe fruits and vegetables, but not over ripe. Canning jars are made from high-tempeed glass to with stand the changing temperatures that occur during the canning process. Because of the temperature changes, it is recommended that you do not use commercial jars, such as salad dressing jars or other similar jars. These jars have a tendency to crack easily during the canning process. Also, make sure you always check your jars before you start to can; discarding any jars that are cracked or chipped.

Imperfect jars can promote botulism, a bacteria growth that can cause grave illness, even death.

There are basically three ways to can food. There is the water bath method, the pressure canning method and the steam canning method. The latter method is not recommended because of safety issue.

WATER BATH CANNING METHOD

This method is used for fruits, tomatoes, butters, pickles, relishes and any other food that is high in acid. Before preparation of the food to be canned, place the water bath canner, with sufficient water to cover the jars, at least 1-inch over the top. This permits water, as it boils, to circulate around the jars to uniformly heat the food for proper preservation.

PRESSURE CANNING METHOD

This method is used to process low acid foods, because this method is the only way to get the heat high enough to insure the safety of low acid foods from botulism. because of safety issue.

FREEZING PEACHES IN DRY SUGAR PACK

Wash and peel peaches; cut in halves or slices; remove pits. Place peaches into freezer containers, leaving ½ inch head space. Dissolve ascorbic acid in cold water (½ teaspoon per quart of fruit); sprinkle over peaches. Add 2/3 cup sugar per quart of fruit. Cover tightly; freeze. Thaw in refrigerator before serving.

FREEZING PEACHES IN SYRUP

Wash and peel peaches, cut in halves; remove pits. Prepare syrup by combining 3 cups sugar to 4 cups water adding ½ teaspoon ascorbic acid to each quart of syrup. Put ½ cup cold syrup in each freezer container. Cut halves or slices directly into cold syrup. Press fruit down; cover with more syrup, leaving ½-inch head space. Place crumpled foil or plastic wrap on top to hold fruit below level of syrup. Cover tightly; freeze.

TO FREEZE HERBS

Select young, tender leaves; wash thoroughly in several changes of water. Blanch in boiling water about 10 seconds, then chill in ice water about 1 minute; drain. Pat leaves dry with paper towels. Place in freezer bag or container desired, in quantities you need for your recipes. Label and freeze.

TO USE FROZEN HERBS: Cut leaves in small pieces while still frozen, then use as desired.

CANNING FRESH PEACHES

Peel, halve and pit peaches; pack, cut side down, into hot, sterilized jars, overlapping halves. Leave ½-inch head space. Cover with medium syrup, (by combining 1 cup sugar with 2 cups water) to within ½ inch from the top of jar. Seal; process in boiling water bath, 25 minutes for pints and 30 minutes for quarts.

BREAD & BUTTER PICKLES

6 medium onions
6 quarts cucumbers, sliced
1 cup salt
1½ quarts white vinegar
6 cups granulated sugar
1/3 cup mustard seed
1½ tablespoons celery seed
¼ teaspoon cayenne pepper

Slice onions, then in a large mixing bowl, combine together, onions, sliced cucumbers and salt; let stand for about 3 hours; drain. In a sauce-pan, combine remaining ingredients. Over medium heat, bring to a boil; cook for 5 minutes. Add cucumber mixture; reduce heat to simmer for 4 to 5 minutes. Pack into 8 hot, sterilized pint jars, leaving a ½ inch; seal jars immediately.

PICKLED BEETS

*1 can beets, sliced
½ cup white vinegar
2 tablespoons granulated sugar
½ teaspoon ground ginger
½ teaspoon allspice
¼ teaspoon salt
1 medium onion, sliced,
    separated into rings
    (optional)

Drain beets, reserving ¾ cup beet juice. In a saucepan, combine together, beet juice, vinegar, sugar, ginger, allspice and salt; mix well. Over medium heat, bring mixture to a boil, remove from heat, pour over beets. Refrigerate overnight in a covered bowl. If desired, add onions just before serving, *Substitute 1 pound fresh beets, cooked. Add water to beet juice to measure ¾ cup liquid, if necessary.

CORN COB JELLY

7 dried shelled field corn
2 quarts water
2 boxes Sure-Jell
5 cups granulated sugar

In a large kettle, boil cobs in water for 20 minutes; strain, then combine liquid with Sure-Jell, in a large kettle. Bring mixture to a rolling boil, stirring constantly; add sugar, bring back to a rolling boil; cook for

2 minutes. With a ladle, remove foam from top of mixture. Remove from heat, spoon into clean, sterilized jars. Yield 7 (8 ozs. each) jars.

CORN RELISH

8 cups corn, cut from cob
4 cups cabbage, chopped
1 cup red pepper, chopped
2 large onions, chopped
1 cup granulated sugar
2 tablespoons dry mustard
1 tablespoon mustard seed
1 tablespoon celery seed
4 cups cider vinegar
1 cup water

In a large saucepan, combine together, all ingredients; mix well. Over low heat, simmer mixture for 20 minutes. If desired, add more sugar and salt to taste. Pack corn relish, hot, into sterilized pint jars, leaving ½ inch head space, adjust lids. Process 10 minutes, in water bath. Yield 6 pints.

PICCALILLI

6 pounds green tomatoes
(about 24 medium)
6 medium green peppers
6 medium sweet red peppers
3 medium onions
4 cups white vinegar
3½ cups granulated sugar
2 cups white vinegar
¼ cup pickling salt
½ cup mustard seeds
1 tablespoon celery seeds
1½ teaspoons allspice
1½ teaspoons ground
   cinnamon

Wash, trim and quarter
vegetables. Chop or coarsely
grind vegetables in a food
processor or food grinder;
drain, discard liquid. In a large
saucepan, pour 4 cups vinegar
over vegetables; heat to boiling
Remove from heat; pour into
sterilized pint jars; seal. Cold
pack for 20 minutes.

END OF THE GARDEN PICKLES

**PREPARE 1 CUP EACH of the
FOLLOWING VEGETABLES:**
cucumbers, sliced
green peppers, chopped
cabbage, chopped
celery, chopped
onions, sliced
green tomatoes, chopped
carrots, sliced OR chopped
beans, cut in 1-inch pieces

In a large container, combine
together, cucumbers, peppers,
cabbage, tomatoes and
onions. Next prepare salt brine,
as follows: add ½ cup pickling
salt to 2 quarts water; pour
over vegetables; let stand
over night. Next day, drain salt
brine from vegetables; put
them in large saucepan; set
aside. Meanwhile, combine
carrots and green beans;
cook in water, over medium
heat until tender; remove
from heat; drain well. Add to
cucumber mixture, along with
the following ingredients: 2
tablespoons mustard seed, 1
tablespoon celery seed, 2 cups
cider vinegar, 2 cups sugar
and 2 tablespoons turmeric;
mix well. Over medium-high
heat, bring to boil; cook for 10
minutes; remove from heat.
Pack into hot, sterilized jars;
adjust lids. Proceed in boiling
water bath for 10 minutes. Yield
6 pints.

REFRIGERATOR DILL PICKLES

Pickles, enough to fill * 1 gallon
  jar or crock
1 garlic bulb, broken into cloves
  & peeled
1 cup pickling salt
1 quart whie vinegar
3 quarts water
Fresh dill

*If desired, you can use quart
canning jars Scrub pickles,
place in container desired.
Cut several cloves of garlic
in half and a clump of fresh
dill. In a medium saucepan,
combine together, salt, vinegar
and water. Bring mixture to a
boil; cook for about 1 minute.
Remove from heat, pour vinegar
mixture over pickles; cover
immediately. Store in refrigerator
for 2 or 3 weeks before serving.

FREEZER COLESLAW

1 medium head cabbage,
  shredded
1 medium green pepper,
  chopped
1 tablespoon salt
1 medium carrot, grated
1 cup white vinegar
1 teaspoon mustard seed
¼ cup water
1 teaspoon celery seed
2 cups granulated sugar

In a large mixing bowl, mix salt
with cabbage, green pepper
and carrot; set; let stand for 1
hour, then drain. Meanwhile,
in a small saucepan, combine
together, vinegar, mustard
seed, water, celery seed and
sugar. On medium-high heat,
bring mixture to a boil; cook
for 1 minute; remove from from
heat. Pack cabbage mixture
into desired freezer containers.
Pour boiled vinegar mixture
over cabbage, leaving 1-inch
headspace; freeze. Yield 2½
pints.

PEACH MARMALADE

1 small orange, quartered &
  seeded
1 lemon, quartered & seeded
¼ cup water
3 lbs. peaches, peeled, pitted
  & sliced
1 pkg. (1¾ ozs.) fruit pectin
  powder
5 cups granulated sugar

Slice orange and lemon
quarters into thin slices. In a
medium saucepan, combine
fruit slices and water. Cover
and place over medium heat;
bring mixture to a boil; remove
from heat. Then combine
together, all fruit, pectin &
sugar: mix well. Over high
heat, bring mixture to a full
rolling boil, uncovered, stirring
constantly, boil hard for 1
minute. Remove from heat;
using a metal spoon, ladle
mixture into sterilized pint jars,
leaving ½ inch headspace;
seal immediately.

TO CAN CABBAGE

Cut cabbage in chunks. Pack in hot sterilized quart jars. Add 1 teaspoon salt. Fill jars to within 1-inch of top with water; seal jars. Place jars in cold packer, cover jars with water. Over medium heat bring water to a rolling boil; boil for 20 minutes. Remove jars from cold packer and let cool.

FREEZER TOMATO PUREE

Approximately 12 large tomatoes will yield 6 to 7 cups of puree'. Wash and core tomatoes, remove any bruised spots. It is not necessary to peel or slice them; put whole tomato with hole side down in a large stock pot. Pour enough water to prevent tomatoes from sticking to the pot. Cover; cook on low heat, about 30 minutes, or until very soft, do not stir while cooking. As tomatoes are cooking, drain excess liquid, if any, or add more water, if necessary. When tomatoes are done, remove from heat; let cool. With a slotted spoon, place tomatoes in a food blender, processor or food mill; filling only one-half full at a time. Puree' for about 30 seconds or until smooth. Pour puree' into a strainer placed over a large bowl; use spoon, if necessary, to push juicy pulp through strainer. Place desired amount into freezer container, leaving ½ inch headspace, label, date and freeze.

GRAPE BUTTER I

5 cups Concord grapes
4 cups granulated sugar

Wash and sort grapes; place in medium saucepan with a little water to prevent sticking. Ass sugar; mix well; bring to a boil; then reduce heat to simmer, for 20 minutes, or until desired thickness; stirring constantly. Remove from heat; cool slightly. Strain by pressing through sieve or use food mill. Pour into hot, sterilized pint jars, leaving ¼ inch head space. Process in boiling water bath for 10 minutes. Let jars cool. then store in cold place. Yield about 2 to 3 pints.

CANTALOUPE PICKLES

4 cantaloupes, quartered,
   seeds & rind removed
3 cups granulated sugar
3 cups apple cider vinegar
1½ cups apple juice
6 cinnamon sticks, broken
2 tablespoons whole cloves
5 thin slices fresh ginger root

Cut cantaloupe into 1 inch cubes. Combine together, sugar, vinegar and apple juice; mix well. Over medium heat, bring to a boil; stirring occasionally. Tie spices in spice bag; add to syrup; boil for 10 minutes. Add melon; reduce heat, then simmer for 15 minutes, stirring occasionally. Remove from heat and remove spice bag. Fill hot, sterilized jars with mixture, leaving ½ inch headspace. Process in boiling water canner, for 10 minutes for pints and 5 minutes for half-pints.

OVEN APPLE BUTTER

6 pounds apples, peeled &
   cored
6 cups granulated sugar
1 cup white vinegar
1 tablespoon cinnamon
1 teaspoon ground cloves

Prepare apples, by peeling, then core; using food grinder, blender or food processor, puree' apples. Place pureed apples, or apple sauce, along with remaining ingredients into a shallow baking pan. Bake for ½ hour at 350 degrees, then for 3 to 5 hours. Keep the oven door ajar so moisture is released. Stir applesauce every 30 minutes. Pour into hot, sterilized pint jars, leaving ¼ inch head space; cover with lid.

DILL PICKLES

4 pounds pickling cucumbers
(4 to 5" long)
4 tablespoons salt
1½ tablespoons mustard seed
3 cups white vinegar
3 cups water
¾ cup dillweed
6 bay leaves

Wash cucumbers; cut in half. In saucepan, combine together, salt, mustard seed, vinegar and water; bring to a boil. Pack cucumbers into sterilized pint jars, then cover with boiling vinegar mixture. Add 2 tablespoons of dillweed and1 bay leaf to each jar; seal. Process for 10 minutes in a boiling water bath. Yield 6 pints.

GREEN TOMATO JELLY

2½ cups green tomatoes, diced
2½ cups granulated sugar
1 pkg. raspberry gelatin

In a saucepan, combine
together, diced tomatoes and
sugar; mix well. Over medium
heat, cook for 6 minutes; stirring
occasionally; add gelatin; cook
6 more minutes. Remove from
heat, put in desired sterilized
jars; cover. Store in cool place.

RHUBARB FREEZER JAM

5 cups rhubarb, cut in pieces
4cups granulated sugar
1 small pkg. strawberry gelatin
1 cup crushed pineapple, with
    juice

In a 4-quart saucepan,
combine together, all
ingredients; mix well. Over
medium heat bring to a boil;
cook for 20 minutes. Skim foam
off the top. Remove from heat;
cool Put in desired containers
and freeze. Yield 6 cups

PESTO

2 cups fresh basil, loosely packed
4 cloves garlic, peeled
2 tablespoons pine nuts
½ cup Parmesan cheese, grated
¾ cup olive oil
2 tablespoons butter

In a blender or food processor,
combine basil, garlic, pine nuts

and cheese. While processing,
pour oil through the feed tube
in a thin stream. Process until
smooth, then scrape into bowl;
beat in butter. Yield enough
pesto for 1 pound pasta.

RED BEET EGGS

½ cup white vinegar
½ cup granulated sugar
½ teaspoon salt
¼ teaspoon celery seed
1 can (16 ozs.) beets, undrained
12 hard-boiled eggs, peeled

In a large saucepan, combine
together, vinegar, sugar, salt
and celery seeds; bring to boil,
over medium heat. Place beets
beet juice and hard-boiled
eggs, in a large container. Pour
hot mixture over eggs. Cover
and refrigerate 24 hours before
serving.

STRAWBERRY VINEGAR

2 pints fresh strawberries
1 quart cider vinegar
1 cup sugar

Remove stems from
strawberries; cut in half; set ¼
cup aside. In a large bowl place
remaining berries; pour vinegar
over them. Cover; set side for
1 hour. Transfer berries and
vinegar to a large saucepan;
add sugar. Over medium-
high heat, bring mixture to a
boil. Reduce heat to simmer,
covered for 10 minutes

BARBEQUE RELISH

10 large cucumber
10 green tomatoes
6 large onions
6 red peppers & 3 green
   peppers (or 9 green)
1 bunch celery

Grind together, all vegetables, add ½ cup salt; let stand over night; next day; drain. Meanwhile, in a large saucepan, combine together, 2 quarts white vinegar, 1/3 all-purpose flour, 1 tablespoon dry mustard, 1 teaspoon celery seeds, 1 teaspoon turmeric and 2½ granulated sugar, bring to a boil, reduce heat to simmer, add vegetables, cook for 15 to 20 minutes, do not boil. Spoon mixture into clean, sterilized pint jars; leaving ½ inch headspace; seal. Yield 9 to 10 pints.

CITRUS JELLY

1 can (6 ozs.) frozen grapefruit concentrate, thawed
3 tablespoons lime juice
1¼ cups water
3 cups granulated sugar
½ bottle (3 ozs.) liquid pectin

In a large saucepan, combine together, grapefruit juice, lime juice and water; add sugar; mix well. Over medium heat, bring to a boil, stirring constantly, until sugar dissolves. Add pectin, continue to boil for 1 minute, stirring constantly. Remove from heat; skim off foam with ladle. Spoon mixture into hot, sterilized pint jars, leaving ½ inch headspace; adjust lids. Yield 4 pints.

CHILI SAUCE

4 to 5 pound ripe tomatoes
1 large onion
¾ cup granulated sugar
1¼ cups apple cider vinegar
1 teaspoon mustard seed
½ teaspoon ground ginger
½ teaspoon nutmeg
¼ teaspoon curry powder

Prepare tomatoes, by washing, peeling and coarsely chopping tomatoes; measure 8 cups. In a large saucepan, over medium heat, bring mixture to a boil. Reduce heat; simmer gently, uncovered, until very thick, about 2 hours. As mixture thickens, stir frequently, to prevent sauce from sticking or scorching. When thick, as desired, remove from heat; spoon into clean sterilized pint jars, leaving ½ inch headspace. Process for 15 minutes, in boiling water bath. Yield about 2 pints.

HOT DOG RELISH-I

3 pounds green tomatoes
4 tart apples
3 green OR red peppers
1½ tablespoons pickling salt
1½ teaspoons black pepper
1½ teaspoons ground
    cinnamon
½ teaspoon ground cloves
2 cups white vinegar

Prepare tomatoes, by washing, removing stem ends; cut in quarters. Wash apples core, cut in quarters. Wash peppers, remove seeds; skin onions, cut in quarters. Put vegetables through food chopper or food processor, using coarse blade; set aside. Combine remaining ingredients; mix thoroughly. Over medium heat, bring mixture to a boil; add vegetables, simmer uncovered, stirring occasionally, for about 30 minutes, or until mixture thickens. Spoon into hot, sterilized jars; seal immediately, Yield 4 to 5 pints.

HOMEMADE MINCEMEAT

2 pounds lean pork
2 cups molasses
4 cups white vinegar
4 cups dried apples, cooked
2 cups granulated sugar
1 tablespoon allspice
1 box (15 ozs.) raisins

In a large saucepan, over medium heat, bring water to a boil; add pork and cook pork until tender. Remove pork from water; cool, then dice in small pieces. In the saucepan, combine the remaining ingredients; add diced pork. Bring to a boil then reduce heat; stirring constantly, cook for 15 minutes. Remove from heat; skim grease from surface. Spoon mixture into clean, sterilized jars; seal.

ONION RELISH

14 onions, peeled & quartered
6 green peppers
6 hot red peppers
4 cups white vinegar
3 cups granulated sugar
2 tablespoons salt

Grind all vegetables in food processor or blender, using coarse blade setting. In a large saucepan, over medium heat, cook the vinegar, sugar and salt, bring to a rolling boil. Add vegetables; lower heat to simmer and simmer for 15 minutes. Pour into hot, sterilized pint jars; adjust lids. Yield 3 pints.

SOUR CHERRY JAM

4½ cups sour cherries
7 cups granulated sugar
1 bottle (6 ozs.) liquid pectin
3 teaspoons almond extract
    (optional)

Sort, wash, stem, pit and drain
fully, ripe sour cherries. Put
cherries through blender or
food processor, to coarsely
chop. Place prepared cherries
in a medium-size saucepan;
add sugar; mix thoroughly. Put
over high heat; bring to a rapid
boil; stirring constantly. Boil for
10 minutes; add liquid pectin;
return to full boil for 1 minute.
Remove from heat; add
almond extract; skim off foam.
Pour mixture into sterilized
jelly glasses, leaving ½ inch
headspace; seal immediately.
Yield about 9 (8 ozs.) glasses.

RHUBARB-STRAWBERRY MARMALADE

3 cups rhubarb, diced
2 cups strawberries
1 medium orange, juice & rind,
    grated
2½ cups granulated sugar

Wash, trim and dice rhubarb,
sort, wash and hull strawberries.
Place rhubarb and strawberries
in a large saucepan; add
orange juice and rind; mix
well. Let stand for 1 hour, in a
cool place. Add sugar; mix
thoroughly. Bring to a boil, over
high heat, stirring frequently;
boil for 2 minutes or until slightly
thickened. Remove from
heat skim off foam; discard.
Pour hot mixture into sterilized
jelly glasses; leaving ½ inch
headspace; seal immediately.
Yield 3 to 4 (8 ozs.) jelly glasses.

ZUCCHINI JAM

6 cups zucchini, peeled &
    grated
6 cups water

In a large saucepan, combine
together, zucchini and water,
over medium heat, cook for 8
minutes. Remove from heat;
drain; set aside. In another
saucepan, place the following
ingredients; mix well.

6 cups granulated sugar
½ cup lemon juice
1 can (16 ozs.) crushed
    pineapple, drained

Boil for 1 minute; remove
from heat; add 2 boxes of
your favorite gelatin, peach
is very good. Stir until gelatin
is dissolved; add drained
zucchini; mix thoroughly. Put in
desired containers and freeze.

AUTUMN CHUTNEY

1½ cup granulated sugar
1½ cups cider vinegar
¼ cup fresh ginger, peeled &
   slivered
1 tablespoon mustard seeds
1 teaspoon salt
¼ teaspoon crushed red
   pepper
2 large pears, peeled & cut in
   wedges
2 large tart apples, peeled &
   cubed
2 onions, peeled & cut in
   wedges
1 red pepper, cut in 1-inch
   pieces
½ cup golden raisins

In a 5-quart Dutch Oven or
a large saucepan, combine
together, sugar, vinegar, ginger
and spices; mix well. Add
pears, apples, onions, pepper
and raisins; mix thoroughly.
Over high heat, bring to a
boil; reduce heat to simmer,
uncovered, for 1 hour, or
until mixture thickens slightly;
stirring occasionally. Remove
from heat let cool; cover and
refrigerate until well chilled.
Serve with roasted meats or
poultry. Yield 4 cups.

TO CAN: Remove from heat,
spoon into hot, sterilized pint
jars, leaving ½ inch headspace.
Adjust lids and seal

RADISH JELLY

2 cups radishes, finely chopped
2½ cups granulated sugar
¾ cup water
1¼ ozs. dry pectin
2 teaspoons prepared
   horseradish

In a large saucepan, combine
together, radishes, sugar and
water; cook over medium-
high heat. Bring to a boil,
stirring constantly, until sugar
dissolves, then add pectin.
Bring mixture to a rolling
boil, stirring constantly, boil
for 1 minute. Remove from
heat; skim off foam; stir in
horseradish; mix well. Spoon
mixture into sterilized pint jars;
leave 1-inch head-space; seal
immediately. Cool, then store in
the refrigerator. Yield 2 pints.

RHUBARB JAM

10 cups rhubarb, cut in ½" pieces
8 cups granulated sugar
3 pkgs. (3 ozs. each) strawberry
   gelatin

Combine together, rhubarb
and sugar in a large saucepan;
let set for 5 minutes. Then
over medium heat, bring to a
boil, cook for 10 minutes. Add
gelatin, then cook for 2 minutes
longer, or until gelatin has
dissolved. Remove from heat;
put in hot, sterilized jars, leaving
½ inch headspace; seal. Yield
about 5½ pints.

CUCUMBER RELISH

1 peck large cucumbers
6 large onion
3 cups granulated sugar
1/3 cup pickling salt
1 tablespoon celery seed
'2 tablespoons mustard seed
3 cups whie vinegar

Prepare cucumbers, by washing and peeling; prepare onions by peeling, then put chunks of cucumber and onions in food processor; process to desired consistency. Place in large bowl; sprinkle salt over mixture; let stand 1 hour; drain well. In a large saucepan, combine together, remaining ingredients; mix well. Cook over low heat for 25 minutes, stirring occasionally. Remove from heat; pour into hot, sterilized pint jars, leaving ½ inch headspace; seal Store in a cool place.

PEACH BUTTER

8 cups peach pulp
4 cups granulated sugar

To prepare pulp: Wash, scald in boiling water for 1 minutes (makes it easier to peel). Use a food processor or blender to puree peaches to desired consistency. Measure pulp, place in a large saucepan; add sugar; mix well. Cook over low heat until mixture thickens, about 30 minutes. As mixture thickens, stir often to prevent sticking. Remove from heat; pour into hot, sterilized pint jars, leaving ½ inch headspace. Adjust lids; process 10 minutes, in boiling water bath. Yield 4 pints.

PEACH LEATHER

Peel peaches, remove pit, then force through sieve. To each 4 cups of pulp, add 1-2/3 cups granulated sugar; mix well. In a saucepan, bring to a boil; cook for 2 minutes on high heat, stirring constantly. Spread thin layer evenly on cookie sheet; cover loosely with cheesecloth. Dry in sun for 3 to 4 days, or leather can be rolled up. Cut into strips; sprinkle with sugar; store in air-tight container.

PEACH CHUTNEY

4 quarts peaches, peeled and finely chopped
1 cup onions, chopped
1 cup raisins
1 clove garlic, minced
1 whole hot red pepper
3 cups brown sugar, packed
¼ cup mustard seeds
2 tablespoons ground ginger
1 teaspoon salt
5 cups white vinegar

In a large saucepan, combine together, all above ingredients. Bring to a boil, over medium heat; stirring constantly; reduce heat to simmer. Cook, uncovered, stirring often, for 2 hours, or until thick; remove red pepper and dispose. Spoon chutney into hot, sterilized pint jars, leaving ½ inch headspace, cover with lids. Process in boiling water bath, for 10 minutes. Yield 6 pints.

COLESLAW RELISH

16 cups cabbage, shredded (about 4 lbs.)
4 cups onions, chopped (about 4 large)
1 cup green pepper, diced
1 cup red pepper, diced
2/3 cup salt
2 cups granulated sugar
1 teaspoon celery seeds
2 cups white vinegar

In a large bowl, combine together, cabbage, onions, green and red peppers and salt; mix well. Pour ice water in to cover vegetables. Cover bowl; let stand overnight. Drain vegetables well; pack into hot, sterilized jars. In a medium-size saucepan, combine together, sugar, celery seeds and vinegar; mix well. Over medium heavy, bring sugar mixture to boiling, stirring constantly. Remove from heat, pour into jars, leaving ½ inch headspace; seal. Yield 12 eight ounce jars.

FREEZER PICKLES

7 cups pickles, thinly sliced
1 cup onions, thinly sliced

Place pickles and onions in a large mixing bowl sprinkle 1 tablespoon salt over the top; mix well. Let stand for 5 minutes, then drain well. Meanwhile prepare vinegar mixture.

VINEGAR MIXTURE

1 cup white vinegar
1½ cups granulated sugar
1 teaspoon celery seed

Place ingredients in a saucepan; bring to a boil; cook for 1 minute or until sugar completely dissolved, stirring constantly. Remove from heat; let cool completely before adding to pickles. Use the size freezer containers you desire. Place pickles in container; add cooled vinegar mixture, leaving ½ inch headspace, cover and freeze.

GREEN TOMATO MARMALADE

24 medium green tomatoes
3½ pounds granulated sugar
4 medium oranges

Wash, core and peel tomatoes; cut into thin slices. Wash and peel oranges; cut peel into thin strips. Cut oranges into thin slices. Combine tomato slices, orange peels, orange slices and sugar, into a large saucepan; mix well. Let stand, covered, overnight. In the morning, place saucepan over low heat, uncovered; gradually bring mixture to a boil; stirring occasionally. Reduce to simmer; cook gently for 2 hours, or until thick. Spoon immediately into hot, sterilized jelly jars; seal. Yield 6 pints.

HONEY PEACH BUTTER

10 pounds peaches, peeled & chopped
½ cup water
4½ cups granulated sugar
1½ cups honey

In a large saucepan, cook peaches with water until soft. Press through a sieve, or use a blender or food processor to puree'. Measure 12 cups of pulp, return to saucepan. Add sugar and honey; cook over low heat, stirring often, for about 1¼ hours, or until mixture

thickens. Remove from heat; pour into hot, sterilized pint jars; leaving ½ inch headspace. Adjust lids; process for10 minutes, in a boiling water bath. Yield 6 pints

REFRIGERATOR RELISH

8 cups cucumbers, unpeeled, sliced
1 cup onions, chopped
1 cup green peppers, chopped
½ teaspoon salt

In a large mixing bowl, combine together, cucumbers, onions and green peppers. Sprinkle salt over vegetables; mix well. Let set for 1 hour Meanwhile prepare dressing.

DRESSING:

2 cups granulated sugar
1 cup white vinegar
1 teaspoon celery seed
1 teaspoon mustard seed

In a mixing bowl, combine together, sugar, vinegar, celery and mustard seeds; mix well. Pour over relish, chill in refrigerator before serving.

RED PEPPER RELISH I

4 red bell peppers
½ cup white vinegar
1 cup granulated sugar
½ teaspoon salt

Coarsely chop or grind peppers; place in a medium saucepan, along with vinegar, sugar and salt. Over medium heat, bring mixture to simmer, cook for 45 minutes, stirring often. Remove from heat; allow to cool. Pour into freezer containers; freeze until ready to use.

TO SERVE: Bring relish to room temperature and serve. One way to serve is to pour over a softened block of cream cheese; serve with crackers.

GRAPE JELLY

3½ pounds concord grapes
7 cups granulated sugar
1½ cups water
1 box Sure-Jell pectin

Discard stems; wash; use potato masher to crush grapes. Measure 5 cups mashed grapes into a medium saucepan, along with water, over medium heat; bring to a boil. Reduce heat; cover; simmer for 10 minutes. Add sugar and pectin; mix thoroughly; bring to a rolling boil, on high heat, stirring constantly Boil for 1 minute, remove from heat; skim off any foam; discard foam. Spoon jelly into hot sterilized jars; adjust lids. Process in a hot water bath for 5 minutes. Remove jars from canner; let stand at room temperature for 24 hours. Store in a cool, dark place up to a year. Refrigerate opened jars up to 3 weeks. Yield about 4 pints.

OLD FASHION CABBAGE RELISH

1 head cabbage
10 green tomatoes12 green peppers
6 red peppers
4 cups onions
½ cup pickling salt
6 cups granulated sugar
1 tablespoon celery seed
2 tablespoons mustard seed
1½ teaspoons turmeric
4 cups apple cider vinegar
2 cups water

Coarsely chop all vegetables; place in large mixing bowl. Sprinkle with salt; let stand overnight. In the morning, rinse vegetables thoroughly with water to remove salt; drain well; set aside. In a large saucepan, combine together, the remaining ingredients. Over medium heat, bring mixture to a boil; reduce heat to simmer; cook for 5 minutes. Place vegetables in hot, sterilized pint jars. Pour hot liquid over vegetables to fill jars within, ½ inch from the top. Seal jars with lids. Yield 8 pints.

HOT TOMATO SALSA

8 cups tomatoes, peeled and
    diced
8 to 10 mixed peppers, green
    peppers, yellow peppers &
    *jalapeno, chopped
3 medium onions, chopped
1/2 cup white vinegar
1 cup tomato paste
1 tablespoon garlic, minced
1 tablespoon black pepper
1 tablespoon salt

In a large saucepan, combine
together, all the above
ingredients; mix well. Over
medium heat, bring mixture
to a boil, stirring occasionally.
Reduce heat to low; simmer
for about 1½ hours, stirring
occasionally. Remove from
heat; spoon into hot, sterilized
jars, leaving ½ inch headspace;
seal with lids. Process in a
boiling water bath, for 10
minutes.

NOTE: When preparing hot
peppers, wear latex gloves or
wash hands thoroughly, after
chopping peppers. Take care
not to touch or rub eyes.

ZUCCHINI PICKLE

2 cups cider vinegar
1½ cups granulated sugar
½ teaspoon turmeric
¼ teaspoon ground cloves
2 teaspoon mustard seeds
2 teaspoon celery seeds
¼ teaspoon ground ginger
1 teaspoon salt
1 medium onion, sliced thin
1 pound zucchini, sliced thin

In a large saucepan, combine
together, vinegar, sugar,
turmeric, cloves, mustard and
celery seeds, ginger and salt.
Over high heat, bring mixture
to a boil. Reduce heat to low;
simmer for 10 minutes. Then
bring back to boil; add sliced
onions; cook for 1 minute, add
the zucchini slices; cook for 2
minutes more, stirring to keep
vegetables submerged in
liquid. Remove from heat; let
cool. Put in desired containers;
refrigerate. Serve as you would
any bread and butter pickle.
Yield about 4 cups.

PINEAPPLE PICKLE

1 can (20 ozs.) sliced pineapple
1 cup vinegar
1 cup brown sugar, packed
2 sticks cinnamon
20 whole cloves

Drain juice from pineapple;
place juice into a medium
saucepan. Add remaining
ingredients EXCEPT pineapple.
Over medium heat, bring to
a boil; then reduce heat to
simmer; cook for 10 minutes.
Add pineapple slices; simmer
for another 15 minutes. Remove
from heat; let cool; chill before
serving. Good with most meats.

PINEAPPLE JAM

2 tablespoons cold water
1 envelope unflavored gelatin
1 teaspoon cornstarch
1 can (20 ozs.) crushed
    pineapple
½ cup water
¼ cup granulated sugar, more
    or less to taste

Place 2 tablespoons cold water in blender container; sprinkle with gelatin. Let gelatin soften for 1 minute, then sprinkle cornstarch on top. Heat ½ cup water to boiling; add to blender, Cover; blend, using on/off pulses, just until gelatin granules are well-blended. Add pineapple with juice and sugar; cover, blend just until combined. Store in jars in refrigerator.

RHUBARB-CRAB APPLE JAM

2 cups rhubarb, cut into ½ inch
    pieces
2 cups crab apples, quartered
Granulated Sugar

Place unpeeled crab apples in large saucepan with water. Over medium heat, bring crab apples to a boil; reduce heat to simmer; cook until tender. Strain crab apples, using cheese cloth or jelly bag. Meanwhile bring rhubarb to a boil, in a small amount of water. Cook rhubarb, over medium heat until tender; remove from heat and strain. Combine equal amounts of strained crab apples juice and rhubarb juice. Add ¾ cup sugar for each cup of fruit juice. Boil mixture rapidly until jelly sheets on a spoon. Remove from heat put in pint jars. Yield about 3 to 4 pints.

TOMATO BUTTER

5 pounds tomatoes
1 cup white vinegar
3 cups granulated sugar
1 small stick of cinnamon
¼ oz. ginger root
½ teaspoon whole cloves

Prepare tomatoes by, peeling and slicing tomatoes; place in a medium saucepan, along with vinegar and sugar. Tie all spices in a spice bag or make one, by using a piece of cheesecloth, gathered and tied with a piece of string. Add to mixture; cook over medium heat until thick, as desired; remove from heat. Remove spice bag, then pour into hot, sterilized pint jars; seal, leaving ½ inch headspace. Yield 4 pints.

TOMATO SALSA

4 cups tomatoes (about 6 large) peeled, cored, & chopped
2 cups green OR yellow mild peppers, seeded & chopped
1 cup *hot peppers, seeded & chopped
1 cup onions, peeled & chopped
1 teaspoon salt
3 cloves garlic, minced
1½ cups apple cider vinegar

In a large saucepan, combine together, all ingredients. Bring mixture to a boil; reduce heat to simmer; cook for 25 minutes Pour hot salsa, leaving ½ inch headspace. Adjust lids; process 30 minutes in a boiling water bath canner. Yield about six 8 ounce jars.

*NOTE: When working with hot peppers, it is best to wear latex gloves. Do not touch or rub your eyes.

CHERRY PIE FILLING

6 pounds fresh sour cherries
3 cups granulated sugar, divided
½ cup cornstarch OR 1 cup tapioca
1 teaspoon almond extract
¼ teaspoon red food coloring (optional)

Wash and sterilize 6 pints, keep hot until needed. Prepare lids as manufacturer directs. Wash cherries, remove stems and pits. In a large saucepan, combine together, cherries and 2 cups sugar. Let stand for 15 minutes or until juice begins to flow. Attach a candy thermometer to the side of the saucepan so bulb is covered with cherry mixture, stir frequently Bring mixture to a boil, over medium heat. Continue boiling until mixture reaches 212 degrees; then set aside. Meanwhile, in a small mixing bowl, combine remaining 1 cup sugar and cornstarch. Stir into cherry mixture, mix well; add almond extract and food coloring. Continue cooking, stirring constantly, until temperature is again, at 212 degrees. Remove from heat; spoon cherry pie filling into hot jars, leaving ½ inch headspace. As a precaution, use a wooden spoon by inserting into the middle of each jar to release any trapped air. Wipe rims of jars with a clean, damp cloth; adjust lids. Place in canner; process in boiling water bath, for 15 minutes for pints, and 20 minutes for quarts.

SANDWICH SPREAD

12 green bell peppers, stem
   removed and seeded
12 red bell peppers, stem
   removed and seeded
12 green tomatoes
½ cup onions, chopped
1 cup self-rising flour
2 cups granulated sugar
1½ to 2 cups white vinegar
2 cups dry mustard
1 tablespoon salt
1 teaspoon celery seeds
1 quart mayonnaise

In a food processor, grind all
vegetables. Remove from
processor; drain well. Reserve
liquid for thinning, if necessary.
In a large sauce pan, combine
together, all ingredients,
EXCEPT mayonnaise. Cook
over medium heat, for 10
minutes. Remove from heat;
add mayonnaise, mixing well.
Spoon into hot, sterilized jars,
leaving ½ inch headspace;
seal Yield 12 pints.

HOW TO MAKE SAUERKRAUT?
(Easy and Quick Recipe)

Shred cabbage in the amount
desired; pack into clean,
sterilized quart canning
jars, not too tightly. With a
wooden spoon handle make
a hole down through the
middle of sauerkraut. Add 1
teaspoon of salt, then fill jar

with boiling water, leaving
½ inch headspace of top of
jar. Seal jar tight immediately.
Sauerkraut will be ready to use
in 4 to 6 weeks.

CHUNKY APPLESAUCE

24 large apples, peel, core &
   cut in chunks
½ cup water
2 tablespoons lemon juice
1 cup granulated sugar
3 teaspoons cinnamon
½ teaspoon nutmeg
1 teaspoon vanilla extract

Put prepared apples in large
saucepan with water and
lemon juice. Cook covered,
until apples are tender, about
20 minutes, stirring occasionally.
Add sugar and remaining
ingredients; mix well. continue
to cook until sugar dissolves.
Remove from heat, spoon hot
mixture into sterilized pint jars
to within ½" of top; Clean rims;
seal; process in water bath, for
20 minutes. Yield 5 pints.

PICKLED RED CABBAGE

1 firm head red cabbage
¼ cup pickling salt
4 cups white vinegar
1 cup granulated sugar
¼ cup pickling spice (wrapped
    in cheese-cloth & secured
    with string) (optional)

Shred cabbage with a sharp knife; add salt; mix well. Cover; let stand for 12 hours or overnight. Drain using a colander; rinse well in cold water. In large saucepan, combine I together, vinegar and sugar. Over medium heat, bring mixture to a boil. Add spice bag, if desired; reduce heat to simmer; cook for 15 minutes. Add drained cabbage; bring to a boil (cabbage will turn a bright pink). Pack into hot, sterilized quart jars, leaving ½ inch headspace. Seal immediately. Label; store in cool, dry, dark place. Yield about 10 cups.

ZUCCHINI RELISH

10 cups zucchini, chopped
4 cups onion, chopped
2 red peppers
2 green peppers

Grind all ingredients together; add 5 tablespoons salt. Let stand overnight; next day drain, rinse with cold water. squeeze out as much water as possible.

SYRUP

2½ cups white vinegar
5½ cups granulated sugar
1 teaspoon nutmeg
1 teaspoon turmeric
½ teaspoon pepper

In a medium saucepan, combine together, all syrup ingredients. Over medium heat, bring to a boil, cook for 8 minutes. Remove from heat; pour over zucchini mixture. Place in sterilized pint jars, leaving ½ inch headspace. Adjust lids; process 5 minutes in boiling water bath.

TOMATO SAUCE

¼ cup butter OR margarine
1 cup onions, chopped
1 clove garlic, minced
¼ cup all-purpose flour
1 can (10½ ozs. condensed
    chicken broth
1 can (16 ozs.) tomatoes,
    drained & chopped
Salt (optional)

In a medium saucepan, over low heat, melt butter; sauté onions and garlic until golden, about 5 minutes. Stir in flour; mix well; cook, stirring constantly, for 1 minute. Gradually, blend in chicken broth; add tomatoes; cook until thickened. If desired, add salt to taste. Yield 6 servings.

PICKLED BOLOGNA

¾ pound bologna, 1 piece
1 small onion, thinly sliced
½ cup apple cider vinegar
2 tablespoons vegetable oil
2 tablespoons green pepper,
   diced
2 tablespoons pimiento, diced
1 clove garlic, minced
½ teaspoon salt
Dash of black pepper
Dash of paprika

Remove casing from bologna,
cut bologna into bite-size
pieces. Place in a bowl with
onion, set aside. Meanwhile
combine vinegar with the
remaining ingredients; place in
a jar. Cover with lid; shake well.
Pour dressing over bologna and
onions; cover and refrigerate
for 24 hours. Mix ingredients
occasionally.

ZUCCHINI CHIPS

4 quarts zucchini, thinly sliced
2½ cups onions, thinly sliced
1½ cups red pepper strips,
   (2x1/8")
½ cup pickling salt
3 tablespoons mixed pickling
   spices
2 teaspoons whole cloves
1 quart white vinegar
2½ cups granulated sugar
¼ cup mustard seeds
1 teaspoon curry powder
   (optional)

In a large bowl, combine
together, zucchini, onions
and red pepper. Sprinkle with
salt; add cold water to cover.
Refrigerate for 2 hours; drain
well. Tie pickling spices and
cloves in cheesecloth bag.
In a large saucepan (8 qt.),
over high heat, bring vinegar,
sugar mustard seeds, curry
powder and spice bags to a
boil. Add vegetables; return
to heat; simmer for 5 minutes,
stirring frequently. Ladle into
hot, sterilized pint or quart jars,
leaving ½ inch headspace.
Adjust lids.

STRAWBERRY LEATHER

9 to 10 cups strawberries
Add honey, granulated sugar
   or brown sugar, TO TASTE

In a large saucepan, bring
strawberries, slowly to a boil.
over medium heat, stirring
constantly. Boil 1 minute;
remove from heat; let cool
slightly, then puree' in food
processor or blender; set aside.
Meanwhile, prepare 2 jell roll
pans or cookie sheets, by lining
them with clear plastic wrap,
securing edges with tape.
Pour strawberry purée onto
prepared pans, spreading
evenly to about 1/8 inch thick.
Place in food dehydrator, if you
have one, otherwise, place in
oven with the lowest possible

heat (140 to 150 degrees).
Keep the oven door open
about 1", using a wedge. This is
done to allow the moisture to
evaporate and for strawberries
to dry thoroughly. Drying time
can vary from 8 to 24 hours,
or possibly longer. Leather is
dry when it can be peeled
off the plastic easily. To store,
roll in plastic wrap, seal
tightly. Leather will keep at
room temperature for about
1 month. in the refrigerator,
for about 3 months, or in the
freezer for about 1 year. Yield 2
large rolls.

EASY HORSERADISH SPREAD

1 cup horseradish, grated
½ cup white vinegar
¼ teaspoon salt

Wash horseradish roots
thoroughly; remove brown
outer skin with peeler. Put
roots through food chopper,
with plenty ventilation made
available. The fumes from
grating the horseradish are
powerful, actually it would be
best to do this grating outside.
Combine the ingredients; mix
well. Pack the mixture into
container, seal tightly; store in
the refrigerator.

PEAR RELISH

1 cup granulated sugar
1 cup white vinegar
½ teaspoon salt
¼ teaspoon cayenne pepper
6 pears, cored and finely
   chopped
3 green peppers, cored,
   seeded & diced
1 sweet red pepper, cored,
   seeded & diced
2 large onions, peeled & diced

In a large saucepan, combine
together, sugar vinegar,
salt and pepper; bring to
a boil. Add pears, green &
red peppers and onions;
return to boil, then reduce
heat to simmer. Cook for 25
to 30 minutes or until mixture
thickens; stir occasionally.
Remove from heat; spoon into
hot, sterilized pint jars, leaving
½ inch headspace; seal.
Process in a water bath for 10
minutes Yield about 5½ pints.

OKRA PICKLES

2 pounds fresh okra
3 cups water
1 cup white vinegar
¼ cup pickling salt
2 teaspoons dillseed
½ teaspoon red pepper,
   crushed

Wash okra thoroughly; drain. Pack into hot sterilized pint jars, leaving ½ inch headspace; set aside. In a medium saucepan, combine together, remaining ingredients; mix well. Over medium heat, bring mixture to a boil; cook for 1 minute. Remove from heat, carefully pour hot liquid over okra in jars, leaving ½ inch headspace. Process in boiling water bath for 10 minutes. Yield 4 pints.

STRAWBERRY JAM

2 quarts ripe strawberries
7 cups granulated sugar
1 pkg. (1¾ ozs.) powder fruit
   pectin

Wash and stem strawberries, in a large bowl, crush strawberries. Measure 4½ cups, berries and juice; put in a saucepan, add pectin; mix well. Over high heat, bring mixture to a hard boil, stirring constantly. Add sugar; mix thoroughly, again bring mixture to a hard boil, cook

for 1 minute, stirring constantly. Remove from heat; skim off foam with a metal spoon. Cool slightly; ladle into sterilized jelly glasses. Seal at once with paraffin, 1/8 inch thick or metal lids. Yield about 8 half pints.

FIG PRESERVES

7 cups granulated sugar
¼ cup lemon juice
1½ quarts hot water
2 quarts ripe figs, peeled
2 lemons, thinly sliced

In a large saucepan, combine together, sugar lemon juice and hot water; cook over medium heat until sugar dissolves. Add figs; continue to cook for 10 minutes, stirring occasionally. Add lemon slices; cook rapidly, for another 10 to 15 minutes or until figs are clear. (If syrup becomes too thick, then add boiling water, ¼ cup at a time). Remove from heat; cover; let stand 12 to 24 hours, in a cool place. Pack into sterilized pint jars, leaving ½ inch headspace; seal jars. Process in boiling water bath for 5 minutes.

CHILI SAUCE

14 medium ripe tomatoes,
    cored & chopped
3 red sweet peppers, cored,
    seeded & diced
2 medium onions. peeled &
    diced
2½ cups white vinegar
1½ cups granulated sugar
Salt to taste

In a large saucepan combine together, all ingredients; mix well. Cook over low heat, for 1½ hours, stirring occasionally. When thicken, remove from heat, spoon into sterilized pint jars; seal.

CANTALOPE PRESERVES

3 pounds, ripe cantalope
4 cups granulated sugar
Juice of 1 lemon

Peel cantalope; cut into thin slices, 1 inch long. In a large bowl, place cantalope; add sugar; let stand over night. Next day, in a large saucepan, place mixture; add lemon juice, cook until mixture is clear. Remove from heat; ladle into hot sterilized pint jars; seal. Yield about 2 pints.

PICKLED EGGS

5 medium beets, cooked,
    peeled & quartered
1½ cups cider vinegar
5 tablespoons granulated sugar
2 cloves garlic, minced
1½ teaspoons pickling spice
¾ teaspoon salt
8 hard-cooked eggs, shelled

In a medium mixing bowl, combine together, beets, vinegar, sugar, garlic pickling spice and salt. Let stand for 45 minutes. Place the shelled eggs in a large jar; add beet mixture; cover. Refrigerate for 3 to 7 days, before serving. Yield 8 servings.

ELDERBERRY JAM

3 cups elderberries, washed
¼ cup water
1½ cups granulated sugar

Combine together, all ingredients in a large saucepan, bring to a boil, reduce heat to boil gently for 20 to 30 minutes or temperature reaches 225 degrees on a thermometer. Pour into desired containers; seal.

TANGY SWEET MUSTARD

1 cup granulated sugar
½ cup all-purpose flour
3 tablespoons dry mustard
1 tablespoon turmeric
2 cups white vinegar

In the top of a double boiler, combine together, dry ingredients; mix well. Add vinegar; over medium heat, cook until thick. Remove from heat; pour hot into sterilized pint jars; leaving ½ inch headspace; seal firmly tight. Process in a hot water bath for 5 minutes.

PRESERVED TURNIPS

¼ cup whole mixed pickle
   spices
2 quarts white vinegar
2 cups granulated sugar
4 quarts turnips, cooked, slices
   or chunks

Tie spices in piece of cheesecloth. In a large saucepan, combine together, spice bag with sugar and vinegar; mix well. Bring to a boil, over medium heat; cook mixture for 5 minutes. Remove spice bag; add cooked turnips; bring to a boil again; cook for 1 minute. Remove from heat; pack into hot sterilized pint jars; seal. Process in a water bath for 5 minutes, or use fresh after standing for a few hours.

CHOW CHOW RELISH

3 large onions
5 green tomatoes
6 green peppers
2 cups green beans, cut in ½"
   pieces
2 cups cauliflower, cut in small
   clumps
2 cups fresh corn kernels
¼ cup pickling salt
3 cups granulated sugar
1 tablespoon mustard seed
1½ teaspoons celery seed
¾ teaspoon turmeric
2 cups white vinegar
1 cup water

Use a coarse blade of a food grinder or food processor, grind onions, tomatoes & green peppers. In a large mixing bowl, combine together, onion mixture along with green beans, cauliflower and corn, mix well. Sprinkle with pickling salt, cover; let stand at room temperature overnight. Rinse and drain mixture in the morning. Meanwhile, in a mixing bowl, combine sugar, mustard and celery seeds, turmeric, vinegar and water; mix thoroughly. Pour over vegetables; place in a 4 quart casserole. Cook, covered, over high heat, for 25 minutes, or until mixture boils, then cook 5 minutes more. Seal in hot sterilized pint jars; refrigerate. Relish will keep up to 2 months in refrigerator

APPLE CHUTNEY

4 medium onions, finely diced
2 cloves garlic, minced
8 large apples, pared, diced in
   1/4" pieces
½ cup raisins, coarsely diced
½ cup dried apricots, coarsely
   chopped
1 teaspoon salt
2 teaspoons cinnamon
1 teaspoon ground ginger
1 teaspoon ground cloves
½ teaspoon dry mustard
2½ cups brown sugar
1 cup cider vinegar

In a large saucepan, combine together, all ingredient; mix well. Cook over medium heat, for about 1 hour or until mixture thickens; stirring occasionally. Remove from heat and spoon immediately into hot sterilized jars; seal. Yield 5 cups.

FRUIT JUICE JELLY

4 cups unsweetened apple,
   grape or orange juice
1 pkg. powdered fruit pectin
¼ cup lemon juice
4½ cups granulated sugar

In a large saucepan, combine your choice of fruit juice, pectin and lemon juice; mix well. Bring mixture to a full rolling boil. Cook uncovered for 1 minute, stirring constantly. Remove from heat; immediately pour mixture into hot, sterilized half pints, leaving ½ inch headspace; seal tightly. Yield 6 half pints.

BLACKBERRY JELLY (old recipe)

Crush or grind 2 quarts of ripe berries; squeeze out juice through jelly bag. Measure 3½ cups juice; add 1 package of Sure Jell Pectin; bring to a boil Add 5 cups of granulated sugar; bring to a boil again. Cook hard for 1 minute; remove from heat; pour into ½ pint jars; leaving ½ inch headspace; seal.

TACO SAUCE

3 cups tomatoes, peeled &
   chopped
3 cups jalapeno pepper,
   seeded & finely chopped
   (Caution-it is important to
   gloves when preparing
   peppers)
¾ cup onions, chopped
½ teaspoon salt
3 cloves garlic, minced
1½ cups white vinegar

In a medium saucepan, combine together, all ingredients; mix well. Over medium heat, bring mixture to a boil, reduce heat to simmer. over, cook for 5 minutes. Remove from heat, pack into hot, sterilized pint jars; seal firmly tight. Process in hot water bath for 30 minutes, starting time when water stars to boil.

VARIETY MELON FREEZER JAM

2 cups melon, watermelon,
  cantelope or honeydew, cut
  in 1-inch chunks
4 cups granulated sugar
¼ cup water
1 box pectin

Mash melons, either by hand
or put in blender to puree'.
Measure melon, place in bowl.
Add sugar; mix well, then
allow to set for 10 minutes.
In the meantime, in a small
saucepan, boil water and
pectin, mixed together;
cook for 1 minute. Remove
from heat, stir into fruit; mix
thoroughly. Spoon into desired
containers, leaving ¼ inch
headspace. Allow to set at
room temperature for 24 hours
before placing in the freezer.
Yield 5 cups jam.

HOW TO FREEZE RHUBARB!

Remove leaves; (Note:
leaves are toxic.) trim stems
from stalks. Wash stalks; cut
into 1-inch pieces. Place
cut rhubarb into desired
containers, allowing ½ inch
headspace, tightly seal bag or
container; freeze.

PERSIMMON RELISH

1 cup (2 medium) persimmon,
  diced
½ cup onion, diced
½ * jalapeno' pepper, cored,
  seeded & diced
2 tablespoons lime juice
3 teaspoons cilantro, chopped
Pinch cayenne pepper
Salt to taste

* It is best to wear gloves when
preparing jalapeno' pepper.
Do not touch eyes!

In a small mixing bowl, combine
together, all ingredients; mix
well. Refrigerate before serving.
Yield about 1½ cups relish.

RHUBARB RELISH

2 cups *rhubarb, fresh OR
  frozen, chopped
2 cups onion, chopped
2½ cups brown sugar, packed
1 cup white vinegar
½ teaspoon salt
½ teaspoon ground cinnamon
½ teaspoon allspice
¼ teaspoon ground cloves
¼ teaspoon black pepper

*Careful rhubarb leaves are
toxic. In a medium saucepan,
combine together, all
ingredients; mix well. Over
medium heat, cook for
30 minutes, or until thickened,
stirring occasionally. Remove

from heat, let cool, then store in refrigerator. Relish is good to serve with chicken, pork or beef. Yield 3½ cups.

SWEET CHERRY JAM

2 cups sweet cherries,
    prepared (about
1½ pounds, unprepared)
2 tablespoons lemon juice
4¼ cups granulated sugar
    (keep separate)
¾ cup granulated sugar
1 box Sure-Jell Fruit Pectin

Stem and pit cherries. Finely chop by hand or use food grinder. Measure exactly 2 cups prepared cherries; place in a large bowl. Add lemon juice, along with sugar; mix well and let stand 10 minutes, stirring occasionally. Meanwhile, mix water and pectin together. Place in a small saucepan; bring mixture to a boil, over high heat. Cook for 1 minute, stirring constantly. Remove from heat; then place into mixture. Stir constantly until sugar dissolves and is no longer grainy, about 3 minutes. (Note: A few sugar crystals may remain.) Prepare desired containers with lids, by sterilizing in hot boiling water. Fill each container to within ½ inch of top; cover and let stand at room temperature for 24 hours. Store in refrigerator, for up to 3 weeks or freeze up to 1 year. Thaw in refrigerator. Yield about 5 cups jam.

FREEZER CONCORD GRAPE JELLY

2 cups grape juice (about 3
    pounds grapes)
5¼ cups granulated sugar
¾ cup water
1 box powder fruit pectin

Mash grapes, 1 layer at a time, about 3 pounds of concord grapes. Place crushed grapes in a jelly bag and squeeze out juice. Place juice in a container; add sugar; mix well and let stand for 10 minutes. Meanwhile, combine water and pectin, place in small saucepan; mix well. Cook over medium heat; bring to a boil, cook for 1 minute, stirring constantly. Remove from heat; stir into juice until sugar is dissolved. Pour jelly into pint-size containers or less; cover with tight-fitting lids. Let stand at room temperature until set (may take up to 24 hours) then store in freezer. You can store jelly in the refrigerator, but only up to 3 weeks. Yield 5 eight ounce containers.
NOTE: You can extract juice by using a potato masher or food mill. This method gives a higher yield of juice, however it will produce a cloudier jelly.

BLANCHING—VITAL PART OF FOOD SAFETY

An important step in freezing such garden vegetables as peas, beans and corn is blanching. It is a necessary step to preserve freshness and color, in these vegetables. It's an extra step, but not blanching the vegetables will shorten their freezer span. to one or two months. It is best to blanch the vegetables you plan to freeze to be safe.

TOMATO KETCHUP

4 quarts ripe tomatoes, peeled, cored, & coarsely chopped (zbout 2 dozen medium)
1 large onion, peeled & chopped
1 medium-sized red pepper, cored, seeded & finely chopped
1 cinnamon stick, broken in several pieces
2 cloves garlic, peeled & minced
1½ teaspoon cloves
1½ cups apple cider vinegar
¾ cup granulated sugar
1 teaspoon salt
2 teaspoons paprika

Place prepared tomatoes, onions red pepper, in a large saucepan, over medium heat. Bring to a boil, uncovered; cook for 45 minutes or until soft. Press through a fine sieve, extracting as much liquid and pulp as possible. Return liquid to low heat; simmer, uncovered for 2 to 3 hours, or until the volume of the mixture is reduced by one-half. Stir mixture occasionally to prevent scorching. Meanwhile, tie cinnamon, garlic and cloves in a cheesecloth bag, made by taking a square of cheesecloth and tie 4 corners together with twine. Place vinegar in a small saucepan; drop in spice bag; simmer slowly, uncovered, for 30 minutes or until volume is reduced by half. When tomato mixture is very thick; add spiced vinegar, sugar, salt and paprika. Once again, over medium heat, bring mixture to a boil, uncovered, cook, stirring frequently, for about 30 minutes or until thick as you desire. Remove from heat; using a wide-mouth funnel, pour hot ketchup into hot, sterilized pint jars, leaving ½ inch headspace. Seal jars; process in boiling water bath for 10 minutes. It is best to wait a month before serving. Yield 3 pints.

HONEY JELLY

2½ cups honey
½ cup liquid pectin
¾ cup water

Combine together, honey and water; bring to a boil, over

medium heat. Add pectin, stirring constantly, bring to a full boil; cook for 1 minute. Remove from heat; skim foam from top; pour into sterilized jelly glasses; leaving ½ inch headspace; seal with lid or wax (follow manufacturer's directions).

MIXED PICKLE RELISH (MICROWAVE METHOD)

1 cup cucumber, peeled, seeded & chopped
½ cup onion, chopped
1 cup tart apple, chopped
1½ cups red or green pepper, seeded & chopped
1 tablespoon pickling salt
1 tablespoon fresh ginger, minced
1 clove garlic, minced
¼ teaspoon allspice
¾ cup granulated sugar
2 teaspoons dry mustard
½ cup white vinegar

In a 3-quart glass or ceramic mixing bowl, combine together, cucumbers, onions, apple, peppers and salt. Toss to mix well; let stand in refrigerator, covered, for 2 hours, stirring occasionally Place colander in sink; pour vegetable mixture in it to drain, for at least 1 hour, toss occasionally.

Place drained vegetables in 1½-quart microwave safe bowl; add ginger, garlic and allspice. Combine sugar with dry mustard, then slowly stir in vinegar, until smooth; pour over vegetable mixture; mix well.

MICROWAVE METHOD

Microwave uncovered on high, until mixture boils and thickens slightly, about 20 to 30 minutes. Stir every 5 minutes after mixture starts to boil. Spoon mixture into jar with lid; refrigerate, at least, 8 hours before serving. Relish will keep 2 months in the refrigerator. Yield 2 cups relish.

HORSERADISH RELISH

1 cup *horseradish, grated
½ cup white vinegar
¼ teaspoon salt

Wash horseradish roots thoroughly; remove brown outer skin with a vegetable peeler. The roots may be grated or cut in small cubes and put through a food processor or blender. Place in a bowl; combine ingredients; mix well. Pack into hot, sterile jars, leaving ½ inch headspace; seal tightly. Store in refrigerator.

*NOTE: Be sure to grate or grind horse-radish in adequate ventilation.

DILLED ZUCCHINI

16 cups (about 6 pounds)
  zucchini, washed, trimmed &
  sliced thin
2 cups celery, sliced thin
2 cups onions, chopped
1/3 cup salt
Ice cubes
2 cups granulated sugar
2 tablespoons dill seeds
2 cups white vinegar
6 cloves garlic, halved

In a large mixing bowl,
combine together, zucchini,
celery, onions and salt. Place
a layer of ice cubes over top
of vegetables; cover. Let stand
for 3 hours, then drain well. In
a large saucepan, combine
together, sugar, dill seeds
and vinegar, over medium
heat, bring to a boil, stirring
constantly. Add vegetables;
bring back to a full rolling boil,
stirring several times. Cook
for 1 minute, remove from
heat. Ladle into hot, sterilized
pint jars; place 1 or 2 pieces
of garlic in each jar; seal.
Process in boiling water bath
for 10 minutes. Store in cool dry
place. Yield 6 pints.

TOMATO PRESERVES

8 pounds green tomatoes
6 cups brown sugar, packed

1 TEASPOON EACH cinnamon,
mace and cloves
1 quart white vinegar

In a food processor or blender,
grind tomatoes; place in
large saucepan with brown
sugar. Over medium heat,
bring to boiling; add spices
and vinegar. Reduce heat
to simmer; cook for 1 hour;
Remove from heat; ladle into
sterilized jars; seal.

GREEN TOMATO CHOW CHOW

1 quart green tomatoes
3 green peppers
2 red peppers
2 carrots
½ head cabbage
1 large onion
Salt over vegetables

1 TEASPOON EACH, celery seed
and mustard seed
2 cups granulated sugar
2 cups white vinegar

Grind together, the first 6
ingredients, sprinkle with salt.
Let stand for 2 to 3 hours;
drain; rinse well. Add celery &
mustard seed, sugar & vinegar;
mix well. No cooking necessary.
Put in jars with lids; keep in
refrigerator

PUMPKIN BUTTER

6 pounds pumpkin
2 tablespoon ground cinnamon
2 tablespoons ginger
1 teaspoon allspice
5 pounds brown sugar
5 fresh lemons, juice & rind,
   grated
2 cups water

Remove seeds; peel; put through fine blade of a food grinder. In a large bowl, combine together, pumpkin puree`, the spices, sugar, lemon juice and lemon rind; mix thoroughly. Let pumpkin puree` sit, covered overnight. In the morning, add water; over medium heat, bring mixture to a boil; reduce heat to simmer until soft and to desired consistency. Pour in to hot sterile jars, size as desired; seal.

JALAPENO' HONEY MUSTARD

1 cup dry mustard
¼ cup all-purpose flour
½ cup water
½ cup mustard seeds
1 cup apple cider vinegar
1 cup honey
1 teaspoon salt
2 to 4 tablespoons jalapeno'
   peppers, seeded and
   chopped

In a saucepan, combine together, mustard and flour, mix until well-blended. Whisk in water; let stand for 10 minutes. Add mustard seeds, vinegar, honey and salt. Over medium heat, bring to a boil; reduce heat to simmer, stirring constantly. Cook for 2 minutes; remove from heat; stir in peppers; bottle and refrigerate, for not more than 2 months.

ZUCCHINI JELLY

5 cups zucchini, peeled &
   chopped
4 cups granulated sugar
1 can (20 ozs.) crushed
   pineapple, undrained
1 box (6 ozs.) strawberry gelatin

In a large saucepan, bring above combined ingredients to a rolling boil, over medium heat. Boil for 20 minutes; remove from heat; add gelatin; mix until dissolved. Place in jelly jars; seal. Yield about 8 cups jelly.

KITCHEN FLOOR PICKLES

Use a gallon jar or crock, pack tightly, small to medium-sized cucumbers. Add 2 tablespoons alum, 2 tablespoons pickling salt, 1 cup whole pickling spice and 4 cups white vinegar Fill the rest of the container with water; Cover and let set for 1 month.

BEET RELISH

1 can (16 ozs.) whole beets
¼ cup prepared horseradish
¼ cup granulated sugar
¼ cup white vinegar
¼ cup water
1 tablespoon onions, grated
1 teaspoon salt
¼ teaspoon pepper

Chop beet finely, by hand or in food processor. In large mixing bowl, combine together, beets and all remaining ingredients; mix well. Place a cover over bowl; place in refrigerator for at least one day, before serving. If desired, add more sugar or vinegar to taste. Serve with roasts, sausages or a as an appetizer. Yield about 3 cups relish.

PICKLING SPICE (How to make?)

1 clean jar, 12 ozs. or less
2 tablespoons whole mustard seeds

1 tablespoon whole allspice
2 teaspoons coriander seeds
1 teaspoon red pepper flakes
1 teaspoon dried ground ginger
1 bay leaf. crumbled
1 medium cinnamon stick
2 whole cloves

Clean and dry completely a jar; thoroughly eliminate all residual odors from the jar and lid. Combine together, whole mustard seeds and whole allspice into jar, along with coriander seeds and red pepper flakes. Shake to mix. Add ground ginger to mixed seeds, along with pepper flakes; shake jar again. Sprinkle a crumbled bay leaf over top of mixture. Break a medium cinnamon stick in half; drop both pieces into jar, along with any crumbs. Drop in 2 whole cloves, the final spice. You can use this mix immediately or seal the jar tightly for storage. Use mix within a month.

TO CAN APPLES

Prepare apples, remove the core, peel and slice, place apples in a light syrup, by combining 2 cups granulated sugar and 4 cups water; bring to a boil; cook for 5 minutes.

Remove apple slices, using a slotted spoon; place in hot sterilized canning jars; add ¼ teaspoon ascorbic acid to each jar. Pour hot syrup over apple slices, leaving ½ inch head space; seal jars and place in a hot water bath; process for 15 minutes for pints; 20 minutes for quarts. A bushel of apples will make 15 to 20 quarts.

TO FREEZE APPLES

Prepare apples as in above recipe (To Can Apples), EXCEPT add ½ teaspoon ascorbic acid, to each cup of granulated sugar used as you pack prepared apples, in desired freezer containers. Label, date and freeze.

TO FREEZE VEGETABLES

Asparagus, cut in desired lengths; blanch 2 to 4 minutes

Beans, String, cut, slice or leave whole; blanch 3 to 4 minutes.

Beans, Lima, shell, sort, wash; blanch 2 to 3 minutes.

Broccoli, trim, split lengthwise; blanch 3 to 5 minutes

Brussel Sprouts, trim, leave whole; blanch 4 minutes.

Carrots, peel, cut in slices or dice; blanch 3 minutes.

Cauliflower, break into flowerlets, blanch 4 minutes.

Celery, trim, cut in 1 inch slices; blanch 3 minutes.

Corn, husk, remove silk, blanch 4 minutes, cool & cut from cob.

Greens, all kinds, wash well, discard damaged leaves & stems; blanch 2 minutes; drain.

Okra, trim stem, do not break pod blanch 3 to 4 minutes

Parsnips or turnips, peel & cut into ½ inch cubes or slice; blanch 2 minutes.

Peas, Green or Blackeye, shell, sort, wash; blanch 1 to 2 minutes.

Peppers, trim, cut out stem & seed; may be frozen without blanching

Squash, Acorn, Hubbard, Zucchini, peel, seed, cube or slice, blanch 3 to 4 minutes.

All above vegetables can be frozen in pro-portions, as desired. Blanching is important, because it stops the active enzymes that lead to spoilage. Vegetables should be well-drained & packed without liquid; use plastic freezer bags OR containers, with lids. Label and date.

TO FREEZE FRUITS—Use ascorbic and citric acid mixture, according to manufacturer's instructions (at grocers, where canning supplies are). The pears and pineapple should be packed to freeze with syrup. The other fruits may be packed dry; label & date.

TO MAKE SYRUP: Boil sugar & water until sugar dissolves. (Medium syrup—2 cups sugar and 4 cups water.) (Heavy syrup—4¾ cups sugar and 4 cups water).

SWEET PICKLE CHIPS

1 quart Kosher dill pickles
2 cups granulated sugar
1 small onion, chopped fine
2 tablespoons white vinegar

Drain all liquid from pickles. Use same jar, place drained pickles back into jar. Add 1 cup sugar and ¼ of onion; repeat the procedure for the second half of pickles. Add vinegar last. Cover jar with lid tight; turn upside down for 24 hours.

HOMEMADE PECTIN

4 pounds under ripe Granny
    Smith's apples, washed & cut
    into eighths (Do not core or
    peel.)
8 cups water

Place apples and water in a large stock pot; cover; bring to a boil. Reduce heat to simmer; cook for 20 minutes or until apples are tender. Remove from heat; let cool slightly. pour pulp and juice through a jelly bag, or line a large bowl with a dampened cheesecloth, gather corners of cheesecloth, tie in a knot. Suspend from cabinet knob or handle to allow to drip in a container overnight. Next day, measure apple juice into a large saucepan. Bring to a boil over high heat; cook apple juice until reduced by half. Remove from heat; let cool, then refrigerate, but use it within 4 days or pour into containers and freeze up to 6 months. Yield 3 cups pectin.

TOMATO PICKLE RELISH

9 large tomatoes
3 large onion
3 green peppers
1 large red pepper
2 stalks celery
1½ cups granulated sugar
1½ cups white vinegar
1 tablespoon salt
1 tablespoon mustard seed
½ tablespoon celery seed
Black pepper to taste

Put tomatoes, onions, green and red peppers tables, then put in large saucepan; add remaining ingredients; cook over medium heat; bring to boil, cook for 1 hour. Remove from heat; pour into sterilized pint jars; seal while hot.

DANDELION JELLY

2 cups dandelion blossoms
1 quart water
1 pkg. (1¾ ozs.) powder fruit
    pectin
5½ cups granulated sugar
2 tablespoons lemon extract

In a saucepan, combine together, blossoms & water; bring to a boil, cook for 4 minutes. Remove from heat, then strain, reserving 3 cups of liquid. Discard blossoms; put dandelion liquid in saucepan; add pectin mix well. Again bring to a boil; add sugar; return to a boil, stirring constantly; cook for 1 minute. Remove from heat; add extract and food coloring; skim off foam. Pour hot liquid into sterilized half-pint jars, leaving ¼ inch headspace; adjust lids. Process in a boiling water bath, for 5 minutes. Yield about 6 half-pints.

NOTE: When harvesting buds, blossoms o or leaves from dandelions, be sure that the dandelions have not been treated with chemicals. Always rinse and dry before cooking.

ZUCCHINI MARMALADE

2 pounds of zucchini
Juice of 2 lemons
1 can (13½ ozs.) crushed
    pineapple, drained
1 package powdered pectin
5 cups granulated sugar
2 tablespoons crystallized
    ginger, chopped

Peel zucchini; slice; place in medium saucepan with lemon juice, lemon peel and pineapple. Bring to a boil, over medium high heat; lower heat. Simmer, uncovered for 15 minutes. Add pectin; bring again to a boil. Stir in sugar and ginger; continue at full boil, for a minute, stirring constantly. Remove from heat; skim off foam. Allow mixture to cool 5 minutes. Skim again, if necessary. Ladle into hot, sterilized pint jars; seal with paraffin. Yield 5 pints.

ZUCCHINI JAM

6 cups zucchini, peeled &
    grated
6 cups granulated sugar
2 tablespoons lemon juice
1 can (20 ozs.) crushed
    pineapple, drained
2 packages (3 ozs. ea.) apricot
    gelatin

In a large saucepan, place zucchini and 1 cup water; bring to a boil, over medium heat, for 5 minutes. Add sugar, lemon juice and pineapple; cook for an additional 5 minutes. Add gelatin and cook for 5 minutes more. Seal in jars, as desired.

ZUCCHINI FREEZER JAM

6 cups zucchini, peeled and
    grated
5 cups granulated sugar
½ cup lemon juice
1 pkg. (6 ozs.) gelatin, your
    choice
1 cup crushed pineapple

In a large saucepan, cook
zucchini, covered with water;
cook for 5 minutes, over
medium heat; drain. Add
lemon juice, pineapple and
sugar; bring to boiling; boil
hard for 5 minutes. Remove
from heat; add gelatin; mix
until dissolved. Place in freezer
containers and freeze.

TO PREPARE PUMPKINS TO BOIL—

slice open the pumpkin; clean
out the seeds and membrane.
Cut pumpkin in pieces. Use
appropriate cooking kettle,
place pumpkin in; cover
with water; cook until tender.
Remove from heat; drain; peel
outer skin, then mash by putting
in food processor.

TO BAKE—slice pumpkin in half;

remove seeds and membrane.
Place halves, cut side down,
in a baking dish. Bake in a 325
degree oven, for about 1 hour,
or until tender. Remove from
oven; peel skin, then mash
pumpkin. Refrigerate until
ready to use.

NEW CANNING INSTRUCTIONS FOR PUMPKIN

It is no longer recommended to
can pumpkin in a water bath If
you want to preserve pumpkin,
it is suggested that you do it
by freezing or you can cube
the pumpkin, then can in a
pressure canner, at 10 pounds
pressure (240 degrees) for 55
minutes, in pint jars 90 minutes
in quart jars.

TOMATO PASTE

8 quarts tomatoes, cored,
    peeled
& chopped (or 4 dozen
    tomatoes)
1½ cups green peppers,
    chopped
2 bay leaves
1 tablespoon pickling salt

In a large saucepan, combine
together, tomatoes, peppers,
bay leaves and salt. Over low
heat, simmer until mixture
thickens, about 2 hours, stirring
frequently. When thicken,
remove from heat, pour into
sterilized pint jars. At 10 pounds
pressure in pressure canner.
process for 45 minutes for ½
pints and 50 minutes for pints.
Yield 4 ½ pints.

GREEN TOMATO RELISH

12 large green tomatoes,
    (about 12 cups) chopped
8 red bell peppers (about 2
    cups) chopped
2 large green peppers (1½
    cups) chopped
2 cups cider vinegar
1½ cups brown sugar, packed
1 teaspoon pickling salt
½ cup prepared mustard

Wash vegetables, remove
stems and seeds from peppers;
chop vegetables. In a large
saucepan, bring vinegar and
sugar to a boil; add salt and
mustard, mix well. Add the
vegetables, again bring to a
boil over high heat, uncovered.
Lower heat to simmer; cook
20 to 30 minutes, stirring
frequently. Place in clean, hot
pint jars; process in a boiling
water bath for 10 minutes. Yield
about 6 pints

FREEZER PEAR JAM

4 cups *pears (about 2¼ lbs.)
1 medium apple
1 teaspoon ascorbic acid
    crystals
¼ teaspoon cinnamon
3¼ cups granulated sugar
1 pkg. fruit pectin

Prepare fruit, by washing,
peeling and coring, then chop
or grind. Measure 4 cups into
a large bowl; add ascorbic

acid crystals and cinnamon;
mix well. Combine pectin and
¼ cup sugar, then add to fruit,
mixing thoroughly; set aside for
30 minutes, stirring occasionally.
add remaining sugar; mix
until dissolved Spoon jam into
sterilized freezer containers;
cover immediately. Let stand at
room temperature overnight,
then place in freezer. Stoe a
small amount in the refrigerator,
no longer than 3 weeks. Yield
5½ cups. *To prevent pears
from browning while preparing,
place in cold water; drain, par
dry before chopping.

PEAR CHUTNEY

3 medium-size pears
1 tablespoon lemon juice
1 cup red seedless grapes, cut
    in half
2 tablespoons honey
2 tablespoons Dijon-style
    mustard
5 tablespoons olive oil
1 small onion, chopped
¼ cup raisins
1 tablespoon mustard seeds
½ teaspoon ground allspice

Peel, core and cut pears into
½ inch pieces, toss with lemon
juice. Add grapes, honey and
mustard; mix well; set aside.
Heat oil in a skillet; add onions;
cook until tender. Add raisins,
mustard seeds and allspice; mix
well. Add to fruit mixture; mix
thoroughly. Yield 6 servings.

CAJUN MUSTARD

2 ozs. dry mustard
¼ cup cold wa
1 tablespoon all-purpose flour
3 tablespoons white wine
  vinegar
1 tablespoon honey
1 clove garlic, minced
1 tablespoon hot red pepper
  flakes

1 TEASPOON EACH
ground cumin
dried thyme
coarse black pepper
paprika

In a bowl, combine the dry mustard and flour. Gradually stir in ¼ cup cold water; let stand 15 minutes. Mix in remaining ingredients; mix thoroughly. Use in sandwiches or salads.

JALAPENO JELLY

5 medium *jalapeno chillies,
  chopped
½ cup green peppers,
  chopped
½ cup red bell peppers,
  chopped
6 cups granulated sugar
2½ cups apple cider vinegar
1 bottle (6 ozs.) liquid pectin

* Use gloves when handling jalapeno chillies; avoid touching eyes.

Discard the stem ends of jalapenos, any part of blackened skin, plus remove seeds, part or all of them. Chop chillies, then measure ¼ cup, more if desired. In a blender or food processor, combine together, chillies, green and red peppers; process until chopped fine. Transfer to a large saucepan; add sugar and vinegar; mix well. Over high heat, bring to a boil, cook for 1 minutes, stirring constantly. Add pectin, mix thoroughly. Return to boil, cook for 1 minute, stirring, then remove from heat; skim foam. Pour into prepared half-pint jars, leaving ¼-inch headspace; cover with lids. Then place in a water bath, cook for 15 minutes. Store in cool, dark place. Yield 6 to 7 half-pints jars of jelly.

NECTARINE JAM

8 pounds nectarines, sliced into
  ½ pieces (do not peel)
1 cup granulated sugar
1 cup honey
2 tablespoons lemon juice

Rinse whole nectarines; dry, then slice fruit. In a large bowl, combine together, nectarines and sugar. Let stand at room temperature, for 3 hours. or cover and refrigerate overnight. Then drain fruit for 1 hour. Put drained syrup in large skillet,

over high heat, bring syrup
to a boil, Cook syrup until it is
reduced by half and becomes
very syrupy, about 7 minutes.
Add fruit; cook for 10 minutes,
stirring often. Fruit will soften
and skin will come off. Process
mixture in blender or processor
until smooth. Puree will thicken
jam so that it does not need
to be cooked any further.
Add honey and lemon juice;
mix well. Place mixture back
in skillet and return to simmer
over medium heat. Ladle into
hot sterilized jars; seal, then
process in a hot water bath for
5 minutes. Yield 6½ pint jars.

APRICOT LEATHER

3 ounces dried apricots
¾ cup water
1 tablespoon granulated sugar
½ teaspoon vanilla extract
3 tablespoons lemon juice

In a large bowl, combine
together, all ingredients;
mix well. Cover tightly with
plastic wrap; microwave on
high power, for 8 minutes.
Prick plastic to release
steam. Remove mixture
from microwave; pour into a
blender or food processor;
puree' until smooth. Line a
11x14 inch microwave dish with
parchment paper. Spread ¾
cup of cooled mixture over
the parchment. Microwave

uncovered on high power for
10 minutes. Reduce power
to 50 percent; microwave 10
minutes more. Remove from
microwave; let stand until
completely cool and dry. Peel
from paper; cut in strips.

PICKLED ONIONS

4 quarts small onions
¼ cup mixed pickling spice
2 quarts white vinegar
2 cups granulated sugar

Peel onions; put in large bowl;
add salt; let stand overnight. In
the morning put in colander;
rinse thoroughly with cold
water to remove all salt; drain.
Tie spices loosely in piece of
cheesecloth. In a medium
saucepan, combine vinegar,
sugar and spice bag. Over
medium heat, bring mixture
to a boil; cook for 10 minutes.
Remove from heat; discad
spices. Pack onions into hot,
sterilized jars; pour hot vinegar
mixture over top of onions.
Adjust lids; process in boiling
water bath for 5 minutes. Yield
8 pints.

PICKLED FISH

5 cups water
1 cup salt
6 cups white vinegar
6 cups granulated sugar
3 tablespoons pickling spice
12 to 13 pounds dressed fish
Sliced white onions

Skin and fillet fish. Soak for 48 hours in 5 cups water combined with 1 cup salt, mixing fish often. Rinse fish in cold water; place fish in a bowl, then add vinegar; to cover fish. Let stand another 48 hours. (Fish will turn white.) Combine together, 6 cups vinegar, sugar and spice, in a large saucepan. Bring to a boil; remove from heat; cool. Put a slice of onion in bottom of each jar, then put fish in the jar. Pour vinegar mixture over fish; add more onion; let set for 7 days. Jars need not be tightly sealed, however they should be refrigerated.

PINEAPPLE RELISH

2 cups * ripe pineapple, diced in ½ inch chunks
½ cup red bell pepper, diced in ¼ inch pieces
1 tablespoon lime juice
1 tablespoon granulated sugar
1 tablespoon fresh mint, chopped
2 teaspoons fresh ginger, peeled and minced

In a bowl, combine together, all ingredients; mix well. Refrigerate, covered for at least 6 hours, for flavors to blend. Yield 2 cups relish.

*Leave pineapple out of the refrigerator for a day before using, so it is ripe as possible.

PICKLED GREEN BEANS

4 pounds green beans
8 dried chili peppers, about 2" long
4 teaspoons mustard seeds
4 teaspoons dill seeds
8 cloves garlic
5 cups white vinegar
5 cups water

Prepare green beans by cutting into ½" lengths to fill pint jars. Pack bean into hot, sterilized pint jars. Add 1 chili pepper, ½ teaspoon mustard seeds, ½ teaspoon dill seeds and 1 clove garlic. In a large saucepan, combine together, vinegar and water; bring to a boil. Remove from heat; pour boiling

HAMBURGER PICKLES

5 quarts cucumber slices,
    unpeeled (about 20 cups)
2 red bell peppers, cut in 1"
    pieces
4 cups granulated sugar
2 cups apple cider vinegar
3 tablespoons kosher salt
1 tablespoon celery seed
1 tablespoon mustard seed
1 tablespoon dill seed
2 large onions, sliced thin

Put cucumber slices and peppers in a gallon container; set aside. In a bowl combine together, remaining ingredients; mix well. Pour over cucumber mixture; cover tightly and refrigerate at least 1 week before serving. Keep up to 1 year in the refrigerator. Yield 1 gallon.

CHOW CHOW

1 gallon cabbage, chopped
12 onions, chopped
12 green bell peppers, chopped
12 red bell peppers, chopped
2 quarts green tomatoes,
    chopped
5 cups granulated sugar
4 tablespoons ground mustard
1 tablespoon turmeric
1 tablespoon ground ginger
4 tablespoons mustard seeds
3 tablespoons celery seeds
2 tablespoons mixed whole
    spices
2 to 3 quarts white vinegar

In a large bowl, combine together, all chopped vegetables; add ½ cup pickling salt. Let stand all night. Next day, drain mixture, tie mixed spices in a bag made with a piece of cheesecloth. Add sugar and spices to vinegar, in a large sauce pan, over medium heat. Bring to a simmer; cook for 20 minutes, then add remaining ingredients. Cook until hot and well-seasoned. Remove spice bag; pack hot chowchow into hot sterilized pint jars, leaving ½" headspace; seal immediately.

TOMATO CHUTNEY

1 large fresh tomato (about 1¼
    cups)
2 tablespoons hot pepper jelly
2 tablespoons onion, minced
2 tablespoons fresh cilantro
leaves, chopped
1 tablespoon lime juice
½ teaspoon salt
¼ teaspoon pepper

Core tomato, then chop; place in a medium bowl; add remaining ingredients; mix well. Cover bowl and let stand in refrigerator, for several hours. Remove from refrigerator an hour before serving. Yield about 1¼ cups.

APPLE MARMALADE

1 orange
1 lemon
¼ cup water
8 cups tart apples, peeled and
   thinly sliced (about 2 lbs.)
5 cups granulated sugar
1¼ cups water

Remove rind from orange and lemon; cut into strips 1 inch long. In a medium saucepan, simmer rinds in ¾ cup water until tender, about 15 minutes. Remove from heat; drain; set aside. In a large bowl, combine together, apples, orange and lemon, which have been chopped; mix well; set aside. In a large saucepan, combine sugar and 1¼ cups water. Over low heat, cook slowly until sugar dissolves. Add fruit mixture; Bring mixture to a rolling boil, over medium heat, boil for 10 minutes. Remove from heat; add cooked rind; mix thoroughly. Remove any foam from top of mixture. Pour into hot, sterilized jars; seal, cool and label. Store in cool dry and dark place. Yield about 7 cups.

CORN RELISH

20 medium ears of sweet corn
2½ cups white vinegar
1½ cups granulated sugar
2 cups water
1 cup medium green bell
   peppers, chopped
1 cup medium red bell
   peppers, chopped
1 cup onions, chopped
1 cup celery, chopped
2 teaspoons salt
2½ teaspoons celery seed
½ teaspoon turmeric

In a large saucepan, cook corn covered in water, over medium heat. Bring to a boil; boil for 5 minutes. Remove from heat; cool. Cut from cob; measure 10 cups; place in a large saucepan. Add remaining ingredients; mix thoroughly. Over medium heat, bring to simmer; simmer for 20 minutes. Pack in hot sterile pint jars, leaving ½ inch headspace. Process in boiling water bath for 15 minutes. Yield about 6 pints.

MILD CHILI SAUCE

1 peck tomatoes, scalded &
   peeled
12 medium onions, peeled
6 green bell peppers, cored
4 red bell peppers, cored
5 cups granulated sugar
4 cups white vinegar
2 teaspoons mustard seeds
½ cup salt (more or less to
   taste)

With a food processor or with a hand grinder, grind all the vegetables' add salt mix well. Place vegetables into cheese cloth & let drip over night. Next day squeeze out any excess liquid. Place in mixing bowl; add remaining ingredients; mix thoroughly. Spoon into hot, sterile canning jars, leaving ½ inch headspace, Seal jars and store in a cool place.

PICKLED OKRA

2 pounds fresh okra
5 pods hot red or green
    peppers
5 cloves garlic, peeled
1 quart white vinegar
½ cup water
6 tablespoons salt
1 tablespoon celery seed OR
    mustard seed (optional)

Wash okra; pack in 5 hot, sterilized pint jars. Put 1 pepper pod and 1 garlic clove in each jar. Bring remaining ingredients to a boil, over medium heat. Remove from heat; pour over okra; leaving ½ inch headspace; seal.

NOTE: If pepper pods are not available, use ¼ teaspoon crushed, dried hot pepper, for each jar.

RASPBERRY FREEZER JELLY

3 ½ to 4 quarts raspberries (OR
    enough to make 3 cups of
    juice)
6 cups granulated sugar
¾ cup water

1 box OR tablespoons Sure-Jell
    powdered fruit pectin

Wash raspberries, then place in a blender or food processor to puree'. Filter juice by pouring it into hanging jelly bag or substituting 4 layers of cheesecloth allowing juice to drip into a large bowl overnight. Do not squeeze jelly bag, jelly will be cloudy. Measure 3 cups juice into a mixing bowl, if you are short, add water to make exact 3 cup measure. Blend sugar into juice; mix well.

Let stand at room temperature, for 15 minutes. Meanwhile, combine water and pectin, put in a saucepan; bring to a boil; boil hard for 1 minute, stirring constantly. Remove from heat; add to juice; mix thoroughly for 3 minutes. Place juice into desired containers, leaving ½ inch headspace. Cover immediately. Let jelly stand at room temperature, for 24 hours. Jelly may be soft, but will firm in the freezer. If desired, store 1 container in refrigerator, but wait 1 week before using. Yield 8 eight ounce containers.

APPLE RELISH

3½ cups applesauce
1 cup mixed dried fruits,
    chopped
1/3 cup golden raisins
½ cup light brown sugar,
    packed
½ teaspoon salt
2 teaspoons lemon juice

In a large saucepan, combine together, all ingredients; mix well. Over low heat, bring to a simmer, cook for 30 to 35 minutes. Remove from heat, chill before serving. Serve with all kinds of meat, etc.

PEAR BUTTER

1 gallon pears, peeled
1 No. 2 can crushed pineapple
1 pound dried apricots (which
    have been soaked for 8
    hours)
Granulated sugar

Grind all ingredients or use a blender or food processor. Then add 1 cup sugar for each cup of pulp. Place in a saucepan, bring to a boil, over medium heat; cook for 12 to 15 minutes. Put in desired size sterilized jars, leaving ½ inch head— Process in hot water bath for 20 minutes.

PEACH PRESERVES

4 cups peaches, peeled, pitted
    & sliced
1 package pectin (i.e. Sure Jell)
2 tablespoons lemon juice
7 cups granulated sugar

In a large saucepan, combine together, peaches, pectin and lemon juice; mix well. Bring to a rolling boil, over medium heat, stirring occasionally. Add sugar, stirring to dissolve; return to a rolling boil, cook for 1 minute, stirring constantly. Remove from heat; skim foam, if necessary. Carefully ladle hot preserves into hot, eight ounce jars, leaving ¼ inch headspace. Wipe jar rims clean; seal. In a hot water bath, process jars in boiling water; cook for 20 minutes. Yield 8 to 9 (8 oz.) jars.

FIG JAM

6 pounds ripe figs (weigh after
    peeling)
1 large can pineapple,
    shredded
Juice of 3 lemons
4½ pounds of granulated sugar
1 tablespoon EACH ground
    cinnamon, cloves and
    allspice

Mash peeled figs to fine pulp; place in large bowl. Add remaining ingredients; mixing thoroughly. Over medium heat, cook until mixture thickens and sugar is dissolved, stirring constantly. Remove from heat; spoon into hot sterilized jars, leaving ½ inch headspace; seal jars. Store in cool, dry place.

GOOSEBERRY JELLY (old recipe)

Wash gooseberries; to each pound of fruit, use 1½ cups of cold water, then place in a saucepan with water. Over medium heat, cook until gooseberries burst open. Then remove from heat; strain in a jelly bag. Weigh juice, place in saucepan, over medium heat, bring to a boil; cook for 15 minutes. Remove from heat; add equal amount of sugar, as there is of juice. Heat again to boiling until sugar is dissolved and juice has thickened, stirring constantly. Remove from heat, skim foam, ladle in hot, sterilized jars; seal.

PICKLED PIG'S FEET

4 pig's feet
Cold water
1 large onion, sliced
1 medium carrot, peeled & halved
1 stalk celery
1 clove garlic

4 to 6 sprigs parsley
½ teaspoon salt
3 cups cider vinegar
2 cups water
6 whole cloves
½ teaspoon black peppercorns
¼ teaspoon whole allspice
1 small bay leafs

Scrub pig's feet thoroughly clean. With a sharp knife, split feet lengthwise, beginning between the toes. Place in a large saucepan; cover with cold water, add onion, carrot, celery, garlic, parsley and salt. Over low heat, bring to a simmer; cook for 3 to 4 hours. Meanwhile, combine together, vinegar and 2 cups water, place in a medium saucepan, bring to a boil. Remove from heat; add remaining ingredients. Drain cooked pig's feet; place in a crock or any other nonplastic, nonmetal container. Cover feet with vinegar mixture. Cover container; refrigerate for 3 days, before serving.

VIDALIA ONION RELISH

14 to 16 medium onions OR 24
   cups ground onions OR 1½
   gallons
½ cup pickling salt
1 quart apple cider vinegar
4½ cups granulated sugar
1 teaspoon turmeric
1 teaspoon pickling spice
1 tablespoon pimento, chopped

Place ground onions in a large
bowl, add salt and let stand
30 minutes, then squeeze juice
from mixture; discard juice. Put
onions in a large saucepan
remaining ingredients; mix
well. Bring to a boil; cook for
30 minutes, stirring often. Pack
onions and liquid to cover into
hot, sterilized pint jars, leaving
½ inch headspace. Wipe rims
clean; adjust. lids; process 10
minutes in boiling water bath.
Yield 8 to 10 pints.

HOMEMADE PIZZA SAUCE

2 sticks butter OR margarine
½ cup onions, finely chopped
8 cups tomatoes, cooked
½ cup celery, finely chopped
¼ teaspoon parsley
4 tablespoons oregano
1 tablespoon salt
1 teaspoon celery salt
½ cup granulated sugar

Prepare tomatoes, by placing
them in a blender or food
processor and puree'; set aside.

Ina large skillet, melt butter;
add onions and celery; cook
for 5 minutes. Add tomatoes
and remaining ingredients;
mix thoroughly. Simmer for
30 minutes or until sauce
thickened. Ladle into hot,
sterilized pint jars, leaving a ½
inch headspace; cover with lids.
Process in a pressure canner for
10 minutes, at 240 degrees.

TOMATO MARMALADE

12 cups tomatoes, peeled &
   sliced (or 3 quarts)
6 cups granulated sugar
1 teaspoon salt
2 oranges
2 lemons
2 cups water
4 sticks of cinnamon
2 teaspoons whole cloves

In a large saucepan, combine
together, tomatoes, sugar, salt;
& spices; mix well. Peel orange
and lemon, slice & remove
seeds; add to tomato mixture.
Slice orange & lemon peels
very thin, then place in a small
saucepan, with water; bring
to a boil. Cook for 5 minutes;
drain and add peels to tomato
mixture. Over medium heat,
bring to a boil, then cook
briskly, stirring constantly, for
about 50 minutes, or until
mixture thickens. Remove &
discard spices. Pour into hot,
sterilized pint jars, leaving ½
inch headspace; seal jars
tightly. Yield 5 pints.

PICKLED BANANA PEPPER RINGS

3 pounds banana peppers
2 cups white vinegar
1 cup water
2 tablespoons granulated sugar
1 tablespoon pickling salt
4 cloves garlic

Wash peppers; cut into ¼ inch thick rings; remove core and seeds. In large saucepan, combine together, vinegar, water, sugar and salt; mix well. Over medium heat, bring to a boil, then add peppers; return to a boil. Remove from heat; place 1 clove in ach hot, sterilized pint jars. Immediately fill jars with pepper rings, leaving ½ inch headspace. Pour hot vinegar mixture over peppers, again leave ½ inch headspace. Wipe rims clean and adjust lids. Process in boiling water canner for 5 minutes. Yield 4 pints.

SWEET CHERRY RELISH

4 cups fresh sweet cherries, pitted
2 cups seedless raisins
1 cup brown sugar, packed
¼ cup honey
1 cup white vinegar
2 teaspoons cinnamon
½ teaspoon ground cloves
½ teaspoon nutmeg
1½ cups pecans, chopped

Wash and pit cherries. In a large saucepan, combine together, all ingredients EXCEPT pecans. Over low heat, cook slowly for 1 hour. Stir in pecans, cook 3 minutes more. Pour into hot, sterilized pint jars, leaving ½ inch headspace, clean rims; seal jars. Process 10 minutes in hot water boiling water bath. Yield 2 pints.

TO DRY CORN

In a large kettle, plunge whole ears of corn, that has been shucked, into boiling water, cook for 2 minutes. Remove corn from boiling water, then plunge into ice water to stop further cooking. Next, cut corn off the cob and spread to a single layer of 1½ inch, on a baking sheet. Set oven at a warm temperature (200 degrees). Place corn in oven for 2 or 3 days, or until thoroughly dry. Store in air-tight containers when dry.

HOW TO USE DRY CORN

Add to 1 cup dried corn, 2 cups cold water. Soak for 2 hours; do not drain. Add ½ teaspoon salt; then in a covered saucepan, cook over low heat, until kernels are tender, about 50 to 60 minutes. Add butter, if desired.

LEATHER BRITCHES (Pole Beans)

Thread a large needle with heavy thread, knotted at one end; string beans on the thread, enough for one meal. Hang the strings in a warm, dry place, like an attic. When dried, remove beans from string; soak in water overnight. The next day, over medium heat, bring beans to a boil; reduce heat to simmer, cook for 3 hours or until beans are tender.

TO MAKE THE BEST PICKLES

-Choose cucumbers grown especially for pickling. For best flavor and texture, use cucumbers and pickles with 24 hours after picking. Remove 1/16-inch from blossom end of cucumbers. Use pure granulated pickling salt. Alum and lime are not necessary for crisp pickles.

PICKLED CARROTS

1 pound carrots, cut into 3-inch
   julienne strips
¾ cup water
2/3 cup white vinegar
¾ cup granulated sugar
1 (3 inch) cinnamon stick
   broken
3 whole cloves
1 tablespoon mustard seeds

Place 1 inch water in a saucepan; add carrots; bring to a boil, then reduce heat; cover, simmer for 3 to 4 minutes or until carrots are crisp-tender. Drain; rinse in cold water. Place in a bowl; set aside. In a saucepan, combine water, vinegar, sugar, cinnamon, whole cloves and mustard seeds. Over medium-high heat; bring to a boil, then reduce heat to simmer, uncovered for 10 minutes. Remove from heat; cool and pour over carrots; cover. Refrigerate for 8 hours or overnight. Discard cloves and cinnamon. Yield 6 to 8 servings

COMMON PICKLE PROBLEMS

SOFT—Cucumbers too mature or yellow. Blossoms or stems were not removed.

SLIPPERY—Vinegar solution too weak. Insufficient heat to destroy micro-organisms, (do not start counting processing time until water returns to boiling).

SHRIVELED—Too much time between harvesting and pickling. Too much salt, sugar or vinegar at the start of pickling process. Vinegar solution too strong.

HOLLOW—Over-mature cucumbers. (If cucumbers float during washing, use for relish or chunk-style pickles.

DARK—Minerals in water, especially iron. Using iodized salt. Cooking too long with spices.

NO-COOK PEACH JAM

2 cups fresh peaches, peeled & mashed
2 cups granulated sugar
1 (3 ozs) liquid fruit pectin
2 tablespoons lemon juice

In a bowl, combine together, peaches and sugar; mix well. Let stand 10 minutes, stirring occasionally. Add pectin and lemon juice; mix constantly for 3 minutes. Spoon into desired freezer container.

PEACH LEATHER

Peel Freestone Peaches, then force through sieve or food mill. In a saucepan, place peach pulp, then to each 4 cups of pulp, add 1-2/3 cups granulated sugar; mix well. Bring to a boil; cook for 2 minutes, over high heat, stirring constantly. On a cookie sheet, spread evenly, a thin layer. Cover loosely with cheesecloth. Dry in sun, for 3 to 4 days, or until leather can be rolled. Cut into strips, then roll; sprinkle—with powder sugar,

if desired. Store in an airtight container.

APPLE PIE FILLING

6 to 8 Granny Smith's apples (or any other tart apple)
2/3 cup granulated sugar
1 tablespoon cornstarch
1 tablespoon lemon juice
¼ teaspoon lemon peel
½ teaspoon salt
½ teaspoon nutmeg
¼ teaspoon allspice
½ teaspoon cinnamon
2 to 3 tablespoons butter OR margarine

Core and peel apples; cut into slices, about ½ inch thick. Place apples in a bowl; set aside. In a small bowl, combine sugar and cornstarch. toss the sugar mixture over the apples. Add lemon juice, peel, salt, nutmeg, allspice and cinnamon; toss to combine. if necessary add more sugar. Transfer apple filling to pie pan, which has bottom crust. Cut butter into small pieces; spread evenly over top of filling. Top with crust (see pie chapter for baking directions).

CHERRY PIE FILLING

6 pounds fresh sour cherries
3 cups granulated sugar
½ cup cornstarch
1 teaspoon almond extract
¼ teaspoon red food coloring

Wash cherries; remove stems and pits. In an eight quart pot, combine together, cherries & 2 cups sugar; mix well. Let stand 15 minutes or until juices begin to flow. Attach a candy thermometer to the side of the pot so that bulb is covered with cherry mixture. Over medium-low heat bring mixture to a boil; stirring frequently. Continue boiling until mixture reaches 212 degrees. In small bowl, combine together, the remaining 1 cup sugar and cornstarch, then add to cherry mixture. Add almond extract and food coloring; stirring constantly. Continue cooking until temperature, again, reaches 212 degrees. Ladle hot filling into hot, sterilized jars, leaving ½ inch headspace. Wipe rims clean; attach lids; place in canner. Process in a boiling water bath for 15 minutes for pints or 20 minutes for quarts.

FROZEN PICKLES

4 cups, cucumbers, unpared & sliced thin
1 cup green & red sweet peppers, diced
1 cup onions, diced
1 teaspoon salt
1 tablespoon celery seed
1¼ cups granulated sugar
1 cup white vinegar

In a large mixing bowl, combine together, all ingredients; mix well to evenly coat. Refrigerate; for 5 days; mix each day. Then put into freezer containers; freeze. Yield 3 small containers.

TO CAN TOMATO SOUP

14 quarts ripe tomatoes
1 stalk celery, diced
7 medium onions, diced
3 bay leaves
14 sprigs of parsley
14 tablespoons all-purpose flour
14 tablespoons butter OR margarine
4 tablespoons salt
8 tablespoons granulated sugar
2 teaspoons pepper

In a large kettle, combine together, tomatoes, onions, celery, parsley and bay leaves. Cook over medium heat until celery is tender. Remove from heat; put mixture through a sieve; put back in kettle and bring back to boiling. In a small bowl, rub flour and butter into a smooth paste, thinned with a little tomato mixture. Add to boiling soup, stir to prevent scorching; add salt, pepper and sugar. mix well. Remove from heat; fill quart jars leaving ½ inch of headspace. Adjust lids; process in a water bath for 15 minutes.

REFRIGERATOR PICKLES
(No cooking needed)

6 cups pickles, sliced
1 cup green peppers, sliced
1 cup onions, sliced
1 cup white vinegar
2 cups granulated sugar
1 teaspoon celery seed
2 teaspoons salt

In a large *container, with lid, combine together, all ingredients; mix well. Put in refrigerator; ready to serve in 24 hours. *It is best to use a glass container, such as a gallon jar.

GRAPE BUTTER II

2 pounds Concord grapes
1½ tablespoons orange peel, grated
1 cup water
2¼ cups granulated sugar
½ teaspoon cinnamon
¼ teaspoons ground cloves
Pinch of nutmeg

Wash grapes; drain; pull from stem. Crush pulp from skins; set skins to the side. Place pulp in a large saucepan; cook pulp slowly, over low heat, for about 10 minutes or until soft. Remove from heat; put through a sieve, to remove seeds. Return pulp to saucepan; add orange peel and water. Cook 10 minutes, stirring frequently. Add skins, heat to boiling; add sugar and spices; mix well. Reduce heat; cook over low heat until mixture thickens; stirring frequently. When mixture thicken, pour into hot, sterile jars; leaving ½ inch headspace; seal at once.

FRUIT JUICE JELLY

4 cups unsweetened apple OR grape juice
1 pkg. powdered fruit pectin
¼ cup lemon juice
4½ cups granulated sugar

In a large saucepan, combine together, your choice of fruit juice, pectin and lemon juice. Bring to a full rolling boil over medium heat. Add sugar; mix well, then return to a full rolling boil. Cook for 1 minute, stirring constantly. Remove from heat; quickly ladle fruit syrup into hot, sterilized half pint jars, leaving ½ inch headspace; seal tightly. Yield 6 half pints.

KOHLRABI PICKLE CHIPS

1½ to 2 pounds of small kohlrabi
3 small onions, peeled & sliced thin
¼ cup pickling salt
1 quart ice water
2 cup white vinegar
2/3 cup granulated sugar
1 tablespoon mustard seeds
1 teaspoon celery seeds
¼ teaspoon turmeric

Soak prepared kohlrabi and onions in a mixture of pickling salt and water for 3 hours. Drain and rinse vegetables; place in a bowl. In a saucepan, combine together, remaining ingredients; mix well. Bring to a boil; cook for 3 minutes. Remove from heat, pour over vegetables; let cool. Cover and refrigerate for 3 days before serving. Store in refrigerator. Yield about 1 quart.

HOW TO CAN MEAT!
(An old recipe)

Remove bones, gristle and most of the fat. Cut meat in serving size or for easier packing in jars. Precook in oven or boil until red or pink color disappears. Pack meat in jars, with ½ teaspoon salt, into hot, sterilized jars. Add broth, gravy or meat juice. Adjust lids; process at 10 pounds (pints) for 75 minutes and (quarts) for 90 minutes. This process is for a pressure cooker.

TO CAN TOMATOES

As a precaution, you should add ½ teaspoon citric acid, (not ascorbic) OR 2 tablespoons lemon juice to each quart of tomatoes when canning tomatoes. However, there is no need to add either to tomato sauce, because sauce is more concentrated and have a higher acid content.

TO FREEZE STRAWBERRIES

Wash berries in cold water; drain and remove hulls,

TO FREEZE DRY WITH SUGAR

Slice, quarter or leave whole. Measure berries; place in large bowl. Add ¾ cup granulated sugar for each quart of berries. Gradually sprinkle over berries or mix gently. Place in freezer containers, leaving headspace of ½ inch for pints and 1 inch for quarts; freeze.

TO USE SYRUP PACK

Make a sugar syrup by boiling, over medium heat, 4½ cups of sugar and 4 cups water. Cook until sugar dissolves. Yield 6½ cups. You will need ½ to 2/3 cup for each pint container. Refrigerate syrup until ice cold. Pack sliced, quartered or whole berries into freezer containers, pour chilled syrup over berries, leaving headspace of ½ inch for pints and a inch for quarts. Do not use crushed berries with syrup.

TO FREEZE STRAWBERRIES WITHOUT SUGAR

Leave berries whole, either freeze individually on a cookie sheet, then pack in freezer containers; label and date. Or pack into desired containers then freeze. Use this method when sugar is restricted, however, the quality of the strawberries are maintained much better when sugar is added. You can cut the amount of sugar in the other methods to ¼ cup per quart. To finish all methods, leave head space of ½ inch for pints and 1 inch for quarts. Twelve quarts of strawberries will yield about 19 pints of frozen berries.

CANNING GREEN BEANS

1 gallon fresh green beans
½ cup white vinegar
2 tablespoon salt
2 tablespoons granulated sugar

Prepare green beans by washing, then cutting into 1 inch pieces. Place beans in a saucepan; cover with cold water; add remaining ingredients. Over medium heat, bring mixture to a boil; cook for 25 minutes. Remove from heat; put beans in hot, sterile jars. Use the liquid that the beans were cooked in; cover beans, leaving ½ inch headspace; seal jars; let cool. If desired, when using beans, you can rinse beans with water to remove vinegar out.

RHUBARB RELISH

8 cups onions, chopped
8 cups rhubarb, sliced (about 3 pounds
1 cup granulated sugar
3 cups white vinegar
2 teaspoons salt
1 teaspoon pepper
2 teaspoons ground cloves
2 teaspoons cinnamon

Boil onions in water for 2 minutes; drain. In a large saucepan, combine together, all the ingredients, including drained onions. Simmer for 30 minutes or until mixture thickens, stirring occasionally. Place mixture into hot, sterilized jars, leaving ½ inch headspace; seal. A good relish to serve with and fish.

FREEZER CORN

12 cups corn, cut off cob
½ cup butter OR margarine
1 teaspoon salt
½ cup granulated sugar
¾ cup milk

In a large saucepan, combine together all the above ingredients EXCEPT corn. Place over low heat until the butter melts. Add cut corn; bring to a boil; boil for 1 minute. Remove from heat; cool, then portion, as desired, in freezer bags; date and freeze.

TO FREEZE GRAPES

Select firm ripe grapes; wash and stem. Seedless grapes may be left whole, grapes with seeds should be split and seeds removed. Grapes used for juice or jelly may be frozen without sugar. Leave a ½ inch headspace in containers, then freeze. Grapes used in jams or pies should be frozen in a sugar syrup, consisting of 3 cups granulated sugar and 4 cups water; mix until sugar dissolves. Pack grapes in containers, leaving ½ inch headspace; seal and freeze.

TO CAN GRAPES

Wash and stem and halve grapes; remove seeds. Pack tightly into canning jars, without crushing. Add boiling syrup, which consist of 3 cups granulated sugar and 4 cups water, brought to a rolling boiling, over medium heat. Cover grapes, leaving ½ inch headspace; seal Process pints or quarts, for 29 minutes, in a boiling water bath. water should cover jars by 1 inch.

HOT DOG RELISH II

1 large yellow Bermuda onion, finely chopped
2 tablespoons cider vinegar
2 tablespoons granulated sugar
¼ teaspoon salt

1 jar (4 ozs.) pimiento, drained & chopped

In a medium bowl, combine together, all temperature, for 30 minutes, before serving. Mixture will keep for 1 week, covered and refrigerated. Yield 1 cup

PICKLED RAMPS (aka Wild leeks)

1 pound ramps, cleaned
½ cup water
1½ cups white vinegar
2 tablespoons salt
2 tablespoons honey

In a saucepan, combine together, all ingredients, EXCEPT ramps. Over high heat, bring mixture to a boil; then remove from heat. Meanwhile, prepare ramps, by cleaning, either use the whole ramp or the bulbs only. Pack ramps in to hot sterilized pint jars, then add pickling brine with ¼ teaspoon alum to each jar leaving ½ inch headspace; seal, then put in water bath for 5 minutes.

MIXED FRUIT COCKTAIL

3 pounds peaches
3 pounds pears
1½ pound seedless green grapes
1 jar (10 ozs.) of Maraschino cherries
3 cups granulated sugar
4 cups water
Cherries, wash, stem & pit

Dip ripe, firm peaches in boiling water, dip in cold water, slip off skins; cut into ½ inch cube, then place peaches in a strong ½ lemon and ½ vinegar solution. Stem and wash grapes, place in lemon/vinegar solution with peaches. Peel, halve and core pears; cut into ½ inch cubes, also, place in lemon/vinegar solution; set aside. In a saucepan, combine together sugar and water, mix well, then over medium heat, bring to a boil. Meanwhile, drain mixed fruit; place ½ cup hot syrup in each hot, sterilized pint jar; fill jar with mixed fruit, add a few cherries. fill jar with more hot syrup, leaving ½ inch headspace; adjust lids. Process pint jars, for 20 minutes in hot water bath.

DRYING VEGETABLES

General instructions for drying vegetables are as follows. Wash, trim and cut into serving slices, strips or cubes. The same instructions apply to all vegetables, except onions and herbs, which should be blanched or precooked. You can harvest food dried on the vine, like some farmers do, or dry foods in a dehydrator unit, then you can use an oven. Following is a list of vegetables that are suitable for drying: Asparagus, Beans such as lima, snap and pole, Beets, Broccoli, Brussel Sprouts, Cabbage, Carrots, Celery, Corn, Mushrooms, Onions, Peanuts, peas, Peppers, Pumpkin and Winter Squash, Rhubarb, Spinach, Swiss Chard Kale, Summer Squash, Zucchini and Tomatoes. All herbs can be dried, plus some fruits, such as apples, plums and cherries. The basic techniques for drying vegetables is to first to blanch them for 10 to 15 minutes. Blanching stops the ripening process of the vegetable, plus prevents color changes. If you do not blanch your foods before the drying process, you could end up with moldy, discolored food.

General instructions for drying vegetables is to wash, trim, either cut in slices or strips, approximately 1/8 inch thick or in cubes, about 3/8 inch on each side. You will need a cooking utensil with a lid, you will need 1 gallon of water for each pound of vegetable (use 2 gallons of water for leafy vegetables). It would be helpful if a wire basket were used.

PICKLED HERRING

2 whole salted herrings
2 large onions, sliced
1 cup cider vinegar
4 peppercorns
4 whole allspice
1 teaspoon granulated sugar

Soak herrings in cold water for at least 24 hours; change water every 8 hours. Save the milch from the herring. Skin & remove bones; cut each herring into 4 pieces. Arrange a layer of onions on a deep platter, then layer herrings on top of onions. Meanwhile boil vinegar; set aside to cool. Rub milch through sieve; mix with vinegar and sugar; pour over herring. If desired, serve with whole boiled potatoes.

ROSE JELLY (old recipe)

8 cups, wild unsprayed rose
    petals, picked in the early
    recipe
10 cups cold water
½ cup strained fresh strawberry
    juice
7 pounds granulated sugar
2 cups liquid fruit pectin
24 rose leafs, washed (optional)

Wash and drain rose petals; place in large enamel pan with the cold water. Bring to a boil; simmer gently for 15 minutes. Strain through a jelly bag or through several thicknesses of cheese-cloth. Add strawberry juice; mix well. Add water if necessary, to make up 2 quarts; return to pan. Add sugar; bring to a boil, stirring until sugar dissolves. When the mixture is boiling rapidly, pour and stir in the pectin all at once. Pour into hot, sterilized jelly jars, if desired, decorate the surface of each jar with a rose leaf. Seal with 2 thin layers of melted paraffin; let stand, undisturbed until cool, then store in a cool, dark place. Yield about 2 dozen six ounce jars.

VIOLET JELLY

2 cups wild violets, lightly
packed, washed
Juice of 1 lemon
1 box Sure-Jel
4 cups granulated sugar

Place violets in a quart jar; add boiling water. Let stand for 24 hours; strain mixture, reserving 2 cups violet water. In a saucepan, combine together, violet water, lemon juice and Sure-Jel; mix well. Over high heat, bring to a boil; then add sugar; mix thoroughly. Cook until mixture sheets from spoon. Pour into hot, sterilized jelly jars, leaving ½ inch head space; seal.

QUEEN ANNE'S LACE JELLY

4 cups water
18 large Q. Anne's Lace
  blossoms
¼ cup lemon juice
1 pkg. powder pectin
3½ cups granulated sugar
Red food color (optional)

In a large saucepan, bring
water to a boil. Remove from
heat; add blossoms, pushing
them down into the water;
cover. Let steep for 30 minutes.
Remove cover; let mixture cool
slightly, about 15 minutes. Strain
liquid through a dampened
cheese-cloth, discarding
blossoms. Measure 3 cups of
liquid in to saucepan; add
lemon juice and pectin. Over
high heat, bring to a rolling boil,
stirring constantly; add sugar.
Cook until mixture returns to
rolling boil, continue stirring;
boil for 1 minute. Remove from
heat, if desired add red food
color Skim foam, then pour into
jars, leaving ¼ inch headspace;
seal.

FRUIT LEATHERS

2 cups fruit, peeled & chopped

Preheat oven at 200 degrees.
Line rimmed cookie sheet
with plastic wrap. Puree' fruit
in blender or food processor,
then spread evenly in prepared
cookie sheet. Bake 3 to 4 hours,
with ven door ajar, checking
occasionally, until no longer
moist, to touch. Remove from
oven; let cool. Roll up; place in
container.

Chapter 4

NEW AND OLD DESSERTS

IN TRYING TIMES, DON'T QUIT TRYING!

OLD AND NEW DESSERTS

Whether dessert after your next dinner is a new one taken from the latest women's magazine. Or an old one that your grandmother made when you were a child, desserts are great. Most desserts are easy to make, some take a little time to make. The following dessert recipes have been chosen for variety and especially for your enjoyment.

BLACK WALNUT BRITTLE

½ cup light corn syrup
2 cups granulated sugar
1/3 cup water
1 teaspoon vanilla extract
¼ teaspoon salt
1 tablespoon butter OR
    margarine
1 cup black walnuts

In a medium saucepan, combine together, corn syrup, sugar, water, salt and butter, Bring mixture to a boil; cook until sugar dissolves; add walnuts. Lower the heat to simmer; cook, stirring constantly, until a small amount of candy separates into hard brittle threads when dropped into cold water or (300 degrees on a candy thermometer). Remove from heat; add vanilla; mix well. Pour onto a buttered cookie sheet; let cool completely. Then break into pieces. Yield 1¼ pounds.

ROCKY ROAD ICE CREAM

3 cups milk
3 cups half & half cream
9 squares (1 oz. ea.) semisweet
    chocolate
2¾ cups granulated sugar
½ teaspoon salt
6 cups heavy whipping cream
3 cups miniature marshmallows
2¼ cups mini chocolate chips
1½ cups pecans, chopped
6 teaspoons vanilla extract

In a large saucepan, combine milk and half & half; heat to 175 degrees. Add chocolate squares, sugar and salt; stir until chocolate is melted and sugar is dissolved. Remove from heat; cool by placing mixture in refrigerator for about 1 hour. When cooled completely, place in a large mixing bowl; stir in remaining ingredients; mix thoroughly. Place in desired containers and freeze for 2 to 4 hours before serving. Yield about 4½ quarts.

EGGNOG FUDGE

½ cup butter OR margarine
¾ cup eggnog
2 cups granulated sugar
1¼ cups white chocolate bars,
broken into pieces
½ teaspoon nutmeg
1 jar (7 ozs.) marshmallow
  crème
1 cup pecans, chopped
  (optional)
1 teaspoon rum extract

In a large saucepan, combine together butter, eggnog and sugar. Over medium-high heat, bring to a full boil, stirring constantly. Reduce heat to medium; continue to boil and stirring frequently for 8 to 10 minutes or until mixture reaches 234 degrees on a candy thermometer. Remove from heat; add chocolate and nutmeg; stir until smooth. Add marshmallow crème, pecans and rum extract; mix well. Pour mixture into a square pan, lined with foil; cool completely. Cut into 1½ inch squares, or as desired Store in an airtight container; refrigerate up to 1 week.

FUNNEL CAKES

3 large eggs
1 cup milk
2 cups all-purpose flour
1 tablespoon granulated sugar
1 teaspoon baking powder
¼ teaspoon salt
Oil for deep frying
Powder sugar, sifted OR maple
  syrup

Pour about 1½ inches oil into skillet, if electric, heat to 375 degrees. In the mean time, beat all ingredients, EXCEPT powder sugar, in a large mixing bowl, until smooth. When oil is hot, fill a large funnel, with batter, holding forefinger over the open end. Remove forefinger to let batter dribble into the center of skillet, moving funnel in a spiral to make an 8 or 9-inch round cake. Cook until golden, on both sides. Remove cake with slotted spatula; place on paper towels. Sprinkle with powder sugar or place on plate and drizzle with maple syrup.

HOMEMADE FROZEN CUSTARD

4 cups milk
4 large eggs
1¼ cups granulated sugar
1/3 cup cornstarch
Pinch of salt
1 can (14 ozs.) sweetened
    condensed milk
2 tablespoons vanilla extract

In a large saucepan, bring milk to a boil, over medium-high heat Meanwhile, beat eggs; add sugar, cornstarch and salt; mix well. Gradually add a small amount of hot milk; then return mixture to saucepan to cook. Stir constantly for 6 to 8 minutes, or until mixture thickens. Gradually stir in condensed milk and vanilla; mix well. Chill in refrigerator for 3 to 4 hours. Pour into desired containers. Freeze several hours before serving. Yield about 1½ quarts.

RHUBARB COBBLER

¾ cup granulated sugar
2 tablespoon cornstarch
4 cups rhubarb, chopped
1 tablespoon water
1 tablespoon butter OR
    margarine, diced
1 teaspoon ground cinnamon
1 cup all-purpose flour
1 tablespoon granulated sugar
1½ teaspoons baking powder
¼ teaspoon salt

¼ cup butter OR margarine
¼ cup milk
1 large egg, beaten

Combine together, sugar and cornstarch; mix well. Add to chopped rhubarb, with water. Place rhubarb in a medium saucepan; cook over medium heat; bring to a boil. Cook and stir for 1 minute; pour rhubarb mixture into a greased 13x9" baking pan. Dot with butter; sprinkle with cinnamon; set aside. In a bowl, combine together, by sifting, flour, 1 tablespoon sugar, baking powder and salt. Cut in ¼ cup butter until coarse crumbs form; set aside. Mix together milk and beaten egg, then add to dry ingredients, stirring just to moisten. Drop by teaspoon on top of rhubarb; sprinkle with sugar. Bake at 400 degrees, for 20 minutes.

SWEET POTATO PUDDING

2 cups sweet potatoes, cooked
    & mashed
½ cup brown sugar, firmly
    packed
3 tablespoons butter OR
    margarine, melted
2 large eggs, separated
¾ cup unsweetened orange
    juice
¼ teaspoon ground nutmeg
¼ teaspoon ground cloves
Dash of salt
2 tablespoon granulated sugar

In a large mixing bowl,
combine together, potatoes,
brown sugar, margarine and
egg yolks; mix well. Gradually
add orange juice, nutmeg
and cloves; mix well; set aside.
Beat egg whites until foamy;
add salt; beat until soft peaks
form. Fold egg whites into
potato mixture. Pour into a 1½
quart baking dish, sprayed
with cooking spray. Place
baking dish in a large shallow
pan, adding hot water in the
pan to a depth of 1 inch. Bake
at 350 degrees, for 1 hour or
until center is set and edges
are browned. Remove dish
from water; let cool 15 minutes
before serving. Yield 8 to 10
servings.

CRACKER PUDDING

2 quarts milk
2 large eggs
2 teaspoons vanilla extract
1¼ cups granulated sugar
1½ pkgs. club crackers, crushed

In a large saucepan, heat milk
over low heat. Meanwhile, in a
small mixing bowl, beat eggs
with vanilla and sugar. Remove
hot milk from heat; add egg
mixture gradually to hot milk;
mix well. Add crushed crackers,
mix until thickens. Refrigerate
until ready to serve.

PEACH FRITTERS

½ cup granulated sugar
2 large eggs, well beaten
1/3 cup butter OR margarine
2 cups all-purpose flour
3 teaspoons baking powder
½ teaspoon salt
1 cup milk
½ teaspoon lemon juice
½ teaspoon vanilla extract
1½ cups peaches, chopped

In a large bowl, cream butter
& sugar; add eggs; beat
thoroughly. In another bowl, sift
together, dry ingredients; add
to butter mixture, then add milk
slowly; mix well. Fold in peaches,
lemon juice and vanilla. Drop
by spoonful into hot oil; fry until
golden brown. If desired, serve
with whipped cream.

APPLE MUFFINS

¼ cup shortening
½ cup granulated sugar
1 large egg, beaten
½ cup milk
1½ cups all-purpose flour
½ teaspoon cinnamon
½ teaspoon salt
3 teaspoons baking soda
1 cup tart apples. Chopped

TOPPING

1/3 cup brown sugar, packed
½ teaspoon cinnamon
1/3 cup nuts, chopped

Preheat oven at 375 degrees. In a medium mixing bowl, cream together, shortening, sugar and egg, until light and fluffy. In a another bowl, sift together dry ingredients. Add dry ingredients and milk alternately to creamed mixture; mix well Fold in apples, then spoon into well-greased muffin pans, filling 2/3 full; set aside. Prepare topping, then spoon over tops of muffins. Bake for 20 to 25 minutes, or until tested done.

COCONUT ICE CREAM

1¾ cups granulated sugar
½ teaspoon salt
4 cups milk
1½ coconut, flaked, divided
4 cups whipping cream
1 tablespoon vanilla extract

In a large saucepan, combine together, sugar, salt and milk. Over medium heat, cook until mixture begins to boil. Add ½ cup coconut. Remove from heat; let stand for 30 minutes. Strain, discarding coconut. Place milk mixture in a large bowl; add whipping cream, vanilla and remaining coconut. Freeze in an ice cream freezer according to manufacturer's directions, or transfer to a 2 quart freezer container. Cover and freeze for at 4 hours before serving. Yield 2 quarts.

CARROT MUFFINS (with Cream Cheese Filling)

1 can (14½ ozs.) carrots, sliced, drained
1¾ cups all-purpose flour
1 cup granulated sugar
1¼ teaspoons baking soda
½ teaspoon salt
½ teaspoon cinnamon
Pinch of ground allspice, cloves & nutmeg
1 large egg
1/3 cup vegetable oil

FILLING

1 pkg. (8 ozs.) cream cheese, softened
1 large egg
¼ cup granulated sugar

Place carrots in food processor or blender; cover; process until smooth. In a large bowl combine together, flour, sugar, baking soda, salt and spices; set aside. In a small bowl, whisk the pureed carrots, egg and oil; mix well. Add carrot mixture to dry ingredients; mix just until moistened; set aside. Prepare filling, by beating together all the filling ingredients until smooth. Fill a greased muffin tin 1/3 full of batter, then place a tablespoonful of filling in the center of each muffin; top with batter. Bake at 350 degrees, for 20 to 25 minutes or until tested done. Remove from oven and let cool for 5 minutes before removing from pan. Yield 12 muffins.

BASIC MUFFIN RECIPE (with Cream Cheese Filling & Streusel Topping)

2½ cups all-purpose flour
½ cup granulated sugar
1 tablespoon baking powder
½ teaspoon salt
1 cup milk
½ cup butter OR margarine, melted
1 large egg, beaten

Preheat oven to 400 degrees F. In a medium bowl, combine together, by sifting, flour, sugar, baking powder and salt; set aside. In a large mixing bowl, combine milk, melted butter, beaten egg and vanilla; mix well. Add dry ingredients gradually to milk mixture Mix only until all dry ingredients are moistened. Do not over mix. Grease muffin tin and fill each cup ½ full with batter; add cream cheese mixture, about 2 tablespoons onto batter, then top cream cheese with more muffin batter to fill muffin tin about ¾ full. Add streusel evenly on top of batter. Bake muffins for 20 to 25 minutes, or until tested done.

Remove from oven; let cool for 10 minutes; remove from tin; let cool completely. Yield 10 to 12 muffins.

CREAM CHEESE FILLING

1/3 cup granulated sugar
1 large egg
½ teaspoon vanilla extract

In a small bowel, beat together, above ingredients, until well-blended.

STREUSEL

½ cup granulated sugar
½ cup all-purpose flour
½ cup butter OR margarine

In a small mixing bowl, combine together, all ingredients, with a fork until crumbs, the size of peas, form. Spread evenly on top of batter.

APPLE OR BLACKBERRY MUFFINS

1½ cups all-purpose flour
¼ cup granulated sugar
2 teaspoons baking powder
½ teaspoon cinnamon
¼ teaspoon salt
1 large egg
½ cup milk
¼ cup vegetable oil
1 cup apples, chopped OR 1
   cup blackberries

In a large mixing bowl, combine together, flour, sugar, baking powder, cinnamon and salt; set aside. In another bowl, beat eggs; add milk and oil; mix well. Add fruit, then add flour, all at once and stir only just until batter is moistened; do not over mix. Lightly grease muffin tin; fill 2/3 cup full; bake at 400 degrees F., for 25 to 30 minutes Yield 12 muffins.

RICE MUFFIN

1½ cups all-purpose flour
2 teaspoons baking powder
½ teaspoon salt
2 tablespoons granulated sugar
3 tablespoons shortening,
   softened
2 cups rice, cooked
1 large egg
1 cup milk

In a medium mixing bowl, sift dry ingredients together. Cut in shortening; add rice, egg & milk. Mix only until moistened. Lightly grease muffin tin; fill ½ full; bake at 425 degrees F., for about 25 minutes, or lightly browned. Yield 12 muffins.

CAKE MIX MUFFINS

1 box (9 ozs.) yellow cake mix
¼ cup cold water
1 large egg, beaten
1 tablespoon sour cream

In a large mixing bowl, combine together, all the ingredients. Mix only just until blended. Fill muffin tins ¾ full. Bake at 400 degrees, for about 15 minutes, or until tested done. Yield 10 to 12 muffins.

FRESH LEMON ICE CREAM

2 cups whipping cream OR Half
   & Half
1 cup granulated sugar
1 to 2 tablespoons lemon peel,
   grated
1/3 cup fresh lemon juice

In a medium bowl, combine
together, cream and sugar,
mix until sugar is thoroughly
dissolved. Mix in peel and
juice. Pour into ice cube tray
or desired container. Freeze
several hours or until firm.

PUMPKIN CREAM CHEESE MUFFINS

1¼ cups all-purpose flour
1 teaspoon pumpkin pie spice
½ teaspoon baking soda
1 large egg, slightly beaten
¾ cup brown sugar, packed
2/3 cup pumpkin puree'
¼ cup vegetable oil
1 pkg. (3 ozs.) cream cheese,
   softened
1 large egg white only
2 teaspoons granulated sugar
1/3 cup pecans, chopped

In a medium mixing bowl,
sift together, flour, spice and
baking soda; set aside. In
another bowl, combine whole
egg, brown sugar, pumpkin
and oil; mix well. Add to flour
mixture, mixing only until batter
is moistened; set aside. In
another bowl, combine cream
cheese, egg white and sugar;
mix until smooth and creamy.
In a muffin tin, with or without
paper cups, spoon pumpkin
batter ½ full. Spoon 1 rounded
teaspoon of cream cheese
mixture on top of batter. Add
a dollop of pumpkin batter on
top of cream cheese, spreading
carefully to the edges. Sprinkle
with chopped pecans; bake at
350 degrees, for about 20 to 25
minutes, or until tested done.
Yield 12 muffins.

BLUEBERRY MUFFINS

¼ cup butter OR margarine
¾ cup granulated sugar
1 large egg
1½ cups all-purpose flour
2 teaspoons baking powder
½ teaspoon salt
½ cup milk
1 cup blueberries, fresh OR
   *frozen
*If using frozen blueberries,
   drain excess liquid.

In a medium mixing bowl,
cream together, butter and
sugar; add egg; beat until
smooth and creamy. Add dry
ingredients, alternately with
milk. Gently fold in the berries;
spoon batter into greased
muffin tin ¾ full. Bake at 375
degrees, for 15 to 20 minutes.
Yield 12 muffins.

BANANA NUT MUFFINS

2½ cups all-purpose flour
¾ cup granulated sugar
1 teaspoon baking powder
1 teaspoon baking soda
½ teaspoon salt
3 large eggs, beaten
2/3 cup butter OR margarine,
    melted
2/3 cup buttermilk
1¼ cups bananas, mashed (3
    medium)
2/3 cup nuts, chopped

In a large mixing bowl, sift together flour, sugar, baking powder, soda and salt. In a smaller bowl, beat eggs; add melted butter and buttermilk; mix thoroughly. Add mashed bananas; mix well. Make a well in the dry ingredients; add egg mixture, mix lightly. Fold in nuts; spoon batter into greased tins. Bake at 350 degrees, for 20 to 25 minutes or until golden brown. Yield 24 muffins.

KOLACHE'-TYPE MUFFINS FILLING

½ cup prunes, pitted, chopped
    finely
1 tablespoon margarine,
    melted
1 tablespoon granulated sugar
½ teaspoon cinnamon
¼ cup nuts, chopped

In a small bowl, place pitted prunes; cover with water. Soak overnight, next day; drain; chop finely and stir together, melted margarine, sugar, cinnamon and nuts; set aside.

MUFFINS

1½ cups all-purpose flour
1/3 cup granulated sugar
1½ teaspoons baking powder
½ teaspoon baking soda
¼ teaspoon allspice
1 large egg
2 tablespoons margarine,
    melted
1 cup buttermilk
Cinnamon sugar (optional)

In a medium mixing bowl, sift together, dry ingredients. Beat together, egg, melted margarine and buttermilk. Then add egg mixture to dry ingredients; mix well. Spoon batter into lightly greased muffin tin 1/3 full. Add 1 tablespoon prune filling; cover with more batter to fill muffin tin 2/3 full. If desired, sprinkle cinnamon sugar on top. Bake at 400 degrees, for 15 to 20 minutes. Yield 12 muffins.

ZUCCHINI MUFFINS

3 cups all-purpose flour
1 teaspoon baking powder
1 teaspoon baking soda
½ teaspoon salt
1 teaspoon cinnamon
1 cup granulated sugar
4 large eggs
1 cup vegetable oil
2 cups zucchini, grated
1 teaspoon vanilla extract
1 cup nuts, chopped (optional)
½ cup raisins (optional)

In a large mixing bowl, sift dry ingredients together; set aside. In another bowl, combine sugar and eggs, beat for 2 minutes. Gradually add oil, beating constantly, for 2 to 3 minutes. Add zucchini and vanilla; mix well. Fold in nuts, raisins and dry ingredients; mix just until moistened. Do not over mix. Spoon batter into greased muffin tins; bake at 400 degrees, for 20 minutes, or until tested done. Remove from oven, let cool in tins for 10 minutes, before serving. Yield 24 muffins.

ROCKY ROAD MUFFINS

4 ozs. semisweet chocolate
1 oz. unsweetened chocolate
1/3 cup butter OR margarine
¾ cup sour cream
½ cup brown sugar, packed
¼ cup light corn syrup
1 large egg
1 teaspoon vanilla extract
1½ cups all-purpose flour
Pinch of salt
1 teaspoon baking soda
2/3 cup nuts, chopped
2/3 cup miniature marshmallows

In a double boiler, melt first three ingredients In a small mixing bowl, beat together, sour cream, brown sugar, corn syrup, egg and vanilla; set aside. In a large mixing bowl, mix remaining ingredients thoroughly, EXCEPT nuts and marshmallows. Add melted chocolate to sour cream mixture; mix well. Add gradually to flour mixture; mix thoroughly. Fold in nuts and marshmallows; batter will be lumpy. Spoon batter into greased muffin tins, ¾ full. Bake at 400 degrees, for 18 to 20 minutes, or until tested done. Yield 16 muffins.

PINEAPPLE MUFFINS

1 large egg
1 cup unsweetened pineapple
    juice
¼ cup shortening, melted
2 cups all-purpose flour
½ teaspoon salt
4 teaspoons baking powder
¼ cup granulated sugar
½ cup crushed pineapple,
    well-drained
2 tablespoons granulated sugar
1 teaspoon orange peel, grated

In a large mixing bowl, beat together, egg and pineapple juice; add shortening. In a separate bowl, combine together, flour salt, baking powder and sugar. Mix until just moistened; fold in drained pineapple. Fill greased muffin tins two-thirds full. Sprinkle with 2 tablespoons sugar and grated orange peel. Bake at 400 degrees, for 25 minutes, or until golden brown. Yield 12 muffins.

NOTE: Muffins bake best on the middle shelf of oven.

PINEAPPLE UPSIDE-DOWN MUFFINS

¼ cup butter OR margarine, melted
1/3 cup brown sugar, packed
1 cup crushed pineapple, drained
1½ cups all-purpose flour
½ cup granulated sugar
¼ teaspoon salt
½ teaspoon baking soda
1 teaspoon baking powder
1 teaspoon cinnamon
2 large eggs, beaten
1 cup buttermilk
2 tablespoons butter OR margarine, melted

Grease muffin tin; spoon one-fourth cup melted butter evenly into each muffin cup. Sprinkle brown sugar over butter, then put pineapple evenly over brown sugar mixture; set aside. In a large mixing bowl, combine together all dry ingredients; mix well; set aside. In another mixing bowl, beat eggs with buttermilk and 2 tablespoons butter. Gradually add egg mixture into dry ingredients; mix only until mixture is just moistened. Spoon batter over pineapple mixture ¾ full. Bake at 375 degrees, for 20 to 25 minutes, or until golden brown. Remove from oven and immediately invert muffin tin on to a platter. Yield 12 muffins

MICROWAVE APPLESAUCE MUFFINS TOPPING

2 tablespoons all-purpose flour
1 tablespoon brown sugar
¼ teaspoon cinnamon
1 tablespoon butter OR margarine, melted

In a small mixing bowl, combine together, all above ingredients; mix well; set aside.

BATTER

¾ cup all-purpose flour
¾ teaspoon baking powder
¼ teaspoon baking soda
½ teaspoon cinnamon
¼ teaspoon ground cloves
¼ cup nuts (optional)
1 large egg
1/3 cup applesauce
¼ cup buttermilk
3 tablespoons vegetable oil

In a medium mixing bowl, sift together, dry ingredients; add nuts. In another bowl, beat egg with applesauce, buttermilk and oil; mix well. Add egg mixture to dry ingredients, mix together just until moistened. Spoon batter into 6 microwave muffin cups with paper liners. Top each muffin with 1 tablespoon of brown sugar mixture. Bake on high 2½ to 4 minutes until done, stopping microwave to rotate pan every minute Yield 6 muffins.

PEANUT BUTTER AND JELLY MUFFINS

2 cups all-purpose flour
½ cup granulated sugar
2½ teaspoons baking powder
½ teaspoon salt
¾ cup peanut butter
2 large eggs, lightly beaten
¾ cup milk
¼ cup strawberry preserves

In a large mixing bowl, combine together, flour, sugar, baking powder and salt; add peanut butter, cut with a pastry blender until mixture resembles coarse meal. In another bowl, combine eggs and milk; add to dry ingredients, mix until just moistened. Spoon batter 1/3 full in muffin pan; top each muffin with ¾ teaspoon strawberry preserves. Spoon remaining batter into muffin pans, filling 2/3 full. Bake at 400 degrees for 15 to 20 minutes, or until lightly brown. Remove from pans immediately. Yield 16 muffins.

EGGNOG MUFFINS

3 cups all-purpose flour
½ cup granulated sugar
3 teaspoons baking powder
½ teaspoon salt
½ teaspoon ground nutmeg
1 large egg
1¾ cups eggnog
½ cup vegetable oil
½ cup raisins
½ cups pecans, chopped

In a large bowl, combine flour, sugar, baking powder, salt and nutmeg. In another bowl, combine egg, eggnog and oil; mix well, then stir into dry ingredients; mix until just moistened. Fold in raisins and pecans. Fill paper-lined muffin tins, 2/3 full. Bake at 350 degrees for 20 to 25 minutes, or until a toothpick comes out clean. Cool for 5 minutes before removing from pans. Yield: 16 muffins.

BLUEBERRY SOUR CREAM MUFFINS

4 large eggs
2 cups granulated sugar
1 cup vegetable oil
1 teaspoon vanilla extract
4 cups all-purpose flour
½ teaspoon salt
1 teaspoon baking soda
2 teaspoons baking powder
2 cups sour cream
3 cups blueberries, fresh OR
    frozen

In a large mixing bowl, beat eggs and while beating eggs, gradually add sugar, then slowly add oil; add vanilla; mix well. Add salt, baking soda and baking powder; mix thoroughly. Add flour alternating with sour cream. Gently fold in fresh or frozen blueberries. Spoon into greased muffin tin. Bake at 400 degrees for 20 minutes, or until tested done.

BANANA OATMEAL MUFFINS

1 cup all-purpose flour
1½ cups oatmeal, uncooked
1½ cups whole wheat flour
1 cup granulated sugar
1/3 cup wheat germ
2 teaspoons baking soda
½ teaspoon salt
2 teaspoons cinnamon
3 large eggs
1 can (8 ozs.) crushed
   pineapple, undrained
2 cups bananas, mashed
½ cup vegetable oil

In a large mixing bowl, combine together, all the above dry ingredients. Then make a well in the center of mixture. Add remaining ingredients; stir together just until batter is moist. Spoon batter into a greased muffin pan, filling 2/3 full. Bake at 350 degrees for 20 to 25 minutes or until tested done. Yield 2½ dozen muffins.

ALL-BRAN MUFFINS

2 cups all-bran
½ cup molsses
1½ cups buttermilk
1 large egg, unbeaten
1 cup all-purpose flour
½ teaspoon salt
1 teaspoon baking soda
1 teaspoon cinnamon
Pinch of ginger
Pinch of nutmeg
1 tablespoon vegetable oil
½ cup raisins (optional)
½ cup nuts (optional)

In a large mixing bowl, combine together, all-bran with molasses and buttermilk; mix well and let stand for about 15 minutes. Add eggs; mix well; set aside. Meanwhile sift together, all dry ingredients. Combine with all-bran mixture; add oil; stir until just mixed; do not over mix. Fold in raisins & nuts, if desired. Fill greased muffin pans, ½ full; bake at 400 degrees, for about 20 minutes. Yield 12 muffins.

CAPPUCCINO MUFFINS
(with Expresso Spread)

½ cup butter OR margarine,
   melted
1 large egg, beaten
¾ cup granulated sugar
1 teaspoon cinnamon
2 cups all-purpose flour
2½ teaspoons baking powder
½ teaspoon salt
1 cup milk
2 tablespoons instant coffee
1 teaspoon vanilla extract
¾ cup mini chocolate chips

In a medium mixing bowl, cream butter with sugar; add egg; mix well. In another bowl, sift together, sugar, cinnamon, flour, baking powder and salt. Add dry ingredients alternately with milk with instant coffee dissolved in milk and vanilla; mix thoroughly. Fold in chocolate chips. Fill muffin tin ¾ full; bake at 375 degrees for 18 to 20 minutes, until tested done.

EXPRESSO SPREAD

4 ounces cream cheese,
    softened
1 tablespoon granulated sugar
½ teaspoon instant coffee
¼ cup mini chocolate chips
½ teaspoon vanilla extract

Combine all ingredients; mix
well; spread evenly on cooled
muffins.

CABBAGE MUFFINS

1¾ cups all-purpose flour
2 teaspoons celery seed
1 tablespoon baking powder
2 cups cabbage, grated
½ teaspoon salt
2 large eggs
1 tablespoon granulated sugar
¾ cup milk
2 teaspoons onion flakes
1 teaspoon celery flakes
6 tablespoons butter OR
    margarine, melted

In a large mixing bowl,
combine together, flour, baking
powder, salt, sugar, onion and
celery flakes; mix well. Add
grated cabbage; set aside.
Meanwhile, in another bowl,
beat eggs, milk and melted
butter together; add to dry
ingredients; mix batter only until
just moistened. Spoon into a
greased muffin tin, ¾ full. Bake
at 400 degrees, for about 20
minutes, or until tested done.

KITCHEN SINK MUFFINS

2 cups all-purpose flour
1¼ cups granulated sugar
2 teaspoons baking soda
2 teaspoons cinnamon
½ teaspoon salt
2 cups carrots, grated
½ cup raisins (optional)
½ cup nuts, chopped (optional)
½ cup coconut
1 medium apple, peeled,
    cored & grated
3 large eggs
1 cup vegetable oil
2 teaspoons vanilla extract

In a large mixing bowl,
combine together, all dry
ingredients. Add carrots, raisins,
nuts, coconut and apple; mix
well; set aside. In a another
bowl, beat eggs; gradually add
oil, then vanilla; mix thoroughly.
Add egg mixture into flour
mixture; mix just until batter is
moistened. Spoon batter into
a greased muffin tin, filling ¾
full. Bake at 350 degrees for 20
minutes or until tested done.
Yield about 14 muffins.

RASPBERRY STREUSEL MUFFINS
STREUSEL TOPPING

½ cup all-purpose flour
½ cup quick oatmeal
1/3 cup granulated sugar
½ teaspoon ground cinnamon
Pinch of salt
6 tablespoons butter OR
margarine

MUFFIN BATTER

½ cup butter OR margarine, softened
½ cup granulated sugar
1 large egg
2 cups all-purpose flour
½ teaspoon baking powder
½ teaspoon baking soda
½ teaspoon ground cinnamon
¼ teaspoon salt
½ cup milk
½ cup sour cream
1 teaspoon vanilla extract
1 cup fresh OR frozen raspberries, thawed and drained

Preheat oven to 400 degrees; grease 12-count muffin pan. Prepare streusel, then in a medium-sized mixing bowl, combine together, flour. oatmeal, sugar, cinnamon and salt. With a pastry blender, or two knives, cut butter into flour mixture, until mixture resembles coarse crumbs; set aside. In a large mixing bowl, with electric mixer, on medium speed, beat butter and sugar, until light and fluffy. Add egg, beating until well mixed. In a medium bowl, combine together, flour, baking powder, baking soda, cinnamon and salt; set aside. In a small bowl, combine together, milk, sour cream and vanilla. With the electric mixer on low speed, beginning and ending, with flour mixture, alternately, beat the flour mixture and the milk mixture into the butter mixture, just until combined. Gently fold in raspberries. Divide the batter among the muffin cups, filling each cup 2/3 full. Generously sprinkle streusel topping over muffins. Bake muffins for about 20 to 25 minutes, or until tested done. Cool muffins in pan for 5 minutes, then remove from tin. If desired, sprinkle with powder sugar. Yield 12 muffins.

SWEET POTATO MUFFINS

1½ cups all-purpose flour
1 cup granulated sugar
3 teaspoons baking powder
3 teaspoons orange peel, grated
1½ teaspoons ground ginger
1 teaspoon baking soda
¼ teaspoon salt
2 large eggs, slightly beaten
1 cup sweet potatoes, mashed
¼ teaspoon cinnamon
1 tablespoon granulated sugar

In a large bowl, combine together, flour, 1 cup sugar, baking powder, orange peel, ginger, baking soda and salt; set aside. In another bowl, combine eggs and sweet potatoes; stir into dry ingredients, just until moistened. Spoon into greased muffin pan 2/3 full; set aside. In a small bowl, combine cinnamon and 1 tablespoon sugar; mix well; sprinkle over batter. Bake at 400 degrees, for 15 to 20 minutes, or until tested done. Remove from oven; let cool 5 minutes before removing muffins from pan. Yield 12 muffins.

BROWN SUGAR MUFFINS

½ cup shortening
1 cup brown sugar, packed
1 large egg
1 cup milk
2 teaspoons vanilla extract
2 cups all-purpose flour
1 teaspoon baking soda
½ teaspoon salt

In a medium mixing bowl, cream together, shortening and brown sugar. Add egg, milk and vanilla; set aside. Combine together dry ingredients; add to creamed mixture; mix just until moistened, do not over mix. Fill muffin tins ¾ full; bake at 400 degrees, for 15 to 20 minutes, or until tested done. Remove from oven; let cool for 5 minutes before removing from pan. Yield 1 dozen.

MICROWAVE CORN MUFFINS

½ cup all-purpose flour
½ cup yellow cornmeal
½ teaspoon baking soda
Pinch of salt
½ cup plain yogurt
2 tablespoons vegetable oil
2 tablespoons maple syrup
1 egg white, beaten

Line six 2½ inch microwave safe muffin pan, with paper baking cups; set aside. In a large mixing bowl, combine together, flour, cornmeal, baking soda and salt. Stir in yogurt, oil and maple syrup, just until combined, do not over mix. Gently fold in beaten egg white. Divide the batter among the prepared muffin cups. Microwave the muffins on high (100 percent), for 2½ to 3½ minutes, or until tested done. Rotate the muffin pan midway, if the microwave does not have a carousel. Cool muffins for 5 minutes before removing from pan.

APRICOT MUFFINS

2 cups all-purpose flour
½ cup granulated sugar
2 teaspoons baking powder
½ teaspoon salt
2 large eggs
1 cup milk
¼ cup vegetable oil
½ to ¾ cup dried apricots,
    chopped
2 teaspoons orange peel, grated

In a large mixing bowl, combine together, flour, sugar, baking powder and salt; set aside. In another bowl, combine eggs, milk oil; mix well. Stir into dry ingredients, just until combined. Do not over mix. Fold in apricots and orange peel. Fill paper-lined muffin pan, 2/3 full. Bake at 400 degrees, for 15 to 20 minutes, or until tested done. Remove from oven; let cool 5 minutes before removing from muffin pan. Yield about 1 dozen muffins.

PEACH MUFFINS

1 cup peaches, chopped
1 teaspoon lemon juice
1 cup milk
1 large egg
¼ cup margarine
2/3 cup granulated sugar
¼ teaspoon cinnamon
3 teaspoons baking powder
2 cups all-purpose flour

Place chopped peaches in bowl, sprinkle with lemon juice; set aside. In another bowl. combine together, milk, egg, margarine, sugar, cinnamon and baking powder; mix well. Add flour last, mix thoroughly, then fold in peaches. Fill greased muffin tin 2/3 full; bake at 400 degrees, for about 20 minutes, or until tested done. Yield 12 muffins.

RICOTTA CHEESECAKE

Nut Crust (recipe follows)

FILLING

3¾ cups ricotta cheese
2 large whole eggs
3 large egg whites
1 cup buttermilk
½ cup granulated sugar
2 teaspoons vanilla extract
2 tablespoons lemon juice
Grated peel of ½ lemon

Preheat oven to 325 degrees. Grease a 9-inch spring form pan.

Press Nut Crust in an even layer over bottom & side of pan. Bake crust for 10 to 15 minutes or until light golden brown. Remove from oven to cool, meanwhile increase oven temperature to 375 degrees. In a large mixing bowl, combine together, all ingredients; mix thoroughly. Pour mixture into prepared crust. Place a large pan of water in the bottom of oven. Bake for 50 minutes or until set.

NUT CRUST: In a bowl, combine together, 1 cup all-purpose flour. ¼ cup light brown sugar, packed & ¼ cup nuts,. Cut in ¼ cup butter OR margarine, with 2 forks, until well-blended.

BAKED CUSTARD

2 large eggs
1/3 cup granulated sugar
¼ teaspoon salt
Nutmeg (optional)

Scald 2 cups of milk, stirring constantly. Remove from heat; cool slightly. Mean while, in a medium mixing bowl, beat together, eggs, sugar and salt; add cooled milk to egg mixture, beating thoroughly. Pour into custard cups; set in a pan of hot water. Sprinkle evenly on top with a little nutmeg, if desired. Bake at 350 degrees, for 20 to 30 minutes, or until tested done Serve hot or cold. Yield about 4 servings.

FRUIT SALAD CHEESECAKE

1 can (20 ozs.) crushed
   pineapple, drained
1 cup granulated sugar
2 envelopes unflavored gelatin
1 pkg. (8 ozs.) cream cheese
   cubed
1½ cups crisp macaroons,
   crushed
2 tablespoons butter OR
   margarine, melted
2 cups seedless grapes, cut in
   half
1 can (11 ozs.) mandarin
   oranges, drained
1 jar (10 ozs.) maraschino
   cherries, drained and
   chopped
½ cup pecan OR walnuts, finely
   chopped
2 cups whipped topping

In a small saucepan, over
medium heat, cook pineapple
and sugar, for 5 minutes. In
a another small bowl, place
cold water, then sprinkle with
gelatin; mix; let stand for 1
minute. Then stir into warm
pineapple mixture. Reduce
heat to low; add cream
cheese; cook, stirring until
cheese is melted and mixture
is well-blended; set aside.
Combine together, macaroon
crumbs and butter. Press
crumbs onto the bottom of a
greased 9" spring form pan; set
aside. Stir in grapes, oranges,
cherries and nuts into cream
cheese; Then fold in whipped
topping into cream cheese
mixture. Pour into prepare pan;
cover; refrigerate overnight.
Remove sides of pan before
serving. Yield 12 servings.

HOMEMADE VANILLA ICE CREAM

2¼ cups granulated sugar
6 tablespoons all-purpose flour
½ teaspoon salt
6 cups milk
6 large eggs, beaten
6 cups whipping cream
4½ tablespoons vanilla extract

In a large saucepan, combine
together, sugar, flour and salt.
Gradually stir in milk. Cook over
low heat, stirring constantly until
mixture thickens. Remove from
heat; add small amount of hot
mixture to beaten eggs; mix
well. Add egg mixture to hot
mixture in saucepan; cook for 1
minute more, stirring constantly.
Remove from heat; cool;. add
whipping cream and vanilla;
mix well. Put in ice cream
freezer and freeze according to
manufacturer's directions. Yield
1 gallon.

VARIATIONS: Add 2 cups
fresh diced strawberries,
peaches or fruit your choice
OR 1 cup chocolate syrup; mix
thoroughly before putting ice
cream into freezer.

NO-BAKE BROWNIES

2 cups semisweet chocolate
    chips
1 can (14 ozs.) sweetened
    condensed milk
1 pkg. (8½ ozs.) chocolate
    wafers, finely crushed
1 cup nuts, divided

In a double boiler, over
hot water, not boiling, melt
chocolate chips, stir until
smooth. Add sweetened
condensed milk. chocolate
wafer crumbs and ½ cup
chopped nuts; mix until well-
blended. Press into foiled-lined
8-inch square pan, then press
remaining nuts into the top
of brownie. Let stand at room
temperature until firm. Cut into
2-inch squares. Yield 16 2-inch
brownies.

RHUBARB ICE CREAM

2 cups rhubarb, chopped
1 cup granulated sugar
1 cup water
1½ cups miniature marshmallows
Red food coloring (optional)
2 teaspoons lemon juice
1 cup heavy cream, whipped

In a medium saucepan,
combine rhubarb, sugar and
water; bring to a boil; reduce
heat to simmer for 10 minutes.
Add marshmallows; mix until
melted. Add food coloring, if
desired and lemon juice. Cool;
refrigerate until mixture has
chilled; fold in whipped cream.

Pour mixture into a freezer
container; cover and freeze.
Yield 3 servings.

BLUEBERRY MUFFINS (with cream cheese)

1½ cups blueberries
1 pkg. (8 ozs.) cream cheese,
    softened
1 teaspoon vanilla extract
¼ cup sour cream
2 tablespoons powder sugar
2 cups all-purpose flour
¾ cup granulated sugar
1 tablespoons baking powder
½ teaspoon salt
¾ cup milk
1 tablespoon lemon juice
½ cup vegetable oil
1 large egg, beaten

Preheat oven to 400 degrees.
Place liners in muffin tin.
In a medium mixing bowl,
combine together, cream
cheese, vanilla, sour cream
and powder sugar; mix until
well-blended and smooth; set
aside. In a large bowl, combine
flour, sugar. baking powder
and salt; mix thoroughly; set
aside. In a small bowl, combine
milk, lemon juice, oil and egg;
mix well. Add to flour mixture;
mix just until combined; fold in
blueberries. Spoon batter half
way in muffin cup, then put
a spoonful of cream cheese
mixture on batter, top with
more batter, to fill muffin cup
¾ full. Bake for 20 minutes or
until muffin tests done. Yield 15
muffins.

WHOOPIE PIES (with filling)

2½ cups all-purpose flour
1 cup granulated sugar
1½ teaspoons baking soda
½ teaspoon salt
2 teaspoons cream of tartar
½ cup shortening
1 cup milk
2 large eggs
1 teaspoon vanilla extract
1 cup unsweetened cocoa

In a medium mixing bowl, sift together the dry ingredients. Add remaining ingredients; beat with electric mixer, at medium speed, (or by hand) for 2 minutes. Drop by teaspoonfuls onto a greased baking pan. Bake at 350 degrees for 8 to 10 minutes, or until tested done.

WHOOPIE PIE FILLING

1 cup milk
4 tablespoons all-purpose flour
¾ cup shortening
1 cup powder sugar
1 teaspoon vanilla extract

In a saucepan mix together, milk and flour; cook over medium heat. Cook until mixture thickens; stirring constantly. Remove from heat; set aside to cool. Beat shortening until creamy; add cooled milk mixture; beat until well-mixed. Gradually add powder sugar and vanilla; mix well. Use about ¼ cup filling for each whoopie pie.

GRAPE SHERBET

1¾ cups grape juice
3 tablespoons lemon juice
½ cup granulated sugar
1¾ cups cream (i.e. Half and Half)

In a large mixing bowl, combine together, all ingredients; mix well. Put in desired freezer container; freeze. Allow to ripen for 2 to 4 hours before serving. Yield 1 quart.

HEAVENLY HASH

2 cups cold, rice, cooked
1 can (8 ozs.) pineapple tidbits, drained
¼ cup maraschino cherries, drained & quartered
1½ cups miniature marshmallows,
1 cup heavy cream, whipped

In a large mixing bowl, combine rice with pineapple, cherries and marshmallows. Refrigerate, covered for 1 hour. Then fold in whipped cream just before serving. Top with additional cherries.

STRAWBERRY ICE CREAM

6 cups strawberries
Juice of 1 lemon
½ cup granulated sugar
½ cup water
3 egg yolks
2 cups light cream (i.e. half & half)
Powder sugar to taste

Chop strawberries coarsely; mix with lemon juice' set aside. In a small saucepan, cook sugar and water, over low heat, stirring until sugar dissolves. Boil, stirring constantly, until syrup spins a thread (230 to 234 degrees on candy thermometer); set aside. In a medium bowl, beat egg yolks until well mixed; then gradually beat in the syrup, until mixture is cool and thick. Add strawberries; add powder sugar, if more sweetness is desired. Pour into freezer container. Yield about 1½ quarts.

FRIED ICE CREAM

1 pint ice cream, any flavor
½ cup cornflakes OR cookie crumbs, finely crushed
1 teaspoon ground cinnamon
2 teaspoons granulated sugar
1 large egg
Vegetable oil for frying
Honey
Whipped cream

Scoop out 4 to 5 balls of ice cream, about the size of a baseball. Return to freezer to firm. In a medium bowl, combine together, cornflakes, cinnamon and sugar; mix well. Roll frozen ice cream balls in half of crumb mixture; freeze once more. In another bowl, beat egg, then dip ice cream balls in egg, then roll again in remaining crumbs. A thick coating of cornflake crumbs will insure success. If the coating isn't thick enough, then repeat dipping in egg, then roll in crumbs once more. preheat oil to 350 degrees. Place a frozen ice cream ball on a slotted spoon, lower in hot oil for 1 minute. Immediately remove from oil; place on place on serving plate. If desired, drizzle with honey, top with whipped cream. Continue to fry ice cream balls, one at a time until done. They will be crunchy on the outside and just beginning to melt on the inside. Yield 4 to 5 servings.

FRESH FRUIT ICE CREAM

1 can (14 ozs.) Sweetened
    Condensed Milk
1 tablespoon vanilla extract
1 to 1½ cups ripe fresh fruit,
    mashed (such as raspberries,
    strawberries, bananas or
    peaches)
2 cups whipping cream,
    whipped

In a large mixing bowl,
combine together milk and
vanilla; fold in fruit. Then fold
in whipped cream. Pour into a
2-quart container. Freeze until
firm.

CRANBERRY SHERBERT

1 cup water
2 cups fresh cranberries
1 cup granulated sugar
¼ cup cold water
1 envelope unflavored gelatin
½ lemon, peeled & seeded
1 orange, peeled & seeded

In a saucepan, combine
together, 1 cup water,
cranberries and sugar; mix well.
Over medium heat, bring to
simmer; cook until cranberry
skins pop. Then place ¼
cup cold water and gelatin
in blender; add cranberry
mixture, lemon and orange.
Blend mixture until liquefied
smooth; pour in freezer tray and
freeze. Yield 1 quart sherbert.

PUMPKIN NUT CAKE

1 package white cake mix
1 large egg
½ cup canned pumpkin
¼ cup water
½ teaspoon ground cinnamon
¼ teaspoon nutmeg
1/3 cup nuts, chopped

In a large mixing bowl,
combine together, cake mix,
egg, pumpkin, water and
spices. Beat with electric
mixer at medium speed, for
2 minutes, or by hand for 4
minutes. Pour batter into a
8x8x2" baking pan. Top with
nuts; bake at 350 degrees,
for 20 to 25 minutes. Yield 9
servings.

APPLE SHERBERT

2 apples, peeled, cored and
    sliced
2 oranges, peeled, sectioned
    and seeded
2 tablespoons lemon juice
¼ cup honey
1 banana, peeled and sliced
6 cups apple cider, chilled.

In a blender or food processor,
place all ingredients, EXCEPT
apple cider. Cover and process
mixture until smooth. Pour into
an ice cube tray and freeze.

PUMPKIN NUT ROLL

3 large eggs
1 cup granulated sugar
¾ cup all-purpose flour
1 teaspoon baking powder
2 teaspoons cinnamon
1 teaspoon ginger
½ teaspoon nutmeg
½ teaspoon salt
1 teaspoon lemon juice
2/3 cup canned pumpkin
1 cup walnuts, chopped

Beat eggs on high; gradually add sugar, beating until well mixed. Add remaining ingredients, EXCEPT pumpkin; blend well. Fold in pumpkin. Spread batter in a greased floured cookie sheet or jelly roll pan. Top with nuts; bake at 375 degrees, for 15 minutes, or until tested done. Turn cake out on a clean towel, sprinkle with powder sugar. Start at the narrow end of cake and roll up towel and cake together. Let cool, then unroll for filling.

FILLING INGREDIENTS & DIRECTIONS

1 cup powder sugar, sifted, 8 ounces cream cheese, 4 tablespoons butter OR margarine, and ½ teaspoon vanilla extract—Beat together all ingredients, until smooth. Spread filling on inside of cake. Roll cake up and place seam side down; chill before serving.

PUMPKIN CUSTARD

1½ cups canned pumpkin
2/3 cup brown sugar, packed
1 teaspoon lemon peel, grated
3 large eggs, beaten
1½ cups milk, scalded
1 tablespoon cornstarch
1 teaspoon ground cinnamon
½ teaspoon ground ginger
¼ teaspoon cloves
¼ teaspoon nutmeg

In a medium mixing bowl, combine together all ingredients; mix well. Pour into buttered baking dish. Bake at 350 degrees, for 45 minutes. Yield 4 to 6 servings.

PUMPKIN ICE CREAM

2 cups milk, scalded
2 large eggs
1 cup granulated sugar
Pinch of salt
2 cups pumpkin, canned
1 cup cream
½ teaspoon vanilla extract
2 teaspoons cinnamon
1 teaspoon nutmeg
½ teaspoon allspice
¼ teaspoon ginger
1 cup nuts, chopped (optional)

Scald milk in double boiler; set aside. In a medium mixing bowl, combine the remaining ingredients, EXCEPT cream and nuts; mix well. Add to hot milk; cook over medium heat, for 4 minutes. Remove from heat; cool slightly; stir in cream; mix well. Fold in nuts; put in desired container and freeze until stiff.

LADY FINGERS

4 large egg whites (½ cup)
¼ teaspoon cream of tartar
5 tablespoons granulated sugar
2 large egg yolks
Pinch of salt
1 teaspoon vanilla extract
5 tablespoons granulated sugar
1¼ cups cake flour
½ teaspoon baking powder

In a large mixing bowl, beat egg whites to a foam; add cream of tartar, and gradually add 5 tablespoons sugar, continue beating until mixture is very stiff, but not dry. In another bowl, beat egg yolks, salt and vanilla until light, gradually add 5 tablespoons sugar; beat until thick. Fold egg yolk mixture into egg whites, then fold in the flour and baking powder. Form 3 inch fingers on a well-greased cookie sheet; bake at 450 degrees, for 6 to 8 minutes. Remove from oven, sprinkle or sift powder sugar over Lady Fingers, then remove from cookie sheet immediately. Yield about 3 dozen Lady Fingers.

CRULLERS (Doughnut)

4 tablespoons shortening
1 cup granulated sugar
2 large eggs, beaten
3 cups all-purpose flour
1 teaspoon cinnamon
½ teaspoon salt
3 teaspoons baking powder
¾ cup milk
Powder sugar

In a large mixing bowl, cream shortening with sugar; add eggs, one at a time, beating well after each addition. set aside. In another bowl, sift together, flour, cinnamon, salt and baking powder; add ½ of dry flour mixture with shortening mixture; mix well. Add milk and remaining flour mixture to make a soft dough. On a lightly floured surface, roll out dough to about ½ inch thick, then cut into strips about 4 inches long and ½ inch wide; roll in hands and twist each strip, bringing ends together. Let set for about 30 minutes; fry in deep fat until a golden brown on each side. Remove from and drain on paper towels, then roll in powder sugar.

FUDGESICLES

1 small pkg. Instant Chocolate Pudding Mix
¼ cup granulated sugar
4 cups milk

In a large mixing bowl, combine together, all ingredients; mix thoroughly. Pour into paper cups, molds or ice cubes trays. Freeze for 30 minutes, then insert wooden sticks or plastic teaspoons into center of each cup. Freeze until completely hardened.

EASY BANANA ICE CREAM

2 cups bananas, mashed
1½ cups buttermilk
1 container (9 ozs.) frozen
   whipped topping
1 cup granulated sugar
1½ teaspoons vanilla extract

Blend all ingredients thoroughly in a blender or food processor. Place ice cream in desired freezer container; freeze.

PIZZELLES
(Recipe to use with Pizzelle Maker)

6 large eggs
3½ cups all-purpose flour
1½ cups granulated sugar
1 cup butter OR margarine,
   melted
4 teaspoons baking powder
2 tablespoons vanilla extract

In a large bowl, beat eggs, adding sugar gradually; continue beating until smooth. Add cooled, melted butter and vanilla; set aside. In another bowl, sift together, flour and baking powder; add to egg mixture; mix well. Meanwhile, warm up pizzelle maker. When warm, drop 2 spoonfuls onto center of pizzelle iron. Cover; bake as manufacturer directs (do not lift cover while baking). When done, lift cover; loosen pizzelle with fork; repeat until batter is used up. Yield about 30 pizzelles. Store in tightly covered container.

CHOCOLATE PIZZELLES

½ cup unsweetened cocoa
½ cup granulated sugar
½ teaspoon baking powder

Add cocoa, sugar and additional baking powder ingredients to the pizzelle recipe above. Sift with flour, then add to egg mixture.

HOT FUDGE SAUCE

6 squares (1 oz. each)
   unsweetened Chocolate
¼ cup butter OR margarine
2 cups granulated sugar
1 cup cream (i.e Half and Half)
1 can (14 ozs.) sweetened
   condensed milk

In a saucepan, over medium heat, melt the chocolate and butter, stirring constantly until chocolate melts. Then add sugar and cream, stirring until thickened. Gradually add milk, cook for 20 minutes more, stirring occasionally. Remove from heat and let cool. Yield 4 cups.

CHOCOLATE ECLAIRS (with Filling & Chocolate Frosting)

1 cup water
½ cup butter OR margarine
1 cup all-purpose flour, sifted
4 large eggs (at room
   temperature)

In a medium saucepan, over medium heat; cook water and butter. When boiling point is reached; add flour, all at once. Cook, stirring vigorously, until mixture is thick and smooth and forms a ball, in the center of the pan. Remove from heat; let cool slightly. Add eggs, one at a time, beating thoroughly, after each addition, until mixture is smooth and has a satin-like sheen. Put dough through a pastry tube or shape heaping tablespoons, into 4 inches by 1 inch, rounding sides and oiling dough on top, on an ungreased cookie sheet. Bake at 400 degrees, for 45 to 60 minutes. Lift eclairs off cookie sheet with a spatula; place on wire rack Immediately prick once with a fork, on one side, where eclairs will be cut later, to insert filling after they have cooled. Fill with Custard Filling (recipe following next page). Yield 8 eclairs.

NOTE: To make cream puffs, drop batter about 2 tablespoons, on cookie sheet, 2" apart. Bake like eclairs; cool, slit puffs, fill with custard & frost.

CHOCOLATE ECLAIRS FILLING

½ cup granulated sugar
½ teaspoon salt
6 tablespoons all-purpose flour
1 cup milk
1 cup light cream
4 large egg yolks
2 teaspoons vanilla extract

In a saucepan, combine together, sugar, salt and flour; add milk and cream; mix well. Cook over low heat, stirring until mixture comes to a boil; cook for 1 minute; remove from heat, stir a little mixture into beaten egg yolks, then add egg yolks into mixture in saucepan. Bring to boiling point; remove from heat; add vanilla; mix well; set aside to cool.

CHOCOLATE FROSTING

Melt 3 squares unsweetened chocolate and 1 tablespoon butter OR margarine, in a double boiler, over hot water. Meanwhile, in a saucepan, combine 1/3 cup granulated sugar & 4 tablespoons water; bring just to the boiling point. Do not boil. Cool until lukewarm, then add to chocolate, stir to blend. Fill eclairs with filling, then frost.

NUT ROLL

1 pkg. active dry yeast
½ cup warm milk, not hot
1 tablespoon granulated sugar
3 large egg yolks, lightly beaten
2 to 2½ cups all-purpose flour
¼ teaspoon salt

NUT FILLING

3 large egg whites
¾ cup granulated sugar
1 cup walnuts, finely chopped
½ cup butter OR margarine, softened
Peel from ½ lemon, grated
1 teaspoon lemon juice
Melted butter OR margarine
1 cup light raisins

Grease a 13x9x2 inch baking pan; set aside. Soften yeast in milk; add sugar. When yeast bubbles, add to egg yolks. In a large bowl, combine together, flour and salt, cut in butter. Slowly beat in yeast mixture, beating until dough leaves sides of bowl. Cover; refrigerate overnight Next day, beat egg whites until stiff, but still glossy. Fold in sugar, lemon peel and juice. Divide dough in half; roll out one half on a lightly floured surface to 13x5½ inches Spread lightly with melted butter; sprinkle with half of raisins, then spread lightly with half the filling, not quite to the edges. Roll up from the long side; place on 1 side of the baking pan. Repeat to make second roll; place besides the first roll, not touching. Brush tops with milk, prick tops with fork. Cover; let rise in draft-free warm area, for 1½ hours Then in a preheated oven at 350 degrees, bake for 45 minutes or until tested done. Remove from oven cool, before slicing. Yield 2 nut rolls.

DOUGHNUTS (with variations)

4¼ cups all-purpose flour, sifted
3 ½ teaspoons baking powder
½ teaspoon salt
½ teaspoon nutmeg
¼ teaspoon cinnamon
3 large eggs
1 teaspoon vanilla extract
¾ cup granulated sugar
3 tablespoons butter OR
    margarine, softened
¾ cup milk

In a mixing bowl, sift together, sifted flour, baking powder, salt and spices; set aside. In another bowl, beat eggs; add vanilla and sugar; beat well. Add softened butter; then add milk, alternately with dry ingredients; mix to form soft dough. Turn dough onto a lightly floured surface; knead lightly for ½ minute. Roll out dough to 1/3 inch thick. Cut with floured doughnut cutter. Remove trimmings. Lift each doughnut with a wide spatula & ease into hot oil (375 degrees). Put as many into oil as can be turned easily. Fry about 3 minutes until completely brown on both sides. Lift from oil with a long fork. Do not pierce; drain on paper towels. Form trimmings into balls; deep-fry as doughnuts or reroll; cut more doughnuts. Serve plain, sugared or frosted (see variations below.) Yield about 2dozen doughnuts.

VARIATIONS
DROPPED DOUGHNUTS

Make the preceding doughnut recipe. Drop by spoonfuls into oil or shortening (375 degrees); turn as soon as they rise to the top, then fry golden brown. Remove with slotted spoon; drain on paper towels. If desired, frost, then dip in flaked coconut or when cool, sprinkle with powder sugar.

SUGARED DOUGHNUTS
While doughnuts are still warm, dip into a bowl of granulated sugar or a mixture of ½ cup sugar and ½ teaspoon cinnamon.

FROSTED DOUGHNUTS
While doughnuts are still warm, dip into the following frostings.

PLAIN Mix together 1¾ cups sifted powder sugar, 3 tablespoons hot water, 2 teaspoons butter, melted and ½ teaspoon vanilla.

CHOCOLATE DOUGHNUTS—
Add to Plain Frosting 1 square melted chocolate & additional 2 teaspoons hot water; mix well.

ITALIAN SPUMONI

1½ pints vanilla ice cream
Rum flavoring to taste
6 maraschino cherries
1½ pints pistachio ice cream
1/3 cup pistachio nuts, chopped
¾ cup whipping cream
1/3 cup instant (dry) cocoa
1 pkg. (10 ozs.) frozen red
   raspberries, thawed & drained
½ cup whipping cream
¼ cup powder sugar

Chill 2-quart metal mold in freezer. Stir vanilla ice cream just to soften; add rum flavoring. Refreeze until workable; spread quickly in a layer over bottom & sides of mold, bringing ice cream all the way to the top. (If it tends to slip, refreeze until workable). Circle cherries around bottom; freeze. Stir pistachio ice cream to soften; stir in nuts. Refreeze until workable, then quickly spread over first layer; freeze. In a bowl, combine together, ¾ cup whipping cream and cocoa; whip to peaks. Quickly spread over pistachio layer; freeze. Drain raspberries, puree' in blender or food processor. In a bowl, combine together ½ cup whipping cream, sugar & dash of salt; whip to peaks. Fold in pureed raspberries, then pile into mold; smooth top. Cover with foil; freeze 6 hours. Remove from freezer; peel off foil; invert on chilled plate; lift off mold; cut in wedges. Yield 12 to 16 servings.

PINEAPPLE NUT CAKE (with Frosting)

2 large eggs
2 cups granulated sugar
2 cups all-purpose flour
1 stick margarine, softened
2 teaspoons vanilla extract
2 teaspoons baking soda
½ cup nuts, chopped
1 can crushed pineapple, with
   juice

In a medium mixing bowl, mix all ingredients together until thoroughly mixed and smooth. Pour batter into greased 9x13x2" baking pan. Bake at 350 degrees, for 35 to 45 minutes, or until tested done. Remove from oven and let cool, while making the frosting, if desired. Yield 10 to 12 servings

FROSTING

¼ cup margarine, softened
1 pkg. (8 ozs.) cream cheese,
   softened
1¾ cups powder sugar
1 teaspoon vanilla extract
½ cup nuts, chopped (optional)

In a medium mixing bowl, cream together, softened margarine and cream cheese until smooth and creamy. Gradually add sugar, beating on low speed of an electric mixer; add vanilla; mix thoroughly. Spread on cooled cake; sprinkle with nuts, if desired.

INTRODUCTION TO CAKES-
PLAIN AND FANCY

Here are some simple guidelines to help you make a cake. First of all, assemble all the ingredients together before you begin so you can go from one step of the recipe to the next easily, without too much time elapsing while putting the cake together. Be sure to cream the butter, margarine or shortening with the sugar until it's light and fluffy. This procedure traps air bubbles and guarantees that your cake will rise well. Also it is important to follow directions that call for adding dry and liquid ingredients alternately. The point is to create a smooth batter without losing air bubbles. It helps to grease and flour the cake pan well or use a piece of wax paper cut to fill the bottom of the cake pan.

The finishing touch is the frosting. It best to frost a cake as soon as it is thoroughly cooled; this will keep your cake fresh and moist. If it is going to be a 2-layer cake, then place the first layer upside layer down on a serving plate. Brush any loose crumbs; frost the first layer, or put a filling on the top of the first layer. Add the second layer of cake, right side up and frost cake completely.

A flexible spatula, about eight inches long is handy to have when frosting a cake.

*HOECAKES (type of cornbread)

*(Name was derived by, in the old day, field hands cooked these cakes, over fire on garden hoes.)

1½ cups cornmeal
½ cup all-purpose flour
¼ cup vegetable oil
1¼ cups buttermilk
½ cup granulated sugar
2 large eggs, beaten
½ teaspoon salt
1 teaspoon baking soda

In a medium bowl, combine together, flour, sugar, salt and baking soda. Add beaten eggs, oil and buttermilk; mix together, only until ingredients are moistened. Pour about ¼ cup of batter into a heavily oiled skillet. Fry over medium-high heat for 1 to 2 minutes or until golden, on each side. Drain on paper towels. Serve immediately.

APPLE SNACK CAKE

2 cups all-purpose flour
1½ cups granulated sugar
1 teaspoon salt
1 teaspoon baking soda
1 teaspoon ground cinnamon
3 large eggs, slightly beaten
1 cup vegetable oil
3 cups apples, peeled & sliced
½ cup nuts (optional)

Combine all dry ingredients together, in a large mixing bowl. Add eggs with oil; mix thoroughly. Fold in apple slices and nuts. Put in an ungreased 9x13x2" pan; bake at 350 degrees F. for 35 to 45 minutes or until tested done. Yield about 10 to 12 servings.

TO TOAST COCONUT FOR CAKES
Put coconut in pie pan, then place in oven at 350 degrees. Stir often from edges to brown easily.

TEXAS SHEET CAKE (with Frosting)

1 cup water
1 cup butter OR margarine
4 tablespoons unsweetened
   cocoa
2 cups all-purpose flour
2 cups granulated sugar
½ teaspoon salt
2 large eggs
½ cup sour cream
1 teaspoon baking soda

In a medium saucepan, combine water, butter and cocoa; bring to a boil, stirring occasionally. Boil one minute; remove from heat; cool. In a medium mixing bowl, combine flour and sugar. Add cooled chocolate mixture to dry ingredients; mixing thoroughly. Add eggs, sour cream and baking soda; mix well. Place in a greased 11x17" cookie sheet; bake at 350 degrees F. for 20 minutes, or until tested done. (Frosting is following). Yield 12 to 15 servings.

FROSTING

½ cup butter OR margarine
6 tablespoons milk
4 tablespoons unsweetened
   cocoa
1 box powder sugar

In medium saucepan, bring butter, milk and cocoa to a boil; boil one minute Remove from heat; cool slightly. Add powder sugar; beat until smooth and creamy; spread over warm cake

BLACKBERRY CAKE

½ cup butter OR margarine
1 cup granulated sugar
2 large eggs, beaten
4 tablespoons water
1 cup frozen blackberries, with
   juice

1 teaspoon baking soda
½ teaspoon ground cloves
2 cups all-purpose flour
1 teaspoon ground cinnamon

In a medium bowl, cream butter with sugar until light and fluffy. Add eggs, 1 at time, beating well after each addition. Add water & blackberries with juice. In another bowl, sift dry ingredients together. Add dry ingredients to butter mixture; mix well. Pour batter into 2 greased and floured cake pans. Bake at 350 degrees F. for 35 to 40 minutes, or until tested done. If desired, serve with whipped topping. Yield 8 to 10 servings.

HOW TO MAKE CAKE FLOUR:

For each cup of cake flour you need, put 2 tablespoons of cornstarch into a 1 cup regular all-purpose flour, then sift 3 times to thoroughly mix. Make enough for the recipe that calls for cake flour, or make enough to have on hand. Store in-an air-tight container to use in any recipe calling for cake flour.

WHITE TEXAS SHEET CAKE

1 cup water
1 cup butter OR margarine
2 cups, plus 2 tablespoons
   granulated sugar
2 cups, plus 2 tablespoons all-
   purpose flour
½ teaspoon salt
2 large eggs, beaten
1 teaspoon baking soda
½ teaspoon lemon extract
Grated rind of 1 lemon

In a small saucepan, bring water and butter to a boil; remove from heat. While mixture is hot, add flour, sugar and salt; mix thoroughly. Add eggs, sour cream and baking soda, beating until well mixed. Add lemon extract and rind. Pour batter into greased jelly roll pan or cookie pan with sides. Bake at 375 degrees F. for 20 to 25 minutes, or until tested done. Yield 12 to 15 servings.

CAKE FROSTING

½ cup butter OR margarine
6 tablespoons milk
3½ cups powder sugar, sifted
½ teaspoon lemon extract
Grated rind of 1 lemon
1 cup nuts, chopped (optional)

In a small saucepan, bring butter and milk to a boil; remove from heat; cool. Add powder sugar gradually, along with lemon extract and rind; beat thoroughly. Fold in nuts. Frost cake while warm.

BANANA CAKE (with Cream Filling & Chocolate Frosting)

½ cup shortening
1½ cups granulated sugar
2 large eggs
½ cup *sour milk
1 teaspoon baking soda
2 teaspoons baking powder
2 cups all-purpose flour
1 cup bananas, mashed
(***SOUR MILK**—mix ½ teaspoon lemon juice OR vinegar in ½ cup milk.)

In a medium mixing bowl, cream shortening with sugar until light and fluffy. Add eggs, one at a time, beating well after each addition. In another mixing bowl, combine dry ingredients; add to shortening mixture, stir until well-blended. Add mashed bananas. Pour batter into 2 greased and floured 9" cake pans. Bake at 350 degrees F., for 30 to 35 minutes, or until tested done. Prepare filling while cake is baking and cooling.

CREAM FILLING

½ cup granulated sugar
2 tablespoons cornstarch
Pinch salt
2 large eggs, beaten
1 cup milk, scalded
2 teaspoons butter
1 teaspoon vanilla extract

Combine sugar, cornstarch, salt and beaten eggs. Scald milk; add to sugar mixture; cook in double boiler, until mixture thickens, about 2 minutes, stirring constantly. Remove from heat; cool slightly; add butter and vanilla. Spread filling between cooled cake layers. If desired, frost with chocolate frosting (recipe following), or leave plain. Yield 10 to 12 servings.

CHOCOLATE FROSTING

1 cup butter OR margarine, softened
2 pkgs, (16 ozs. EACH) powder sugar
½ cup unsweetened cocoa
1 tablespoon vanilla extract
About ½ cup milk, more if necessary

In a large bowl, with an electric mixer, on medium speed, combine and beat all ingredients until well-mixed and creamy. Yield enough frosting to cover 2 layers of cake.

BROWN SUGAR CAKE (with icing)

1 cup butter OR margarine
2 cups brown sugar, packed
2 large, whole eggs & 2 eggs
  separated
2-2/3 cups all-purpose flour
1 teaspoon baking powder
1 cup brown sugar, packed
  (for icing)
1 teaspoon baking soda
1 teaspoon ground cloves
1 teaspoon ground cinnamon
½ teaspoon salt
1 cup buttermilk
½ cup nuts, chopped (optional)

In a medium mixing bowl, cream butter and brown sugar, until smooth and creamy. Add 2 whole eggs and 2 egg yolks; beat until thoroughly mixed. In another bowl, sift together, flour, baking powder, spices and salt; set aside. Mix together buttermilk and baking soda; then add to sugar mixture, alternating with flour mixture, mixing thoroughly. Pour into 2 lightly greased, cake pans; set aside. In a small mixing bowl, beat 2 egg whites, with electric mixer, on high speed, until stiff. Gradually add 1 cup brown sugar; fold in nuts. Spread evenly, on top of cake batter; bake at 350 degrees, for 25 to 30 minutes, or until tested done. Yield 8 to 10 servings.

EASY CHOCOLATE CAKE

3 cups all-purpose flour
4 heaping tablespoons
  unsweetened cocoa
½ teaspoon salt
2 teaspoons baking soda
2 cups granulated sugar
1 cup vegetable oil
2 teaspoons vanilla extract
2 cups warm water

Sift together, in a large bowl, flour, cocoa, salt, baking soda and sugar. Add oil, vanilla and water; mix thoroughly. Pour batter into 2 lightly greased and floured cake pans. Bake at 350 degrees, for 30 to 40 minutes, or until tested done. If desired frost as you wish, or leave plain. It is a moist cake. Yield 8 to 10 servings.

CHOCOLATE ZUCCHINI CAKE

3 cups all-purpose flour
½ cup unsweetened cocoa
1 teaspoon baking soda
½ teaspoon baking powder
1 teaspoon ground cinnamon
1 teaspoon salt
1½ cups vegetable oil
3 cups granulated sugar
4 large eggs
1 teaspoon vanilla extract
3 cups zucchini, peeled &
  grated

In a medium mixing bowl, sift together, flour, cocoa, baking soda, baking powder, cinnamon & salt; set aside. In another bowl combine oil and sugar; mix thoroughly. Add eggs, one at a time, beating well after each addition. Add 1/3 of the flour mixture at a time, to sugar mixture, mixing thoroughly after each addition. Add vanilla; fold in zucchini; mix only until blended. Prepare a bundt pan, by lightly greasing & dusting lightly with flour. Pour batter into bundt pan; bake at 350 degrees F. for 1 hour, or until tested done. Remove cake from oven; cool cake for 10 minutes; remove from pan to a wire rack; cool completely before slicing. Yield 12 to 15 servings.

ZUCCHINI CAKE

1½ vegetable oil
3 cups granulated sugar
4 large eggs
3 cups all-purpose flour
1 teaspoon baking soda
2 teaspoon baking powder
½ teaspoon salt
1½ teaspoons ground cinnamon
3 cups zucchini, peeled & grated
1 cup nuts, chopped (optional)

In a large mixing bowl, mix oil and sugar; blend thoroughly. Add eggs, one at a time, beating well after each addition. Add dry ingredients to sugar mixture, mixing until well blended. Fold in grated zucchini and nuts; mix thoroughly. Pour batter into lightly greased 9x13x2" baking pan. Bake at 300 degrees F., for 1 hour, or until tested done. Frost cake, if desired. Yield about 10 to 12 servings.

MANDARIN ORANGE CAKE (with Special Frosting)

1 box yellow cake mix
1 cup vegetable oil
3 large eggs
1 can mandarin oranges, undrained

In a medium mixing bowl, combine ingredients until well blended. Grease & flour a 9x13x2" cake pan. Bake 350 degrees, for 30 to 35 minutes, or until tested done. Frost cake with frosting below. Yield 10 to 12 servings.

SPECIAL FROSTING

1 pkg. instant vanilla pudding
1 cup milk
1 can (15 ozs.) crushed pineapple, drained
1 container (9 ozs.) Whipped Topping

In a medium mixing bowl, combine ingredients; mix only until blended thoroughly. This frosting must be refrigerated.

SWEET POTATO CAKE

2½ cups *cake flour
1 teaspoon ground cinnamon
1 teaspoon nutmeg
1½ cups vegetable oil
2 cups granulated sugar
4 large eggs
¼ cup warm water
1½ cups uncooked sweet
  potatoes, finely grated
1 teaspoon vanilla extract
½ cup raisins (optional)
1 cup nuts, chopped (optional)

Preheat oven to 350 degrees; grease three 8-inch round cake pans. In a medium mixing bowl, sift together, flour, cinnamon and nutmeg; set aside. In another bowl, combine oil and sugar; add eggs, one at a time, beating well after each addition. Add warm water gradually fold in flour mixture; add grated sweet potatoes, vanilla and, if desired, add raisins and nuts. Pour batter into cake pans; bake for 30 to 40 minutes, or until tested done. When cake layers have cooled, frost as desired. Yield 8 to 10 servings.
*Cake Flour—See Index.

ORANGE UPSIDE-DOWN CAKE

4 medium oranges
12 tablespoons butter OR
  margarine
1 cup brown sugar, packed
1½ cups all-purpose flour
1½ teaspoon baking powder
¼ teaspoon salt
2/3 cup granulated sugar
2 large eggs
1 teaspoon vanilla extract
½ cup milk

Preheat oven to 350 degree. Grate 1 tablespoon orange peel (zest). Peel oranges; remove all white pith. Cut sections of orange away from membrane. Combine 4 tablespoons of butter and brown sugar; place into a 9" round cake pan, in the oven. When butter has melted and sugar is well-blended; arrange orange sections in sugar mixture; set aside. Combine together, by sifting, flour, baking powder & salt; set aside. In a medium mixing bowl, mix together remaining butter and sugar; eggs beating until light and fluffy. Beat in orange peel, eggs and vanilla. Add flour alternately with milk, mixing thoroughly. Spread batter evenly over oranges. Bake for 30 to 35 minutes, or until tested done. Remove from oven; let cool for 5 minutes, then immediately invert cake onto a heat proof plate. Yield 6 servings.

OLD FASHION JELLY ROLL

2/3 cup all-purpose flour
1 teaspoon baking powder
3 large eggs, beaten
½ cup granulated sugar

Preheat oven to 425 degrees F. Combine together, flour and baking soda; mix well; set aside. In a medium mixing bowl, mix together, eggs and sugar, until light and fluffy. Add flour mixture to egg mixture, stir until well-blended. Pour batter into greased jelly roll pan; bake for about 10 minutes, or until tested done. Remove from oven, turn onto waxed paper or foil, sprinkle lightly with sugar. Spread evenly, with jam of your choice, or other filling; roll lengthwise. Wrap with waxed paper, foil or plastic wrap; let cool completely. Yield about 6 to 8 servings.

ORANGE CHIFFON CAKE

3 medium oranges
1 cup walnuts, chopped
2¼ cups cake flour
1½ cups granulated sugar
1 tablespoon baking powder
¼ teaspoon salt
6 large eggs, separated
½ cup vegetable oil
1 teaspoon vanilla extract
1 tablespoon butter OR
   margarine
1 cup powder sugar

Grate peel (zest) from oranges. Squeeze 1 cup juice from oranges. Chop walnuts; place nuts in an ungreased 10" angel food cake pan; set aside. In a medium bowl, combine, by sifting, flour, 1 cup sugar, baking powder and salt; set aside. Separate eggs; in another bowl, beat egg yolks, ¾ cup orange juice, ½ of grated orange peel, oil and vanilla, with electric mixer on high speed, until well-mixed. Gradually add flour mixture into egg yolk mixture; beat until smooth. In another mixing bowl, beat egg whites, until form soft peaks. Gradually add remaining sugar; continue beating at high speed until egg whites form stiff peaks. Fold egg whites into batter; pour in cake pan; bake at 325 degrees, for 1 hour, or until tested done; remove from oven. Melt butter in a saucepan, over low heat. Remove from heat; stir in powder sugar, remaining zest and enough orange juice to make thin glaze. Pour over cooled cake. Yield 16 servings.

STRAWBERRY TAPIOCA

2 pkgs. (10 ozs, each) frozen
   strawberries, thawed & sliced
¼ cup quick-cooking tapioca
¼ teaspoon salt
2 tablespoons lemon juice
1/3 cup whipping cream

Drain berries, reserving liquid.
Add water to liquid to make 2
cups. In a medium saucepan,
over medium heat, cook liquid
with tapioca & salt, stirring
constantly, until mixture comes
to a boil. Remove from heat;
cool stirring occasionally. When
cold, add berries & lemon
juice; cover & refrigerate.

TO SERVE: In a small bowl, with
electric mixer, at medium
speed, beat whipping cream
until stiff peaks form. Then fold
into straw berry mixture; serve.
Yield 6 to 8 servings.

CHERRY UPSIDE-DOWN CAKE

1 can (1 lb. 6 ozs.) cherry pie
   filling
1-2/3 cups all-purpose flour
1 cup granulated sugar
¼ cup unsweetened cocoa
1 teaspoon baking soda
½ teaspoon salt
1 cup water
½ cup vegetable oil
1 teaspoon vinegar
½ teaspoon vanilla extract
Whipped topping (optional)

Preheat oven to 350 degrees.
Spread cherry pie filling evenly
in bottom of ungreased 9"
square baking pan; set aside.
In a medium mixing bowl, sift
together flour, sugar, cocoa,
baking soda and salt. butter
until well-blended; Add eggs,
Add water, vinegar & vanilla;
stir until batter is well-mixed and
smooth. Pour batter evenly over
cherries; bake 40 to 45 minutes,
or until cake is tested done.
Remove from oven; invert cake
on heat proof platter. If desired,
serve with whipped topping.
Yield about 9 servings

BLUEBERRY SWIRL COFFEE CAKE

2 cups granulated sugar
1 cup butter OR margarine
2 large eggs
½ teaspoon vanilla extract
1 cup sour cream
2 cups all-purpose flour
1½ teaspoons baking powder
¼ teaspoon salt
1 cup fresh blueberries
½ teaspoon cinnamon
½ cup light brown sugar,
   packed
½ cup pecans, finely chopped

In a large mixing bowl,
combine together, sugar,
butter, eggs, vanilla and sour
cream; mix thoroughly. In
another bowl, sift together,
flour, baking powder and
salt. Add dry ingredients to

sugar mixture; mix well. Fold in blueberries. In a small mixing bowl, combine together, cinnamon, brown sugar and nuts. Lightly grease a tube or bundt pan, then in layers, put part of batter in pan, then evenly sprinkle crumb mixture over batter. Add remaining batter, then remaining crumb mixture. Insert a knife into batter, gently swirl batter. Bake at 350 degrees, for about 45 minutes. or until tested done.

PEACH SPICE CAKE

1½ cups peaches, mashed (Use fresh OR canned peaches.)
1½ cups granulated sugar
2/3 cup shortening
3 large eggs, beaten
2-3/4 cups all-purpose flour
3 teaspoons baking powder
1 teaspoon baking soda
½ teaspoon salt
2 teaspoons ginger
1 teaspoon cloves

In a large mixing bowl, cream sugar and shortening until creamy. Add eggs mashed peaches; mix thoroughly. In a separate bowl, sift together, flour, baking powder, baking soda, salt and spices. Grease 3 round cake pans; bake at 375 degrees for 25 to 30 minutes. Frost cake as desired. Yield 8 to 10 servings.

TRADITIONAL LAMB CAKE (use with lamb mold)

2¼ ups all-purpose flour
1¼ cups granulated sugar
1 tablespoon baking powder
½ teaspoon salt
½ cup shortening
1 cup milk
3 large eggs, beaten
1 teaspoon vanilla extract

In a medium mixing bowl, combine ingredients together; mix well. Grease and flour lamb mold. Place on cookie sheet, face down. Fill 1 half of mold with batter, cover with the other half; place in middle of oven. Bake at 350 degrees, for 30 to 45 minutes, or until tested done. Yield 1 lamb cake.

PINEAPPLE UPSIDE-DOWN CAKE

¼ cup butter OR margarine
1 can pineapple slices, drained
2/3 cup brown sugar, packed
Maraschino Cherries, drained
1¼ cups all-purpose flour
1 cup granulated sugar
Whipped topping (optional)
1½ teaspoon baking powder
½ teaspoon salt
¾ cup milk
1/3 cup shortening
1 large egg
1 teaspoon vanilla extract

Preheat oven to 350 degrees; place butter in 9" baking pan, in the oven until butter is melted. Drain pineapple, reserving 2 tablespoons syrup; stir syrup in butter; sprinkle evenly with brown sugar. Arrange pineapple slices in butter mixture. Place a cherry in center of each pineapple slice. In a medium mixing bowl, beat remaining ingredients, EXCEPT whipped topping, with electric mixer, for 3 minutes, on high speed, scraping bowl with spatula occasionally until batter is smooth and creamy. Pour batter evenly over pineapple slices. Bake for about 35 to 40 minutes, or until tested done. Remove from oven; immediately invert cake on heat proof platter. If desired, serve with whipped topping. Yield about 9 servings.

CHOCOLATE-CHERRY-UPSIDE-DOWN CAKE

TOPPING

¼ cup butter OR margarine
½ cup light brown sugar, packed
¼ cup almonds, slivered
2 cups tart *red cherries, pitted

CAKE

¼ cup butter OR margarine
2/3 cup granulated sugar
1 large egg

1 teaspoon vanilla extract
1¼ cups all-purpose flour
½ teaspoon baking powder
½ teaspoon salt
2/3 cup milk
Whipped cream OR topping (optional)
Toasted almonds, slivered (optional)
Preheat oven to 350 degrees F.

FOR TOPPING: place butter in 9" round cake pan. Put in oven to melt butter, about 2 to 3 minutes. Remove from oven; stir in brown sugar; sprinkle with almonds; top with cherries; set aside.

FOR CAKE: in a medium mixing bowl, cream butter with sugar until fluffy. Add egg and vanilla; beat thoroughly; set aside. Sift together, flour, baking powder and salt; add dry ingredients, alternately with milk, beating well after each addition. Spread batter, evenly over topping mixture. Bake for 40 to 45 minutes, or until tested done. Remove from oven and cool on wire rack, for 10 minutes. Invert cake onto heat proof serving platter.

TO SERVE, Garnish with whipping cream and almonds, if desired. Yield 8 to 10 servings.

*NOTE:
Substitute 1 can peaches, sliced, or pineapple slices for cherries.

CARROT CAKE (with Cream Cheese Frosting)

½ cup butter OR margarine, softened
1 cup granulate sugar
2 large eggs, beaten
½ teaspoon lemon peel
2 cups carrots, grated
2 cups all-purpose flour
2 teaspoons baking powder
½ teaspoon salt
½ teaspoon ground cinnamon
½ cup nuts, chopped (optional)

In a medium mixing bowl, cream butter and sugar together, until light and fluffy. Add eggs, lemon peel and carrots, mix thoroughly. In another bowl, sift flour, baking powder, salt and cinnamon together. Add sifted, dry ingredients to butter mixture, beating until well mixed. Pour batter into a greased 8" square baking pan. If desired, sprinkle nuts on top of batter. Bake at 350 degrees, for 35 to 40 minutes, or until tested done. Yield about 9 servings.

CREAM CHEESE FROSTING

1 pkg. (3 ozs.) cream cheese, softened
¼ cup butter OR margarine, softened
2 cups powder sugar
1 teaspoon vanilla extract

Blend cream cheese and butter thoroughly; add sugar and vanilla; mix together, until smooth and creamy.

WHIPPED CREAM CAKE (with Whipped Cream Frosting)

1 cup whipping cream
2 large eggs, beaten
1 cup granulated sugar
1 teaspoon vanilla extract
1½ cups all-purpose flour
¼ teaspoon salt
2 teaspoons baking powder

With electric mixer, on high speed, beat whip cream until holds its shape. Add eggs, continue beating until light and fluffy. Add sugar, beating until well-mixed; add vanilla. Add flour, salt and baking powder, mixing thoroughly. Pour batter into 2 lightly greased and floured cake pans. Bake at 350 degrees, for 25 to 30 minutes, or until tested done. Remove from oven and cool completely before frosting. Frost with Whipped Cream Frosting, (recipe following) or frost as you desire. Yield 8 to 10 servings.

WHIPPED CREAM FROSTING

1 cup whipped cream
1 cup powder sugar
1 pkg. (3 ozs.) cream cheese
1 teaspoon vanilla extract

With electric mixer, beat whipped cream on high speed, until holds its shape; set aside. In a small bowl, cream sugar, cream cheese and vanilla until smooth and creamy. Fold in whipped cream. If desired, you can substitute whipped topping, instead. Frost Whipped Cream Cake, or use for top of fresh fruit or gelatin dishes, etc., or as you desire.

PEANUT BUTTER CAKE
(with Peanut Butter Frosting)

3 large eggs, divided
1-2/3 cups granulated sugar, divided
1½ cups milk, divided
3 squares unsweetened chocolate, (1 ounce each), finely chopped
½ cup shortening
1 teaspoon vanilla extract
2 cups cake flour
1 teaspoon baking soda
½ teaspoon salt

In a saucepan, combine 1 egg, 2/3 cup sugar, ½ cup milk and chocolate. Cook over medium heat, stirring constantly until chocolate is melted and just begins to boil. Remove from heat; set aside to cool. In a medium mixing bowl, cream shortening and remaining sugar thoroughly. Add remaining eggs, one at a time, beating well after each addition; add vanilla. In

another bowl, sift flour, baking soda and salt. Add flour mixture to creamed mixture, alternately with remaining milk; mix well. Add cooled chocolate mixture, mixing thoroughly. Pour into three greased and floured 9" round cake pans. Bake at 325 degrees, for 25 to 30 minutes, or until tested done. Cool for 10 minutes before removing from pans to wire rack.

PEANUT BUTTER FROSTING

2 pkgs. (8 ozs. ea.) cream cheese, softened
1 can (14 ozs.) sweetened condensed milk
1½ cups peanut butter
¼ cup peanuts, chopped, (opt.)
3 milk chocolate candy bars (opt.)

In a medium mixing bowl, beat softened cream cheese until light and fluffy. Gradually add condensed milk and peanut butter, beating until well mixed. Spread between layers, top and sides of cooled cake layers. If desired, sprinkle top with chopped peanuts & garnish with candy bars. Yield 12 to 14 servings.

BLUEBERRY UPSIDE-DOWN CAKE

1 tablespoon butter OR
   margarine
1 teaspoon cornstarch
1 teaspoon granulated sugar
1 teaspoon lemon peel, grated
2 cups fresh OR frozen
   blueberries, drained

BATTER

¼ cup butter OR margarine
½ cup granulated sugar
1 large egg
1 teaspoon vanilla extract
½ teaspoon lemon extract
1 cup all-purpose flour
½ teaspoon baking powder
1/3 cup milk
Whipped Topping (Optional)

Preheat oven to 375 degrees.
Put butter in 9" round cake
pan until melted. In a medium
mixing bowl, combine
cornstarch, 1 teaspoon sugar,
& lemon peel; add blueberries;
mix gently altogether, until
berries are coated. Spread
evenly over melted butter in
cake pan; set aside. In a large
mixing bowl, beat the butter
and remaining sugar, with
electric mixer, on high speed,
until light and fluffy. Add egg,
vanilla and lemon extract, beat
thoroughly. In another bowl,
combine flour and baking
powder, by sifting together.
Add flour mixture to butter
mixture alternately with milk;

mix well. Pour batter gently
over blueberries. Bake for 35
to 40 minutes, or until tested
done. Remove from oven and
immediately invert cake pan
onto a heat proof plate. If
desired, serve with whipped
topping. Yield about 8 or 9
servings.

NO-BAKE FRUIT CAKE

1 package (16 ozs.) graham
   crackers finely crushed
   (about 5 cups)
½ teaspoon ground cinnamon
½ teaspoon allspice
¼ teaspoon ground cloves
¾ cup seedless raisins
1 cup dates, pitted & chopped
1½ cups mixed candied fruit
1 cup walnuts, chopped
½ cup orange juice
1/3 cup light corn syrup

In a large mixing bowl,
combine together graham
cracker crumbs, cinnamon,
allspice, cloves, raisins, dates,
candied fruit and walnuts.
In a separate small bowl, stir
together orange juice & corn
syrup, until well-blended. Add
to crumb mixture, blending
until moistened. Press firmly into
foil-lined loaf pan, cover tightly.
Store in refrigerator 2 days
before serving. Yield 1 loaf or
about10 to 12 slices.

APRICOT UPSIDE-DOWN CAKE

1 can (17 ozs.) apricot halves
1½ teaspoon vanilla extract
2/3 cup brown sugar, packed
Maraschino cherries (optional)

BATTER

1¼ cups all-purpose flour
1 cup granulated sugar
1½ teaspoons baking powder
½ teaspoon salt
¾ cup milk
1/3 cup shortening
1 large egg
1 teaspoon vanilla extract

Preheat oven to 350 degrees.
Put butter in 9" round cake
pan; melt in heated oven.
Drain apricots, reserving 2
tablespoons syrup. Stir syrup
into melted butter, along with
vanilla. Sprinkle brown sugar
evenly over butter mixture;
arrange apricots in butter
mixture. If desired, place
cherries, in between apricots.
In a medium mixing bowl,
combine together, all batter
ingredients; mix thoroughly.
Pour batter gently over
apricot mixture; bake for 40
to 45 minutes, or until tested
done. Remove from oven and
immediately invert cake pan
onto a heat proof plate. If
desired, serve with whipped
topping. Yield 8 or 9 servings.

YANKEE"S BLUEBERRY CAKE

¼ cup butter OR margarine
1 cup granulated sugar
1 large egg
2½ cups all-purpose flour
1 tablespoon baking powder
¼ teaspoon ground nutmeg
1 cup milk
3 cups blueberries, fresh OR
    frozen, thawed
Cream Cheese Frosting (below)

In a large mixing bowl, cream
butter; gradually add sugar,
beating well with an electric
mixer, on medium speed; then
add egg. In another bowl,
combine flour, baking powder
and nutmeg; add to creamed
mixture, alternately with milk;
mix well after each addition.
Add blueberries. Pour batter
into a greased and floured, 10
inch Bundt baking pan. Bake
at 350 degrees, for 45 minutes,
or until tested done. Allow
cake to cool for 5 minutes, then
remove from pan and let cool
completely, before frosting
cake Yield 8 to 12 slices.

CREAM CHEESE FROSTING

1 (8 oz.) package cream
    cheese, softened
½ cup powder sugar, sifted
1 tablespoon milk
½ teaspoon vanilla extract

In a small mixing bowl, beat
cream cheese until light and
fluffy; add powder sugar, along
with remaining ingredients.

BLACK WALNUT CAKE
(with Sour Cream Filling)

3½ cups all-purpose flour
5 teaspoons baking powder
1 teaspoon salt
1¼ cups shortening
1 teaspoon almond extract
1 teaspoon vanilla extract
1¾ cups granulated sugar
4 large egg yolks
1½ cups milk
4 large egg whites
1¼ cups black walnuts,
    chopped

Sift together, flour, baking powder and salt; set aside. In a large bowl, cream shortening with extracts. Gradually add 1½ sugar, beating until light and fluffy. Add yolks, one at a time, beating well after each addition. Add flour mixture, alternately, with milk, beating until smooth after each addition, ending with flour; set aside. Beat egg whites until frothy; add remaining ¼ cup sugar, beating until egg whites are glossy, but not dry. Lightly fold egg whites into batter; mix well. Fold in nuts. Pour batter into 2 well-greased cake pans. Bake at 350 degrees, for 35 to 45 minutes, or until tested done. Cool layers for 15 minutes. Frost as desired.

BLACK WALNUT CAKE SOUR CREAM FILLING

2 large eggs
2/3 cup granulated sugar
Pinch of salt
1 cup sour cream
½ teaspoon vanilla extract

In the top of a double boiler, beat eggs until well mixed, gradually add sugar, along salt and sour cream. Cook over boiling water until thickened, stirring constantly, for about 15 minutes. Cool slightly; add vanilla; mix well. Yield enough filling for one 9" 2-layer cake.

MOCHA FROSTING

½ cup butter OR margarine
2 cups powder sugar
1½ tablespoons unsweetened
    cocoa
1 tablespoon instant coffee

In a medium mixing bowl, cream butter; add powder sugar gradually. Beat with electric mixer at medium speed until smooth and creamy. Add cocoa and coffee gradually, beat until of right consistency to spread; about 1 or 2 minutes.

PEACH MERINGUE CAKE
(with Filling)
BATTER

4 tablespoons butter OR
    margarine
½ cup granulated sugar
½ teaspoon vanilla extract
4 large egg yolks
1 cup all-purpose flour
1 teaspoon baking powder
5 tablespoons milk

Preheat oven to 350 degrees; grease and flour two 9" round cake pans. In a medium mixing bowl, cream butter with sugar, until light and fluffy. Beat in vanilla and egg yolks, one at a time, beating well after each addition. Sift flour and baking powder together. Add to butter mixture, alternately with milk, mixing thoroughly. Divide batter into prepared cake pans; set aside; to prepare meringue.

MERINGUE

4 large egg whites
Pinch of salt
1 cup granulated sugar
2 tablespoons almonds, sliced

In a medium bowl, combine egg whites and salt; beat, with electric mixer, on high speed, until stiff. Gradually add sugar; mix thoroughly. Spread evenly on top of batter in each cake pan. Sprinkle sliced almonds on top of only one pan of cake batter. Bake for 35 to 40

minutes, or until tested done. Remove from oven and let cool on wire racks.

FILLING

2 cups fresh peaches, sliced
1 tablespoon powder sugar
1 cup whipping cream

In a small mixing bowl, whip cream with electric mixer, until soft peaks form. Remove cake without almonds from cake pan; place on serving plate, meringue side up. Spread entire amount of whipped cream, evenly, on top of cake. Top with about 1½ cups of sliced peaches. Remove second layer, with almonds from cake pan; place on top of peaches and cream layer, meringue side up. Spread remaining peaches on top. Refrigerate leftovers Yield 8 to 12 servings.

CHOCOLATE SAUERKRAUT CAKE
(with Chocolate Frosting)

½ cup butter OR margarine
1½ cups granulated sugar
3 large eggs
1 teaspoon vanilla extract
2 cups all-purpose flour
½ cup unsweetened cocoa
¼ teaspoon salt
1 teaspoon baking soda
1 cup water
1 can (8 ozs.) sauerkraut,
    drained & finely cut

In a medium mixing bowl, with electric mixer, on medium-high speed, beat butter and sugar, until light and fluffy. Beat in eggs, one at a time, beating well after each addition; add vanilla; set aside. In another bowl, sift together, flour, cocoa, salt, baking powder and baking soda. Add to creamed mixture, alternately with water; beating well after each addition. Rinse drained sauerkraut with water; drain again thoroughly. With kitchen shears, or sharp knife cut or dice sauerkraut Fold into creamed mixture. Pour batter into greased and floured 13x9x2 inch baking pan. Bake at 350 degrees, for 35 to 40 minutes, or until tested done. Remove from oven; cool, if desired, cover cake with chocolate frosting (recipe follows next page). Yield 10 to 12 servings.

CHOCOLATE FROSTING

1 pkg. (6 ozs.) semisweet
    chocolate chips
¼ cup butter OR margarine
½ cup sour cream
1 teaspoon vanilla extract
¼ teaspoon salt
2½ cups powder sugar

In a saucepan, melt chocolate chips and butter, over low heat; cook until melted. Remove from heat; blend in sour cream,

vanilla and salt. Gradually mix in powder sugar, beating until frosting is of spreading consistency. Add a little more powder sugar, if necessary.

DEVIL'S FOOD CAKE (with Sour Cream Frosting)

Unsweetened cocoa powder
2¼ cups cake flour, sifted
2 teaspoons baking soda
½ teaspoon salt
½ cup butter OR margarine
2½ cups brown sugar, packed
3 large eggs
3 ounces unsweetened
    chocolate, melted
½ cup buttermilk
1 cup boiling water
2 teaspoons vanilla extract

Preheat oven to 375 degrees F. Prepare 3-9" round cake pans; grease and lightly dust with unsweetened cocoa; set aside. In a medium mixing bowl, sift together, flour, baking soda and salt; set aside. In another bowl, with an electric mixer, on high speed, beat butter until light and smooth. Add sugar gradually, beating well after each addition. Add eggs, one at a time, beating well, after each addition. Blend in melted chocolate. Add sifted flour mixture alternately with buttermilk; mix thoroughly. Stir in boiling water and vanilla.

Pour batter into cake pans; bake for 25 to 30 minutes, or until tested done. Remove from oven; cool in pans for ten minutes. Remove from pans and let cool completely, while preparing frosting. Prepare Sour Cream Frosting (next page). Yield about 10 servings.

SOUR CREAM FROSTING

1½ cups sour cream
1½ teaspoons vanilla extract
Pinch of salt

In the top of a double boiler, melt chocolate over hot water, not boiling. Remove from heat; beat in sour cream, vanilla and salt. Beat mixture until creamy and holds its shape. Place a layer on serving plate; spread frosting evenly on each layer, as you stack them on top of each other. Frost sides of cake.

EASY BLACKBERRY CAKE

1 box spice cake mix
1 can (28 ozs.) blackberry pie filling
4 large eggs
1 can Sour Cream Frosting

In a large mixing bowl, combine together, cake mix, pie filling and eggs; mix thoroughly. Pour into a greased 9x13-inch pan; bake at 350 degrees F., for 30 to 35 minutes.

When cool, if desired, frost cake. Yield about 12 servings.

EASY CHOCOLATE-CHERRY CAKE (with Chocolate Frosting)

1 pkg. chocolate cake mix
1 can (21 ozs.) cherry pie filling
2 large eggs
1 teaspoon almond extract
Chocolate Frosting (below)

In a large mixing bowl, beat together, all the ingredients until thoroughly mixed. Place batter into a greased 13x9 baking pan; bake at 350 degrees, for 30 to 35 minutes, or until tested done. Cool cake if desired, frost with Chocolate Frosting

CHOCOLATE FROSTING

1 package (6 ozs.) chocolate chips
½ cup half and half cream
2½ cups powder sugar, sifted
¼ cup butter OR margarine

Combine first 3 ingredients in a medium saucepan; cook over medium heat, stirring until chocolate melts. Remove from heat; add powder sugar, mixing well. Place saucepan in a large bowl of ice. Beat at speed with an electric mixer until frosting holds its shape and loses its gloss. Add a little more cream, if needed, to make a good spreading consistency. Yield 2½ cups.

CHOCOLATE SNACK CAKE

1½ cups all-purpose flour
2 heaping tablespoons cocoa
¼ teaspoon salt
1 teaspoon baking soda
1 cup granulated sugar
½ cup vegetable oil
1 teaspoon vanilla extract
1 cup warm water

In a medium mixing bowl, sift together all dry ingredients. Make a well in center of mound; add oil, vanilla and warm water; mix well. Grease and flour a 9x13x2" baking pan; bake at 350 degrees, for 30 minutes or until tested done. Frost cake, if desired or leave plain. Yield 10 to 12 pieces

CARROT TUNNEL CAKE
(with cream cheese frosting)

CAKE

3 large eggs
1¾ cup granulated sugar
3 cups carrots, shredded
1 cup vegetable oil
2 cups all-purpose flour
2 teaspoons baking soda
2 teaspoons ground cinnamon
1 teaspoon salt
½ cup pecans, chopped
    (optional)

FILLING

1 package (8 ozs.) cream
    cheese, softened
¼ cup granulated sugar
1 large egg

FROSTING

1 package (8 ozs.) cream
    cheese, softened
¼ cup butter OR margarine,
    softened
2 teaspoons vanilla extract
4 cups powdered sugar

In a large mixing bowl, beat eggs and sugar until well-mixed. Add carrots and oil; beat until blended; set aside. In a separate bowl, combine flour, baking soda, cinnamon and salt, by sifting together. Add dry ingredients to carrot mixture; mix well. Stir in pecans. Pour 3 cups batter, into a greased and floured 10-inch fluted tube baking pan. In a medium mixing bowl, beat softened cream cheese and sugar. Add egg; mix well. Spoon filling evenly over batter. Top with remaining batter.

CHOCOLATE CAKE (with Whipped Cream Filling & Chocolate Frosting)

1 cup unsweetened cocoa
2 cups boiling water
1 cup butter OR margarine, softened
2½ cups granulated sugar
4 large eggs
2¾ cups all-purpose flour
2 teaspoons baking soda
½ teaspoon baking powder
½ teaspoon salt
1½ teaspoon vanilla extract

Combine cocoa and boiling water; set aside. Beat butter at medium speed with an electric mixer about 2 minutes or until light and creamy. Gradually add sugar, beating 5 to 7 minutes. Add eggs, 1 at a time, beating well, after each addition. In a separate bowl, combine flour, baking soda, baking powder and salt; add butter mixture alternately with cocoa mixture, beginning and ending with flour mixture. Beat at low speed, just until blended after each addition. Gently stir in vanilla. Pour batter into 3 greased cake pans. Bake at 350 degrees, for 20 to 25 minutes or until tested done. Cool in pans for 10 minutes; remove from pans and cool completely on wire racks. Spread Whipped Cream Filling between layers; spread Chocolate Frosting on top and sides of cake. Yield 10 to 12 servings.

WHIPPED CREAM FILLING

1 cup whipping cream
1 teaspoon vanilla extract

In medium bowl, beat on high speed with electric mixer, whipping cream & powder sugar, beating until soft peaks form. Cover and chill. Yield about 2 cups filling.

CHOCOLATE CAKE CHOCOLATE FROSTING

1 package (6 ozs.) chocolate chips
½ cup half and half cream
2½ cups powder sugar, sifted
¼ cup butter OR margarine

Combine first 3 ingredients in a medium saucepan; cook over medium heat, stirring until chocolate melts. Remove from heat; add powder sugar, mixing well. Place saucepan in a large bowl of ice. Beat at low speed with an electric mixer until frosting holds its shape and loses its gloss. Add a little more cream, if needed, to make a good spreading consistency. Yield 2½ cups frosting.

APPLE CAKE

½ cup brown sugar, packed
3 large eggs
3 cups all-purpose flour
2 teaspoons ground cinnamon
½ teaspoon salt
3½ cups apples, peeled, cored
   & diced
1 cup walnuts, chopped
   (optional)
2 teaspoons vanilla extract

In a large mixing bowl, combine together, oil, granulated sugar and brown sugar; mix well. Add eggs, one at a time, beating well after each addition. In a separate bowl, sift together dry ingredients; add to oil mixture a little at a time, stirring well after each addition. Fold in apples, nuts and vanilla Pour into a greased and floured 10-inch tube pan. Bake at 325 degrees F., for 1½ hours or until cake done. Cool in pan 10 minutes remove cake to a wire rack to cool completely.

PUMPKIN NUT CAKE

1 package white cake mix
1 large egg
½ cup canned pumpkin
¼ cup water
½ teaspoon ground cinnamon
¼ teaspoon nutmeg
1/3 cup nuts, chopped

In a large mixing bowl, combine together, cake mix, egg, pumpkin, water and spices Beat with electric mixer at medium speed, for 2 minutes, or by hand for 4 minutes. Pour batter into a 8x8x2" baking pan. Top with nuts; bake at 350 degrees, for 20 to 25 minutes. Yield 9 servings

GERMAN CHOCOLATE UPSIDE DOWN CAKE

1 cup flaked coconut
1 cup pecans, chopped
1 German Chocolate Cake Mix
1 pkg. (8 ozs.) cream cheese,
   softened
1 cup butter OR margarine,
   softened
1 box (16 ozs.) powder sugar
Lightly grease a 9x13x2" baking
   pan.

Sprinkle coconut in bottom of pan; sprinkle pecans over coconut; set aside. Prepare cake mix as directed on box. Pour cake batter over coconut and pecans; set aside. In a medium mixing bowl, beat, with electric mixer, on medium speed, cream cheese and butter until smooth and creamy. Gradually add powder sugar, continue beating until smooth. Spoon cream cheese mixture carefully over top of cake. Bake at 350 degrees for 45 to 50 minutes, or until cake is tested done. Yield 12 to 15 servings.

RHUBARB UPSIDE-DOWN CAKE DOWN CAKE

2 tablespoons butter OR
    margarine
1 cup brown sugar, packed
2 cups fresh rhubarb, diced
¼ cup vegetable oil
1 cup granulated sugar
1 large egg
2 cups all-purpose flour
2½ teaspoons baking powder
½ teaspoon salt
1 cup milk
Whipped Topping (optional)

Preheat oven to 375 degrees F. Melt butter in a square baking pan; add brown sugar and rhubarb; mix well; set aside. In a medium size mixing bowl, combine oil and sugar; add egg; beat well. In a separate bowl, sift together flour, baking powder and salt. Add dry ingredients alternately with milk to the sugar mixture; mix well. Pout mixture over rhubarb bake cake for 40 to 45 minutes, or until tested done. Invert cake immediately, onto platter. If desired, serve with whipped topping. Yield. about 6 servings.

HIDDEN SURPRISE CARROT CAKE (with Cream Cheese Frosting)

3 large eggs
1¾ cups granulated sugar
3 cups carrots, shredded
1 cup vegetable oil
2 cups all-purpose flour
2 teaspoons baking soda
2 teaspoons ground cinnamon
1 teaspoon salt
½ cup pecans, chopped
    (optional)

In a medium mixing bowl, beat eggs and sugar until light and fluffy. Add carrots and oil; beat until well blended. In a separate bowl, combine flour, baking soda, cinnamon and salt by sifting. A little at a time, add flour mixture to carrot mixture; mix well. Fold in nuts, if desired. Spoon in 3 cups batter into greased and floured 10-inch fluted tube pan. Place filling on top.

TO MAKE FILLING: Beat together, 1 package (8 ozs.) cream cheese, softened and ¼ cup granulated sugar until well-blended. Add 1 large egg; mix well. Spoon over 3 cups batter, Top with remaining batter. Bake at 350 degrees, for 55 to 60 minutes or until tested done. Remove from oven; cool for 10 minutes before removing from pan to a wire rack to cool completely.

TO MAKE FROSTING: In small mixing bowl, beat 1 package (8 ozs.) softened cream cheese, ¼ cup softened butter OR margarine and 2 teaspoons vanilla extract until smooth and creamy. Gradually add 4 cups powdered sugar. Mix until well-blended. Frost cake; cover and refrigerate until serving. Store in refrigerator. Yield 12 to 15 slices.

SOUR CREAM POUND CAKE

1 cup unsalted butter
3 cups granulated sugar
½ cup vegetable oil
6 large eggs
1 teaspoon baking powder
3 cups all-purpose flour
½ teaspoon salt
1 cup sour cream
1 teaspoon vanilla extract
2 tablespoons lemon juice

Preheat oven at 350 degrees. In a large mixing bowl, cream butter and sugar; add oil. Add eggs, one at a time, beating well after each addition; set aside. In a separate bowl, mix together, flour, baking powder and salt. Add to egg mixture, the flour mixture, alternately with sour cream, mixing well after each addition. Pour in to a greased and floured bundt pan. Bake for 1 hour or until tested done. Yield 12 to 15 servings.

PEACH COFFEE CAKE (with filling)

CAKE

2¼ cups all-purpose flour
¾ cup granulated sugar
¾ cup cold butter
¾ cup sour cream
½ teaspoon baking powder
½ teaspoon baking soda
1 large egg
1 teaspoon almond extract

FILLING

1 package (8 ozs.) cream cheese
¼ cup granulated sugar
1 large egg
¾ cup peach preserves

In a large mixing bowl, combine flour and sugar; cut in butter until mixture resembles coarse crumbs; set aside 1 cup for topping. To the remaining crumb mixture, add sour cream, baking powder, baking soda, egg and almond extract; beat until blended. Press onto the bottom and 2" up the sides of a greased 9" spring form pan. Combine filling ingredients together, EXCEPT preserves; mix well. Put filling into prepared crust; top with preserves. Sprinkle with reserved crumb mixture; top with almonds. Place pan on a baking sheet; bake at 350. degrees, for 45 to 50 minutes, or until filling is set and crust is golden brown Cool on a wire rack for 15 minutes. Carefully run a knife around edge. of pan to loosen cake, then remove sides of pan. Cool for 1½ hours before slicing. Store in refrigerator. Yield 12 to 14 servings.

CHOCOLATE MAYONNAISE CAKE (with Brown Sugar Frosting)

CAKE

2 cups all-purpose flour
1 cup granulated sugar
3 tablespoons unsweetened
  cocoa
2 teaspoons baking soda
1 cup water
1 cup mayonnaise
1 teaspoon vanilla extract

In a large mixing bowl, combine by sifting, flour, sugar, cocoa and baking soda. Add water, mayonnaise and vanilla, beat at medium speed with electric mixer, until thoroughly blended. Pour into a greased 9" square baking pan. Bake at 350 degrees, for 30 to 35 minutes or until tested done. Cool completely before frosting. Yield 10 to 12 servings.

BROWN SUGAR FROSTING

¼ cup butter OR margarine
½ cup brown sugar, packed
2 tablespoons milk
1¾ cups powdered sugar

In a small saucepan, melt butter on low heat, add brown sugar; cook, stirring constantly, until bubbly. Remove from heat and stir in milk. Gradually add powder sugar; beat by hand until frosting is of spreading consistency. Enough to frost above cake.

EGGNOG CAKE (with frosting)

CAKE

½ cup butter (do not substitute),
  softened
1¼ cups granulated sugar
3 large eggs
½ teaspoon vanilla extract
½ teaspoon rum extract
2 cups all-purpose flour
2 teaspoons baking powder
1 teaspoon salt
1 cup eggnog

In a large mixing bowl, cream butter and sugar until well-blended. Add eggs, one at a time, beating well after each addition. Add extracts; mix well; set aside. In a separate bowl, combine together, by sifting, flour, baking powder and salt, add to creamed mixture alternately with eggnog, mixing well after each addition. Pour into 2 greased 9" round baking pans. Bake at 350 degrees, for 30 to 35 minutes or until tested done. Cool for 10 minutes before removing from pans to wire racks.

FROSTING

¼ cup all-purpose flour
¼ teaspoon salt
1½ cups eggnog
1 cup butter, softened
1½ cups granulated sugar
1½ teaspoons vanilla extract

Combine in a medium saucepan, flour and salt. Gradually stir in eggnog until smooth. Bring to a boil over medium heat, cook, stirring constantly for 2 minutes or until thickened. Remove from heat; cool to room temperature. In a large mixing bowl, cream butter and sugar until well-blended. Add eggnog mixture and vanilla; mix on high with an electric mixer until light and fluffy. Spread frosting between layers, on top and sides of cake. Store in refrigerator Yield about 12 slices

CRANBERRY CAKE

3 large eggs
2 cups granulated sugar
¾ cup butter OR margarine, softened
1 teaspoon almond extract
2 cups all-purpose flour
2½ cups fresh cranberries, chopped
2/3 cup pecans, chopped
Whipped Cream (optional)

In a large mixing bowl, beat eggs with sugar, until slightly thickened and light in color, about 5 minutes. Add butter and extract; beat 2 minutes more. Stir in flour just until moistened. Fold in cranberries and pecans. Spread batter in a greased 13x9x2" baking pan. Bake at 350 degrees, for 45 to 50 minutes or until tested done. Serve with whipped cream, if desired. Yield 16 to 18 servings.

BLUEBERRY DUMP CAKE

2½ cups crushed pineapple, undrained
3 cups fresh or frozen *blueberries
1 package yellow cake mix, (dry)
½ cup butter OR margarine, melted
*(If using frozen blueberries, thaw first.)

Lightly grease 13x9x5" baking pan. Layer evenly into baking pan, undrained pineapple, blueberries, sugar and dry cake mix. Do not stir. Drizzle melted butter evenly over cake mix; sprinkle with pecans. Bake at 350 degrees F., for about 45 minutes. Yield about 20 servings.

STRAWBERRY NUT ROLL CAKE

6 large eggs, separated
¾ cup granulated sugar, divided
1 cup walnuts, ground fine
¼ cup dry bread crumbs
¼ cup all-purpose flour
Pinch of salt
Powdered sugar

CAKE DIRECTIONS

In a large mixing bowl, beat egg whites until soft peaks form. Gradually add ¼ cup sugar, beating until stiff peaks form; set aside. In another mixing bowl, beat egg yolks and remaining sugar until thick and lemon-colored. Combine walnuts, bread crumbs, flour and salt; add to egg white mixture. Line a greased 15x10x1" baking pan with wax paper; lightly grease wax paper. Spread batter evenly in pan. Bake at 375 degrees, for 15 minutes or until cake springs back when lightly touched. Cool for 5 minutes. Invert cake onto a kitchen towel, dusted with powdered sugar. Gently peel off waxed paper. Roll up cake in the towel, jelly-roll style, starting with short side. Cool on a wire rack. Slice 6 large straw-berries in half; set aside for garnish. Thinly slice remaining berries; set aside.

FILLING & DIRECTIONS

1 pint strawberries
1 cup whipping cream
2 tablespoons granulated sugar
1 teaspoon vanilla extract

In a separate bowl, beat whipping cream until soft peaks form. Gradually add sugar and vanilla, beating until stiff peaks form. Unroll cake; spread with filling to within ½ inch of edges. Top with sliced straw berries; roll up again. Place seam, side down, on serving platter. Chill until serving. Dust cake with powdered sugar, if desired. Garnish with reserved strawberries. Keep refrigerated. Yield 12 servings.

PUMPKIN DUMP CAKE

1 can (29 ozs.) pumpkin
1 can (12 ozs.) evaporated milk
3 large eggs
1 cup granulated sugar
1 teaspoon salt
3 teaspoons ground cinnamon
1 box yellow cake mix
1 cup pecans, chopped
¾ cup margarine, melted

Preheat oven to 350 degree. In a large mixing bowl, combine together, the first 6 ingredients until well-blended; pour batter into a greased 9x13x2" baking pan. Sprinkle dry cake mix evenly on top of batter; add pecans. Pour melted margarine evenly over top. Bake for 50 minutes or until tested done. Yield 12 servings. If desired, serve with whipped cream.

LEMON MERINGUE CAKE

CAKE

1 package (18¼ ozs.) lemon OR
  yellow cake mix
3 large eggs
1 cup water
1/3 cup vegetable oil

In a large mixing bowl,
combine together, cake mix,
eggs, water and oil. Beat
on low speed of an electric
mixer, until ingredients are just
moistened. Beat on high for 2
minutes or until well-blended.
Pour into 2 greased and floured
9-inch round baking pans. Bake
at 350 degrees, for 25 to 30
minutes or until tested done.
Cool in pans for 10 minutes;
remove from pans to wire racks.

FILLING

1 cup granulated sugar
3 tablespoon cornstarch
¼ teaspoon salt
½ cup water
¼ cup lemon juice
4 large egg yolks, beaten
4 teaspoons butter OR
  margarine
1 teaspoon lemon peel, grated

FOR FILLING—Combine
together, sugar, cornstarch and
salt in a saucepan. Stir in water
and lemon juice until smooth.
Bring to a boil, over medium
heat; cook and stir constantly
until thickened, about 1 to 2
minutes. Remove from heat;
set aside. In a medium bowl,
beat egg yolks until light and
lemoncolored. Stir a little
amount of hot mixture into
eggs, then add all egg yolk
mixture to saucepan, stirring
constantly while bringing
mixture to a gentle boil. Stir for
2 minutes. Remove from heat;
stir in butter and lemon peel;
set aside. Cool completely.

MERINGUE

4 large egg whites
¼ teaspoon cream of tartar
¾ cup of granulated sugar

In a medium bowl, beat egg
whites and cream of tartar until
foamy. Gradually beat in sugar
on high speed until stiff peaks
form.

TO ASSEMBLE CAKE—Split
each cooled cake in two
layers. Place bottom layer on
a serving plate; spread 1/3 of
filling. Repeat layers twice. Top
with 4th cake layer. Spread
meringue over top and sides.
Bake at 350 degrees, for 10 to
15 minutes or until meringue is
lightly browned. Keep cooled
cake in refrigerator. Yield 12 to
14 servings.

MAPLE NUT CAKE

2 large eggs, separated
½ cup granulated sugar
2¼ cups cake flour
3 teaspoons baking powder
½ teaspoon salt
1/3 cup vegetable oil
1 cup milk
1 teaspoon maple flavoring
½ cup nuts chopped
1 cup brown sugar

In a medium mixing bowl, beat egg whites until frothy. add ½ cup sugar gradually, beating on medium speed of electric mixer until thick and glossy; set aside. In a separate bowl, sift together, flour, baking powder and salt. Add ½ of the milk, brown sugar and oil; beat for 1 minute, scraping sides often. Add remaining milk, egg yolks and flavoring; beat 1 minute until well mixed. Fold in egg whites; gently mix thoroughly; fold in nuts. Pour into greased 9x13x2 inch baking pan; bake at 350 degrees, for 30 to 35 minutes, or until tested done. Yield 12 to 15 pieces.

MISSISSIPPI MUD CAKE
(with frosting)

1 cup butter OR margarine, softened
2 cups granulated sugar
4 large eggs
1½ cups self-rising flour*

½ cup unsweetened cocoa
1 cup pecan, chopped
1 jar (7 ozs.) marshmallow crème

In a large mixing bowl, cream butter and sugar. Add eggs, one at a time, beating well after each addition. In a separate bowl, combine together, by sifting, flour and cocoa; gradually add to creamed mixture. Fold in pecans. Spoon into greased 13x9x2" baking pan. Bake at 350 degrees, for 35 to 40 minutes or until tested done. Cool for 5 minutes; (cake will fall in center). Spoon marshmallow crème evenly over top of cake. Cool completely. Frost cake with the following frosting below.

FROSTING

½ cup butter OR margarine, softened
3¾ cups powdered sugar
3 tablespoons baking cocoa
4 to 5 tablespoons milk
1 cup pecans, chopped

In a large mixing bowl, cream butter. Add powdered sugar, cocoa, vanilla and enough milk, by beating until frosting is of spreading consistency. Spread frosting evenly over marshmallow crème. Store in refrigerator. Yield 16 to 20 servings.

TO MAKE SELF-RISING FLOUR

For each ½ cup of self-rising flour, place ¾ teaspoon baking powder and ¼ teaspoon salt in a ½ cup measuring cup. Add all-purpose flour to measure ½ cup self-rising flour.

NO EGGS CHOCOLATE CAKE

3 cups all-purpose flour
2 cups granulated sugar
1/3 cup baking cocoa
2 teaspoons baking soda
½ teaspoon salt
¾ cup vegetable oil
2 tablespoons lemon juice
2 cups water

In a large mixing bowl, combine together, by sifting dry ingredients. Add oil, lemon juice and water; mix thoroughly. Pour into an ungreased 9x13x2 inch baking pan; bake at 350 degrees, for about 35 minutes, or until tested done. Yield 12 to 15 pieces.

BUTTERNUT SQUASH LAYER CAKE (with Brown Sugar Frosting)

½ cup butter OR margarine, softened
1 cup granulated sugar
1 cup brown sugar, packed
2 large eggs
1 cup butternut squash, cooked & mashed
1 teaspoon maple flavoring
3 cups cake flour*
4 teaspoons baking powder
¼ teaspoon baking soda
½ cup milk
1 cup walnuts, chopped (optional)

In a large mixing bowl, cream butter and sugars. Add eggs, one at a time, beating after each addition. Add squash and maple flavoring; mix well. In a separate bowl, combine flour, baking powder and baking soda; add to creamed mixture alternately with milk. Fold in nuts. Pour into 2 greased and floured 9-inch round baking pans. Bake at 350 degrees, for 25 minutes or until tested done. Cool 10 minutes before removing sugar from pan. Frost with Brown Sugar Frosting when cool.

BROWN SUGAR FROSTING

1½ cups brown sugar, packed
3 large egg whites
6 tablespoons water
¼ teaspoon cream of tartar
1/8 teaspoon salt
1 teaspoon vanilla extract

In medium saucepan, combine brown sugar, egg whites, water, cream of tartar and salt. Beat for 1 minute over low heat; continue beating for about 8 to 10 minutes, or thermometer reaches 160 degrees. Pour frosting into a large mixing bowl; add vanilla. Beat on high speed until stiff peaks form, about 3 minutes. Spread between layers, over top and sides of cake Refrigerate. Yield 10 to 12 servings.

PINEAPPLE CAKE (with Cream Cheese Frosting)

2 cups all-purpose flour
2 cups granulated sugar
2 large eggs, beaten
2 teaspoons baking soda
1 can (20 ozs.) crushed
    pineapple, with juice

Preheat oven to 350 degrees. In a large mixing bowl, combine together, all ingredients; mix well. Pour batter in 13x9x2 inch baking pan. Bake for 30 minutes, or until tested done. Allow cake to cool about 10 minutes, then while still warm frost with Cream Cheese Frosting (below)

CREAM CHEESE FROSTING

1 pkg. (8 ozs.) cream Cheese,
    softened
1 stick butter OR margarine,
    softened
1 cup powder sugar
1 teaspoon vanilla extract
1 teaspoon milk

In a medium mixing bowl, combine together, all ingredients; blend thoroughly. Enough frosting for above cake.

GERMAN CHOCOLATE CAKE (with Coconut-Pecan Frosting)

1 pkg. German Sweet
    Chocolate
½ cup boiling water
1 cup butter OR margarine
2 cups granulated sugar
4 large egg yolks
1 teaspoon vanilla extract
2½ cups all-purpose flour
½ teaspoon salt
1 teaspoon baking soda
1 cup buttermilk
4 large egg whites. stiffly
    beaten

Melt chocolate in boiling water; set aside to cool. In a medium mixing bowl, cream butter and sugar until fluffy. Add egg yolks, one at a time, beating well after each addition. Blend in vanilla and cooled chocolate; set aside. Sift flour, baking soda and salt together; add flour mixture alternately with buttermilk to chocolate mixture, beating after each addition until smooth. Fold in beaten egg whites; pour into 3 cake pans. Bake at 350 degrees, for 35 minutes, or until tested done. When cake is cool, frost with Coconut-Pecan Frosting.

COCONUT-PECAN FROSTING

1 cup evaporated milk (not
   condensed)
1 cup granulated sugar
1 pound shredded coconut
3 large egg yolks (slightly beaten)
½ cup butter OR margarine
1 teaspoon vanilla extract
1½ cups flaked coconut
1 cup pecans, chopped
   (optional)

In a medium saucepan,
combine together, milk, sugar,
egg yolks and butter; mix
well. Cook over medium heat,
stirring constantly, until mixture
thickens, about 15 minutes. Do
not boil. Remove from heat;
add vanilla, fold in coconut and
pecans. When mixture is room
temperature, spread over each
layer of cake, then stack layers.

IMPOSSIBLE COCONUT CAKE (with pecans)

2 cups milk
¾ cup granulated sugar
½ cup biscuit mix
4 large eggs
¼ cup butter OR margarine
1½ teaspoons vanilla extract
1 can (4 ozs.) flaked coconut
½ cup pecans, chopped

Place milk, sugar, biscuit mix,
eggs, butter and vanilla in a
blender. Cover; blend on low
speed, for 3 minutes. Pour into
greased 9" round or 8" square
cake pan. Let stand at room
temperature for 5 minutes.

Sprinkle with coconut and
pecans. Bake at 350 degrees,
for 40 minutes or until tested
done. Yield 6 to 8 servings.

RHUBARB CAKE

½ cup butter OR margarine,
   softened
1½ cups brown sugar, packed
1 cup sour cream
2 cups all-purpose flour
1 teaspoon baking soda
½ teaspoon salt
1 teaspoon vanilla extract
1 cup rhubarb, cut-up into ½
   inch pieces

In a medium mixing bowl,
cream together, butter and
brown sugar; add sour cream;
mix well. In another bowl, sift
together, flour, baking soda
and salt. Add butter mixture
into flour mixture; mix well. Add
vanilla. Fold in rhubarb; mix
thoroughly. Spread batter into
a 9x13 baking pan; sprinkle with
topping (recipe follows).

TOPPING

¾ cup brown sugar, packed
1 teaspoon cinnamon
2 tablespoons butter OR
margarine, softened

Combine together, above
ingredients, sprinkle evenly over
top of cake batter; bake at
350 degrees, for about 35 to 45
minutes, or until tested done.
Yield about 10 to 12 servings.

SWEET POTATO CAKE

1 package yellow cake mix
2 cups sweet potatoes, cooked
   & mashed
2/3 cup dark brown sugar,
   packed
2 tablespoons apricot jelly
½ teaspoon nutmeg
1 teaspoon cinnamon
1/3 cup plus 2 tablespoons sour
   cream
3 large eggs
½ teaspoon baking soda

In a medium mixing bowl, combine together, sweet potatoes, brown sugar and spices; beat until thoroughly mixed. Add cake mix, plus remaining ingredient; beat for 2 minutes. Pour into greased and floured two 9-inch cake pans. Bake at 350 degrees, for 25 to 35 minutes, or until tested done. Frost as desired.

NUT FILLING

½ cup brown sugar, packed
2 tablespoon all-purpose flour
½ cup evaporated milk
1/3 cup walnuts OR pecans,
   finely chopped
½ teaspoon vanilla extract
Pinch of Salt

In a medium saucepan, combine together brown sugar and flour; add milk; mix well. Add butter; cook over medium heat, stirring constantly until mixture thickens. Remove from heat, add nuts, vanilla and salt. Chill in refrigerator for 2 hours. Yield enough filling for one 2-layer cake.

POWDER SUGAR FROSTING

1 large egg white
½ cup shortening
¼ cup butter OR margarine
1 teaspoon vanilla

In a medium mixing bowl, beat together, egg white, shortening, butter and vanilla. Beat on medium speed of electric mixer, until well-blended. Gradually add powder sugar beating until light and fluffy. Yield enough frosting to cover one 2-layer cake, or 12 cupcakes.

BUTTERSCOTCH GLAZE

1 cup granulated sugar
½ cup buttermilk
¼ cup corn syrup
¼ cup margarine
2 cups powder sugar, sifted
½ teaspoon baking soda
½ teaspoon vanilla extract

In a small saucepan, combine together, all ingredients. Over medium heat, bring mixture to a boil; boil for 10 minutes, stirring constantly. Pour over warm cake, especially good served on carrot cake.

GREEN TOMATO CAKE
(w/Cream Cheese Frosting

3 cups all-purpose flour
2 cups granulated sugar
3 cups green tomatoes, grated
   & drained
½ teaspoon salt
1¼ cups vegetable oil
3 large eggs
2 teaspoons vanilla extract
1 teaspoon ground cloves
2 teaspoons baking soda
1 teaspoon cinnamon

In a large mixing bowl, sift
together, all dry ingredients.
Add oil, eggs, vanilla; beat well.
Add tomatoes; mix thoroughly.
Pour into greased 9"x13" baking
pan. Bake at 350 degrees, for
about 1 hour, or until tested
done.

CREAM CHEESE FROSTING
Cream ¾ butter (or margarine)
with 1 pkg. (8 ozs) cream
cheese. Add 1 teaspoon
vanilla; along with 1½ cups
powder sugar (add gradually);
beat until well-blended,.

CHERRY COFFEE CAKE

CAKE
½ cup butter OR margarine
1 cup granulated sugar
2 large eggs
½ cup milk
1 teaspoon vanilla extract
2 cups all-purpose flour
2 teaspoons baking powder

TOPPING

1/3 cup all-purpose flour
¼ cup granulated sugar
1 teaspoon cinnamon
3 tablespoons butter OR
   margarine
1 can (24 ozs.) cherry pie filling

Preheat oven to 350 degrees.
Grease and flour an 8x11 inch
baking pan; set aside. In a
medium mixing bowl, combine
together, butter, sugar, eggs
and vanilla; mix well. Add flour
and baking powder alternately
with the milk; mix thoroughly.
Place half of the batter in the
prepared pan. Put cherry
pie filling on top, then add
remaining batter on top of pie
filling; set aside. Meanwhile
prepare topping by combining
flour, sugar, cinnamon and
butter until mixture is crumbly.
Sprinkle on top of cake. Bake
cake for 1 hour or until tested
done. Yield about 12 servings.

EASY PUDDING CAKE

1 pkg. plain cake mix
1 pkg. Jell-o Brand Instant
   Pudding and Pie Filling, any
   flavor
4 large eggs
1 cup water
¼ cup vegetable oil

In a large mixing bowl,
combine together, all
ingredients. Beat on medium
speed of electric mixer for 3
minutes. Pour batter into a
greased, floured 10-inch tube
pan. Bake at 350 degrees, for
50 to 60 minutes, or until tested
done. Cool for 15 minutes,
before removing from pan.
Frost cake, if desired.

NOTE: Cake can be baked in
a 13x9-inch pan for 45 to 50
minutes.

HOW TO MAKE SOUR MILK—mix
½ teaspoon lemon juice OR
vinegar in ½ cup milk.

SOUR CHERRY CAKE (with frosting)

1¼ cups granulated sugar
½ cup butter OR margarine,
   softened
¾ cup *sour milk (see
   preceding page)
2 large eggs
2 cups all-purpose flour, sifted
1 teaspoon baking soda
¼ teaspoon salt

1 teaspoon cinnamon
1 cup sour cherries, pitted &
   stemmed

Grease two 8" cake pans; dust
with flour. In a large mixing
bowl, cream together, butter
and sugar; add eggs, one
at a time, beating well after
each addition; set aside. In a
separate bowl, sift together,
flour, baking soda, salt and
cinnamon. Add butter mixture
to flour mixture, alternately with
milk, beating well after each
addition. Fold in cherries; bake
at 350 degrees, for 30 minutes,
or until tested done. Meanwhile
prepare frosting.

SOUR CHERRY FROSTING
2 tablespoons butter OR
   margarine, softened
2½ cups powder sugar, sifted
1 teaspoon vanilla extract
¼ cup sour cherries

Cook cherries in a small
amount of water & sugar, over
low heat to form a syrup. Bring
to a boil. stir ring constantly.
Remove from heat; strain
cherries; set aside. In a small
bowl, combine ingredients,
then add enough cherry
juice to obtain a spreadable
consistency.

APRICOT CREAM FILLING

1 tablespoon all-purpose flour
¼ cup granulated sugar
Dash salt (optional)
½ cup milk
1 large egg
2/3 cup dried apricots, cooked
   & diced
½ teaspoon lemon juice

In top of a double boiler, combine together, flour, sugar and salt; gradually add milk. Cook over medium heat, stirring constantly, until thick. Meanwhile beat egg; then add to creamed mixture; cook for 3 minutes. Remove from heat; add apricots and lemon juice; cool. Yield enough to fill 2-8" cake layers.

BANANA FILLING

3 tablespoons all-purpose flour
3 tablespoons granulated sugar
½ cup milk
2 teaspoons lemon juice
½ cup bananas, mashed
3 tablespoons butter OR
   margarine, melted
Dash salt

In top of a double boiler, combine together, flour and sugar; gradually add milk. Cook over medium heat, stirring constantly, until thick. Meanwhile mix lemon juice and bananas; add to milk

mixture; remove from heat; cool. Add butter and salt; mix well. Yield enough to fill 2-8" cake layers.

SHORTCUT COFFEE CAKE

2 cups pancake mix
¼ cup granulated sugar
1 teaspoon cinnamon
½ cup evaporated milk.
   undiluted
½ cup warm water
1 large egg
¼ teaspoon baking powder

In a large mixing bowl, combine together, all the above ingredients; mix well. Pour into greased 9-inch square baking pan;. set aside while making the topping.

TOPPING

¼ cup dark brown sugar,
   packed
2 tablespoons butter OR
   margarine
½ cup nuts, finely chopped
½ cup raisins (optional)

In a small mixing bowl, combine topping ingredients; mix well. Place topping on top of cake; swirl mixture through cake batter with knife. Bake at 350 degrees for 30 to 45 minutes or until tested done. Serve warm.

CHERRY 7 UP CAKE

¾ cup shortening
2 cups granulated sugar
3 cups cake flour
5 large egg whites, room
  temperature
2 teaspoons baking powder
¼ teaspoon salt
7 oz. bottle of 7-Up Cherry Pop

In a medium mixing bowl,
cream shortening and sugar,
until smooth and light. Add flour,
baking powder and salt; mix
well. Add 7-up; mix until well-
blended; set aside. In another
bowl, beat egg whites until stiff,
but not dry; fold into batter.
Grease and flour two cake
pans; fill with batter. Bake at 350
degrees for 35 to 40 minutes,
or until tested done. Frost if
desired. Yield 6 to 8 serving.

CHOCOLATE ECLAIR CAKE
(made with graham crackers)

1 box (16 ozs.) honey graham
  crackers
2 pkgs. (3¾ ozs. each) instant
  vanilla pudding
3 cups milk
1 carton (12 ozs.) whipped
  topping
1½ cups powder sugar, sifted
6 tablespoons unsweetened
  cocoa
2 tablespoons butter OR
  margarine
3 tablespoons milk

2 teaspoons light corn syrup
1 teaspoon vanilla extract

Place whole graham crackers
in a single layer on the bottom
of 9x13x2 inch baking pan. In a
medium mixing bowl, combine
pudding mix with 3 cups of milk,
stirring until thickened. Fold in
whipped topping; mix gently.
Spread half the pudding on
graham crackers. Add another
layer of graham crackers;
evenly cover with remaining
pudding. Top with third layer of
crackers; set aside. In a small
saucepan, combine together,
remaining ingredients; mix well.
Over low heat, cook until sugar
dissolves, stirring constantly.
Remove from heat, let cool
slightly, then pour over top layer
of crackers. Refrigerate at least
24 hours before serving. Yield
about 16 to 24 servings.

HAWAIIAN WEDDING CAKE
(with Cream Cheese Frosting)

2 cups all-purpose flour
2 cups granulated sugar
2 teaspoons baking **powder**
2 large eggs, lightly beaten
1 cup mixed nuts, finely chopped
1 cup shredded coconut
1 can (20 ozs.) crushed
  pineapple, undrained

Preheat oven to 350 degrees.
Grease and flour cake pans
or 13x9x2 inch baking pan. In

a large mixing bowl, combine together, flour, sugar and baking powder. Fold into flour mixture, eggs, nuts, coconut and crushed pineapple with juice; mix well. Pour batter into prepared pan (s). Bake for 35 to 40 minutes, or until tested done. Cool completely; frost if desired.

CREAM CHEESE FROSTING

1 cup cream cheese, softened
¼ cup butter, softened
1 teaspoon vanilla extract
1½ cups powder sugar

In a medium mixing bowl, beat together, all the ingredients, with electric mixer, at high speed; beat until smooth and creamy. Spread over cooled cake.

CINNAMON BUNDT CAKE

1 cup butter, softened
1¼ cup granulated sugar
2 large eggs
1 cup sour cream
2 cups all-purpose flour
½ teaspoon salt
1 teaspoon baking soda
1½ teaspoon baking powder
¾ cups nuts, chopped
2 tablespoons granulated sugar
1 teaspoon cinnamon
1 teaspoon vanilla extract

In a large mixing bowl, combine together, butter, sugar and eggs; beat until mixture

is light and fluffy Blend in sour cream; set aside. In another bowl, combine together, by sifting dry ingredients, then add dry ingredients along with vanilla

BROWN SUGAR POUND CAKE

3 cups all-purpose flour
1 teaspoon baking powder
½ teaspoon salt
1½ cups butter OR margarine, softened
1 pound light brown sugar
1½ teaspoon vanilla extract
5 large eggs, room temperature
1 cup milk
1½ cup nuts, chopped (pecans OR walnuts)
2 teaspoons powder sugar

In a medium mixing bowl, sift together, flour, baking powder and salt; set aside. In a large mixing bowl, beat together, butter, brown sugar and vanilla, until light and fluffy, for 2 minutes. Add eggs, one at a time, beating well after each addition. Add dry ingredients alternately with milk, blending well after each addition. Fold in nuts; pour batter into greased 10" fluted tube pan. Bake at 325 degrees, for 1 hour 20 minutes, or until cake tests done. Remove cake from oven; cool on rack. If desired, sprinkle powder sugar over cooled cake. Yield 16 servings.

CARAMEL PECAN POUND CAKE

1 cup butter, softened
2¼ cups brown sugar, packed
5 large eggs
3 teaspoons vanilla extract
3 cups all-purpose flour
½ teaspoon baking powder
½ teaspoon salt
1 cup milk
1 cup pecans, finely chopped
Powder sugar

In a large mixing bowl, cream butter; gradually add sugars, beat until light and fluffy. Add eggs, one at a time, beating well after each addition; stir in vanilla; set aside. Meanwhile, in another bowl, combine flour, baking powder and salt. Add to creamed mixture alternately with milk; mix until well-blended; fold in pecans. Pour into greased and floured 10" tube pan. Bake at 325 degrees, for 1½ hours, or until tested done. Remove from oven; let cool for 10 minutes, before removing cake from pan. Cool completely; sprinkle with powder sugar. If desired, serve with fruit. Yield 16 servings.

CARAMEL FROSTING

¼ cup butter OR margarine, softened
2 cups powder sugar
3 tablespoons milk
¼ teaspoon salt
¾ teaspoon vanillas extract
3 tablespoons brown sugar
½ teaspoon maple flavoring

In a medium mixing bowl, combine together, all ingredients. Mix well for spreading consistency. If necessary, add more powder sugar or milk to obtain spreading consistency. Yield enough frosting for one 2-layer cake or 12 cupcakes.

DECORATOR'S FROSTING

2 cups powder sugar
½ teaspoon vanilla extract
About 2 tablespoons milk
Food coloring (optional)

In a bowl, beat together, sugar, vanilla and enough milk, until smooth and of spreading consistency. If desire, tint with a few drops of food coloring. Place in decorator's tube; pipe onto cake, etc., or do it by hand.

MARSHMALLOW FROSTING

1 cup granulated sugar
¼ cup light corn syrup
¼ cup water
2 large egg whites
¼ teaspoon salt
¼ teaspoon cream of tartar
1 teaspoon vanilla

In the top of a double boiler, combine together all ingredients, EXCEPT vanilla. Over simmering water, beat until soft peaks form, about 5 to 7 minutes. Remove from heat, add vanilla; mix well. Let cool; then frost cake.

BUTTER FROSTING

½ cup vegetable shortening
½ cup butter OR margarine
1 teaspoon vanilla extract
2 tablespoons milk
4 cups powder sugar

In a medium mixing bowl, cream shortening and butter until smooth and creamy; add vanilla and milk; mix well. Add sugar, 1 cup at a time, beating well after each addition. Good frosting for decorating, it holds up well.

SEVEN MINUTE FROSTING

2 large egg whites
1½ cups granulated sugar
1/3 cup cold water
2 teaspoons corn syrup
1 teaspoon vanilla extract

In the top of a double boiler, combine together, egg whites sugar, water and corn syrup. Beat with hand beater or electric mixer at medium speed, about 1 minute or until well mixed. Place over boiling water; cook while beating mixture, for 7 minutes or until frosting stands in stiff peaks. Remove from water; add vanilla; beat 1 more minute or until frosting is thick enough to spread. Yield enough frosting for a 2-layer cake.

NOTE: If desired, you can take 1½ cups of coconut, shredded, spread over frosting.

ORANGE FROSTING

¼ cup butter OR margarine
2 cups powder sugar
2 tablespoons milk
¼ teaspoon salt
¾ teaspoon vanilla extract
3 tablespoons orange juice
1 teaspoon orange peel,
   grated

In a mixing bowl, cream together, butter; add sugar gradually; mix well. Add milk, salt, vanilla, orange juice and peel. Mix until of spreading consistency. Yield enough frosting for one 2-layer cake or—12 cupcakes.

COFFEE FROSTING

¼ cup butter OR margarine
½ cup brown sugar, packed
1½ instant coffee
3 cups powder sugar, sifted
3 to 4 tablespoons evaporated milk, undiluted
2/3 cup walnuts, finely
   chopped

In a saucepan, over medium heat, combine together, butter and brown sugar. Bring to a boil, then remove from heat; add instant coffee; mix well. Add powder sugar alternately with evaporated milk; mix until of good spreading consistency. Fold in walnuts. Yield enough frosting for a 2-layer cake.

PENOCHE FROSTING

1 cup light brown sugar, packed
1/2 cup granulated sugar
1/3 cup milk
¼ cup butter OR margarine
1 tablespoon corn syrup
¼ teaspoon salt
1 teaspoon vanilla extract

In a medium saucepan, combine together, sugars, milk, butter, corn syrup and salt; mix well. Over low heat, bring to a full boil, stirring constantly. Boil for 1 minute, remove from heat; cool to lukewarm; add vanilla. Beat frosting until thick enough to spread, about 8 to 10 minutes. Yield enough frosting for a 2-layer cake.

FOR THE PERFECT CHEESECAKE!

1. Have all ingredients at room temperature OR warm cream cheese 10 minutes in oven at 200 degrees OR 2 minutes in a microwave oven. Eggs can be warmed by setting eggs in their shells into a bowl of warm water.

2. It is best to oil the spring form pan, this will keep the cake from sticking to the sides, which can cause the cake to crack as it cools.

3. Do not open the oven door during the first 30 minutes of baking time.

4. Make cheesecake at least 1 day ahead to allow flavor to ripen.

5. Cheesecakes may be refrigerated for up to a week, OR wrapped securely and can be frozen for up to a month. Thaw overnight, in the refrigerator.

PINA COLADA CHEESECAKE

1-9" graham cracker crust
1 pkg. (8 ozs.) cream cheese, softened
3 large eggs
½ cup granulated sugar
½ teaspoon vanilla extract
1 tablespoon rum
1 can (8 ozs.) crushed pineapple, drained
½ cup sour cream
½ cup flaked coconut

In a large mixing bowl, beat cream cheese, eggs, sugar and vanilla, until smooth and creamy. Stir rum into pineapple, then add to cream cheese mixture. Pour into prepared crust; bake at 350 degrees, for 30 minutes, or until tested done. Remove from oven; spread sour cream, evenly over the top; sprinkle with coconut. Return to oven and bake 5 minutes more. Cool before serving. Yield 8 servings.

WHITE CHOCOLATE CHEESECAKE

1 cup chocolate wafer crumbs
3 tablespoons butter OR
    margarine, melted
3 pkgs. (8 ozs. each) cream
    cheese, softened
½ cup granulated sugar
3 large eggs
6 ounces white chocolate
    chips, melted
½ cup sour cream
½ teaspoon vanilla extract

Combine crumbs and butter;
mix well. Press onto bottom of a
9" spring form pan. Bake at 350
degrees, for 10 minutes; remove
from oven; set aside. In a large
mixing bowl, with an electric
mixer at medium speed, beat
cream cheese and sugar, until
well-blended. Add egg, one at
a time, mixing well after each
addition; set aside. Meanwhile,
melt white chocolate in double
boiler over hot water, then
blend white chocolate, sour
cream and vanilla into cream
cheese mixture; pour into crust.
Bake at 350 degrees, for 50
minutes. Loosen cake from rim
of pan; cool completely before
removing from pan. Chill 1 hour
before serving, Yield 10 to 12
servings.

BLUEBERRY SWIRL CHEESECAKE

CRUST
1 cup graham cracker crumbs
1 cup plus 3 tablespoons
    granulated sugar, divided

3 tablespoons butter OR
    margarine, melted

Preheat oven to 325 degrees.
Combine together, crumbs,
3 tablespoons sugar and
butter; mix well. Press firmly
onto bottom of a foil-lined 13x9
inch baking pan. Bake for 10
minutes; set aside.

FILLING

4 pkgs. (8 ozs. each) cream
    cheese, softened
1 teaspoon vanilla extract
1 cup sour cream
4 large eggs
2 cups blueberries, fresh or
    frozen, thawed

Meanwhile, in a large mixing
bowl, beat with electric mixer
on medium speed, beat cream
cheese, remaining cup of
sugar and vanilla until well-
blended. Add eggs, one at a
time, beating well after each
addition. Pour into crust; set
aside. Puree' blueberries in
a food processor or blender.
Gently drop spoonfuls of
pureed blueberries over batter,
then using a knife cut through
batter for marble effect. Bake
for 45 minutes or until tested
done. Cover and refrigerate for
at least 4 hours before serving.
Yield 16 servings.

BANANA SPLIT CHEESECAKE

CRUST
2 cups graham cracker crumbs
1/3 cup butter OR margarine, melted
¼ cup granulated sugar

FILLING
3 large eggs
1 tablespoon instant coffee
1 tablespoon banana extract
3 pkgs. (8 ozs. each) cream cheese, softened
¾ cup granulated sugar
1 teaspoon vanilla extract
½ cup bananas, mashed

TOPPING
1 cup strawberries, halved
1 banana, sliced & tossed with 1 tea-spoon lemon juice
1 can (8 ozs.) pineapple chunks, drained

GARNISH
2 to 4 squares semisweet chocolated, melted (Optional)
½ cup nuts, chopped (Optional)

Preheat oven to 350 degrees. Line a 13x9 inch baking pan, with foil; set aside. Prepare crust by mixing crumbs, butter and sugar in a medium-size bowl; mix well. Press mixture evenly into the bottom of the prepared baking pan.

Prepare filling by combining together, eggs, instant coffee and banana extract in small bowl, beat until well-blended; set aside. Using an electric mixer on medium speed, beat cream cheese, sugar and vanilla together until thoroughly mixed. Add egg mixture; mix well. Fold in mashed banana. Spread filling evenly over crust. Bake for 30 minutes, or until tested done. Remove from oven and cool completely. Arrange strawberries, sliced banana and pineapple chunks on top of cake. If desired, drizzle melted chocolate over fruit; sprinkle with nuts. Refrigerate overnight before serving. Yield 12 large servings.

CRUST

1 cup chocolate wafer crumbs
¼ cup (½ stick) butter OR margarine, softened
Combine crumbs and butter; press onto the bottom of 9-inch spring form pan. Yield 1 crust.

CHEESECAKE

3 pkgs. (8 ozs. each) cream
  cheese, softened
1½ cups granulated sugar
1 carton (8 ozs.) sour cream
2 teaspoons vanilla extract
½ cup unsweetened cocoa
2 tablespoons all-purpose flour
3 large eggs

Prepare crust; set aside.
Preheat oven to 450 degrees.
In a large mixing bowl, beat
cream cheese and sugar until
well mixed. Add sour cream
and vanilla; mix well. Add
cocoa and flour, then add
eggs, one at a time, beating
just until blended; pour into
crust. Bake for 10 minutes, then
reduce oven temperature to
250 degrees, continue baking
for 40 minutes. Remove from
oven; loosen cake from sides
of pan, use a butter knife. Yield
about 10 to 12 servings.

PEACH CHEESECAKE

1 cup vanilla wafer crumbs,
  (about 24 wafers)
½ cup pecans, finely chopped
¼ cup butter OR margarine,
  melted
4 pkgs. (8 ozs. each) cream
  cheese, softened
1 can (14 ozs.) sweetened
  condensed milk (not
  evaporated milk)
2 medium peaches, peeled,
  seeded & pureed (about 1
  cup pureed))
3 large eggs
1 tablespoon all-purpose flour
Fresh peaches

Preheat oven to 300 degrees.
On the bottom of a 9-inch
spring form pan, combine
together, crumbs, pecans
and butter; press firmly; set
aside. In a large mixing bowl,
beat cheese until light & fluffy.
Gradually beat in sweetened
condensed milk until smooth.
Add pureed peaches, eggs
and flour; mix well. Pour batter
into prepared pan; bake for
1 hour and 15 minutes or until
tested done. Turn off oven;
remove cake from oven; run
knife around edge of pan.
Return to oven with door slightly
open. When cool remove side
of spring-born pan. Garnish
with peach slices; refrigerate
leftovers. Yield about 10 to 12
servings.

PRALINE CHEESECAKE CRUST

1 cup graham cracker crumbs
3 tablespoons granulated sugar
3 tablespoons butter, melted

FILLING

3 pkgs. (8 ozs. each) cream
    cheese, softened
1 cups dark brown sugar,
    packed
2 tablespoons all-purpose flour
3 large eggs
1½ teaspoons vanilla extract
½ cup pecans, finely chopped
Maple syrup and Pecan halves

Combine together, cracker
crumbs, sugar and butter;
then press into bottom of a
9-inch spring form pan. Bake
at 350 degrees for 10 minutes.
Meanwhile, in a large mixing
bowl, combine together,
cream cheese, brown sugar
and flour, mixing at medium
speed with electric mixer,
until well-blended. Add eggs,
one at a time, mixing well
after each addition. Stir in
vanilla; fold in pecans; pour
in crust. Bake at 450 degrees
for 10 minutes; reduce oven
temperature to 250 degrees,
continue baking for 30 minutes.
Remove cake from oven; cool,
then loosen cake from rim of
pan. Brush with maple syrup
and top with pecan halves.
Yield 10 to 12 servings.

FILLING

1½ cups dry cottage cheese
½ cup granulated sugar
3 tablespoons heavy cream
Grated peel of 1 lemon
3 large eggs, beaten, plus 1
    egg yolk

CRUST

1 cup butter OR margarine,
    softened
1 cup granulated sugar
1 large egg
1/3 cup milk
3 cups all-purpose flour
½ teaspoon baking soda
1 teaspoon vanilla extract

In a medium mixing bowl,
combine together, cottage
cheese, sugar, cream, lemon
peel and eggs; mix well; set
aside. Meanwhile, in another
bowl, cream butter; add sugar
gradually; mix well. Beat in
egg; add milk; mix thoroughly.
Sift together, flour and baking
soda, then fold into butter
mixture; add favoring. On a
lightly floured surface, roll 1 inch
thick; line dough in a cake pan.
Place filling in prepared cake
pan. Bake at 350 degrees, for
30 to 40 minutes, or until tested
done. Yield 8 to 10 servings.

BURNT SUGAR CHIFFON CAKE (with Burnt Sugar Frosting)

2 cups all-purpose flour
1¼ cups granulated sugar
1 tablespoon baking powder
½ teaspoon salt
½ cup vegetable oil
7 large eggs, separated
¼ cup water
½ cup Burnt Sugar Syrup
   (recipe next page)
1 teaspoon vanilla extract
¼ teaspoon cream of tartar

Burnt Sugar Frosting (recipe next page) Preheat oven to 325 degrees. In a medium mixing bowl, combine together, flour, sugar baking powder and salt. Add oil, egg yolks, water, Burnt Sugar Syrup and vanilla. Start on low speed of electric mixer, then increase speed slowly, beat at medium speed until very smooth, about 2 minutes. Wash beaters, then beat egg whites and cream of tartar until stiff, but not dry. Gently fold egg yolk mixture into egg white mixture until well-blended. Pour batter into ungreased 10-inch tube bake in preheated oven for 1½ hours, or until top springs back when lightly touched. Invert pan, cool completely. When cool, remove from pan and frost with Burnt Sugar Frosting,

BURNT SUGAR SYRUP

¾ cup granulated sugar
1 cup boiling water

In a small saucepan, melt sugar, over medium heat, stirring constantly, until sugar syrup turns a deep golden brown. Remove from heat; slowly pour in boiling water, stirring constantly until well-blended. Remove from heat; cool and refrigerate any excess syrup. Yield 1 cup syrup.

BURNT SUGAR FROSTING

1 cup granulated sugar
1/3 cup water
1 tablespoon light corn syrup
2 large egg whites
1½ tablespoons Burnt Sugar
   Syrup
1 teaspoon vanilla extract

In a small saucepan, combine sugar, water and corn syrup; cover; cook over medium heat until mixture boils rapidly. Uncover; continue to boil to 240 degrees on candy thermometer. While mixture is boiling, beat egg whites until stiff, but not dry. Remove syrup mixture from heat; pour hot syrup slowly into egg whites, beating constantly. Add burnt sugar syrup and vanilla; beat on high speed until stiff peaks form and is of spreading consistency.

$100 MAYONNAISE CAKE (1940's)

2 cups all-purpose flour
1 cup granulated sugar
4 tablespoons unsweetened
　cocoa
1½ teaspoons baking soda
¾ cup mayonnaise
1 cup water
1 teaspoon vanilla extract

In a medium mixing bowl, sift together all the dry ingredients. Add mayonnaise, water and vanilla; mix well. Pour batter into a greased cake pan (8x8x2 in.); bake at 350 degrees, for about 35 o 40 minutes, or until tested done. Frost with favorite frosting, if desired. Yield about 8 servings.

SAUERKRAUT APPLE CAKE
(with Cream Cheese Frosting)

4 large eggs
1 cup sugar & ½ cup brown
　sugar, packed
1 can (14 ozs.) sauerkraut,
　rinsed & drained
1 lge. tart apple, cored, peeled
　& grated
1 cup vegetable oil
1 cup walnuts, chopped
2 cups all-purpose flour
2 teaspoons baking powder
2 teaspoons ground cinnamon
1 teaspoon baking soda
½ teaspoon salt
½ teaspoon nutmeg

In a large mixing bowl, beat together, eggs and both sugars, until fluffy; set aside.

Squeeze sauerkraut until dry, finely chop; add to egg mixture; mix well. Stir grated apple into egg mixture; add oil and walnuts; mix thoroughly. In another bowl, combine together, flour, baking powder, cinnamon, baking soda, salt and nutmeg; mix well. Mix thoroughly into egg mixture. Grease and flour (2) 8 inch cake pans. Pour batter into pans; bake at 350 degrees, for 35 to 40 minutes or until tested done. Cool in pans for 10 minutes, before inverting onto a wire rack to cool completely. Frost with Cream Cheese Frosting. Yield 10 to 12 servings.

CREAM CHEESE FROSTING

1 pkg. (8 ozs.) cream cheese,
　softened
3 tablespoons whipping cream,
　divided
4½ cups powder sugar
1 tablespoon orange peel,
　grated
½ teaspoon ground cinnamon
1 teaspoon vanilla extract
Walnuts, chopped (optional)

In a small mixing bowl, beat cream cheese, whipping cream and sugar; until fluffy. Add orange peel, cinnamon and vanilla; mix well. Spread frosting between layers, then frost entire cake. If desired, garnish cake with chopped walnuts. Store covered in refrigerator.

ORANGE CHIFFON CAKE
(with Orange Glaze)

2 cups all-purpose flour
1½ cups granulated sugar
4 teaspoons baking powder
1 teaspoon salt
6 large eggs, separated
¾ cup orange juice
½ cup vegetable oil
2 tablespoons orange peel,
   grated
½ teaspoon cream of tartar

ORANGE GLAZE

½ cup butter OR margarine
2 cups powder sugar
2 to 4 tablespoons orange juice
½ teaspoon orange peel.
   Grated

In a large mixing bowl,
combine together, flour, sugar,
baking powder and salt. Add
egg yolks, orange juice, oil and
orange peel; beat until smooth,
about 5 minutes. In another
mixing bowl. beat egg whites
and cream of tartar, until stiff,
but not dry. Fold egg whites
into orange mixture. Spoon
into an ungreased 10 inch tube
pan; bake at 350 degrees, for
45 to 50 minutes or until tested
done. Remove from oven and
immediately invert pan to cool
When cool, remove cake from
pan. FOR GLAZE: Melt butter
in a small saucepan, add
remaining ingredients. Stir until
smooth; pour over top of cake,
allowing it to drizzle down sides.
Yield 16 servings.

GRAPEFRUIT CAKE
(with Grapefruit Frosting)

2/3 cup butter OR margarine
1¾ cups granulated sugar
2 large eggs
3 cups *cake flour, sifted
2½ teaspoon baking powder
½ teaspoon salt
½ cup grapefruit juice
¾ cup milk
1 teaspoon grapefruit peel,
   grated
1½ teaspoon vanilla extract

In a large mixing bowl, cream
butter; gradually add sugar;
beat well. Add eggs, one
at a time, beating well after
each addition. In another
bowl, combine together, dry
ingredients; add to creamed
mixture alternately with
grapefruit juice, ending with
flour mixture. Gradually add
milk, along with peel and
vanilla; mix well. Grease 2 cake
pans; bake at 350 degrees
for 25 minutes or until tested
done. Remove from oven; cool
10 minutes, then remove from
pans and completely cool
before frosting cake

GRAPEFRUIT FROSTING

1½ cups granulated sugar
2 large egg whites
1 tablespoon light corn syrup
Pinch of salt
1/3 cup grapefruit juice
1 tablespoon grapefruit peel
2 teaspoons vanilla extract

In the top of a double boiler, combine together, the first 5 ingredients. First, beat at low speed of electric mixer, for 30 seconds or mixed thoroughly. Place over boiling water; continue beating mixture, on high speed, until stiff. Remove from heat; add grapefruit peel and vanilla beat 1 to 2 minutes more. Frost cooled cake. Yield about 10 to 12 servings.

CHOCOLATE-PECAN MERINGUE CAKE

4 large eggs, separated
½ teaspoon Cream of Tartar
1 cup granulated sugar
1 pkg. Betty Crocker Super
    Moist Devil Food Cake Mix
½ cup pecans, chopped
1-1/3 cups water
1/3 cup vegetable oil
1½ cups whipping Cream,
    chilled
1½ teaspoons vanilla extract
3 tablespoons granulated sugar
Whole pecans

Preheat oven to 350 degrees; grease and flour 2 round cake pans. In a small bowl, beat egg whites and cream of tartar, until foamy. Add sugar; 1 tablespoon at a time; continue beating until stiff and glossy. Do not underbeat; set aside. In a large mixing bowl, combine together, cake mix, egg yolks, chopped pecans, water and oil; beat on low speed with electric mixer, scraping the bowl constantly until moistened. Then beat on medium speed, scraping the bowl frequently, for about 2 minutes. Pour batter into prepared cake pans, then spread half of the meringue over batter in each cake pan, to within ¼ inch of the edge. Bake for 40 to 50 minutes, or until meringue is light brown. (Meringue will crack.) Remove from oven; let cool 10 minutes.

In a small mixing bowl, beat whipping cream, 3 tablespoons sugar and vanilla, until stiff. Fill layers with half of the whipped cream mixture, spread remaining mixture over the top. Garnish with whole pecans; refrigerate at least 4 to 5 hours. Also refrigerate any remaining cake. Yield about 10 to 12 servings.

PEACH UPSIDE DOWN CAKE
FRUIT LAYER

¾ cup brown sugar, packed
1/3 cup flaked coconut
2 tablespoons butter OR
  margarine
¼ teaspoon cinnamon
2 cups peaches, peeled &
  sliced
1 teaspoon lemon peel, grated
Combine together, brown
  sugar, butter and cinnamon
  and pat with fingers, into
  a buttered 9-inch square
  baking pan.
Arrange peach slices on top;
  sprinkle with lemon peel; set
  aside.

CAKE

¼ cup butter OR margarine
¾ cup granulated sugar
1 teaspoon vanilla extract
1 large egg
1½ cups all-purpose flour
1 tablespoon baking powder
½ teaspoon salt
2/3 cup milk

In a medium mixing bowl,
cream together, butter and
sugar. Blend in vanilla and
egg, beat well; set aside. In
another bowl, mix together, dry
ingredients; mix well. Add to
creamed mixture, alternately
with milk, beating well. Spoon
mixture over fruit layer in cake
pan. Bake at 325 degrees, for

35 to 40 minutes, or until tested
done. Remove from oven and
immediately invert onto serving
plate. Let sit for 2 to 3 minutes,
before re moving pan. Serve
warm or cold. Yield bout 9
servings.

RED BEET CAKE (with Almond Topping)

1 cup vegetable oil
2 cups granulated sugar
4 large eggs
2 cups all-purpose flour
2 teaspoons baking powder
1½ teaspoon baking soda
1 teaspoon ground cinnamon
3 cups fresh beets, uncooked &
  shredded
1 cup walnuts, chopped
1 teaspoon vanilla extract

In a mixing bowl, combine
together, oil and sugar; beat
at medium speed with electric
mixer until well-blended. Add
eggs, one at a time, beating
well after each addition.
In another bowl, combine
together, flour, baking powder,
baking soda and cinnamon;
add to egg mixture, mix well.
Fold in beets, walnuts and
vanilla. Pour into greased and
floured 13x9x2 inch baking
pan; bake at 350 degrees, for
45 minutes or until tested done.
Cool completely in pan. serve
with Almond Topping, recipe
below. Yield about 12 servings.

ALMOND TOPPING

1 pkg. (8 ozs.) cream cheese, softened
½ cup whipped cream
1 teaspoon almond extract

Combine together, beat at medium speed with electric mixer until well-blended. Yield 1½ cups.

CASSATA CAKE(with Ricotta Filling)

9 large egg yolks
2 tablespoons cold water
1½ cups granulated sugar
2 cups cake flour
1 teaspoon baking powder
1 teaspoon lemon peel, grated
1 teaspoon lemon extract
1 teaspoon vanilla extract
½ teaspoon almond extract
6 large egg whites
½ teaspoon cream of tartar

Preheat to 350 degrees; grease a 13x9-inch baking pan. In a large mixing bowl, beat egg yolks with water until smooth Beat in 1 cup sugar until mixture is light and lemon-colored. On low speed of electric mixer, gradually beat in flour and baking powder; mix well. Add lemon peel, lemon, extract, vanilla and almond extracts. In another bowl, with clean beaters, beat egg whites until frothy, add cream of tartar and continue beating until soft

peaks form. Gradually beat in the remaining ½ cup sugar; beat until stiff, but not dry. Fold in yolk mixture. Pour batter into prepared cake pan; bake about 30 minutes or until tested done. Remove from oven; let cool in pan for 10 minutes; turn out of pan onto rack; cool completely. Using a long sharp knife, cut cake into two layers. Fill with Ricotta Custard Filling and Frosting.

RICOTTA CUSTARD FILLING

2 cups ricotta cheese
½ cup powder sugar
8 ounces milk chocolate, chopped
¼ cup walnuts, chopped
1 teaspoon vanilla extract
1 cup whipped cream

In medium mixing bowl, stir together, cheese and sugar; add chocolate, walnuts and vanilla; mix well. Fold cheese mixture into whipped cream. Yield 5 cups filling.

CASSATA FROSTING

¼ cup granulated sugar
3 tablespoons all-purpose flour
½ cup milk
1 large egg
1 cup butter OR margarine
¼ cup powder sugar
1 teaspoon vanilla extract

In a small saucepan, combine together, sugar and flour; set aside. Whisk together milk and egg; then whisk into sugar mixture. Cook over low heat, stirring constantly,. until mixture thickens. Remove from heat; let cool 10 minutes, then refrigerate. Meanwhile beat together butter, powder sugar and vanilla, until light and fluffy. With a electric mixer on highest speed, add chilled milk mixture, a spoonful at a time; beat until light and fluffy.

CHOCOLATE CHIP BARS

½ cup butter OR margarine, melted
½ cup granulated sugar
½ cup brown sugar, packed
1 large egg
½ teaspoon vanilla extract
1 cup plus 2 tablespoons all-purpose flour
½ teaspoon baking soda
½ teaspoon salt
½ cup nuts, chopped
1 cup chocolate chips

In a medium mixing bowl, cream butter and both sugars, until well-blended. Add remaining ingredients; mix thoroughly. Put batter into a lightly greased 9x13 inches baking pan. Fold in chocolate chips. Bake at 375 degrees, for 12 to 15 minutes, or until tested done. Remove from oven, cool; cut into squares, as desired.

ANGEL FOOD CAKE

1 cup cake flour, sifted
1¼ cups granulated sugar
1 cup large egg whites (about 10)
¼ teaspoon salt
1 teaspoon cream of tartar
1 teaspoon vanilla extract
¼ teaspoon almond extract

Sift flour and 1/4 cup sugar twice. In a large mixing bowl, beat egg whites and salt, with electric mixer on high speed until foamy. Add cream of tartar; beat until stiff, but not dry. Gradually add sugar, 2 or 3 tablespoons at a time, reduce speed until sugar is well-blended. Fold in flavorings; gradually add flour mixture into egg white mixture; mix gently, until all is well-blended. Turn batter into an ungreased 9-inch tube pan. Bake at 325 degrees, for 1 hour, or until tested done. Invert pan to allow cake to cool, about 1 hour, before removing from pan. Serve plain, frost or sprinkle over top, with powder sugar. Yield about 10 servings.

CHOCOLATE ANGEL FOOD CAKE

1½ cups large egg whites
  (about 10)
1 teaspoon cream of tartar
1 teaspoon vanilla extract
1¾ cups granulated sugar
1 cup cake flour, sifted
½ teaspoon salt
¼ cup unsweetened cocoa

Chocolate Butter Frosting (recipe below) In a mixing bowl, beat egg whites until frothy; add cream of tartar. Continue beating until egg whites are stiff, but not dry; add vanilla. In another bowl, sift together dry ingredients, 2 or 3 times. Gradually fold dry ingredients into egg white mixture; mix well. Bake in an ungreased tube pan, at 325 degrees, for 1 hour, or until tested done. Remove from oven, invert pan, to allow cake to cool, about 1 hour, before removing from pan.

CHOCOLATE BUTTER FROSTING
Melt 2 squares unsweetened chocolate with ½ cup butter, in top of double boiler. In a large mixing bowl, combine 1½ pounds of powder sugar, ½ cup milk & 1½ teaspoons vanilla extract; add chocolate mixture; beat until fluffy.

PUMPKIN-PINEAPPLE CAKE

3 cups all-purpose flour
2 cup granulated sugar
½ teaspoon salt
2 teaspoon baking powder
2 teaspoons cinnamon
½ teaspoon ginger
¼ teaspoon nutmeg
1 cup vegetable oil
1 can (15 ozs.) crushed
  pineapple, undrained
2 teaspoons vanilla extract
3 large eggs, beaten
2 cups pumpkin, uncooked &
  grated
1 cup pecans, chopped
  (Optional)

In a large mixing bowl, combine together, all the dry ingredients; mix well. Add oil, pineapple and vanilla; mix thoroughly. Add eggs, grated pumpkin and nuts; mix well. Grease and flour a 10-inch tube cake pan. Pour in batter; bake at 350 degrees, for 1 hour and 15 minutes, or until tested done. Yield 10 to 12 servings

DUMP CAKE

1 pkg. Duncan Hines Yellow
  Cake Mix
1 can (20 ozs.) crushed
  pineapple, undrained
1 can (21 ozs.) cherry pie filling
1 cup nuts, chopped
½ cup butter OR margarine,
  melted

Preheat oven to 350 degrees,
Grease a 13x9x3 inches baking
pan. Dump crushed pineapple
into baking pan, spread evenly.
Next dump in pie filling; spread
evenly. Dump dry cake mix
on top of cherry layer; spread
evenly. Sprinkle nuts over cake
mix; drizzle melted butter over
top. Bake for 50 minutes or
until tested done. Yield 10 to 12
servings.

LINZER TORTE

1 cup butter OR margarine
1 cup granulated sugar
1 tablespoon orange OR lemon
peel, grated
2 large egg yolks
1½ cups all-purpose flour
1 teaspoon baking powder
2 teaspoons cinnamon
½ teaspoon cloves
¼ teaspoon salt
1 cup nuts, ground
1 cup tart preserves

In a mixing bowl, cream
together, butter with sugar;
add peel and egg yolks, one
at a time, beating well after
each addition. In another
bowl, sift together, flour, baking
powder, spices and salt.
Gradually add dry ingredients
into butter mixture; mix well.
Fold in nuts, (dough will be
stiff) mix with hands until all
ingredients are are thoroughly
combined. Pat 2/3 dough in
the bottom of a 9-inch cake
pan, if possible, use a cake
pan with a removable bottom.
Spread preserves evenly over
top. Roll out remaining dough;
cut into 8 strips, ¾ inch wide,
then place lattice fashion on
top of preserves. Bake at 350
degrees, for 50 to 60 minutes or
until tested done. Yield 10 to 12
servings.

PINEAPPLE SHEET CAKE/PIE

2 can (No. 2½) crushed
   pineapple
2/3 cup granulated sugar
2½ tablespoons cornstarch
2 cups all-purpose flour
½ pound butter OR margarine
1 cake active yeast
2/3 cup lukewarm milk
4 teaspoons granulated sugar
3 large egg yolks, beaten

In a saucepan, combine
together, crushed pineapple,
2/3 cup sugar and cornstarch.
cook over medium heat, stirring
until thick; set aside to cool. In
another bowl, cut butter into
flour, as for pie dough. Crumble
yeast into lukewarm milk; add 4
teaspoons sugar. Let stand until
mixture bubbles; add to flour
mixture; mix well. Stir in beaten
egg yolks, then knead dough
lightly. Divide dough in half;
on a lightly floured surface, roll
dough to fit a 15-inch cookie
sheet. Spread pineapple filling
on top; roll out other half of
dough; place over filling. Bake
at 350 degrees, for about 30
minutes, or until tested done.

APPLE CRISP

1¾ cups granulated sugar
1 cup vegetable oil
3 large eggs
2 cups all-purpose flour
1 teaspoon cinnamon
1 teaspoon baking soda
½ teaspoon salt
3 cups apples, peeled & sliced
½ cup nuts, chopped (optional)

In a medium mixing bowl, beat
together, sugar, oil and eggs;
set aside. In another bowl,
combine together, remaining
ingredients. Add to sugar
mixture; mix well. Fold in apples
and nuts; put in an greased
9x13 baking pan. Bake at 350
degrees for 30 to 45 minutes, or
until tested done.

PUMPKIN SHEET CAKE

1 can (16 ozs.) pumpkin
2 cups granulated sugar
1 cup vegetable oil
4 large eggs, slightly beateb
2 cups all-purpose flour
2 teaspoons baking soda
1 teaspoon ground cinnamon
½ teaspoon salt

FROSTING

1 pkg. (3 ozs.) cream cheese,
  softened
5 tablespoons butter OR
  margarine, softened
1 teaspoon vanilla extract
1¾ cups powder sugar
3 to 4 teaspoons milk
Nuts, chopped (optional)

In a large mixing bowl,
combine together, pumpkin,
sugar and oil; mix well. Mix
in slightly beaten eggs. In a
another bowl, combine flour,
baking soda, cinnamon and
salt; add to pumpkin mixture;
beat until well-blended. Pour
into a greased 15x10x1 inch
baking pan. Bake at 350
degrees, for 25 to 30 minutes,
or until tested done. Meanwhile
pre pare frosting, by beating
cream cheese, butter and
vanilla, until smooth. Gradually
add sugar; mix well; Add milk
until frosting reaches desired
spreading consistency. Frost

cooled cake; sprinkle with nuts.
Yield 20 to 24 servings.

EASY PUDDING FROSTING

1 pkg. (4-serving size) Instant
Pudding, any flavor
¼ cup powder sugar
1 container (8 ozs.) Cool Whip,
  thawed
1 cup cold milk

In a small bowl, combine
together, pudding mix, sugar
and milk. Beat at the lowest
speed of electric mixer, until
well-blended, about one
minute. Fold in Cool Whip, then
spread on cooled cake; cover
and refrigerate.

WORLD WAR I—ARMY CAKE

In a saucepan, combine together, 1 box raisins and 3 cups water; bring to a boil. Cook for 15 minutes, then remove from heat; drain; set aside. Reserve water.

1 cup walnuts, chopped
2 cups granulated sugar
2 cups cold water (use all or part of raisin water)
1 teaspoon cinnamon
½ teaspoon salt
5 cups all-purpose flour. sifted
½ cup *lard
1 teaspoon ground cloves
1 teaspoon nutmeg
*You can substitute shortening for lard.

In a large mixing bowl, cream lard & sugar set aside. In a another bowl, combine all dry ingredients; mix well. Then alternately, add lard mixture, with dry ingredients and water; mix well, Fold in nuts and raisins, if desired, you can also, add mixed fruit or candied cherries (about ½ cup each). Place batter in a greased floured cake pan. Bake at 325 degrees, for 1½ hours, or until tested done.

30 DAY FRIENDSHIP CAKE
(An alternative to a traditional Fruitcake)

Prepare starter.
3½ cups granulated sugar
1 can (29 ozs.) peaches & juice
In a bowl, add sugar and peaches together, do not refrigerate. Stir everyday for 10 days.

ON DAY 1:
1½ cups starter.
2½ cups granulated sugar
1 can (29 ozs.) sliced peaches. In a large container, stir mixture, then cover loosely. Stir every day, for 9 days.

ON DAY 10:
Add 2 cups granulated sugar 1 can (14 ozs.) chunk pineapple & juice Mix together; cover loosely. Stir everyday for 9 days.

ON DAY 1:
1½ cups starter.
2½ cups granulated sugar
1 can (29 ozs.) sliced peaches. In a large container, stir mixture, then cover loosely. Stir every day, for 9 days.

ON DAY 10:
Add 2 cups granulated sugar 1 can (14 ozs.) chunk pineapple & juice Mix together; cover loosely. Stir everyday for 9 days.

LADY BALTIMORE CAKE
(with frosting)

1-1/3 cups cake flour
2 teaspoons baking powder
3 large egg whites
Pinch of salt
1 cup granulated sugar, divided

½ cup butter OR margarine,
   softened
1 teaspoon vanilla extract
½ cup milk
Whole candied red cherries &
   candied green pineapple,
   cut into small pieces
Nuts

Preheat oven at 350 degrees.
Sift together, flour and baking
powder; set aside. In a large
bowl, beat egg whites with
salt until foamy; add 1/3 cup
sugar gradually. Beat until stiff
but not dry; set aside. Cream
butter with the remaining sugar
and vanilla until fluffy. Add
flour mixture, alternately with
milk, until smooth and well-
blended. Fold in egg white
mixture gently, but thoroughly
Divide batter between 2
greased, floured 8-inch cake
pans. Bake for 20 to 25 minutes
or until golden brown. Remove
from oven; cool pans for 5
minutes, then invert pans;
cool completely. Meanwhile,
prepare frosting,

FROSTING

1 cup granulated sugar
½ teaspoon cream of tartar
Pinch of salt
1/3 cup hot water
3 large egg whites
5 figs, cut in small pieces
2/3 cup raisins
2/3 cup nuts, chopped

In a small saucepan, combine
together, sugar, cream of
tartar, salt and water; mix
well. Bring to a rapid boil, over
medium-high heat; cook until
soft-ball stage (240 degrees
on candy thermometer)
Meanwhile, beat egg whites
with electric mixer, until stiff,
but not dry. Pour hot syrup in
a fine stream into egg whites,
while beating continually at
high speed, until frosting holds
stiff peaks, is shiny and smooth;
cool. Fold in figs, raisins and
nuts. Spread about 1¼ cups
frosting between layers. Spread
remaining frosting on top
and sides of cake. If desired,
decorate center with cherries,
pineapple and nut halves.

PUMPKIN ROLL (with Cream Cheese Filling)

CAKE

¾ cup all-purpose flour
½ teaspoon baking powder
½ teaspoon baking soda
½ teaspoon ground cinnamon
½ teaspoon ground cloves
¼ teaspoon salt
3 large eggs
1 cup granulated sugar
2/3 cup pumpkin, cooked
1 cup walnuts, chopped
   (optional)
Powder sugar

FILLING

1 pkg. (8 ozs.) cream cheese,
   softened
1 cup powder sugar, sifted
6 tablespoons butter OR
   margarine, softened
1 teaspoon vanilla extract

Preheat oven at 375 degrees. Grease and flour, 15x10 inches, jelly roll pan; line with wax paper. In a small bowl, combine together, flour, baking powder, baking soda, cinnamon, cloves and salt; mix well; set aside. In a large mixing bowl, beat eggs and sugar until thickened. Add pumpkin; mix well; then gradually add flour mixture; mix thoroughly. Spread evenly in prepared pan; if desired, sprinkle with nuts. Bake for 12 to 15 minutes or until cake tests done. Remove from oven.

Carefully peel wax paper off; immediately place cake onto a towel, sprinkled with powder sugar; roll cake and towel together. starting with the narrow end. Let cake cool on a wire rack.

In a small mixing bowl, beat cream cheese, powder sugar, butter and vanilla, until smooth. Carefully unroll cake, remove towel and spread cream cheese mixture over cake. Reroll cake; then wrap in plastic wrap. Refrigerate at least 1 hour; then sprinkle with powder sugar before serving, if desired. Yield about 10 servings.

Chapter 5

GLORIOUS PIES
AND PIECRUSTS

THE BEST VITAMIN FOR MAKING FRIENDS—B 1!

GLORIOUS PIES!

Let's make a pye. Before the turn of the Twentieth Century, words were often spelled the way they sounded. Today we spell pye-P-I-E. Folks had pies for breakfast, lunch and supper and probably in between. There are fruit pies, custard pies, cream pies, cheese pies, meat pies and vegetable spies. Also, there are chiffon and meringue pies.

In the olden days, filled dumplings were dropped in a boiling liquid to be cooked. These were known as "pot pies". Pies were made with all kinds of plain, everyday ingredients a woman used in the kitchen, like buttermilk, vinegar and oatmeal. Pie is one of the most versatile table foods that can be served.

Since the invention of refrigeration, pies can be made days ahead of time, even months. Plus, there are more varieties of pies to choose from to make for the evening meal, or for special occasions, or a tasty light pie while you're dieting.

Pies are not expensive to make at home, however when time is important, you can buy pie crusts that are ready made. One suggestion that may help you is, by taking two prepared pie crusts, fill the one with fruit, and take the other crust and invert it over the filled portion. Lift off the tin from the pie crust gently, then seal, flute just as if you prepared the dough yourself. Put some slits in the top to allow steam to escape as the pie is baking. There is other prepared dough that you can buy, plus, buy packaged graham cracker crumbs, or prepared graham cracker crumb pie crust in a tin, so let's make a pie.

The End.

TEN PIE MAKING TIPS

1. Handle pie dough as little as possible because too much handling of the pie dough makes it tough

2. For a flaky top crust, brush with a little water.

3. An 8-inch pie yields approximately 6 servings and a 9-inch pie yields about 8 servings.

4. Always seal meringue to edges of pie to prevent shrinkage of the meringue

5. Sprinkle fine bread crumbs on the bottom crust to avoid leaking from fruit pies.

6. To prevent soggy bottom crust, brush the bottom crust with an egg white.

7. If you have leftover pie dough, roll it very thin; place in muffin tin. Fill with 2 teaspoon jam (any flavor) and garnish. with coconut, or any other filling you desire.

8. You can also, roll leftover pie dough thin and cut with cookie cutters. Sprinkle with cinnamon and granulated sugar, a mixture of half and half.

9. To freeze pies, note that fruit, mince meat and chiffon pies freeze well, but custard and meringues do not.

10. When freezing pies be sure to place pies in airtight freezer container.

PINEAPPLE COCONUT PIE

Pastry for single 9" pie desire.
Bake at 400 degrees F. for 10
  to 12 minutes, or until lightly
  browned.
1/3 cup Parmesan Cheese,
  grated
1½ cups granulated sugar
5 tablespoons butter OR
  margarine, melted
4 large eggs
1 can (20 ozs.) crushed
  pineapple, drained
1 cup coconut, flaked

In a medium mixing bowl,
combine sugar and melted
butter. Add eggs, one at a
time, beating well after each
addition. Fold in pineapple
and coconut; mix well. Pour
mixture in to pie crust; bake at
350 degrees for about 1 hour,
or until golden brown Yield 8
servings.

IMPOSSIBLE ZUCCHINI PIE

2 cups zucchjni, chopped
1 cup tomatoes, chopped
½ cup onions, chopped
1¼ cups milk
3 large eggs
½ teaspoon salt
¼ teaspoon pepper
¾ cup Bisquick Baking Mix

Preheat oven to 400 degrees;
grease a pie pan. Layer the first
four ingredients, in the bottom
of pie pan. In a medium
mixing bowl, beat together,
the remaining ingredients, for
1 minute. Pour over mixture in
the pie pan; bake for 30 to 35
minutes, or until tested done.
Cool for 5 minutes, before
serving. Yield 6 to 8 servings.

RHUBARB PIE

Pastry for single crust 8" pie
1 cup granulated sugar
¼ cup all-purpose flour
3 cups rhubarb, cut in ½" pieces
1 tablespoon butter OR
  margarine

In a medium mixing bowl,
combine sugar and flour.
Add rhubarb; mix gently. Put
rhubarb mixture into pastry
lined pie tin; dot with butter.
Cover with top crust; seal,
flute and cut slits in top to
allow steam to escape while
baking. Bake at 400 degrees
for about 45 minutes, or until
lightly browned. Yield about 6
servings.

RHUBARB-PINEAPPLE PIE

Pastry for 2-crust 8" OR 9" pie
1 cup crushed pineapple,
    drained
1 tablespoon cornstarch
2 cups rhubarb, cut in ½" pieces
1 cup granulated sugar

In a medium mixing bowl,
combine all ingredients; mix
thoroughly. Put rhubarb mixture
into pastry lined pie tin; dot with
butter. Cover with top crust;
seal and flute; cut slits in top to
allow steam to escape while
baking. Bake at 400 degrees
for about 45 minutes, or until
lightly browned. Yield about 6
to 8 servings.

RHUBARB-STRAWBERRY PIE

1½ pint fresh strawberries
3 cups fresh rhubarb
Pastry for 2-crust 9" pie
1½ cups granulated sugar
6 tablespoons tapioca
1 tablespoon butter OR
    margarine

Wash, drain, hull and slice
strawberries; wash, drain and
cut rhubarb in ½" pieces. In a
large mixing bowl, combine the
fruit, sugar and tapioca; mix
well; set aside while preparing
pastry. Divide pastry in half.
On lightly floured surface roll
dough to fit pie pan. Fill with
fruit; dot with butter. Roll other
half dough out; lift onto pie,
seal, flute and cut slits in the
top to allow steam to escape
while baking. If desired, brush
top crust with a little milk and
sprinkle with sugar. Bake at 400
degrees, for 60 to 65 minutes,
or until lightly browned. Yield
about 8 servings.

RHUBARB PIE (with raisins)

Pastry for 2-crust 9" pie
3 cups rhubarb, cut in 1" pieces
½ cup seedless raisins
1 cup granulated sugar
½ teaspoon ground cinnamon
¼ cup all-purpose flour

In a medium mixing bowl,
combine cut rhubarb, raisins,
sugar, cinnamon and flour
Mix well; pour mixture into a
prepared pie crust. Bake at
400 degrees, for 10 minutes
Reduce heat to 350 degrees,
for 30 minutes, or until lightly
browned. Yield about 8
servings.

RHUBARB CREAM PIE
(with crumb topping)

Pastry for single 9" pie, UNBAKED
1 cup granulated sugar
2 tablespoons all-purpose flour
¼ teaspoon salt
1 cup sour cream
1 large egg
1½ teaspoons vanilla extract
3½ cups fresh rhubarb, diced

CRUMB TOPPING

1/3 cup all-purpose flour
1/3 cup granulated sugar
¼ cup margarine

Preheat oven to 425 degrees F. In a large mixing bowl, combine sugar, flour and salt. Add sour cream, egg and vanilla, beat until smooth. Fold in rhubarb; mix well. Pour into prepared crust. Bake for 15 minutes; reduce heat to 350 degrees, bake for 30 minutes longer. Meanwhile, prepare crumb topping, by combining flour and sugar in a small mixing bowl. Cut in margarine, with a fork; mix until crumbly. Increase oven temperature to 400 degrees, sprinkle crumb topping evenly over rhubarb; bake for 10 minutes more, or until lightly browned.

RHUBARB-PEACH PIE

Pastry for 2-crust 9" pie
2 cups rhubarb, sliced ½ inch pieces
¼ cup flaked coconut (optional)
1¼ cups granulated sugar
1 can (8½ ozs.) peaches, drain; reserve juice
3 tablespoons tapioca
1 teaspoon vanilla extract
3 tablespoons butter OR margarine

Slice peaches; combine in a medium bowl, with rhubarb, coconut, sugar and tapioca; mix well. Add reserved peach juice and vanilla; mix well. Put mixture into pastry lined pie pan; dot with butter Cover with top crust, seal, flute and cut slits in the top to allow steam to escape while baking. Bake at 325 degrees F., for about 45 to 50 minutes, or until lightly browned. Yield about 8 servings.

RHUBARB MERINGUE PIE

Pastry for single crust 9" pie
1 tablespoon butter OR
     margarine
4 cups rhubarb, cut in 1 inch
     pieces
1¼ cups granulated sugar
Pinch of salt
2 large eggs, separated
¼ cup cream
2 tablespoons cornstarch
¼ cup granulated sugar

Preheat oven at 400 degrees.
In the meantime, melt butter
in a medium saucepan; add
rhubarb, 1¼ cups sugar &
salt. Cook over medium heat,
stirring constantly until rhubarb
is tender, about 10 minutes. In a
small bowl, combine egg yolks,
cream, and cornstarch; add
to rhubarb mixture. Continue
to cook, stirring constantly until
thickened. Remove from heat;
when cool put into pastry lined
pie tin. Prepare meringue by
beating egg whites until stiff,
but not dry. Add ¼ cup sugar
gradually into egg whites while
beating until sugar is thoroughly
mixed. Place meringue on
cooled filling making sure
meringue is spread to edge of
crust. Bake in preheated oven
to brown meringue, about 2
minutes. Yield 8 servings

LEMON MERINGUE

Pastry for 1-8" OR 9" pie, BAKED
1 cup granulated sugar
¼ cup cornstarch
1 cup water
2 large egg yolks, slightly
     beaten
2 tablespoons butter OR
     margarine
1 teaspoon lemon peel
1/3 cup lemon juice

In a medium saucepan,
combine together, sugar
and cornstarch; stir while
gradually adding water. Cook
over medium heat, stirring
constantly, until mixture boils
and thickens. Boil for one
minute; remove from heat
and stir ½ of the hot mixture
gradually into egg yolks; mix
well. Return to the stove and
boil one more minute. Remove
from the heat; stir in butter,
lemon peel and lemon juice.
Pour mixture into baked pie
crust; spoon meringue over
hot pie filling, making sure
meringue covers the pie filling
to the edge of crust. Bake at
400 degrees until a delicate
brown, about 10 minutes; cool
completely, then refrigerate
until ready to serve, Yield 6 to 8
slices.

PECAN FUDGE PIE

Pastry for single 9" pie, UNBAKED
2 squares (1 oz. each)
    unsweetened chocolate
¼ cup butter OR margarine
1 can (14 ozs.) sweetened
    condensed milk
½ cup hot water
2 large eggs, beaten
1 teaspoon vanilla extract
Pinch of salt
1¼ cups pecan halves OR
    pieces

Preheat oven to 350 degrees.
In a medium saucepan, over
low heat, melt chocolate and
butter. Stir in condensed milk,
hot water and mix thoroughly.
Remove from heat; stir in
remaining ingredients. Pour
into prepared pie crust; bake
for 40 to 45 minutes or until
tested done. Remove from
oven; refrigerate for at least 3
hours before serving If desired,
serve with whipped topping
and pecan halves. Refrigerate
leftovers. Yield 8 servings.

PEACH PIE

Pastry for 2-crust 8" pie
2/3 cup granulated sugar
3 tablespoons all-purpose flour
½ teaspoon ground cinnamon
3 cups fresh peaches, peeled
    and sliced
1 tablespoon butter OR
    margarine

In a medium mixing bowl,
combine beaten eggs; sugar,
flour and cinnamon; add
peaches and mix gently. Put
into pastry lined pie pan; dot
with butter. Cover with top
crust; seal, flute and cut slits on
top crust to let steam escape
while baking. Bake at 400
degrees, for 35 to 45 minutes
or until lightly browned. Yield
about 6 servings.

PEACH CREAM PIE

Pastry for single 9" pie
6 medium peaches, peeled &
    sliced
½ cup granulated sugar
3 tablespoons all-purpose flour
¼ teaspoon salt
¾ cup whipping cream

Arrange sliced peaches in pie
crust. In a small mixing bowl,
combine sugar, flour & salt;
add cream; mix together until
smooth. Pour over peaches;
bake at 400 degrees F. for 40
to 45 minutes, or until filling is
set and crust is lightly browned.
Serve warm or cold. Refrigerate
leftovers. Yield leftovers. Yield 6
to 8 servings.

APPLE PIE

Pastry for 2-crust 8" OR 9" pie
6 cups apples, peeled & sliced
¾ cup granulated sugar
½ teaspoon ground cinnamon
2 tablespoons all-purpose flour
¼ teaspoon salt
1 tablespoon butter

In a large mixing bowl, sift together the dry ingredients and mix gently with sliced apples. Line pie pan with pastry, fill with apple mixture, dot with butter; cover with top crust. Seal, flute and cut slits on top crust to let steam escape while baking. Bake at 400 degrees, for 35 to 45 minutes or until lightly browned. Yield about 6 to 8 servings.

PEACH PIE FILLING
(Quantity recipe)

6 quarts fresh peaches, sliced
7 cups granulated sugar
2 cups plus 3 tablespoons Clear Jel
5¼ cups cold water
1 teaspoon cinnamon (optional)
1 teaspoon almond extract (optional)
1¾ cups bottled lemon juice

Peel and slice peaches; place in large mixing bowl, with 1½ quarts water and lemon juice (to prevent browning); set aside for 30 minutes. In a large saucepan, put 1 gallon of water, along with drained peaches; bring to a boil. Cook for 1 minute; stirring constantly. Remove from heat; cool slightly. Place filling in a prepare pie shell. Bake according to recipe directions.

*SOUR CHERRY PIE

Pastry for double 8 OR 9" pie
4 cups sour cherries, pitted
1½ cups granulated sugar
5 tablespoons all-purpose flour
Pinch of salt
¼ teaspoon almond extract
2 tablespoons butter OR margarine

Sort, rinse, drain cherries; remove stems and pits. In a medium mixing bowl sift together, sugar, flour and salt; add cherries and mix gently with fork. Add almond; blend well. Put cherry mixture in pastry line pie tin; dot with butter. Cover with top crust. Seal, flute and cut slits on top to allow steam to escape while baking. Bake at 400 degrees, for 35 to 45 minutes or until lightly browned. Yield about 6 to 8 servings.

NOTE: You can substitute Sweet Cherries for the Sour Cherries, with one exception decrease the sugar to 1 cup.

PEACH CRUMB PIE

Pastry for single 9" pie, UNBAKED
2 cups fresh peaches, diced
1 cup granulated sugar
1 tablespoons all-purpose flour
1 large egg, beaten

Peel, pit and dice fresh peaches. Add sugar, flour and well beaten egg; mix gently. Spoon peach mixture into unbaked pie crust; top with crumb mixture.

CRUMB MIXTURE—Combine together in a small mixing bowl, ½ cup all-purpose flour, ¼ cup granulated sugar and 2 tablespoons butter OR margarine. Mix until mixture resembles coarse crumbs. Spread crumb mixture evenly over peaches. Bake at 400 degrees. for 35 to 45 minutes, or until lightly browned. Yield 8 servings.

FRENCH APPLE PIE

Pastry for single 8" pie
About 5 cups apples, peeled & sliced
½ cup granulated sugar
½ teaspoon cinnamon

In a large mixing bowl, sift together the dry ingredients and mix gently with sliced apples. Line pie pan with pastry, fill with apple mixture. Prepare Crumb Topping In a small bowl, combine the following ingredients, 1/3 cup butter, 1/3

cup brown sugar, packed and ¾ cup all-purpose flour. Mix with fork until mixture is like coarse crumbs. Sprinkle crumb mixture evenly over top of apples. Bake at 400 degrees, for about 50 minutes or until lightly browned. If desired, serve with ice cream Yield about 6 servings

LARGE QUANTITY PUMPKIN PIE

8 pie shells, 9-inch each, UNBAKED
16 large eggs, beaten
4 cans (29 ozs. each) pumpkin
½ cup dark corn syrup
9 cups granulated sugar
1¼ cups all-purpose flour
1 cup nonfat dry milk
4 teaspoons salt
4 teaspoons EACH ground ginger, cinnamon and nutmeg
1 teaspoon ground cloves
2 quarts (8 cups) milk.

Beat eggs in large mixing bowl, combine together with beaten eggs, pumpkin and corn syrup. In another bowl, combine together the dry ingredients; place half dry ingredients in each of the 2 large bowls. Stir one-half of pumpkin mixture into each bowl of dry ingredients. Mix until smooth; gradually stir in half of milk into each bowl until smooth and well mixed. Divide evenly among pie crusts; bake at 350 degrees, for 60 to 65 minutes or until tested done. Cool on wire racks, store in refrigerator. Yield 8 pies or 6 to 8 servings each pie or 48 to 64 servings.

ELDERBERRY PIE

Pastry for 2-crust 8" pie
2 tablespoon all-purpose flour
1 cup granulated sugar
3 cups elderberries
½ cup sweet OR sour cream

Wash, sort and drain elderberries. Combine elderberries, flour, sugar and cream; mix well. Pour fruit into prepared pie pan. Cover with top crust; seal, flute; cut slits in the top to allow steam to escape while baking. Bake at 400 degrees, for 35 to 45 minutes, or until lightly browned. Yield about 6 to 8 servings.

CHERRY-PINEAPPLE PIE

Prepared graham cracker crust
1 can (8 ozs.) crushed
    pineapple, divided
1 pkg. (8 ozs.) cream cheese,
    softened
1 teaspoon vanilla extract
1 can (21 ozs.) cherry pie filling,
    divided
1 cup heavy cream

Drain pineapple; reserve 2 tablespoons juice; set aside. In a large mixing bowl, place reserved juice; stir in ¼ cup pineapple and ½ cup pie filling; set aside. In another bowl, add sugar gradually to cream, while beating, on high speed of an electric mixer. Beat until soft peaks form; fold into cream cheese mixture. Pour into pie crust; top center with remaining pie filling; circle outer edge of pie with remaining pineapple. Chill in refrigerator until firm. Yield 6 to 8 servings.

BLACKBERRY PIE

Pastry for 2-crust 9" pie
3 cups fresh blackberries
1 cup granulated sugar
2 tablespoons all-purpose flour
2 tablespoons lemon juice
Pinch of salt
1 tablespoon butter OR
    margarine

In a large mixing bowl, combine blackberries, flour, lemon juice and salt; mix thoroughly. Put into pastry lined pie pan; dot with butter. Cover with top crust, seal, flute and cut slits in top crust to allow steam to escape while baking. Bake at 400 degrees, for 35 to 45 minutes or until lightly browned. Serve with ice cream or plain. Yield about 8 slices

APPLE PECAN CRUMB PIE

Pastry for single 8" pie, UNBAKED
2/3 granulated sugar
¼ cup all-purpose flour
¾ teaspoon ground cinnamon
¼ teaspoon ground nutmeg
6 cups apples, peeled & sliced

Preheat oven at 400 degrees. In a large mixing bowl, gently toss together sugar, flour, cinnamon, nutmeg and apples. Spoon into unbaked pie crust; set aside. Prepare crumb topping; recipe follows.

CRUMB TOPPING

½ cup brown sugar, packed
½ cup all-purpose flour
1/3 cup butter OR margarine,
    softened
1/3 cup pecans

In a small mixing bowl, combine brown sugar and flour; mix thoroughly. Cut in butter with a fork; stir in pecans. Sprinkle evenly over apples. Bake for 40 to 50 minutes, until lightly browned. Yield 6 servings.

CHERRY PIE (with Chocolate Cookie Crust)

CRUST—for 9-inch pie
2 cups chocolate chip cookie
    crumbs
½ cup butter OR margarine,
    melted

Combine cookie crumbs and butter, mix with a fork, until well-blended. With the back of a spoon or hand, press mixed crumbs evenly into a pie pan. Chill until firm, about 30 minutes.

FILLING

1 pkg. (8ozs.) cream cheese,
    softened
½ cup sour cream
2 tablespoons cherry preserves

In a medium mixing bowl, combine together, cream cheese, sour cream and preserves with an electric mixer. Beat on medium speed, until filling is smooth and creamy. Spread filling evenly into pie crust; chill while preparing topping.

TOPPING

½ cup cherry preserves
¼ cup granulated sugar
2 tablespoons water
2 cups fresh Bing cherries,
    pitted

In a medium saucepan, melt cherry preserves with water, over very low heat. Add fresh cherries, stirring constantly, while cherry mixture simmers gently, for 5 minutes. Remove from heat; cool slightly, then spoon evenly over filling. Brush any remaining glaze over top of cherries. Cover, refrigerate for at least 1 hour before serving. Yield 8 servings.

VANILLA CREAM PIE

Pastry for single crust 8" pie, BAKED
½ cup granulated sugar
½ teaspoon salt
2 tablespoons cornstarch
2 cups milk
2 large egg yolks, slightly beaten
2 teaspoons butter OR margarine
1 teaspoon vanilla extract
1¼ cups crushed pineapple, drained

In a medium saucepan, combine sugar, salt cornstarch and milk; mix well. Bring mixture to a boil over medium heat. Boil for 1 minute stirring constantly. Remove mixture from heat; stir ½ of the hot milk mixture into egg yolks stirring until thoroughly mixed; then add remaining hot milk mixture. Return mixture back to the saucepan; continue to cook for 1 more minute, stirring constantly. Remove mixture from heat; blend in butter and vanilla. Pour into baked pie shell; chill for 2 hours before serving. Garnish with whipped topping, if desired. Yield about 6 servings.

CHERRY CHEESE PIE

*Pastry for single 9" pie, BAKED
1 pkg. (8 ozs.) cream cheese, softened
1 can (14 ozs.)**sweetened condensed milk
½ cup lemon juice
1 teaspoon vanilla extract
1 can (21 ozs.) cherry pie filling

In a large mixing bowl, beat cream cheese with electric mixer on medium-high speed, until smooth and fluffy. Gradually add condensed milk, beating until well mixed. Mix in lemon juice and vanilla. Pour cheese mixture into baked pie crust. Chill for 2 hours or until set. Top with pie filling before serving. Refrigerate leftovers. Yield 8 servings.

***NOTE**—If desired, you may use a graham cracker crust instead of regular pie crust.
***NOTE**—Do not use canned evaporated milk.

APRICOT PIE (Fresh)

Pastry for 2-crust 8" pie
5 cups apricots, peeled &
 sliced
1 teaspoon lemon juice
2/3 cup granulated sugar
3 tablespoons all-purpose flour
¼ teaspoon ground cinnamon
1 tablespoon butter OR
 margarine

In a large mixing bowl,
combine apricots and lemon
juice; mix well. In a separate
bowl, combine sugar, flour and
cinnamon; stir into apricots;
mix thoroughly. Put into pastry
lined pie pan; dot with butter.
Cover with top crust; seal, flute
and cut slits in top crust to allow
steam to escape while baking.
Bake at 400 degrees, for 35
to 45 minutes or until lightly
browned. If desired, serve with
ice cream.

IMPOSSIBLE CHERRY PIE

1 cup milk
2 tablespoons butter OR
 margarine, softened
¼ teaspoon almond extract
2 large eggs
½ cup Bisquick Baking Mix
1 can (21 ozs.) cherry pie filling
Streusel (recipe below)

Preheat oven to 400 degrees;
grease pie pan; set aside. In a
medium mixing bowl, combine
milk, butter, almond extract,
eggs, Bisquick Baking Mix
and sugar; beat with electric
mixer, on medium speed,
until smooth. Pour filling into
prepared pie pan; Bake for 25
minutes; remove from oven.
Spread streusel evenly over
cherry filling, return to oven;
continue baking until streusel is
brown, about 10 minutes. Yield
about 8 servings.

STREUSEL

2 tablespoons firm butter OR
 margarine
½ cup Bisquick Baking Mix
½ cup brown sugar, packed
½ teaspoon ground cinnamon

In a small mixing bowl, with a
pastry blender or 2 knives, cut
butter into baking mix, brown
sugar and cinnamon, until
crumbly.

APRICOT CHEESE PIE

Pastry for single 9" pie, BAKED
1 can (15 ozs.) sweetened
   condensed milk
½ cup lemon juice
1 teaspoon vanilla extract
1 pound can *apricots, in
   heavy syrup, sliced
2 teaspoons cornstarch

Beat softened cream cheese until light and fluffy; gradually beat in condensed milk, until well blended. Add lemon juice and vanilla; mix well. Pour cheese mixture into baked pie crust; chill for 2 hours. Meanwhile, drain apricots thoroughly, reserving syrup, if needed, cut in slices. In a small saucepan, stir cornstarch into syrup, on medium heat. Cook until syrup boils, cooking constantly until mixture thickens. Remove from heat and let cool. Arrange apricots on top of cream cheese filling. Spoon thickened syrup over apricots. Chill until glaze has set, for about 2 hours, before serving. Yield 8 servings.
*NOTE—You can substitute canned peaches for apricots.

APRICOT PIE (using dried apricots)

Pastry for single 9" pie,
UNBAKED

FILLING

2 cups sour cream
1½ cups granulated sugar
¼ cup all-purpose flour
½ teaspoon salt
¾ teaspoon almond extract
2 large eggs
1½ cups dried apricots

In a medium mixing bowl, combine sour cream, sugar, flour, salt, almond extract and eggs; beat thoroughly. Cook apricots in small amount of water, covered for 5 minutes, or until soft. Drain; cut in small pieces; fold into cream mixture. Pour into unbaked pie crust; bake at 400 degrees, for 20 minutes. Remove pie from oven, sprinkle topping evenly over top. Return pie to oven, continue baking for 20 minutes longer, or until lightly browned. Cool in refrigerator before serving. Yield 8 servings.

TOPPING

½ cup light brown sugar
½ cup all-purpose flour
¼ cup butter OR margarine

In a small mixing bowl, combine topping ingredients together, mix until well blended and crumbly. Proceed as above recipe directs.

BANANA SPLIT PIE

9" graham cracker crust
2 bananas, thinly sliced
1 quart ice cream, your choice
¾ cup fudge sauce
1/3 cup nuts, chopped

Line bottom of pie crust with
sliced bananas; cover with
ice cream. Freeze 2 hours, or
until firm. Remove from freezer;
top with fudge sauce. Sprinkle
nuts on top; top with whipped
topping. Yield 8 servings.

NO ROLL PIE CRUST

1½ cup plus 3 tablespoons all-
    purpose flour
1½ teaspoon granulated sugar
½ teaspoon salt
½ cup vegetable oil
3 tablespoons cold milk

In a medium mixing bowl, mix
dry ingredients with fingers
until well-blended; set aside.
Combine together oil and milk;
with fork beat until creamy.
Pour over flour mixture; mix
with fork until completely moist.
Transfer mixture to pie pan; pat
dough with fingers, first up the
sides of pan, then across the
bottom. Flute edges; fill shell
with favorite filling. Bake at
400 degrees for about 25 to 30
minutes or until lightly browned.
Yield 1 single pie crust.

PINEAPPLE PIE

Pastry for 2-crust 8" pie
1½ cups crushed pineapple,
    well drained
2 tablespoons butter OR
    margarine, melted
1/3 cup granulated sugar
1/3 cup milk
2 large eggs, beaten
1 teaspoon cornstarch

Beat eggs until light and fluffy;
add sugar, beating until mixed;
add butter. Dissolve cornstarch
in milk; add to egg mixture.
Stir in drained pineapple and
lemon juice; mix thoroughly.
Put into pastry lined pie pan;
dot with butter. Cover with top
crust, seal, flute and cut slits
in top crust to allow steam to
escape while baking. Bake
at 400 degrees, for 35 to 45
minutes or until lightly browned.
Yield about 6 servings.

YOU CHOOSE FRUIT CHIFFON PIE

Pastry for single 9" pie, BAKED
½ cup cold water
1 envelope unflavored gelatin
½ cup granulated sugar
½ cup lemon juice
3 large egg whites
½ cup corn syrup
2 cups *fruit

*FRUIT—Use fresh peaches, diced and raspberries OR blueberries and banana, OR crushed pineapple, drained and strawberries, sliced, OR oranges, diced and seedless grapes OR you choose. In a double boiler, combine water with gelatin; let set for 2 minutes to soften gelatin. Add sugar; mix well. Over hot water, on low heat, cook mixture, stirring constantly until it dissolves completely. Remove from heat; stir in lemon juice; let cool. In a medium mixing bowl, add salt to egg whites; beat egg whites on high of electric mixer until stiff, but not dry. Gradually. add corn syrup, beating until smooth and glossy. Fold gelatin mixture into beaten egg whites gently mix thoroughly. Refrigerate until mixture mounds on spoon, about ½ hour. Spoon lightly into baked pie crust; over the fruit; refrigerate until ready to serve. If desired, top with whipped topping. Yield 8 servings.

PINEAPPLE MERINGUE PIE

Pastry for single crust 8" pie, BAKED
¾ cup granulated sugar
3 tablespoons cornstarch
1/3 cup water
¾ cup (drained) pineapple juice
2 large egg yolk, slightly beaten
2 tablespoons butter OR margarine
2 teaspoons lemon juice
1 teaspoon lemon peel, grated

In a medium saucepan, mix together, sugar, cornstarch, water and pineapple juice (Note -If reserved pineapple juice is not equivalent to ¾ cup, add some water). Cook over medium heat, stirring constantly until mixture thickens; boil one minute.Slowly stir one-half of the mixture into slightly beaten egg yolks; mix thoroughly.Return mixture to saucepan; continue to cook 1 minute longer, stirring constantly. Remove from heat; blend in butter, lemon juice and lemon peel.Add pineapple, mix thoroughly pour into baked pie shell.Cover with meringue, (recipe following) making sure meringue covers pie to edges, to prevent shrinkage.

MERINGUE

2 large egg whites
4 tablespoons granulated sugar
½ teaspoon vanilla extract

Beat eggs with electric mixer until frothy Add sugar gradually; continue beating egg whites until stiff. Cover pie with meringue, making sure meringue seals filling to the edge of pie. Brown pie in oven at 400 degrees, for 1 to 2 minutes, or until meringue has lightly browned.

CARROT PIE

Pastry for single crust 9" pie, UNBAKED
1 cup evaporated canned milk
2 large eggs
1 cup granulated sugar
1 tablespoon nutmeg
½ tablespoon cinnamon
2 tablespoons butter OR margarine
3 cup carrots, cooked & mashed
Butter OR margarine

Cook carrots until tender, drain and mash with fork. Blend in milk, sugar, nutmeg and cinnamon. Add eggs, one at a time, beating well after each addition. Pour mixture into unbaked pie shell; dot with butter. Bake at 350 degrees until light brown and tested done. Serve with whipped topping, if desired, Yield 6 to 8 servings.

GOOSEBERRY PIE

Pastry for 2-crust 8" OR 9" pie
3 cups fresh gooseberries
1½ cups granulated sugar
½ cup granulated sugar
Pinch of salt
1 teaspoon vanilla extract

Clean and pick over gooseberries; crush ¾ cup gooseberries; add sugar, tapioca and salt Mix in the remaining gooseberries. Put in a saucepan, cook over medium heat, stirring constantly, about 5 minutes, or until mixture thickens. Remove from heat; pour into pastry lined pie pan; dot with butter. Cover with top crust; flute edges. Cut slits in top crust to allow steam to escape while baking. Brush with milk for a golden brown crust. Bake at 400 degrees for about 45 minutes or until crust is golden brown. Remove from oven; cool on wire rack. Yield 8 servings.

VINEGAR PIE

Pastry for single crust 9" pie,
    BAKED
3 large egg yolks, beaten
1 cup granulated sugar
¼ teaspoon salt
1¾ cups boiling water
¼ cup apple cider vinegar
¼ cup cornstarch
¼ cup cold water
1 teaspoon lemon extract
3 egg whites (for meringue)

Place beaten egg yolks in top
of double boiler; add sugar
and salt. Gradually add boiling
water, stirring constantly. Add
vinegar and cornstarch, which
has dissolved in the ¼ cup
cold water, Cook over boiling
water until mixture thickens,
about 10 minutes. Remove from
heat; add lemon extract. Blend
thoroughly; pour hot mixture
into baked pie shell. Let cool to
lukewarm; top with meringue,
spreading to edges to prevent
meringue from shrinking. Bake
at 400 degrees, for about 10
minutes or until meringue is
lightly browned. Remove from
oven; cool. Refrigerate until
serving, Yield about 8 servings.

BANANA MERINGUE PIE

Pastry for single crust 8" OR 9"
    pie, BAKED
1 cup canned evaporated milk
1 cup water
1½ tablespoons cornstarch
¼ cup granulated sugar
2 large eggs, beaten
½ teaspoon vanilla extract
Pinch of salt
3 bananas, mashed

Combine milk, water,
cornstarch and sugar in a
double boiler. Over medium
heat bring mixture to a boil;
cook for about 5 minutes, or
until mixture thickens. Remove
from heat; cool slightly; add
beaten eggs and vanilla; set
aside. Allow mixture to cool
completely. Slice bananas into
baked pie shell; pour cooled,
thicken mixture over bananas.
Cover with meringue.

IMPOSSIBLE PECAN PIE

1½ cups pecans, chopped
¾ cup brown sugar, packed
¾ cup milk
¾ cup corn syrup
½ cup Bisquick Baking Mix
¼ cup butter OR margarine,
    softened
4 large eggs
1½ teaspoon vanilla extract

Preheat oven to 350 degrees
F. Grease 9" pie pan; sprinkle
chopped pecans in pie pan;
set aside. In a medium mixing
bowl, beat together, brown
sugar, milk, corn syrup, Bisquick,
butter and vanilla until smooth,
for about 1 minute. Pour mixture
into pie pan; bake for 50 to 55
minutes or until tested done.
Yield 8 servings.

BANANA FUDGE PIE

¾ cup chocolate chips
1 container (8 ozs.) whipped
    topping
2 large eggs, beaten
¼ cup granulated sugar
2 medium bananas, sliced

Preheat oven to 350 F. In
a saucepan, melt ½ cup
chocolate chips, over low
heat; remove from heat. Stir
in 1 cup whipped topping,
beaten eggs and sugar; mix
well. Pour chocolate mixture
into prepared pie crust. Bake for
25 to 30 minutes, or until crust is
lightly browned. Remove from
oven and let cool, on wire rack,

for 10 minutes. Refrigerate for 1
hour; then layer sliced bananas
over top of chocolate; top with
remaining whipped topping If
desired, garnish with banana
slices, dipped in lemon juice,
so they don't turn brown and
sprinkle remaining chocolate
chips on top. Yield 8 servings.

BANANA CREAM PIE

Pastry for single 9" pie, BAKED
1 cup milk
1 cup evaporated milk, undiluted
3 tablespoons all-purpose flour
1 tablespoon cornstarch
¼ teaspoon salt
2 large egg yolks, slightly beaten
2 bananas, sliced
Meringue (recipe follows)

Scald milk and evaporated
milk in the top of a double
boiler. Remove from heat; set
aside. In a small mixing bowl,
sift together flour, cornstarch,
sugar and salt. Add to scalded
milk; cook for 15 minutes, stirring
constantly, or until mixture is
thick and smooth. Beat egg
yolks slightly; pour a little of hot
mixture in egg yolks; mix well.
Return mixture with egg yolks,
to top of double boiler; cook for
1 minute more. Remove from
heat; set aside to cool. Add
vanilla. Spread sliced bananas
in bottom of baked pie crust.
Pour cooled milk mixture over
bananas. Prepare meringue;
cover pie, with meringue to
edges. Bake at 325 degrees
F. for 12 to 15 minutes, or until
lightly browned. Yield 8 servings.

MERINGUE

2 egg whites
6 tablespoons granulated sugar
½ teaspoon vanilla extract

In a small mixing bowl, beat egg whites, with electric beater, on high speed. Beat egg whites until foamy; gradually add sugar. Continue beating until egg whites for stiff peaks, but not dry. Add vanilla; proceed as recipe directs.

BUTTERNUT SQUASH PIE

Pastry for single 8" pie
1 cup brown sugar, firmly packed
1 tablespoon all-purpose flour
½ teaspoon salt
1/8 teaspoon (or a pinch) EACH
    ground cloves, nutmeg,
    allspice & ginger.
¼ teaspoon ground cinnamon
1½ cups squash, cooked &
    mashed
1 large egg, beaten
1½ cup milk, scalded

Combine together, sugar, flour, salt, spices and squash; mix thoroughly. Add beaten egg to milk, cooled to lukewarm; blend well. Add to squash mixture; mix thoroughly. Pour into unbaked pie shell. Bake at 400 degrees, for about 30 to 40 minutes or until tested done. Yield 6 servings.

NOTE—Butternut Squash Pie Crust recipe is on next page

should you desire to use instead of plain pastry.

BUTTERNUT SQUASH PIE CRUST

3 cups all-purpose flour
1 large egg
1 cup butternut squash, peeled,
    seeded, cooked and mashed

Place ingredients in food processor until dough forms a ball. If desired, do so by hand. Add more flour, if necessary. Makes 2-8" pies; bake at 400 degrees, for about 20 minutes.

SHOOFLY PIE (AMISH)

Pastry for 2-8" pies
2 cups all-purpose flour
½ cup granulated sugar
½ teaspoon baking soda
¼ cup shortening
1 cup light molasses
1 teaspoon baking soda
1 cup hot water

In a medium mixing bowl, combine flour, sugar, ½ teaspoon baking soda. Cut in shortening with a pastry blender or 2 knives until mixture resembles crumb-like texture. Divide crumbs evenly between 2 pastry lined pie pans; spread in smooth layers; set aside. In a small mixing bowl, combine molasses, 1 teaspoon baking soda and hot water. Pour over crumbs. Bake at 350 degrees F. for about 35 to 40 minutes or until tested done. Yield 2 pies= about 12 servings.

FRESH RASPBERRY PIE

Pastry for 8" pie, BAKED
1/4 cup granulated sugar
1 tablespoon cornstarch
1 cup water
1 pkg. (3 ozs.) raspberry gelatin
4 cups fresh *raspberries
Whipped topping

In a small saucepan, combine sugar and cornstarch. Add water; on medium heat, bring to a boil, stirring constantly. Cook for 2 minutes; remove from heat; stir in gelatin, mix until gelatin is dissolved. Cool for 15 minutes. Place raspberries in pie crust; slowly pour gelatin mixture over berries. Cover and refrigerate until set; about 3 hours. Garnish with whipped topping. Yield 8 servings

NOTE—*If desired, you can use frozen raspberries, instead of fresh, drain, use liquid for some of the water.

CHERRY CHIFFON PIE

Pastry for 9" pie
2 cups frozen cherries, drained, reserving juice
5 tablespoons granulated sugar
1/2 cup water
1 tablespoon lemon juice
1 pkg. cherry flavored gelatin
1/4 teaspoon almond extract
1 cup canned evaporated milk, chilled

Thaw frozen cherries; drain, reserving juice; set aside. Cut cherries in half. In medium saucepan, combine cherries, cherry juice, sugar, water and lemon juice. Cook over low heat for about 5 minutes; remove from heat. Place gelatin in a medium mixing bowl, pour cherry mixture over gelatin; stir until gelatin is dissolved; add almond extract. Refrigerate until slightly thickened. In a small mixing bowl, beat evaporated milk, with electric mixer, at high speed until stiff peaks form; fold into cherry mixture; mix until well blended. Pile lightly into baked pie shell; chill at least 3 hours before serving. Yield 6 to 8 servings.

RASPBERRY PIE (with fresh peaches)

Pastry for single 9" pie, BAKED
4 medium fresh peaches, peeled & sliced
1-1/3 cups granulated sugar
4 teaspoons lemon juice
1/4 cup cornstarch
1/3 cup water
3 cups fresh raspberries

In a large saucepan, combine peaches, sugar and lemon juice. Mix cornstarch and water together, then add to peach mixture. Bring to a boil over medium heat, stirring constantly, until mixture thickens, about 1 minute. Remove from. heat; cool to lukewarm; fold in raspberries. Spoon into baked pie crust; refrigerate for 2 hours before serving. Yield 8 servings.

RASPBERRY CHIFFON PIE

CRUST

¼ cup butter OR margarine,
   melted
1 cup graham cracker crumbs,
   finely ground
2 tablespoons granulated sugar

Melt butter; combine
with cracker crumbs; mix
thoroughly. Pat prepared
crumbs evenly on bottom and
side of a 8" pie pan. Refrigerate
while making the filling.

FILLING

1 pint fresh raspberries
2/3 cup granulated sugar
Pinch of salt
1 tablespoon lemon juice
2 teaspoons unflavored gelatin
½ cup cold water
1 cup whipped cream
1 teaspoon vanilla extract

Hull; wash berries; drain well;
cut into pieces or mash. In
a medium mixing bowl, mix
berries with sugar, salt and
lemon juice. In small sauce
pan, soften gelatin in cold
water for 5 minutes; stir over
low heat, only until gelatin
has dissolved. Remove from
heat; add to raspberry mixture.
Fold in whipped cream; add
vanilla; blend thoroughly. Chill
for 1 hour or until firm, before
serving. Yield 6 servings.

BLACK RASPBERRY PIE

Pastry for single 9" pie, BAKED

GLAZE

1 cup granulated sugar
1 cup water
2 tablespoons blackberry
   gelatin
1 quart fresh, black raspberries
3 tablespoons cornstarch
2 tablespoons corn syrup

In a saucepan, over medium
heat, combine sugar, water,
cornstarch, corn syrup and
gelatin; bring to a boil; stirring
constantly. Boil for 1 minute,
or until sugar is completely
dissolved. Remove from heat;
set aside. Sort and wash
berries, drain and dry on a
paper towel. Put berries in
baked pie crust; pour glaze
mixture over berries. Chill
in refrigerator to set, before
serving. Yield 8 servings.

BLACK RASPBERRY CREAM PIE

9" graham cracker crust
1 large egg white, beaten
1 cup whipping cream
1 pkg. (8 ozs.) cream cheese,
  softened
1 jar (10 ozs.) black raspberry
  jam

Fresh black raspberries, for garnish, (optional) Preheat oven to 375 degrees. Brush pie crust with egg white; bake for 5 minutes. Cool on wire rack. In a medium mixing bowl, beat whipping cream, with an electric mixer, on medium-high speed, until stiff peaks form. In a large mixing bowl, beat cream cheese until smooth; add raspberry jam; beat on low speed until well combined. Fold in whipped cream; spoon mixture into pie crust. Cover; refrigerate until firm or overnight. Garnish with fresh black raspberries, if desired. Yield 8 servings.

OLD FASHION PEAR PIE

Pastry for 2 crust 9" pie
½ cup granulated sugar
½ cup all-purpose flour
¼ teaspoon mace
½ teaspoon ground cinnamon
10 medium Bartlett pears,
  peeled & sliced
1 tablespoon butter OR
  margarine
1 large egg white
1 tablespoon granulated sugar

In a medium mixing bowl, combine together; ½ cup sugar, flour, mace, and cinnamon. Add sliced pears; mix to coat pears with sugar mixture; set aside Put in pastry-lined pie pan; cover with top crust; crimp edges. Brush pastry with egg white; sprinkle with sugar. Cut slits in the top crust, to allow steam to escape while baking. Bake at 400 degrees, for 35 to 40 minutes, or until golden brown. Yield 8 servings.

STRAWBERRY CHIFFON PIE (with Graham Cracker OR Vanilla Wafer Crust)

1 graham cracker OR vanilla
   wafer crust
2 cups fresh strawberries
1 envelope unflavored gelatin
1/3 cup cold water
½ cup granulated sugar
Pinch of salt
Juice of 1 lemon
2 large egg whites, stiffly beaten
3 tablespoons granulated sugar
1 container whipped topping

Dissolve gelatin in 1/3 cup cold water; mix until dissolved. In a medium saucepan, combine berries, gelatin with water, ½ cup sugar and salt. On low heat, cook ingredients, but do not boil, stirring constantly. Cook for 1 or 2 minutes; remove from heat; add lemon juice; mix well; refrigerate until mixture has thickened. Fold whipped topping into berry mixture; set aside. In a small mixing bowl, beat egg whites, with electric mixer, at high speed until stiff peaks form; gradually add 3 tablespoons sugar. Fold into berry mixture. Pile lightly into prepared pie crust; chill before serving. Yield 6 servings.

CRUST

2 cups crumbs
½ cup butter OR margarine,
   softened
2 tablespoons granulated sugar

In an 8" pie pan, combine crumbs, butter and sugar with a fork; mix thoroughly. Press crumbs on bottom and side of pie pan.

DATE PIE

1 pound dates
2 large eggs
2 tablespoons granulated sugar
Pinch of salt
2 cups milk

In a medium saucepan, cook dates in water to cover. When tender, remove from heat, drain, then put through a food mill. Place dates in a bowl; beat eggs; add to dates with sugar, salt and milk; mix well. Pour into uncooked pie shell. Bake at 400 degrees, for 45 minutes or until mixture is set. Yield 6 to 8 servings.

AVOCADO CHIFFON PIE

9" graham cracker crust
1 envelope unflavored gelatin
6 tablespoons granulated sugar
2 large eggs, separated
1½ cups milk
1 avocado. peeled, pitted &
    mashed
¼ cup lemon juice

In medium saucepan, mix gelatin with 4 tablespoons sugar; blend in egg yolks beaten with milk. Let stand a minute, cook mixture over low heat until gelatin is completely dissolved, about 5 minutes. With wire whisk or rotary beater, blend in avocado and lemon juice. Pour mixture into large bowl; chill until mixture mounds slightly when dropped from spoon. In medium mixing bowl, beat egg whites until soft peaks form; gradually add remaining sugar beating until stiff, but not dry. Fold egg whites into avocado mixture. When thoroughly mixed, pour into prepared crust. Brush top with additional lemon juice; if desired, top with whipped topping. Yield about 8 servings.

PUMPKIN PIE

Pastry for single 9" pie,
    UNBAKED
2 large eggs, slightly beaten
1 can (16 ozs.) pumpkin
¾ cup granulated sugar
½ teaspoon salt
1 teaspoon ground cinnamon
½ teaspoon ginger
¼ teaspoon cloves
1 can (13 ozs.) evaporated milk

Preheat oven at 425 degrees. In a medium mixing bowl, combine together, eggs, slightly beaten, pumpkin, sugar, salt, spices, and evaporated milk; mix thoroughly. reduce temperature to 350 degrees. Bake for additional 45 minutes, or until knife inserted in the center of the pie, comes out clean. Remove from oven; put on wire rack to cool. If desired, serve with whipped topping. Yield 8 servings.

PUMPKIN CHIFFON PIE

Pastry for single 9" pie,
 UNBAKED
1 envelope unflavored gelatin
¾ cup brown sugar
½ teaspoon salt
1 teaspoon ground cinnamon
½ teaspoon nutmeg
3 large eggs, separated
¾ cup milk
2 cups canned pumpkin
¼ cup granulated sugar

Preheat oven to 400 degrees, bake prepared pie crust, for 12 minutes, or until golden brown. Remove from oven; set aside. In a medium saucepan, mix gelatin, brown sugar, salt, cinnamon and nutmeg; blend in egg yolks, beaten with milk. Let stand for 1 minute; cook mixture over low heat until gelatin is completely dissolved, about 5 minutes. With wire whisk or rotary beater, blend in pumpkin. Pour mixture into large bowl; chill until mixture mounds slightly when dropped from spoon. In medium mixing bowl, beat egg whites until soft peaks form; gradually add remaining sugar beating until stiff, but not dry. Fold egg whites into pumpkin mixture. When thoroughly mixed, pour into prepared crust. If desired, top with whipped topping. Yield about 8 servings.

GREEN TOMATO PIE

1 cup granulated sugar
½ cup brown sugar, packed
2 tablespoon all-purpose flour
¼ cup white vinegar
1 tablespoon butter OR
 margarine
1 teaspoon cinnamon
¼ teaspoon ground cloves
3 cups green tomatoes, sliced
1-9" double pie pastry

Place sliced tomatoes in prepared pie pastry; set aside. In a bowl, combine together, remaining ingredients; mix well. Pour over top of tomatoes, then place top crust on; seal edges; prick top with fork, to allow steam to escape while baking. Bake at 425 degrees, for 15 minutes, then lower the temperature to 350 degrees, bake for 30 to 40 minutes or until golden brown. Yield 6 to 8 servings.

PEPPERMINT CHIFFON PIE

CRUST (9" pie)

1-2/3 cup chocolate sandwich
    cookie crumbs (about 18
    cookies)
3 tablespoons butter OR
    margarine, melted

In a medium mixing bowl,
combine cookies and melted
butter; mix well. Press on
bottom and sides of pie pan;
chill.

FILLING

1 pkg. (10½ ozs.) miniature
    marshmallows
1 cup milk
¾ teaspoon peppermint extract
8 drops red food coloring
1/3 cup granulated sugar
1 cup heavy cream, whipped
Whipped cream

In a medium saucepan,
combine marshmallows and
milk. Cook over medium heat,
stirring constantly, until mixture
is melted. Remove from heat;
cool. Stir in peppermint extract
and coloring. Pour into mixing
bowl; refrigerate and chill until
mixture thickens. In a medium
mixing bowl, beat egg whites
until foamy; gradually add
sugar; continue beating until
egg whites are stiff and glossy.
Fold marshmallow mixture into
stiff egg whites.; mix well. Fold
in whipped cream; refrigerate
until mixture mounds well when
dropped from spoon. Pour
mixture into prepared cookie
crust. Refrigerate for 8 hours or
overnight before serving. Yield
8 servings.

CHOCOLATE CHEESE PIE

Pastry for single 9" pie
1 pkg. (3 ozs.) cream cheese,
    softened
¼ cup granulated sugar
1 teaspoon vanilla extract
½ cup chocolate syrup
1 container (12 ozs.) whipped
    topping
Chocolate curls (optional)

In a mixing bowl; with an
electric mixer, on medium
speed, cream cheese, sugar
and vanilla, until well blended.
Gradually add syrup, beating
until smooth. Fold gently one-
half of whipped topping into
cheese mixture. Pour mixture
into prepared pie crust; chill
before serving Use remaining
whipped top ping when you
serve pie. If desired, you can
garnish top with chocolate
curls. Yield 8 servings.

PLUM (RED OR BLACK) PIE

Pastry for single 8" pie, UNBAKED
4 cups plums, pitted & sliced
½ cup granulated sugar
¼ cup all-purpose flour
¼ teaspoon salt
¼ teaspoon ground cinnamon
1 tablespoon lemon juice

Wash, pit and slice plums. In a large mixing bowl, combine plums, sugar, flour, salt, cinnamon and lemon juice; mix well. Pour plum mixture into prepared pie shell; set aside. Prepare Spicy Topping, below,

SPICY TOPPING

½ cup all-purpose flour
½ cup sugar
¼ teaspoon ground cinnamon
¼ teaspoon ground nutmeg
¼ cup margarine

Combine dry ingredients; mix well. Mix in margarine with fork until crumbly. Spread evenly over plum mixture; bake at 400 degrees, for 30 minutes or until golden brown. Yield 6 servings.

COCONUT MERINGUE PIE

Pastry for single 9" pie, BAKED
6 tablespoons granulated sugar
5 tablespoons all-purpose flour
¼ teaspoon salt
2 cups milk
3 large egg yolks, lightly beaten
2 teaspoons vanilla extract
1 cup flaked coconut

In a medium saucepan, combine sugar, flour and salt; gradually add milk. Cook over medium-high heat, stirring constantly, until mixture boils. Reduce heat; cook for 2 minutes or until thickened. Remove from heat; stir a small amount of milk mixture into egg yolks; return mixed egg yolks to saucepan; continue cooking to a gentle boil. Boil for 2 minutes, stirring constantly. Remove from heat; add vanilla and coconut; mix thoroughly. Pour into baked pie shell; spread with meringue (recipe next page). Chill completed pie for 2 hours before serving. Store leftover in the refrigerator. Yield 6 to 8 servings.

MERINGUE

3 large egg whites
¼ teaspoon cream of tartar
6 tablespoon granulated sugar
½ cup flaked coconut

In a medium mixing bowl, beat egg whites and cream of tartar on medium speed of electric mixer, until soft peaks form. Gradually add sugar, 1 tablespoon at a time, beating on high, until stiff peaks form. Spread over hot filling, sealing edges to crust. Sprinkle coconut on top of filling. Bake at 350 degrees, for 12 to 15 minutes or until golden. Cool on wire rack for 10 minutes.

PEAR PIE (with Streusel Topping)

Pastry for single 9" pie, UNBAKED

STREUSEL TOPPING

2/3 cup all-purpose flour
1/3 cup light brown sugar,
   packed
1/3 cup butter OR margarine

In a small mixing bowl, combine together, flour & brown sugar, cut butter, with a pas try blender, or 2 knives, until mixture is like coarse cornmeal; set aside.

FILLING

¼ cup granulated sugar
¼ teaspoon ground ginger
4 teaspoons flour
5 pears, peel & cored
4 teaspoons lemon juice
¼ cup light corn syrup

Preheat oven to 400 degrees. Prepare pie crust; set aside. In a small bowl, combine sugar, ginger & flour; sprinkle about a third of mixture over bottom of pie crust. Peel and core pears, slice thinly into bowl; arrange one-half of sliced pears in pie crust. Sprinkle with 1/3 of sugar mixture over pear slices. Add remaining pears; sprinkle with remaining sugar mixture. Drizzle lemon juice and corn syrup over top. Cover with streusel topping; bake for 15 minutes. Reduce heat to 350 degrees and bake an additional 30 to 35 minutes, or until lightly browned. Yield 8 servings.

TANGERINE CHIFFON PIE

Pastry for single 9" pie, BAKED
1 tablespoon unflavored gelatin
¼ cup granulated sugar
Pinch salt
½ cup cold water
4 large egg yolks, slightly beaten
1 can (6 ozs.) frozen tangerine
   juice, thawed
4 large egg whites
1/3 cup granulated sugar
1 cup whipped topping

In the top of a double boiler, thoroughly combine gelatin, ¼ cup sugar and salt; blend in water. Mix in beaten egg yolks. Cook over simmering water until gelatin dissolves and mixture thickens slightly, stirring constantly, about 5 minutes. Remove from heat; stir in thawed, undiluted tangerine concentrate; blend well. Refrigerate until mixture mounds by dropping from a spoon. In a medium mixing bowl, beat egg whites until soft peaks form; gradually add 1/3 cup sugar, beating until stiff peaks form. Fold egg whites and half of the whipped topping, into gelatin mixture; blend thoroughly. Pile into cooled pie shell; chill until firm before serving. Top with remaining whipped topping; garnish with fresh tangerine or orange sections, if desired. Yield 8 servings.

DATE MERINGUE PIE

Pastry for single 9" pie, UNBAKED
16 ounces dates, cut up
4 large eggs, separated
1 cup nuts, chopped
¾ cup granulated sugar
½ teaspoon ground cinnamon
1 cup milk
4 tablespoons granulated sugar

In a large mixing bowl, add egg yolks to cut up dates; mix well. Add nuts, sugar, cinnamon and milk; mix thoroughly. Pour into unbaked pie crust. Bake at 450 degrees for 10 minutes; reduce heat to 350 degrees; bake for 30 more minutes. Remove from oven; set side. Make meringue by beating egg whites at high speed with electric mixer. Gradually add sugar, beating until stiff peaks form. Cover with meringue, sealing to edges. Return to oven for 15 to 20 minutes more, or until meringue is lightly browned. Yield 8 servings.

CRANBERRY CHIFFON PIE

Pastry for single 9" pie, baked
1 envelope unflavored gelatin
½ cup cold water
2 cups fresh cranberries
2 large egg whites
1 cup granulated sugar
1 tablespoon lemon juice
¼ teaspoon salt
Whipped topping
1 tablespoon granulated sugar

Soften gelatin in cold water. Combine gelatin mixture and cranberries in a medium saucepan. Cook on high heat for 5 minutes or until skins of cranberries pop and gelatin is dissolved, stirring occasionally. Remove from heat; set aside to cool. In a large mixing bowl, combine egg whites, sugar, lemon juice, salt and cranberry mixture. Beat until mixture hold firm peaks, about 8 to 10 minutes. Spoon into baked pie shell; chill 4 to 5 hours before serving. Spoon whipped topping on top of pie in mounds, if desired. Yield 8 servings.

BROWN SUGAR PIE

Pastry for single 9" pie, UNBAKED
2 cups light brown sugar, firmly
    packed
¼ cup butter OR margarine,
    softened
3 large eggs, beaten
¼ cup milk
1 teaspoon vanilla extract

Beat eggs until light and fluffy. In a medium mixing bowl, combine together, brown sugar, butter, beaten eggs, milk and vanilla; mix thoroughly. Pour into unbaked pie crust; bake at 325 degrees F. for 45 minutes, or until solid. Serve warm Yield 8 servings.

NOTE: If desired, you can put a layer of pecans in pie crust, before putting in batter.

ZUCCHINI PIE

Pastry for double 9" pie, UNBAKED
3 cups zucchini, shredded
1 teaspoon ground cinnamon
3 teaspoons lemon juice
1 cup granulated sugar
3 tablespoons all-purpose flour
1 tablespoon butter OR
    margarine

In a medium mixing bowl, combine together all the above ingredients, EXCEPT butter; mix well. Spoon mixture into an unbaked prepared pie crust. Place butter on top of zucchini, put top crust on, seal and flute. Bake at 400 degrees, for 35 to 45 minutes, or until lightly browned. Yield 8 servings.

ONION PIE

Pastry for single 8" OR 9" pie
2 tablespoons butter OR
    margarine
2 cups Vidalia onions, thinly sliced
2 large eggs
¾ cup milk
½ teaspoon salt
Dash of pepper
¼ cup sharp Cheddar Cheese,
    grated
Paprika
Parsley (optional)

Sauté onions in butter until clear, but not brown; spoon in crust. In a small mixing bowl, beat thoroughly, eggs with milk, salt, pepper; pour over onions. Sprinkle evenly with cheese and paprika. Bake at 350 degrees, for 30 minutes, or until tested done. Sprinkle with parsley before serving. Yield 6 to 8 servings.

MUSHROOM PIE

Pastry for single 9" pie
½ pound small mushrooms
½ cup onions, chopped
3 tablespoons butter OR
    margarine
½ teaspoon salt
¼ teaspoon paprika
3 large eggs, lightly beaten
1 cup sour cream, at room
    temperature

Preheat oven to 425 degrees F. Trim and rinse mushrooms; dry on paper towels; slice. Melt butter in medium-sized skillet; add mushrooms and onions; on low heat, sauté until mushrooms are golden brown, about 5 minutes. Season with salt and paprika; drain and set aside Bake pie shell for 8 minutes. Meanwhile, blend eggs with sour cream. Spread drained mushroom mixture, in bottom of pie crust. Pour egg mixture over mushroom mixture. Reduce oven temperature to 350 degrees; bake for 25 to 30 minutes more, or until custard is firm at the edges. Remove from oven and let cool for 5 minutes before serving. Yield 8 servings.

CHOCOLATE CREAM PIE

Pastry for single 9" pie
¼ teaspoon salt
4 tablespoons all-purpose flour
2 cups milk
½ cup granulated sugar
4 tablespoons unsweetened
    cocoa
3 large egg yolks
1 teaspoon vanilla extract
1 tablespoon butter OR
    margarine

In a saucepan, combine together, salt, flour, milk, sugar, cocoa and egg yolks; mix thoroughly. Cook over medium heat until mixture thickens, about 5 minutes. Remove from heat; let cool slightly, add vanilla and butter. Pour into prepared pie crust; refrigerate for 2 hours or more. Just before serving, if desired, top with whipped cream and nuts. Refrigerate leftovers. Yield 8 servings.

GROUND CHERRY PIE

Pastry for 2-crust 8" pie
2½ cups ground cherries
½ cup brown sugar, packed
1 tablespoon all-purpose flour
2 tablespoon water

Wash ground cherries; dry on paper towels and put in unbaked pie crust. In a small mixing bowl, mix sugar and flour; sprinkle evenly over cherries.

Sprinkle water on top; *cover with top crust. Flute, seal and cut slits in the top to allow steam to escape while baking. Bake at 425 degrees, for 15 minutes; reduce temperature to 375 degrees F., continue baking for 20 to 25 minutes more, or until tested done. Yield 6 to 8 servings.

*NOTE—If desired, You can use crumbs on top, instead of a top crust. Mix 3 tablespoons all-purpose flour, 3 tablespoons brown sugar and 2 tablespoons butter OR margarine, until crumbly. Spread evenly over cherries.

BUTTERMILK PIE

Pastry for 2-crust 8" OR 9" pies
3¾ cups granulated sugar
4 tablespoons all-purpose flour
6 large eggs
1 cup buttermilk
1 cup butter OR margarine,
    melted
2 teaspoons vanilla extract

Preheat oven to 450 degrees F. Melt butter. In a large mixing bowl, combine together, sugar, flour, eggs, melted butter and vanilla; mix until well-blended. Pour batter into prepared pie crust. Bake for 10 minutes; reduce heat to 350 degrees; bake an additional 40 to 50 minutes, or until center is firm. Yield 6 to 8 servings.

BLUEBERRY PIE

Pastry for 2-crust 9" pie
5 cups fresh *blueberries
1 tablespoon lemon juice
1 cup granulated sugar
1/3 cup all-purpose flour
Pinch of salt
½ teaspoon ground cinnamon
2 tablespoons butter OR
  margarine
1 large egg, slightly beaten
1 teaspoon granulated sugar

In a medium mixing bowl, sprinkle berries with lemon juice. In another bowl, sift together, sugar, flour, salt and cinnamon. Add to blueberries; mix well. Pour mixture into prepared pie crust; cover with top crust; seal and crimp edges. Cut slits in the top crust to allow steam to escape while baking. Brush top with slightly beaten egg; sprinkle with 1 teaspoon sugar. Bake at 400 degrees, for 30 to 35 minutes, or until golden brown. Yield 8 servings.

*NOTE—You can substitute two packages (14 ounces each) frozen blueberries, thawed and drained. Increase flour to ½ cup.

CHOCOLATE CHIFFON PIE

9-inch graham cracker pie
  crust
1 tablespoon unflavored
  gelatin
1 cup granulated sugar
Pinch of salt
1 cup milk
2 squares (2 ozs.) of
  unsweetened chocolate
2 cups heavy cream, whipped

Shaved chocolate for garnish (optional) Combine gelatin, sugar and salt in the top of double boiler. Add milk and chocolate, cut in small pieces or grated. Place over simmering hot water, cook stirring constantly until gelatin and sugar are dissolved and chocolate is melted. Remove from heat, cool slightly, then refrigerate until mixture mounds on spoon. Fold in whipped cream; spoon into prepared pie crust; chill before serving. If desired, garnish with shaved chocolate pieces. Yield 8 servings.

RED GRAPE PIE

Pastry for double 9" pie, UNBAKED
7 cups seedless red grapes
¼ cup tapioca
½ cup granulated sugar
1 teaspoon vanilla extract
½ teaspoon ground cinnamon
1 tablespoon butter OR margarine

Measure 1½ cups of grapes; put in blender or food processor to liquefy. Add tapioca, sugar, vanilla and cinnamon; mix thoroughly. Let set for 15 minutes; meanwhile, place remaining grapes in a prepared pie crust. Spoon liquefied grape mixture evenly over grapes in the pie crust; dot with butter. Cover with top crust, seal, flute and put slits in the top crust, to allow steam to escape while baking. Bake at 450 degrees F. for 15 minutes. Reduce heat to 350 degrees and continue baking for 35 to 45 minutes more, or until lightly browned. Yield 8 servings.

PISTACHIO PUDDING PIE

Pastry for single 9" pie
1 box (3 ozs.) instant pistachio pudding
1 cup evaporated milk, undiluted
1 container (8 ozs.) whipped topping

In a medium mixing bowl, combine together, pudding mix and milk; mix well. Fold in ½ of whipped topping. Pour into baked pie crust. Top with remaining whipped topping; refrigerate 1 hour before serving. Yield 8 servings.

JALAPENO PIE (aka Quiche')

1 pie crust (9"), UNBAKED
1 jar (12 ozs.) whole jalapeno peppers, drained & seeded
2 cups Monteray Jack Cheese, shredded
4 large eggs
¼ teaspoon salt
2 tablespoons fresh cilantro, chopped

Cut peppers lengthwise into thin slices. Arrange slies on bottom of piecrust; combine together, eggs & salt; beat until fluffy. Place cheese over peppers, then add eggs on top Bake, uncovered, at 350 degrees, for 25 minutes; or until tested done; remove from oven, if desired sprinkle with cilantro. Yield 6 servings.

GREEN GRAPE PIE

CRUST

1½ cups graham cracker
　crumbs
¼ cup brown sugar, packed
6 tablespoons butter OR
　margarine, melted

FILLING

½ cup granulated sugar
½ cup cornstarch
Pinch of ground cinnamon
1 quart fresh, seedless green
　grapes
¼ cup water
1 cup sour cream
1 teaspoon vanilla extract

In a 8" pie pan, combine
cracker crumbs, brown sugar
and melted butter; mix well.
Press crumbs on bottom and
side of pie pan. Place pie
crust in the refrigerator; chill
for 1 hour. Remove stems
from grapes. In a sauce pan,
combine granulated sugar,
cornstarch and cinnamon. Add
grapes and water. Stir mixture
over low heat until thickened,
about 5 minutes. Remove from
heat; cool 10 to 15 minutes;
pour grape mixture into
prepared pie crust; chill in the
refrigerator and before serving,
top with sour cream mixed with
vanilla. Lightly sprinkle over sour
cream, with brown sugar. Yield
8 to 10 servings.

GRAPE JUICE PIE

Pastry for single 9" pie, BAKED
¾ cup granulated sugar
½ cup tapioca
1-1/3 cups grape juice
1 large egg, beaten
2 tablespoons butter OR
　margarine
2 tablespoons lemon juice

In a saucepan, combine sugar
and cornstarch; stir in grape
juice. Cook over medium heat,
until thick and bubbly, stirring
constantly. Remove from heat;
set aside to cool for 1 minute.
Beat egg, then pour a small
amount of hot mixture into the
beaten egg; mix well. Return
egg mixture to saucepan,
add butter and lemon juice.
Return to heat, continue
cooking, stirring constantly
for about 1 minute. Remove
from heat; pour into baked
pie crust. Refrigerate 2 hours
before serving. If desired, serve
with whipped cream. Yield 8
servings.

ORANGE MERINGUE PIE

Pastry for single 9" pie, BAKED
1 cup orange juice
1 cup orange sections, cut in
    pieces
2 tablespoons orange peel,
    grated
1 cup granulated sugar
5 tablespoons cornstarch
3 egg yolks, beaten
2 tablespoons lemon juice
2 tablespoons butter OR
    margarine

In a medium saucepan,
combine together, orange
juice, orange sections, peel,
sugar and cornstarch. Cook
on low heat, stirring constantly,
until mixture is clear, about
5 to 7 minutes. Remove from
heat; add a little hot mixture
to beaten egg yolks. Return
mixture to heat; cook about
5 minutes more. Remove from
heat; blend in lemon juice
and butter. Pour into baked
pie crust. Cover filling with
meringue. Yield 8 servings.

MERINGUE

3 egg whites
¼ teaspoon cream of tartar
6 tablespoon granulated sugar

In a medium mixing bowl,
beat egg whites and cream
of tartar on medium speed of
electric mixer, until soft peaks

form. Gradually add sugar, 1
tablespoon at a time, beating
on high, until stiff peaks form.
Spread over hot filling, sealing
edges to crust. Bake at 350
degrees, for 12 to 15 minutes or
until lightly brown. Cool on wire
rack for 1 hour. Refrigerate.

RICOTTA CHEESE PIE

2½ cups Ricotta cheese
¼ cup milk
1 cup powder sugar, sifted
2 teaspoons almond extract
¾ cups Maraschino cherries,
    cut up
½ cup chocolate chips
½ cup almonds, sliced
*Pastry for single 9" pie

*NOTE—You may use traditional
or chocolate piecrust, if you
prefer. In a medium mixing
bowl, combine cheese, milk,
sugar and almond extract; mix
well. Fold in cut-up cherries,
chocolate chips and almonds.
Spoon into prepared crust.
Refrigerate any leftovers. Yield
about 6 to 8 servings.

KENTUCKY LEMON PIE

Pastry for single 9" pie, UNBAKED
5 large eggs
1½ cups light corn syrup
1 cup granulated sugar
3 fresh lemons, juiced
Peel of 1 lemon, grated
¼ cup butter OR margarine,
    melted

In a medium mixing bowl, beat eggs well; add corn syrup, sugar, lemon juice and grated peel. Add melted butter; mix thoroughly. Pour into prepared pie crust; bake at 375 degrees, for 10 minutes. Reduce heat to 350 degrees, continue to bake for 35 to 40 minutes, or until golden brown. Yield 8 servings

SWEET POTATO PIE

Pastry for single 9" pie
4 cups sweet potatoes, cooked
    & mashed
½ cup light brown sugar,
    packed
¼ cup butter OR margarine,
    melted
½ teaspoon nutmeg
¼ teaspoon cinnamon
3 large eggs, beaten with ¼
    cup milk
Whipped Topping

Preheat oven to 325 degrees. Boil sweet potatoes in jackets until tender; drain, peel and mash. Measure 4 cups and place in a large mixing bowl; blend in sugar, butter, nutmeg and cinnamon. Add eggs beaten with milk; mix thoroughly. Pour into pie crust; bake for 35 to 40 minutes, or until lightly browned. Remove from oven and cool on wire rack. If desired, top with whipped topping. Yield 8 servings.

SWISS CHEESE PIE

Pastry for single 8" OR 9" pie
12 slices bacon
¼ pound Swiss Cheese, grated
4 large eggs
2 cups cream, (i.e. Half and
    Half)
½ teaspoon salt (optional)
Pinch of nutmeg
2 tablespoons granulated sugar
Pepper to taste

Fry bacon until crisp; cool and crumble. Spread crumbled bacon evenly on bottom of pie crust. Grate cheese, spread over bacon. In a small mixing bowl, beat eggs, cream, salt, nutmeg, sugar and pepper, until well mixed. Pour egg mixture over cheese and bacon. Bake at 425 degrees, for 15 minutes; reduce heat to 300 degrees, and bake an additional 35 to 40 minutes, or until tested done. Serve hot. Yield 6 to 8 servings.

APPLE CIDER PIE

CRUST

2 cups all-purpose flour
2/3 cup shortening
½ teaspoon salt
6 tablespoon cold apple cider

In a medium mixing bowl, combine flour and salt. Cut in shortening, with a pastry blender or 2 knives, until mixture resembles coarse crumbs. Sprinkle apple cider over mixture, 1 tablespoon at a time, mixing with a fork, until dough forms. Cover dough while making filling.

FILLING

6 inches cinnamon stick
8 cups apples, peeled & sliced
1 tablespoon lemon juice
1 cup raisins (optional)
1/3 cup granulated sugar
2 tablespoons all-purpose flour
3 tablespoons butter OR
    margarine
Milk
2 tablespoons honey
1 tablespoons cornstarch

In a saucepan, combine apple cider and cinnamon stick, cook over medium heat; bring to gentle boil; boil uncovered for 20 minutes, or until cider is reduced to 1 cup. Strain through a cheesecloth lined sieve. Discard cinnamon set cider aside. Meanwhile, put apple slices in a saucepan, along with 2 tablespoons cooked cider mixture. Cook over low heat, covered, until tender, but not soft. Remove from heat; add raisins. Combine sugar and flour; add to apples, mix thoroughly; set aside. Prepare pastry by dividing dough in half. Roll dough out on a lightly floured surface, to fit 9" pie pan Put apple filling in crust; roll out other ½ dough Dot filling with 1 tablespoon butter; cover pie; seal and flute edges. Cut slits in top crust, to allow steam to escape, while pie is baking Brush top crust with milk. Bake at 400 degrees, for 25 to 30 minutes, or until crust is a golden brown. Remove from oven and place on wire rack to cool.

TO SERVE—prepare sauce by combining remaining cider mixture, remaining 2 tablespoons butter, honey and cornstarch Cook over low heat, stirring constantly, until thick and bubbly, for about 2 minutes. Serve pie with sauce. Also, if desired, serve with ice cream Yield 8 servings.

CANDY BAR PIE,

Pastry for single 9" pie
5 Snickers candy bars, cut into
    ¼" pieces
12 ounces cream cheese,
    softened
½ cup granulated sugar
2 large eggs
1/3 cup sour cream
1/3 cup peanut butter
2/3 cup semisweet chocolate
    chips
2 tablespoons whipping cream

Place candy bar pieces in the pie crust; set aside. In a large mixing bowl, beat, with electric mixer, on medium speed, softened cream cheese & sugar until smooth. Add eggs, sour cream & peanut butter, beat on low speed, just until well-blended. Bake at 325 degrees, for 35 to 40 minutes, or until tested done. Remove from oven & cool on a wire rack. Meanwhile in a small saucepan, melt chocolate chips and cream, cooled filling. Refrigerate 2 hours before serving, or over night. Cut with a warm knife. Yield 8 to 10 servings.

OHIO SLICED LEMON PIE

Pastry for 2-crust 8" pie
2 OR 3 large lemons
3 teaspoons lemon peel
1¼ cups granulated sugar
4 large eggs

Preheat oven to 400 degrees; prepare pie crust._Grate lemon for peel; set aside. Peel lemons, removing all membrane; cut lemons into very thin slices. Remove seeds. In a medium bowl, combine_lemon slices, lemon peel and sugar. Let stand for_20 minutes, stirring occasionally. Beat eggs well; stir eggs into lemon mixture, gently mix thoroughly Pour into prepared bottom pie crust; top with crust, seal, flute and cut slits in top crust. (This allows steam to escape while baking.) Bake for 35 to 40 minutes or until golden brown. Yield about 6 servings.

CURRANT PIE

Pastry for double 8" OR 9" pie
3 cups red currants
1½ cups granulated sugar
¼ cup quick-cooking tapioca
Pinch of salt
¼ teaspoon almond extract
Powder sugar

Preheat oven to 400 degrees.
Remove stems; wash and dry
on paper towels. In a medium
mixing bowl, combine sugar,
tapioca and salt; add currants
and almond extract. Toss lightly
until berries are coated with
mixture. Put currant mixture
in prepared pie crust. Top
with pastry; dot filling with 1
tablespoon butter; cover pie;
seal and flute edges. Cut slits
in top crust, to allow steam to
escape, while pie is baking.
Brush top crust with milk. Bake
at 400 degrees, for 25 to 30
minutes, or until crust is a
golden brown. Remove from
oven and place on wire rack to
cool. If desired, before serving
pie, sprinkle powder sugar on
top. Yield 8 servings.

KEY LIME PIE

Pastry for single 9" pie, BAKED
2 large egg yolks, lightly beaten
1 can (14 ozs.) sweetened,
    condensed milk
½ cup fresh lime juice
1 cup whipping cream
2 tablespoons powder sugar,
    sifted

In a medium mixing bowl, beat
egg yolks with sweetened
condensed milk, until just
blended Add lime juice; beat
until mixture thickens slightly,
about 2 to 3 minutes. Pour
into baked and cooled pie
crust. Refrigerate until well
chilled. Whip cream; fold in
sugar. Spread over chilled pie,
covering to edges. Return to
refrigerator, covered; chill for
several hours, or over night,
before serving. Yield 8 servings.

LEMON ICE CREAM PIE

Single graham cracker crust
3 pints vanilla ice cream,
   softened

TOPPING

½ cup granulated sugar
3 tablespoons butter OR
   margarine
½ teaspoon lemon peel, grated
3 pints vanilla ice cream,
   softened
2 tablespoons fresh lemon juice
1 large egg, slightly beaten

Spoon ice cream into pie crust;
pack firmly. Freeze several
hours or overnight. In a small
saucepan, combine sugar,
butter, lemon peel and lemon
juice; heat to boiling, stirring
occasionally. Remove from
heat; take a small amount
of mixture and add to egg,
mix slightly then return both
the egg mixture and sugar
mixture to cook over low heat.
Stir constantly, until thickened,
about 1 minute; remove from
heat; set aside to cool. Just
before serving, spoon half of
the topping mixture over ice
cream. Cut into serving pieces,
then spoon additional topping
over each serving. Yield about
6 to 8 servings.

BUTTERSCOTCH PIE

Pastry for single 9" pie, BAKED
6 tablespoons butter OR
   margarine
1 cup dark brown sugar,
   packed
1 cup boiling water
3 tablespoons cornstarch
2 tablespoons all-purpose flour
½ teaspoon salt
1-2/3 cups milk
3 large egg yolks
1 teaspoon vanilla extract
Whipped Topping

In a heavy 10-inch skillet over
medium-high heat, brown
butter (do not burn). Add
brown sugar; cook, stirring
constantly until mixture is
bubbly. Remove from heat;
gradually add water, stirring
until sugar is completely
dissolved; set aside. In a
medium saucepan, mix
cornstarch, flour and salt; stir in
milk.

Add brown sugar mixture,
stirring constantly, over medium
heat. Bring to a boil; cook for 1
to 2 minutes, or until mixture has
thickened. Remove from heat;
gradually stir about half of the
hot mixture into egg yolks, then
return egg yolk mixture back
into saucepan. Return to heat;
cook over low heat for 1 minute

(do not boil), stirring constantly. Remove from heat; stir in vanilla. Pour into baked pie crust; cover pie; place in refrigerator to cool. Refrigerate for at least 3 hours before serving. If desired, serve with whipped topping. Refrigerate leftovers. Yield 8 servings.

LIME MERINGUE SHELL PIE

3 large egg whites
¼ teaspoon cream of tartar
¼ teaspoon salt
¼ cup granulated sugar

In a medium mixing bowl, beat egg whits, cream of tartar and salt, with electric beater on high speed, until foamy. Gradually add sugar, beating until stiff, glossy peaks form, but not dry. Spread meringue in a well greased 9" pie pan. Bake at 275 degrees, for 1 hour, or until crisp. Remove from oven; set aside to cool.

WHITE CHOCOLATE BANANA CREAM PIE

Pastry for single 8" pie, BAKED
1 banana, sliced
½ cup walnuts, divided
1 box (3 ozs.) *instant vanilla pudding
1 can (12 ozs.) evaporated milk
2/3 cup white chocolate, grated
2 cups whipped topping, thawed

*OR banana instant pudding, your choice

Arrange banana slices on bottom of baked pie crust; sprinkle with ¼ cup of chopped walnuts; set aside. In a medium mixing bowl, combine milk and pudding mix; mix thoroughly; pour over bananas. In a small bowl, gently fold 1/3 cup white chocolate into whipped topping. Spread evenly over pudding mixture. Sprinkle top with remaining white chocolate and nuts. Refrigerate at least 1 hour before serving. Yield 6 servings.

CHESS PIE

Pie crusts 2-9", UNBAKED
¾ cup butter OR margarine, softened
6 large eggs
1½ teaspoons vanilla
2 tablespoons cornmeal
3 cups granulated sugar

In a medium mixing bowl, cream together, butter and sugar. Add eggs, one at a time, beating well after each addition. Add vanilla and cornmeal. Pour half of the mixture into each pie crust; bake at 325 degrees for 1 hour. Yield 2 pies or about 8 slice per pie.

NO CRUST GERMAN CHOCOLATE PIE

2 ounces German sweet
   baking chocolate
½ cup butter OR margarine
1 teaspoon vanilla extract
3 large eggs, beaten
1 cup granulated sugar
3 tablespoons all-purpose flour
¼ teaspoon salt
1 cup walnuts, chopped
Whipped cream

In a small saucepan, combine chocolate and butter; melt over low heat. Remove from heat; add vanilla; set aside to cool. In a small mixing bowl, combine eggs, sugar, flour and salt. Beat with electric mixer on low speed, just until blended. (Do not over beat) Fold in cooled choclate mixture and nuts. Pour mixture into a lightly greased and floured 9-inch pie pan. Bake at 350 degrees, for 1 hour, or until tested done. Remove from oven and let cool. Refrigerate pie over-night before serving. If desired, top with whipped cream. Yield 8 servings.

MODERN BLACK FOREST PIE

Chocolate Pastry for single 9"
   pie
1 jar (7 ozs.) marshmallow
   crème
2 squares unsweetened
   chocolate, melted
1 teaspoon vanilla extract
2 tablespoons maraschino
   cherry juice
1 cup heavy cream, whipped
½ cup maraschino cherries, cut
   in quarters

Over low heat, melt chocolate. In a medium mixing bowl, combine marshmallow crème, vanilla and melted chocolate; mix until well-blended. Mix in cherry juice; set aside. Meanwhile, whip cream until soft peaks form Fold whipped cream and cherries in chocolate mixture, mix thoroughly. Pour into prepared. pie crust; refrigerate or freeze, for at least 1 hour, before serving. If desired, garnish with additional cherries. Yield 8 servings.

MACADAMIA-DATE PIE

Pastry for single 9" pie
1 cup dates, pitted & chopped
¾ cup boiling water
1 egg, beaten with 2 teaspoons
   cream
3 large, whole eggs + 1 egg
   white
½ cup granulated sugar
½ cup brown sugar, packed
2 tablespoons butter OR
   margarine, melted
½ teaspoon ground cinnamon
¼ teaspoon nutmeg
Pinch of cloves
1 teaspoon vanilla extract
2/3 cup macadamia nuts,
   chopped coarse
Whipped topping (optional)

Prepare pastry; line pan.
Preheat oven to 350 degrees.
In a heat proof bowl, combine
cut-up dates and boiling
water; set aside and let sit, until
water becomes lukewarm.
Meanwhile, make glaze, by
beating egg yolk together with
cream. Brush rim of pie crust
with some of the glaze. Pour
remaining glaze into a large
mixing bowl; add whole eggs,
egg white, sugars, beating on
high speed of electric mixer.
Add butter, spices and vanilla,
beating until well mixed. Fold
in date mixture and nuts. Pour
mixture into prepared pie crust.
Bake for 45 minutes, or until

filling is set. Remove from oven
and let cool on rack. If desired,
serve with whipped topping.
Yield 8 servings.

SOUTHERN PECAN PIE

Pastry for single 9" pie,
   UNBAKED
3 large eggs, slightly beaten
1 cup corn syrup
3 tablespoons margarine,
   melted
½ cup granulated sugar
1 teaspoon vanilla extract
1½ cups pecan halves
Pinch of salt

In a medium mixing bowl,
combine above ingredients
together, EXCEPT nuts, until well
blended. Fold in pecan halves;
pour into prepared pie crust.
Bake at 350 degrees, for 50 to
60 minutes, or until tested done.
Yield 8 servings.

CHOCOLATE PECAN PIE
Decrease sugar to 1/3 cup
granulated sugar and add 4
ounces semisweet chocolate,
melted.

MAPLE PECAN PIE
Instead of corn syrup, replace
with 1 cup maple syrup,
Decrease vanilla extract to ½
teaspoon.

MANGO PIE (with Macadamia Nuts)

CRUST - 9"

1½ cups chocolate graham
    cracker crumbs
½ cup macadamia nuts, finely
    chopped
4 tablespoons butter OR
    margarine, melted
2 tablespoons granulated sugar

Place cracker crumbs into 9" pie pan; add melted butter, nuts and sugar. Mix with fork; spread evenly and pat on bottom and sides of pie pan. Bake at 350 degrees, for about 8 minutes; set aside to cool.

FILLING

1 ripe mango, peeled
2 envelopes unflavored gelatin
2/3 cup granulated sugar
¼ teaspoon salt
3 large eggs, separated
1¼ cups milk
2 teaspoons vanilla extract
¾ cup macadamia nuts,
    coarsely chopped
4 tablespoons granulated sugar
2 cups whipped cream

Peel mango; cut one-half of mango into slices for garnish. Coarsely chop the remaining mango. In a saucepan, combine gelatin, 2/3 cup sugar & salt together; set aside. Beat egg yolks and milk together; add to gelatin mixture. Cook over medium heat, stirring constantly, until gelatin is completely dissolved & mixture begins to thicken, about 8 to 10 minutes. Remove from heat; add vanilla; set aside to cool slightly, but not to set.

Meanwhile, if you desire, toast nuts by placing nuts on a *greased nonstick skillet. Stir nuts constantly, with a wooden spoon, to evenly brown nuts; (toasting heightens the flavor of nuts). Add ½ cup nuts and chopped mango to gelatin mixture; mix well. In a medium mixing bowl, beat egg whites until soft peaks form. Gradually add the 4 tablespoons of sugar; beat until stiff, but not dry. Gently fold into cooled mixture; set aside. Whip cream and fold ½ of cream gently, into gelatin mixture Refrigerate the remaining whipped cream. Pour filling into baked pie crust; refrigerate several hours, or overnight, before serving. Garnish top of pie with remaining whipped cream and mango slices. Yield 8 servings.

NOTE: Use Pam Non-Stick Spray, if you prefer.

OATMEAL PIE

9' pie shell, UNBAKED
3 large eggs
¾ cup white corn syrup
¾ cup oatmeal
2 tablespoons water
¾ cup butter OR margarine,
    melted
¾ cup granulated sugar
½ cup coconut

In a medium mixing bowl, beat eggs; add cooled melted butter; mix well. Add remaining ingredients; mix thoroughly. Pour into pie shell; bake at 350 degrees, for 40 minutes. Yield 6 to 8 servings.

PINEAPPLE CHEESE PIE

Pastry for 9" pie, UNBAKED

PINEAPPLE LAYER

1/3 cup granulated sugar
1 tablespoon cornstarch
1 can (8 ozs.) crushed
pineapple, with juice

In a small saucepan, combine sugar, cornstarch and pineapple with juice. Cook over medium heat, stirring constantly, until mixture thickens, about 3 to 5 minutes. Remove from heat; cool; set aside.

CREAM CHEESE LAYER

1 pkg. (8 ozs.) cream cheese,
    softened
½ cup granulated sugar
½ teaspoon salt
2 large eggs
½ cup milk
½ teaspoon vanilla extract
¼ cup pecans, chopped

In another bowl, cream together, cream cheese, sugar and salt; blend well. Add eggs, one at a time, beating well after each addition. Blend in milk and vanilla. Spread cooled pineapple mixture over the bottom of prepared pie crust. Next, spread cream cheese mixture evenly over pineapple mixture. Sprinkle pecans on top. Bake at 400 degrees, for 10 minutes. Reduce heat to 325 degrees, continue to bake for 35 to 40 minutes more, or until lightly browned. Remove from oven; cool, then cover and chill in refrigerator, about 2 hours, before serving. Refrigerate leftovers. Yield 8 servings.

JERUSALEM ARTICHOKE PIE

1-9" graham cracker crust
¾ cup brown sugar, packed
1 envelope unflavored gelatin
1 teaspoon pumpkin pie spice
3 large eggs, divided
½ cup milk
1¼ cups J. artichokes, peeled,
    cooked & mashed
1/3 cup granulated sugar

Combine together, brown
sugar, gelatin, spice, 3 egg
yolks, slightly beaten and
milk. in a medium sauce
pan. Cook over low heat
until mixture reaches boiling,
stirring constantly. Remove
from heat; add J. artichokes
into brown sugar mixture. Chill
in refrigerator until mixture
mounds slightly, about 1 hour.
In a medium bowl, beat 3 egg
whites until soft peaks appear,
then gradually add 1/3 cup
sugar, beat until stiff, but not
dry. Fold the slightly stiffened
J. artichoke mixture into egg
whites. Place into prepared
crust; chill for about 1 hour;
serve. Yield about 8 servings.

ALMOND-DATE-FUDGE PIE

1 8" piecrust, UNBAKED
1 cup almonds,
    slivered,.*toasted
4 ounces German sweet
    chocolate
2 tablespoons butter OR
    margarine
3 large eggs, slightly beaten
1 cup dark corn syrup
1/3 cup granulated sugar
1 cup dates, chopped

*(To toast almonds. Spread
in shallow pan; toast in oven
at 400 degrees until lightly
browned, about 12 to 15
minutes.) Melt chocolate with
butter, in a small saucepan over
low heat, stirring constantly.
In a medium mixing bowl,
combine together, beaten
eggs, corn syrup and sugar;
mix well. Add chocolate
mixture, dates and almonds;
mix thoroughly. Pour filing into
prepared pie crust; bake at
350 degrees, for 50 minutes or
until filling is completely puffed
across the top. Cool pie to
room temperature. Garnish
with whipped topping and
additional almonds, if desired.
Yield 1 pie or about 6 slices.

RUTABAGA PIE

1 (9-inch) pie crust, unbaked
1½ cups rutabaga, cooked &
   mashed
1 cup light brown sugar,
   packed
2 tablespoons unsulphured
   molasses
2 large eggs, lightly beaten
1¼ cups light cream
½ teaspoon ginger
1 teaspoon cinnamon
½ teaspoon nutmeg
¼ teaspoon cloves
½ teaspoon salt
1 teaspoon vanilla extract
Whipped topping

In a medium-size mixing bowl,
beat all ingredients together
until well mixed. Pour into
prepared pie crust; bake 15
minutes at 450 degrees, then
reduce temperature to 350
degrees. Bake for 35 minutes or
until pie is set. Do not overbake!
When cool, top with whipped
topping, if desired. Yield 1 pie
or about 8 slices.

DELIGHTFUL WATERMELON PIE

Pastry for single 9" pie, BAKED
1 container (12 ozs.) whipped
   topping, thawed
1 box (4 ozs.) watermelon
   flavored gelatin
¼ cup water
2 cups watermelon balls or
   cubes

In a large mixing bowl, thawed
whipped topping, gelatin and
water together. Fold in the
watermelon balls; mix gently.
Spoon into prepared pie crust.
Cover and chill for at least 2
hours before serving. Yield 8
servings. Refrigerate leftovers.

FRENCH SILK PIE
(updated version, no eggs)

Single pie crust, BAKED
¼ cup granulated sugar
3 tablespoons cornstarch
1½ cups milk
1 cup semi-sweet chocolate
  chips
1 teaspoon vanilla extract
1½ cups whipping cream
2 tablespoons powdered sugar

In a medium saucepan, combine sugar and cornstarch. Gradually add milk; cook over medium heat until mixture boils, stirring constantly. Reserve 1 tablespoon chocolate chips for garnish. Add remaining chips and vanilla into sugar mixture, stirring until melted and smooth. Pour into large mixing bowl, cover with plastic wrap; set aside to cool to room temperature. In a separate large bowl, combine whipping cream and powdered sugar; beat until soft peaks form. Reserve 1½ cups for topping. Beat cooled chocolate mixture at medium speed with electric mixer, until light and fluffy, about 1 minute. Fold chocolate mixture into whipped cream only until blended. Spoon evenly into cooled crust. Top with reserved whipped cream. Chop reserved chips; sprinkle over top. Refrigerate 2 to 3 hours before serving. After serving, refrigerate any remaining pie. Yield 10 servings

CLASSIC WALNUT PIE

3 large eggs, lightly beaten
1 cup granulated sugar
2 tablespoons all-purpose flour
1 cup corn syrup
2 tablespoons butter OR
  margarine, melted
1 teaspoon vanilla extract
1½ cups large pieces of walnuts
1 (9-inch) pie crust, UNBAKED

Preheat oven to 400 degrees. In a medium-size bowl, combine together, all ingredients; EXCEPT walnuts; blend well. Pour ingredients into unbaked, prepared pie crust; arrange walnuts on top. Bake for 15 minutes, then reduce heat to 350 degrees; bake an additional 35 to 40 minutes or until center appears set. Cool completely. Yield 8 servings.

GERMAN CHOCOLATE PIE

1 pastry shell, 9-inch, unbaked
1 package (4 ozs.) German
    chocolate
¼ cup butter OR margarine
1 can (12 ozs.) evaporated milk
1½ cups granulated sugar
3 tablespoons cornstarch
1/8 teaspoon salt
2 large eggs, lightly beaten
1 teaspoon vanilla extract
½ cup pecans, chopped
1-1/3 cups coconut, flaked

In a saucepan, melt chocolate and butter over low heat, to stirring to mix well. Remove from heat; gradually blend in milk; set aside. In a medium bowl, combine sugar, cornstarch and salt. Stir in eggs and vanilla. Gradually stir in chocolate mixture. Pour into pastry shell. Combine pecans and coconut; sprinkle over filling. Bake at 375 degrees, for 45 to 50 minutes or puffed and browned. Cool for 3 or 4 hours. Refrigerate to chill before serving (filling will firm as it cools). Yield 6 to 8 servings.

IMPOSSIBLE LASAGNA PIE

½ cup creamed cottage
    cheese
¼ cup Parmesan Cheese,
    grated
1 pound ground beef, cooked
    & drained
1 teaspoon oregano
½ teaspoon basil
1 can (6 ozs.) tomato paste
1 cup mozzarella, shredded
1 cup milk
2/3 cup Bisquick Baking Mix
2 large eggs
½ teaspoon salt
¼ teaspoon black pepper

Preheat to 400 degrees; grease 9" pie pan. Layer cottage and Parmesan Cheeses in pie pan. In a medium mixing bowl, combine together, ground beef, herbs, tomato paste and ½ cup mozzarella; mix well. Spoon mixture on top of cheeses. In another mixing bowl, beat milk, Bisquick, eggs, salt and pepper, by hand for about 2 minutes. Pour over ground beef mixture. Bake for about 30 to 35 minutes, or until tested done. Sprinkle with remaining mozzarella. Yield about 6 servings.

COOKIE SHEET APPLE PIE

3¾ cups all-purpose flour
1½ teaspoons salt
¾ cup shortening
3 large eggs, lightly beaten
1/3 cup milk
8 cups apples, peeled & sliced
1½ cups granulated sugar
1 teaspoon ground cinnamon
½ teaspoon nutmeg
1 cup cornflakes, crushed
1 large egg white, beaten

In a large mixing bowl, combine flour and salt; cut in shortening until mixture resembles coarse crumbs. Add eggs and milk; mix to form dough. Chill for 20 minutes. Divide in half; roll one half to fit the bottom and sides of a greased 15x10x1 inch baking pan. Arrange apples on bottom crust. In a small bowl, combine together, sugar, cinnamon, nutmeg and cornflakes until well mixed. Sprinkle evenly over apples. Roll remaining dough out to fit top of pie. Seal edges; cut slits in top to allow steam to escape. Brush with beaten egg white. Bake at 400 degrees, for 15 minutes; reduce heat to 350 degrees and bake for 25 to 30 minutes or until golden brown. Yield 16 to 20 servings.

HONEY PECAN PIE

9-inch pie shell, UNBAKED
½ cup honey
½ cup brown sugar, packed
3 large eggs, beaten
1 cup pecans

In a small saucepan, combine honey and brown sugar; cook slowly over low heat. to form a smooth syrup; add butter; mix well. Add beaten eggs and pecans; mix thoroughly. Pour into pie shell; bake at 400 degrees, for 8 to 10 minutes. Reduce heat to 350 degrees; bake 30 minutes more or until a knife comes out clean when inserted in the center. Yield about 8 servings.

DUTCH APRICOT PIE

1 single pastry, 9-inches
¾ cup granulated sugar
2 tablespoons quick-cooking
   tapioca
4 cups fresh apricots, sliced
1 tablespoon lemon juice

TOPPING INGREDIENTS

2/3 cup all-purpose flour
½ cup granulated sugar
½ cup pecans, chopped
¼ cup butter OR margarine,
   melted

In a medium bowl, combine sugar and tapioca; mix well. Add apricots and lemon juice; mix lightly to coat. Let stand 15 minutes. Line a 9-inch pie tin with pastry. Trim pastry to ½ inch over lapping edge of pie tin; flute edges. In a small bowl, combine together, flour, sugar and pecans. Stir in butter. Sprinkle evenly over filling. Cover edges loosely with foil. Bake at 350 degrees, for 25 to 30 minutes or until crust is golden brown. Cool on wire rack. Store in refrigerator. Yield 6 to 8 servings.

OLD-FASHION CUSTARD PIE

Pastry for double-crust pie,
   9-inches
4 large eggs
2½ cups milk

½ cup granulated sugar
1 teaspoon vanilla extract
1 teaspoon almond extract
1 teaspoon salt
1 teaspoon ground nutmeg

Line pie tin with bottom pastry. Bake at 400 degrees, for 10 minutes. Mean while, beat eggs in a large mixing bowl. Add remaining ingredients; mix well Pour into prepared crust. Cover edges with foil and bake for 20 to 25 minutes or until a knife inserted in center comes out clean. Cool completely. Store in refrigerator. Yield 6 to 8 servings.

PARTY-TIME PECAN PIES

8 pastry shells, 9 inches each,
   UNBAKED
12 large eggs, beaten
1 cup dark brown sugar,
   packed
5 cups granulated sugar
2 cup dark corn syrup
1-1/3 cups honey
1 cup butter OR margarine,
   melted
3 tablespoons vanilla extract
12 to 15 cups pecans, chopped

In large mixing bowl, combine together, the first 7 ingredients; mix well. Fold in nuts. Pour 2¼ cups filling into each pie shell. Bake at 300 degrees, for 40 to 50 minutes. Yield 6 to 8 slices per pie OR about 64 servings.

RED TOMATO PIE

1 pie crust, 9-inch, BAKED
5 medium tomatoes, peeled, &
  sliced
½ cup mayonnaise (not salad
  dressing)
1 clove garlic, peeled & crushed
½ cup Parmesan Cheese,
  grated
¼ teaspoon black pepper
2 tablespoons fresh basil*,
  chopped
¼ cup Ritz cracker crumbs
2 teaspoons butter OR
  margarine
*OR 2 teaspoons dry basil.

Arrange tomatoes in baked
pie crust. In a small mixing
bowl, combine together,
mayonnaise, garlic, parmesan
cheese, pepper and basil;
blend well. Spread this mixture
evenly over the tomatoes.
Sprinkle evenly with cracker
crumbs; dot with butter Bake in
a preheated 425 degrees oven
for 15 to 20 minutes. Yield 6 to 8
servings.

HONEY WHIPPED CREAM TOPPING

1 cup whipping cream
Almonds, toasted & slivered
  (optional)
1½ tablespoons honey

In a chilled medium mixing
bowl, with chilled beaters from
an electric mixer, whip on high
speed until stiff peaks form.
Blend in honey; spoon over
pie and sprinkle with toasted
slivered almonds, if desired.
Yield 2 cups. Use topping on
desired pie.

PUMPKIN ICE CREAM PIE

1 pie shell, 9-inch, BAKED
1 quart vanilla ice cream,
  slightly softened
1 cup canned pumpkin
¾ cup granulated sugar
¾ teaspoon pumpkin pie spice
½ teaspoon salt
1 cup whipped topping
½ cup walnuts, chopped
  (optional)

Chill crust in freezer for about
30 minutes. Spoon softened
ice cream evenly onto bottom
of crust; return to freezer.
Meanwhile, combine together
in a medium mixing bowl,
pumpkin, sugar, spice and
salt. Fold in whipped topping.
Spread evenly over ice cream;
top with nuts, if desired.
Return to freezer in a covered
container until completely
harden. Yield 6 to 8 servings.

CRANBERRY PIE FILLING

3 quarts (12 cups) cranberries
5 cups granulated sugar
5 cups water
2 cups raisins
1 cup quick-cooking tapioca
1 teaspoon salt
1 tablespoon orange rind, grated

Combine together, all ingredients; EXCEPT orange rind. Place ingredients in a large saucepan, let stand for 15 minutes. Over medium heat, bring to a boil; boil for 10 minutes, stirring occasionally. Remove from heat, stir in orange rind. Let stand for 10 minutes to slightly thickened. Filling may be frozen. Yield enough filling for 4 (9-inch) pies.

CHOCOLATE PEANUT BUTTER PIE

1 cup granulated sugar
6 tablespoons all-purpose flour
½ teaspoon salt
2 cups milk
3 egg yolks, beaten
1 teaspoon vanilla extract
2 tablespoons peanut butter
1 square (1 oz.) semisweet
    chocolate, melted
1-9-inch graham cracker crust
Whipped Cream
Peanuts, chopped (optional)

In the top of a double boiler, over hot water, but not boiling water, combine together, sugar, flour and salt. Gradually add milk; cook for 10 minutes, stirring constantly. Pour a small amount of the hot milk mixture into beaten egg yolks, return mixture to double boiler. Cook for 5 minutes, stirring constantly. Remove from heat; stir in vanilla; cool for 10 minutes. Divide mixture in half; to one portion, stir in peanut butter; mix well. Stir in melted chocolate to the remaining portion. Allow mixture to cool completely. Fill pie crust with peanut butter mixture, then chocolate mixture. Chill in refrigerator, for 2 to 3 hours. If desired, just before serving, top with whipped cream and peanuts. Store leftovers, covered in refrigerator. Yield 6 to 8 servings.

PUMPKIN CHEESE PIE

1 graham cracker crust, 9-inch
1 package (12 ozs.) cream
    cheese, softened
1 teaspoon lemon peel, grated
¾ cup granulated sugar
1 cup cooked pumpkin
¼ teaspoon vanilla extract
3 large eggs, beaten

In a medium mixing bowl, combine all ingredients; blend thoroughly. Pour mixture into pie crust; bake at 350 degrees, for about 35 to 40 minutes, or tested done. Cool completely and serve with whipped topping, if desired. Yield 6 to 8 servings.

COCONUT CREAM PIE

1 package (3 ozs.) cream
    cheese
2 tablespoons granulated sugar
½ cup milk
1-1/3 cups flaked coconut
1 container whipped topping,
    thawed
1 prepared graham cracker pie
    crust, 8-inch

Combine together in a blender container, cream cheese, sugar, milk and flaked coconut. Cover and blend at low speed for 30 seconds. Place mixture in a medium mixing bowl; fold in whipped topping. Spoon into pie crust. Freeze until firm, about 4 hours. Let stand at room temperature 5 minutes before serving. Refrigerate leftovers. Yield 6 to 8 servings.

CHERRY CREAM PIE

CRUST

1 cup all-purpose flour
1 cup walnuts, finely chopped
½ cup butter OR margarine,
    softened
¼ cup brown sugar

FILLING

1 package (8 ozs.) cream
cheese, softened
1 cup powder sugar
¼ teaspoon almond extract
½ cup heavy whipped cream
1 can (21 ozs.) cherry pie filling

In a small bowl, combine flour, walnuts, butter and brown sugar. Place mixture in a 13x9x3 inch baking pan. Bake at 375 degrees, for 15 minutes, stirring once. Measure 1 cup crumbs; set aside. Press the warm remaining crumb mixture into a greased 9-inch pie tin, firmly pressing crumbs onto the bottom and side of pie tin. Chill for 30 minutes. In a small mixing bowl, beat the cream cheese, powder sugar and almond extract until smooth. Spread evenly over the bottom of pie crust. Gently fold whipped cream into the cherry pie filling; spread evenly over cream cheese layer. Sprinkle with reserved crumbs. Chill for at least 4 hours before serving. Yield 6 to 8 servings.

PUMPKIN PIE with Honey-Whipped Cream Topping

1 pie shell, 9-inches, UNBAKED
1 can (1 lb) pumpkin
¾ cup brown sugar, paked
2 teaspoons cinnamon
¾ teaspoon ground ginger
½ teaspoon nutmeg
¼ teaspoon mace
Pinch of ground cloves
¾ teaspoon salt
4 large eggs, slightly beaten
1½ cups evaporated milk

In a large mixing bowl. combine together, pumpkin and sugar, Blend in spices and salt, Add eggs, one at a time, mixing well after each addition, Gradually stir in evaporated milk. Pour into prepared pie crust. Bake at 350 degrees, for 40 to 45 minutes or until tested done. If desired, top with Honey Whipped Cream Topping. Yield 6 to 8 servings.

HONEY WHIPPED CREAM TOPPING

1 cup whipping cream
Almonds, toasted & slivered
    (optional)
1½ tablespoons honey

In a chilled medium mixing bowl, woth chilled beaters from an electric mixer, whip on high speed until stiff peaks form, Blend in honey: spoon over pie and sprinkle with toasted slivered almonds, of desired. Yield 2 cups.

GOOSEBERRY MERINGUE PIE

1 pastry shell, 9-inches, baked
2 cups canned, fresh or frozen
    gooseberries
2 tablespoons water
½ cups granulated sugar
3 tablespoons cornstarch
1 cup milk
2 large eggs, separated

In a covered saucepan over medium heat. cook gooseberries and water for 3 to 4 minutes or until tender. Stir in ¾ cup sugar: set aside. In another saucepan. combine together, ½ cup sugar and cornstarch. Gradually add milk, stir until smooth;:bring to a boil. Cook and stir constantly over medium-high heat until thickened. Reduce heat: cook and stir 2 minutes. longer; remove from heat. In a small mixing bowl, beat egg yolks, then add egg yolks to hot filling in pan. Bring to a gentle boil, stirring constantly, for 2 minutes more. Remove from heat: stir into gooseberry mixture; mix together: gently. Spoon into pastry shell: set aside. In another small mixing bowl. beat egg whites with electric mixer until soft peaks form. Gradually add remaining sugar beating on high until stiff peaks form. Spread meringue evenly over hot filling, to edges of crust. Bake at 350 degrees, for 10 to 15 minutes or until golden brown. Refrigerate leftovers, Yield 6 to 8 servings.

PEANUT BUTTER PRALINE PIE

CRUST

1 ½ cups vanilla wafer crumbs
6 tablespoons unsweetened
   cocoa
1/3 cup sugar
¼ cup butter OR margarine,
   melted

In a medium bowl, combine
crumbs cocoa and powder
sugar; stir in butter mix well.
Press evenly onto bottom and
sides of a 9 inch pie tin: Bake
at 350 degrees, for 10 minutes;
cool on wire rack.

PRALINE LAYER

¼ cup brown sugar packed
2 tablespoons granulated sugar
1 tablespoon cornstarch
1/3 cup butter OR margarine,
   cubed
2 tablespoons water
½ cup pecans, chopped

In a saucepan, combine
together, the sugars,
cornstarch, butter and water.
Bring to a boil in chopped
pecans, Pour into crust;
cover and refrigerate, while
preparing filling.

FILLING

1 pkg. instant vanilla pudding
2 cups milk
1 pkg. peanut butter chips
1 cup whipped topping
Pecan halves
Additional whipped topping

In a medium saucepan,
combine pudding mix &
milk, mix until smooth, Cook
over medium heat, stirring
constantly, until mixture comes
to a boil. Remove from heat;
stir in: peanut butter chips &
1 cup whipped topping; mix
until smooth. Pour evenly over
praline layer, then cover &
refrigerate until ready to serve.
If desired, garnish with pecan
halves & additional whipped
topping. Yield 8 servings.

APPLE CREAM CHEESE PIE

Pastry for single 9" pie, Baked
4 cups apples peeled, cored & thinly sliced
2 tablespoons granulated sugar
2 tablespoons lemon juice
¼ cup butter OR margarine
1 pkg (8oz) cream cheese, softened
1½ cups cold milk, divided
1 pkg (3/4 ozs) instant vanilla pudding
1 tsp lemon peel, grated
¼ cup strawberry preserves, melted

In a large skillet, sauté apples, sugar and lemon juice, in butter: cook until apples are tender. Remove from heat: set aside to cool. In a medium bowl. beat the cream cheese until smooth. with electric mixer, on medium high speed. Gradually add 1 cup milk, dry pudding mix and lemon peel. Add remaining milk. Beat until thickened. Spread mixture evenly, into pie crust. Arrange apples over filling. Brush with melted strawberry jelly. Cover and refrigerate for 1 hour before serving. Brush with additional jelly, if desired. Yield 6 to 8 servings.

NO-TOP APPLE PIE

1-piecrust (9 inch), UNBAKED
6 cups apples, cored, peeled & sliced
2/3 cup granulated sugar
2 tablespoons all-purpose flour
1 teaspoon lemon peel, grated
2 teaspoons lemon juice
½ teaspoon cinnamon
¼ teaspoon nutmeg
Pinch of salt
1 tablespoon butter OR margarine
Light corn syrup

Preheat oven at 425 degrees. In a large mixing bowl, combine together, all ingredients EXCEPT butter and corn syrup; toss gently. Place in piecrust; dot with butter. Cover top of pie with foil; bake for 40 to 45 minutes; remove foil. Bake uncovered for 10 to 15 minutes more or apples are tender and crust is browned. Remove from oven; drizzle corn syrup over top of hot pie. Serve warm or cold. Yield 6 to 8 servings.

PEACH PIE (with Sour Cream Topping)

1 pie crust, 9 inch UNBAKED
2 ½ cups fresh peaches, peeled
   & sliced
1 large egg beaten
½ teaspoon salt
½ teaspoon vanilla extract
1 cup sour cream
¾ cup granulated sugar
2 tablespoons all-purpose flour

TOPPING
½ cup butter or margarine
1/3 cup granulated sugar
1/3 cup all-purpose flour
1 teaspoon cinnamon

Preheat oven to 375 degrees. Peel & slice peaches. In a large mixing bowl, combine together, peaches and remaining ingredients; mix gently. Spoon into an unbaked pie shell. Bake in preheated oven, for 30 minutes or until pie is slightly brown. While the pie is baking. prepare topping. In a medium mixing bowl. blend together,. butter, sugar, flour and cinnamon with a pastry cutter or fork. Blend until crumb mixture is the size of small peas. Sprinkle topping evenly over top of pie. Bake an additional 15 minutes. Cool completely on wire rack before serving. Yield 6 to 8 servings.

NO BAKE PUMPKIN PIE

1 pie crust.9 inch, BAKED
2 tablespoons butter
¼ cup granulated sugar
½ cup brown sugar, packed
1 cup evaporated milk
½ teaspoon salt
2 ½ tablespoons cornstarch
1 ½ cups pumpkin, cooked &
   mashed
1 teaspoon pumpkin pie spice
1 cup milk
2 large eggs. beaten
Whipped topping

(Its a no bake pie, however there is cooking in this recipe. You can substitute a premade graham cracker crust) In a medium saucepan, combine butter and sugars, add evaporated milk. cornstarch & salt. Cook stirring constantly, for about 5 minutes. or until mixture begins to thicken. Remove from heat; blend in pumpkin, spices and milk. Add beaten eggs & continue cooking for 2 minutes more. Pour into pie shell;. chill in refrigerator until ready to serve. If desired, serve with whipped topping. Yield 6 to 8 serving.

IMPOSSIBLE CHERRY PIE

1 cup milk
2 tablespoons margarine,
    softened
¼ teaspoon almond extract
2 large eggs
½ cup Bisquick Baking Mix
¼ cup granulated sugar
1 can (21 ozs.) cherry pie filling
Streusel (see below)

Preheat oven to 400 degrees;
grease pie pan; set aside. In a
medium mixing bowl, combine
all ingredients, EXCEPT cherry
pie filling and streusel; beat
until smooth and creamy. Pour
mixture into prepared pie pan.
Spoon pie filling evenly over
top. Bake 25 minutes; then
spread streusel on pie; return
pie to oven to brown, bake
about 10 minutes more. Cool
on rack. Refrigerate leftovers.
Yield 6 to 8 servings.

STREUSEL

Using a pastry blender or 2
knives, cut 2 tablespoons firm
margarine into ½ cup Bisquick
Baking Mix, ½ cup brown
sugar, packed and ½ teaspoon
ground cinnamon until mixture
resembles coarse crumbs.

CARROT CREAM PIE
(with Honey Topping)

Pastry for 9-inch one-crust pie

FILLING

2 cups carrots, cooked &
    mashed
¾ cup granulated sugar
1½ teaspoons pumpkin pie
    spice
¼ teaspoon salt
2 large egg yolks
1 whole large egg
2 cans (5.33 ozs. each)
    evaporated milk

TOPPING

2 large egg whites
¼ cup honey

Preheat oven to 425 degrees;
prepare pastry; set aside. In
a small saucepan, combine
honey & brown sugar; cook
slowly over low heat, to form
a smooth syrup; add butter.
Add beaten eggs and pecans;
pour into pie shell. Bake at 400
degrees, for 8 to 10 minutes.
Reduce heat to 350 degrees;
bake 30 minutes more, or until
knife comes out clean when
inserted in center. Yield about 8
servings.

IMPOSSIBLE COCONUT PIE

2 cups milk
1 cup coconut, flaked
¾ cup granulated sugar
½ cup Bisquick baking mix
¼ cup butter OR margarine
4 large eggs
1½ teaspoons vanilla extract

Preheat oven to 350 degrees. Lightly grease 9-inch pie pan. In a medium mixing bowl, combine all ingredients; mix until well-blended. Pour into pie pan; bake 50 to 55 or until knife inserted in center of pie comes out clean. Yield about 6 to 8 slices

GOOSEBERRY CREAM PIE.

1 cup cream
1 cup granulated sugar
2 tablespoons all-purpose flour
2 large eggs, beaten
2 cups gooseberries
Pastry for double-crust pie

In a medium mixing bowl, combine together, all ingredients, EXCEPT gooseberries; mix thoroughly. Place berries in pie shell; cover with cream mixture. Put on top crust; bake at 350 degrees, for 50 to 60 minutes. Yield about 6 to 8 servings.

PUMPKIN MERINGUE PIE

9-inch pie shell, UNBAKED
3 large eggs, separated
1 can (16 ozs.) pumpkin
½ cup granulated sugar
¼ cup brown sugar, packed
1½ teaspoons pumpkin pie
  spice
½ teaspoon salt
1 teaspoon vanilla extract
1 jar (7 ozs.) marshmallow
  crème

In a large mixing bowl, beat egg yolks slightly. Add pumpkin, sugars, spice, salt and vanilla; mix well. Pour into prepared pie shell; bake at 425 degrees, for 15 minutes. Reduce temperature to 350 degrees, continue baking for 45 minutes more, or until tested done. Remove from oven; set aside to cool. Meanwhile, beat egg whites until soft peaks form. Gradually add marshmallow crème, beating until stiff peaks form. Spread meringue on top of pie, sealing to edge of pie. Bake at 350 degrees, for 15 minutes, or until lightly browned. Yield 8 to 10 servings.

GRAPENUTS PIE

1-9-inch pie shell, UNBAKED
½ cup Grapenuts Cereal
½ cup lukewarm water
1 cup brown sugar, firmly
    packed
1 cup dark corn syrup
¼ cup butter OR margarine
3 large eggs
1 teaspoon vanilla extract

Soak cereal in water until water is absorbed. In a medium saucepan, combine together, sugar, corn syrup and butter. Bring to a boil. stirring constantly until sugar is dissolved. Remove from heat; set aside. Beat eggs until foamy. Mix a small amount of sugar mixture into eggs, then add remaining mixture into eggs; mix well. Add softened cereal and vanilla; mix thoroughly. Pour mixture into pie shell; bake at 375 degrees, for 45 to 50 minutes, or until set. Serve warm or cold. Yield about 6 to 8 slices.

SUGAR CREAM PIE

Pastry for single 9" pie UNBAKED
4 tablespoons all-purpose flour
2 tablespoons cold butter or
    margarine
1 cup granulated sugar
1 cup whipping cream
1 cup milk
1 teaspoon vanilla extract
Nutmeg (optional)

Blend flour, butter, sugar and salt mix until smooth. Add whipping cream; gently blend together. Put mixture into prepared pie crust. Mix milk with vanilla; pour over the top of the cream mixture. but do not stir. Sprinkle with nutmeg. Bake at 300 degrees, for 1½ hours, or until tested done. Remove from oven, cool completely. Store in refrigerator. Yield 8 servings.

CRANBERRY CREAM CHEESE PIE TOPPING

Pastry for single 9" pie BAKED
1 pkg.(3 ozs) raspberry-flavored
   gelatin
1/3 cup granulated sugar
1-1/4 cups cranberry juice
1 can (8ozs) jellied cranberry
   sauce
1 pkg (3ozs) cream cheese,
   softened
¼ cup granulated sugar
1 tablespoon milk
1 teaspoon vanilla extract
½ cup frozen whipped topping,
   thawed

In a medium mixing bowl, combine gelatin and sugar: set aside. In a saucepan bring cranberry juice to a boil over medium high heat. Remove from heat: pour over gelatin mixture, stirring to dissolve. stir in cranberry sauce. Chill in refrigerator until slightly thickened. Meanwhile in another mixing bowl, combine softened cream cheese, sugar, milk and vanilla, beat with electric mixer. at medium speed, until light and fluffy. Fold in the whipped topping; Spread evenly in baked pie crust. Beat cranberry topping until frothy: pour over filling and refrigerate over night Yield 8 servings.

GEORGIA STRAWBERRY PIE

Pastry for single 9" pie BAKED
¾ cup granulated sugar
1 cup 7-up pop
3 tablespoons cornstarch
1 quart fresh strawberries
Whipped topping (optional)

FILLING

In a medium saucepan, combine together, sugar, 7-up and cornstarch. Cook over medium heat stirring constantly, until mixture thickens. remove from heat and set aside to cool. In the meantime,. wash and hull strawberries. Pour 7-up mixture over berries: mix gently; spoon into baked pie crust. Cover and refrigerate several hours before serving. If desired, serve with whipped topping. Yield 8 servings.

CHOCOLATE MOCHA PIE (WITH CHOCOLATE WALNUT CRUST

Crust for 9" pie
1 cup all-purpose flour
¼ cup light brown sugar. packed
½ teaspoon salt
6 tablespoons butter or margarine
½ cup walnuts, chopped
1 ounce unsweetened chocolate, grated
1 tablespoon cold water
1 teaspoon vanilla extract

In a medium mixing bowl, combine together flour, sugar and salt. Cut in butter that has been cut in pieces., with a pastry blender or use 2 knives. along with chopped nuts grated chocolate: mix until mixture is crumbly. Add water and vanilla. tossing lightly, with a fork only until mixture holds together. Cover dough and refrigerate for 1 hour. Meanwhile, prepare filling,

FILLING

¾ cup butter or margarine, softened
1 ¼ cups powder sugar
3 large eggs
2 ounces unsweetened chocolate melted
2 teaspoons instant coffee
Topping (recipe below)
Walnut halves for garnish (optional)

Preheat oven to 350 degrees. In a medium mixing bowl. blend together, butter and sugar until light and fluffy. Add eggs one at a time. beating well after each addition. Melt chocolate over boiling water, in a double boiler, blend melted chocolate and coffee in butter mixture. blend thoroughly. Roll out chilled dough, on a lightly floured surface. Fit dough in a 9" pie pan: (if dough does not roll easily press into pie pan with hands.) Bake pie crust in preheated oven for 12 to 15 minutes or until lightly browned. Spoon filling into cooled pie crust: refrigerate 1 hour before serving. Yield 8 servings

TOPPING

In a mixing bowl. beat 1 cup heavy cream, 1½ tablespoons unsweetened cocoa and 3 tablespoons granulated sugar, until stiff peaks form Spread evenly over top of pie.

SALAMI PIE

Pastry for single 9" pie, BAKED
6 ounces Muenster cheese,
   shredded
1 large egg, beaten
¾ cup all-purpose flour
½ teaspoon salt
Pinch of pepper
1 cup milk
¼ cup salami, chopped
½ teaspoon oregano

Reserve 3 tablespoons cheese.
set aside In a medium mixing
bowl. combine together, all
ingredients: mix well. Pour into
prepared piecrust; bake at 200
degrees, for 30 minutes until
lightly browned. or tested done.
Top with reserved cheese: bake
for 2 minutes more, or until
cheese melts. Yield 6 servings.

SAUERKRAUT CREAM PIE

Piecrust—8 or 9" UNBAKED
½ cup sauerkraut, drained
½ cup butter OR margarine,
   softened
2 cups granulated sugar
5 large eggs
1 cup milk
1 teaspoon vanilla extract
2 tablespoons lemon juice
2 tablespoons yellow cornmeal
2 tablespoons all-purpose flour

Preheat oven at 350 degrees.
Roll out piecrust on a floured
surface; line 2 pie pans; set
aside. Drain sauerkraut; rinse
with cold water, then squeeze
dry; set aide. In a mixing
bowl, cream butter and sugar
thoroughly. Add eggs, milk,
vanilla and lemon juice; blend
well. In a small bowl, combine
together, flour and cornmeal,
then add to egg mixture; mix
well. Fold in sauerkraut; pour
into prepared piecrust. Top with
crust; seal flute & cut slits on
top. Bake for 55 to 60 minutes.
Yield 6 to 8 servings.

IMPOSSIBLE BLT PIE

9-inch pie shell, BAKED
12 slices bacon, cooked crisp &
   crumbled
1 cup Swiss Cheese, shredded
1½ cups milk
½ cup mayonnaise OR salad
   dressing
4 large eggs
1 cup Bisquick Baking Mix
Salt and pepper to taste
Lettuce, coarsely shredded
Tomatoes, thinly sliced

Preheat oven to 400 degrees;
grease 9 inch pie pan; layer
bacon and cheese in pie pan.
In a medium mixing bowl,
combine together, remaining
ingredients, EXCEPT lettuce and
tomatoes. Beat for 1 minute, or
until smooth. Pour into pie tin and
bake for 30 to 35 minutes, or until
tested done. Remove from oven
and cool for 5 minutes. Garnish
with lettuce and tomatoes. Yield
about 6 servings.

BUTTERNUT SQUASH CREAM PIE

1 medium butternut squash
  (about 2 lbs.)
¼ cup hot water
1 pkg. (8 ozs.) cream cheese,
  softened
¼ cup granulated sugar
2 tablespoons caramel ice
  cream topping
1 teaspoon ground cinnamon
½ teaspoon salt
½ teaspoon ground ginger
¼ teaspoon ground cloves
1 pkg. (5.1 ozs.) Vanilla Instant
  Pudding Mix
¾ cup plus 2 tablespoons milk
Whipped cream & flaked
  coconut

Cut squash in half, discard
seeds. Place squash cut side
down, in a microwave safe
dish, add hot water. Cover;
microwave for 12 to 15 minutes,
or until tender. When cool
enough to handle, scoop out
pulp & mash; set aside 1½ cups
squash. Save remaining squash
for another use. In a mixing
bowl, beat cream cheese until
smooth; stir in squash, until well-
blended. Add sugar, caramel
topping, cinnamon, salt, ginger
and cloves; beat until well
mixed. Add pudding mix and
milk; beat on low speed for 2
minutes. Spoon mixture into
a baked pie shell; refrigerate
for at least 3 hours. If desired,
garnish with whipped cream
and coconut. Yield 6 to 8
servings.

PRETZEL PIE CRUST

¾ cup butter OR margarine,
  softened
3 tablespoons brown sugar
2½ cups pretzels, finely crushed

In medium mixing bowl,
combine together, the above
ingredients; mix well. Place
ingredients in pie pan; press
evenly up sides; bake at
350 degrees, for 10 minutes.
Yield 1-9" pie crust. month, in
a covered container in the
refrigerator. Yield 8 single or 4
double

- 302 -

HOMEMADE PASTRY MIX

7 cups all-purpose flour, sifted
3 teaspoons salt
1¾ cup shortening

In a large mixing bowl, combine flour and salt; with pastry blender or with a fork, mix shortening into flour. Mix until mixture forms crumbs the size of peas. This mixture will keep for a pie crusts.

DIRECTIONS FOR 1 SINGLE CRUST

1¼ cups of mix, plus 2 to 4 tablespoons
water

Add water to mix, a tablespoon at a time. mix quickly until dough forms a ball, then on a lightly floured surface, roll dough to 1/8 inch thick, allowing ½ inch to extend over edge of pie pan.

HICKORY NUT PIE

2-9" pie shells, UNBAKED
3 cups granulated sugar
2¼ cups corn syrup (light)
5 tablespoons all-purpose flour
5 tablespoons butter OR margarine, melted
2½ cups hickory nuts, chopped
10 large eggs, beaten
1 cup cold water

In a large mixing bowl, combine together, sugar, corn syrup, flour, butter, eggs and water; mix well. Fold in nuts; pour into unbaked pie shells. Bake at 350 degrees for 45 minutes or until tested done. Remove from oven and cool completely. Refrigerate until ready to serve. Yield 3 pies or 18 to 24 servings.

BLACK WALNUT PIE

1 pie shell, UNBAKED
3 large eggs
2/3 cup granulated sugar
Pinch of salt
1 cup dark corn syrup
1/3 cup butter OR margarine, melted
1 cup black walnuts

In a medium mixing bowl, beat thoroughly, eggs with sugar, salt, syrup and melted butter. Add black walnuts; mix well. Pour into unbaked pie shell; bake at 350 degrees, for 50 minutes, or until tested done. Yield 6 to 8 servings.

POTATO PIE CRUST

1 cup mashed potatoes
½ teaspoon salt
1 teaspoon baking powder
1 large egg, beaten
2 tablespoons, shortening,
   melted
Flour

In a mixing bowl, combine
together, first 5 ingredients;
add flour enough to make a
soft dough. On a lightly floured
surface, roll ½ of dough to
about 1/8 inch thick. Line pie
pan, fill as desired, then other
half dough to top filling. Press
to seal, prick with fork to allow
steam to escape as pie bakes.
Bake as directions direct.

IMPOSSIBLE *ASPARAGUS PIE

1 can (8 ozs.) water chestnuts,
   drained and coarsely
   chopped
1 pkg. (10 ozs.) frozen asparagus,
   thawed, cut in pieces and
   drained
1 jar (2 ozs.) pimientos,
   chopped & drained
½ cup onions, chopped
1½ cups, (6 ozs.) sharp cheddar
   cheese, shredded
1½ cups milk
3 large eggs
¾ cup Bisquick Baking Mix
½ teaspoon garlic powder
¼ teaspoon black pepper

1 jar (2 ozs.) pimientos,
chopped and drained,
for garnish (optional)

Preheat oven to 400 degrees.
Lightly grease pie plate; reserve
¼ cup of water chestnuts. Layer
remaining water chestnuts,
pimientos, onions and cheese;
set aside. In a medium
mixing bowl, beat remaining
ingredients, EXCEPT reserved
¼ cup water chestnuts, until
smooth. Pour into prepared pie
pan; bake for 40 to 45 minutes,
or until tested done. Remove
from oven and let cool. If
desired, garnish with reserved
¼ cup water chestnuts and
1 jar pimientos. Yield 6 to 8
servings.

*SUBSTITUTE 1 pkg. (10 ozs.)
broccoli spears, thawed,
drained & cut into 1" pieces,
instead of asparagus.

SUMMER SQUASH PIE

1-9 inch pie shell, BAKED
2½ cups zucchini, sliced (¼ inch slices)
2½ cups yellow summer squash, sliced
(¼ inch slices)
1 teaspoon vegetable oil
½ teaspoon salt
¼ teaspoon dried thyme
¼ teaspoon garlic powder
¼ teaspoon paprika
¼ teaspoon pepper
2 large tomatoes, sliced
1 cup cheddar OR mozzarella cheese, shredded
¾ cup mayonnaise

In a large skillet, sauté zucchini and yellow squash, in oil, for 10 minutes, or until tender. Sprinkle with seasonings; mix well. Spoon into pie shell; top with tomatoes; set aside. In a small bowl, combine the cheese with mayonnaise; spread over top of pie. Bake at 350 degrees, for 25 minutes, or until golden brown. Refrigerate leftovers. Yield 6 to 8 servings.

PUMPKIN CHIFFON PIE

1-9" pie shell, BAKED
3 large egg yolks, beaten
¾ cup brown sugar, packed
1½ cups pumpkin, cooked and mashed
½ cup milk
1 teaspoon cinnamon
½ teaspoon nutmeg
1 tablespoon unflavored gelatin
¼ cup cold water
3 large egg whites
¼ cup granulated sugar

In a medium mixing bowl, combine beaten egg yolks, brown sugar, pumpkin, milk and spices; mix well. Place ingredients in the top of double boiler. Cook on medium heat, stirring constantly. Soften the gelatin in ¼ cup cold water; stir into hot mixture until dissolved. In a small bowl, beat egg whites until soft peaks appear. Add sugar gradually; continue beating until stiff. Fold egg whites into cooled pumpkin mixture. Pour into pie crust; chill covered in refrigerator, until set. If desired, serve with whipped topping. Yield 6 to 8 persons.

EASY PUMPKIN CHIFFON PIE

1-9" pie shell, BAKED
2 large packages Vanilla Instant Pudding
1 cup milk
1 can (16 ozs.) pumpkin
1 regular size container Cool Whip
1 teaspoon pumpkin pie spice

In a medium mixing bowl, mix pudding and milk, until slightly thickened. Add pumpkin, one-half container of Cool Whip and pumpkin pie spice; mix thoroughly. Pour into baked pie crust. Top pie with other half of Cool Whip. Chill for several hours before serving. Yield 6 servings.

PUMPKIN PIE VARIATIONS

MAPLE PUMPKIN PIE—

Cool pie about 30 minutes, Drizzle 2 tablespoons maple-flavored syrup on warm pie; sprinkle with 2 tablespoons pecans. Serve warm.

PUMPKIN PIE
(with Rum Whipped Topping)

Cool pie about 1 hour. Mix 8 ozs. whipped cream cheese, 2 tablespoons powder sugar and 1 tablespoon rum or ½ teaspoon rum flavoring. Spread topping on warm pie.

OLD FASHION RAISIN PIE

1 carton (16 ozs.) sour cream
1½ cups granulated sugar
3 tablespoon all-purpose flour
3 large egg yolks
1 cup raisins
3 egg whites
½ teaspoon Cream of Tartar
¾ cup granulated sugar
1-9-inch pie shell, BAKED

In a medium saucepan, combine together, sour cream, 1½ cups sugar, flour, egg yolks and raisins. Over medium heat, cook, stirring constantly, until thickened. Remove from heat; but keep warm; set aside.

FOR MERINGUE: Place egg whites and Cream of Tartar in a large mixing bowl. Beat with an electric mixer, on medium speed, until soft peaks form. Gradually add ¾ cup sugar, 1 tablespoon at a time, with electric mixer on high speed, at about 4 minutes or until mixture forms stiff glossy peaks. Pour warm filling into baked pie crust; spread meringue over filling. Bake at 350 degrees for 15 minutes; remove from oven. Cool for 1 hour, then chill in refrigerator for 3 to 4 hours before serving. Yield 8 serving.

TRADITIONAL PIE CRUST

2 cups all-purpose flour, sifted
1 teaspoon salt
¾ cup shortening
4 to 5 tablespoons cold water

In a medium mixing bowl, combine flour & salt; cut in shortening with pastry blender or with 2 knives, until mixture is the consistency of coarse cornmeal. Sprinkle 1 tablespoon cold water on flour mixture, mixing lightly with fork Continue adding water, 1 tablespoon at a time until dough is moist enough to hold together when pressed gently with fork Shape dough in to a smooth ball with hands and then roll on a floured surface

BASIC NO ROLL PIE CRUST

2 cups all-purpose flour
½ teaspoon salt
¾ cup shortening, part butter, if
   desired
3 to 4 tablespoons cold water

In a medium mixing bowl, combine flour and salt. Cut in shortening using a pastry blender or 2 knives, until mixture resembles course cornmeal. Add water gradually to flour mixture; stir with fork until mixture holds together. Press mixture firmly and evenly against sides and bottom of a 9" pie pan. Fill with your favorite filling; bake at 400 degrees, for about 20 minutes or until tested done. Yield about 8 slices.

CHOCOLATE PIE CRUST

1 cup all-purpose flour
½ teaspoon salt
4 tablespoons granulated sugar
4 tablespoons unsweetened
   cocoa
1/3 cup shortening
½ teaspoon vanilla extract
3 to 4 tablespoons water

In a medium mixing bowl, sift together, flour, salt, sugar and cocoa. Cut in shortening with pastry blender or 2 knives; blend thoroughly. Add vanilla and water; mix with fork until dough holds together. Shape into ball; take half dough and roll between 2 pieces of waxed paper to about 1/8" thick and 1 or 2" larger than pie pan. Remove wax paper, then fold dough in half; place in pie pan; unfold. Proceed as pie recipe directs. Yield 1-double pie crust OR 2 single pie crusts.

CHOCOLATE COCONUT PIE CRUST

1 pkg. (4 ozs.) sweet cooking
   chocolate OR
2 squares semi-sweet
   chocolate
2 tablespoons butter OR
   margarine
2 cups flaked coconut

In saucepan, melt chocolate and butter over low heat, stirring constantly until chocolate is melted. Remove from heat. Stir in coco-nut; mix well. Spread and press on bottom and sides of a 9" pie pan. Refrigerate until ready to use. Yield about 8 servings.

CHOCOLATE COCONUT PIE CRUST

1 pkg. (4 ozs.) sweet cooking
   chocolate OR
2 squares semi-sweet chocolate
2 tablespoons butter OR
   margarine
2 cups flaked coconut

In saucepan, melt chocolate and butter over low heat, stirring constantly until chocolate is melted. Remove from heat. Stir in coco-nut; mix well. Spread and press on bottom and sides of a 9" pie pan. Refrigerate until ready to use. Yield about 8 servings.

CORNFLAKE PIE CRUST

1½ cups cornflakes, finely
   crushed
1/3 cup granulated sugar
1/3 cup butter OR margarine,
   melted

In a small mixing bowl, combine all ingredients; mix with fork until well blended. Press crumb mixture on bottom and sides of a 9-inch pie pan. Refrigerate until pie crust sets, about 15 minutes. Proceed as pie recipe directs. Yield 1-8" or 9" pie crust.

FAT-FREE GRAHAM CRACKER PIE CRUST

1 cup fat-free graham cracker
   crumbs
3 tablespoons *orange
   marmalade, melted
¼ teaspoon ground cinnamon
1 tablespoon granulated sugar

Preheat oven to 350 degrees F. Lightly spray a 9-inch pie pan with nonfat cooking spray. In a medium mixing bowl, combine together crumbs, melted orange marmalade, cinnamon and sugar; mix until blended. Press crumb mixture in pie pan; bake for 8 to 10 minutes. Proceed as pie recipe directs.

*__NOTE__—Apple butter or apricot preserves can be substituted for orange marmalade.

OTHER CRUST VARIATIONS

Use vanilla wafer crumbs, chocolate cookie crumbs OR cereal flake crumbs instead of graham cracker crumbs. Also ground nuts can be used.

GRAHAM CRACKER
WHEAT GERM PIE CRUST

½ cup wheat germ
¾ cup graham cracker crumbs
1/3 cup butter OR margarine,
    melted
3 tablespoons granulated sugar

Combine all ingredients
together; mix well. Press into 9"
pie pan; chill before you fill with
your favorite filling.

CAJUN PIE CRUST
(for turnovers or pasties)

¾ cup unsalted butter, softened
1-1/3 cups granulated sugar
1 teaspoon vanilla extract
1 large egg
4½ cups all-purpose flour
2 teaspoons baking powder
1 teaspoon salt
½ cup milk

In a large mixing bowl, beat
with an electric mixer, butter,
sugar, vanilla and egg until
light and fluffy; set aside. In
a separate bowl, combine
together, by sifting flour, baking
powder and salt. Add flour
mixture to butter mixture, a little
at a time, alternately with milk.
Stir until mixture holds together
and forms a ball. Refrigerate for
2 hours or overnight. Proceed
as recipe directs. Depending
on size, yield is about 8 to 10
turnovers or pasties.

MORE PIE CRUST VARIATIONS

-Add 1 teaspoon celery seeds
to plain pie crust; good with
vegetable pies.

-Add ½ cup cheddar cheese,
grated, to plain crust; use when
making apple pie.

-Add 1½ teaspoons lemon OR
orange peel, grated; enhances
lemon meringue pie.

-Add 2 tablespoons nuts, finely
ground; compliments almost
any pie.

-Add 2 tablespoons sesame
seeds to plain crust.

GRAHAM CRACKER PIE CRUST

1½ cups graham cracker
    crumbs, finely ground
½ cup butter OR margarine,
    melted
¼ cup granulated sugar

In a medium mixing bowl,
combine crumbs and sugar
together; with a fork, stir in
butter. Press crumbs on bottom
and sides of 9" pie pan. Chill
for 20 minutes; add filling.
Refrigerate any leftovers.

NUTTY GRAHAM CRACKER PIE CRUST

Prepare crust above, except reduce cracker crumb to 1 cup and add ½ cup finely chopped nuts.

GINGERSNAP COOKIE PIE CRUST (with pecans)

(Good pastry for pumpkin pies)
4 ounces pecan halves or
  pieces
8 ounces gingersnap cookies
1 teaspoon ground cinnamon
1 stick unsalted butter, cut into
  pieces

Grind nuts and cookies until finely ground. In a large mixing bowl, combine nuts, cookie crumbs and cinnamon. Cut in butter with pastry blender or use fork; mix until well blended. Press mixture onto bottom and sides of two pie pans, add prepared pumpkin filling. Yield enough for 2-8" pies.

SPICY GRAHAM CRACKER PIE CRUST
Prepare crust above then add 1 teaspoon ground cinnamon and ½ teaspoon nutmeg.

HONEY GRAHAM CRACKER PIE CRUST
Prepare crust above then add 2 tablespoons honey in place of sugar.

LARGE QUANTITY PIE CRUSTS (Makes 12 double crusts OR 24 single crusts)
(Use 14 ounces dough to make 9" pies, OR 11 ounces dough to make 8" pies. Yield 96 servings.)

CRUST
5 pounds all-purpose flour
2 tablespoons salt
8¼ cups shortening
3 cups cold water

In a large mixing bowl, combine flour and salt; cut in shortening with pastry blender, OR 2 knives, 1 cup at a time until mixture resembles coarse crumbs. Gradually add water, stirring until mixture is moist enough to hold together. Refrigerate dough for 4 hours. Proceed as pie recipe directs.

BOILED PIE CRUST

1 cup shortening
½ cup boiling water
2 cups *cake flour
Pinch of salt

In a medium mixing bowl, whip shortening and water until light and creamy. Add salt and flour, stirring with fork until mixture holds together. Refrigerate about 3 hours, or overnight. Proceed as pie recipe directs. Yield 2 single 9" pie crusts OR 1 double 9" crust.

PLAIN PIE CRUST READY-MIX (Needs no refrigeration.)

6 cups all-purpose flour
1 tablespoon salt
2-1/3 cups shortening

In a large bowl, combine flour and salt; cut in shortening with pastry blender OR 2 knives. Mixture should resemble coarse crumbs. Store in covered, airtight container up to 6 months.

TO USE PIE CRUST READY-MIX

FOR SINGLE 9" PIE CRUST

1½ cups of pie mix
2 to 3 tablespoons water

Put pie mix into a medium mixing bowl; sprinkle water over pie mix, a tablespoon at a time. Blending with a fork until dough comes together to form a ball. On a lightly floured surface, roll dough out to 1/8" thickness; proceed as pie recipe directs.

FOR DOUBLE 9" PIE CRUST

2½ cups pie mix
4 to 6 tablespoons water

Proceed as above single pie recipe directs.

CHEDDAR CHEESE PIE CRUST

1-2/3 cups all-purpose flour
½ teaspoon salt
1 cup sharp Cheddar Cheese, grated
½ cup shortening
4 to 6 tablespoons cold water

In a medium mixing bowl, sift flour and salt together. Add cheese; mix lightly with fork. Cut in shortening, using pastry blender or 2 knives until mixture resembles coarse crumbs. Add water, 1 tablespoon at a time, mixing until dough holds together. Continue as pie recipe directs. Yield 1 double 8" OR 9" pie crust.

PRETZEL PIE CRUST

¾ cup margarine, softened
3 teaspoons brown sugar
2½ cups pretzels, finely crushed

In a medium mixing bowl, combine ingredients together; mix until well-blended. Press mixture on bottom and sides of 8" pie pan. Bake at 350 degrees, for 10 minutes. Fill as desired. Yield about 6 servings.

LEMON PIE CRUST

2 cups all-purpose flour
1½ teaspoon salt
½ cup vegetable oil
2 tablespoons *lemon juice
2 tablespoons water
*If desired, use 4 tablespoons
   lemon
juice and no water.

In a medium mixing bowl,
sift together, flour and salt;
gradually add oil; mix well. Add
lemon juice and water; mix until
dough sticks together. Proceed
as pie recipe directs.

BANANA PIE CRUST

2 cups graham cracker crumbs
¼ cup brown sugar, packed
1 stick butter OR margarine,
   softened
1 ripe banana, mashed

Preheat oven to 375 degrees.
In a medium mixing bowl,
combine cracker crumbs
and brown sugar; add butter
and mashed banana; mix
thoroughly. Press the mixture
into a 9" pie pan; bake for
about 15 minutes, or until
brown. Remove from oven; cool
completely before filling.

PECAN PIE CRUST

1¾ cups all-purpose flour
1 teaspoon salt
2/3 cup shortening
2/3 cup pecans, finely chopped
About 7 tablespoons cold water

In a medium mixing bowl,
combine together, flour and
salt. Cut in shortening, with
pastry blender, or 2 knives, until
mixture resembles coarse meal.
Add pecans; mix well. Sprinkle
cold water, 1 tablespoon at
a time, mixing with fork, until
mixture forms a ball of dough.
Roll dough out on a lightly
floured surface. Place in a 9" pie
pan; trim. Chill in refrigerator,
when preparing filling. Proceed
as pie recipe directs.

OATMEAL PIE CRUST

1 cup oatmeal
1/3 cup all-purpose flour
1/3 cup brown sugar, packed
¼ teaspoon salt
1/3 cup butter OR margarine,
   softened

In a medium mixing bowl,
combine together, oatmeal,
flour, brown sugar and salt;
blend well Add butter; cut
in flour mixture with a pastry
blender or 2 knives until it is
crumbly. Press crumbs on
bottom mix with fork until it
holds together.

BULK PIE CRUSTS

Makes 12-2 crust pies OR 24 single crust pies. Use 14 ounces dough for 9" pie OR 11 ounces dough for 8" pie. Yield 96 servings.

CRUST

5 pounds all-purpose flour
8¼ cups shortening
3 cups cold water
2 tablespoons salt

In a large mixing bowl, combine flour and salt; cut in shortening until mixture resembles coarse crumbs; add water, a little at a time, mixing until dough holds together. (It is easier to handle dough, if you refrigerate dough for 4 hours.) Proceed as pie recipe directs.

MICROWAVE PIE CRUST

1/3 cup shortening
2 tablespoons margarine, softened
1 cup all-purpose flour
½ teaspoon salt
3 tablespoons water

In a medium mixing bowl, cream together, shortening and margarine; add flour and salt; mix well until mixture resembles coarse granules. Add water; mix until dough forms a ball. On a floured surface roll out dough to fit an 9-inch pie pan. Pie crust must be microwaved before putting in filling, or crust will not bake properly. This recipe is only good to use for single pastry pies. Microwave at high for 5 to 7 minutes rotating ½ turn every 3 minutes. Use caution because crust will not brown, but when cooked the crust will appear dry.

EGG PIE CRUST

2 cups all-purpose flour, sifted
½ teaspoon salt
2/3 cup shortening
1 large egg, slightly beaten
2 tablespoons cold water
2 teaspoons lemon juice

Sift flour with salt into a medium mixing bowl. Cut in shortening with pastry blender or 2 knives until crumbly. Combine water with lemon juice; add 1 tablespoon at a time mixing with a fork until dough comes together. Continue by following pie recipe directions

WALNUT PIE CRUST

1½ cups walnuts, finely ground
3 tablespoons butter OR margarine
2 tablespoons granulated sugar

Combine together, ingredients; blend well Press in 9" pie tin; bake at 325 degrees for 10 minutes. Yield 1 pie crust.

SOUR CREAM PIE CRUST

1 cup all-purpose flour
½ teaspoon baking powder
½ teaspoon salt
Pinch of sugar
6 tablespoons butter OR
    margarine, cold and cut into
    small pieces
4 to 5 tablespoons sour cream

In a medium mixing bowl, combine together, dry ingredients; mix well. Add butter, with a fork mix ingredients until it looks like cornmeal. Stir in sour cream until moist enough to hold together. Knead briefly; cover and chill at least for 1 hour. Prepare as pie recipe directs.

CHOCOLATE GRAHAM CRACKER PIE CRUST

1¼ cups chocolate graham
    crackers finely ground
¼ cup granulated sugar
6 tablespoon butter OR
    margarine

Use same directions as for regular graham cracker crust (See index.)

BUTTER PIECRUST

2½ cups all-purpose flour
½ teaspoon salt
¼ teaspoon baking powder
1 tablespoon granulated sugar
1 cup (2 sticks) unsalted butter
3 to 6 tablespoons cold water

In a large mixing bowl, combine together, by sifting, flour, salt baking powder and sugar. Cut butter into small pieces; add to flour mixture using a fork, mix until mixture resembles coarse meal. Add 1 table spoon water at a time, mixing with fork until dough sticks together and form a ball. Chill for 1 hour. Yield 2-9-inch piecrusts.

VINEGAR PIE CRUST

1 large egg
1 tablespoon white vinegar
½ cup cold water
4 cups all-purpose flour
1 tablespoon granulated sugar
1 teaspoons salt
1¾ cups shortening

In a small bowl, beat egg slightly; add vinegar and cold water; set aside. In a large mixing bowl combine flour, sugar and salt; cut in shortening with a pastry blender until mixture resembles coarse meal. Add egg mixture, mix quickly with a fork until the dough can be gathered into a ball. Turn dough onto a lightly floured surface and continue as pie recipe directs. Yield enough dough for 2 double crust pies.

SWEET POTATO PIE CRUST

1 cup all-purpose flour
1 teaspoon baking powder
½ teaspoon salt
1 cup sweet potatoes, cooked
   & mashed
1/3 cup butter OR margarine,
   melted
1 large egg, well beaten

In a medium bowl, combine together, all ingredients; mix until dough is formed. On a floured surface, roll out dough to fit desired pie pan.

PIE CRUST FOR TURNOVERS

4 cups all-purpose flour
1 tablespoon baking powder
½ teaspoon baking soda
Dash of salt
1/3 cup shortening
1 large egg, beaten
1 cup buttermilk

In a large mixing bowl, combine all dry ingredients; cut in shortening, mix until resembles small crumbs. In a separate bowl, mix beaten egg and buttermilk; add to dry ingredients; mix thoroughly. On a lightly floured surface roll dough, cut desired size circles; place filling on half of circle; fold dough over filling. Use fork to press edges together. Bake

at 400 degrees for 20 to 25 minutes or until golden brown. Yield about 12 to 14 turnovers.

COCONUT PIE CRUST

1/3 cup butter OR margarine,
   softened
3 tablespoons granulated sugar
1 large egg yolk
1 cup all-purpose flour
1 cup coconut, chopped

In a 9-inch pie pan, combine together, all ingredients mix thoroughly. Press mixture up sides of pan and evenly across bottom. Bake at 350 degrees, 25 minutes or as pie recipe directs. Yield 1 pie.

CANNOLLI PIE

Chocolate pie crust, ready-made
1¼ pounds (2½ cups) ricotta
   cheese
¼ cup milk
1 cup powder sugar
2 teaspoons almond extract
1 to 2 drops red food coloring
¾ cup maraschino cherries,
   quartered
½ cup milk chocolate shaved
½ cup almonds, sliced

Preheat oven to 375 degrees.
Bake pie crust for 5 minutes;
cool. In a mixing bowl,
combine together, by beating
ricotta cheese, milk, powder
sugar, almond extract and
food coloring; beat well. Fold
in cherries, chocolate and
almonds. Spoon into pie crust;
chill before serving. Refrigerate,
covered, any leftovers. Yield 6
to 8 servings.

DEWBERRY PIE

Fill 1-9" pie pastry with
prepared (washed & sorted)
dewberries. In a small mixing
bowl, combine together, 1 cup
granulated sugar, ¼ cup all-
purpose flour and a pinch of
salt; mix well. Sprinkle evenly
over berries; dot with butter
OR margarine. Put top crust in
place, with a fork perforate top
to allow steam to escape while
baking. Bake at 400 degrees,
for 45 minutes, or until golden
brown. Yield 6 to 8 servings.

SWEETBREAD PIE

1 pie shell, BAKED
1 pound beef sweetbreads
4 ounces fresh mushrooms,
   sliced
3 tablespoons butter OR
   margarine
2 cups white sauce, medium
   thick
1 tablespoon capers, drained
¾ cup potato chips, slightly
   crushed

Soak sweetbreads in cold,
salted water for 1 hour. Drain
water, then use fresh water, with
a little salt and vinegar added.
In a saucepan, over medium
heat; bring to a boil, then
reduce temperature to simmer.
Cook until tender. Meanwhile,
sauté mushroom in skillet for 2
to 3 minutes; set aside. Prepare
white sauce (see index for
recipe). When sweetbreads are
tender and cooled, cut into ½
inch cubes, discarding coarse
tubes. Add to sauce, along with
mushrooms and capers; mix
lightly. Pour sweetbread mixture
into baked pie shell; sprinkle
crushed potato chips evenly,
on top; bake at 400 degrees
for 5 minutes. Yield about 6
servings.

NO WEEP MERINGUE

½ cup cold water
2 tablespoons granulated sugar
1 tablespoon cornstarch
3 large egg whites
1 teaspoon vanilla extract

In a medium saucepan, combine together, water sugar and cornstarch; mix well. Over medium heat, bring mixture to a boil; cook until thick, stirring constantly. Remove from heat; set aside; let cool. Meanwhile, beat 3 large egg whites, room temperature, until stiff. When the sugar mixture is cool, then beat the egg whites into the mixture; add 1 teaspoon vanilla extract. Spread over pie filling, sealing to the edge of crust. Yield enough meringue for 1 pie.

FOOLPROOF MERINGUE

3 large egg whites, room
    temperature
Dash salt
1 cup Marshmallow Creme

In a medium mixing bowl, beat egg whites until soft peaks form. Then gradually add Marshmallow Creme, beating until stiff peaks form. Spread over pie filling, sealing to the edge of the crust. Bake at 350 degrees, for 12 to 15 minutes, or until light brown. Yield enough meringue for 1 pie.

COMMON PASTRY PROBLEMS

When the dough is tough.

A. Too much water; over mixing; not enough
B. shortening; or too much flour when rolling out.

When the dough is crumbly.

A. Not enough water or too much fat.

DANDELION MERINGUE PIE

CRUST
2/3 cup whole wheat pastry flour
2/3 cup rice flour
3 tablespoons butter OR margarine
3 tablespoons vegetable oil
2 tablespoons cold water

FILLING
4 large egg yolks
2/3 cup honey
2 tablespoons whole wheat flour
1½ cups milk1 cup dandelion leaves, cooked, chopped & squeezed dry
½ cup pine nuts OR sunflower seeds
2 teaspoons orange peel, grated

MERINGUE
4 large egg whites
2 tablespoons honey

TO MAKE CRUST

In a mixing bowl, combine together, wheat and rice flours; cut in butter with pastry blender or 2 knives. Add oil; mix until dough looks crumbly. Stir in water, mix until dough gathers into a bal; add more water, if necessary. Press dough into a lightly greased 9-inch pie pan.

TO MAKE FILLING

In a medium saucepan, combine together, egg yolks, honey and flour. Gradually add milk; mix well. Cook over low heat, stirring constantly until thickened. Do not let mixture scorch. If lumps form, pour mixture through a strainer. Puree' dandelion leaves in a blender or food processor. Add to filling; stir un nuts and orange peel. Pour mixture into piecrust; bake at 350 degrees, for 20 minutes.

TO MAKE MERINGUE

In a mixing bowl, beat egg whites until stiff. Gradually add honey very slowly or the egg whites will collapse. Remove the pie from oven, then mound the meringue over the top, spreading meringue to crust. Return to oven, for an additional 10 to 15 minutes, or until golden. Yield 6 to 8 servings.

BAKED ALASKA PIE

CRUST

1 cup all-purpose flour
3 tablespoons powder sugar
½ cup butter OR margarine,
  softened
1/3 cup nuts, chopped

In a mixing bowl, combine together, flour, sugar and butter; mix until well-blended. Add nuts; press into bottom and sides of a 9-inch pie pan; then prick with fork. Bake at 350 degrees, for 15 to 18 minutes or lightly browned. Remove from oven, cool, then refrigerate.

FILLING

2 pints cherry ice cream,
  softened
1 pint vanilla ice cream,
  softened

Spoon 1 pint of cherry ice cream into chilled crust; pack down with back of spoon. Freeze, then repeat with vanilla ice cream and remaining cherry ice cream. Cover with was paper; freeze until firm.

MERINGUE

2 large egg whites
¼ teaspoon cream of tartar
¼ cup granulated sugar

Beat egg whites until foamy; add cream of tartar; beat until soft peaks form. Add sugar 1 tablespoon at a time to keep soft peaks. Just before serving spread meringue over ice cream, sealing edges to crust. Place pie on wooden board and bake at 500 degrees for 1 to 3 minutes or lightly brown. Serve immediately.

SOME COMMENTS . . . .

Some pie crusts in this booklet are made the old traditional way and many are new and different. Pies are easy to make and of course, today when costs are high, they are economical. Whether you make the pie a meal or have pie for dessert, it is always a family favorite.

Chapter 6

MISCELLANEOUS MEATS

NOTHING IS GOOD OR BAD,
BUT THINKING MAKES IT SO!

POLISH KIELBASA

5 pounds pork, coarsely ground
1½ tablespoons salt
1 teaspoon black pepper
1 teaspoon marjoram
3 cloves garlic, finely chopped
1 cup water

In a large mixing bowl. combine together, all ingredients; mix thoroughly. Rinse the sausage casing real good, then stuff meat mixture into the casing.

TO COOK, cover partially with water; simmer for 1½ hours, adding more water when necessary. Half way through cooking, turn sausage over.

HOMEMADE HOT SAUSAGE

27 pounds pork, cut in chunks
9 tablespoons salt
8 tablespoons dried sage
4 tablespoons black pepper
3 tablespoons red pepper (add more if desired)

Mix ingredients with meat before grinding; mix again until thoroughly blended. Stuff into sausage casing or make sausage patties.

NOTE—This recipe is over 200 years old.

ITALIAN SAUSAGE

5 pounds pork butt, coarsely ground
1 tablespoon salt
1 tablespoon black pepper
5 cloves garlic, minced
1 tablespoon fennel seeds
1 teaspoon anise seeds
1 cup cold water

(NOTE): Add 1 tablespoon crushed hot pepper for hotter tasting sausage.) In a large mixing bowl, combine together, all the ingredients; mix until blended thoroughly. Stuff into sausage casing or make sausage patties.

SUMMER BOLOGNA

80 pounds beef, ground
20 pounds pork, ground
1 cup salt
2 cups brown sugar, packed
4 tablespoon pepper
1 ounce of mace

Use food grinder or food processor to grind meat, Place meat in a large mixing bowl, add remaining ingredients; mix together thoroughly. Use store-bought on casings or 8-inch in diameter muslin bags. Stuff casings lightly with sausage stuffer. Hang on hooks in smoke house. Smoke continuously for 2 weeks.

SUMMER SAUSAGE

5 pounds hamburger
5 teaspoons Morton
   Tenderquick Salt
1 teaspoon garlic salt
2 teaspoons mustard seed
1 teaspoon black pepper
2 teaspoons hickory smoked
   salt
About 3 drops liquid smoke

In a large mixing bowl,
combine together, all
ingredients; mix thoroughly.
Place in refrigerator uncovered.
On the second day stir
ingredients completely; cover
and refrigerate. On the third
day, mix ingredients; cover
and refrigerate. On the fourth
day, mix, then divide in 5 long
rolls. Place on a broiler pan so
grease goes in the bottom of
pan; bake at 200 degrees, for 8
hours.

(NOTE)—This is a snack luncheon
meat.

RED-EYE GRAVY

Fry han OR Canadian Bacon in
skillet until done, but not hard.
Remove from skillet; then add 1
cup cold, weak coffee. Bring to
a boil, over medium heat; pour
into a bowl; serve hot.

HOMEMADE BOLOGNA (old commercial recipe)

45 pounds ground beef
5 pounds ground pork
1 pound Morton Tenderquick
   Salt
2 ounces ground coriander
   seeds
4 tablespoons liquid smoke
2 ounces black pepper
8 pounds cold water
1 teaspoon powder mace
1 teaspoon saltpeter
½ cup salt

In a large container,
mix together, meat and
tenderquick; mix well. Cover
and let cure in a cool place
for 48 hours. After curing meat,
grind twice; add seasoning
and water; mix thoroughly, for
30 minutes. Stuff meat tightly
into beef casing, then allow to
hang in a cool place overnight.
In a large kettle of hot water,
put in meat and cook about
60 to 90 minutes, or until tested
done. Remove from hot water
and plunge into ice water to
cool.

SOUTH AFRICAN SAUSAGE

3 pounds beef
2 pounds bacon
1 teaspoon black pepper
1 teaspoon salt
½ teaspoon ground nutmeg
1 teaspoon coriander seeds
½ cup white vinegar

Coarse grind meats with seasoning, in a blender, food processor or meat grinder. Stuff into sausage casings. Cook as you would any fresh sausage. ingredients with meat mixture; mix

AMISH BBQ SAUCE

1 can Cream of Mushroom
  Soup
1 cup ketchup
1 tablespoon Worcestershire
  Sauce
½ cup onions, chopped

Combine together, all the above ingredients; mix well. Pour over meat and bake at 375 degrees for 2 hours or until tested done.

HOMEMADE HOT DOGS

1 pound raw pork, finely
  ground
½ pound raw beef, finely
  ground
Pinch of marjoram
Pinch of mustard
½ teaspoon salt
1 black pepper
½ cup water

In a large bowl, combine ground meats; mix thoroughly; set aside. In another bowl, combine together remaining ingredients; mix well. Combine remaining well. (Note: Color of meat will not be pink like store-boughten hot dogs). Stuff into casing, forming 4 to 6 links. Refrigerate 3 to 5 days to cure. Yield 1½ pounds.

TO COOK: Simmer in water for 20 to 30 minutes.

BROWN SUGAR GLAZE

1 cup brown sugar, packed
2 tablespoons all-purpose flour
½ teaspoon dry mustard
1 teaspoon ground cloves
¼ cup white vinegar

Combine together, all ingredients; mix well. Brush glaze on meat during cooking. Yield about 1/3 cup glaze.

POLISH *SAUSAGE PIZZA

½ cup onions, chopped
4 slices of bacon, cut in ½ inch
  pieces
1 jar (16 ozs.) sauerkraut, well
  drained
1 tablespoons caraway seeds
  (optional)
1 jar mushrooms, drained &
  sliced
1½ cups Swiss cheese, shredded
½ pound Polish Sausage
  (kielbasa) sliced
Pizza Crust

In a medium saucepan, over
medium-high heat, cook
bacon and onion until light
brown, stirring frequently.
Reduce heat to low; add
sauerkraut and caraway seeds;
simmer for 3 minutes. Stir in
mushrooms; cook for 1 minute.
Remove from heat; Spread
mixture over crust (made from
scratch or bought). Sprinkle
cheese evenly, over top. Place
sliced sausage over cheese;
bake at 425 degrees, for 15 to
20 minutes, or until edges are
golden brown and cheese is
melted. Yield about 8 servings.

*REUBEN PIZZA

Same as above recipe, EXCEPT
substitute sliced corned
beef, cut in pieces, top with
Thousand Island Salad Dressing,
amount as you desire.

PECAN CHICKEN CASSEROLE

1 cup chicken, cooked & diced
1 can *Cream of Mushroom
  Soup
2 tablespoons onions, chopped
½ cup pecans, chopped
1½ cups rice, cooked
½ teaspoon salt
¼ teaspoon pepper
1 tablespoon lemon juice
½ cup mayonnaise
¼ cup water
3 large eggs, hard cooked
  (If desired, reserve some
  chopped egg for garnish.)

*If you choose, substitute can
of Cream of Chicken Soup for
Mushroom Soup. In a medium
mixing bowl, combine together,
chicken, soup, vegetables, rice,
nuts and seasoning; blend well.
Mix in lemon juice, mayonnaise
and water. Chop eggs; add
to chicken mixture. Place in a
greased casserole. Bake at 400
degrees for 25 minutes or until
bubbly. Remove from oven;
let stand 15 minutes before
serving. Garnish with remaining
chopped egg. Yield 4 servings.

PORK CHOPS (with Sauerkraut)

4 pork chops
Salt and pepper to taste
2 tablespoons vegetable oil
1 jar (32 ozs.) sauerkraut with
   caraway seeds
2 tablespoons brown sugar
4 medium-size potatoes,
   peeled & cut in half
2 tablespoons butter OR
   margarine
¼ cup water

Season to taste, pork chops
with salt and pepper. In a large
skillet, heat oil; lightly brown
pork chops. Drain sauerkraut
thoroughly; place in medium
mixing bowl. Add brown sugar;
mix well. Place potatoes in
bottom of 3-quart casserole dish.
Spread sauerkraut mixture over
potatoes. Place pork chops on
top; dot with butter. Add water;
cover; bake at 325 degrees, for
about 3 hours, or until tested
done. Yield about 3 to 4 servings.

TURKEY STUFFING

3 tablespoons butter OR
   margarine
2 medium onions, diced
2 stalks celery, diced
1 loaf bread, dried and cubed
½ teaspoon pepper
½ teaspoon salt
2 tablespoons dried sage
1 can (14,5 ozs.) chicken broth

In a medium-sized skillet, melt
butter sauté onions and celery,
until tender. In a large mixing
bowl, combine together, bread
cubes, pepper, salt and sage;
toss lightly. Add onions and
celery; mix gently. Pour chicken
broth slowly over bread mixture;
mix thoroughly. Place stuffing in
a 3-quart casserole dish. Bake
at 350 degrees, for about 45
minutes, or until lightly brown.
NOTE: This recipe makes
enough to loosely stuff a 12
pound turkey.

PECAN FRIED CHICKEN

2 pounds chicken pieces, your
   choice
1½ cups pecans, finely chopped
1 cup all-purpose flour
1 cup cornmeal
1 teaspoon salt
1 teaspoon black pepper
1 teaspoon cayenne pepper
4 large eggs
½ cup butter OR margarine
4 cups vegetable oil

Cut up chicken into pieces,
wash, dry with paper towels. In
a large mixing bowl, combine
together all dry ingredients; mix
well. In another bowl, mix eggs
and melted butter. Dip chicken
pieces into egg mixture, then
roll in dry ingredients to coat
thoroughly. Repeat procedure
a second time for each chicken
piece, to make thick-coated
pieces. Place vegetable oil in a
large skillet, heat until hot. Add
chicken pieces. a few at a time.
Fry about 10 to 12 minutes,
on each side; drain on paper
towels; serve.

COCA-COLA BEEF ROAST

About 3 pounds English or
   chuck roast
1 bottle Chili Sauce
1 envelope Onion Soup Mix
12 ounces Coca-Cola
Cooked noodles OR
   hamburger buns

In a crockpot, combine
together, all ingredients. Cook
on low heat for 7 to 8 hours;
shred cooked beef. Combine
with cooked noodles OR serve
meat on buns. Yield about 6
servings.

EASY COCKTAIL SAUCE

1 cup chili sauce
1/3 cup horseradish
1/3 cup ketchup
1½ teaspoons Worcestershire
   Sauce

Combine together, all
ingredients; mix thoroughly.
Chill mixture before serving.
Yield about 1-2/3 cup sauce.

CHERRY SAUSAGE

1 cup tart cherries
2 pounds lean pork
1 teaspoons salt
1 teaspoon dried sage
½ teaspoon thyme
1½ brown sugar
Pepper to taste

Remove fat from pork; cut into
1" cubes. In a food processor,
place cherries, process until
cherries are finely diced.
Place in small bowl; set aside.
In a large mixing bowl, mix
cubed pork with remaining
ingredients. Divide mixture
in half; put ½ of mixture in
food processor, process until
desired texture is reached.
Return to bowl; add cherries;
mix thoroughly or until evenly
combined. Get ready to fry,
by making patties, or freeze to
cook later.

HAM PATTIES

Combine 2 cups of ham,
cooked & ground, ½ cup soft
bread crumbs, ¼ cup green
onions, chopped, ½ cup milk,
1 large egg, slightly beaten
& a dash of pepper; mix well.
Shape into 4 patties. Brown
slowly in a small amount of
shortening. If desired, heat 1
cup sour cream just until hot.
Top patties with sour cream &
green onion tops, chopped.
Yield 4 servings.

MEATLOAF FOR A CROWD

8 large eggs, beaten
1 can (46 ozs.) V8 Juice
2 large onions, finely chopped
4 stalks celery, finely chopped
4 cups seasoned bread crumbs
2 envelopes onion soup mix
2 teaspoons pepper
8 pounds ground beef
¾ cup ketchup
1/3 cup brown sugar, packed
¼ cup prepared mustard

In a very large bowl, combine together, eggs, V8 Juice, onions, celery, bread crumbs, onion soup mix and pepper; mix well. Crumble ground beef over mixture; mix thoroughly. Shape into 4 loaves; place each loaf into a 13x9x2 inch baking pan. Bake, uncovered, at 350 degrees, for 45 minutes or until tested done. Meanwhile, in a small bowl, combine ketchup, brown sugar and mustard. Spread over meat loaves. Yield 4 meat loaves, about 8 servings each OR total 32 servings.

BURRITOS

3 pounds ground meat
1 medium onion, diced
3 cans Cream of Mushroom Soup, undiluted
½ can green chili peppers, chopped
1 teaspoon chili powder
1 teaspoon garlic salt
1 teaspoon cumin
1 teaspoon oregano
3 pkgs. flour tortillas

In a large skillet, fry ground meat until brown; drain grease. Add remaining ingredients EXCEPT tortillas. Put about 2 tablespoons of mixture, if desired, top with cheese, then roll up; wrap in foil. Bake at 325 degrees for 30 minutes. Yield about 12 servings.

SWEET & SOUR PORK CHOPS

3 tablespoons all-purpose flour
½ cup brown sugar, packed
¼ teaspoon salt
¼ cup soy sauce
1/3 cup white vinegar
¾ cup water
1 small onion, chopped
1 small green pepper, sliced (optional)
5 to 6 pork chops

In a medium bowl, combine together, flour, brown sugar and salt; mix well. Coat pork chops in mixture, then arrange pork chops in 8x12 inch baking dish. Sprinkle remaining flour mixture over chops set aside. Meanwhile, combine soy sauce, vinegar and water;; pour over chops. Top with chopped onion & sliced green pepper, if desired. Bake at 350 degrees for 60 to 75 minutes, or until tested done

HOMEMADE BEEF JERKY

Partially freeze about 3 pounds of lean beef (partially freezing the meat makes it easier to slice thin). Slice round or flank steak, ¼ inch thick and about 4 to 6 inches long. Remove fat, then combine:

1 teaspoon salt
1 teaspoon onion powder
1 teaspoon garlic powder
¼ teaspoon black pepper
1/3 cup soy sauce
1/3 cup A-1 sauce

Lay meat strips in a plastic bag; add marinade; gently force air from bag, Lay bag flat in a shallow pan, place in refrigerator for 24 hours. While meat is marinating, turn bag over several times. Next day drain meat, then lay meat strips to dry on paper towel, then place meat strips in shallow pan and place in oven, at 150 degrees. Do not allow oven temperature to go over 150 degrees. Meat is done when it is brittle and chewy, about 4 hours. Store in covered container.

QUICK & EASY SAUERBRAUTEN

2 pound chuck roast
2 medium onions
2 cups vinegar
4 cups water
¾ cup granulated sugar
½ teaspoon salt
2 teaspoons pickling spice

In a large kettle, brown meat in shortening: add the remainder of ingredients; bring to a boil, turn heat down to simmer; cook until tender. Remove from heat, strain gravy, then return to heat and thicken. Serve with mashed potatoes or noodles. Yield 4 to 6 servings.

CITY CHICKEN ON A STICK

1½ pounds pork and veal, combined, cut in cubes
1 large egg
1 cup bread dry crumbs OR cracker crumbs

Cut meat into 1 inch cubes; put on wooden skewers. Then dip meat into egg, then coat meat with crumbs; set aside, brown meat over medium heat quickly, reduce heat. Add a little water; cover skillet tightly, simmer for 1 hour, or until meat is tender. Yield 4 servings.

BEEF HAMBURGERS

1½ pounds ground meat
1 medium onion, chopped
1 teaspoon dry mustard
2 tablespoons sour cream
Dash of Worcestershire Sauce
Salt and pepper to taste
1 egg, lightly beaten

In a large mixing bowl, combine together, all the ingredients; mix thoroughly. Shape into patties, then in a large skillet, over medium heat, fry hamburgers, on both sides, until tested done, about 20 to 35 minutes.

LIVER AND ONIONS

1 pound liver, sliced about ½"
   thick
¼ cup shortening
2 cups onions, thinly sliced
3 tablespoons butter OR
   margarine

Coat liver pieces in flour; in a skillet, melt shortening, brown liver, over medium heat, 2 to 3 minutes on each side, if desired, season with salt and pepper. Sauté onions in butter until tender; add more water if necessary.

HOMEMADE PORK SAUSAGE

10 ounces ground lean pork
6 ounces ground pork fat
1 teaspoon salt
½ teaspoon pepper
Butter for frying

In a large bowl, combine together, all ingredients, EXCEPT butter; mix thoroughly until well-blended. Cover with plastic wrap; chill overnight, to allow flavors to blend. Shape into 2½ inch patties, using about ¼ cup mixture for each patty. In a large skillet, melt about 1 teaspoon butter, over medium heat. Add patties; cook about 5 minutes per side, or until brown and cooked through; remove from heat; drain. Yield about 6 patties.

CORNED BEEF HASH

2 cups corned beef, cooked
2 cups potatoes, cooked &
   diced
2 tablespoons butter OR
   margarine
1 tablespoon vegetable oil
1 cup onions, finely chopped
½ cup liquid from corned beef
   OR beef broth
1 tablespoon Worcestershire
   sauce

Chop corned beef into small pieces. Place meat in a small bowl; add potatoes; set aside. Combine butter and oil in a medium-size skillet, over medium heat. Add onions; fry for 5 minutes, then add corned beef, potatoes, broth and Worcestershire sauce; mix all ingredients thoroughly. Lower heat and cook for 30 minutes; mixing now and then, making sure hash is not sticking. Invert hash onto a plate and serve. Yield about 4 servings.

HAM LOAF

2 pounds ground pork
1 pound ground ham
2 large eggs
1 cup milk
1 cup cracker crumbs

In a medium mixing bowl, combine together, the above ingredients; mix thoroughly. Put into ungreased baking pan; set aside. In a small bowl, combine ½ cup brown sugar, packed, ½ cup vinegar and 1 tablespoon dry mustard; mix well. Pour sauce over top of ham loaf before baking. Use remaining sauce for basting ham loaf during baking. Bake at 250 degrees, for 3 hours.

PORK CHOPS (with Honey Glaze)

6 pork chops
1/3 cup all-purpose flour
1/3 cup honey
2 tablespoons lemon juice
½ teaspoon Worcestershire Sauce
½ teaspoon celery salt

Trim any excess fat from pork chops. Fry trimmings, then discard; save drippings Dredge chops in flour, then brown meat in hot grease, on both sides. Remove from heat and place in 9-inch square baking pan. In a small mixing bowl, combine together, remaining ingredients. Pour over pork chops; cover tightly with foil; bake at 375 degrees, for 1 hour, or until tested done

COUNTRY-STYLE SPARERIBS (with sauce. on the grill)

4 pounds country-style ribs
1 tablespoon butter OR margarine
1 clove garlic, minced
2 tablespoons onions, chopped
¾ cup ketchup
1 teaspoon chili powder
2 tablespoons brown sugar
2 tablespoons Worcestershire sauce
1 tablespoon prepared mustard
1 teaspoon celery seed
Dash of hot pepper sauce (optional)
1 tablespoon lemon juice

In a large saucepan with a cover, bring ribs to a simmer over medium heat. Cook for about 1 hour, you can do this a day ahead, if desired. In another saucepan, melt butter; add garlic and onions, then add remaining ingredients; bring to a boil; remove from heat; set aside. Drain ribs, grill over medium coals, about 10 minutes on each side, brushing often with sauce until well-coated. If the ribs were chilled before cooking, grill.15 to 18 minutes on each side. May substitute any meat for the ribs, i.e. chicken, steak, etc. Yield 6 to 8 servings.

BUTTERMILK FRIED CHICKEN (with gravy)

1 broiler-fryer chicken (about
   2½ to 3 pounds), cut up
1 cup buttermilk
1 cup all-purpose flour
½ teaspoon salt
Black pepper to taste
Vegetable oil for frying

GRAVY

3 tablespoons all-purpose flour
1 cup milk
1½ to 2 cups water

Place chicken in a single layer in a large container; pour buttermilk over cut-up chicken, Cover and refrigerate for 1 hour. Meanwhile, combine flour salt and pepper, in a medium mixing bowl; mix thoroughly. Drain chicken, then dredge in flour, one at a time; shake off excess flour. Place chicken on a large platter; let dry for 15 minutes. In a large skillet, heat about 1/4-inch oil, over medium heat. When oil is hot, fry chicken until browned on all sides. Reduce heat to simmer; cover skillet; let cook for about 45 minutes, turning occasionally. When chicken is tested done, uncover skillet and cook for 5 minutes longer. Remove chicken to platter and keep warm. Drain all but ¼ cup of drippings in skillet. Stir in flour; over low heat cook mixture until bubbly. Gradually add milk and 1½ cups water; stirring constantly until thickened. Cook 1 minute more, if needed add more water. Season with salt and pepper. Server with chicken. Yield 4 to 6 servings.

CHITTERLINGS (An old recipe)

A large intestine of a hog is used. The intestine is turned inside out and is thoroughly cleaned and cut into pieces, 5 or 6 inches in length. The slices are then rolled in corn meal or cracker crumbs and are slow-cooked by, either frying in a small amount of fat or broiling until crisp. Chitterlings are eaten hot, if desired, with chopped raw onions on top.

COUNTRY HAM (with Red Eye Gravy)

3 slices (1/4 inch thick) center-
   cut cured country-style ham
1 cup brewed coffee

Score fatty edges of ham slices; place in large skillet. Over low heat, slowly fry ham until slightly brown on each side. Remove ham to platter; increase heat to high. Pour coffee into skillet; scrape bottom of skillet; mix thoroughly. Boil until liquid is reduced to a glaze. Pour glaze over ham and serve. Yield about 8 servings.

VEAL SCALLOPINI

1½ pounds veal round steak
¼ cup all-purpose flour,
    1 teaspoon salt,
dash pepper &1 teaspoon
    paprika
1 can (3 ozs.) mushrooms, sliced
1 teaspoon beef-flavored gravy
    base
½ cup tomato sauce
2 tablespoons green pepper,
    chopped
4 ounces medium noodles,
    cooked
Parmesan Cheese

Cut meat into serving pieces;
coat with seasoned flour.
Brown in a little hot shortening,
then place in 9x9x2-inches
baking dish. Drain mushrooms,
reserving liquid. Add water to
mushroom liquid to make ½
cup; heat to boiling. Then add
beef-flavored gravy base; pour
over meat. Bake, covered, at
350 degrees, for 30 minutes.
Meanwhile, combine together,
tomato sauce, green pepper
and mushrooms; place over
meat; bake uncovered, for
15 minutes more. Baste meat
with sauce, just before serving.
Serve over hot, buttered
noodles; sprinkle with Parmesan
Cheese. Yield 4 to 6 servings.

PEPPER STEAK

1 pound beef round OR chuck,
    fat trimmed off
¼ cup soy sauce
1 clove garlic
½ teaspoon ground ginger
¼ cup vegetable oil
1 cup green onions, thinly sliced
1 cup green peppers, cut into
    1-inch squares
2 stalks celery, thinly sliced
1 tablespoon cornstarch
1 cup water
2 tomatoes, cut into wedges

With a sharp knife cut beef
across grain into thin strips.
In a medium mixing bowl
combine together, soy sauce,
garlic, ginger; add beef strips;
mix well; set aside. Prepare
vegetables; set aside. In a
large skillet or wok, heat oil,
over high heat; add beef.
Stir meat until browned, then
reduce heat to simmer for 30
to 40 minutes, or until tested
done. Add vegetables; EXCEPT
tomatoes, stir to mix with
meat, over medium heat, for
10 minutes, or the vegetables
are tender crisp. Meanwhile
mix cornstarch with water;
add to pan; stir and cook until
thickened. Add tomatoes
and heat through. Remove
from heat and serve. Yield 4
servings.

HOMEMADE SALAMI

2 pounds ground beef
½ teaspoon black pepper
1 teaspoon dry mustard
½ teaspoon garlic powder
1 teaspoon fennel
3 tablespoons Morton
    Tenderquick Salt

In a medium mixing bowl, combine together, all the above ingredients; mix thoroughly. Shape into 2 logs or rolls; wrap in foil; twist ends. Refrigerate for 24 hours. Do not remove foil; place in saucepan cover with water and boil for 60 minutes. Remove roll from saucepan; unwrap 1 end foil to drain roll. Retwist foil, then refrigerate until ready to slice and serve. May be frozen.

TEXAS BARBEQUE

4 to 6 cups beef OR pork,
    cooked & sliced
1 medium onion, chopped
2 tablespoons butter OR
    margarine
2 tablespoons vinegar
4 tablespoons brown sugar
1 cup ketchup
3 tablespoons Worcestershire
    sauce
½ teaspoon prepared mustard
1 cup water
½ teaspoon salt
½ teaspoon black pepper

1 tablespoon Tabasco
    (optional)
12 buns

In a large skillet, combine together, all ingredients, EXCEPT buns. Over low heat, simmer, covered, for 1 hour. Serve on buns or as desired.

CLASSIC BARBEQUE SAUCE

2 tablespoons vegetable oil
¼ cup onions, finely chopped
1 cup chili sauce
1/3 cup water
¼ cup dark corn syrup
¼ cup cider vinegar
1 tablespoon Worcestershire
    sauce
½ teaspoon salt

In a skillet, heat oil over medium heat; add onions, cook for 5 minutes, stirring frequently. Stir in remaining ingredients; bring to a boil; reduce heat and simmer 10 minutes. Brush on sausage, meat or poultry during last 15 to 20 minutes of cooking. Yield about 2 cups barbeque sauce.

BARBEQUE FOR A CROWD

5 pounds rump roast
5 pounds roast beef

BBQ SAUCE

½ cup margarine, melted
4 medium onions, chopped
8 cloves garlic, minced
1 cup Worcestershire Sauce
1 cup vinegar
4 dashes red pepper
2 teaspoons salt
8 cups boiling water
4 cups ketchup
4 teaspoons dry mustard
8 teaspoons chili powder

Cook roasts for about 6 hours at 325 degrees, until tested done. It would be best if you cover the beef roast with aluminum foil to keep outside from becoming crisp. Remove from oven; drain fat from meat; shred meat. Put in a bowl; set aside. Prepare barbeque sauce, by sautéing onions & garlic in margarine, in a large saucepan, over medium heat, until tender. Add remaining sauce ingredients; bring to a boil, then add shredded meat. Reduce heat; cook to desired consistency. Serve in buns or over rice. Yield about 35 servings in buns or 16 to 18 servings over rice. Can be frozen.

HONEY-BARBEQUE WINGS

3 pounds chicken wings
½ cup honey
1 teaspoon dry mustard
1 teaspoon paprika
1 teaspoon chili powder
½ teaspoon salt
½ teaspoon pepper
¼ cup water
3 tablespoons ketchup
2 tablespoons butter OR
   margarine
3 tablespoons lemon juice OR
   vinegar
2 tablespoons Worcestershire
   sauce
2 cloves garlic, minced

Preheat oven to 325 degrees. Prepare wings by removing tips and cutting wings in half. In a medium-size saucepan, combine together, the sauce ingredients; mix well. Over medium heat, bring to a boil, remove from heat; cool slightly, then dip wings in sauce; lay them in a roasting pan. Cover wings with remaining sauce; bake for 45 minutes, basting often. Turn wings over; bake for 15 to 20 minutes more, or until wings are well-browned. Yield about 4 servings.

BUFFALO CHICKEN WINGS (with Blue Cheese Dipping Sauce)

2 pounds chicken wings
1 large egg
1 cup vegetable oil
2 cups cider vinegar
½ teaspoon pepper
Cayenne pepper to taste
1 clove garlic, minced
Pinch of nutmeg
Pinch of celery seed
Dash coriander
Dash ground cloves

In a medium mixing bowl, beat egg; beat in oil; then add remaining ingredients; mix well; set aside. Cut chicken wings in half, at the joint; remove wing tips; (reserve for use when making chicken stock). Dip wings into sauce; place in shallow roasting pan. Bake at 500 degrees, for about 10 minutes, reduce heat to 400 degrees, turning and basting with sauce, several times, until wings reach desired crispness. Remove from oven, drain; place on serving dish. Serve with Blue Cheese Dipping Sauce, or one of your choice.

BLUE CHEESE DIPPING SAUCE

In a medium bowl, combine together, 2 tablespoons onions, chopped, 1 clove garlic, minced, ¼ cup fresh parsley, chopped, 1 cup mayonnaise, ½ cup sour cream, 1 tablespoon lemon juice, 1 tablespoon vinegar and ¼ cup blue cheese, crumbled, mix well. If desired, add cayenne pepper to taste. Cover and chill before serving.

POLISH SAUSAGE PATTIES

5 pounds pork butt OR steak, trimmed
5 teaspoons dried marjoram
2 teaspoons salt
1 teaspoon garlic powder
¼ teaspoon pepper
2 cups water

In a food processor, coarsely grind pork; place in large mixing bowl. Add the next 4 ingredients; mix thoroughly. Add water; mix well. Shape into patties, 4 inches each. Fry in a skillet over medium heat for 20 to 25 minutes or until tested done. Yield about 20 patties.

NOTE: Patties can be frozen OR sausage can be stuffed into casings, to make links.

PEANUT BUTTER CHICKEN NUGGETS

½ cup peanut butter
½ cup orange juice
Salt to taste
2 pounds boneless, skinless
    chicken breast
4½ cups cornflakes (about 1½
    cups crushed)
2 teaspoons paprika

Preheat oven to 400 degrees. In a large mixing bowl, combine together, peanut butter, orange juice and salt; set aside. Cut chicken breasts into chunks, about 1"x2". Add to peanut butter mixture; toss to coat; set aside. Crush cornflakes, then combine with paprika. Spread the cornflake mixture on a large plate. Lift chicken chunks from peanut butter mixture; let excess drop off. Roll chicken in crumb mixture until well-coated on all sides. Put on ungreased baking pan; bake 8 to 10 minutes, turning once; Yield about 40 nuggets.

ENCHILADAS, CHICKEN OR TURKEY

2 cups chicken OR turkey,
cooked & cut in bite-size pieces
1 cup green pepper, diced
1 jar (8 ozs.) mild salsa, divided
1 pkg. (8 ozs.) cream cheese
8 (6") flour tortillas
¾ lb. Velvetta Cheese, cubed
¼ cup milk

In a medium saucepan, combine cooked chicken, green pepper, ½ jar salsa, and cream cheese. Over low heat, cook until smooth. Spoon 1/3 cup mixture onto a tortilla; roll up and put seam side down. place in a lightly greased 9x13 baking pan; set aside. Meanwhile, over low heat or in microwave, melt cheese spread and milk; mix until smooth. Pour evenly over tortillas; cover with foil. Bake at 350 degrees, for 20 minutes or when thoroughly heated. If desired, pour remaining salsa over tortillas; serve. Yield 4 to 6 servings.

CAJUN STIR FRY

1 pound lean ground chuck
2 cups onions, chopped
1 cup celery, chopped
1 cup green peppers, chopped
8 cups cabbage, shredded
1 can (12 ozs.) tomatoes, dice &
    chile peppers
3 beef bouillon cubes
2 tablespoons vegetable oil
¼ cup water
Rice

In a large saucepan, put
vegetable oil, in with ground
chuck; cook over medium
heat, stirring until meat browns.
Add bouillon cubes, onions,
celery and green peppers.
Cook, stirring constantly, for 15
minutes. Add tomatoes and
water; cook for a few minutes
more, then add cabbage.
Cover; cook until cabbage is
tender; stir often. Serve over
rice.

EASY CHICKEN POT PIE

2 cups chicken, cooked &
    diced
2 cans Cream of Mushroom
    Soup, undiluted
1 can mixed vegetables,
    drained
1 double 9" pie crust

In a mixing bowl, combine
together, all ingredients, mix
well. Place in bottom crust. Top
with crust; with fork, press to
seal crusts. Cut slits in top crust
to allow steam to escape while
baking. Bake at 350 degrees,
for 40 to 50 minutes, or until
golden brown. Yield 6 to 8
servings.

CHICKEN OR TURKEY FRITTERS

1½ sup all-purpose flour
2 teaspoons baking powder
½ teaspoon salt
1 large egg, beaten
1 cup milk
½ cup chicken OR turkey,
    chopped
¼ cup onions, finely chopped
Shortening for deep frying

In a medium mixing bowl,
combine together flour, baking
powder and salt; mix well
set aside. In another bowl,
combine remaining ingredients;
add to dry ingredients; mix just
until moistened. Drop batter by
tablespoonful into shortening
heated to 365 degrees. Fry
a few at a time until golden
brown, turn once. Drain on
paper towels If desired, serve
with Pimiento-Cheese Sauce
(recipe follows).

PIMIENTO-CHEESE SAUCE

In a skillet, melt 3 tablespoons shortening. Stir in 2 tablespoons flour; gradually add 1½ cups milk with ½ teaspoon salt. Cook over low heat, stir constantly until mixture is thick and bubbly. Remove from heat; add ½ cup sharp American cheese and 2 ounces pimiento, drained and diced If necessary, reheat sauce

TURKEY GRAVY

Drippings from turkey
½ cup all-purpose flour
4 cups stock from giblets and
    turkey bones OR water
Giblets, cooked & chopped
    (optional)
Salt and pepper to taste

Pour drippings from roasting pan into a measuring cup. Return ½ cup drippings to roasting pan. Over low heat, add flour; whisk mixture for 2 or 3 minutes. Remove from heat, gradually mix in stock. Return to heat; bring to a boil; stirring constantly. Reduce heat to simmer; cook for 5 minutes, stirring frequently. If desired, add giblets near end of cooking. Yield 4 cups of gravy.

PEPPERONI SAUSAGE

4 to 5 pounds ground beef
1 envelope Good Seasons
    Italian Salad
Dressing, dissolved in ½ cup
    water
1 tablespoon hickory-smoked
    salt
2 tablespoons Morton's Tender
    Quick Salt
1 tablespoon mustard seeds
1 tablespoon black pepper,
    coarse ground
1 teaspoon anise seeds
½ teaspoon anise extract
1 teaspoon cumin powder
1 teaspoon garlic powder
1 tablespoon Worcestershire
    Sauce
1 tablespoon liquid smoke

In a large mixing bowl, combine together, all the above ingredients; mix thoroughly. Cover and refrigerate. for 3 days; each day mix well. On the last day, divide mixture into fourths. Shape in to loaves, about 13 inches long, lay on the 18 inch side of a 12x18-inch piece of nylon netting. Roll up tightly; tie ends with string. Place on a broiler pan with a rack; bake at 225 degrees, for 6 hours. When done, remove the netting immediately, if not, when cool, it will stick to the meat. Cool, wrap meat & refrigerate or freeze for later use.

HAMBURGER-TATER TOT CASEROLE

1 pound hamburger
¼ cup onions, chopped
1 pkg, frozen Tater Tots
1 can Cream of Mushroom Soup
¾ cup milk

Preheat oven to 350 degrees. In a medium skillet, cook hamburger with onions. Stir hamburger with a fork to break up large pieces. Cook over medium heat until hamburger is browned; remove from heat; drain grease. Place hamburger mixture in a baking dish or casserole. Add Tater Tots; mix well. In a small mixing bowl, combine together, soup and milk; mix thoroughly. Pour soup mixture over hamburger mixture; mix well. Bake at 350 degrees, for 30 minutes. Yield about 4 servings.

CAJUN BARBEQUED STEAK

½ cup ketchup
¼ cup water
2 tablespoons soy sauce
1 tablespoon vinegar
1 tablespoon brown sugar
1 clove garlic, minced
Pinch of EACH cayenne pepper, black pepper
white pepper
chili powder
2 pounds boneless chuck
    shoulder steak
1½ teaspoon tenderizer

In a small saucepan, combine together, all ingredients EXCEPT steak and tenderizer; mix well. Over medium heat, simmer for 10 minutes; set aside, but keep warm. Moisten steak with water; sprinkle evenly, on both sides, with tenderizer; pierce meat with fork, on both sides. Broil or grill steak, 5 to 6 inches from heat, for 25 to 30 minutes, turning and basting frequently with sauce.

LARGE QUANTITY CHICKEN CASSEROLE

10 cups chicken, cooked and
    diced
10 cups celery, chopped
2 bunches green onions with
    tops, sliced
2 cans (4 ozs. each) green
    chilies, chopped
1 can (5¾ ozs.) ripe olives,
    drained, pitted and sliced
2 cups almonds, slivered
5 cups (20 ozs.) cheddar cheese,
    shredded and divided
2 cups mayonnaise
2 cups sour cream
5 cups potato chips, crushed

In a large mixing bowl, combine together, the first 6 ingredients; add 2 cups cheese. In a separate bowl, mix well, mayonnaise and sour cream. Add to chicken mixture; toss gently to mix. Spoon into 2 greased 13"x9"x3" baking dishes. Sprinkle with potato chips; top with remaining cheese. Bake, uncovered, at 350 degrees, for 20 to 25 minutes or until heated through. Yield 24 servings.

CHICKEN TURNOVERS FILLING (Yield about 30 turnovers)

2 tablespoons butter OR
    margarine
2 tablespoons onions, finely
    chopped
1½ cups chicken, cooked &
    shredded
1 pkg. (3 ozs.) cream cheese
¼ teaspoon salt
¼ teaspoon thyme
¼ teaspoon pepper
3 tablespoons chicken broth

PASTRY

1-1/3 cup all-purpose flour
½ teaspoon salt
½ teaspoon paprika
½ cup butter OR margarine
2 to 4 tablespoons water

In a skillet, melt butter; add
onion. Cook over medium
heat, until softened, about
5 minutes. Add remaining
filling ingredients. Continue
cooking, stirring occasionally,
until cream cheese is melted
and heated through, about
2 to 3 minutes; remove from
heat; set aside. In a medium
bowl, combine together, all dry
pastry ingredients. Cut in butter
until crumbly; add water; shape
into a ball. On a lightly floured
surface, roll dough to 1/16 inch
thick; cut with floured 2½ inch
round cookie cutter. Place 1
teaspoon filling on one half of

circle; fold other half over. Press
edges with fork to seal; place
on cookie sheets. Bake at 375
degrees, for 15 to 20 minutes, or
until golden brown.

CHICKEN STEW (with Dumplings)

2½ to 3 pounds chicken thighs
5 cups water
4 potatoes, peeled & cut in
    bite-size pieces
3 carrots, sliced
¼ cup celery, diced
1 medium onion, chopped
1 bag (10 ozs.) peas
½ teaspoon salt
Pinch of pepper

In a large saucepan, cook
chicken in water, until tender,
about 30 to 45 minutes.
Remove from heat, remove
chicken; set aside to cool.
Keep broth to cook vegetables,
while you debone chicken,
cut in pieces, add chicken
to vegetables; cook until
vegetables are tender.
Meanwhile prepare dumplings.

DUMPLINGS

1-1/2 cups all-purpose flour
2 teaspoons baking powder
¾ teaspoon salt
3 tablespoons butter OR
    margarine, softened
¾ cup milk
¼ cup fresh parsley, chopped

In a medium mixing bowl, combine together, all ingredients; mix well. Drop by rounded tablespoons, into hot stew. Cook uncovered, for 10 minutes, then cover, continue cooking until dumplings are done, for 8 to 10 minutes.

CHILI CON CARNE

1 pound ground beef
6 cups onions, chopped
¾ cup green pepper, chopped
1 can (16 ozs.) tomatoes,
    chopped
1 can (16 ozs.) kidney beans,
    drained
1 can (8 ozs.) tomato sauce
½ teaspoon salt
1 to 2 teaspoons chili powder
1 bay leaf

In a large skillet, brown meat, onion and green pepper until meat is lightly brown and vegetables are tender. Add remaining ingredients; cover, simmer for 1 hour. Re move bay leaf and serve. Yield about 4 servings.

SCRAPPLE

1 cup cornmeal
½ teaspoon salt
Dash of pepper
1 cup cold water
3 cups boiling water
½ pound pork sausage
2 teaspoons green onions,
    diced

In a small mixing bowl, combine cornmeal, salt, pepper and 1 cup cold water. In a large saucepan, bring to a boil, 3 cups water, when boiling, pour the cornmeal mixture into boiling water. Cook until thickened, stirring constantly. Reduce heat to low; cover; continue cooking about 5 minutes, stirring occasionally. Add pork sausage, that has been cooked, drained and crumbled; add onions; mixing well. Place mixture in a loaf pan; cool slightly; cover and refrigerate several hours or overnight.

TO SERVE: Cut into ½ inch slices; fry on lightly buttered skillet until golden brown, about 10 minutes on each side. Yield 6 servings.

HOME-STYLE POT ROAST

3 pounds boneless pot roast
2 tablespoons shortening
1 can of beef broth
2 medium onions, cut in quarters
½ teaspoon salt
Pinch of pepper
1 bay leaf
6 medium-size potatoes, cut in
   half
6 medium carrots, cut in 2"
   pieces
½ cup water
¼ cup all-purpose flour

In a large saucepan, brown meat on all sides in shortening; when meat is browned; pour off fat. Add broth, onions and seasonings; cover; cook over low heat for 2 hours. Add potatoes and carrots; cook for 1 hour more or until tender; stirring occasionally. Remove bay leaf. In a small bowl, gradually blend water into flour until smooth, then slowly stir into sauce; continue to cook, stirring often, until sauce has thickened. Yield 6 to 8 servings.

BEEF TURNOVERS

½ pound ground beef
1 tablespoon instant onion
   flakes
1 teaspoon Italian seasoning
½ teaspoon garlic salt
Pinch of pepper
1 can (4 ozs.) mushroom pieces,
   well drained
1 pkg. (11 ozs.) piecrust mix
1 large egg, lightly beaten

In a medium hot skillet, crumble ground beef, stir to brown lightly. Remove from heat; drain off fat; add seasonings and mushrooms; set aide or refrigerate until ready to use. Preheat oven to 400 degrees. Prepare piecrust according to package directions. On a floured surface, roll ½ of dough to 1/8 inch thickness. Take a 3 inch round cookie cutter or a glass; cut out circles. Refrigerate remaining dough. On half of each circle, place 1 teaspoon of meat mixture; brush edges with egg. Fold dough over filling; with fork press edges to seal. Place on lightly greased cookie sheet; brush with egg. Repeat with remaining dough and filling. Bake until golden brown, about 15 minutes. Yield about 36 turnovers.

SWEDISH MEATBALLS

1 pound ground beef
1/3 cup onions, chopped
½ cup bread crumbs
1 large egg
½ teaspoon salt
¼ teaspoon garlic powder
1 teaspoon Worcestershire
    Sauce
1 cup beef bouillon
1 cup sour cream

In a large bowl, combine together, the first 7 ingredients; mix well. Shape into balls; brown in medium skillet; pour bouillon over meatballs; over low heat. simmer for 20 minutes. Add sour cream; stir until well-mixed. Heat through, but do not boil, mixture may curdle. Serve over noodles or rice. Yield 6 servings.

VEAL PARMIGIANA

3 tablespoons butter OR
    margarine
½ cup cracker crumbs
¼ cup Parmesan Cheese,
    grated
½ teaspoon salt
Pinch of pepper
1 pound veal cutlets OR veal
    steak,
¼ inch thick
1 large egg, slightly beaten
1 can (8 ozs.) tomato sauce
½ teaspoon oregano, crushed
½ teaspoon granulated sugar
¼ teaspoon onion salt
2 thin slices mozzarella cheese,
    halved

In 10x6x1½ inch baking dish, melt butter; set aside. In a small bowl, combine together, crumbs, Parmesean cheese, salt and pepper; set aside. Cut veal into serving pieces; dip into egg. Roll in crumb mixture. Place in baking dish; bake at 400 degrees, for 20 minutes, turn over; bake, for 15 to 20 minutes longer or until tender. Meanwhile, combine together, tomato sauce, oregano, sugar and onion salt; over medium heat, bring to a boil, stirring frequently. Pour sauce over meat; top with mozzarella cheese. Return to oven for about 3 to 5 minutes or until cheese melts. Yield 4 servings.

STUFFED CABBAGE

1 pound ground beef
1 pound ground pork
2 medium onions, diced
2 large heads cabbage
1 cup rice, partially cooked
1 can (12 ozs.) tomato paste
2½ cups water
Salt and pepper to taste

Remove core from cabbages, then place whole cabbage in boiling water for 20 minutes; drain, and let cool. When cool, peel off leaves, one at a time; set aside. To prepare each leave for wrapping, cut off the thick rib at the base of the leave. Cook the rice about ½ the usual time, drain; and cool. In a large mixing bowl, combine together, the rice, meats, onions, salt and pepper; mix thoroughly. Place 1 to 2 tablespoons of the mixture in the center of a cabbage leaf. Fold the bottom of the leaf in first over the filling, then fold each side, over the middle, then roll to the top edge of the leaf to finish. Stack in a large roasting pan, seam side down. In a separate bowl, combine together, tomato paste and water. Sauce should have the consistency of soup. Pour over cabbage rolls; bake at 350 degrees, for 1½ hours, basting occasionally. Yield about 30 to 35 cabbage rolls.

PUMPKIN SLOPPY JOES

2 pounds ground beef
1 medium onion, finely chopped
1 cup ketchup
½ cup tomato juice
1 teaspoon chili powder
½ teaspoon salt
¼ teaspoon EACH ground cloves, nutmeg and black pepper
2 cups pumpkin, cooked
Hamburger buns, split

In a large skillet, over medium heat, cook meat and onion until meat is no longer pink; remove; drain grease. Add remaining ingredients, except pumpkin; mix well. Bring to a full boil; stir in pumpkin. Reduce heat; cover; simmer for about 15 minutes. Serve on buns. Yield 6 to 8 servings.

COUNTRY FRIED STEAK (with gravy)

1½ to 2 pounds round steak,
   1-inch thick
½ teaspoon salt
Dash of pepper
¼ to ½ cup all-purpose flour
2 tablespoons shortening
1 small onion, chopped
2 cups water

Cut steak into serving pieces, season with salt and pepper. Dredge with flour; brown in hot shortening; add onions Cook over medium heat until meat is browned on both sides. Remove meat; stir 2 tablespoons flour into drippings; add water to make gravy. Cover, simmer over low heat for 2 hours, or until tender. Yield 4 to 6 servings.

PORK CHOPS (with Mushroom Gravy)

½ cup all-purpose flour
1 teaspoon paprika
½ teaspoon salt
¼ teaspoon pepper
6 to 8 boneless pork chops, 1
   inch thick
¼ cup butter OR margarine
1 medium onion, chopped
½ cup green pepper, chopped
1 can (4 ozs.) mushrooms,
   drained
2 cups milk
2 tablespoons lemon juice
Hot, mashed potatoes

In a large plastic bag, combine together, flour, paprika, salt and pepper; shake to mix. Add chops, one at a time; toss to coat; set remaining flour mixture aside In a large skillet, sauté chops in butter until golden brown; then transfer to a 13x9x2 inch baking dish. In the same skillet, sauté the onions, green pepper and mushroom until tender. Stir in remaining flour mixture; gradually add milk, mix until blended. Bring mixture to a boil; cook for 5 minutes, or until thickened, stirring constantly. Remove from heat; stir in lemon juice; pour over chops; cover and bake at 350 degrees, for 50 to 60 minutes, or until meat is tested done. Serve with potatoes. Yield 6 to 8 servings.

CORN DOGS

1 cup all-purpose flour
¾ cup cornmeal
2 tablespoons granulated sugar
1 tablespoon dry mustard
2 teaspoons baking powder
½ teaspoon salt
1 cup milk
1 large egg, beaten
2 tablespoons shortening, melted
12 hot dogs
12 wooden skewers

In a tall container, combine together flour, cornmeal and sugar, mix well. Add. remaining ingredients; mix thoroughly until smooth. Place a wooden skewer in each hot dog; dip hot dog into batter; let excess drip off. Deep fry in hot shortening until golden brown. Yield 12 corn dogs

CHICKEN FRIED STEAK

1 large round steak, cut in
   serving-size pieces
1 large egg
1 tablespoon water
1 cup all-purpose flour, plus 2
   more tablespoons
Oil for frying
Salt and pepper to taste
1½ cups milk

In a medium bowl, combine together, egg and water; dip meat into egg mixture. Then dredge in the 1 cup flour,

shaking off excess. Heat ½-inch oil in a large skillet until hot. Brown meat on both sides. Season with salt and pepper. Lower heat, partially cover skillet. Simmer gently, for 15 minutes or until tender. Remove meat to a warm platter; set aside. In a small bowl, combine 2 tablespoons flour with milk; add to drippings in skillet; over low heat, stir until mixture thickens. Serve over steak.

HOMADE TURKEY SAUSAGE

1 pound turkey meat, cut in
   chunks
1½ teaspoon dried sage
1 teaspoon dried thyme
½ teaspoon salt
½ to ¾ teaspoon red pepper
   (optional)
½ teaspoon marjoram
¼ teaspoon garlic powder
Pinch of black pepper

Place all ingredients in blender or food processors; process until it is ground, as you desire. Make into patties; use immediately or can be frozen. Fry patties in large skillet with a little oil, on both sides, until lightly browned or tested done. Yield 4 to 5 patties.

CHICKEN FINGERS (with Honey Mustard Sauce)

4 skinless chicken breast (about 4 ozs, each)
1 cup all-purpose flour
½ teaspoon salt
¼ teaspoon pepper
¾ cup milk
1 cup vegetable oil for frying

Cut chicken into ½ x 2-inch strips. Mix flour, salt and pepper in a shallow bowl. Dip chicken in milk; roll in flour mixture to coat well. Place chicken on waxed paper. Pour ¼ inch oil into a large skillet; heat over medium-high heat. Place chicken in an even layer in hot oil. Fry, turning once, for about 5 minutes on each side or until golden brown and crisp. Drain on paper towels. Serve with Honey Mustard Sauce (Recipe below) Yield about 6 servings.

HONEY MUSTARD SAUCE

½ cup honey
¼ cup Dijon Mustard
In a small bowl, blend honey and mustard.

MUFFULETTA SANDWICH

Olive oil
3 slices baked ham, thinly sliced
3 slices Provolone cheese
6 slices Genoa-style salami
3 slices Swiss cheese
1 round loaf Italian bread, or use hoagie buns or sub rolls
¼ cup Olive Salad (recipe below)

Split bread, brush with olive oil. Alternate slices of meat and cheese on one side of bread. Top with Olive Salad; cover with other side of bread. Yield 2 to 3 servings.

OLIVE SALAD

½ cup pimiento-stuffed olives
½ cup black olives, chopped
½ cup celery, finely chopped
¼ cup carrots, finely chopped
¼ cup cauliflower, diced (optional)
1 tablespoon green pepper, chopped
1 tablespoon parsley, chopped
2 teaspoons garlic, minced
1 tablespoon onions, finely chopped
1 cup olive oil
1/3 cup vegetable oil
Pinch oregano and pepper

Mix all ingredients together in a quart jar. Refrigerate for about 1 hour

HERO SANDWICH

4 Italian loaves, 12 inches long
   OR
8 small Italian rolls, 6 inches long
Mayonnaise
About 2½ cups lettuce
Salt and pepper to taste
8 ounces pork lunch meat, sliced
8 ounces bologny
8 ounces Swiss cheese, sliced
2 medium tomatoes, sliced thin
8 paper-thin slices of onions

Green Pepper, cut in strips
(optional) Cut loaves
lengthwise; spread cut surfaces
with mayonnaise, layer
lettuce, lunch meats, cheese,
tomatoes, onions and green
pepper. Cut loaves in half
crosswise; serve with bottled
Italian dressing, if desired.

ROAST LEG OF LAMB

5 to 6 pounds leg of lamb
Salt
Butter
¼ cup currant or grape jelly
1/3 cup hot water
Garlic (optional)

Remove fell from meat (thin
paper-like coverings); rub meat
salt and butter. Cut several slits
in the leg; if desired, insert sliver
of garlic Place leg of lamb,
fat side up on rack in roasting
pan. Roast uncovered at 325
degrees, for 3 hours to 3½ or
well-done. During last hour,
baste with currant or grape jelly
mixed with hot water. Yield 5 to
6 servings.

SLOPPY JOE TURNOVERS

1 pound ground beef
¼ cup onions, chopped
½ cup ketchup
¼ cup sour cream
½ teaspoon salt
¼ teaspoon garlic powder
1 can (12 ozs.) refrigerated
   biscuits
2 tablespoons butter OR
   margarine (optional)

In a large skillet, over medium
heat, cook ground beef and
onions, until ground beef is
brown and crumbly. Drain in
a colander. Return ground
beef mixture to the skillet.
Add ketchup, sour cream, salt
and garlic powder; mix well.
Preheat oven to 375 degrees.
On a lightly floured surface, pat
or roll each biscuit into a 4-inch
square. Arrange biscuit squares
on an ungreased cookie sheet.
Spoon ¼ cup of beef mixture in
the center of each square. Fold
over the corner of each square
to form a triangle. Seal edges
with a fork; cut three ½ inch
slits in the top of each turnover.
Bake for 15 to 20 minutes, or
until golden brown. Remove
from oven, if desired, brush with
melted butter. Yield 5 servings.

HAM LOAF (with topping)

¾ pound ham, ground
¾ pound pork, ground
1/3 cup onions, chopped
1/3 cup dry bread crumbs
¼ cup milk
2 large eggs
1 tablespoon prepared mustard
1½ teaspoons parsley flakes
½ teaspoon pepper

TOPPING

¼ cup brown sugar, packed
4 tablespoons pineapple juice,
    divided
1 teaspoon prepared mustard

In a large mixing bowl,
combine together, all ham loaf
ingredients; mix thoroughly.
Place in a loaf pan; set aside. In
a small bowl, combine brown
sugar, 1 tablespoon pineapple
juice and mustard; mix well.
Spread evenly over ham loaf,
then sprinkle with remaining
pineapple juice on top. Yield 4
to 6 servings.

ALL KINDS OF MEAT FILLINGS!

HAM—1 cup ham, cooked &
ground

½ tablespoon onions, minced
½ teaspoon dry mustard
2 tablespoons mayonnaise—
    Mix well.

HAM AND CHEESE—½ boiled
ham, ground, ½ cup American
cheese, ground 2 tablespoons
sweet OR dill pickle, ½
teaspoon onions, minced and
mayonnaise to moisten; mix
well.

HAM SALAD—¾ cup cooked
ham, chopped 1 tablespoon
onion, chopped, 1 hard-boiled
large egg, chopped, ¼ cup
green pepper, chopped and ¼
cup mayonnaise; mix well.

BACON—7 slices bacon, crisp &
chopped, 1 pimiento, chopped
and ¼ cup mayonnaise; mix
well.

LAMB—1¼ cups lamb, cooked
& chopped, ½ teaspoon
salt, ¼ teaspoon pepper, ½
tablespoon onion, minced, 1
teaspoon mint leaves, minced
1 tablespoon lemon juice; mix
well

CHICKEN CACCIATORE

6 pieces chicken breast
1 medium onion, chopped
1 medium green pepper,
   chopped
Garlic powder to taste
1 small bottle of spaghetti
   sauce

In a large skillet, heat oil, over medium heat. Place chicken in hot oil; sprinkle garlic powder to desired taste; sauté until chicken is browned; add onions, green pepper and spaghetti sauce. Simmer for 25 minutes or until chicken is tender. Serve over rice, spaghetti or noodles. Yield about 6 servings.

CHICKEN PAPRIKAS (with Dumplings)

4 or 5 pound chicken, cut-up in
   serving size
1 onion, chopped
¼ cup shortening
Salt and pepper to taste
1 tablespoon paprika
1½ cups water
1 pint sour cream
Dumplings (see next recipe)

In a large skillet, sauté onions in shortening until tender. Add seasonings and paprika; mix well. Add chicken pieces; cook for 10 minutes; add water; cover; simmer slowly until tender. Remove chicken from skillet; keep warm Add sour cream into sauce; mix thoroughly. Add cooked dumplings, then arrange chicken on top of dumplings; heat through. Yield 4 to 6 servings.

CHICKEN PAPRIKAS DUMPLINGS

1-1/2 cups all-purpose flour
2 teaspoons baking powder
¾ teaspoon salt
3 tablespoons butter OR
margarine, softened
¾ cup milk
¼ cup fresh parsley, chopped

In a medium mixing bowl, combine together, all ingredients; mix well. Drop by rounded tablespoons, into hot stew. Cook uncovered, for 10 minutes, then cover, continue cooking until dumplings are done, for 8 to 10 minutes.

TEXAS HASH

2 large onions, sliced
2 green peppers, chopped
3 tablespoons shortening
1 pound ground beef
2 cups canned tomatoes
½ cup rice, uncooked
1 teaspoon chili powder
½ teaspoon salt
¼ teaspoon pepper

In a skillet, sauté onions and green peppers; add ground beef, cook until meat falls apart. Add remaining ingredients; mix well. Place mixture in a large casserole, cover; bake at 375 degrees, for 45 minutes. Yield 8 servings.

CREAMY CHICKEN FILLING

¼ cup butter OR margarine
1 cup fresh mushrooms
2 tablespoons green pepper, diced
¼ cup celery, chopped
¼ cup all-purpose flour
½ teaspoon salt
Dash of cayenne
1½ cup milk
1 cup chicken broth
2 cups chicken, cooked & cut in bite-size pieces
1 tablespoon parsley, chopped
1 tablespoon pimiento, diced
2 large egg yolks
2 teaspoons lemon juice

In a saucepan, melt butter; add mushrooms celery & green pepper, over medium heat, cook for 5 minutes. Combine together, flour, salt & cayenne; add to vegetables; cook for 5 minutes. Add milk, chicken broth, a little at a time. Add chicken, parsley and pimiento; cook until heated through. Add a little *hot mixture to egg yolks, then add yolks to the chicken mixture with lemon juice. Lower the heat, stirring until the mixture has thickened. Serve with toast or as you choose.

***NOTE:** Adding a little hot mixture to egg yolks will prevents eggs from curdling.

STUFFED PORK CHOPS

4 double pork chops
4 slices Swiss Cheese
1 jar (2½ ozs.) mushrooms
Salt and pepper to taste
2 tablespoons shortening
2 tablespoons all-purpose flour
2 cups water

Slit chops to bone, insert cheese and mushrooms; seal with toothpicks. Sprinkle with salt and pepper. In a large dry skillet, brown chops, then transfer to a casserole. Make gravy by combining, shortening, flour and water. Pour gravy over chops; cover; bake at 350 degrees, for 1 hour and 15 minutes. Uncover for the last 15 minutes.

CHICKEN LOAF

4½ tablespoon butter OR
   margarine
½ cup all-purpose flour
1 cup chicken broth
½ cup milk
1 tablespoon onions, chopped
2 tablespoons green pepper,
   chopped
3 cups soft bread crumbs
4 cups chicken, cooked &
   chopped
Salt to taste

In a bowl, combine together,
4 tablespoons butter, flour,
broth and milk; mix thoroughly;
set aside. In a skillet, add ½
tablespoon butter; cook onions
and green pepper until tender.
In a bowl, combine together,
the sauce, cooked vegetables,
bread crumbs and chicken; mix
well. Season to taste with salt.
Place mixture into a greased
loaf pan; bake at 350 degrees,
for 1 to 1½ hours or until loaf is
well-browned.

COUNTY FAIR HOT DOGS

2 packages hot dogs (20 count)
1 cup self-rising flour
1 teaspoon granulated sugar
1 teaspoon chili powder
½ teaspoon salt
1 to 1½ cup yellow cornmeal
1 tablespoon prepared mustard
2 large eggs, beaten
1¼ cups milk
Wooden skewers

In a large bowl, combine
together, flour, sugar, chili
powder, salt; and cornmeal;
set aside. In another bowl,
combine. mustard, eggs and
milk; mix well. Add to dry
ingredients; mix, but do not
over mix. Stick skewers in one
end of hot dog, leave room to
hold. Wipe hot dogs dry with
paper towels. Dip them into
batter (Note—Batter will stick
better if hot dogs are dry).
Let excess drip off, then deep
fry at 375 degrees, for about
3 minutes, turning to brown
evenly.

HOG JOWL & TURNIP GREENS

1½ to 2 pounds hog jowl
2 quarts turnip greens (tops)
1 teaspoon salt
½ teaspoon pepper

In a large saucepan, place
hog jowl, cover with water.
Bring to boiling over medium
heat. Cook about 40 minutes
or until meat is tender. Remove
meat and keep warm. Add
turnip greens and seasoning
to pan. of liquid; cover; cook
over low heat, for 30 minutes or
until turnip greens are tender.
Remove greens; drain. Cut
greens in serving pieces, then
place around hog jowl Serve
in bowls with pot liquor. Yield
about 4 servings.

BARBEQUE PORK CHOPS

12 pork chops
3 medium onions, sliced,
    separated in rings
2 cups tomato juice
2 tablespoons white vinegar
1 teaspoon dry mustard
1 tablespoon Worcestershire
    Sauce
½ cup onions, chopped
½ teaspoon chili powder
½ teaspoon salt
Dash of pepper

In a large skillet, brown pork chops on both sides. Arrange in a roaster or large casserole, then cover each chop with slice onion rings; set aside. Meanwhile, in a medium saucepan, combine together, all sauce ingredients. Over medium heat, bring sauce to a boil; reduce heat to simmer. Cook for 10 minutes, then remove from heat. Pour over pork chops; cover. Bake at 350 degrees, for 30 minutes, then remove cover And bake for 15 minutes more or until meat is tender. Yield about 6 servings.

CREAMED CHIPPED BEEF

1½ tablespoons butter OR
    margarine
1 green onion, including top,
    diced
2 ozs. dried beef. cut in pieces
1½ tablespoons all-purpose
    flour
¾ cup milk

Dash of hot pepper sauce (optional) In a medium saucepan, melt butter; add green onions. Cook over low heat, for 1 minute. Add dried beef; toss with fork until coated with butter. Add flour; mix thoroughly. Continue cooking over low heat, for about 5 minutes, stirring often. Remove from heat; add milk and pepper sauce; mix well. Return to heat, at medium heat, bring mixture to a boil. Reduce heat to simmer, cook for 5 minutes. If mixture is too thick, add a little more milk.

STUFFED PORK CHOPS

DRESSING

1 cup bread crumbs
¼ celery, chopped
¼ cup onions, chopped
Milk, enough to moisten dressing
2 tablespoons parsley
¼ teaspoon salt
Pinch of paprika
1 can of Cream of Mushroom
    Soup, with 1/3 can milk
6 rib OR loin chops, about ¾
    inch thick with a pocket cut
    & excess fat removed

Prepare dressing, then fill pockets (which your butcher should be glad to fill your order to slit pockets in the meat) with dressing; fasten pockets with toothpicks. In a large skillet, brown meat, then place in a 9x13 inch baking pan. Dilute soup with milk; cover chops with soup mixture. Cover the pan with foil; bake at 350 degrees, for 1 hour or until meat is tender. Yield 6 servings.

*CHICKEN CRUNCH CASSEROLE

2½ cups chicken, cooked & diced
3 cups potato chips, crushed
1 can Cream of Mushroom Soup, undiluted
1 cup milk
¼ cup sharp cheese, grated
Paprika

In a medium saucepan, combine together, cooked chicken, soup and milk, bring to a boil. Remove from heat; set aside. Spread 1½ cups crushed potato chips in the bottom of a greased 2-quart casserole. Pour chicken mixture, evenly, over the top of chips. Cover with remaining chips; sprinkle cheese and paprika over top. Bake at 350 degrees, for 25 to 30 minutes. Yield 6 servings.

*You may use turkey instead of chicken

HEARTY CHEESEBURGER (on the grill)

1 pound ground meat
¼ cup steak sauce (like A1)
¼ cup sweet pickle relish
1 medium onion, sliced
1 medium tomato, sliced
4 single cheese slices
4 bread rolls, split
Lettuce leafs

Shape meat into four ¼ inch thick patties. Mix 2 tablespoons steak sauce with relish; refrigerate. Grill patties and onions for 5 to 7 minutes on each side or until patties are cooked through and onions are tender; brushing occasionally with steak sauce. Top burgers with cheese singles, place in buns, top with relish mixture. Yield 4 servings.

PHILLY STEAK SANDWICH

4 tablespoons butter OR margarine
3 to 4 large onions, sliced
2 cans (8 ozs. each) sliced mushrooms
12 slices sandwich steak
6 slices American, Provoline OR Monteray Jack cheese
6 steak rolls
Toasted

In a large skillet, melt butter; add onions; cook until tender. Add mushrooms; cook until heated through. Remove vegetables from skillet, then fry steaks. Cut cheese slices in half; place on top of each steak. Cover, cook just until cheese melts slightly. Place 2 steaks on each roll. Spoon onions and mushrooms on top of cheese. Yield 6 servings.

REUBEN SANDWICH

1 cup sauerkraut, well-drained
¼ cup Thousand Island Salad
   Dressing
1 pound corned beef
16 slices rye bread
8 slices of Swiss Cheese
Butter OR margarine

Combine together, sauerkraut
and Dressing; mix well. Place
meat on 1 slice bread; spread 2
tablespoons sauerkraut mixture.
Top with cheese slice, then slice
of bread. Butter both sides of
bread; then grill until bread is
toasted and cheese is melted.
Yield 8 sandwiches.

CAPON (with Chestnut Stuffing)

6 or 7 pound capon
1 cup butter OR margarine
4 small onions, finely chopped
6 tablespoons celery, diced
1 pound *chestnuts, cooked,
   peeled
& coarsely chopped
8 cups day old bread, trimmed
& cubed
1 teaspoon salt
½ teaspoon pepper
½ cup parsley, chopped

In a small skillet, sauté onions
& celery in butter; cook for
5 minutes. Add mix to bread
cubes, along with remaining
ingredients. Toss lightly until
well-mixed. (If mixture is too dry,
add 2 or 3 tablespoons milk.)
Stuff capon's body & neck
cavities loosely, sew up & truss.
Place breast side up on rack
in shallow roasting pan. Rub
capon with butter or margarine;
add ½ cup water to pan. Cover
capon loosely with foil; roast at
325 degrees, for 3½ to 4 hours
or until tested done. Let capon
stand about 20 minutes before
carving.

NOTE: To cook chestnuts, slit
each twice on convex side with
sharp knife, place in boiling
water; boil for 20 minutes.
Remove a few chestnuts at a
time, with a slotted spoon; then
strip off shells and inner skins
while still hot.

HEADCHEESE

1 hog's head
1 hog's tongue
Salt and pepper

Clean and scrape hog's head;
wash thoroughly. Wash and
trim tongue. In a large kettle,
place head and tongue; cover
with slightly salted water. Over
medium heat, bring mixture to
simmer. Cook until meat falls
from bone. Remove from heat;
drain meat, then shred and
season with salt and pepper.
Pack tightly in a bowl, cover
and weigh it down. Let stand
for 3 days in a cold place. Yield
6 to 8 lbs.

SOME NOTES ON "TONGUE"

Tongue is sold fresh, pickled, corned or smoked. Wash tongue thoroughly, in warm water. Remove blood vessels and clotted blood from fresh tongue. Soak pickled or smoked tongue in water several hours before cooking.

FRESH TONGUE

Cover with water; add 1 teaspoon salt for each quart of water, in a saucepan. Over medium heat, simmer until tender. Allow 3 to 4 hours for a large tongue and 1 to 1½ hours, for pork, lamb or veal tongues.

PICKLED TONGUE

Cover tongue with cold water, in a saucepan, bring to a boil, over high heat. As soon as tongue boils; pour off water, then cover with fresh water, reduce heat to simmer, cook for 4 to 5 hours or until tender.

SMOKED TONGUE

In a saucepan, cover mild-cured tongue with cold water; heat to boiling, then reduce heat to simmer. Cook for 4 to 5 hours or until tender.

WILD GAME DRESSING RATTLESNAKES

Place dead rattlesnake on cutting board; hold firmly behind the head; cut off head and rattler; discard. Strip off skin; make a long slice on the underside; remove all organs. Cut snake into chunks; refrigerate until ready to use or can be frozen.

BREADED ALLIGATOR

Cut meat into bite-size strips; dip in flour, to coat, then dip into a mixture of 1 large egg and ¼ cup milk; mix thoroughly. Dip in seasoned bread crumbs. Pan fry or deep fry, at 350 degrees, for about 5 minutes or until golden brown,

SNAKES

Cut around the neck, then down the stomach to skin the snake. The skin pulls off very easy, the entrails, literally drop out, making the snake one of the easiest animals to clean. Cut into pieces, then parboil snake meat for about 20 minutes. Remove from heat; drain, then dredge in flour fry like chicken.

OVEN BARBEQUE RABBIT

1 rabbit, dressed, cut up
6 tablespoons butter OR
    margarine
Salt and pepper to taste
1 small onion, chopped
1 clove garlic, minced
2 tablespoons brown sugar
2 tablespoons Worcestershire
    Sauce
4 tablespoons ketchup
Few drops of liquid smoke
    (optional)

Melt butter in a large skillet; add rabbit; sauté for 20 minutes or until brown, on all sides. Transfer rabbit to a baking pan, salt and pepper to taste. Pour drippings from skillet over rabbit; set aside. Make sauce by combining remaining ingredients, then cover meat with sauce. Cover & bake at 350 degrees, for 25 minutes. Uncover; baste meat once more, then bake for 15 minutes more to brown.

TEXAS RATTLESNAKE CHILI

2 tablespoons vegetable oil
½ cup onions, chopped
½ cup green pepper, chopped
1 clove of garlic, minced
1 pound lean ground beef
1 cup rattlesnake meat, cubed
2 tablespoons chili powder
½ teaspoon salt
1 teaspoon cayenne pepper

3½ cups tomatoes OR 2 cans
    (14½ ozs.).
tomatoes, undrained
2/3 cup tomato paste OR 1 can
    tomato paste (6 ozs.)
2 cups water

In a large saucepan heat oil; add onions, green pepper and garlic until tender. Add meat, cool until tender, about 5 minutes. Stir in seasonings, tomatoes and tomato paste; bring to a boil, then reduce heat to low; simmer for 2 hours. Yield 6 servings.

ALLIGATOR STEW

2 tablespoons vegetable oil
4 cups alligator meat, cut in
small chunks
½ cup onions, chopped
½ cup green pepper, chopped
½ cup celery, chopped
2 tablespoons parsley, minced
1 can (10 ozs.) tomatoes
Salt and pepper to taste

Place oil and alligator in a large saucepan; add remaining ingredients. Cover; cook over medium heat for 35 to 40 minutes.

NOTE: Alligator is available year around in 4 cuts, tail, legs, torso and jaw. Use fresh alligator meat within two to three days of purchase; freeze up to one year.

ROAST PHEASANT

1 pheasant
1 quart boiling water
3 stalks celery
1 medium onion
½ teaspoon salt
Pinch of pepper
4 strips of bacon
1 cup water

Clean and cut up pheasant; place in pan. Pour boiling water over bird, plus into the cavity. Put celery stalk & onion into the cavity, do not close. Rub bird with salt and pepper. Place in roasting pan; arrange bacon strips over breast. Add 1 cup of water; roast in oven, with temperature at 350 degrees, bake until tested done.

WILD DUCK

1 wild duck
1 stalk celery,
½ of apple
1 small onion
3 strips of bacon
2 tablespoons bacon fat
Salt and pepper

Clean duck thoroughly, inside and out. Soak duck in strong salt water for 2 or 3 hours. Remove duck from water; dry thoroughly. In the cavity of the duck, put the celery stalk, ½ apple and onion. Season outside of duck with salt and pepper. With toothpicks, fasten the strips of bacon across the breast. Place duck, breast side down, in a large roasting pan, uncovered. Add bacon fat; roast duck at 375 degrees, bake until the duck sizzles and turns brown. Then put lid on; reduce temperature to 300 degrees. Baste every 20 minutes, continue roasting for 3 hours, during the last half hour, remove lid; turn duck on its back to brown.

GENERAL NOTE ABOUT RABBITS AND SQUIRRELS!

Skin and clean thoroughly, then cut into serving pieces. Rabbits and squirrels should be soaked in salt water to take away their gamey taste. Add some white vinegar to the brine, it will have a tenderizing effect on the meat. Squirrels or rabbits may be prepared by the same methods applied to chicken.

HINTS TO HELP TO PREPARE VENISON!

To clean the dressed meat, wipe down the venison with a (white) vinegar-soaked cloth. Do not use water because it tends to toughen the meat fibers, Vinegar will pick up hairs and clotted blood as well. Age the venison by hanging it in cold dry place. After aging of the meat, then cut into steaks & roasts. If you prefer less gamey flavor in your venison, soak in a brine as you would rabbits and squirrels. Use the ratio of 1 cup of (white) vinegar to 1 quart of brine; refrigerate for about 2 days. Remember to turn the meat every few hours, while soaking venison.

ROAST SQUIRREL

3 squirrels, skinned & cleaned
¼ cup lemon juice
½ cup milk
4 tablespoons onions, grated
Bacon fat
¼ cup vegetable oil
2 cups bread crumbs
1 cup mushrooms, sliced
   (sautéed in butter)
Salt and pepper to taste

In a large saucepan, combine together, oil with lemon juice; pour over squirrels. Let stand for 45 minutes; set aside. In a medium bowl, combine bread crumbs with milk to moisten.

Add sautéed mushrooms, onions, salt and pepper; mix well. Stuff squirrel; place in roaster; brush with bacon fat. Roast uncovered, at 325 degrees, for 1½ to 2 hours or until tender.

PAN FRIED RABBIT

3 pounds rabbit
1½ teaspoons seasoned salt
¼ teaspoon black pepper
¾ cup all-purpose flour
¼ cup margarine
1½ cups water
2 teaspoons instant chicken
   bouillon
3 tablespoons all-purpose flour
1 cup milk

Wash; dry meat and cut into serving pieces. at a time; shake to coat meat. Heat margarine in a large skillet; brown rabbit on both sides. Mix water and bouillon; add to skillet, about ½ cup, at a time, over a period of 1 hour. Simmer, covered, turning rabbit over as you add liquid. When rabbit is tender, remove from pan; keep warm; set aside. If liquid has cooked down to less than 1 cup, add enough water to make a cup. Mix the 3 tablespoons of flour with a little milk. Slowly add the milk mixture to the skillet, stirring constantly, to keep gravy from getting lumpy. Simmer and stir until smooth and thick Yield 4 servings.

BUFFALO CHILI

2 tablespoons chili powder
½ teaspoon hot pepper sauce
3 cloves garlic
1 bay leaf
1¾ cups beef stock
1 pound buffalo meat, cut into
1" chunks
1 tablespoon all-purpose flour
½ teaspoon dried oregano
½ teaspoon ground coriander
½ teaspoon ground cumin
Pinch of allspice
1 tablespoon vegetable oil

In a blender or food processor, place chili powder, garlic, bay lead and ¾ cup beef stock, blend until smooth. Add remaining stock; set aside. In a large bowl, combine together, buffalo meat, flour, and spices; toss well. In a large skillet, heat oil, then add buffalo mixture; sauté over medium heat until meat pieces are almost all brown. Add chili powder mixture; bring to a boil. Reduce heat; simmer for 30 minutes, or until meat is tender. If necessary, add more stock. Yield 4 servings.

MISC. BARBEQUE SAUCES

FOR HOT DOGS

2 tablespoons vegetable oil
½ cup celery, diced
½ cup green pepper, diced
½ medium onion, diced
½ cup chili sauce
Dash of tabasco
1 can (8 ozs.) tomato sauce

In a saucepan, combine together, oil celery, green pepper and onions, over medium heat, cook until lightly browned. Reduce heat to simmer; add remaining ingredients; cook for 5 minutes.

FOR PORK

1 tablespoon vegetable oil
½ cup green olives, chopped
Pinch of curry powder
2 teaspoons capers
1 can (8 ozs.) tomato sauce

In a saucepan, heat oil over low heat, sauté olives and capers, until lightly browned. Add remaining ingredients; simmer for 5 minutes.

MARINADE FOR GAME

2 cups dry red wine
2 tablespoons vegetable oil
1 teaspoon salt
½ teaspoon pepper
¼ teaspoon thyme leaves
2 medium onions, thinly sliced
1 clove garlic

In a large container, combine together, all ingredients. Add venison or other game; cover refrigerate overnight. Yield enough marinade for 5 pounds of meat.

SAUCE FOR GAME MEAT!

½ cup red currant jelly
¼ cup ketchup
¼ cup red wine
½ teaspoon Worcestershire
   Sauce

In a small saucepan, cook all the ingredients over low heat, stirring constantly, until mixture is smooth and jelly has melted. Serve with any game or wild birds. Yield 1 cup or enough for 8 servings.

LET'S GO FISHING . . . .

Since fat-free and low cholesterol are a big issue these days, fish is eaten more often. Fresh fish can be kept in the refrigerator, at 35 to 40 degrees, for one to two days before cooking. Fish, like chicken, if kept too long is highly susceptible to bacteria.

Prepared fish that is breaded can be stored for three to four days, in the refrigerator, and in the freezer for about three months.

Frozen raw fish can be kept in the freezer, at 0 degrees, in its' original wrapper up to six months, any longer, fish has the tendency to dry out.

When fish is breaded or topped with a sauce, keep in mind, that all white fish fillets, can be interchanged in recipes. If the recipe calls for cod, you can replace it with some of these fish, such as perch, halibut or whiting. These are just a few in the long list of white fish.

MARYLAND CRAB CAKES

1 pkg. (6 ozs.) crab meat.
   (if frozen, thaw)
2 large egg whites
2 tablespoons green onions,
   finely chopped
2 tablespoons mayonnaise
1 tablespoon fresh parsley.
   chopped
2 teaspoons Dijon-style mustard
2 teaspoons fresh thyme
½ teaspoon Worcestershire
   sauce
½ cup seasoned bread crumbs,
   divided
¼ cup cornmeal
2 tablespoons olive oil
Lemon wedges (optional)

In a mixing bowl, combine together, egg whites, onions, mayonnaise, parsley, mustard, thyme, Worcestershire sauce and ¼ cup bread crumbs; add crab meat; mix well. Shape into patties about ¾ inch thick. In another bowl, combine together, remaining crumbs & cornmeal. Dip each patty into mixture, then fry in olive oil, over medium heat, for about 3 minutes, on each side, or until golden brown. Serve with lemon wedges, if desired.

FRIED FISH (with 7-up batter)

6 fish fillets
1 cup pancake mix
1 large egg, slightly beaten
1 small bottle 7-up
Salt and pepper to taste
Shortening for frying

In a medium mixing bowl, combine together, pancake mix, egg and 7-up; mix well. Batter will be thin; set aside. Dredge fish in dry pancake mixture; let set for 20 minutes. Sprinkle with salt and pepper to taste; then dip in batter. Fry on each side until golden brown. Batter will puff up. Yield about 4 servings.

SIMPLE CHEESE SAUCE

1 can (10.5 ozs.) Cream of
    Mushroom Soup
¼ cup milk
4 ounces of cheddar cheese,
    grated

Combine together, all the above ingredients, in a small saucepan. Cook over low heat, stirring constantly, only until heated through and the cheese is melted. <u>Do not boil</u>.

COATING FOR FISH I

2 cups all-purpose flour
1 teaspoon paprika
2 teaspoons dried marjoram,
    crumbled
2 teaspoons dried thyme,
    crumbled
4 teaspoons onion powder
1 teaspoon dried rosemary,
    crumbled
1 teaspoon salt

In a medium mixing bowl, you can either crumble the herbs, or put in blender for a few seconds to blend well. Combine all ingredients together; mix well Will keep for 6 months. Enough to coat about 30 fish.

COATING FOR FISH II

2 cups all-purpose flour
2 teaspoons dried tarragon
1 teaspoon dill weed
2 teaspoons parsley flakes
2 teaspoons black pepper
2 teaspoons salt
2 teaspoons onion powder
1 teaspoon paprika

Use same directions as Fish Coating I, (above).

BEER-BATTERED FISH

½ cup buttermilk baking mix
½ cup all-purpose flour
½ teaspoon salt
¼ teaspoon black pepper
1 teaspoon paprika
1 cup *beer
1½ to 2 pounds fresh fish fillets
Flour for dredging
Oil for cooking

In a medium mixing bowl, combine together, the first six ingredients; mix well. Wash and dry fish fillets; remove all bones; dredge with flour. The flour will help the batter to stick to the fish better. Dip fish in batter; let excess batter drip from fish. Then deep fry in hot oil, a few pieces at a time, until golden brown. Test with a fork, if fish flakes easily, it is ready to serve. Actual time is determined by the thickness of fillets. Yield about 6 servings.

*COOKING WITH BEER

Beer is as versatile as cooking with wine, the biggest difference is the cost of cooking with beer. It is minimal compared to cooking with wine. When cooking with beer, it should be used at room temperature and it should be allowed to become flat, so that you can get an accurate measurement. A good way to insure flatness is to open the beer the day before you use it in a recipe.

COATING FOR FISH III

1 cup cracker crumbs, finely crushed
1 cup cornmeal
¼ garlic powder (more or less, as desired)
1 teaspoon celery seed
1 tablespoon paprika

Combine together all ingredients; mix well.

DEEP FRIED PERCH

1 pound Perch fillets, cut into 3" pieces
½ cup all-purpose flour
2 teaspoons baking powder
½ teaspoon salt
Pepper to taste
1 large egg, beaten
½ cup milk
Vegetable oil for deep frying

In a medium mixing bowl, sift together, all dry ingredients. Add egg and milk; mix well. Dip fish pieces into batter; deep fry until golden brown. Drain on paper towels. Yield about 4 servings.

CHEESE-TOPPED CATFISH

2 tablespoons mayonnaise
2 teaspoons milk
1 teaspoon honey
¼ teaspoon cayenne pepper
1 large egg white, at room
　temperature
½ cup cheddar cheese,
　shredded
6 catfish fillets (about 4 ounces
　each)
Vegetable cooking spray

In a small mixing bowl,
combine together, the first
4 ingredients; mix well; set
aside. In another bowl beat
egg white, at high speed of
an electric mixer, until stiff
peaks form. Fold egg white
into mayonnaise mixture; fold
in cheese. Place fish fillets on
a rack of a broiler pan coated
with vegetable cooking spray.
Broil 6 inches from heat for 10
to 12 minutes, or until fish flakes
easily when tested with a fork.
Spread egg white mixture over
fillets; broil 3 minutes more, or
until lightly browned. Yield 6
servings.

EASY TUNA CASSEROLE

1 pkg. (1 lb.) Tator Tots
1 can Cream of Mushroom
　Soup
1/3 soup can of milk
2 tablespoons dry onions,
　minced
1 can (6 ozs.) tuna fish
Cheddar cheese, grated

Place tator tots in a glass
baking dish. In a mixing bowl,
combine together, soup, milk,
onions and tuna; mix well. Pour
soup mixture over tator tots;
top with desired amount of
cheddar cheese. Bake at 350
degrees, for 25 minutes. Yield
about 4 servings.

LEMON BATTER

¼ cup lemon juice
1 cup all-purpose flour
½ cup cornstarch
Salt to taste
1¼ cup cold water
6 fish fillets
Flour for dredging

In a medium mixing bowl,
with a wire whisk, combine
together all ingredients. Whisk
ingredients thoroughly. Place
covered bowl in the refrigerator
for about 1 hour. Meanwhile,
dredge the fillets in flour When
batter is chilled dip fish fillets in
batter. Deep fry in hot cooking
oil until brown on both sides.
Drain on paper towels. Yield
about 2 cups batter.

LOBSTER FRITTERS

1½ cups all-purpose flour
2 teaspoons baking powder
¼ teaspoon salt
¼ teaspoon paprika
1 large egg, beaten
¾ cup milk
1½ cups lobster meat, cooked & ground

In a medium bowl, sift together, dry ingredients. In another bowl, combine egg, milk & lobster meat; mix well, then add to dry ingredients; mix thoroughly. Drop by spoonfuls into hot oil; fry until brown for 3 to 5 minutes. Yield about 4 servings.

HUSH PUPPIES

1 cup raw potatoes, grated
1 cup onions, grated
2 cups cornmeal
1 cup all-purpose flour
1 cup buttermilk
2 teaspoons baking powder

In a medium mixing bowl, combine all ingredients together; mix thoroughly. Drop by teaspoon into hot skillet with grease. Fry on both sides until golden brown. Drain on paper towels.

LOBSTER ORLEANS

2 medium onions, diced
2 tablespoon butter OR margarine

1 cup lobster meat, cooked & flaked
Flour
1 cup sour cream
Salt and pepper to taste

In a skillet, brown onions in butter. Dredge lobster meat in flour; add to onions. Cook for about 5 minutes, but do not brown. then put cream over lobster; simmer for 15 to 20 minutes; season to taste; serve on toast. Yield about 4 servings.

FISH CAKES

2 cups fresh OR canned fish
½ cup cracker crumbs, finely crushed
1 large egg
1 tablespoon lemon juice
½ teaspoon seasoned salt
¼ teaspoon pepper
¼ teaspoon dill weed
Milk
2 to 4 tablespoon margarine

In a medium mixing bowl, combine together, the first seven ingredients. If using fresh fish, put through food processor or blender, grind before mixing with other ingredients. Add enough milk to hold fish mixture together; shape into patties. Heat 2 tablespoons of margarine in a medium-size skillet. Fry patties until browned on both sides; add more margarine as needed. Yield about 2 servings.

LEMON SAUCE

½ cup butter OR margarine
¼ cup lemon juice
½ cup almonds, slivered

In a small saucepan, melt
butter; add lemon juice and
almonds. When butter has
melted and sauce is heated
through, pour over prepared
fish. Yield about ¾ cup sauce.

GRILLED MACKEREL

2 - 1 pound mackerel, boned
    and split in half, plus melted
    butter for grill
½ cup butter OR margarine,
    softened
1 tablespoon Dijon Mustard
1 teaspoon lemon juice
Salt and Pepper to taste

Grease broiler rack with melted
butter. Place mackerel, skin
side down. Brush fish with
melted butter; broil about 2"
from heat for 6 minutes. In the
meantime, in a small mixing
bowl, combine together
remaining ingredients. Remove
fish from grill; place on platter
and serve with favorite

RAINBOW TROUT (with pecans)

5 tablespoons butter OR
    margarine, softened
½ cup pecans, chopped
2 tablespoons onions, minced

1 teaspoon lemon juice
Dash of pepper sauce
Salt and pepper to taste
½ cup dry bread crumbs
1¼ pounds trout fillets

Place 4 tablespoons of butter,
pecans, onions, lemon juice
and pepper sauce in a blender
or food processor. Process
or blend until well mixed; set
aside. In a medium mixing
bowl, combine together, bread
crumbs, salt and pepper.
Dredge fillets in bread crumbs.
Melt remaining butter in a large
skillet; place fillets in a single
layer. Over medium heat, fry
for 2 minutes on each side, or
until browned. Transfer fillets
to plates; top each fillet with
2 spoonfuls of pecan mixture.
Yield 4 servings.

HOMEMADE TARTAR SAUCE I

1½ cups salad dressing (i.e.
    Miracle Whip)
¼ cup sweet relish, undrained
    (or to taste)
2 tablespoons onions, minced

In a medium mixing bowl,
combine together, all
ingredients; mix well. Put in a
glass jar, with lid; refrigerate for
one to two hours before using.
Yield about 1¾ cups sauce.

HOMEMADE TARTAR SAUCE II

1 cup mayonnaise
¼ cup sweet pickle relish
1 teaspoon granulated sugar
1 tablespoon onion, minced
½ teaspoon prepared mustard

In a small mixing bowl, combine together, all ingredients; mix thoroughly. Yield 1½ cups.

RICE STUFFING FOR FISH

1½ cups rice, cooked
½ cup onions, chopped
1 stalk celery, chopped
¼ cup mushrooms, sliced
2 tablespoons butter OR margarine
1 teaspoon garlic powder
Salt and pepper to taste
¼ cup white wine

In a medium mixing bowl, combine together, all the ingredients; mix well. Stuff the whole fish; wrap in foil; grill until fish is cooked. Turn over after 30 minutes.

HOMEMADE SEAFOOD SAUCE

1 cup ketchup
3 tablespoons lemon juice
1 tablespoon prepared horseradish
3 drops hot pepper sauce
½ teaspoon celery salt

In a mixing bowl, combine together, all ingredients; blend thoroughly. Put in a glass jar with lid; refrigerate for one to two hours before using. Yield about 1¾ cups sauce.

SAVORY STUFFING (for fish)

2 teaspoons butter OR margarine
¼ cup carrots, shredded
¼ cup celery, chopped
2 tablespoons onions, finely chopped
1 teaspoon lemon peel, grated
¼ teaspoon salt
Pinch of dried thyme
Dash of pepper
3 tablespoons water
2 cups bread crumbs, soft

In a skillet, melt butter; add carrots, celery and onions. Over medium heat, cook until tender, about 5 minutes. Remove from heat; add remaining ingredients; mix well.

FRIED SHARK

1 pound shark fillets
1 cup all-purpose flour
1 large egg, beaten
Salt and pepper to taste
1 tablespoon dried parsley
1 cup bread crumbs
½ cup butter OR margarine
Lemon wedges (optional)

In a small mixing bowl, combine together, egg, salt and pepper; set aside. In another bowl, combine bread crumbs and parsley; set aside. Dredge each fillet in flour, next dip in egg mixture, then roll in bread crumbs. In a large skillet, melt butter; fry fillets until browned, on both sides. If desired, serve with lemon wedges. Yield 3 to 4 servings.

HONEY MUSTARD SWORDFISH

4 swordfish fillets
½ cup honey
2 teaspoons prepared mustard
½ cup brown sugar, packed

In a small mixing bowl, combine together, honey, mustard and brown sugar; mix well. Spread on swordfish steaks; let marinade for at least 2 hours. You can, broil or bake on a slightly greased baking pan, or grill until fish flakes easily. Yield 4 servings.

SALMON LOAF

1 can (14¾ ozs.) salmon
1 cup milk, scalded
1 cup dry bread crumbs
Salt to taste (optional)
1 tablespoon butter OR
   margarine
1 tablespoon dried onion flakes
½ cup fresh mushrooms, sliced
1 tablespoon dried parsley
   flakes
2 large egg yolks, beaten
1 teaspoon lemon juice
2 large egg whites, beaten
Bread crumbs

Remove skin and bones from salmon; discard. Place milk in a medium saucepan, (rinse pan first in cold water), this procedure keeps the milk from sticking to the pan. Over medium heat, scald milk (bring to a boil), but be careful so milk does not boil over. As soon as milk boils, remove from heat; add bread crumbs, salt and butter; mix well. Add salmon, onion flakes, mushrooms, parsley flakes, egg yolks and lemon juice; blend together. Fold in beaten egg whites; place mixture into a loaf pan. Top with bread crumbs, bake at 375 degrees, for 45 to 55 minutes, or until tested done. Yield about 4 to 6 servings.

TUNA FISH PATTIES

1 slice *white bread
1 large egg, beaten
1 can (6 ozs.) tuna fish
½ cup onions, diced
*You can use ¾ cup cracker
   crumbs
in place of white bread.

Soak bread in beaten egg, then combine with tuna fish and onions; mix well. Divide into 4 medium-sized patties. Fry patties in large skillet, with a little vegetable oil. Brown on both sides; drain patties on paper towels. Serve hot. Yield 4 servings.

SALMON PATTIES

1 can (16 ozs.) pink salmon
1½ teaspoons baking powder
1 large egg
1/3 cup onions, chopped
½ cup all-purpose flour
Shortening for frying
Drain salmon, reserving liquid.

Remove skin, bones and discard. Add baking powder to 2 tablespoons of reserved liquid; set aside. In a medium mixing bowl, combine together, salmon, remaining liquid, egg and onions; add flour; mix well. Combine baking powder mixture with salmon mixture; mix thoroughly. Form into patties; fry in shortening until brown, on both sides.

FISH HASH

3 tablespoons butter
1 large onion, chopped
3 cups potatoes, cooked &
   diced
2 cups fish filets, cooked &
   flaked
2 tablespoons parsley
1 teaspoon Worcestershire
   Sauce
1 teaspoon horseradish
½ teaspoon dried dillweed
Few dashes of Tabasco Sauce
Salt and pepper to taste
1/3 cup heavy cream

In a medium skillet, over medium heat, melt butter. Add onion; sauté' until tender. Add potatoes; cook for 5 minutes, then add flaked fish; mix well. Add remaining ingredients; mix thoroughly. Pour cream over fish mixture; cook until hash is crusty on the bottom. Remove from heat; serve. You can serve as a luncheon or light supper and with tomato relish, chili sauce, a tossed salad or for breakfast or brunch with muffins and fresh fruit. Yield 6 servings

MUSTARD SAUCE

½ cup mayonnaise
2 tablespoons Dijon Mustard
¼ to ½ teaspoon dry mustard
  (or to taste)
3 tablespoons milk

In a small mixing bowl, beat all ingredients together; serve with fish. Yield 4 servings.

OYSTER STIR-FRY

1 tablespoon cornstarch &
  water
1½ tablespoons vegetable oil
1 clove garlic, minced
2 tablespoons green onions,
  chopped
1 tablespoon fresh ginger,
  peeled & minced
¾ pound oysters, shucked &
  drained
1/3 cup orange juice
2 tablespoons soy sauce

In a small bowl, mix cornstarch and 1 tablespoon water; set aside. In a skillet, heat oil; add garlic, onion and ginger; stir-fry for about 1 minute. Add oysters, orange juice and soy sauce; stir-fry for an additional 30 seconds. Add cornstarch mixture; cook until sauce thickens, about 1 minute more. Serve immediately with rice. Yield about 4 servings.

CATFISH CHOWDER

Large firm catfish bones
5 cups water
1 teaspoon salt
4 medium potatoes, diced
1 can (16 ozs.) tomatoes, diced
2 onions, diced
¼ teaspoon pepper
2 pounds catfish fillets, diced
1 tablespoon lemon juice
1 tablespoon fresh parsley

In a large saucepan, combine together, catfish bones, water and salt. Bring to a boil, then reduce heat; simmer for 10 minutes. Remove and discard bones. Add potatoes, tomatoes, onions and pepper to saucepan. Bring to a boil; reduce heat to simmer, until potatoes are tender. Add fish and cook until it flakes. Add lemon juice and parsley just before serving.

SALMON TOSS SALAD

½ cup mayonnaise
Pinch of chili powder
Pinch of curry powder
Pinch of coriander
3 tablespoons lemon juice
1 can salmon, drained
½ cup green bell pepper,
    chopped
¼ cup green onions, sliced
½ cup *almonds, slivered
2 apples, peeled, cored &
    cubed
Lettuce OR spinach leaves
*OR pecans, chopped

In a small mixing bowl,
combine together, mayonnaise
and spices; mix thoroughly.
Add 1 tablespoon of lemon
juice; set aside. Drain salmon,
skin, and remove bones; flake
salmon. In another bowl,
combine salmon, bell pepper,
green onions and nuts. Peel,
core cube 1 apple, place
in a separate bowl; sprinkle
with remaining lemon juice.
Pour mayonnaise mixture
over salmon mixture, add
apple cubes; mix thoroughly.
Refrigerate at least 2 hours.
Serve on a bed of lettuce or
spinach leaves. Garnish with
slices of the remaining apple.

CAJUN-STYLE CATFISH

1 tablespoon paprika
1 teaspoon salt
¾ teaspoon pepper
1 teaspoon onion powder
½ teaspoon dried thyme leaves
1 teaspoon garlic powder
½ teaspoon marjoram
6 catfish fillets
½ pound butter OR margarine,
    melted
6 tablespoons butter OR
    margarine
Lemon wedges

Get grill ready; meanwhile, in
a small mixing bowl, combine
all seasoning ingredients; mix
thoroughly. Dip fillets in melted
butter, then sprinkle evenly
with seasoning mix on both
sides. Place each fillet on an
18x18 inch section of heavy
duty-aluminum foil. Add 1
tablespoon butter to top of
each fillet; wrap in foil. When
grill coals are white hot, place
wrapped fish on the grill, about
6 inches above the heat. Cook
for 10 to 15 minutes or until fish
flakes easily. If desired, serve
with lemon wedges.

CRAWFISH PIE

Pie crust for double 9-inch pie
1 medium onion
3 stalks celery
6 cloves garlic
1 can (12 ozs.) evaporated milk
1 can Cream of Mushroom Soup
1 pound crawfish tails
5 tablespoons cornstarch

Preheat oven to 350 degrees. In a large skillet, sauté onion, celery and garlic, in butter. Add milk and soup to skillet; bring to boil, add crawfish. Bring to a boil again, add cornstarch; mix. Lower heat; cook for 10 minutes more, or until thoroughly thickens. Place crawfish mixture in prepared pie crust; dot with butter. Top with crust, seal edges; with a knife put slits on top, to allow air to escape while baking. Bake for 20 minutes, or until tested done. Yield 6 to 8 servings

CRAB CAKES

1 pound crab meat
1 tablespoon prepared mustard
2 cups cracker crumbs
2 large eggs, beaten
6 dashes hot sauce (optional)
½ cup onions, finely chopped
¼ cup mayonnaise
Salt and pepper to taste
Dash of Worcestershire Sauce

In a large mixing bowl, combine together, all ingredients EXCEPT 1 cup cracker crumbs; mix well. Make into patties, 3 inches in diameter. Bread with remaining cracker crumbs. In a skillet, fry patties in hot oil, over low heat, until brown on both sides. Yield about 10 patties at 3 inches in diameter.

BASIC MICROWAVE COOKING FOR FISH

1. Allow 3 minutes cooking time, on high, for every pound of fish.
2. Since seconds make a difference in microwave cooking, it is important to check cooking progress before the end of designated time.
3. To tell if the fish is done, test with fork, if it flakes easily, then the fish is done.
4. In preparing seafood in dishes, cover with plastic wrap, leaving one corner turned back to allow steam to escape. Recipes requiring a bread or crumb coating should be cooked uncovered or lightly covered with a paper towel to prevent sogginess and spattering.
5. Rotate the dish during cooking to insure even heat distribution.
6. Seafood can be baked, broiled, poached or steamed, but frying is not recommended.
7. The last suggestion is, since seafood cooks much faster than other meals, you should prepare seafood item last in your meal preparation.

CATFISH, (with Black Walnut Crust & Maple Sauce)

4 catfish fillets, about ½ inch thick (about 1½ pounds)
Salt and pepper to taste
¼ cup milk
1 large egg
2 cups cornflakes, finely crushed
¼ cup black walnuts, finely chopped
1 tablespoon butter OR margarine
¼ cup maple syrup
¼ cup butter OR margarine, softened

Rinse fish, pat dry with paper towels. Season with salt and pepper. In a shallow dish, beat together, milk and egg with a fork; set aside. In another shallow dish, combine together cornflakes and walnuts. Dip fish fillets in milk mixture, then dip in mixture, turning to coat evenly. In a large skillet, melt the 1 tablespoon butter, over medium heat. Cook fish, half at a time, in hot butter, for 4 to 6 minutes per ½ inch thickness of fillet or until golden, turning once. If necessary, reduce heat to prevent overbrowning.

FOR MAPLE SAUCE—In a small saucepan, bring maple syrup to boiling, over medium heat. Remove from heat; add butter; mix until well-combined.

TO BAKE FISH—Bake, uncovered, at 450 degrees, for 4 to 6 minutes, or until fish flakes easily. Yield 4 servings.

TUNA STEAK FRY

4 tuna steaks, ¾ inch thick
½ cup all-purpose flour
1 tablespoon curry powder
Salt and pepper to taste
2 tablespoons oil (for marinade)
1 tablespoon ginger root, grated
8 scallions, finely chopped
1 clove garlic, chopped
¼ teaspoon tabasco sauce

Marinade tuna steaks, by mixing oil, ginger, scallions, garlic and tabasco sauce, together, for at least 1 hour. In a mixing bowl, combine together, remaining ingredients; mix well; Dredge tuna steaks in flour mixture. In a large skillet, with a little walnut oil, over medium heat, place steaks' cook for 3 to 4 minutes, turn over and cook other side until golden brown, or tested done. Yield 4 servings.

*WALLEYE HASH

2 tablespoons butter OR
   margarine
3 small potatoes, partially
   cooked, peeled & thinly
   sliced
½ cup onions, chopped
½ cup red bell pepper, diced
Salt and pepper to taste
1 cup walleye, cooked, flaked
   or diced
¼ cup cilantro, chopped

In a large skillet, melt butter;
add potatoes, onions and
peppers. Season with salt and
pepper to taste. Cook over
medium heat until onions are
tender. Continue cooking,
pressing down with spatula
to create a layer that holds
together. Top with diced or
flaked walleye, then using a
large spatula flip mixture over;
cook for 2 minutes or until
tested done. Yield 2 servings

*NOTE: Can use chicken or
other meat in place of fish.`

BASIC COOKING METHODS FOR FISH

1) BAKING—To keep moist,
cover with sauce or melted
butter or margarine (if counting
calories add 3 tablespoons
water, cover with foil and bake
at 350 degrees, for 30 minutes,
or until fish flakes easily

2) BROILING—Fish should be at
least 1 inch thick; place fish 3 to
4 inches below heat; broil until
fish flakes easily. Baste fish and
flour in a plastic bag. Add a
few pieces of basting sauce to
keep moist

3) GRILL—Fish should be at
least 1 inch thick; place about
4 inches from moderately hot
coals. Baste often to keep moist.
When done fish will flake easily

4) FRYING Dredge fish lightly in
flour; fry in oil (if using an electric
skillet, set temperature about
350 degrees; cook 2 to 3 minutes
per side, or until fish is browned.

OVEN FRIED SNAPPER

2 pounds snapper fillets
½ cup vegetable oil
1 teaspoon salt
2 to 3 cloves garlic, minced
1 cup Parmesan Cheese
1 cup dry bread crumbs

Rinse fish with cold water; pat
dry with paper towels. Cut fish
in 6 equal size servings. In s
glass baking dish, combine oil,
salt and garlic. Place fish in oil
mixture, making sure both sides
of are moistened with mixture;
let marinade for 20 minutes.
Remove fish; roll in Parmesan
Cheese, then in bread crumbs.
Place on a well-greased cookie
sheet. Bake at 400 degrees
for 12 to 15 minutes or until fish
flakes easy. Yield 6 servings.

STUFFED WALLEYE

4 walleye fillets (about 6 ozs. each)
4 bacon strips, halved
¼ cup onions, chopped
2 stalks celery, finely chopped
1 can (6 ozs.) crabmeat, drained, flaked & cartilage removed
¼ cup butter OR margarine
4 cups seasoned stiffing, crushed
1½ cups boiling water
½ teaspoon salt
Pinch teaspoon pepper
Pinch teaspoon cayenne pepper

In a large skillet, cook bacon over medium heat, for 3 to 5 minutes or until crisp; drain on paper towels. In the same skillet, sauté onions, celery and crab meat in butter, until vegetables are tender. Transfer to a large mixing bowl; add crushed stuffing, water and spices; toss to moisten. Place fillets in a greased 15x10x1 inch baking pan Spoon stuffing mixture over fillets; top each fillet with 2 pieces of bacon. Bake, uncovered, at 425 degrees, for 20 to 25 minutes or until fish flakes easily with a fork. Yield 4 servings.

SNAKE RIVER TROUT

6 whole trout, filleted
Juice of 1 lemon
Salt and pepper to taste
5 large egg whites, at room temperature
1 1/3 cups mayonnaise
1 1/3 cups Monterey Jack cheese
½ cup green onions, chopped
¼ teaspoon garlic powder
4 medium onions
¼ cup fresh parsley, minced
2 tablespoons dill
½ teaspoon cayenne pepper

Divide fillets in half; place in well-greased broiling pan. Sprinkle with lemon juice, salt and pepper. Broil on each side until fish begins to flake. In a medium mixing bowl, beat egg whites until stiff. Fold in mayonnaise and remaining ingredients. Spread generously on each fillet; broil again until lightly browned. Place fillets on a serving platter; garnish with fresh parsley sprigs.

FISH FRY ON THE GRILL FOR 12 PERSONS

8 pounds assorted fish & seafood
SUCH AS:
2 pounds shrimp
1 pound scallops
2 pounds haddock OR scrod
2 pounds bass
1 pound trout
4 tomatoes
4 medium onions
3 lemons
½ pound margarine
1 teaspoon seasoned salt
2 teaspoons garlic powder
1 teaspoon celery salt
2 tablespoons paprika

Prepare fish, by removing the skin; prepare vegetables by slicing tomatoes and onions; set aside. Next make a shallow tray out of foil to fit grill rack, triple thick. Arrange shrimp, single layer, in the center of foil tray. Make a circle of assorted fish around the shrimp. Scatter scallops over fish; place tomatoes and onions around the top of the fish. Squeeze lemon juice over the top. Sprinkle evenly with salts, garlic powder and paprika; cover with additional foil; grill for 25 minutes, or until tested done. Serves 12.

SIMPLE BAKED FISH

Clean amount of fish desired; sprinkle with salt and pepper. Put strips of bacon over each fish. Bake at 350 degrees F., for 25 to 35 minutes, or until fish flakes easily. Serve with butter or margarine and lemon juice.

BARBEQUE FISH

1½ pounds fish fillets.
1/3 cup vegetable oil
½ cup onions, diced
Salt and pepper to taste
2 tablespoons lemon juice
1 tablespoon honey
1 tablespoon Worcestershire
   Sauce
¼ cup water

Heat oil in large frying skillet; sauté onions until golden brown. Remove onions; cut fillets into serving size pieces. Fry both until lightly browned; spread cooked onions over fish. Season fish with salt and pepper to taste. In a small bowl, combine together, the remaining ingredients; pour over fish. Cover skillet; simmer over medium heat for 10 minutes. Yield about 3 to 4 servings.

TUNA TURNOVERS

2 cans tuna fish, water packed, drained
½ cup Cheddar cheese, shredded
1/3 cup mayonnaise OR salad dressing
¼ cup onions, chopped
¼ cup celery, chopped
1 can Pillsbry Grands Refrigerated Biscuits
1 large egg, beaten

Preheat oven to 350 degrees. In a medium bowl, combine together, tuna, cheese, mayonnaise, onion and celery; mix well; set aside. Separate biscuits; roll each one into a 6-inch circle. Spoon about ¼ cup tuna mixture onto the center of each biscuit. Fold dough in half over the filling; press edges with a fork to seal. Make 2 or 3 half inch cuts on each top. Brush each top with beaten egg, then place on ungreased cookie sheet. Bake for about 20 minutes or until golden brown. Serve immediately. Yield 8 turnovers.

FISH STUFFING

½ cup onions, chopped
4 tablespoons butter
½ cup mushrooms, sliced
2 cups dried bread crumbs
1 tablespoon tarragon OR dill weed
1 teaspoon lemon rind, grated
Fish or chicken stock
1 whole fish, prepared & ready to stuff
Thin sliced bacon

In a medium-sized bowl, mix together, onion, butter, mushrooms, bread crumbs, tarragon and lemon rind. Add enough stock to moisten bread crumbs. Place fish on baking pan, stuff fish; place bacon slices on top of fish. Bake at 425 degrees, for 10 minutes for each inch of the depth of fish.

SHRIMP CREOLE

1 cup onions, sliced
½ cup celery, diced
1 clove garlic, minced
3 tablespoons butter OR margarine
1 teaspoon granulated sugar
½ teaspoon salt
1 tablespoon all-purpose flour
2 teaspoons chili powder (or more to taste)
1 cup water
2 cups tomatoes
1 tablespoon vinegar
2 cups shrimp

In a medium skillet, sauté onions, celery and garlic in butter for 10 minutes. Add sugar, flour, salt, chili powder and water; simmer uncovered for 15 minu8tes, or until heated through. Serve over cooked rice. Yield about 5 servings.

BAKED, NOT FRIED FISH

1 pound walleye, perch OR
   pike fillets
¼ cup milk
1 cup potato chips, crushed
¼ cup Parmesan Cheese,
   grated
¼ teaspoon dried thyme
1 tablespoon dry bread crumbs
2 tablespoons butter OR
   margarine, melted

Prepare fish by cutting fish
into serving size pieces. Place
milk in a small mixing bowl.
In another bowl, combine
together, potato chips,
Parmesan Cheese and thyme;
mix well. Dip fish in milk, then
coat with potato chip mixture.
In a greased 8" square baking
pan, sprinkle evenly with bread
crumbs. Place fish over crumbs;
drizzle fish with butter. Bake
uncovered, at 500 degrees,
for 12 to 15 minutes or until fish
flakes easily with a fork.
Yield 4 servings.

FISH STOCK

2 pounds white fish
1¼ quarts cold water
2 peppercorns
1 clove garlic
Sprig of parsley
1 bay leaf
1 tablespoon carrots, diced
1 tablespoon celery, diced
1 tablespoons onion, diced

Prepare fish by cutting fish into
small pieces. Combine fish
and remaining ingredients in
a large saucepan. Over low
heat, simmer for 1 to 2 hours.
Strain stock through several
thicknesses of cheesecloth.
Reheat to serve hot or use
as stock in soup, chowder or
creamed mixtures. It enhances
the flavor. Yield 1 quart stock.

FRIED CATFISH

4 catfish fillets
¾ cup yellow cornmeal
¼ cup all-purpose flour
2 teaspoon salt
1 teaspoon cayenne pepper
¼ teaspoon garlic powder
Vegetable oil

In a medium bowl, combine
together, cornmeal, flour, salt,
cayenne pepper and garlic
powder; mix well. Coat catfish
with mixture, shaking off excess.
In a large skillet, fill half-full with
vegetable oil. Add catfish in
single layer; fry until golden
brown, about 5 to 6 minutes,
depending on size. Remove
from skillet; drain on paper
towels. Yield 4 servings.

TUNA TACOS

2 cns (6½ ozs. each) tuna fish,
    drained
½ cup taco sauce
1 avocado, thinly sliced
1½ cups lettuce, shredded
1 cup Monterey Jack cheese,
    shredded
8 taco shells

In a small bowl, combine
together, tuna fish and taco
sauce; mix well. In each taco
shell, place equal amounts of
tuna fish, avocado, lettuce and
cheese. Yield 4 servings.

GOLDEN FRIED SHRIMP

1½ pounds raw, shell-on shrimp
    (26 to 30 count)
2 egg whites
1 egg yolk
¼ cup all-purpose flour
½ cup saltine crackers, crushed
Oil for frying

Butterfly shrimp; wash under
cold running water. In a shallow
bowl, combine eggs, by mixing
well. In another bowl, combine
flour and cracker crumbs. Dip
each shrimp in egg mixture,
then roll in cracker mixture.
Repeat procedure until all
shrimp are covered. Heat oil
until 365 degrees; fry shrimp
for 2 to 3 minutes, until golden
brown. Drain on paper towels.
Yield 6 servings.

EASY SALMON CHOWDER

3 slices bacon, cut into about
    ¼" pieces
1 medium onion, chopped
1 clove garlic, minced
¾ teaspoon ground cumin
¼ teaspoon hot-pepper flakes
    (optional)
2 tablespoons all-purpose flour
3½ cups chicken stock or
    canned broth
1 can (14¾ ozs.) salmond
    rained, reserve liquid
1¾ cups tomatoes in juice
½ cup white wine (optional)
½ teaspoon salt
1 small sweet potato, peeled &
    cubed
½ cup green pepper, chopped
¾ cup corn, drained

In a soup kettle, fry bacon
until crisp; add onions, garlic,
cumin and pepper flakes.
Cook over low heat for 5
minutes; add flour; mix well;
cook an additional 1 minute.
In the meantime, add stock
to reserved salmon juice, to
equal 3-2/3 cups. Gradually
stir stock mixture in soup kettle;
add tomatoes with juice,
wine, salt, sweet potatoes and
green peppers; bring to a boil.
Reduce heat to simmer for 15
minutes. Add corn and salmon;
cook until heated through,
for about 2 minutes. Yield 5
servings.

FISH AND CHIPS

6 medium-sized potatoes
3 pounds haddock fillets
½ cup all-purpose flour
½ teaspoon salt
Pinch of pepper
Vegetable oil for frying

BATTER

1 cup all-purpose flour
½ teaspoon baking powder
½ teaspoon salt
1 large egg
1 cup milk

Prepare potatoes by cutting lengthwise ½ inch slices, then cut each slice crosswise into ½ inch strips. Rinse in cold water; pat dry with paper towels; set aside. Cut haddock fillets into 12 pieces. In a medium bowl, combine together, flour, salt and pepper. Dip each fillet into flour mixture, coating fillet completely; set aside. In another bowl, combine together, 1 cup flour, baking powder, salt, egg and milk. Beat until batter is smooth. Refrigerate potatoes, fish and batter, separately, for at least 30minutes or until ready to cook. Cover with foil or plastic wrap. Meanwhile, get deep fryer ready, or large sauce pan; put enough oil in to measure 3 inches deep. Heat to 375 degrees, then fry potato strips until golden brown; drain on paper towels.
Keep potatoes warm. Dip floured fillets into batter; deep fry for 5 to 8 minutes, or until golden brown; drain on paper towels. Serve immediately. Yield 6 servings.

SHRIMP SAUCE

1 cup orange marmalade
4 tablespoons brown mustard
4 tablespoons horseradish

In a small mixing bowl, combine together, mix thoroughly; serve. Yield about 1½ cups.

RATTLESNAKE CORN RELISH

2 pounds fresh OR frozen cut
    corn
2 pounds rattlesnake meat,
    cooked & sliced
4 medium tomatoes, diced
4 Jalapeno peppers, diced
1 red onion, diced
6 green onions, sliced
1 bunch Cilantro, chopped
1 tablespoon black pepper
1 tablespoon salt

In a large mixing bowl, combine together, all ingredients; chill in refrigerator for 1 hour before serving.

EASY PHEASANT BAKE

1 whole pheasant
¼ cup butter OR margarine
½ cup all-purpose flour
Salt and pepper to taste
1 can Cream of Mushroom
    Soup
1½ cups half and half cream

Cut pheasant into serving pieces. In a medium skillet, over medium-high heat, melt butter. Dip pheasant pieces into flour, then brown on both sides, in melted butter. Season with salt and pepper. Remove meat from heat; set aside. Meanwhile, combine soup and half and half; blend well; pour over pheasant pieces in skillet. Bake covered, at 325 degrees F., for 1½ hours, or until tender.

BARBEQUED RABBIT OR SQUIRREL

2½ to 3 lbs. rabbit OR squirrel
    meat
1 cup milk
1 cup all-purpose flour
½ teaspoon seasoned salt
¼ teaspoon black pepper
3 to 4 tablespoons margarine
1 can tomato soup
1/3 cup Worcestershire sauce
1 teaspoon chili powder
2 to 3 drops hot pepper sauce
    (optional)

½ teaspoon garlic powder
¼ cup brown sugar, packed
2 stalks celery, finely chopped
1 cup water

Wash and dry meat; cut into serving pieces. Combine together, flour, salt and pepper; place in a plastic bag. Moisten meat with milk, then place meat, a few pieces at a time, in the bag. Shake bag for meat to coat. Heat three tablespoons of margarine, in a large skillet; cook meat until browned, on both sides. Add more margarine as needed. Place browned meat in a single layer in a baking pan. Combine the remaining ingredients in a small mixing bowl; mix thoroughly. Pour over meat; bake at 350 degrees, for 1 to 1½ hours, or until tender. Baste frequently during baking time. Yield 4 to 6 servings.

SAVORY TOMATO SAUCE

½ cup onions, chopped
¼ teaspoon garlic powder
1 tablespoon vegetable oil
2 cans (16 ozs. each) stewed
    tomatoes
1 can (8 ozs.) tomato sauce
1 can (6 ozs.) tomato paste
1½ cups water
1 teaspoon dried basil
2 teaspoons celery flakes
1 tablespoon dried parsley
2 teaspoons instant beef
    bouillon
Black pepper to taste
1 can (4 ozs.) mushrooms, sliced

In large saucepan, sauté
onions and garlic powder in
hot oil, over medium heat.
Mash tomatoes into small
pieces with fork; add to onions.
Add remaining ingredients to
saucepan; reduce heat to low.
Simmer covered for 30 minutes.
Pour over meatballs, then
simmer meatballs and sauce,
covered for about 45 minutes.
Stir occasionally; serve over
hot spaghetti, or use in another
favorite recipe.

SMELT WITH SALSA

3 tablespoons vegetable oil,
    divided
2 pounds smelt
1 small onion, chopped
1 clove garlic. minced
1 medium tomato, chopped

½ green pepper, chopped
1 can (15 ozs.) black beans,
    drained and rinsed
1 can (15 ozs.) whole kernel
    corn, drained
Salt and pepper to taste

Brush 2 tablespoons oil on fish;
cook fish over hot coals for 10
minutes or until flakey.

FOR SALSA: Heat remaining oil
in a large skillet, over medium
heat. Add onions, garlic,
tomato & pepper; sauté for
10 minutes; add remaining
ingredients; cover. Reduce
heat to simmer; cook for 5
minutes. Top smelt with salsa.
Yield 6 servings.

NOTE: It is not necessary to fillet
or debone the smelt, because
even the backbone is soft
enough to eat.

OYSTERS AU GRATIN

6 slices toast, buttered
2 large eggs, beaten
½ teaspoon salt
1 teaspoon prepared mustard
½ teaspoon paprika
½ cup milk
2 cups oysters, drained
Parmesan cheese, grated

Trim crust from bread; cut
each slice in fourths; set aside.
In a mixing bowl, combine
together, eggs, salt, mustard,
paprika and milk; mix well. In a
buttered casserole, layer bread
in bottom, then cover with a
layer of oysters. Sprinkle with
cheese. Repeat layering, then
cover the last layer with egg
mixture. Top with more grated
cheese. Place casserole in a
pan of hot water; bake at 350
degrees, for 30 minutes or until
brown on top. Yield 6 servings.

FRIED CALF BRAINS

1 pound brains
2 tablespoons all-purpose flour
Salt and pepper to taste
2 tablespoons fat (i.e. butter,
    oil, etc.)

Precook brains, by placing
in cold water, for 30 minutes,
then remove membranes. In a
saucepan, over medium heat,
simmer for 15 minutes, in water,
with ½ teaspoon salt and 1
teaspoon lemon juice OR white
vinegar has been added for
each quart of water. Drain; roll
in flour, season and brown in
fat. Yield 4 servings.

ROAST BEAVER

1 small beaver, skinned &
    cleaned
Salt and pepper
Pinch of Chervil
2 medium onions, sliced
1 bay leaf
Bacon fat

Trim excess fat; cut in serving
sizes; brown in bacon fat,
salting as meat is turned,
pepper, if desired. Place
meat in roasting pan, put
onions on top. Roast in oven,
at 350 degrees, for 2½ to 3
hours or about 20 minutes per
pound. Make pan gravy from
drippings, using flour and water
paste, salt and pepper to taste;
add bay leaf, over low heat,
bring to simmer; cook until
gravy is thickened. Add chervil
before serving. Yield about 8
servings.

COUNTRY-STYLE GROUNDHOG

1 groundhog, skinned &
   cleaned
½ cup all-purpose flour
¼ teaspoon salt
¼ teaspoon pepper
¼ teaspoon baking soda
4 tablespoons oil
½ teaspoon granulated sugar
½ cup warm water

Soak groundhog overnight,
in salt water, to remove wild
flavor. Cut meat into serving
pieces; set aside. In a small
bowl, combine together,
flour, salt, pepper and baking
soda' mix well. Rub into meat;
brown in hot oil, over medium
heat. Sprinkle with sugar, then
reduce heat to simmer; add
water; cover. Cook for 45
minutes or until tender remove
cover last 10 minutes to brown.
Yield 4 servings.

BARBEQUED BEAR

2 to 3 pound bear roast
Salt and pepper
1 clove garlic
2 tablespoons brown sugar
1 tablespoon paprika
1 teaspoon dry mustard
¼ teaspoon chili powder
Pinch of cayenne pepper
2 tablespoons Worcestershire
   Sauce
¼ cup white vinegar
1 cup tomato juice
¼ cup ketchup
½ cup water

Place bear roast in roasting
pan; season with salt, pepper,
rub meat with garlic. Roast
meat at 350 degrees, for 1
hour or until well done. Cut into
thin slices; set aside. In a skillet,
combine together, remaining
ingredients, over low heat,
simmer for 15 minutes, then add
meat. Cook for 1 hour. Yield 6
to 8 servings.

HASENPFEFFER

1 dressed rabbit, cut into
   serving pieces
2 cups water
2 cups white vinegar
1 medium onion, sliced
1 teaspoon salt
½ teaspoon pepper
1 teaspoons ground cloves
1 teaspoon bay leaves,
   crushed

Butter OR margarine for frying
Place rabbit pieces in a large
jar, with all the ingredients.
Let stand in a cool place for 2
days. Remove meat; reserve
pickling liquid, then in a large
skillet, brown meat in hot butter.
Turn meat often. Gradually
add 1 cup pickling liquid, cover
and let simmer for 1 hour or
until meat is tender. Thicken
sauce and use as gravy. Yield 4
servings.

OPPOSSOM W/ SWEET POTATOES

1 oppossom, skinned & cleaned
4 cups water
Salt and pepper
4 to 6 red peppers, chopped
4 large sweet potatoes, pared
  & sliced

In a large saucepan, combine
together, all ingredients,
EXCEPT sweet potatoes. Bring to
a simmer, cook for 30 minutes.
Remove oppossom to baking
pan, keep cooking liquid until it
is reduced by about half. Add
liquid and sweet potatoes to
baking pan with oppossom.
Bake at 350 degrees, for 1 hour
or until meat is tender. Yield
about 4 servings.

HOPPING JOHN

8 ozs. raw blackeye peas
½ pound ham bone
1 medium onion, chopped
½ teaspoon salt
¼ teaspoon pepper
1 cup instant rice
1 can (16 ozs.) tomatoes
  (optional)

In a saucepan, combine
together, peas, ham bone,
onions, salt and pepper. cook
over medium heat, for 1 hour
and 15 minutes. Add rice, then
add water to cover rice; bring to
a boiling point, cover; remove
from heat. Let stand until rice
is tender. Add tomatoes. Yield
about 6 servings.

MARYLAD STUFFED "HOG MAW"

1 hog's stomach
1 pound loaf bread
1 quart potatoes, peeled &
  diced
1 pounds pork sausages
2 medium onions, diced
Salt and pepper to taste
2 tablespoons parsley, diced

Enlarge opening at lower end
of stomach, turn inside out.
Scrape out inside lining. Wash
in warm water, then turn right
side out. Sew shut at upper
end; dice bread. Let dry over
night, or dry in oven at low
heat. In a large bowl, combine
together thoroughly, bread and
remaining ingredients. Pack
loosely into hog's stomach; sew
opening shut. Place in roaster;
add enough water to cover
bottom of pan, cover tightly.
Cook at 350 degrees, for about
2½ hours. Yield 8 to 10 servings.

FROG LEGS

The hind legs of the frog are
the only part that is eaten. Frog
leg's have a taste similar to
chicken. To prepare frog legs,
cut them from the body; then
wash in cold water. Turn the skin
down, then strip off like a glove.
Cover with boiling water; drain
quickly; dry with paper towels;
use as desired.

FRIED FROG LEGS

Season prepared legs with salt and pepper; dip into cracker crumbs, crushed fine or bread crumbs. Dip into slightly beaten egg, then again in to crumbs. Let stand for 15 to 20 minutes; fry in hot, deep fat (375 degrees), for about 3 minutes or until browned. Allow 2 legs per person. If desired serve with tartar sauce.

TO DRESS AND TRUSS RABBITS

To skin and dress a rabbit or hare, cut off the forefeet, at the first joint, cut skin around the first joint of the hind leg, loosen it and with a sharp knife, slit the skin on under side of the leg, at the tail. Loosen the skin; turn it back until it is removed from the hind legs.

Tie hind legs together; hang rabbit on a hook. Draw the skin over the head, slipping out the forelegs whey they are reached. Cut off the head, then remove the entire skin. Wipe with a damp cloth. Slit down the front; remove entrails, saving the heart and liver. Wipe inside carefully, then wash inside and out with acidulated water, using 1 tablespoon to each cup of water. Rinse and wipe thoroughly. If blood has settled in any part of meat, cut out with a sharp point of knife where it is black. Prepare as desired.

ROAST RABBIT

1 dressed rabbit
Salt and pepper
2 tablespoons butter OR
  margarine

Wash dressed rabbit thoroughly under running water; dry with paper towels. Sprinkle with salt and pepper on inside. Fill with desired stuffing; fasten opening securely, then spread with butter. Again sprinkle with salt and pepper. Roast in uncovered pan, at 325 degrees, for 1¾ hours or until tender. Yield 4 to 6 servings.

FRIED RABBIT

2/3 cup all-purpose flour
1 teaspoon paprika
2 wild rabbits, dressed (about
    4 lbs.)
OR 1 (about 6 lbs.) domestic
    rabbit
¾ cup vegetable oil
½ teaspoon salt
Pepper to taste

Combine together, flour and
paprika, to dredge rabbit
pieces. In a 12-inch skillet, over
medium-high, in vegetable
oil, cook rabbit, a few pieces
at a time, until browned on
all sides. Remove pieces to a
platter, as they are browned,
when complete, return meat
to skillet. Sprinkle with salt &
pepper. Reduce heat to low;
cover; cook for 45 minutes, or
until tender. If wild rabbit, yield
6 servings, if domestic rabbit,
yield 8 servings.

Chapter 7

SOUPS, STEWS, CHILIES & CHOWDERS NOODLES AND DUMPLINGS

IT IS BETTER TO HOLD YOUR HAND
THAN TO POINT A FINGER!

GREAT SOUPS, STEWS, CHOWDERS NOODLES & DUMPLINGS

Soup is great on a cold wintery day; it can be served hot or cold. It is very nourishing and filling, and easy to prepare. There are so many different kinds of soup, most soups

VICHYSSOISE

2 tablespoons butter OR
  margarine
½ cup leeks, chopped (white
  part)
2/3 cup water
½ teaspoon chicken stock base
1 can (10½ ozs.) Condensed
  Cream of Potato Soup,
  undiluted
1 cup Half & Half
½ cup milk

Chives, chopped for garnish
In a skillet, over medium heat, cook leeks in butter, for 5 minutes. Add chicken stock base & water; heat to boiling. Reduce heat to simmer; cover. Cook for 10 minutes, then add remaining ingredients; mix well; chill in refrigerator. Just before serving, place mixture in a blender, process for 30 seconds or until smooth. If desired, garnish with chives. Yield 4 servings.

VEGETABLE SOUP

1 cup onions, chopped
1 cup celery, chopped
2 tablespoons butter
6 cups beef broth
1 cup potatoes, peeled and
  cubed
1 cup turnips, peeled and
  chopped
2/3 cup carrots, chopped
2 tablespoons fresh parsley,
  minced
¼ teaspoon dried thyme
1 cup cabbage, shredded

In a large saucepan, sauté onions and celery in butter until tender. Add broth, potatoes, turnips, carrots, parsley and thyme. Bring to a boil over medium heat; reduce heat to simmer for 30 minutes. Add cabbage; simmer uncovered, for 10 minutes more. Yield 6 servings.

FRENCH ONION SOUP

4 medium onions, peeled and
   sliced
1 tablespoon butter
1 quart beef broth
½ teaspoon Worcestershire
   Sauce
Salt and pepper to taste
Pieces of toasted bread
Parmesan Cheese, grated

Brown onion slices in butter in
a medium saucepan, over low
heat. Add broth, Worcestershire
Sauce, salt and pepper;
simmer until onions are tender.
Pour into a casserole, arrange
toasted bread on top of soup,
sprinkle with grated Parmesan
cheese. Place under broiler at
400 degrees; broil until cheese
melts and browns. Yield 4
servings.

BUTTERNUT SQUASH SOUP

1 medium butternut squash,
   washed and cut in half
1 cup milk
½ tablespoon all-purpose flour
1 tablespoon vegetable oil
½ teaspoon cardamom

Place squash halves on a
cookie sheet, cut side up. Bake
uncovered, at 350 degrees
until tender. When tender,
remove skin, seeds and strings.
Puree squash in blender; set
aside. In a medium saucepan,
over low heat cook milk, flour
and oil; add cardamom and
salt; stirring constantly. When
mixture is heated to boiling
point, add squash; mix well,
serve. Yield 3 to 4 servings.

VEGETABLE NOODLES

¼ cup pureed *vegetable
1 large egg, slightly beaten
¼ teaspoon salt
2 cups all-purpose flour

*(Use spinach, asparagus, peas
or tomatoes).
Cook vegetable until soft;
drain. Puree' in blender or
food processor. Place pulp in
a medium-sized bowl; add
egg, salt and flour; knead to
a smooth dough. Let stand
covered for ½ hour. On a lightly
floured surface, roll dough
very thin. Let stand to dry and
when no longer sticky, cut in
desired width. Drop into salted
boiling water. Boil for 10 to 15
minutes or until tender; drain.
To use noodles another day,
dry completely, then store in
covered container until ready
to use.

POTATO KLUZSKI (Noodles)

¾ cup raw potatoes, finely
    grated
1½ cups all-purpose flour
1 large egg
¼ teaspoon salt

In a mixing bowl, combine
together, all ingredients; mix
well. In a large saucepan, bring
4 quarts of water, with a little
salt, to boiling. Drop batter by
spoonfuls into boiling water;
cook for. 15 minutes. Remove
with slotted spoon; serve.

HOMEMADE NOODLES

4 large eggs, beaten
1 teaspoon salt
2 tablespoon butter OR
    margarine, melted

Add enough all-purpose flour
to make a stiff dough. Roll out
on a floured surface to 1/8 inch
thickness; cut as desired with
sharp knife; dry completely,
then store in covered container,
or use immediately, as desired.

QUICK NOODLES

1 large egg
1 cup baking mix (i.e. Bisquick)

In a small mixing bowl, beat
egg; add baking mix; mix
until dough forms. On a lightly
floured surface, roll dough
into paper-thin rectangle. Cut
dough crosswise into ¼ inch
strips. Spread noodle so they
can dry, at least 8 hours. When
dry, store dried noodles in a
tightly covered container. Yield
3 cups uncooked noodles.

TO COOK: Heat water over
medium heat; with ½ teaspoon
salt. Bring water to a boil; Add
desired amount of noodles;
cook uncovered, until tender,
about 6 to 8 minutes. Remove
from heat, drain in colander;
serve.

TURNIP SOUP

2 cups turnips, cooked &
    mashed
1 cup potatoes, cooked &
    mashed
4 cups scalded milk
4 tablespoons butter OR
    margarine
2 tablespoons all-purpose flour
1 teaspoons salt
1 tablespoon onions, minced
Watercress (optional)

In the top of a double boiler,
combine together, turnips,
potatoes and milk; set aside.
In a small skillet, melt butter;
blend in flour, salt and onion;
add turnip mixture gradually,
stirring constantly. Cook for 20
minutes. If desired, garnish with
watercress. Yield 6 servings.

OX TAIL SOUP

1 ox tail
Salt and pepper
1 teaspoon all-purpose flour
1 teaspoon butter OR
    margarine
6 cups beef stock
1 medium carrot, diced
2 medium turnips, diced
½ cup celery, diced
½ cup onions, diced
½ teaspoon salt
Pinch of pepper
1 teaspoon Worcestershire
    Sauce
1 teaspoon lemon juice
Water

Cut ox tail in pieces; sprinkle with salt and pepper; dredge in flour. Fry in butter for 10 minutes. In a large saucepan, place beef stock with ox tail; over medium heat simmer for 2 hours or until tender. Meanwhile, sauté cut vegetables in the same butter as ox tail, for 2 to 3 minutes; set aside. Strain stock and remove bones; return stock to heat; add vegetables. Simmer until vegetables are tender, about 30 to 45 minutes. Add remaining ingredients and water. if needed. Yield 4 servings

ZUCCHINI CORN CHOWDER

3 ears of corn, cut from cob OR
    2 cans corn
4 strips bacon, cooked &
    crumbled
3 cups zucchini, peeled &
    sliced
1 cup onions, diced
¾ cup green pepper, diced
1 clove garlic, minced
1 cup water
½ teaspoon salt
¼ teaspoon tarragon
2 cups milk
2 large eggs, beaten

Combine together, zucchini, onions, green pepper and garlic; sauté in bacon grease; add water and salt and spices. Bring mixture to a boil, then reduce heat to simmer; cook for 10 minutes. Combine milk with eggs; mix thoroughly; add to zucchini mixture, continue to simmer until mixture thickens. Do not allow to boil. When serving, sprinkle with bacon bits. Yield 6 servings.

SPLIT PEA SOUP

1 ham bone
1 pkg. (16 ozs.) split peas
2 carrots, thinly sliced
1 medium onion, chopped
¼ teaspoon whole allspice
¼ teaspoon peppercorns
1 bay leaf
Salt to taste

In a large saucepan, over medium heat, combine together, ham bone, split peas, carrots, onions and 7 cups water. Bring mixture to boiling. Meanwhile, tie allspice, peppercorns and bay leaf, in a cheesecloth bag; add to ham bone mixture. Reduce heat to simmer; cook for 1 hour, covered or until tender. Remove from heat; discard spice bag. Remove bone; cut meat in pieces; return meat to soup. Yield 6 servings.

POTATO SOUP

6 potatoes, peeled and diced
1 carrot, shredded
2 tablespoons parsley, chopped
¼ cup onions, chopped
3 chicken bouillon cubes
4 tablespoons all-purpose flour
1 cup sour cream
1 can (4 ozs.) mushroom pieces, drained
Salt and pepper to taste

In a large saucepan, combine together, potatoes, carrots, parsley, onion and bouillon cubes. Cover with water, over medium heat, bring to a simmer; cook until potatoes are tender. Meanwhile, combine flour with sour cream; mix well. Gradually add to vegetable mixture, blending well. Add mushrooms, salt and pepper; simmer until heated through. Yield about 6 servings.

POTATO DUMPLINGS

4 medium potatoes, peeled & cubed
½ teaspoon salt
1 large egg
½ cup parsley, chopped
1/3 cup all-purpose flour
Salt and pepper to taste

In a large saucepan, place potatoes and ½ teaspoon salt and water to cover potatoes; cover. Cook over medium-high heat; bring to a boil; reduce heat to simmer, for 20 minutes, or until potatoes are tender; drain. Mash and let cool, then add remaining ingredients; mix thoroughly. Shape into balls; drop into boiling water; cook for 8 to 10 minutes.

BEET BORSCHT

3 pounds beef stew meat, cut
   in cubes
6 cups water
2 carrots, sliced
2 ribs celery, sliced
1 medium onion, chopped
1 teaspoons salt
½ teaspoon pepper
½ teaspoon dillweed
1 bay leaf
4 cups cabbage, shredded
1 can (16 ozs.) beets, julienne,
   undrained
Juice of 1 lemon
1 cup sour cream

In a Dutch oven, combine
together, beef, water, carrots,
celery, onions and seasonings.
Cover; bake at 250 degrees,
for 3½ hours or until the meat
is tender. Add cabbage, bake
for 30 minutes or until cabbage
is tender. Remove from oven;
discard bay leaf; add beets
and lemon juice. Stir in 1/3 cup
sour cream; mix well. Ladle into
soup bowls; top each bowl,
with dollop of remaining sour
cream. Yield 6 to 8 servings.

CHICKEN SOUP

4 quarts chicken stock
3 cups (about 3 lbs.) chicken,
   diced
1½ cups celery, diced
1½ cups carrots, sliced
1 cup onions, diced
Salt and pepper to taste
3 cubes chicken boullion
   (optional)

In a large kettle, combine
together, chicken stock,
chicken, celery, carrots and
onions. Bring mixture to a boil;
reduce heat to simmer. Cook
for 30 minutes; season to taste.
If desired, add boulion cubes;
cook until cubes are dissolved.
Yield 4 quarts or about 6
servings

TURTLE SOUP

1-1/3 pounds turtle meat
3½ cups water
2 medium onions
1 bay leaf
¼ teaspoon cayenne pepper
½ teaspoon salt
5 tablespoons butter OR
   margarine, cubed
1/3 cup all-purpose flour
3 tablespoons tomato puree
3 tablespoons Worcestershire
   Sauce
1/3 cup chicken broth
2 hard-cooked eggs, chopped
¼ cup lemon juice

In a large kettle, combine turtle meat and water. Over medium heat, bring to a boil; skim off foam as cooking. Chop 1 onion; set aside. Quarter the other onion; add to turtle meat, along with bay leaf, cayenne pepper and salt. Cover; simmer for 2 hours or until meat is tender. Remove meat with a slotted spoon; cut into ½ inch pieces; set aside. Strain broth; set aside. In the same kettle, which has been washed & dried, melt butter over medium heat; add chopped onion. Cook onion until tender; add flour; mix well until bubbly and lightly browned. Whisk in reserved broth; continue cooking until thickened; reduce heat. Stir in tomato puree and Worcestershire Sauce; simmer

uncovered, for 10 minutes. Add remaining ingredients and meat; simmer for 5 minutes or until heated through. Yield 4 to servings.

CREAM OF BROCCOLI SOUP

1 medium bunch broccoli,
   chopped
4 cups water
1 cup onions, chopped
2 cups milk, divided
3 tablespoons butter OR
   margarine
3 tablespoons all-purpose flour
½ teaspoon salt
¼ teaspoon pepper
1 cube chicken bouillon

In a large saucepan, place water over high heat, bring to a boil; add broccoli and onion. Cook uncovered until broccoli is tender. Remove from heat; drain, reserve 2 cups liquid. In a blender place broccoli & onion along with 1 cup milk, cover puree' until smooth; set aside. In the same saucepan, over medium heat, melt butter, stir in flour, salt and pepper until smooth. Add reserved 2 cups liquid, 1 cup milk and bouillon cube; cook until mixture comes to a boil. Add pureed' broccoli mixture; cook only when heated through. Serve soup hot or cold. Yield about 6 cups.

DUMPLINGS (Master Recipe)

1 cup all-purpose flour
1½ teaspoon baking powder
½ teaspoon salt
2 tablespoons shortening
1/3 cup milk
1 large egg, beaten

In a medium-size bowl, combine together, flour, baking powder and salt. Cut in shortening with fork, until mixture is crumbly. Add milk and beaten egg; mix only until flour is dampened, (dough should be lumpy). Drop by spoonfuls, on top of boiling water and/or other hot liquid dishes. Cover tightly and steam for about 12 minutes, without removing the cover. Yield 6 dumplings.

VARIATIONS:

PARSLEY OR SPINACH DUMPLINGS

Add ¼ cup parsley OR spinach, minced to flour and shortening mixture; then add milk and egg.

NOTE: Substitute minced mint leaves in dumplings, served with lamb stew.

WHOLE WHEAT DUMPLINGS

Decrease flour to 2/3 cup; add 1/3 cup whole wheat or graham flour to dry ingredients before cutting shortening.

CORNMEAL DUMPLINGS

Add the 1/3 cup milk to ½ cup cornmeal; set aside and let stand. Reduce flour to 1/3 cup; add the beaten egg to the cornmeal milk mixture; mix well. Fold flour mixture into cornmeal only until flour is dampened. Especially good with stews that have tomatoes in it.

CHEESE DUMPLINGS

Add ½ cup cheese, grated, to flour and shortening mixture; add liquids. Continue as the Master Recipe directs. These dumplings are good with combination of vegetables.

SEED DUMPLINGS

Add ½ to 1 teaspoon poppy OR caraway seeds to dry ingredients. After spooning dumplings into boiling liquid; sprinkle with additional seeds, if desired. Good with cabbage dishes.

MEAT DUMPLINGS

Add ½ cup of chopped or ground meat to the flour and shortening mixture before adding the liquids. Steam covered, on top of vegetables or soup, etc. or on foil over any boiling liquid.

FRUIT DUMPLINGS

Add ½ cup prunes OR apricots; cooked & finely chopped, sweetened, if necessary, to flour and shortening, then add liquids. Great with pork dishes.

POLISH CABBAGE SOUP

½ pound lean pork, cut into
  small pieces
1 tablespoon butter OR
  margarine
1 can (10½ ozs.) beef broth
1 can (10½ ozs.) Condensed
  Tomato Soup
2 soup cans of water
½ cup onions, chopped
4 cups cabbage, shredded
½ teaspoon salt
½ teaspoon paprika
1 bay leaf
Sour cream

In a large skillet, brown pork in butter; add remaining ingredients, EXCEPT sour cream. Cover; cook over low heat, for 30 minutes; stir often. If desired, serve with a spoonful of sour cream.

SOUP BAGS FOR FLAVORING SOUP

Use 2-inch square cheesecloth to make bags to be used as seasoning with 2 quarts liquid. These bags are dropped into boiling soup towards end of cooking and no longer than 1 hour.

Crush and mix all together the following ingredients.

NOTE: Use only <u>dried</u> ingredients.
1 teaspoon parsley
1 teaspoon thyme
1 teaspoon marjoram
¼ teaspoon sage
½ teaspoon savory
¼ teaspoon bay leaf
2 teaspoons celery

POTATO CHOWDER

¼ pound salt pork
1 medium onion, sliced
3 cups potatoes, cut-up &
cooked
2 cups boiling water
1 cup corn, fresh or canned,
cooked
4 cups hot milk
½ teaspoon salt
Pinch of pepper
Parsley for garnish (optional)

Cut pork into small pieces; fry with onions; cook until tender. Add potatoes, boiling water, corn and hot milk. Season with salt and pepper; heat to boiling. Remove from heat; if desired, garnish with parsley. Yield 6 to 8 servings.

TURNIP STEW

1/3 cup salt pork, diced
2 cups potatoes, diced
1 cup turnips, diced
1 cup, carrots, diced
1 medium onion, minced
1 stalk celery, diced
1 green pepper, diced
2 cups thin white sauce (see index)
Salt and pepper to taste

In a medium saucepan, fry pork with vegetables; cook until lightly browned. Add boiling water to cover ingredients; cook until tender. Add white sauce, salt and pepper; mix well. Remove from heat. Yield 6 servings.

CREAM OF MUSHROOM SOUP

4 tablespoons butter OR margarine
½ pound fresh mushrooms, washed and chopped
2 tablespoons all-purpose flour
4 cups chicken stock
½ teaspoon salt
¼ teaspoon pepper
1 cup cream

In a skillet, melt butter; add mushrooms, sauté until tender. Blend in flour; add chicken stock; heat to boiling; cook for 5 chicken stock; heat to boiling; cook for 5 Add seasoning and cream; heat; serve hot. Yield 4 to 6 servings.

POLISH BIGOS (Stew)

1 pound sauerkraut, drained & squeezed
12 ounces fresh mushrooms
2 tablespoons vegetable oil
2 cans (16 ozs. each) whole tomatoes, undrained & cut-up
1 cup water
½ pound sausage (kielbasa), sliced
1 teaspoon caraway seed
1 bay leaf

Drain sauerkraut; soak in cold water for 15 minutes. Again drain in sieve; press out liquid; set aside. Meanwhile, clean and slice mushrooms. In a large saucepan, sauté mushrooms in oil, about 5 minutes. Add tomatoes, and juice, plus remaining ingredients. Bring to a boil; reduce heat to simmer, cover; cook for 15 minutes. If desired, chop sauerkraut, then add to stew, cover; simmer 15 minutes longer. Remove bay leaf. Remove from heat; allow to cool. Refrigerate and serve 24 hours later. It will improve the flavor. Yield 8 cups stew.

CHEDDAR CHEESE SOUP

½ cup *onions, finely chopped
¼ cup *carrots, chopped
¼ cup *celery, chopped
3 cups chicken broth
1 tablespoon cornstarch
2 tablespoons water
1 cup (4 ozs.) sharp cheddar
   cheese, cut in small pieces
1 can (10¾ ozs.) Cream of
   Mushroom Soup
1 jar (8 ozs.) cheese spread (i.e.
   Cheese Whiz)

In a large saucepan, combine together, vegetables and broth; bring to a boil. Reduce heat, cover; simmer for 10 minutes or until vegetables are tender. If desired, (vegetable mixture can be pureed' in blender, until smooth), In a small bowl, combine cornstarch with water; mix well. Stir into vegetable mixture; again bring to a boil; reduce heat to simmer. Add cheddar cheese, soup and cheese spread; mix until cheese has melted and is thoroughly mixed. After the cheese has been added, heat gently; <u>do not boil.</u>

*<u>NOTE</u>: You can replace the above vegetables with 1 cup broccoli or 1 cup cauliflower, chopped. Yield 6 one cup servings.

LOBSTER STEW

2 tablespoons butter OR
   margarine
4 tablespoons all-purpose flour
2 cups light cream
Salt and pepper to taste
½ teaspoon granulated sugar
2 cups lobster meat, cut in small
   pieces

In a medium skillet, melt butter; add flour stirring constantly until smooth. Add cream gradually; cook for 10 minutes over low heat, stirring constantly. Remove from heat; season with salt and pepper; add sugar. Add lobster meat pieces, the stew should be the consistency of a thick white sauce. Yield 4 servings.

MANHATTAN CLAM CHOWDER

2½ tablespoons bacon, diced
1 medium onion, diced
1 medium stalk celery, diced
½ green pepper, diced
1 carrot, diced
1 medium potato, diced
½ teaspoon salt
Pinch of pepper
2/3 cup water
1 cup tomato juice
1 bay leaf
¼ teaspoon thyme
1 can (8 ozs.) clams, minced

In a medium saucepan, cook bacon until brown; add remaining ingredients, EXCEPT clams; mix well. Cover; cook over low heat for 1 hour, then add clams. If necessary to thicken, do so with a little flour. Remove bay leaf before serving.

EASY MINESTRONE

¼ cup butter OR margarine
1 pkg. (10 ozs.) frozen peas, thawed
1 cup carrots, diced
1 cup celery, diced
1 cup onions, chopped
1 tablespoon fresh parsley, chopped
1 teaspoon basil
1 can (28 ozs.) tomatoes
3 cans (13¾ ozs. ea.) chicken broth
1 cup cabbage, shredded
½ pound zucchini, sliced
2 cans kidney beans
½ cup spaghetti, broke in small pieces
Salt to taste
Parmesan Cheese, grated

In a large saucepan, over medium heat, combine together, butter, peas, carrots, celery, onions and parsley; cook for 5 minutes. Add remaining ingredients; cook for 20 minutes or until spaghetti is tender. Salt to taste; if desired serve with cheese. Yield 8 servings.

HOMEMADE NOODLES II

2½ cups flour
3 large eggs
¼ teaspoon salt
¼ teaspoon salt

In a medium mixing bowl, combine together flour, eggs and salt; gradually add cold water mixing until mixture forms dough. Place dough on a floured surface, roll out dough; with a sharp knife, cut dough into strips and place on a clean towel on a flat surface to dry. Noodles dry in about 2 days.

Note: Dough can be used to make soup noodles, or lasagna noodles, or ravioli

EASY TOMATO SOUP

2 cups canned tomatoes,
    pureed OR chopped
Pinch of baking soda
3 cups milk
2 tablespoons butter OR
    margarine
Salt and pepper to taste

In a medium saucepan, over
low heat, cook tomatoes until
warm. Add baking soda; mix
well. Stir in milk and butter;
cook until heated through, but
do not boil. Season to taste.
Yield 4 servings.

HUNGARIAN GOULASH

1½ pounds beef, cut in 1½"
    cubes
2 tablespoons shortening
1 can (10½ ozs.) tomato soup,
    undiluted
½ cup sour cream
¼ cup water
1 cup onions, sliced
1 tablespoon paprika
Pinch of pepper
4 medium potatoes, quartered

In a large saucepan, brown
beef in shortening. When meat
is browned, pour off fat. Add
the remaining ingredients,
EXCEPT potatoes. Cover; cook
over low heat, for 1½ hours; add
potatoes. Cook for 1 more hour
or until meat and potatoes are
tender. Stir occasionally. Yield
about 6 cups.

NAVY BEAN SOUP

1½ pounds Navy Beans
1 medium onion, peeled &
diced
2 pounds shank end of ham
1 large potato, peeled & diced
1 carrot, sliced
1 celery stalk, diced
1 can (8 ozs.) tomato sauce

Soak beans in water overnight.
Drain and rinse. Over medium
heat, in a large saucepan,
cook beans, covered, in water.
for 3 hours. Add onion & ham
shank; cook 2 hours more.
Add potatoes, carrot slices,
celery and tomato sauce; mix
well. Cook for 2 hours more,
uncovered, over low heat.
Serve.

LAMB STEW (with dumplings

2 lbs. breast of lamb, cut in
  2-inch cubes
3 tablespoons vegetable oil
3 cups hot water
Salt and pepper to taste
1 medium onion, peeled &
  chopped
4 carrots, sliced
3 potatoes, peeled & cubed
1 tablespoon green pepper,
  chopped
2 tablespoons parsley,
  chopped (opt.)
1 teaspoon Worcestershire Sauce
2 tablespoons all-purpose flour
¼ cup cold water

In a large skillet, brown meat
in hot vegetable oil; add hot
water, seasoning and onions.
Cover; over low heat, bring to a
simmer; cook for 1½ hours. Add
vegetables; continue cooking,
covered, for 30 minutes. Add
Worcestershire Sauce. Mix 2
tablespoons flour with cold
water; then add to meat
mixture, to thicken the stew. Drop
in dumplings; (recipe follows).

DUMPLINGS Combine together
by sifting 1 cup all-purpose
flour, ½ teaspoon salt, and 1½
teaspoons baking powder, in
a bowl. Add ½ cup milk and 2
tablespoons shortening, melted
OR vegetable oil to make a soft
dough. Drop by tablespoons
onto hot stew; cook for 12
minutes, covered.

BEEF STOCK

3 pounds beef soup bones
1 large onion, peeled &
  chopped
2 carrots, pared & chopped
2 stalks celery, chopped
2 tablespoons dried parsley
2 peppercorns
½ teaspoon salt

In a large saucepan, combine
together, all ingredients, cover.
Cook over low heat, for about
6 hours. When tested done,
remove from heat; strain, let
cool, then refrigerate. Keeps
well for about 5 days. or may
be frozen until ready to use.
Yield about 3½ quarts.

ECONOMIC VEAL STEW

2 pounds veal, cut in 1-inch
  cubes
1 small onion, sliced
¼ cup vegetable oil
1 can (8 ozs.) tomato sauce
1 can water
1 pkg. noodles, cooked
Salt and pepper to taste

In a large skillet, brown veal in
oil, with onions; add tomato
sauce and water; simmer,
covered, for 1 hour. Add
cooked noodles; simmer 30
minutes more. Season to taste.
Yield 6 to 8 servings.

HAM AND BEAN SOUP

2½ cups Navy Beans
1½ pounds smoked ham hocks
2 medium potatoes, cubed
2 carrots, chopped
2 stalks celery, sliced
1 medium onion, chopped
¾ teaspoon dried thyme
½ teaspoon salt
¼ teaspoon pepper

Rinse beans, place in a medium saucepan; add water to cover. Add ½ teaspoon baking soda; bring to a boil; then remove from heat. Drain and rinse beans, return to sauce pan; add 6 cups water and ham hocks. Cover and simmer for 1 hour or until beans are tender. Remove ham hocks; let cool, then cut meat from bone. Return meat to sauce pan; add vegetables and seasoning; cover simmer for 30 minutes or until vegetables are tender. Yield about 4 servings.

CHOP SUEY

1 pound veal, cubed
1 pound pork, ground
Vegetable oil for frying
1 cup onions, minced
1 cup celery, chopped
Salt and pepper to taste
2 cups hot water
1 can bean sprouts, drained OR
1 can Chinese vegetables, drained
¾ cup water
2 tablespoons cornstarch
4 teaspoons soy sauce
1 teaspoon granulated sugar
Cooked rice

In a large skillet, brown meat in a small amount of oil; add onion. Sauté for 5 minutes, then add celery, seasonings and hot water; cover. Over medium heat, cook for 1 hour. Add bean sprouts or Chinese vegetables. In a small bowl, combine ¾ cup water, cornstarch, soy sauce and sugar; mix well. Add to meat mixture; simmer until mixture thickens Serve over cooked rice. Yield 6 servings.

NEW ENGLAND CLAM CHOWDER

Water
1 can (8 ozs.) whole clams,
   drained (reserve liquid)
1 can (6½ ozs.) chopped clams,
   drained (reserve liquid)
¼ pound bacon, diced
1 large onion, sliced
Salt to taste
2 large potatoes, peeled &
   diced
2 cups Half and Half OR milk
1 tablespoon butter OR
   margarine
Dash of hot pepper sauce
   (optional)
Paprika (optional)

Add enough water to reserved
clam broth to measure 2 cups;
set aside. In a saucepan, over
medium heat, cook bacon
until crisp. Remove bacon
with a slotted spoon to paper
towels, to drain. Drain off all,
but 2 tablespoons of bacon
drippings. Add onions; cook,
stirring occasionally, for 5
minutes. Add broth mixture
and salt; bring to a boil. Add
potatoes, cover; reduce heat
to simmer; cook for 15 minutes
or until tender. Add Half &
Half, clams and butter, heat
through. If desired, season
with pepper sauce; sprinkle
with paprika and serve. Yield 4
servings.

CREAMY CARROT SOUP

1 cup onions, chopped
¼ cup butter OR margarine
4½ cups carrots, sliced ¼ inch
   thick
1 large potato, peeled &
   cubed
2 cans (14½ ozs. each) chicken
   broth
1 teaspoon ground ginger
2 cups heavy cream
1 teaspoons dried rosemary
½ teaspoon salt
Pinch of pepper

In a 5-quart Dutch oven, sauté
onions in butter until tender.
Add carrots, potato, broth
and ginger. Cover; cook over
medium heat, for 30 minutes
or until vegetables are tender.
Remove from heat; cool
15 minutes. Puree' in small
batches, in a blender or food
processor until smooth. Return
mixture to Dutch oven; add
cream, rosemary, salt and
pepper. Cook over low heat
until warmed through. Yield 6 to
8 servings.

WON TON SOUP

1½ cups all-purpose flour
½ teaspoon salt
1 large egg, slightly beaten
1/3 cup water
½ pound pork, chopped
½ teaspoon salt
Pinch of pepper
2 teaspoons green onions,
    minced
2 quarts boiling, salted water
4 cups chicken broth
½ cup celery, minced
½ cup ham OR chicken,
    cooked & shredded
1 cup spinach leaves, tightly
    packed and stems removed

TO PREPARE WON TONS: Mix flour and salt; add egg and water; mix well. Turn out on a floured surface; knead to make a soft dough. Cover with a clean towel; let rest 15 minutes. Roll out into paper-thin rectangle, about 8x12". Cut into 24 two inch squares, let stand while preparing meat mixture. Combine together, chopped pork, salt, pepper and onions. Place a spoonful of mixture in center of each square; fold diagonally in half. Press edges firmly together to seal. Drop in boiling water; cook for 15 minutes, then drain. Mean while prepare soup; put chicken broth in a saucepan; add celery; bring to a boil; reduce heat to simmer. Cook 5 minutes; add ham & spinach; cook 1 minute longer. Put 4 Won Tons in each bowl; pour soup on top. Yield 6 servings.

MINESTRONE SOUP

1 tablespoon vegetable oil
½ cup onion, chopped
½ cup celery, chopped
1 clove garlic, minced
1 can (16 ozs.) whole tomatoes,
    crushed
2 cups water
1 cup cabbage, shredded
1 cup carrots, sliced
¾ teaspoon dried basil
1 bay leaf
¼ teaspoon dried oregano
Salt and pepper to taste
½ cup dry elbow macaroni

Heat oil in a soup kettle; add onion, celery and garlic; cook until soft, about 3 minutes. Add remaining ingredients, EXCEPT macaroni. Simmer covered, for 25 minutes; Simmer covered, for 25 minutes; minutes more. Remove bay leaf; minutes more. Remove bay leaf; serve hot. Yield 6 one-cup servings.

GOULASH (with Paprika Dumplings)

1½ pounds beef, cut in 1" pieces
¼ cup all-purpose flour
1 teaspoon salt
1/3 cup shortening
¾ cup onions, chopped
¼ cup green pepper, diced
2 cups canned tomatoes
¼ teaspoon red pepper
1 teaspoon paprika
½ cup celery, diced
1 cup carrots, strips

Dredge beef cubes in flour; brown in shortening. Add onions and green pepper; brown lightly. Add tomatoes and seasonings; cover; cook over low heat. Cook until meat is tender, about 30 minutes; add celery and carrots. Cook an additional 20 minutes. Meanwhile prepare dumplings.

PAPRIKA DUMPLINGS

1 cup all-purpose flour, sifted
1½ teaspoons baking powder
½ teaspoon salt
2 tablespoons shortening, melted
½ cup milk
Paprika

In a small bowl, combine together, all dry ingredients; mix well. Add shortening and milk; mix thoroughly. Drop by spoonfuls onto simmering goulash. Cover; let steam about 12 minutes. Sprinkle dumplings lightly.

SHITAKE MUSHROOM SOUP

¼ pound fresh shitake mushrooms
4 cups water
4 chicken bouillon cubes
2 tablespoons soy sauce
2 tablespoons green onions, thinly sliced
Salt and pepper to taste

In a large saucepan, combine together, water bouillon cubes and soy sauce. Over medium heat, bring to a boil. Meanwhile, rinse mushrooms; cut into bite-size strips; set aside. Stir together 2 tablespoons cornstarch and 2 tablespoons water; mix well. Add mushrooms and cornstarch mixture to soup; reduce heat to simmer; cook, stirring until soup thickens.

HEARTY CHICKEN NOODLE SOUP

1 chicken (about 3 to 4 lbs.),
  cut up
4 quarts cold water
½ teaspoon salt
1 medium onion, chopped
½ teaspoon dried thyme
2 leeks, white & light green
  parts only, chopped
1 large carrot, chopped
1 parsnip, chopped
1 stalk celery, chopped
2 tablespoons fresh tarragon,
  finely chopped
2 tablespoons fresh parsley,
  finely chopped
2 cups wide egg noodles,
  cooked

In a large stock pot, combine together, chicken, water and salt; bring to a boil, over high heat. Add onion and thyme; reduce heat to low, partially cover; cook 1½ to 2 hours or meat is tested tender. Remove chicken; when cool, remove meat from bones; set aside. Meanwhile add chopped vegetables; cook for 10 to 15 minutes or until vegetables are tender. Then add chicken, tarragon & parsley; simmer for about 2 minutes. Add cooked noodles & serve. Yield 8 about two cup servings.

BASIC CHICKEN BROTH

2 chickens (about 3 to 3½ lbs.
  EACH)
Chicken giblets
2 medium carrots, pared
1 large parsnip, pared
1 large onions, chopped
  (1 cup)
2 stalks celery
3 sprigs parsley
1 leek, washed well
12 peppercorns
Water
Salt

In a large stock pot, combine together, all ingredients; add enough water to cover chicken and vegetables. Tie celery, tops, parsley and leek together. Heat slowly to boiling; add salt and pepper corns; reduce heat to simmer. Cook for 1 to 1½ hours or until the meat falls off the bone; strain broth. Refrigerate up to 4 days, or freeze up to 3 to 4 months. Yield about 12 cups broth.

PARSNIP CHOWDER

6 strips bacon, cut into 1-inch
　　pieces
1 large onion, chopped
1½ pounds parsnips, peeled &
　　cut in ½ inch cubes
1½ pounds potatoes, peeled &
　　cut in ½ inch cubes
2½ cups chicken broth
1 bay leaf
2 cups Half & Half Cream
¼ teaspoon pepper
2½ tablespoons butter OR
　　margarine
2½ tablespoon all-purpose flour

In a skillet, over medium
heat, sauté bacon pieces &
onions together until bacon
is done; drain; set aside. In a
large saucepan, combine
together, parsnips, potatoes,
chicken broth and bay leaf.
Cover; simmer for about 25
minutes or until vegetables
are tender. Add Half and Half
and pepper; mix well; bring to
a boil. Meanwhile, in a small
bowl, combine together, butter
and flour into a paste, then
add to soup, half of teaspoon
at a time. Gently mix soup until
thickened, about 10 minutes,
then add bacon and onions;
serve.

Chapter 8

PASTA, DAIRY, CHEESE AND EGG DISHES

DO UNTO OTHERS AS YOU WANT
THEM TO DO UNTO YOU!

PASTA, DAIRY & EGG DISHES

KENTUCKY DERBY EGGS

2 tablespoons butter OR
   margarine
½ cup onions, chopped
2 tablespoons all-purpose flour
1¼ cups milk
1 cup cheddar cheese.
   Shredded
6 hard-boiled eggs, sliced
1½ cups potato chips, crushed
10 slices bacon, cooked &
   diced

Preheat oven to 350 degrees.
In a small skillet, melt butter;
add onions; cook until tender
and browned. Blend in flour;
add milk; cook until mixture
thickens. Add cheese; stir until
melted. Layer half of the sliced
eggs, cheese sauce, crushed
potato chips and bacon, in a
baking dish; repeat layers, then
bake at 350 degrees, for about
30 minutes.

DENVER OMELET

½ cup ham, cooked & diced
¼ cup green pepper, chopped
¼ cup fresh mushrooms, sliced
1 green onion, sliced
1 tablespoon butter OR
   margarine
3 large eggs, slightly beaten

2 tablespoons water
Pinch of salt
Dash of cayenne pepper
1 ounce cheddar cheese,
   shredded

If using electric skillet, preheat
to 300 degrees. Combine
together, ham, green pepper,
mushrooms, onions and butter;
place into skillet. Sauté' for 2
minutes, stirring constantly.
Arrange ham and vegetables,
in an even layer. Meanwhile,
slightly beat eggs, then
combine with water, salt and
cayenne; pour over top of ham
with shredded cheese; cook an
additional 2 minutes. Lift omelet
on to serving platter, or cut in
wedges; serve. Yield 4 servings.

FRIED CHEESE

4 slices Cheddar Cheese, ¾
   inch thick
½ cup all-purpose flour
1 large egg, beaten
2/3 cup bread crumbs
1 cup shortening

Dip slices of cheese in flour,
then in beaten egg and then
in bread crumbs. Fry quickly in
hot shortening until golden.

LAZY DAY PIEROGI

½ pound lasagna noodles
10 medium potatoes, peeled
¾ pound Colby Cheese,
    shredded
2 or 3 medium onions, sliced
2 sticks butter OR margarine

Cook noodles according to
package directions; drain;
set aside. Cook potatoes until
tender; remove from heat;
drain, then mash potatoes with
cheese; set aside. Saute' onions
in melted butter. In a 9x13
inch baking pan, layer half of
noodles, potatoes and onions;
in the melted butter; repeat
with remaining ingredients.
Cover; bake at 350 degrees, for
about 35 to 40 minutes.

FOUR CHEESE LASAGNA

1 pound ground beef
1 medium onion
2 cloves garlic, minced
1 can (28 ozs.) tomatoes, with
    liquid
1 can (8 ozs.) mushrooms,
    sliced, drained
1 can (6 ozs.) tomato paste
½ teaspoon salt
1 teaspoon oregano
1 teaspoon basil
½ teaspoon pepper
½ teaspoon fennel seed

1 carton (16 ozs.) cottage
    cheese

2/3 cup Parmesan Cheese
¼ cup mild cheddar cheese,
    shredded
1½ cups mozzarella cheese,
    shredded & divided
2 large eggs
1 pound lasagna noodles,
    cooked & drained

In a medium skillet, cook
beef, onions and garlic, until
beef is browned and onions
are tender; remove from
heat; drain; set aside. Process
tomatoes in blender until
smooth. Add tomatoes to meat
mixture, along with mushrooms,
tomato paste and seasonings;
simmer over medium heat, for
about 15 minutes; remove from
heat; set aside. In a large bowl,
combine together, cottage
cheese, Parmesan Cheese,
cheddar cheese, ½ cup
mozzarella and eggs.

Spread 2 cups meat sauce in
the bottom of an ungreased
13x9x2 inch baking pan.
Arrange half the noodles over
the sauce Spread cottage
cheese mixture over noodles.
Top with remaining noodles
and meat sauce. Cover;
bake at 350 degrees, for 45
minutes; uncover; sprinkle with
remaining mozzarella. Return to
oven, bake for 15 minutes more
or until cheese melts. Yield 12
servings.

POTATO DUMPLINGS (with Swiss Cheese)

1½ potatoes, cooked, mashed
   & cold
½ cup all-purpose flour
1 large egg yolk
1/3 cup Parmesan Cheese,
   grated
¼ teaspoon nutmeg
Water for cooking dumplings
1 tablespoon salt
2 tablespoons margarine,
   melted
Salt and pepper to taste
¼ cup Swiss Cheese, diced

Place cooked potatoes in a medium mixing bowl; add 1/3 cup flour, egg yolk, Parmesan cheese and nutmeg, if necessary add more flour to get kneading consistency. Form into a roll 1" in diameter, then cut into 1" slices. Bring water to a boil in a medium saucepan, with 1 tablespoon salt. Cook dumplings for 10 to 12 minutes, or just until they float. Remove from heat; drain. Layer dumplings in a single layer, topped with melted margarine, salt and pepper to taste and Swiss cheese. Yield about 3 dozen dumplings.

NO MORE BOIL LASAGNA

½ pound ground chuck
1 jar (32 ozs.) spaghetti sauce
1 container of ricotta cheese
8 ounces lasagna noodles,
   about
10 noodles, <u>uncooked</u>
1 cup water
2 cups mozzarella cheese,
   shredded
1 cup Parmesan Cheese,
   grated
¼ cup green pepper, diced
   (optional)

Over medium heat, brown meat until no longer pink; remove from heat; drain, then layer ingredients, in a 13x9" baking pan. Start with a layer of spaghetti sauce, then lasagna noodles, a layer of meat with green pepper, then a layer of meat with green pepper, then evenly over top, repeat layers. Add 1 cup water; place foil over top; bake at 350 degrees, for 30 to 45 minutes, or until tested done. Yield 6 to 8 servings.

HOME-STYLE MACARONI AND CHEESE

1 pkg. (7 ozs.) elbow macaroni, uncooked
¼ cup butter OR margarine
3 tablespoons all-purpose flour
2 cups milk
1 pkg. (8ozs.) cream cheese, softened
Salt and pepper to taste
2 cups (9 ozs.) Cheddar Cheese, cut in ½ inch cubes
1 cup bread crumbs
2 tablespoons butter OR margarine, melted
2 tablespoons fresh parsley

Preheat oven to 400 degrees. Cook macaroni according to package directions; drain. Mean while. in a large saucepan, melt butter, stir in flour. Cook over medium heat, stirring occasionally, until smooth and bubbly, for about 1 minute. Stir in milk, cream cheese, salt and pepper. Continue cooking, stirring occasionally, until sauce is thickened, about 3 to 4 minutes. Stir in macaroni and cheese. Pour into 2 quart casserole; set aside. In a small bowl, combine together remaining ingredients; mix well. sprinkle over macaroni and cheese. Bake for 15 to 20 minutes or until golden brown and heated through. Yield 6 servings.

EASY PIEROGI

2 cups dry cottage cheese
2 tablespoon granulated sugar
1 cup fine dry bread crumbs
4 large eggs
2 tablespoons butter OR margarine
¼ teaspoon salt
All-purpose flour
1 medium onion, diced

Force cottage cheese through a sieve. In a large mixing bowl, combine together, the remainder of ingredients; mix thoroughly. Form into balls, roll in flour. Bring water to a boil; cook pierogi until tender. Remove from water, then place in a skillet with melted butter or margarine and onions; cook until onions are tender and pierogi are lightly browned. Serve with sour cream.

PIEROGI DOUGH
(Filling recipes are on following pages.)

5 cups all-purpose flour
6 large egg yolks
3 large eggs
¾ cup water
Pinch of salt
¼ pound butter OR margarine
1 cup sour cream (optional)

In a large mixing bowl, combine together, flour, egg yolks, eggs, water and salt; mix until dough forms, then on a lightly floured surface, knead until smooth and elastic. Roll dough out thin, then cut circles with a cup. Place a small amount of filling off center, on each circle of dough. Fold over filling; seal by putting pressure on edges. Bring water to by putting pressure on edges. Bring water to boiling. Drop pierogi into boiling water; cook for about 5 minutes. Remove gently, place in single layer. Melt butter in a large skillet, cook pierogi, until they are browned as you like, on both sides. If desired serve with sour cream.

CHEESE FILLING (for pierogi)

1½ cup dry cottage cheese
¼ teaspoon vanilla extract
1 large egg yolk
1 tablespoon butter OR
   margarine, melted
½ teaspoon salt
1½ tablespoons granulated
   sugar

In a medium mixing bowl, combine ingredients together; mix until smooth. Fill circles of dough with desired amount.

MEAT FILLING (for pierogi)

1 pound of ground beef
1 onion, peeled & chopped
1 tablespoon butter OR
   margarine
1 tablespoon all-purpose flour
Salt and pepper to taste

In a skillet, brown ground beef and onions until done, then drain. Stir in flour, salt and pepper to taste. When still warm, place desired amount on circles of dough.

SAUERKRAUT FILLING (for pierogi)

2 cups sauerkraut, rinsed
2 teaspoons butter OR
   margarine
1 small onion, chopped
Salt and pepper to taste

In a medium skillet, cook sauerkraut with onions in butter, about 5 minutes. Let cool, then proceed to fill rounds of dough.

MUSHROOM FILLING (for pierogi)

1 cup mushrooms, chopped
1 small onion, finely chopped
2 large egg yolks
Butter OR margarine
Salt and pepper to taste

In a small skillet, saute' onions;
in butter; add mushrooms with
seasoning, cover skillet, for
10 minutes. Stir occasionally.
Remove from heat; add egg
yolks, mix well. Cool before
filling dough.

PRUNE FILLING (for pierogi)

2 cup prunes, pitted &
   chopped
1 teaspoon lemon juice
1 tablespoon granulated sugar

Soak prunes in water for
about 10 hours or overnight.
In a medium saucepan, cook
prunes with lemon juice and
sugar, for 10 to 15 minutes.
Remove from heat, cool, then
fill pierogi dough.

POACHED EGG

¼ teaspoon salt
½ teaspoon (white) vinegar
1 large egg

In a shallow pan, heat water
to simmering; add salt, pepper
and vinegar. Break egg in a
cup; slip it carefully into water.
Make a whirlpool with spoon.
Let egg cook below boiling
point, for about 5 minutes or
until white is firm and a film has
formed over the yolk. Remove
egg drain. if desired, serve on
toast.

DEVILED EGGS

6 large eggs, hard boiled
2 teaspoons prepared mustard
¼ teaspoon salt
3 tablespoons mayonnaise OR
   salad dressing
1 tablespoon white vinegar
Pinch of pepper
Paprika

Slice eggs in half lengthwise;
carefully remove yolks. In a
bowl place yolks and mash
with a fork; add remaining
ingredients, EXCEPT paprika;
mix well. Spoon into egg whites;
sprinkle top with paprika. Yield
12 servings.

RICE NOODLES

2 cups rice, cooked
1 tablespoon butter OR
   margarine
2 large eggs

In a medium bowl, combine
together, all ingredients; mix
thoroughly. Drop from spoon
into boiling soup. Cover pan,
cook for 2 to 3 minutes, or until
teated done.

EGG DROPS

2 large eggs, beaten
¼ teaspoon salt
1 tablespoon water
½ cup all-purpose flour

In a bowl, combine together, all ingredients; mix until smooth. Drop from spoon into boiling soup. Cover pan cook for 2 or 3 minutes.

GREEN NOODLES

1½ cups torn spinach leaves
2 tablespoons water
1 large egg
½ teaspoon salt
1¼ cups all-purpose flour

In a saucepan, combine together, spinach and water; cover. Cook over low heat until spinach is very tender. Remove from heat; cool slightly; place spinach and liquid in blender or food processor. Add egg and salt; cover and blend until smooth. Transfer to a mixing bowl; add enough flour to make a stiff dough. Knead on a lightly floured surface for 1 minute. Let rest for about 20 minutes, then roll dough out. Cut strips of dough ¼ inch wide and cut in desired lengths. Spread noodles evenly on a rack or on a cookie sheet and let dry for about 2 hours. Store in an airtight container until needed.

ALFREDO SAUCE WITH PASTA

1 cup whipping cream
3 tablespoons butter OR
    margarine Pasta
2/3 cup Parmesan Cheese,
    grated Salt and pepper to
    taste

Bring a large saucepan of salted water to a boil, to cook the pasta. In a small sauce pan, combine together, 2/3 cup of whipping cream & butter; cook over medium heat for less than a minute; remove from heat. Add pasta to boiling water; cook until tender, but firm, stir occasionally. When pasta is done cooking, drain well; set aside Add pasta to sauce; set pan over low heat; add remaining whip cream, Parmesan Cheese, and pepper; toss to mix. Sauce should be on the thin side. Serve with extra cheese, if desired. Yield 6 servings.

MOZZARELLA STICKS

1 pkg. (8 ozs.) mozzarella
    cheese
3 tablespoons all-purpose flour
2 large eggs
¼ cup water
2/3 cup seasoned bread crumbs
1/3 cup Parmesan cheese
Oil for frying

Put about 1 inch oil in a medium sauce pan or skillet. Over medium heat, bring oil to 365 degrees on cooking thermometer, for about 12 minutes. Meanwhile, cut cheese into strips ½ inch by ½ inch. Line baking sheet with paper towels; set aside. Place flour on a dish; roll cheese strips in flour to coat. In a shallow bowl, combine egg and water. In another shallow bowl, combine bread crumbs, Parmesan cheese and garlic powder. One stick at a time, coat in egg, then in crumbs. Place sticks in single layer on a plate. Fry in small batches, carefully place sticks in hot oil. Cook until golden brown, about 30 seconds. Remove from oil with a slotted spoon and place on prepared lined baking sheet. Yield 4 servings.

DANDELION OMELET

3 strips bacon
4 mushrooms, sliced
1 cup dandelion greens,
    chopped fine
4 large eggs, beaten
½ cup cheese, grated
    (Mozarella, Provolone,
    Muenster, Swiss OR Cheddar)

Fry bacon until crisp; remove bacon reserving fat. Crumble bacon; place in a medium bowl; set aside. Saute' mushrooms and dandelion greens, in mushrooms and dandelion greens, in move with slotted spoon to bowl with bacon. In the same skillet, lightly scramble the eggs. As the eggs near the desired doneness; add cheese and dandelion mixture. The flip the egg over; remove at once to a serving platter. Yield 2 servings.

DANDELION QUICHE

One 9-ich pie shell, UNBAKED
4 cups dandelion greens
2 tablespoons vegetable oil
1 clove garlic, minced
8 ounces mushrooms, sliced
Salt and pepper to taste
1 tablespoon all-purpose flour
3 large eggs
1½ cups milk
2 cups Swiss cheese, shredded

Bake pie shell at 450 degrees, for 5 to 6 Bake pie shell at 450 degrees, for 5 to 6 heat to 325 degrees. Meanwhile, in a large saucepan of boiling salted water; cook greens until well-wilted, about 2 minutes. Drain thoroughly; squeeze out as much liquid as possible. then cool, chop greens coarsely. Heat oil in a skillet, then over medium heat; saute' garlic until softened. Add mushrooms and cooked dandelion greens, add seasoning to taste, cook until liquid has evaporated; add flour; mix well. In a mixing bowl, beat together, eggs and milk; season to taste; add dandelion mixture; sprinkle cheese evenly in the pie shell; add egg mixture. Bake for about 1 hour, or until tested done. Remove from oven; let stand 10 minutes before serving. Yield 6 servings.

RICOTTA CHEESE FRITTERS

½ pound ricotta cheese
½ cup all-purpose flour
2 large whole eggs
1 large egg yolk
Grated peel of 1 lemon
Pinch of salt
1 tablespoon granulated sugar
1 tablespoon rum extract
Powder sugar

In a medium-size bowl, combine together, all ingredients; mix well. Then refrigerate, covered, for several hours, or overnight. Form into balls; meanwhile, in a skillet heat about 1 inch oil; drop fritters into hot oil, cook until browned. Remove with slotted spoon; drain on paper towels. If desired, sprinkle with powder sugar.

HOMEMADE MANICOTTI CREPE NOODLES

1½ cups all-purpose flour
1 cup milk
3 large eggs
½ teaspoon salt

FILLING

1½ pounds ricotta cheese
¼ cup Romano Cheese, grated
1 large egg
1 tablespoon fresh parsley, minced

OR 1 teaspoon dried parsley
flakes
1 jar (28 ozs.) spaghetti sauce
Romano Cheese, shredded
(optional)

In a mixing bowl, combine
together, flour, milk, eggs and
salt; whisk until smooth. Pour
about 2 tablespoons of batter
onto a hot, greased 8" skillet,
spread batter to a 5" circle.
Cook over medium heat until
set; do not brown or turn.
Repeat with remaining batter,
making about 18 crepes. Stack
crepes between waxed paper;
set aside. For filling, in a bowl,
combine together, cheeses,
egg and parsley. Spoon 3
tablespoons down the center
of each crepe; roll up. Pour ½
of the spaghetti sauce into an
ungreased 13x9" baking pan.
Place crepes seam side down,
on top of sauce. then pour
remaining sauce over the top.
Cover & bake at 350 degrees,
for 20 minutes. Uncover: bake
20 minutes longer. Sprinkle with
Romano Cheese, if desired.
Yield about 6 servings.

SPANISH RICE

2 cups tomatoes, chopped
1 small onion, chopped
1 can (4 ozs.) pimiento, drained
1 green pepper, chopped
½ cup Cheddar Cheese,
cubed

½ teaspoon salt
Dash of cayenne pepper
1-1/3 cup instant rice

In a bowl, combine together,
all ingredients; mix well. Place
mixture in a buttered casserole;
bake at 350 degrees for 35
to 40 minutes. Yield about 4
servings.

FRIED NOODLES

2 quarts boiling water
½ pound of thin noodles
1 teaspoon salt
2 cups vegetable oil

Place salt in boiling water; add
noodles; boil about 5 minutes.
Drain noodles in a colander;
rinse with cold water. Again
drain to dry well. Put oil in deep
fryer, heat until hot. Put dried
noodles in hot a few at a time
until they turn delicately brown;
remove noodles with a slotted
spoon; drain. Sprinkle lightly
with salt. Keep warm or reheat
in oven at 400 degrees. Yield 4
servings.

SCRAMBLED EGGS

In a mixing bowl, for each
egg, add 1 tablespoon milk
OR cream, salt and pepper
to taste. Beat egg with fork
until ingredients are blended.
In a skillet, heat ½ tablespoon
butter OR margarine, over
medium heat. Add in egg
mixture; reduce heat to low.
When egg starts to set at
bottom and sides, lift cooked
portion with spatula; turn gently
to cook all portions of egg
evenly, for about 5 to 8 minutes.
Re move to plate and serve at
once.

Chapter 9

NOT THE USUAL RECIPES

ASK AND YOU SHALL RECEIVE;
SEEK AND YOU WILL FIND!

NOT THE USUAL RECIPES!

Some of these recipes are OLD AND NOT the regular kind you see in a cookbook.

HOMEMADE COUGH SYRUP

Green Pine Needles, ends with
   a bit of stems
Cold water
1½ pints corn syrup

In a large kettle put about 20 cups pine needles, which have been cleaned and washed. Next put in enough water to cover needles. Simmer over low heat all day; remove from heat and let set overnight. Next day remove needles and bring mixture to a boil; cook mixture down to 5 pints. Then add corn syrup; continue cooking until scum forms on top. Remove from heat; remove scum with a ladle. Put in desired heat; remove scum with a ladle. Put in desired necessary.

HOMEMADE PESTICIDE

½ to 1 cup of dead insects
1 tablespoon of liquid dish soap
1 tablespoon cayenne pepper
2 cups water

Puree' all ingredients, in preferably an old blender. Strain pulp using cheesecloth or old pantyhose. After mixture is strained, dilute, at the rate of ¼ cup of puree to 1 cup water. Spray in garden when necessary.

FURNITURE POLISH (for old furniture)

1 cup linseed oil
5 cups turpentine
1 cup white vinegar

In a large bottle, combine together, all ingredients; shake well.

TO USE: Apply polish, using a clean cloth, when dry, polish with a soft cloth.

DANDELION COFFEE

½ cup dandelion roots, roasted
   & ground
4 cups water

Bring water to boil; add powdered dandelion root. Simmer gently for 8 to 10 minutes. Strain and serve. Yield 4 servings.

ACORN PANCAKES

1½ cups acorn meal
1 teaspoon baking powder
½ teaspoon salt
½ cup cornmeal
1 tablespoon granulated sugar
¼ cup all-purpose flour
3 tablespoons margarine, melted
1 large egg, beaten
½ cup milk

In a medium mixing bowl, combine together, all dry ingredients. Add margarine, egg and milk; mix well. Cook over medium heat, in a lightly greased skillet, on both sides until browned. Yield about six 4-inch pancakes.

HOMEMADE SOAP

6 pounds of fat, (sheep, cattle
   or hog)
2½ pints of cold water
1 can (13 ozs.) lye
1 cup Borax
Few drops of oil of sassafras
6 pounds clean fat

Slowly pour lye into cold water. Use enamel or irom vessel only. Stir with wooden spoon, keeping as far sway from fumes as possible, until it is dissolved; let mixture cool. Add borax and oil of sassafras; stir to mix before mixture thickens; set aside. Melt fat; let cool completely, then stir as you pour lye and water into fat; mix until it looks like honey,

about 15 to 20 minutes. Pour into a wooden box lined with a cloth rung out in cold water. Cover; let ripen for 24 hours. water. Cover; let ripen for 24 hours.

ANT REPELLANT

2 tablespoons sassafrass leaves
2 cups water

In a small saucepan, combine together, leaves and water, bring to a boil, cook for 5 minutes; remove from heat. Allow to cool; strain mixture. Paint on ant entrances.

COCKROACH REPELLANT

4 tablespoons borax
2 tablespoons all-purpose flour
1 tablespoon cocoa powder

Combine all ingredients using a fork to mix. Spread in cabinets and on roach runways.

HOW TO DRY ELDERBERRIES!

Crush clean berries; place in a thin layer on a cookie sheet. Dry in the oven at 225 degrees for 6 to 8 hours stirring occasionally. Shape into ½ inch cakes & dry for 1 hour longer. Store in a paper bag. In any recipe use 1/3 less of dried berries than of the fresh berries. Then add 1/3 cup water to every cup of dried berries; soak for 15 minutes before using.

HOMEMADE FLYPAPER

Mix pine tar with molasses; brush mixture on piece of cardboard. Hang with string or tack on surface where flies congregate.

HEALTH DRINK TO REDUCE HIGH BLOOD PRESSURE & CHOLESTEROL

2 tablespoons apple cider
  vinegar
2 tablespoons honey
6 ounces water

Combine together; mix well. Drink before breakfast everyday. It should take about a week to see results.

FOR BIRDS ONLY

1½ cups fat, melted & unsalted
2 tablespoons or more peanut
  butter
1½ cups bread crumbs
Desired amount bird seed
½ cup cornmeal
1 cup oatmeal

In a large shallow pan, combine together, all above ingredients; mix thoroughly. Leave in pan or pack into pine cones. Allow to harden before serving.

DOCTOR'S MUSTARD PLASTER

2 tablespoons dry mustard
5 tablespoons all-purpose flour
1 tablespoon lard
1 teaspoon baking soda
Water, enough to make a
  paste.

Spread plaster on a cloth, then fold cloth over to have the paste between two pieces of cloth. If the plaster gets too hot, remove it in 5 minutes, so the skin does not get red and irritated.

HOW TO REPLENISH TOPSOIL!

Even if a plant does not need to be repotted, the topsoil still should be replenished yearly. Remove 2 to 4 inches of the old topsoil, with out harming fragile feeder roots. Refill fresh soil, mixed with fertilizer.

HOMEMADE SCOURING POWDER

1 cup baking soda
1 cup borax
1 cup salt

Combine together, all ingredients; mix well. Store in a covered jar. Use as you would any commercial scouring powder.

HOMEMADE DRAIN CLEANER

2 level tablespoons sodium
   bicarbonate
2 level tablespoons table salt
1 teaspoon baking powder

In a small bowl, mix together all
ingredients Pour into drain; flush
slowly with water.

NOTE: This is not a clogged
drain opener. Regular use will
keep drain fresh & free running.

PLAY DOUGH (DO NOT EAT!)

3 cups all-purpose flour
1½ cups of salt
3 tablespoons vegetable oil
1 cup water
1 tablespoon of food coloring

In a large bowl, combine
together, all ingredients; mix
well. Add food coloring, as
desired. Store in an airtight
container.

ROSE SYRUP

1 cup rose petals
1 cup water
1½ cups granulated sugar
3 whole cloves

Trim away the heel (white part)
of rose Trim away the heel
(white part) of rose Combine
together, petals and water,
in a medium saucepan. Over
medium-high heat, bring to
a boil, cover; reduce heat to
simmer. Cook for 5 minutes or
until sugar dissolves (do not
let mixture boil). Remove from
heat, strain petals boil). Remove
from heat, strain petals syrup
until ready to use. Serve as a
table syrup or to sweeten tea.
Also use syrup to make Rose
Cooler. (Recipe follows). Yield
1-2/3 cups.

ROSE COOLER

½ cup Rose Syrup
2 cups club soda
Fresh rose petals, washed &
   trimmed

Combine together, syrup and
club soda; mix well. Serve over
ice; garnish with a few rose
petals. Yield 2½ cups.

JERUSALEM ARTICHOKE SOUP (aka Sunchokes)

1 pound Jerusalem artichokes, cooked, skinned and diced
1 small onion, chopped
Butter
3 cups chicken stock
6 tablespoons thick cream, plus extra for garnish
Salt and pepper to taste
Cinnamon OR nutmeg

In a heavy saucepan, fry onion in butter, for 2 minutes Add chicken stock; simmer for 40 to 45 minutes, or until tested done. Remove from heat, mash gently with potato masher. Return to heat; add cream, simmer until soup thickens; season to taste. If desired, drizzle with additional cream, sprinkle on top, cinnamon or nutmeg. Serve immediately. Yield 4 to 6 servings.

HOMEMADE DOG BISCUITS I

3½ cups all-purpose flour
1 cup rye flour
1 cup cornmeal
2 cup wheat germ
½ non-fat dry milk
1 teaspoon salt
1 package dry yeast
1 package dry yeast
OR stock flavored with turkey
¼ cup ground chicken, etc. (optional)

In a large mixing bowl, combine together, all the ingredients; mix until mixture forms a ball. It will be sticky. Roll dough out on a lightly floured surface. Cut with desired cookie cutter. Place biscuits on slightly greased cookie sheet. In a small mixing bowl, combine 1 large egg, beaten with 1 tablespoon milk. Bake at 300 degrees, for 40 to 45 minutes. If you desire, shorten the baking time for a softer biscuit.

HOMEMADE DOG BISCUITS II

1½ cups whole wheat flour
1 cup all-purpose flour
1 cup non-fat dry milk
1/3 cup meat fat, melted (beef, lamb or bacon
1 large egg, lightly beaten
1 cup cold water

In a medium mixing bowl, combine together, flour and dry milk; add melted fat, by drizzling and mixing dry ingredients. Add egg and water; mix until dough forms a ball. Roll dough out on a lightly floured surface, to ½ inch thick; on a lightly floured surface, to ½ inch thick; for 50 to 60 minutes, or until crisp. Yield about 36 (2½ inch) biscuits.

HOW TO DRY ROSE HIPS!

Pick rose hips when ripe; peel and slice them. Place on tray and dry in a shady place. When dry, store in a paper bag. When ready to use, grind then in food processor or blender. Use for flavoring in puddings, sauces, vegetables, stews and soups.

BUBBLE BATH

½ cup detergent
1 cup Epsom salts
4 or 5 drops glycerin (available at most drug stores)
Few drops of food coloring
Few drops of cologne

Combine together, all above ingredients; mix thoroughly to insure even distribution of color and fragrance. Place Bubble Bath in clean, attractive jars and/or bottles.

BATH SALTS

Use same ingredients as Bubble Bath recipe, EXCEPT omit the detergent.

*FLAME-RETARDANT FORMULA

3 ounces boric acid
7 ounces borax
2 quarts water

Add a small amount of water to boric acid; make a paste. Mix paste and borax into the water, stirring until solution is clear. Immerse dry fabric or garment into solution; soak for 5 minutes. If fabric is not absorbing water, add 1 teaspoon of detergent for each gallon of water. Wring out fabric by hand; place on a plastic hanger to dry. If fabric needs to be ironed, use a moderately hot iron when fabric is still damp. If the fabric is wet or the iron is too hot, the solution will stick to the iron.

NOTE: This recipe is a simple way to treat washable fabrics for flame-retardancy. This treatment is not permanent (it will come out during the first washing) and will lose effectiveness during storage. All ingredients are available at drug or grocery stores.

DANDELION NOODLES

2 cups dandelion leaves, chopped
1 cup boiling water
2 cups all-purpose flour
1 large egg
2 to 4 tablespoons water

Combine leaves and water; cook until tender, about 15 minutes; drain well. Add remaining ingredients with just enough of water to combine ingredients; mix until stiff dough forms. Roll dough on a floured surface, to ¼ inch thickness. Let dry 3 to 4 hours, then slice into strips. Cook in boiling water until tender, about 20 to 25 minutes. Use noodles as desired. Yield 6 servings.

DANDELION COFFEE

½ cup roots, *roasted & ground
4 cups water

Bring water to a boil; add round dandelion roots. Simmer gently, for 8 to 10 minutes. Strain & serve. Yield 4 servings.

*Roast—Place roots in oven at 400 degrees, until roots are lightly browned, turning roots occasionally.

DANDELION TEA

½ cup dandelion leaves, dried
    & crushed
4 cups water

Bring water to a boil; add leaves; simmer for 10 minutes; strain & serve. Yield 4 servings

DANDELION PANCAKES

6 cups dandelion leaves
1 cup water
½ teaspoon salt
4 tablespoons flour
1 large egg
Cooking oil

Combine leaves, water and salt; bring to a boil. Cook gently for 10 minutes; remove from heat; drain. Replenish with fresh water, again bring to a boil. Cook10 minutes more; drain. Place leaves, flour and egg in blender; blend until smooth. Drop by spoonfuls onto skillet with hot oil. Cook until crisp, turn over. (These pancakes take longer to cook than normal.) Yield 4 servings.

DANDELION WINE

3 quarts boiling water
3 quarts dandelion petals
6 cups granulated sugar
2 oranges, sliced
2 lemons, sliced
1 pkg. dry active yeast

Place petals in a large container, pour boiling water over petals; cover. Let set for 4 days; then strain and discard petals. Combine liquid, sugar, orange and lemon; bring to a boil, over medium heat. Cook gently for 20 minutes. Remove from heat, pour into jug and let cool. Dissolve yeast in 2 tablespoons warm water; add to cooled mixture; cover. Let set for 5 days; then strain, bottle as desired. Allow to age for 1 month, before using. Yield 1 gallon wine.

CATTAIL SOUP

1 cup cattail roots, peeled &
    sliced
½ cup young cattail shoots,
    peeled & laced
4 cups chicken stock
1 stalk celery, sliced
1 stem parsley, diced

In a saucepan, combine
together, cook over low heat,
for about 35 to 40 minutes or
until tender. Yield 4 servings.

HOW TO MAKE ACORN MEAL!

White oak acorns yield the
sweetest fruit. Remove the
tannin by leaching with
water. Grind dried acorns in
a blender, put in a cloth bag,
then place in a pot of water,
changing every hour, do this
for 12 hours. Remove meal from
water; knead bag gently to
remove excess water. Spread
the meal in a shallow baking
pan; place in oven at 225
degrees, for about 2 hours,
stirring occasionally or until dry.

SOY NUTS

3 cups dried soybeans
5 cups water
½ cup vegetable oil
Salt

Soak soybeans overnight in
water. Next day, in a large
saucepan, add soybeans &
fresh water. Bring to a boil, then
lower heat to simmer; cook
for 15 minutes, just to soften
beans. Remove from heat, skim
off foam and hulls that float
to surface; drain well. Spread
soybeans on flat surface; let
dry thoroughly. When dry, heat
¼ cup vegetable oil in large
skillet. Add half of the beans;
sauté until golden brown,
stirring frequently. Repeat with
remaining beans; if desired,
season lightly with salt. Yield
about 3 cups soybeans.

ACORN BISCUITS

½ cup whole wheat flour
½ cup acorn meal
1½ teaspoons baking powder
½ teaspoon salt
2 tablespoons butter OR
    margarine
3 tablespoons milk

Combine together, the dry
ingredients, then cut in butter
and stir in milk; mix until dough
forms. Roll dough on a floured
surface; cut with biscuit cutter.
Place on greased cookie sheet;
bake at 400 degrees, for 10 to
12 minutes. Yield 6 biscuits.

ACORN MUFFINS

½ cup acorn meal
1 teaspoon baking powder
½ teaspoon salt
¼ cup all-purpose flour
¼ cup whole wheat flour
4 tablespoons butter OR
    margarine, melted
1 large egg, beaten
¼ up honey
¼ cup milk
¼ cup raisins

Combine together, dry
ingredients, then add
remaining ingredients; mix just
until moistened. Fold in raisins.
Fill greased muffin pan 2/3 cup
full. Bake at 400 degrees, for 20
to 25 minutes. Yield 6 muffins.

ACORN NOODLES

½ cup whole wheat flour
½ cup acorn meal
1 large egg
1 tablespoon water

Combine together, flour and
acorn meal; stir in egg and
water. Dough will be stiff. Roll
out, on a floured surface to
1/8 inch thick. Let dough dry
completely, for about 1½ hours.
Cut into 2" x ½" strips. Cook
in boiling water, for 15 to 20
minutes or until tender; drain.
Yield 2½ cups.

WALNUT DUMPLINGS

½ cup walnuts, finely ground
2 tablespoons butter OR
    margarine, melted
¼ cup milk
½ cup all-purpose flour

Combine together, all
ingredients; mix until smooth.
Drop by spoonfuls in hot stew
or soup; cover. Cook over low
heat, for about 15 minutes.
Yield 4 servings.

MAPLE BEER

3 gallons boiling water
3 cups maple syrup
½ teaspoon ground ginger
½ pkg. dry active yeast

Combine together, water, syrup
and ginger; mix well. Place
in a crock; set aside to cool.
Dissolve yeast in set aside to
cool. Dissolve yeast in cooled
mixture; cover the crock with
cheesecloth. Let set for 1 week,
then strain and bottle, as
desired. Yield about 3 gallons.

CANDIED VIOLETS

1¼ cups granulated sugar
¼ cup water
½ teaspoon vanilla extract
3 cups violet flowers

Combine together, sugar and water, in a saucepan; bring to a boil. Cook gently for 7 minutes, stirring frequently. Remove from heat; cool. Stir in vanilla; add ½ cup violet flowers in the syrup. When they are covered with syrup, remove with a slotten spoon; place on wax paper. Repeat with remaining flowers. When the violets are dry, then store in a box, in a cool dry place. Yield about 1½ cups.

PAWPAW PIE

6 large ripe pawpaw, sliced
¾ cup granulated sugar
¼ cup apple juice OR cider
3 tablespoons lime juice
1½ teaspoon cinnamon
½ teaspoon allspice
Whipped cream (optional)
1 piecrust (9") UNBAKED

Place pawpaw slices in piecrust; set aside. Combine together, sugar, apple juice, lime juice and spices; mix well. Pour over pawpaw; cover. Bake at 350 degrees, for 45 to 50 minutes, or until crust is light brown. Serve warm; if desired, serve with whipped cream Yield 8 servings.

HOW TO DRY ROSE PETALS!

Spread rose petals on a tray; dry for 5 to 7 days. Store in a paper bag.

ROSE WATER

1 cup water
4 cups fresh rose petals

Bring water to a boil; add rose petals; cover reduce heat to simmer. Cook for 10 minutes; strain and store tightly covered in a glass jar in the refrigerator. Yield 1 cup.

Chapter 10

ALL KINDS OF SALADS AND SALAD DRESSINGS

KNOCK AND IT SHALL BE OPENED TO YOU!

TIPS FOR GREAT SALADS

1. Select greens that are crisp and without discoloration.
2. Wash greens in cool water; pat dry with paper towels. Store in a covered container or plastic bag, refrigerate at least 1 hour before serving.
3. Just before serving, do not cut lettuce, it is best to tear lettuce into bite-size pieces. Cutting with a knife will turn the edges brown.
4. Green salads should not be kept at room temperature any longer than 15 minutes before serving.
5. Toss greens with salad dressing and serve immediately or pass salad dressing at the table. Adding the salad dressing just before eating will prevent soggy salads.
6. And last, pasta, rice and vegetable salads should chill for a few hours to allow flavors to blend.

CAESAR SALAD

DRESSING

¼ cup olive oil
4 teaspoons fresh lemon juice
¼ teaspoon pepper
1 tablespoon anchovy fillets (optional)
1 clove garlic, minced
½ teaspoon Worcestershire sauce

SALAD

8 cups Romaine lettuce, torn in pieces
1 purple onion, sliced thin
½ cup Parmesan Cheese, grated
Croutons (optional)

In a small bowl, combine together, all salad dressing ingredients; mix well. Place lettuce in a large bowl; add dressing; toss to mix. Add onions, cheese and croutons. Yield 6 servings.

BUTTERMILK SALAD DRESSING

1 cup mayonnaise
½ cup sour cream
½ cup buttermilk
¼ cup ketchup
1 teaspoon Worcestershire Sauce
¼ teaspoon garlic salt
¼ teaspoon white pepper
½ teaspoon paprika

In a medium mixing bowl, combine together all the ingredients; blend thoroughly. Chill for 1 hour before serving.

CATALINA SALAD DRESSING

2/3 cup salad oil
1/3 apple cider vinegar
½ cup tomato ketchup
2 tablespoons powder sugar
1 teaspoon granulated sugar
½ teaspoon salt
Dash ground cloves

In a glass jar, combine together, all above ingredients; cover jar; shake vigorously until sugars are dissolved. Refrigerate; shake again before serving over tossed salads. Yield 1½ cups.

POTATO SALAD

2½ cups potatoes, cooked & cubed
1 teaspoon granulated sugar
1 teaspoon white vinegar
¼ cup onions, chopped
½ cup celery, sliced
¼ cup sweet pickle, sliced
1 teaspoon celery seed
¾ cup mayonnaise
2 hard-cooked eggs, sliced

In a large mixing bowl, place cooked potatoes, along with remaining ingredients, EXCEPT eggs; mix gently. Fold in eggs; chill, before serving. Yield about 4 servings.

ALL-PURPOSE PECAN SALAD DRESSING

1 pkg. (3 ozs.) cream cheese
1/3 cup mayonnaise
1/3 cup orange juice
1 tablespoon lemon juice
1 tablespoon granulated sugar
¼ teaspoon salt
1/3 cup pecans, chopped

Soften cream cheese; add remaining ingredients EXCEPT pecans. Beat until well-blended; stir in chopped pecans; chill. Serve with fruit or salad greens. Yield 1-1/3 cups.

CUCUMBER SALAD

1 cup sour cream
3 tablespoons onions, diced
2 tablespoons lemon juice
Salt and pepper to taste
3 large cucumbers, peel & sliced

In a medium mixing bowl, combine together, all ingredients; EXCEPT cucumbers; mix until well-blended; set aside. Peel and slice cucumbers; place in large bowl; add sour cream mixture; gently mix to coat cucumbers. Cover and refrigerate at least ½ hour before serving. Yield about 6 servings.

RED BEET SALAD

4 cups beets, cooked, peeled
   & diced
1 tablespoon vinegar
¼ cup sour cream
¼ cup mayonnaise
1½ teaspoons horseradish
Dash of Salt

Cook, peel and dice beets;
place in a large bowl; set aside.
Combine together, remaining
ingredients; mix well. Pour over
beets; stir gently to coat beets.
Chill, at least 1 hour before
serving.

BLT SALAD

1 medium head lettuce
2 medium tomatoes
½ cup mayonnaise
3 tablespoons milk
1 tablespoon green onions,
   chopped
1 teaspoon Dijon mustard
1 teaspoon lemon juice
½ teaspoon granulated sugar
8 slices bacon, cooked,
   drained & crumbled

Arrange lettuce leaves on 4
individual salad plates. Slice
tomatoes and arrange on top
of lettuce; set aside. In a small
bowl, combine remaining
ingredients, EXCEPT bacon; mix
well. To serve spoon dressing
over salad and garnish with
crumbled bacon. If desired,
add a sprinkling of croutons.

WILTED LETTUCE SALAD

4 cups lettuce, shredded
6 slices bacon, cooked & diced
½ cup water
Salt to taste
1 small onion, minced
¼ cup vinegar
4 tablespoons granulated sugar
Pepper (optional)

Brown bacon in frying pan.
Remove bacon; dice, then
combine with lettuce and
onion; set aside. In a small
saucepan, combine together,
water, vinegar and bacon
fat over medium heat,
bring mixture to a boil. Add
seasoning and sugar, then
pour over lettuce mixture; mix
thoroughly. Serve at once. Yield
6 servings.

SWEET & SOUR SAUCE

1 cup milk
½ cup granulated sugar
1/3 cup white vinegar
5 strips bacon, cut up fine
Salt & pepper to taste

Fry bacon until crisp; drain all
but 2 tablespoons of bacon
grease. In bowl, mix milk, sugar
& vinegar; add bacon; mix
slowly until thickened. Add salt
& pepper to taste. Pour over
lettuce or other greens.

WALDORF SALAD

2 cups apples, unpared &
  diced
1 cup celery, diced
½ cup mayonnaise
½ cup walnuts, chopped

In a medium mixing bowl,
combine together, apples,
celery and mayonnaise;
mix well. Cover and chill in
refrigerator. Just before serving,
fold in nuts. Spoon onto salad
plates. Yield 4 servings.

MAYONNAISE

2 large egg yolks
1 tablespoon lemon juice
1 teaspoon granulated sugar
½ teaspoon Dijon-style mustard
Pinch ground nutmeg
1¼ cups vegetable oil

In a food processor or blender,
place egg yolks, lemon juice,
sugar, mustard and nutmeg;
process until mixture is smooth.
Keep machine running while
adding oil slowly, through lid or
feed tube, until mayonnaise is
thickened.

NOTE: Mayonnaise can be
refrigerated, covered up to 1
week.

PRETZEL SALAD

2¾ cups pretzels, finely crushed
3 tablespoons granulated sugar
1½ cups butter OR margarine,
  melted
1 pkg. (3 ozs.) cream cheese,
  softened
1 cup granulated sugar
2 cups whipped topping
2 pkgs.(3 ozs. each) strawberry
  gelatin
3 cups boiling water

In a small saucepan melt
butter, then combine with
crushed pretzels and 3
tablespoons sugar. Spoon
mixture in a 9x13 inch baking
pan; spread evenly on bottom,
if desired, save some pretzel
mixture for the top. Bake at
350 degrees for 10 minutes; set
aside to cool thoroughly. In a
medium mixing bowl, cream
together, cream cheese and
1 cup sugar; blend well. Fold
in whipped topping; spread
evenly over pretzel mixture.
Meanwhile, dissolve gelatin in
boiling water; add strawberry
gelatin, mix well, then allow
mixture to cool completely.
When cool, slowly pour over
whipped topping. Refrigerate
until set; serve. Yield 12 to 15
servings.

SPAGHETTI SALAD

Breakup 1 box spaghetti in
2" pieces. Cook al dente; let
cool. Cut 3 large peppers in
small pieces. In a large bowl,
combine together, spaghetti,
cut peppers, 2 cups mayonnaise
and 1½ cups Parmesan Cheese
grated; mix well. Refrigerate until
ready to serve.

WATERGATE SALAD

1 box Instant Pistacho Pudding
1 large container Whipped
   Topping
1 large can crushed pineapple,
   undrained
2 cups miniature marshmallows
1 can Mandarin Oranges

In a large mixing bowl,
combine all ingredients; blend
thoroughly. Refrigerate until set,
about ½ hour. Serve.

SWEET MUSTARD DRESSING

1 cup mayonnaise
¼ cup prepared mustard
¼ cup granulated sugar
¼ cup onions, grated

In a small mixing bowl,
combine together, all
ingredients; mix well. Chill
before using, keeps indefinitely
in refrigerator. Dressing good
on hamburger, hot dogs, toss
salad, etc.

RUSSIAN-STYLE SALAD DRESSING

1 can (10¾ ozs.) tomato soup,
   undiluted
½ cup granulated sugar
½ cup vinegar
½ cup vegetable oil
1 small onion, finely chopped
1 tablespoon Worcestershire
   Sauce
1 teaspoon dry mustard
1 teaspoon paprika

In a pint-size jar, with a tight-
fitting lid, combine together,
all ingredients. Cover; shake
vigorously until thoroughly
mixed. Refrigerate at least 2
hours before serving. Store
unused dressing in refrigerator.
Serve over salad greens. Yield
2¾ Cups.

HAM SALAD

2 cups ham, cooked
3 stalks celery
1 large dill pickle
2 tablespoons onions, minced
½ cup mayonnaise OR salad
   dressing
¼ teaspoon dry mustard
½ teaspoon salt
1 tablespoon lemon juice

Put ham, celery and pickle
through coarse blade of food
chopper. In a bowl, combine
together, all ingredients; mix
well. Cover; refrigerate before
serving.

FRENCH SALAD DRESSING

1 cup vegetable oil
½ cup apple cider vinegar
1 tablespoon water
1 teaspoon granulated sugar
1 teaspoon paprika
1 teaspoon dry mustard
½ teaspoon Worcestershire
  Sauce
¼ teaspoon black pepper
Pinch of onion powder
Pinch of garlic powder

In a pint-size jar, with a tight-fitting lid, combine together, all ingredients. Cover; shake vigorously until thoroughly mixed. Refrigerate, for at least 2 hours, before serving. Store unused dressing in refrigerator. Yield 1½ cups.

CRANBERRY SALAD

2 cans wholeberry cranberry
  sauce
1 can (20 ozs.) crushed
  pineapple, undrained
1 red delicious apple, core &
  dice
¼ cup walnuts, chopped
  (optional)

Combine together, all ingredients, in a large mixing bowl; mix well. Chill overnight; stir again before serving.

BASIC VINAGRETTE SALAD DRESSING

1 cup vegetable oil
¾ cup granulated sugar
½ cup red wine vinegar
2 cloves of garlic, minced
½ teaspoon paprika
½ teaspoon salt
¼ teaspoon white pepper

Combine together, all above ingredients; place in a jar with a lid. Shake ingredients until mixed thoroughly and thickened. Serve over salad.

THOUSAND ISLAND SALAD DRESSING

1 cup Miracle Whip Salad
  Dressing
¼ cup granulated sugar
½ cup ketchup
¼ cup sweet pickle relish
2 teaspoons onions, chopped
  fine
Salt to taste

In a medium mixing bowl, combine together all ingredients; mix thoroughly. Yield about 1½ cups of salad dressing.

OLD FASHION FRUIT SALAD

1 can pineapple slices, drained
    & cut up
1 large red apple, diced
2 bananas, sliced
½ cup walnuts, chopped
1/3 cup heavy cream, whipped
2 tablespoons lemon juice
2 tablespoons granulated sugar

In medium mixing bowl. combine together, fruit and nuts; set aside. In another bowl, combine remaining ingredients; mix well. Pour dressing over fruit mixture; mix gently. Yield 4 to 6 servings.

COLE SLAW

5 cups cabbage, finely
    chopped (about 1 small
    head)
2 carrots, peeled & shredded
1 to 2 tablespoon of granulated
    sugar
½ teaspoon salt
¼ teaspoon pepper
1/3 cup mayonnaise OR salad
    dressing

In a large bowl, combine together, cabbage and carrots; sprinkle with sugar, salt and pepper. Toss gently, then stir in mayonnaise; mix well. Cover; refrigerate before serving. Yield about 6 to 8 servings.

EVERYTHING BUT THE KITCHEN SINK SALAD

6 large eggs beaten
1/3 cup granulated sugar
1/3 cup apple cider vinegar
½ teaspoon salt
4 cups macaroni, cooked &
    drained
3 large eggs, hard cooked
1¼ cups ham, cooked, cubed
1 cup Velvetta Cheese, cubed
2 ribs of celery, thinly sliced
1 medium onion, chopped
¾ cup sweet pickle relish
¾ cup stuffed olives, sliced
1/3 cup mayonnaise

In a medium saucepan, combine together, beaten eggs, sugar, vinegar and salt; cook over low heat, for 10 minutes or until mixture has thickened. Remove from heat; set aside and let cool completely, stirring several times. Meanwhile, in a medium mixing bowl, combine together, cooked macaroni, and the remaining ingredients, EXCEPT mayonnaise. Stir mayonnaise into cooked egg mixture, mix well. Pour over macaroni mixture; mix thoroughly. Cover; refrigerate for at least 2 hours before serving. Yield 6 to 8 servings.

FRUIT SALAD

1 can (20 ozs.) pineapple
  chunks
2 large bananas, cut into 1/4-
  inch cubes
1 cup green grapes
1 can (15 ozs.) mandarin
  oranges
1 medium red apple, sliced
1 medium green apple, sliced
½ cup granulated sugar
2 tablespoons cornstarch
1/3 cup orange juice
1 tablespoon lemon juice

Drain pineapple, reserving
juice. Combine the pineapple,
bananas, grapes, oranges
and apples in a large mixing
bowl; set aside. In a small
saucepan, combine sugar and
corn starch. Add the orange
juice, lemon juice reserved
pineapple juice; stir until
smooth. Over high heat, bring
to a boil; reduce heat. Cook for
2 minutes, stirring constantly.
Pour over fruit; mix gently.
Cover; refrigerate until ready to
serve.

REUBEN SALAD

2 tablespoons butter OR
  margarine
3 thick slices pumpernickel
  bread
1 large head lettuce
¾ pound lean corned beef,
  cooked & cut into thin strips
2 cups sauerkraut, rinsed &
  drained
½ pound (or 2 cups) Swiss
  Cheese, cubed
1 cup Russian Salad Dressing
1 teaspoon caraway seeds
  (optional)
Croutons (below)

TO MAKE CROUTONS:

Spread butter on bread; bake
at 300 degrees, for 15 minutes;
remove from oven. Cut into ½
inch cubes.

SALAD DIRECTIONS

Prepare lettuce by tearing
into bite-size pieces. In a
large mixing bowl, combine
together, lettuce, corned beef,
sauerkraut and Swiss cheese,
toss lightly, mixing well. Serve in
individual salad bowls, top with
dressing and croutons; sprinkle
with caraway seeds, if desired.

SWEET POTATO SALAD

½ cup sour cream
½ cup mayonnaise
3 tablespoons honey
2 tablespoons lemon juice
1 teaspoon lemon peel, grated
¼ teaspoon salt
¼ teaspoon black pepper
2 large sweet potatoes, peeled
   & shredded
1 medium tart apple, peeled &
   chopped
1 cup golden raisins (optional)
½ cup pineapple chunks,
   drained
½ cup pecans, chopped
   (optional)

To prepare salad dressing,
combine together, in a small
mixing bowl, sour cream,
mayonnaise, honey, lemon
peel, salt and pepper; mix
well; set aside. Meanwhile,
in another bowl, shred sweet
potatoes, enough to measure
about 4 cups. Measure
1 cup chopped apple.
Combine together, remaining
ingredients; mix well. Add
salad dressing to sweet potato
mixture; mix thoroughly. Cover
and chill in refrigerator for 2
hours, before serving. Yield 8
servings.

ITALIAN SALAD DRESSING

¼ cup white vinegar
3 tablespoons water
2 tablespoons granulated sugar
1 teaspoon lemon juice
½ teaspoon garlic powder
½ teaspoon onion powder
1 teaspoon black pepper,
   coarsely ground
2 teaspoons fresh parsley,
   minced OR
1 teaspoon dried parsley flakes
½ teaspoon fresh basil OR ¼
   teaspoon dried basil
½ teaspoon fresh oregano OR
   ¼ teaspoon dried oregano
½ teaspoon fresh thyme OR ¼
   teaspoon dried thyme
½ cup olive oil

In a bottle or cruet, combine
together, all ingredients,
EXCEPT oil, shake vigorously.
Add oil; shake until well-mixed.
Store covered in the refrigerator
until ready to serve. Yield 1 cup
dressing.

MACARONI SALAD FOR 100 PERSONS

6 pounds ham, cooked & cubed
6 pounds macaroni, cooked & drained
3 pounds cheddar cheese, shredded
2 bags (20 ozs, each) frozen peas, thawed
2 bunches celery, chopped (about 12 cups)
2 large onions, chopped (2 to 2½ cups)
2 cans (5¾ ozs each) ripe olives, pitted, drained and sliced

DRESSING INGREDIENTS

2 quarts mayonnaise
1 bottle French Salad Dressing
¼ cup white vinegar
¼ cup granulated sugar
1 cup light cream
1½ teaspoons onion salt
1½ teaspoons garlic salt
1 teaspoon pepper

In a large container combine together, all salad ingredients; mix well. In another container, combine together, all dressing ingredients; mix thoroughly. Pour over salad mixture; toss gently. Refrigerate before serving.

EGG SALAD FOR 50 PERSONS

3 dozen eggs, hard-cooked & chopped
6 stalks of celery, chopped
3 large carrots, finely shredded
3 small green peppers, diced
3 small onions, diced
2 cans (2¼ ozs. each) olives drained and sliced
3 cups mayonnaise
¾ cup milk
1 tablespoon ground mustard
Salt and pepper to taste
100 bread slices (about 6 loaves)

In a large mixing bowl, combine together, the first six ingredients; set aside. In another bowl, combine together, mayonnaise, milk, mustard, salt and pepper. Mix well until smooth. Stir into egg mixture; cover; refrigerate for at least 1 hour.

FOR SANDWICHES

Spread about 1/3 cup egg salad on one bread slice; top with another bread slice. OR serve with crackers as an appetizer.

FRESH CRANBERRY SALAD

1 pound cranberries
1 can Mandarin oranges,
   chopped
1½ cups granulated sugar
3 pkgs. lemon gelatin
1½ cups celery, chopped
½ cup nuts, chopped

Grind cranberries in food processor, place in bowl with chopped oranges and sugar; let stand for 1 hour. Prepare gelatin according to package directions, using 4½ cups water. Chill until partially thickened; fold in cranberry mixture, celery and nuts into gelatin. Pour mixture into 8½ x 14 inch dish or individual molds; chill until firm. If desired, top with whipped topping. Yield 15 to 18 servings.

FROZEN PEA SALAD

1 pkg. (10 ozs.) frozen peas
1 pkg. (4 ozs.) Hidden Valley
   Ranch Original Salad
   Dressing
1 cup buttermilk
1 carton (8 ozs.) sour cream
1 small onion, chopped
1 small head lettuce, cut in bite
   size pieces
4 large, hard cooked eggs,
   diced
8 to 10 strips bacon, fried,
   drained and cut in bite-size
   pieces
Salt and pepper to taste

Thaw peas; drain well. In a small bowl, place dry dressing mix, buttermilk and sour cream; beat until smooth and creamy. Add onions and salt and pepper; mix well; set aside. In a large mixing bowl, combine lettuce, eggs, bacon and peas; add dressing and toss gently until salad ingredients are coated with dressing. Refrigerate, covered, before serving.

GERMAN POTATO SALAD

8 cups potatoes, cooked &
   sliced (about 3 pounds)
½ teaspoon salt
8 slices bacon, cut into 1"
   pieces
1 cup onions, chopped
1 clove garlic, minced
¾ cup apple cider vinegar
2 tablespoons granulated sugar
½ teaspoon pepper

Cook bacon until brown and crisp. Drain off bacon grease all, but about ¼ cup. Add onions and garlic; cook for 2 to 3 minutes; add vinegar, sugar, salt, pepper and bacon; mix well. Pour vinegar mixture over sliced, cooked potatoes; toss well. Yield 6 servings.

DELICATESSEN COLESLAW

1 cup mayonnaise
1½ tablespoons prepared
    horseradish
2 teaspoons white vinegar
1 teaspoon celery seed
1 teaspoon granulated sugar
½ teaspoon salt
1 large head cabbage,
    shredded

In a small mixing bowl,
combine together, all
ingredients, EXCEPT cabbage;
mix thoroughly. Shred cabbage
into a large bowl, then pour
mayonnaise mixture over
cabbage; mix well. Refrigerate
overnight to ripen before
serving. Yield about 1½ quarts.

DELICATESSEN MACARONI

2 cups elbow macaroni
¾ cup mayonnaise
2 tablespoons white vinegar
2 teaspoons prepared mustard
2 teaspoons granulated sugar
½ teaspoon salt
Pinch of pepper
1½ cups celery, finely chopped
½ cup onions, chopped
3 tablespoons sweet pickle
    relish (optional)

Cook macaroni, according
to package directions; when
cooked, pour macaroni into a
colander; rinse with cold water;
drain well; set aside. In a large
bowl, combine together, all
ingredients; mix thoroughly.
Add drained macaroni; mix
well; cover; refrigerate until
ready to serve. Yield 6 to 8
servings.

TURNIP SLAW

3 cups turnips, peeled &
    shredded
3 tablespoons sour cream
1 tablespoon granulated sugar
1 tablespoon fresh parsley,
    minced
1 tablespoon cider vinegar
1 tablespoon mayonnaise
¼ teaspoon salt

In a large mixing bowl, place
shredded turnips; set aside. In a
small bowl, combine together,
the remaining ingredients; mix
well. Pour over turnips, toss to
coat; cover; refrigerate for 1
hour before serving. Yield 6
servings.

PUMPKIN SALAD

2 cups fresh pie pumpkin,
    uncooked, shredded
1 can (8 ozs.) crushed
    pineapple, undrained
½ cup raisins
1 tablespoon mayonnaise OR
    salad dressing
½ teaspoon granulated sugar
Leaf lettuce, if desired

Place pumpkin in a 1-quart microwave-safe bowl. Cover; microwave on high for 3 minutes; cool. Stir in pineapple, undrained, raisins, mayonnaise and sugar. Refrigerate over night. Serve on leaf lettuce, if desired Yield 4 servings.

7-UP SALAD

2 pkgs. lemon OR lime gelatin
2 cups boiling water
2 cups Seven-up
1 large can crushed pineapple,
    drained
1 cup small marshmallows
2 large bananas, diced

In a mixing bowl, combine together, gelatin, boiling water and 7-up; let cool until partially set. Then add drained pineapple, bananas and marshmallows; mix gently. If desired, place in individual dishes; refrigerate until firm. Yield about 6 to 8 servings.

CELERY SEED SALAD DRESSING

½ cup powder sugar
¼ cup apple cider vinegar
2 teaspoons prepared mustard
½ teaspoon salt
1 teaspoon paprika
1 teaspoon celery seeds
1 cup salad oil

In a medium mixing bowl, combine together, the first 6 ingredients; mix well. Gradually add oil, beating constantly until thickened. Cover and refrigerate, if dressing separates, stir well before serving over fruit salads. Yield 1½ cups.

REFRIGERATOR CUCUMBER SLICES

6 large cucumbers, sliced
3 medium onions, sliced
3 cups granulated sugar
3 cups cider vinegar
3 teaspoons pickling salt
1½ teaspoons mustard seed
½ teaspoon alum

In a large container, combine together, cucumbers and onions; set aside. In a large bowl, combine the remaining ingredients, stirring until sugar is dissolved. Pour over cucumber mixture; mix well. Cover; chill over night; may be refrigerated for up to 2 weeks. Yield 2½ quarts.

COLESLAW DRESSING

¾ cup mayonnaise
3 ounces half & half cream
3 tablespoons granulated sugar
4 teaspoons white vinegar
½ teaspoon celery seed

In a small mixing bowl, combine together, all ingredients; mix until light and fluffy. Pour over shredded cabbage; mix well. Store in the refrigerator. Yield 1 cup.

SUMMER SQUASH SALAD

4 cups zucchini, julienned (cut into sticks)
4 cups yellow squash, julienned
2 cups radishes, sliced
1 cup vegetable oil
1/3 cup cider vinegar
2 tablespoons Dijon mustard
2 tablespoons fresh parsley. diced
1 teaspoon dill weed
1½ teaspoons salt
½ teaspoon pepper

In a large bowl, combine together, zucchini, squash and radishes; toss to mix. In a small bowl, combine remaining ingredients; mix well. Pour over vegetables; cover; refrigerate for ay least 2 hours. Yield 12 to 16 servings.

HONEY SALAD DRESSING

1 large egg, beaten
¼ cup lemon or lime juice
½ cup honey
Dash of salt
Dash of mace
1 cup sour cream

In a saucepan, combine together, beaten egg, juice and honey. Cook over medium heat until mixture thickens; stirring constantly. Remove from heat; add seasonings mix well; let cool. When cool, fold in sour cream. This dressing is good on fruit salads.

POTATO SALAD DRESSING

2 tablespoons all-purpose flour
½ teaspoon salt
½ cup granulated sugar
½ teaspoon celery seeds
2 tablespoons butter OR margarine
2 large eggs, beaten
1 teaspoon prepared mustard
2/3 cup vinegar
1/3 cup water

In a medium mixing bowl, combine together, all dry ingredients; mix well. Add butter, eggs, mustard, water and vinegar. In a double boiler, over medium heat, cook until thick.

COUNTRY POTATO SALAD FOR 100 PERSONS

25 pounds potatoes, cooked & diced
Salt and pepper to taste
3 dozen hard boiled eggs, chopped
2½ quarts salad dressing OR mayonnaise
6 large green peppers, chopped
½ pint cream
7 quarts celery, chopped
3 cups onions, chopped
1 tablespoon prepared mustard
¼ cup white vinegar

In a large container, combine together, potatoes, eggs, celery and onions; mix well. In a large mixing bowl, blend together, remaining ingredients; mix thoroughly. Add to potato mixture; mix well. Yield 3 square plastic dishpans full

BLUE CHEESE SALAD DRESSING

1 cup mayonnaise OR salad dressing
¾ cup buttermilk
1 pkg. (6 ozs.) blue cheese, crumbled
1 teaspoon steak sauce
Hot sauce to taste (optional)
1 tablespoon Italian seasoning
1 tablespoon parsley flakes
1 clove garlic, minced

In a medium bowl. combine together, all ingredients; mix well. Place in a covered container, then refrigerate. Serve on a toss salad or with assorted raw vegetables. Yield about 2½ cups.

CROUTONS (Plain)

4 slices bread, 2 days old
1 to 2 tablespoons butter OR margarine

Remove crusts from bread; cut into small cubes. Brown in oven, at 400 degrees, for 8 to 10 minutes, check often, mix croutons to brown evenly. Remove from oven, then sauté in butter, over medium heat. Serve immediately.

NOTE: You can also make cheese crotons, by sprinkling with Parmesan Cheese after you sauté Croutons. Also you can make croutons out of rye bread, which are good with pea or potato soup.

POPPY SEED SALAD DRESSING

2/3 cup pineapple juice
1 cup granulated sugar
2 teaspoons dry mustard
½ teaspoon salt
2 tablespoons onions, minced
1¾ cup vegetable oil
3 teaspoons poppy seeds

In a blender or food processor, combine together, juice, sugar, mustard, salt and onion. Cover, run on high, until blended. Add oil slowly, continuing to blend. Add poppy seeds; blend thoroughly. Chill before serving. Yield 3¼ cups.

SAUERKRAUT SLAW

1 can (1 lb.11 ozs.) sauerkraut, drained
¾ cup carrots, shredded
½ cup cucumber, diced
2 tablespoons parsley, minced
1 tablespoon onion, chopped
2 tablespoons granulated sugar
Salt to taste
½ teaspoon dry mustard
1 teaspoon celery seed
2 tablespoons French Salad Dressing

In a bowl, combine together, all ingredients; mix thoroughly; cover and refrigerate before serving.

BLUE CHEESE MAYONNAISE

1 cup mayonnaise
1 cup sour cream
¾ cup blue cheese, coarsely crumbled
1 tablespoon apple cider vinegar
1 tablespoon lemon juice
2 dashes hot sauce
1 tablespoon onions, minced
½ teaspoon garlic, minced
2 tablespoons parsley, chopped
Salt and pepper to taste

In a medium mixing bowl, combine together, mayonnaise and sour cream, until well-blended. Add the remaining ingredients; fold in gently. Refrigerate in a covered container until ready to use. Mayonnaise will keep for about a week. Yield about 2 cups.

ROSE VINEGAR

1 cup rose petals
3 whole cloves
2 cups white vinegar

Trim heel (white part) of rose petals.

Wash petals thoroughly; drain. Slightly bruise petals, then place petals and cloves in a wide-mouth canning jar. Put vinegar in a saucepan; bring to a boil; remove from heat. Pour over rose petals, cover at once with metal lids; seal tightly. Let stand at room temperature for 1 week. Strain vinegar into decorative container, if desired, discarding rose petals residue. Seal container; store in a cool, dry place. Yield 2 cups.

ROSE PETAL SALAD

¾ cup rose petals
2 cups leaf lettuce, torn in
  pieces
2 cups Romaine lettuce, torn in
  pieces
Rose Vinegar Dressing (see
  recipe below)
add just before serving. Yield 4
  servings.

ROSE VINEGAR DRESSING

¾ cup vegetable oil
¼ cup honey
¼ cup Rose Vinegar
2 tablespoons poppy seeds
1 tablespoon onion, minced
1 tablespoon Dijon Mustard
½ teaspoon salt

In a blender or food processor, combine together, all ingredients; process on low speed, for 30 seconds. Chill thoroughly. and mix well, before serving. Yield 1-1/3 cups.

7-UP GARDEN SALAD DRESSING (for green salads)

2 small green onions, sliced thin
2 teaspoons paprika
½ teaspoon salt
¼ teaspoon black pepper
Pinch of curry powder
1 tablespoon Worcestershire
  Sauce
1 tablespoon prepared
  mustard
1 cup salad oil
1 bottle (7 ozs.) 7-Up

In a large jar, combine together, all ingredients; seal with a tight-fitting lid. Shake ingredients until thoroughly mixed; chill. Shake before using. Yield 2 cups.

DANDELION SALAD

1 tablespoon vegetable oil
1 teaspoon apple cider vinegar
   OR lemon juice
2 cups young dandelion leaves
¼ cup green onions OR leeks
2 hard-cooked eggs, sliced
½ cup grapefruit OR tangerine
   sections OR mandarin
   oranges
Dandelions blossoms (optional)

In a small bowl, whisk oil and vinegar. In another bowl, combine together, dandelion leaves and onions; add dressing; toss to coat. Arrange on 2 salad plates, top with eggs and fruit. If desired, garnish with dandelion blossoms. Yield 2 servings.

NOTE: When harvesting buds, blossoms or leaves from dandelion, be sure the dandelions have not been treated with chemicals. Rinse and dry dandelions before cooking.

EGGPLANT SALAD

3 medium eggplants (about
   4½ lbs.) skin on, cut into 1½"
   cubes
1 cup olive oil, divided
1 tablespoon salt
4 cloves garlic, peeled, minced
2 medium onions, thinly sliced
Pepper to taste

1 cup fresh basil leaves,
   chopped
Juice of 2 lemons

Preheat oven to 400 degrees. Line roasting pan with foil. Add eggplant, toss with ½ cup olive oil, salt and garlic; Bake for 35 minutes, or until egg plant is soft, but not mushy. Remove from oven; transfer to a large bowl; cool slightly. In a large skillet, heat remaining oil; add onions. Over low heat, cook, covered, until tender. Add onions to eggplant; season to taste with pepper. Add basil and lemon juice; toss well. Serve at room temperature.

CORNED BEEF SALAD

1 can (12 ozs.) corned beef, cut
   into pieces
1 cup celery, diced
4 hard-boiled eggs, diced
½ teaspoon salt
1 pkg. (4 serving size) lemon
   gelatin
1 cup salad dressing

Dissolve gelatin in 1 cup boiling water, then pour into an 5-inch square pan; add the remaining ingredients; mix well. Refrigerate until set. Yield 6 servings.

SPINACH SALAD

1 bag of spinach
1 medium onion, sliced thin
½ pound bacon. fried crisp &
    crumbled
4 hard-boiled eggs, sliced
Italian Salad Dressing to taste

Rinse spinach; gently pat dry
with paper towels. Place in
salad bowl, along with sliced
eggs, onions and crumbled
bacon. Gently toss with desired
amount of dressing; serve.

MANDARIN ORANGE SALAD

1 box (6 ozs.) orange gelatin
1 cup boiling water
2 cups vanilla ice cream
1 container whipped topping
1 can mandarin oranges,
    drained

In a glass serving bowl,
dissolve orange gelatin in
boiling water. Add vanilla
ice cream, stirring until just
melted. Add whipped topping;
beat on medium speed until
blended well. Refrigerate
for about 15 minutes, or until
slightly thickened. Remove
gelatin from refrigerator; add
mandarin oranges, if desired,
save a few to garnish the top.
Refrigerate, covered for several
hours or overnight.

Chapter 11

COOKING & BAKING FORMULAS PLUS CONVENIENT MIXES & SPECIAL HELPS

DO WHAT YOU SHOULD &
YOU WON'T HAVE TIME TO DO
WHAT YOU SHOULDN'T!

BAKING & COOKING FORMULAS

Commercial-made mixes that are purchased from the store are made for your convenience, which is wonderful if you are a busy person. Today you may have noticed that the weekly grocery bill is skyrocketing. Therefore, when the following mixes are made at home, you can save over-half the commercial cost. This is a great savings, plus you avoid the chemical additives and preservatives that are incorporated into the commercial mixes.

FISH STEW SEASONING MIX

½ teaspoon dill
1 teaspoon basil
¼ teaspoon oregano
1 teaspoon lemon balm
1 teaspoon savory
½ teaspoon thyme

In a small bowl, combine together, all ingredients; mix well. Add to stew.

NO UNSWEETENED CHOCOLATE?

Use 3 tablespoons unsweetened cocoa, plus 1 tablespoon shortening or butter in place of 1-ounce chocolate square

PEPPER SPICE (Excellant salt substitute)

3 tablespoons black pepper
1 tablespoon cinnamon
1 tablespoon allspice
1 tablespoon nutmeg
1 tablespoon ground cloves
1 tablespoon cardamon
1 tablespoon ginger

In a small bowl, combine together, all ingredients; mix well. Store in a tightly covered container.

CINNAMON SUGAR

For each cup of granulated sugar, blend in 2 tablespoons ground cinnamon

VANILLA SUGAR

Place 2 cups granulated OR powder sugar in a jar; add 1 vanilla bean. Cover tightly, let stand, at least, for 2 days or more.

NO SALT HERB BLEND

Use this herb blend for soups, stews, salad dressing, vegetables and meats. (Use dried herbs only.)

4 tablespoons oregano
4 tablespoons onion powder
1 to 2 tablespoons garlic powder
4 teaspoons marjoran
4 teaspoon basil
4 teaspoons savory
2 teaspoons thyme
2 teaspoons rosemary
1 teaspoon sage
1 teaspoon black pepper

In a small mixing bowl, combine together, the above ingredients; mix thoroughly. Store in a tightly covered jar. Yield 1 cup.

HOW TO COLOR SUGAR

For each cup of granulated sugar, blend in about 6 drops of food coloring. Use a spatula to blend sugar until evenly tinted.

MILK SUBSTITUTE—Use equal amount of water or fruit juice OR 1 cup pureed zucchini. Use zucchini in baking only.

MAKE YOUR OWN RICE MIX

¾ cup rice
2 teaspoons chicken OR beef soup mix
2 teaspoons parsley
1 teaspoon onion flakes
Pinch of black pepper

Combine together, all ingredients; mix well. Place in a plastic bag; store in cool dry place, for no more than 3 months.

HOW TO USE:—Place mix in 1½ quart casserole; dot with 1 teaspoon butter, then add 1¾ cups boiling water; blend well. Cover tightly with foil; bake at 350 degrees, for 20 to 25 minutes or until liquid is absorbed and rice tender. You can also, combine rice with additional ingredients, according to recipe directions.

NOTE: If using brown rice, increase cooking time to 45 minutes, instead of 20 to 25 minutes.

SELF-RISING FLOUR is a convenient product made from all-purpose flour to which leavening and salt have been added. One cup of self-rising flour contains the equivalent of 1½ teaspoons of baking powder and ½ teaspoon salt.

HOMEMADE CURRY POWDER

2 tablespoons ground
    coriander
1 tablespoon turmeric
1 teaspoon EACH ground
    cumin, fenugreek, ginger,
    and allspice
½ teaspoon EACH: ground
    mace and dried hot red chili
    powder, crushed
¼ teaspoon EACH: powdered
    mustard and black pepper

Combine together all ingredients; mix thoroughly. Store in airtight container; keep in dry place. Yield ¼ cup.

MARINARA SAUCE

2 tablespoons olive oil
1 medium-size onion, peeled
2 cloves garlic, peeled &
    chopped
1 can (28 ozs.) whole tomatoes,
    undrained
1 can (8ozs.) tomato sauce
1 teaspoon Italian Seasoning
    OR ½ teaspoon EACH dried
    oregano & basil

1 teaspoon granulated sugar
½ teaspoon salt
¼ teaspoon pepper

Heat oil in medium-size saucepan, over medium heat. Add onions and garlic; cook for 10 minutes, stirring occasionally. Add tomatoes, that have been cut into bite-size chunks. Then over medium-high heat, bring sauce to a boil; reduce heat to simmer; cook for 20 minutes. Yield 4 cups sauce.

BISCUIT MIX

8 cups all-purpose flour
8 teaspoons baking powder
4 teaspoons salt
1½ cups shortening

Sift dry ingredients thoroughly into a large bowl. Cut in shortening until mixture becomes crumbly. Store in closed container and keep refrigerated. Makes about 9 cups baking mix. (Use as you would as the store-boughten biscuit mix.)

SELF-RISING FLOUR I

8 cups all-purpose flour
5 tablespoons baking powder
2 tablespoon granulated sugar
1 tablespoon salt

Combine all ingredients together in a large bowl; sift three times to thoroughly mix ingredients. Store in a well-sealed plastic bag or other container suitable. Use in any recipe calling for self-rising flour. Yield about 8½ cups.

CAKE FLOUR

For each cup of cake flour you need in a recipe, put two tablespoons of cornstarch into one cup measuring utensil, spoon enough all-purpose flour to reach the one cup mark; sift together three times to thoroughly mix through. Store in an air-tight container.

SELF RISING FLOUR II

4 cups all-purpose flour
2 teaspoons salt
2 tablespoons baking powder

In a medium mixing bowl, combine together, all ingredients; mix thoroughly. (Sifting the ingredients together would be better.) Store in a tightly covered container. It is best if flour is used within 30 days. Use in any recipe calling for self-rising flour. Yield about 4 cups.

SOUR CREAM FILLING FOR A CAKE

¼ cup sour cream
½ cup granulated sugar
1½ cups nuts, finely chopped
    (optional)
Small piece of butter OR
    margarine
½ teaspoon vanilla extract
¼ cup raisins (optional)

In a saucepan, combine together, all ingredients, EXCEPT vanilla and raisins. Over low heat, cook until mixture thickens. Remove from heat; beat for 1 minute; add vanilla and fold in raisins. Yield enough filling for 1 layer cake.

HOW TO MAKE SOUR MILK—mix ½ teaspoon lemon juice OR vinegar in ½ cup milk.

HOW TO MAKE OAT FLOUR?

Place 1 to 1½ cup Quaker oats, uncooked in a blender or food processor, for about 1 minute. Yield about 1 cup ground oat flour. Store in a tightly covered container. in a cool, dry place, up to 6 months. Use for baking, breading, thickening or dredging. When used in baking, substitute up to, but not more than 1/3 of the all-purpose flour called for in a recipe. You can use as a thickener in hot or cold liquid.

MEATLOAF SEASONING MIX

2 cups dry bread crumbs
½ cup instant dry milk
1 teaspoons salt
2 teaspoons poultry seasoning
½ teaspoon black pepper
¼ cup dry minced onions
2 tablespoons parsley flakes

Combine ingredients; mix thoroughly.

TO USE: Combine 1½ lbs. ground meat, 1 egg and the above ingredients; mix well

CORNMEAL MIX (and recipes)

2 cups all-purpose flour
6 cup cornmeal
1 tablespoon salt
1½ cups nonfat dry milk
¼ cup baking powder

Mix dry ingredients together, until well-mixed. Cut in shortening with a pastry blender or 2 knives, until mixture resembles coarse crumbs. Mixture is best stored in a glass jar. Keep tightly closed in a cool, dry place. For best results, use within a month.

CORNBREAD

2 cups cornmeal mix
2 large eggs, beaten
1 cup water

In a small bowl, beat eggs; add water In another bowl, place

cornmeal mix; add ½ of the egg mixture to the cornmeal. Stir until well-blended; add remaining water, beat well. Pour into greased 8x8-inch baking pan. Bake at 400 degrees, for 20 to 25 minutes. Yield 4 to 6 servings.

CORNMEAL PANCAKES

1 cup cornmeal mix
1 large egg, well beaten
½ teaspoon baking soda
½ cup buttermilk

Combine all ingredients; stir until dry ingredients are just moistened. Drop by spoonfuls onto a hot, greased griddle. Cook over medium heat until surface is covered with bubbles. Turn over with spatula, to cook other side to golden brown. Yield 6 medium-sized pancakes.

CORNSTICKS

1 cup cornmeal mix
1 large egg, beaten
¾ cup water

In a small mixing bowl, beat egg; add water. In another bowl, place the cornmeal mix; add ½ of the egg mixture. Stir until well-blended; add remaining egg mixture; beat well. Pour into hot, greased 8x8-inch baking pan. Bake at 400 degrees, for 20 to 25 minutes. Yield 4 to 6 servings.

CORN MUFFINS

2 cups cornmeal mix
1 tablespoon granulated sugar
2 large eggs, beaten
1 cup water
1 tablespoon salad oil

In a medium mixing bowl, combine cornmeal and sugar; set aside. Beat eggs; add water and oil; mix well. Add ½ of the egg mixture to the cornmeal mixture; blend well. Add remaining egg mixture; beat for 1 minute. Fill greased muffin tin 2/3 full. Bake at 400 degrees, for 20 minutes, or until tested done. Yield 12 muffins.

HUSH PUPPIES

2½ cups cornmeal mix
½ cup onion, finely chopped
½ teaspoon salt
1 large egg, beaten
½ cup water

Combine cornmeal mix, onion and salt in a medium bowl. Add beaten egg and water; stir just enough to moisten. Drop by spoonfuls into shallow hot shortening. brown on one side, then turn over with a spatula to brown the other side. Makes 24 hush puppies.

CORNMEAL DROP BISCUITS

2 cups cornmeal mix
1/3 to ½ cup water

Add water to dry mix to make s soft dough, Drop by tablespoons onto greased baking sheet. Bake at 425 degrees, for 12 minutes, or until tested done.

POWDER SUGAR

In a blender, whirl ¼ cup granulated sugar at a time, at highest speed, for about 2 minutes, stopping blender occasionally to push powdered sugar off the container's sides. If using a food processor, you can put up to 1 cup of granulated sugar to process at one time. One cup of granulated sugar will yield about 1½ cups powder sugar. To store sugar without lumping, mix 1½ tablespoons cornstarch into each 1½ cups powder sugar. Homemade powder sugar does not affect your recipe in any way.

FLAVORED INSTANT TEA MIX

1 cup instant orange breakfast
   drink (Tang)
2/3 cup instant tea
1 pkg. unsweetened lemonade
   mix
½ cup granulated sugar
1 teaspoon ground cinnamon
¼ teaspoon ground cloves

Combine together all
ingredients; mix thoroughly.

TO USE: Measure 2 teaspoons of
mix to 1 cup (8 ozs.) hot water.

CELERY SALT

Combine together, ½ cup
table salt with ½ cup dried
celery leaves and ¼ cup
celery seeds. Blend in food
processor or blender until finely
powdered. Use as you would
use commercial celery salt.
Yield 1¼ cups.

CRANBERRY SAUCE

1½ cups water
1½ cups granulated sugar
1 bag (12 ozs.) fresh cranberries

In a saucepan, combine
together, water and sugar;
bring to a boil; over medium
heat. Cook rapidly for 3
minutes; add cranberries.
Stir often; reduce heat to
simmer, cook for 10 minutes

or until cranberry skins pop.
Remove from heat; cool, then
refrigerate, covered. Use within
2 weeks, or freeze to use within
6 months.

SWEETENED CONDENSED MILK I

1 cup evaporated milk
3 tablespoons instant dry milk
1 tablespoon granulated sugar
3/4 cup light corn syrup

Pour approximately ½ cup
of the canned milk into a
small saucepan; blend in the
dry milk and sugar. Place
over medium heat; cook to
thoroughly dissolve sugar,
mixing constantly. Remove
from heat; pour in remaining
canned milk and syrup; blend
well. Use in place of a 15-ounce
can of commercial sweetened
condensed milk.

PUMPKIN PIE SPICE

4 tablespoons cinnamon
1 tablespoon ground ginger
½ teaspoon EACH ground
   cloves, nutmeg and allspice
1 tablespoon cornstarch
1 teaspoon instant tea

Sift all ingredients together at
least 3 times. Blend thoroughly;
store in tightly sealed container.
Keep out of sunlight; use within
1 year. Yield about 1/3 cup of
spices.

TACO SEASONING MIX

1/3 cup instant minced onions
1 tablespoon dried red pepper, crushed
½ teaspoon salt
1 tablespoon instant minced garlic
1 tablespoon curry powder
3 tablespoons chili powder
1 tablespoon cornstarch
2 teaspoons oregano

Combine together, all ingredients; mix well. Store in a jar; cover tightly.

TO USE: Measure out 2 tablespoons for each serving.

SWEETENED CONDENSED MILK II

1 cup instant nonfat dry milk
½ cup boiling water
2/3 cup granulated sugar
3 tablespoons butter OR margarine, melted

In a blender or food processor, combine together, all ingredients; process until smooth and slightly thickened. Store in refrigerator until ready to use. Yield about 1¼ cups (about same size as 14 oz. can.

A GOOD USE FOR SURPLUS ZUCCHINI!

Use as a filler for hamburgers, meat loaf, soups or stuffing, etc.

ZUCCHINI BASIC MIXTURE

1 tablespoon butter OR margarine
1 tablespoon vegetable oil
1 medium onion, finely chopped
1 clove garlic, minced
5 pounds zucchini, peeled & grated
¼ teaspoon salt

In a large skillet, melt butter, add oil, over medium heat. Add onion and garlic; cook until soft. Add zucchini; cook for 3 to 5 minutes, until slightly tender. Season with salt; cool and drain in a colendar for 5 minutes. Store in 2 or 3 cup portions, in suitable containers and freeze. Mixture will last for a few days in the refrigerator and several weeks in the freezer.

NOTE:—You can, also, liquefy zucchini in in a blender or food processor, then use 1 cup of liquefied zucchini as a substitute for 1 cup milk, in baking recipes only

HERMAN STARTER (HOW TO MAKE) (with recipes)

To start Herman—take 2 cups all-purpose flour, 2 cups warm water, ¼ cup granulated sugar and 1 package active dry yeast. Use a glass container or crock large enough to mix all 4 ingredients thoroughly. Let stand overnight in a warm place; cover with lid, but not tightly.

The next day refrigerate Herman, covered. Every day you need to stir the starter, because the batter will rise to the top.

If you are going to share Herman with a friend then you must feed Herman, also, your friend must feed their portion. This is how you do it: take 1 cup flour, 1 cup of milk, ½ cup granulated sugar. Feed Herman on the first day and on the fifth day. Use Herman to bake on the. tenth day. Always keep Herman refrigerated and when you remove a portion of the starter to bake with, you must replenish the starter.

HERMAN CINNAMON ROLLS TOPPING MIX

1 stick butter OR margarine
1 cup brown sugar, packed
½ cup nuts, chopped

In a small bowl, combine together, all ingredients; mix thoroughly. Spread in bottom of 9x13x2 inch baking pan; set aside.

CINNAMON ROLLS

2 cups all-purpose flour
2 cups Herman
½ teaspoon salt
4 teaspoons baking powder
½ cup vegetable oil

Butter OR margarine, cinnamon & sugar In a large mixing bowl, combine together, Herman, flour, baking soda, salt, baking powder and oil. Mix until dough forms a ball, then knead lightly, on a floured surface, until dough is no longer sticky. Roll to ¼ inch thickness; spread with butter. sprinkle evenly with cinnamon and sugar.

There is no exact measurements given for the last 3 ingredients listed, use the amount to your preference. Roll up lengthwise, as for a jelly roll; cut into ½ inch slices. Place cut slices on top of topping mixture, about 1-inch apart. Bake at 350 degrees, for about 30 minutes, or until golden brown. Remove from oven and immediately invert onto a serving platter. Yield about 12 rolls

HERMAN OATMEAL COOKIES

½ cup shortening
1½ cups brown sugar, packed
2 large eggs
1½ cups *sour milk
½ cup Herman
2 cups all-purpose flour
1 teaspoon baking powder
½ teaspoon salt
1 teaspoon cinnamon
3 cups quick-cooking oatmeal
1 cup raisins
½ cup milk

In a large mixing bowl, cream together, shortening and sugar. Add eggs, one at a time, beating well after each addition. Add remaining ingredients; mix thoroughly Drop batter by teaspoonful, on greased cookie sheet. Bake at 375 degrees, for about 10 minutes, or lightly browned.

*How to make sour milk—Mix ½ teaspoon lemon juice or vinegar in ½ cup of milk.

FACTS ABOUT BAKING POWDER!

Baking powder loses its potency if stored too long! It is recommended to store baking powder in a cool place and for not longer than 1 year. If not sure if the baking powder is still good try this test. Stir 1 teaspoon basking powder with 1/3 cup hot water, if the mixture bubbles actively, the powder. is good. However, if the bubble action is weak or there is no bubbling action at all, the powder has lost its leavening power and should be replaced

SOUR DOUGH STARTER

2 cups all-purpose flour
1 package active dry yeast
2 cups warm water

In a large mixing bowl, combine together, all ingredients; mix until well-blended. Let the starter stand uncovered in a warm place (80 to 85 degrees) for 48 hours, or 2 days. Stir from time to time, also, stir well before using. Pour out the amount you need, then replenish starter, by mixing in 1 cup EACH of the flour and warm water. Let the starter stand uncovered, in a warm place, for a few hours, or until the starter bubbles again. Pour it into a crock or glass container, cover it loosely and refrigerate until needed. When ready to bake sour dough bread again, take the starter out of the refrigerator the night before you plan to use it, so it can warm up and start working. You must use the starter, at least, once every 2 weeks and to replenish what you have used. The starter can be used daily.

GRANOLA MIX

5 cups old fashion oatmeal
1½ cups wheat germ
1 cup coconut, shredded
1 cup peanuts, chopped
½ cup whole-bran cereal
   (not flakes)
½ cup brown sugar, packed
½ cup vegetable oil
1/3 cup water
2 teaspoon vanilla extract

In a large mixing bowl,
combine together, first 6
ingredients; mix well; set aside.
In another bowl, combine oil,
water and vanilla; mix well.
Pour over cereal mixture; mix
thoroughly. Spread mixture on
a cookie sheet; bake at 350
degrees, for 1 hour, stirring
every 15 minutes; remove from
oven. Let cool completely; store
in covered container. Yield
about 10 cups mix.

HOMEMADE POULTRY
SEASONING

7 tablespoons ground sage
2 tablespoons parsley flakes
1½ teaspoons black pepper
1¼ teaspoons thyme
1 teaspoon onion powder
¾ teaspoon ground ginger
½ teaspoon garlic powder
¼ teaspoon celery seed

Combine all ingredients; mix
thoroughly; store in air-tight
container. Yield about 2/3 cup.

MEXICAN SEASONING MIX

1 cup instant minced onion
2/3 cup instant beef-flavored
   bouillon
1/3 cup chili powder
2 tablespoons ground cumin
4 teaspoons crushed red
   pepper
4 teaspoons oregano
2 teaspoon garlic powder

In a tightly covered jar,
combine the above
ingredients, shake until well
mixed. Store in a cool dry
place. Use within 3 months.
Yield about 3 cups

HOT COCOA MIX

2½ cups instant nonfat dry milk
1 cup unsweetened cocoa
1 cup granulated sugar
½ cup powdered nondairy
   creamer
¼ teaspoon salt

In a medium mixing bowl,
mix all ingredients thoroughly.
Store in an airtight container
in a cool place. Use within 6
months. Yield 5 cups.

TO MAKE 1 SERVING—Stir 3
tablespoons of mix to 8 ounces
of hot water.

HERB POUCH FOR SOUP OR STEWS

Use a piece of cheesecloth, 2 inches square. Fill with1 teaspoon EACH dried parsley, thyme and, marjoram, then ¼ teaspoon ground sage, ½ teaspoon savory. 1 bay leaf and 2 teaspoons dried celery. Combine and crush slightly; put on cheesecloth; bring 4 corners together, tie with twine. Use pouch with 2 quarts of liquid. Drop each pouch into boiling soup or stew, towards the end of the cooking time, no longer than 1 hour. Remove from soup and stew; discard pouch.

TO ROAST CHESTNUTS

With a sharp knife, make a slit in each nut. Place in boiling water; cook for 3 or 4 minutes. Remove nuts from water; dry thoroughly. Melt 3 tablespoons of butter or margarine in a saucepan; add the chestnuts; cook, stirring thoroughly until very hot. Then with a sharp-pointed knife, both skins can be removed together, leaving the nut whole. Also, you can roast the scored nuts in a very hot oven (450 degrees) about 10 to 15 minutes. Chestnuts can be placed in heavy plastic bags and frozen until ready to be used.

NOTE: It is suggested to slit each chestnut with a sharp knife to prevent the nuts from exploding or popping when roasted.

DIET BUTTER OR MARGARINE

1 envelope unflavored gelatin
2 cups skim milk, divided
1 pound butter OR margarine, softened

Dissolve gelatin in ½ cup skim milk, over low heat, stirring until dissolved; remove from heat; set aside. Slowly add remaining skim milk, plus gelatin mixture to butter OR margarine while beating on high of electric mixer. Continue beating until all milk is absorbed, for about 20 to 30 minutes.

CHOCOLATE SYRUP

1 cup unsweetened cocoa
   or 4 (1 oz. each) squares
   unsweetened chocolate
2 cups granulated sugar
¼ teaspoon salt

In a saucepan, combine together, all ingredients; add 2 cups water; mix well. Simmer over low heat, stirring or beating with rotary beater, constantly until smooth and thick, about 5 minutes. Remove from heat; let cool then add 1 tablespoon vanilla extract; mix thoroughly. Pour into jar with lid; store in refrigerator.

READY GRAVY MIX

1 jar (2½ ozs.) beef OR chicken
   instant bouillon
1½ cups all-purpose flour
½ teaspoon black pepper

In a medium mixing bowl,
combine together all
ingredients; mix thoroughly,
store in a pint jar with tight-
fitting lid, Shake or stir at room
temperature.

HOW TO USE GRAVY MIX!

¼ cup gravy mix
3 tablespoons butter,
   margarine OR pan drippings
1¼ cups water OR milk

In a medium-size skillet, brown
gravy mix & butter; add liquid.
Cook over low heat until thick
and smooth, stirring constantly.
Yield about 2 cups gravy.

SALT SUBSTITUTE

1 teaspoon chili powder
2 teaspoons oregano
2 teaspoons black pepper
1 tablespoon garlic powder
2 tablespoons dry mustard
6 tablespoons onion powder
3 tablespoons paprika
3 tablespoons poultry
   seasoning

Combine together all
ingredients; mix before using
thoroughly; put in a salt shaker
and use as you would salt.

WHITE SAUCE MIX

2 cups instant non-fat dry milk
3 cups flour, sifted
1½ teaspoons salt
1 cup butter OR margarine

In a large mixing bowl,
combine dry milk, flour and
salt. Cut in butter with a pastry
blender or use two knives,
until mixture resembles tiny
peas. Store in tightly covered
container, keep in the
refrigerator. Use in any recipe
that calls for a white sauce or
cheese sauce.

TO MAKE A THIN WHITE SAUCE

Combine 1 cup milk OR water
and 1/3 cup white sauce mix,
in a small saucepan. Cook
over medium heat, stirring
constantly, until bubbly and
thick, about 1 minute.

TO MAKE A MEDIUM WHITE SAUCE

Combine 1 cup milk OR water
and ½ cup white sauce mix.
Cook over medium heat,
stirring constantly, until bubbly
and thick; about 1 minute.

HOW TO MAKE THICK WHITE SAUCE!

Combine 1 cup milk OR water and 1 cup white sauce mix. Cook over medium heat, stirring constantly, until bubbly and thick; about 1 minute.

HOW TO MAKE CHEESE SAUCE!

Add ¾ cup shredded cheese to white sauce after sauce thickens, stirring constantly until cheese melts.

HOW TO MAKE BROWN SUGAR

½ cup granulated sugar
2 tablespoons unsulphured
  molasses

In a small mixing bowl, blend thoroughly; store in airtight container. Yield is the same as ½ cup store-bought brown sugar.

HOW TO MAKE SEASONED CROTONS!

15 slices bread (cut in ½ inch cubes
3 tablespoons vegetable oil
2 tablespoons dried minced onions
2 tablespoons dried parsley flakes
½ teaspoon ground sage

Spread bread cubes evenly on cookie sheet Toast cubes at 300 degrees, until golden brown, for about 40 to 45 minutes, stirring once. Remove cubes from oven; cool slightly. Combine remaining ingredients together. Add to bread cubes; toss lightly to coat. Store in a tightly covered container until needed. Use on salads, casseroles or in soups, etc.

HOMEMADE GRITS

5 cups water
1 teaspoons salt
1 cup regular grits (not quick)
¼ cup milk
Pinch of pepper (optional)
Butter

In a large saucepan, bring water to a boil, over high heat. Reduce heat to medium; add salt. Sprinkle grits, in a fine stream, stirring constantly. Then reduce heat to low, cover and simmer 15 to 20 minutes, until water is absorbed. and grits have thicken, but still are creamy Add milk and pepper. If grits should become lumpy, beat with a whisk. Cover; let stand for 2 minutes. Grits are best, served immediately Top each serving with a pat of butter. Yield 5½ cups or 11 half cup servings.

HOMEMADE PANCAKE SYRUP

2 tablespoons butter OR
    margarine
Pinch of salt
2½ cups water
1 cup brown sugar, packed
3 cups granulated sugar
¼ cup light corn syrup
1 teaspoon maple flavoring

Combine together, all the
ingredients EXCEPT maple
favoring, in 2½ quart saucepan;
bring to a boil, over medium
heat. Boil rapidly for 10 minutes,
stirring frequently. Reduce heat
to low; simmer for another 10
minutes. Remove from heat;
cool; add maple flavoring and
refrigerate. Yield 1 quart.

COFFEE CAKE MASTER MIX

8 cups all-purpose flour
4 cups granulated sugar
4 tablespoons baking powder
1 tablespoon salt
2 teaspoons Cream of Tartar
2 cups shortening

In a large mixing bowl, sift
together, all the dry ingredients;
add shortening. Using a
pastry blender, or 2 knives,
mix in shortening until mixture
appears crumbly, like coarse
cornmeal. Store in a tightly
covered container, at room
temperature. This mix will keep

for 4 to 6 weeks. Yield about 15
cups, enough 6 coffee cakes.

COFFEE CAKE FROM MIX

2½ cups coffee cake mix
2 large eggs
½ cup milk, divided

In a medium mixing bowl,
combine together, the mix,
eggs and ¼ cup milk. Beat for
2 minutes with electric mixer
until light and fluffy, (150 strokes
by hand). At a low speed, add
remaining milk; mix well. Bake
in a lightly greased baking pan,
at 350 degrees, for 35 to 45
minutes, or until tested done.
Yield 9 servings.

SEASONED COATING MIX

2 cups fine bread crumbs
2 tablespoons onion powder
1½ teaspoons salt
½ teaspoon garlic powder
½ teaspoon paprika
½ teaspoon dried thyme
¼ teaspoon black pepper

Crush thyme, then combine
together, all ingredients; mix
thoroughly. Store in tightly
covered container. Use as
needed. to coat fish or chicken

SHAKE AND BAKE COATING

1 cup cornmeal
½ cup all-purpose flour
½ teaspoon paprika
1 teaspoon seasoned salt
Pepper to taste

Combine together, all ingredients; mix well. Coat meat and bake or store in plastic bag or container of your choice; use as the commercial Shake and Bake.

HOMEMADE MUSTARD

¼ cup dry mustard
2 tablespoons water
2/3 cup water
1/3 cup white vinegar
¼ cup granulated sugar
3 tablespoons all-purpose flour
½ teaspoon salt

In a small bowl, combine together, dry mustard and 2 tablespoons water; mix well; set aside. In a saucepan, combine remaining ingredients; cook over low heat, for about 3 minutes or until thick, stirring constantly. Remove from heat; stir in mustard mixture until smooth. Place in desired container with a lid; refrigerate. Yield about 1 cup mustard.

EVAPORATED MILK VERSUS SWEETENED CONDENSED MILK

What is the difference between evaporated milk and sweetened condensed milk?

One difference is that they can not be interchanged in recipes. Sweetened condensed milk is a concentrate of either whole milk or skim milk. It contains almost 50 percent sugar. Evaporated milk is made by removing the water from whole or skim milk to reduce the contents of milk by half.

Evaporated milk should be stored in a cool, dry place where temperature does not exceed 70 degrees and no longer than 6 months. After opening the can the milk should be refrigerated and used within 10 days. **TO USE**— add 1 cup water to every cup of milk, then use as desired.

NOTE: Sweetened condensed is primarily used in candy and dessert recipes.

WARNING in regards to canning apple pie filling. You should be aware that if you do not pressure can the pie filling a danger of botulism can occur. It is thought that processing done in boiling water bath is not sufficient enough. When flour or cornstarch is added to the recipe, to thicken the filling, this increases the time necessary for the filling in the center of the jar to get hot enough to destroy harmful bacteria. This does not occur in hot water bath. Also, by adding flour or cornstarch, it reduces the acidity in the pie filling, again botulism can occur. So, the bottom line is, pressure canning is the better process for canning apple pie filling. And it also, is suggested to eliminate flour or cornstarch and to add the thickening agent at the time you are making the pie

Add water gradually, to form a soft pliable dough. Whole wheat flour may need more water. Knead on a well-floured surface, until smooth and no longer sticky. Cover dough with a damp cloth, as you work. Cut off about 3 tablespoons dough at a time, keeping the rest of the dough covered. Knead into a ball; then with a flour-covered rolling pin, roll the ball out into a very thin circle. Cut into a neat round, using a 10-inch plate, as a guide. Continue until all the dough is used. Stack the tortillas as you make them, lightly flour each one, to prevent sticking. Keep covered with a clean kitchen towel. Heat a large skillet; carefully place 1 tortilla; cook for about 10 seconds per side. Stack and keep covered until all are cooked. Use according to chosen recipe. Yield about 10 tortillas.

FLOUR TORTILLAS

2 cups whole *wheat flour
1 tablespoon salt
6 tablespoons shortening
1 cup hot water

*you can use all-purpose flour. In a medium mixing bowl, combine together, flour and salt; mix well. Rub in shortening with a clean hand, until mixture resembles fine bread crumbs

HOMEMADE PEANUT BUTTER

1 cup peanuts (plain)
Pinch of salt (optional)
1-2 tablespoons peanut oil
1 teaspoon honey OR sugar

Place ingredients in blender or food processor. Run the machine until achieving the smoothness you desire. Yield 1 cup.

CREOLE SEASONING

2 tablespoons onion powder
2 tablespoons garlic powder
1½ cups potato chips, crushed
2 tablespoons sweet basil
1 tablespoon dried thyme leaves
1 tablespoon black pepper
1 tablespoon white pepper
1 tablespoon cayenne
5 tablespoons sweet paprika
2 tablespoons salt
2 tablespoons dried oregano
   leaves

Blend together, all ingredients thoroughly. This recipe can be doubled, if desired. This seasoning can be used on rice or meats.

POTATO CHIP COOKIE MIX

1 cup granulated sugar
2 cups potato chips, crushed
2½ cups all-purpose flour
1 teaspoon baking powder

In a small mixing bowl, combine together, all ingredients; store in a covered jar. you can also give as a gift, by layering ingredients in a quart jar, with directions attached.
(Recipe to make cookies. below.)

POTATO CHIP COOKIES FROM MIX

In a large mixing bowl, place cookie mix; add 2 sticks of butter (or margarine) and 1 teaspoon vanilla. Combine ingredients until thoroughly mixed and dough comes together. Shape dough into balls, the size of walnuts; then flatten with a fork. Place on ungreased cookie sheet; bake at 350 degrees for 15 to 20 minutes, or until lightly brown. Remove from oven; cool on cookie sheet for 10 minutes. Put cookies on a platter to cool completely before storing in covered container Yield 2½ dozen cookies

THICKENING AGENTS

FLOUR—is used by blending with fat before liquid is added in the recipe. Also, flour can be blended with cold liquid before combining with hot mixture. Cook; stirring until mixture thickens and is bubbly.

CORNSTARCH—as flour can be blended with cold liquid. Cook until mixture has thickened and is bubbly, stirring constantly.

TAPIOCA—quick-cooking tapioca is added to the liquid mixture. No soaking is necessary. Cook just to boiling; do not overcook. Cool without stirring.

EGGS—beat eggs slightly, when using as a thickener. Carefully stir a small amount of hot mixture into eggs, then stir eggs into remaining hot mixture. Cook over low heat, stirring constantly.

FRENCH MUSTARD

3 tablespoons dry mustard
1 tablespoon granulated sugar

Mix thoroughly by sifting several times. In a medium saucepan, place mustard mixture; add 1 egg, beating until smooth and creamy. Then add ¾ cup white vinegar, a little at a time, beating well after each addition. Over medium heat, bring mixture a boil, cook mustard mixture for 3 to 4 minutes, stirring constantly. Remove from heat and let cool, when cool, add 1 tablespoon olive oil, mixing thoroughly. Yield about 1 cup.

HOMEMADE PIZZA SAUCE

4 quarts tomatoes, chopped
1 large onion, chopped
1 green bell pepper, chopped
1 small hot pepper diced
   (optional)
1 clove garlic, minced
1 teaspoon oregano
¼ teaspoon basil
½ teaspoon salt
2 tablespoons granulated sugar

In a large kettle, combine all ingredients; bring to a boil; then reduce heat to simmer. Cook, uncovered until mixture becomes thick, as you like. Remove from heat; put in jars, leaving ½ inch head space; seal immediately, or put in desired freezer containers; cool slightly then freeze.

SALT SUBSTITUTE

1 tablespoon oregano leaves,
   crushed
¼ teaspoon ground cumin
¼ teaspoon garlic powder
Pinch of black pepper

Blend spices together thoroughly. This enhances the flavor of hamburger, chicken, cottage cheese, raw or cooked vegetables and salads Add seasoning to foods during preparation or place in salt shaker, for use at the table.

RICOTTA CHEESE

In a large saucepan, bring 1 gallon of fresh goat milk, almost to a boil (90 degrees). Do not scorch. Remove from heat; stir as you add ¼ cup white vinegar. The milk should curdle right away. If not, add more vinegar, a few drops at a time. Let stand undisturbed, until cool, then drain through a colander, about ½ hour Salt, if desired. Freezes well.

FRESH STRAWBERRY FILLING

1 cup whole strawberries
¾ cup powder sugar
Pinch of salt
1 large egg white, unbeaten

Crush strawberries; drain juice. Combine together, crushed berries (will be about ½ cup), sugar, salt and unbeaten egg white in a small bowl. Beat until stiff, about 10 minutes. As the mixture is beaten, it will become stiffer. Besides being used as a filling, this mixture can be used as a frosting.

BARBECUE SAUCE

2 cups ketchup
2 cups vinegar
1 bottle (5 ozs.) Worcestershire Sauce
1 tablespoon dried onions, minced
1 tablespoon hot sauce
1 tablespoon brown sugar
Salt and pepper to taste
1 cup butter OR margarine
2 cloves garlic, minced

In a medium-size saucepan, combine together, all the above ingredients. Cook, over medium heat; bring to a boil; then reduce heat; simmer for 10 minutes, stirring constantly. Remove from heat; cool. Store in refrigerator in a covered container. Yield about 5 cups of sauce.

TRAIL MIX I

2 pounds cashews
2 pounds peanuts
1 pounds M & M's
1 pound raisins
½ pound flaked coconut

Combine together, in a large mixing bowl; mix thoroughly. Yield 6½ pounds.

TRAIL MIX II

1 pound almonds, chopped
1 pound walnuts, chopped
¼ pound sunflower seeds
¼ pound dried apricots, chopped
½ pound raisins
½ pound dried pineapple, chopped
½ pound banana chips
¼ pound M & M's

Toast nuts and seeds in a skillet or oven, until lightly browned. Mix with dried fruits and M & M's. Store in tightly closed container, in a cool place. Yield 4½ pounds.

RANCH-STYLE SALAD DRESSING MIX

1 teaspoon dry parsley
¾ teaspoon black pepper
1 teaspoon seasoned salt
½ teaspoon garlic powder
¼ teaspoon onion powder
Pinch of dried thyme

In a small mixing bowl, combine all ingredients together; mix thoroughly Store in a covered container.

TO USE AS DRESSING: Combine above ingredients with 1 cup mayonnaise and 1 cup buttermilk.

TO USE AS DIP: Combine above ingredients together with 1¾ cups sour cream and ¼ cup buttermilk.

NOTE: The above salad dressing mix recipe is equivalent to 1 packet of commercial ranch dressing.

POTATO SOUP MIX

1¾ cups instant potatoes
1½ cups instant dry milk
2 tablespoons instant chicken bouillon
2 tablespoons minced dry onions
1 teaspoon dried parsley
¼ teaspoon white pepper
¼ teaspoon thyme
Pinch of turmeric
½ teaspoon salt

In a small mixing bowl, combine together, all ingredients; mix thoroughly. Store in covered container. Yield 6 servings.

TO USE POTATO SOUP MIX: For each serving, place ½ cup soup mix in a bowl. Add 1 cup boiling water; mix until blended.

HANDY MUFFIN MIX

1½ cups all-purpose flour
2 teaspoons baking powder
¼ teaspoon baking soda
¼ teaspoon salt
1 cup regular oatmeal
½ cup brown sugar, packed
2 tablespoons lemon peel, grated
½ cup dried cherries, strawberries, apples, prunes OR apricots, diced
1/3 cup walnuts OR pecans. Chopped

Combine together, above ingredients; store in a covered container. Yield 12 muffins.

TO MAKE MUFFINS: In a medium mixing bowl, combine ¼ cup butter OR margarine, melted, 1 cup milk and 1 large egg; beat with electric mixer, on medium speed, until well mixed. Add above ingredients, mix thoroughly. Grease muffin tin; spoon batter in muffin cups ¾ full; bake at 400 degrees, for 20 to 25 minutes, or until tested done. Remove from oven; cool for 10 minutes, before removing muffins from pan; serve warm.

SYRUP—HOW TO MAKE!

2 cups granulated sugar
1 cup water
1 to 2 teaspoons extract or
  flavoring

In a small saucepan, mix together, sugar and water; cover. Over medium-high heat, bring mixture to a boil; remove cover. Boil for 5 minutes; remove from heat; add extract flavoring; mix well. Store in refrigerator Yield 2 cups.

SUGGESTED FLAVORS—Apricot, blueberry, butterscotch, caramel, cinnamon apple, grape, lemon, maple, peach, pineapple, plum, raspberry, strawberry or vanilla

CHINESE FIVE-SPICE

2 tablespoons fennel seeds
2 tablespoons ground
  cinnamon
2 tablespoons whole
  peppercorns
6 whole star anise
2 tablespoons whole cloves

Grind fennel seeds, star anise and cloves in blender or food processor. Grind to fine powder. Use this blend to season meats, poultry to be roasted or broiled; also, can be used in sauces and salad dressings.

DRY HERB MIXES FOR MEATS BEEF

2 tablespoon winter savory
3 tablespoons basil
3 tablespoons sweet marjoram
3 tablespoons parsley
3 tablespoons celery leaves

DIRECTIONS APPLY TO ALL HERB MIXES

Crush dried leaves in a bowl; mix well. Store in jars with tight-fitting lids. Sprinkle 1 to 2 teaspoons herb mix, over meat, before cooking or any other dishes, like gravy.

PORK

2 tablespoons sage
1 tablespoon thyme
1 tablespoon rosemary
1 bay leaf
Direction on preceding page.

VEAL

1 tablespoon tarragon
1 tablespoon basil
1 tablespoon parsley
1 tablespoon chervil
Direction on preceding page.

LAMB

2 tablespoons Rosemary
1 tablespoon parsley
1 tablespoon mint
1 tablespoon thyme

Direction on preceding page.

POULTRY

2 tablespoons tarragon
1 tablespoon basil
2 tablespoons rosemary
Direction on preceding page.

FISH

1 tablespoon parsley
1 tablespoon lemon balm
1 tablespoon basil
1 tablespoon celery leaves

Direction on preceding page.

BUTTER FACTS

TO STORE BUTTER

Keep butter cold and covered. Salted butter should last up to 4 weeks in the refrigerator. Unsalted butter has a shorter shelf life than salted and should be kept in the freezer until ready to use.

TO FREEZE BUTTER

Butter should be wrapped in moisture proof container and will keep for 6 to 9 months in the freezer.

TO SERVE BUTTER

Butter should be taken out of the refrigerator, at least 30 minutes before serving.

TO CLARIFY BUTTER

Clarifying butter is to remove the water and non-fat solids. You do it by, heating the butter in a shallow, heavy pan over low heat. As it cooks, remove the white froth as it forms on top, with a large spoon or ladle, remove from heat and pour off the clear liquid, however be careful not to mix in any of the white solids that have settled to the bottom.

BAKING WITH BUTTER

*Baking with butter keeps baked goods fresher longer.

*When baking with butter, it should be at room temperature or soft enough to blend smoothly with other ingredients.

*To soften butter in the microwave oven, microwave at the lowest power setting, checking every 30 seconds.

*Commercial whipped butter has water and air added to it, therefore it is best not to use it in baking, because it will not provide an accurate measurement.

*Salted or unsalted butter can be used interchangeably in recipes, however using salted butter, you might want to omit the salt called for in the recipe.

BUTTER MEASUREMENTS ARE AS FOLLOWS:

1 pound equals 4 sticks
2 cups= 32 tablespoons.
2 sticks = 1 cup =16 tablespoons
1 stick = ½ cup = 8 tablespoons
½ stick = ¼ cup = 4 tablespoons

HOME-CHURNED BUTTER

2 cups heavy cream

Line a sieve with a single layer of cheese cloth; place sieve over a bowl; set aside Pour the cream into a food processor; process for about 5 minutes or until butter forms a mass and separates from the whey, which appears as a milky liquid. Transfer butter and whey to the sieve; work butter with a wooden spoon or spatula to release more of the whey, until you have a fairly solid mass of butter. Scoop butter from the sieve, then put in plastic wrap, or in a covered container of your choice; refrigerate until ready to serve. If desired, salt to taste.

DID YOU KNOW that you can make butter by using whipping cream and by beating until it separates into water and butter. Pour off the water; scrape butter into a solid mass. Rinse under cold water, then drain. 1 cup whipping creams make about ½ cup butter.

MAITRE D'HOTEL BUTTER

½ cup butter
½ teaspoon salt
Pinch of pepper
1 tablespoon parsley, chopped
1½ tablespoon lemon juice

In a small mixing bowl, cream butter until light and fluffy. Add salt, pepper and parsley; mix well. Slowly stir in lemon juice. Yield ½ cup.

BLENDER-MADE BUTTER

1 cup heavy cream
½ cup ice water

Place cream in blender; cover. Blend until cream thickens around blade. Keep motor. running while pouring ice water through opening in top. Blend 1 or 2 minutes longer until butter forms. Turn into strainer to drain. Then put in desired container; refrigerate.

NOTE—It is best to use cream that is a few days old.

ITALIAN HERB MIXTURE

3 tablespoons leaf oregano
3 tablespoons leaf marjoram
1 tablespoon leaf thyme
3 tablespoons leaf savory
3 tablespoons leaf basil
3 tablespoons rosemary,
  crumbled
1 tablespoon sage

In a small mixing bowl, combine together, mix thoroughly. Store in a tightly covered container. Use for meatballs, salad dressings, eggplant dishes, sautéed chicken and veal. Yield about 1 cup.

EASY ICE CREAM CONES

1¼ cups biscuit mix (i.e. Bisquick)
½ cup graham cracker crumbs
  (about 6 squares)
¼ cup granulated sugar
¼ cup boiling water

2 tablespoons butter OR
  margarine

Foil cones (directions following) Preheat oven to 400 degrees. In a small mixing bowl, combine together, all ingredients, until a stiff dough forms. Shape into ball; divide dough in half. Wrap ½ dough in plastic wrap to prevent drying. Roll remaining half dough into a rectangle about 13x9 inches, on a floured surface; trim. edges to make an even rectangle, 12 x 8 inches. Cut rectangle into six 4-inch square; set aside. Prepare Foil Cones: Cut 12 strips of aluminum foil, 21x5 inches. Fold each strip crosswise into halves; shape into cone with point beginning in center of 6-inch side.

Fold about 1-inch of one corner over each square. For each cone, place Foil Cone on 1 square dough with point of cone at one corner. (Cover remaining squares with plastic wrap to prevent drying.) Roll dough to shape around Foil Cones with folded corner at the top. Moisten edge of dough with a little water; press lightly to seal. Press point lightly to seal; place cones, seam sides down, on ungreased cookie sheet. Bake about 6 to 8 minutes, or until edges are light brown. Cool, then carefully twist to remove Foil Cones. Repeat with remaining half dough. Yield 12 cones.

PUFF PASTRY (with Napoleon recipe)

Chill 1 cup butter OR margarine; reserve 2 tablespoons. Work remaining butter with back of wooden spoon just until pliable. Roll between sheet of waxed paper to a 8x6-inch rectangle. Chill again, for at least 1 hour in refrigerator or 20 minutes in the freezer. In a mixing bowl, cut reserved butter into 1¾ cups, all-purpose flour, sifted, until mixture resembles coarse meal. Gradually add ½ cup ice water, tossing with fork to make a stiff dough; shape into a ball. Knead on lightly floured surface until smooth and elastic, about 5 minutes. Cover dough; let rest for 10 minutes. Then on a lightly floured surface, roll dough into a rectangle, 15x9-inches. Peel wax paper from 1 side of chilled butter; invert on half of dough. Remove wax paper on top; fold dough over to cover butter. Seal edges of dough; wrap in wax paper; chill thoroughly for 1 hour. Unwrap dough, then on a lightly floured surface, roll to 15x9-inch rectangle. Roll from center just to edges; brush off excess flour; fold in thirds, then turn dough and fold in thirds again. Press edges to seal; wrap; chill at least 1 hour Repeat rolling, folding; thoroughly chilling for 2 or 3 times more.

NAPOLEONS (using Puff Pastry)

Roll Puff Pastry into 14x8-inch rectangle, 3/8 inch thick. Cut off all edges; prick dough well with a fork. Cut in 16 (3½x2-inch) rectangles; place on cookie sheets covered with 3 or 4 thicknesses of paper towels; chill well. Brush with mixture of 1 slightly beaten egg white and 1 tablespoon ice water. Bake at 450 degrees, for 6 minutes, then at 300 degrees, for 25 to 30 minutes, until lightly brown and crisp. Remove from pan; cool on rack. Separate each pastry into layers; spread desired filling. Frost with glaze on top with a thinned powder sugar icing. Yield 16 servings.

RHUBARB MINCEMEAT

2 cups rhubarb, chopped
2 cups apples, chopped
1 orange, pulp & grated peel
Juice of ½ lemon
½ cup currants
¼ cup citron
2½ cups brown sugar, packed
½ cup water
½ teaspoon allspice
½ teaspoon ground cinnamon
¼ teaspoon nutmeg

In a saucepan, combine all ingredients; mix well. Bring mixture to a boil, reduce heat to simmer about 30 minutes, or until mincemeat is thick and clear. Spoon into hot sterile jar; seal. Yield enough for 1 pie.

TO MAKE GRAPE JUICE CONCENTRATE!

6 pounds Concord grapes
1½ cups granulated sugar

Wash grapes; remove from stems. Measure 14 cups grapes, then combine with 2 cups water. Place in large saucepan; cover; cook to boiling; then reduce heat to simmer. Cook for 30 minutes or until tender. Remove from heat; strain mixture thru cheesecloth bag. Let juice set for 24 hours, in refrigerator. Strain again, in a large saucepan, place grape juice; add sugar; mix well. Over medium heat; cook to boiling, remove from heat. Pour into hot, sterilized pint jars; let cool; refrigerate, Yield 3 pints.

TO SERVE: Dilute grape juice, amount to taste, in a glass of water.

PANCAKE MIX

10 cups all-purpose flour
2½ cups powder milk (instant)
½ cup granulated sugar
4 tablespoons baking powder
2 teaspoons salt

Sift all ingredients together; store in airtight container. Use within 6 months to insure freshness. Yield about 13 cups.

PANCAKES FROM MIX

1½ cups pancake mix
1 large egg, slightly beaten
1 cup water
2 tablespoons vegetable oil

In a medium mixing bowl, combine together all ingredients; mix well. (If thinner pancakes are desired, add more water.) Fry on a hot oiled griddle; about 3 minutes or until browned, on both sides. Yield about 10 four inch pancakes.

LEMON PEPPER SEASONING

½ cup black pepper
3 tablespoons dried lemon peel
1½ tablespoons coriander
2 tablespoons minced dried onion
2 tablespoons dried thyme

In a small mixing bowl, combine together, all ingredients; mix thoroughly. Store in an airtight container. Yield 1 cup.

CHILI SEASONING MIX

1 tablespoon paprika
2½ teaspoons seasoning salt
1 teaspoon onion powder
1 teaspoon garlic powder
1 teaspoon cayenne pepper
1 teaspoon pepper
½ teaspoon dried thyme
½ teaspoon dried oregano

In a small bowl, combine together, all ingredients; mix thoroughly. Store in an airtight container.

MINCEMEAT FROM SCRATCH

5 to 6 pounds beef, cooked
3 pounds butter OR margarine, melted
4 pounds currants
4 pounds raisins
1 pound citron, finely chopped
4 quarts apples, chopped
1 ounce ground ginger
2 ounces ground cinnamon
1 ounce ground cloves
4 ounces nutmeg
Grated rind & juice of 2 lemons
2 teaspoons salt
2 pounds granulated sugar
1 quart apple cider
1 quart molasses

In a large saucepan cook beef until tender; when cooled, chop by hand or grind very fine. In a large mixing bowl, combine together, melted butter, currants, raisins, citron and apples, cored & chopped.

Add spices, lemon rind, salt and sugar; set aside. Bring apple cider & molasses to a boil, over medium heat; boil for 1 minute. Remove from heat, pour over currant mixture; mix completely. Pack into canning jars, leaving ½ inch headspace. Pressure cook at 10 pounds for 40 minutes.

SHRIMP COCKTAIL SAUCE

¼ cup ketchup
¼ cup chili sauce
2 tablespoons pickle relish
2 tablespoons horseradish cream sauce
1 teaspoon granulated sugar

In a small mixing bowl, combine together, all ingredients; mix well. Refrigerate in a tightly covered container. Use sauce within 30 days. Yield about ¾ cup sauce.

MISCELLANEOUS FOODS FROM SCRATCH

The convenience foods that are purchased from the store are wonderful if they fit your lifestyle, however they are more costly. When the following foods are prepared from scratch, you can save over one-half the commercial cost. And you can eat healthier by not adding preservatives or additives as the food manufacturers do.

ALL-PURPOSE MIX

8 cups all-purpose flour, sifted
1½ cups instant dry milk
¼ cup baking powder
1 tablespoon salt
1½ cups shortening

In a large mixing bowl, combine together, flour, dry milk, baking powder and salt. Cut in shortening with pastry blender or 2 knives until mixture is well blended, and looks like coarse meal. Store in tightly covered container in a cool place. Use within 1 month. Yield 10 cups.

MULTI-PURPOSE MIX

10 cups all-purpose flour
½ cup granulated sugar
1/3 cup baking powder
1 tablespoon salt
2 cups vegetable shortening

In a large mixing bowl, combine together, flour, sugar, baking powder and salt. Cut in shortening with pastry blender or 2 knives until mixture is well blended, and looks like coarse meal. Store in tightly covered container in a cool place. Use within 3 months. Yield 13 cups.

PIE CRUST MIX I

7 cups all-purpose flour, sifted
4 teaspoons salt
2½ cups shortening

In a large mixing bowl, combine flour and salt. Cut in shortening with pastry blender or use 2 knives until mixture resembles small peas. Yield 8½ cups.

FOR ONE 9-INCH PIE CRUST

1½ cups of mix
2 to 3 tablespoons cold water

In a small mixing bowl, sprinkle water over pie mix, 1 teaspoon at a time, blending with a fork, until dough comes together to form a ball. Roll dough out on a lightly floured surface and proceed with pie directions.

FOR DOUBLE 9-INCH PIE CRUSTS

2½ cups pie mix
4 to 6 tablespoons cold water

In a medium mixing bowl, sprinkle water over pie mix, 1 teaspoon at a time, blending with a fork, until dough comes together to form a ball. Take ½ of dough and roll out on a lightly floured surface; proceed with pie directions.

EASY CAKE MIX (with recipes)

7 cups all-purpose flour
6 cups granulated sugar
2½ cups shortening OR part
   butter OR margarine
1½ cups instant powder milk
1¼ cups cornstarch
¼ cup baking powder
2 tablespoons vanilla extract
1½ teaspoons salt

In a large mixing bowl, sift all dry ingredients together. Add vanilla; cut in shortening with pastry blender or 2 knives until mixture is well blended, and looks like coarse meal Store in tightly covered container in a cool place, if using all shortening, otherwise refrigerate. Use within three months. Yield 20 cups mix (Recipes following next page,)

PLAIN 2-LAYER CAKE
(from preceding cake nix)

6 cups cake mix
6 large eggs
1 cup sour cream
¼ teaspoon baking powder

Preheat oven at 350 degrees. In a large mixing bowl, combine ingredients with electric mixer, on low speed. Mix until well-blended and smooth, then beat at medium speed for about 2 minutes. Pour batter into 2 greased 9-inch cake pans. Bake for 25 to 30 minutes or until tested done. Cool in pans for 10 minutes. Remove from pans and cool completely; frost as desired.

CARROT LOAF CAKE (from preceding cake nix)

4 cups cake mix
1 teaspoon cinnamon
4 large eggs
2 cups carrots, shredded
½ cup raisins (optional)
½ cup nuts, chopped (optional)

In a large mixing bowl, combine mix cake mix and cinnamon; add eggs and oil Beat at medium speed with electric mixer until well-blended and smooth. Fold in carrots, raisins and nuts. Pour into greased and floured 9x5x3 inch loaf pan. Bake at 350 degrees, for 30 to 45 minutes, or tested done. Yield about 6 to 8 slices.

CHOCOLATE COOKIE MIX

2 cups all-purpose flour
1 teaspoon salt
1 teaspoon baking soda
1 cup brown sugar, packed
½ cup granulated sugar
1½ cups semisweet chocolate
   chips

In a medium mixing bowl,
combine together the above
ingredients. Store in a 1-quart
container.

DIRECTIONS TO USE MIX:

In a large mixing bowl, cream
1 cup butter or margarine until
light and fluffy; add 1 large
egg and 1 teaspoon vanilla
extract; mix well. Gradually
add cookie mix, stirring until
mixed thoroughly. Drop by
teaspoonfuls of batter, about 2"
apart (cookies spread) onto a
greased cookie sheet. Bake at
375 degrees, for 8 to 10 minutes
or until lightly browned. Yield
about 4 dozen cookies.

MULTI-PURPOSE HERB MIX

1/3 cup nonfat dry milk powder
1 teaspoon salt
1 tablespoon paprika
2 teaspoons dry mustard
2 teaspoons dried oregano,
   crushed
1½ teaspoons dried thyme,
   crushed
1 teaspoon onion powder
1 teaspoon dried dillweed

½ teaspoon garlic powder
¼ teaspoon pepper

In a screw-top jar, combine
together, all ingredients; cover;
shake well. Store in a cool, dry
place. Yield 2/3 cup.

FOR A QUICK DIP

Stir 1 tablespoon of Multi-
Purpose Herb Mix into 1 cup
plain yogurt. Serve with
vegetables. Yield about1 cup.

FOR BURGERS

Combine 1 egg, beaten and
¼ cup milk; mix well. Add ¼
cup fine dry bread crumbs,
1 tablespoon Multi-Purpose
Herb Mix and 1 pound ground
beef OR pork; mix well. Shape
into four ½ inch thick patties.
Panbroil, broil or grill.
Yield 4 servings.

MINT SYRUP

1 cup granulated sugar
2/3 cup water
½ cup mint leaves
¼ cup lemon juice
½ cup orange juice

Combine together sugar and
water, in a small saucepan;
bring to a boil. Boil for 3
minutes; add mint leaves; let
cool. Strain mixture; remove
leaves; add lemon and orange
juices; mix well; chill. This syrup
is good to serve over melons or
other fruit. Keep refrigerated.
Yield 1½ cups

ITALIAN SEASONING

½ cup dried oregano
¼ cup dried basil
2 tablespoons onion powder
1 tablespoon garlic powder
½ teaspoon crushed hot red
    pepper flakes
½ teaspoon black pepper
1 bay leaf, crumbled

Combine above ingredients and whirl in blender, approximately 1 minute. Place in desired container. Use as recipe directs.

CHEF'S SALT

1 cup salt
1 teaspoon paprika
1 teaspoon black pepper
1 teaspoon white pepper
¼ teaspoon celery salt
¼ teaspoon garlic salt

Combine together, all ingredients; mix well. Place in desired container use as an all-purpose seasoning salt in cooking or as table salt. Yield about1½ cups.

BECHAMEL SAUCE

4 tablespoons butter OR
    margarine
4 tablespoons all-purpose flour
½ teaspoon salt
½ teaspoon cayenne pepper
    (optional)
2 cups milk

Melt butter; remove from heat; add flour, salt and cayenne pepper; blend well. Cook over medium heat, stirring constantly, until mixture (roux) bubbles. Cook for 2 to 3 minutes more. Reduce heat to simmer and gently stir in milk; mix well, then bring to a boil, whisk constantly for 1 to 2 minutes. Remove from heat; serve. Yield about 4 servings.

PEANUT BUTTER COOKIE MIX

1½ cups all-purpose flour
1 teaspoon baking powder
¼ teaspoon salt
1 cup brown sugar, packed
1½ cups powder sugar

In a medium mixing bowl, combine together the above ingredients. Store in a 1-quart container.

DIRECTIONS TO USE MIX:

In a large mixing bowl, cream 1 cup margarine, softened, ½ cup peanut butter, 1 egg, beaten and 1 teaspoon vanilla extract; mix well. Gradually add cookie mix, stirring until mixed thoroughly. Shape into walnut-size balls; place 2 inches apart on a lightly greased cookie sheet. Flatten cookies with a fork. Bake at 350 degrees for 8 to 10 minutes or until edges are browned. Remove from oven and let cool for 5 minutes before removing from cookie sheet. Yield about 3 dozen cookies.

INTERNATIONAL COFFEE MIX

½ cup instant coffee
2/3 cup granulated sugar
2/3 cup instant dry milk
½ teaspoon cinnamon

In a large bowl, combine all ingredients; mix well. Store in desired container.

DIRECTIONS to make 1 cup coffee.

1 cup boiling water
2 teaspoons of above coffee mixture
Adjust amount to suit your taste/

BREAD STUFFING

¾ cup onions, finely chopped
1½ cups celery, with leaves, chopped
1 cup butter OR margarine
9 cups soft bread crumbs
½ teaspoon salt
1½ teaspoons dried sage
1 teaspoon dried thyme
½ teaspoon black pepper

In a small skillet, over medium heat, melt butter; cook onions and celery until tender. In a large bowl, combine remaining ingredients; add onions, celery and butter; mix thoroughly. Yield enough stuffing for a large turkey.

SEASONING MIX FOR STUFFING

Combine together; mix well:
½ cup dried celery
½ cup dried sage
½ cup dried parsley flakes
¼ cup dried savory
¼ cup dried marjoram

Store in a covered container.

DIRECTIONS TO USE: Add 2 tablespoons to 4 cups bread crumbs; moisten as usual.

LEMONADE SYRUP BASE

1½ cups granulated sugar
½ cup boiling water

1 tablespoon fresh lemon peel, grated 1½ cups fresh squeezed lemon juice Combine above ingredients; mix well. Store in jar or other desired container.

TO USE: In 1-8 ounces glass, combine ¼ to 1/3 cup lemonade syrup base with ¾ cup cold water; mix well, if desired add ice cubes.

FOR A PITCHER: Combine 2-2/3 cups lemonade syrup base and 6 cups cold water: mix well. Add ice if desired.
NUTMEG—adds robust flavor to fried chicken.

HOMEMADE CHEESE WHIZ

¼ pound butter OR margarine
2 pounds cheddar cheese,
    softened, cut-up
1 cup milk
1 teaspoon granulated sugar

In the top of a double boiler,
combine together above
ingredients, over low heat,
stir to melt. When melted and
mixed smooth, remove from
heat; store in desired container;
refrigerate unused portion.

SPICES TO PERK UP CHICKEN WITHOUT ADDED SALT

Alternative for high sodium
poultry seasonings.

ALLSPICE—great in chicken
stew.

CURRY POWDER—Try sprinkling
¼ teaspoon over fried chicken.

GINGER—Good on stir-fry
chicken.

GROUND MUSTARD—adds zip
to any chicken dish.

PAPRIKA—delicious with baked
chicken.

HOMEMADE HORSERADISH

1 cup *horseradish, grated
½ cup white vinegar
¼ teaspoon salt

Wash horseradish roots
thoroughly; remove brown
outer skin with peeler. The roots
may be grated or put through
a food chopper or blender, cut
in pieces. Combine ingredients;
mix thoroughly; pack into
clean, sterile ½ pint jar. Seal
tight; store in refrigerator.

*WORD OF CAUTION

If possible, work with
horseradish outside, the fumes
are very strong and can make
breathing difficult.

TO BOIL FRESH CHESTNUTS

Use a sharp knife; make a
cross-slit on the flat side of
each chestnut. Place in a
saucepan of cold water.
Bring to a boil; cook for 8 to 10
minutes; remove from heat.
Peel off outer shells and inner
brown skins, taking care to
keep chestnuts whole. For ease
of peeling, leave unpeeled
chestnuts in warm cooking
water until ready to peel.

PIE CRUST MIX II

12½ cups all-purpose flour
1 tablespoon salt
5 cups shortening

In a large mixing bowl, combine flour and salt; mix well. Using a pastry blender, cut in shortening until well-blended and mixture resembles cornmeal. Store in airtight container; label with date and store in cool, dry place. Use mixture within 12 weeks;

NOTE: Can be frozen. Place 2½ cups of mix in freezer bags, label, date and freeze. Use within 12 months. Yield about 16 cups of mix enough for 6 double-crust pies or 12 single-crust pies.

CRUST DIRECTIONS:

1½ cups pie crust mix
¼ cup cold water

In a medium mixing bowl, put the mix & water; using a fork mix until mixture forms a ball of dough. Place on lightly floured surface; roll out dough to desired thickness. Place dough in 9-inch pie tin; bake at 400 degrees, for 20 to 30 minutes or until tested done. Yield for 1 double crust or 2 single crusts

MARZIPAN

2 cups plain almond paste
1 teaspoon almond extract
½ teaspoon salt
1 cup light corn syrup
7 cups powdered sugar

In a large mixing bowl, crumble almond paste; add almond extract and salt. Beat at medium speed, with electric mixer until well-blended. Add corn syrup in a thin stream while beating; beat until smooth Add powder sugar, ½ cup at a time; add the last of sugar, kneading by hand, if necessary. On a clean surface, roll out part of marzipan into a 12-inch circle, about ¼ to ½ inch thick. Use the bottom of a cake pan as a guide, then cut a 12-inch disc for the top. Roll out remaining marzipan and cut into3 strips about 12-inches long and the width to equal the height of the cake. Yield about 3 pounds.

NOTE: Any marzipan that is left can be colored and molded into fruit, vegetable or flower shapes, to decorate the finished cake, or it can be frozen for later use. Wrap it well so it does not dry out

TERIYAKI SAUCE

1 clove garlic, minced
½ teaspoon fresh ginger, minced
½ cup soy sauce
½ cup water

In a small mixing bowl, combine together ingredients; mix well. Use as a marinade, at least 10 minutes, over meat, fish or poultry in your favorite recipe. Yield 1 cup sauce.

PUMPKIN PIE SPICE

2 tablespoons ground
   cinnamon
1 tablespoon ground ginger
½ teaspoon EACH ground
   cloves, nutmeg and allspice
1 tablespoon cornstarch
1 tablespoon instant tea

Sift together, all ingredients, at least 3 times. Blend thoroughly; store in tightly sealed container. Keep out of sunlight and use in 1 year. Yield about 1/3 cup spice.

CHOCOLATE CHIP COOKIE MIX

2 cups all-purpose flour
1 teaspoon salt
1 teaspoon baking soda
1 cup brown sugar, packed
½ cup granulated sugar
1½ cups chocolate chips

In a medium mixing bowl. combine together, flour, salt and baking soda; set aside.

In a covered container, place brown sugar, sugar, chocolate chips; add flour mixture. (It is not necessary to mix ingredients until ready to use.) You can share with someone or give as a gift by layering ingredients in a quart canning jar, or container of your choice.

DIRECTIONS: In a large mixing bowl, thoroughly mix ingredients; set aside. In a separate bowl, cream 1 cup butter OR margarine until light and fluffy; add 1 large egg and 1 teaspoon vanilla extract. Add flour mixture; mix well. Drop by spoonfuls onto a greased cookie sheet, two inches apart. Bake at 375 degrees, for 8 minutes, or until lightly browned. Yield 2 dozen cookies.

STREUSEL MIX

2/3 cup unsalted butter OR
   margarine
¾ cup light brown sugar,
   packed
½ teaspoon salt
1 teaspoon ground cinnamon
1½ cups all-purpose flour

In medium mixing bowl, combine together, all ingredients. Use a fork or clean hand to mix ingredients until butter is completely absorbed and mixture is crumbly. Yield 4 cups.

SHAKE & BAKE MIX

1/3 cup dry powdered milk
1 teaspoon granulated bouillon
½ teaspoon dry mustard
1/3 teaspoon garlic powder
Pinch of poultry seasoning
Pinch of basil
Pinch of seasoned salt
Pinch of black pepper

In a small mixing bowl, combine together all ingredients; mix thoroughly. Use like the commercial Shake and Bake.

STEAK SAUCE

2 cups ketchup
2 garlic cloves, minced
2/3 cup onions, chopped
½ cup EACH lemon juice, water, Worcestershire sauce and vinegar
¼ cup soy sauce
¼ cup dark brown sugar, packed
2 tablespoons prepared mustard

In a large saucepan, combine together, all ingredients; over medium heat, bring to a boil. Cook for about 3 to 5 minutes; remove from heat; let cool. Put in desired container; refrigerate until ready to use.

VANILLA EXTRACT (alcohol-free)

4 to 8 vanilla beans
2/3 cup warm water
2 teaspoons liquid lecithin

Soak beans in water for several hours, then put in blender on high speed until beans are very fine. In s saucepan, over medium heat, covered, bring mixture to a boil. Remove from heat; pour into jar; cover tightly. Let sit overnight; next day, strain, return to blender; add lecithin, blend together on low speed, for 1 minute. Pour into a bottle, with a tight-fitting lid. Store in the refrigerator.

SEAFOOD SEASONING

2 tablespoons mustard seed
2 tablespoons dill seeds
2 tablespoons hot red pepper flakes
2 large bay leaves, crumbled
½ teaspoon whole cloves
½ teaspoon whole allspice
½ teaspoon peppercorns
½ teaspoon ground ginger

Combine together, all ingredients; add to water when boiling seafood, like shrimp or crab.

PICKLING SPICE

1 teaspoon EACH of the
following:
dill seed
fenugreek
mustard seed
whole coriander
celery seed
1 teaspoon dried ginger root,
diced
1 teaspoon allspice
1 cinnamon stick, 1 inch long,
broke in pieces
2 whole bay leaves, crumbled
½ teaspoon peppercorns
½ teaspoon whole cloves
½ teaspoon hot red pepper
flakes

In a mixing bowl, combine
together, all ingredients;
mix well. Use in pickling and
preserving OR enclose in
cheesecloth and use when
cooking soup and stocks,
discard when done cooking.

FRUIT LEATHERS

2 cups ripe fruit, cut up

Preheat *oven to 200 degrees.
Line baking pan, preferably
cookie sheet, with a rim, with
foil. Puree' fruit in a blender or
food processor, then spread
evenly in prepared pan. Bake
for 3 to 4 hours, with oven
door, about 1 inch ajar, so

the moisture can evaporate.
Checking occasionally, until no
longer moist to the touch; cool,
then roll up. Store in a covered
container.

*NOTE: If you have a
dehydrator, follow the
manufacturers directions

CRUMB TOPPING MIX

1-1/3 cups light brown sugar,
packed
1 cup all-purpose flour
1 teaspoons cinnamon
¾ cup butter OR margarine

In a medium mixing bowl,
combine sugar, flour and
cinnamon; mix well. Add butter,
mix with fork until finely mixed.
Store in airtight container, in
cool dry place. Yield 3½ cups
topping mix.

FRESH PUMPKIN PULP

Pumpkins can be boiled or baked to prepare pulp to be used in cooking or baking.

TO BOIL: Slice open the pumpkin. Remove the seeds and membrane. Cut the pumpkin in pieces, place in large saucepan, cover with water; cook over medium heat until tender. Remove from heat; drain and let cool. When cool, peel skin; put pumpkin into food processor, or (Use food mill, or blender) and puree'.

TO BAKE: Slice pumpkin in half and remove seeds and membrane. Place halves, cut side down, on a cooking utensil. Bake at 325 degrees, for 50 to 60 minutes. When tender, remove from oven; cool. Peel off skin, then puree'. Refrigerate the pumpkin pulp until ready to use.

HOMEMADE PUMPKIN PIE FILLING

2 large eggs, slightly beaten
½ cup granulated sugar
½ cup brown sugar, packed
1 tablespoon all-purpose flour
1 teaspoon cinnamon
½ teaspoon salt
¼ teaspoon nutmeg
¼ teaspoon ginger
2 cups pumpkin, cooked
1 can (14 ozs.) condensed milk

In a medium mixing bowl, combine together, the first eight ingredients; mix well. Blend in the cooked pumpkin and gradually add milk; mix thoroughly. Pour into prepared 9" pie shell; bake at 350 degrees, for 50 minutes or until tested done.

HOW TO MAKE YOGURT?

1-1/3 cups instant dry milk
4 cups water
2 tablespoons plain yogurt
   (to use as starter)

Sterilize jar with lid. Heat water to about 180 degrees; Combine together ingredients; mix well. Place in jar, cover; wrap several layers of a towel or other cloth. Let set undisturbed for 6 to 8 hours. After, at least 6 hours minimum, refrigerate yogurt.

APPLE PIE SPICE

½ cup ground cinnamon
1 tablespoon nutmeg
1 tablespoon allspice
1 teaspoon ground cloves
½ teaspoon ground ginger

In a small mixing bowl, blend together, mix thoroughly.

TO USE: Use 1¼ teaspoons apple pie spice per 6 cups sliced apples. Use when you add sugar in recipe of apple pie, applesauce and baked apples. Yield 2/3 cup.

DRIED ONION SOUP MIX

½ teaspoon onion powder
½ teaspoon salt
¼ teaspoon granulated sugar
¼ teaspoon browning sauce
    (i.e. Kitchen Bouquet)
½ cup dried onions, chopped
    or minced

In a small bowl, combine
together, onion powder, salt
and sugar; add browning
sauce. Mix until seasonings are
uniformly brown. Add dried
onions; mix thoroughly, until
color is again uniform. This
procedure will take several
minutes. Yield ½ cup of mix,
which is equivalent to one 1.5
oz. envelope of commercial
dried soup mix.

BOUQUET GARNI
(Using fresh herbs)

3 sprigs fresh chervil (or celery
    leaves)
3 sprigs fresh parsley
½ bay leaf
2 sprigs fresh thyme
Cheesecloth & twine (To make
    cheese-cloth bag.

The above ingredients make 1
serving.

BOUQUET GARNI
(Using dried herbs)

1½ tablespoons dried parsley
    flakes
1 tablespoon celery flakes
1 bay leaf, crumbled
2 teaspoons dried thyme leaves
2 teaspoons marjoran leaves
6 pieces cheesecloth, each
    to measure 4 inches square
    and twine

Combine together, the above
dry ingredients. Place 2
rounded teaspoons on each
cheesecloth square. Store in
tightly covered jar.

TO USE: Immerse 1 bag in soup
or stock, the last 30 minutes of
cooking. Yield 6 bags.

HOMEMADE HONEY
(Recipe from Nova Scotia, 17th Century)

80 blossoms white clover
40 blossoms red clover
5 rose petals, faintly perfumed
10 cups granulated sugar
3 cups water
½ teaspoon powdered alum

In a large saucepan, combine together, sugar, water and alum; over high heat bring to a boil; cook for 5 minutes, stirring constantly. When sugar is dissolved, completely, remove from heat. Place red and white clover, along with rose petals, into a large container. Pour hot syrup over the clover mixture; let stand for 20 minutes. Strain mixture through a cheese cloth; place in desired bottle with a lid. Store in a dry place.

NOTE: When substituting honey in a recipe as the sweetener, remember to reduce oven temperature, by 25 degrees, to prevent over browning.

CANDIED CITRUS PEEL

2 cups orange, lemon or lime peels (OR a combination) cut into ½ inch strips
1 tablespoon salt
1 cup lukewarm water
3 cups cold water
2 cups granulated sugar
Powder sugar

Place peels in a glass or ceramic mixing bowl Dissolve salt in 1 cup lukewarm water, pour over the peels, followed by 3 cups cold water; mix well. Be sure that water covers the peels. Let peels soak for 24 hours at room temperature. Next day, drain peels, rinse in cold water several times; drain. Place peels in a large saucepan, cover with fresh water, over medium heat, simmer for 25 minutes, drain while hot. Sprinkle sugar over peels, stirring to dissolve. If necessary, add a little water to allow cooking over low heat, until the peels absorb all syrup. Be careful not to let peels burn. Remove from heat; spread peels on foil-covered cookie sheet; uncovered, let sit to dry. Turn peels over occasionally while drying. Chop into pieces for baking; dust with powder sugar; store, covered in refrigerator until ready to use. Yield 2 cups.

CANDIED CHERRIES

2 cups fresh cherries, with stems
2 cups granulated sugar
1 cup water

Pit cherries; set aside. In a large saucepan, combine together, sugar and water; bring to a boil. Cook until a candy thermometer reads 230 degrees, or syrup forms a thread when lifted with a clean metal spoon. Remove from heat; add cherries by their stems then return cherries and syrup to cook. Bring to a boil briefly, about 30 seconds set aside. Wet a shallow pan with cold water; place cherries, stems up, in the pan. Meanwhile, continue boiling syrup for another 5 minutes, then pour gently, over cherries; let stand for 12 hours, or simmer until the syrup is set. Place cherries on a rack, uncovered, for 24 hours, or until completely dry to the touch. Store between sheets of wax paper and at room temperature, in a plastic container or bag. If desired, cut in half; remove stems when using cherries in a recipe. Yield 2 cups.

SUGGESTION: Do not prepare candied cherries, if weather is rainy or humid; fruit will not dry properly.

ALMOND PASTE

1½ cups blanched almonds
2/3 cup granulated sugar
2 tablespoon water
1 tablespoon lemon juice
Pinch of salt

Process the almonds, ¼ cup at a time, in a blender, until smooth and paste-like; stop, as needed to push any unground nuts into the blades. Do not do this while machine is on. When nuts are ground to paste, put almonds into mixing bowl; set aside. Combine together, the remaining ingredients, in a small saucepan; over low heat, cook, stirring constantly, until syrup comes to a full boil, and the sugar is dissolved.

Remove from heat; pour over ground almonds; mix well with a wooden spoon. Cool about 5 minutes, then knead with your hands until paste holds together and can be formed into a roll. Wrap the roll tightly in foil, twisting ends to seal, Let ripen in refrigerator for 1 week.

IF USING FOOD PROCESSOR:
Run through blade 4 times; then place all almonds in container; whirl about 1 minute; with the motor still running, gradually pour in the hot syrup through processor's opening, continue processing until mixture forms a ball. With food processor it isn't necessary to knead, proceed to form roll, wrap and refrigerate.

MULTI-PURPOSE HERB MIX

1/3 cup nonfat dry milk powder
1 tablespoon salt
1 tablespoon paprika
2 teaspoons dry mustard
2 teaspoons dried oregano,
    crushed
1½ teaspoons dried thyme,
    crushed
1 teaspoon onion powder
1 teaspoon dried dillweed
½ teaspoon garlic powder
¼ teaspoon pepper

In a dry screw-top jar combine together, all ingredients; cover; shake well. Store in a cool dry place. Yield 2/3 cup mix.

NOTE: Use above mix as you would a store-boughten seasoning mix.

ROASTED PUMPKIN SEEDS

Remove seeds from inside of pumpkin; rinse seeds thoroughly. Dry seeds using paper towels. Spread seeds evenly on ungreased cookie sheet; bake at 350 degrees, for about 10 to 15 minutes or until crisp and slightly browned. If desired, salt to taste.

SANDWICH SPREAD

12 green peppers, seeded
12 red pepper, seeded
12 green tomatoes
½ cup onions, chopped
1 cup self-rising flour
2 cups granulated sugar
1½ to 2 cups white vinegar
2 cups dry mustard
1 teaspoon salt
1 teaspoon celery seeds
1 quart mayonnaise

Grind vegetables in food processor; drain well. Reserve liquid for thinning, if necessary. In a large saucepan, combine together, all ingredients, EXCEPT mayonnaise; cook for 10 minutes. Remove from heat; add mayonnaise; mix well. Put in sterilized jars; seal. Yield 12 pints.

CRACKER JACK

7 quarts popcorn
2 cups brown sugar
2 sticks butter OR margarine
½ cup corn syrup (Karo)
½ cup peanuts (optional)
1 teaspoon baking soda

In a mixing bowl, combine together, brown sugar, butter and corn syrup; mix well. Over medium heat, bring to a boil; cook for 5 minutes. Remove from heat; add baking soda. Pour mixture over popcorn; mix thoroughly; add peanuts. Place on a cookie sheet; bake at 250 degrees, for 1 hour; stir every 15 minutes.

PESTO SAUCE

1½ cups basil leaves, loosely
    packed, tough stems
    removed
½ cup olive oil
2 tablespoons walnuts
2 cloves garlic
Salt to taste
2/3 cup Parmesan Cheese,
    grated
2 tablespoons butter OR
    margarine, Softened

Place basil, oil, nuts, garlic
and salt in a food processor
or blender. Process until well-
blended, scraping down sides
as necessary. Pour sauce into
bowl; add cheese and butter,
beat well by hand. Toss sauce
with hot pasta. Yield about 6
servings.

SPAGHETTI SAUCE MIX

1 tablespoon instant minced
    onions
1 tablespoon parsley flakes
1 tablespoon cornstarch
2 teaspoons green pepper
    flakes
½ teaspoon salt
½ teaspoon instant garlic,
    minced
1 teaspoon granulated sugar
¾ teaspoon Italian Seasoning

Combine together, all
ingredients; put in a covered
container or a plastic bag.
Yield 1 serving.

DIRECTIONS TO USE

1 pound ground meat
1 serving of spaghetti sauce
    mix (above)
1 can (6 ozs.) tomato paste
2 cups water
12 ounces pasta, cooked
Parmesan Cheese for topping

In a medium skillet, over
medium heat, brown meat
until done; drain meat, then
place remaining ingredients
in a medium saucepan;
EXCEPT pasta and cheese.
Cook over medium heat until
warmed though, about 15 to
20 minutes. Meanwhile prepare
pasta according to package
directions; serve.

NOODLE MIX

2 cups egg noodles (medium width)
2 teaspoons chicken OR beef soup mix
2 teaspoons parsley flakes
1 teaspoon onion flakes
Pinch black pepper

In a large bowl, combine together, all ingredients; mix well. Batches may be increased. Store in a plastic bag, in a cool dry place, up to 3 months.

HOW TO USE: Place mix in 1½ quart baking dish; dot with 1 teaspoon butter; add 1½ cups boiling water. Blend well; cover tightly with lid or foil. Bake at 350 degrees, for 25 to 30 minutes or until liquid is absorbed and noodles are firm, but tender. Yield about 4 servings.

HOT & SPICY SEASONING

¼ cup paprika
1 tablespoon dried oregano, crushed
1 tablespoon chili powder
1 tablespoon garlic powder
1 teaspoon black pepper
½ teaspoon red cayenne pepper
½ teaspoon dry mustard

In a small bowl, combine together, all ingredients; mix thoroughly. Store in an airtight container.

GOAT'S MILK CHEESE II (Ricotta)

1 quart goat's milk
2 cups whipping cream
3 tablespoons buttermilk
1 rennet tablet, crushed
½ teaspoon salt

Heat milk, whipping cream and buttermilk to 100 degrees. Do not overheat. Dissolve crushed rennet tablet in 2 tablespoons water. Add to milk mixture; let stand until curd is solid and has separated from whey, 16 to 18 hours. Drain off whey; discard or save for another use. Spoon curds into a sieve that has been lined with a double layer of dampened, cheesecloth. Place sieve over a bowl or pan; allow to drain in refrigerator about 16 hours. When cheese is thoroughly drained; remove from sieve; work in salt. Place in mold or roll into desired shapes. Cover; refrigerate until ready to use. Serve plain or with dry or fresh herbs. Yield 1½ to 2 cups cheese.

TOMATO PASTE

8 pounds plum tomatoes,
  chopped
1 teaspoon salt
1 stalk celery, chopped
½ cup onions, chopped
1 tablespoon parsley, chopped
1 teaspoon oregano
½ teaspoon sweet basil
1 clove garlic, minced
4 whole cloves
½ teaspoon peppercorns
½ teaspoon cinnamon

In a large saucepan, combine together, over medium heat, bring mixture to simmer. Cook until tomatoes are tender, stirring frequently. Put the mixture in a blender or food processor and puree' Place mixture back in saucepan, over low heat, stir frequently to avoid scorching Continue to simmer until mixture is of desired consistency. Put in hot, sterilized pint jars, seal at once. Yield 2 pints.

WHOLE WHEAT MIX & RECIPES

4 cups whole wheat flour
4 cups all-purpose flour
1½ cups nonfat dry milk
1½ cups granulated sugar
½ cup wheat germ
¼ cup baking powder
1 tablespoon salt
1½ cups shortening

In a large mixing bowl, combine together, all ingredients EXCEPT shortening; mix well. Cut in shortening with a pastry blender until mixture is evenly distributed. Store in a airtight container in a cool dry place. Yield about 13¾ cups.

WHOLE WHEAT BREAD

Preheat oven to 350 degrees. In a large mixing bowl, beat 1 large egg with 1¼ cups water. Add 4½ cups Whole Wheat Mix, mix just until dry ingredients are moistened. Place into a greased 9x5x3 inch loaf pan; bake for 50 minutes, or until tested done. Let cool in pan for 5 minutes, loosen sides with spatula. Cool thoroughly before slicing.

WHOLE WHEAT MUFFINS

Prepare batter as for Whole Wheat Bread. Spoon into greased muffin tin, filling 2/3 full. Bake in preheated oven, at 400 degrees, for 15 to 20 minutes, or until tested done.

WHOLE WHEAT PANCAKES

In a medium bowl, beat 1 large egg with 1 cup water. Add 2¼ cups Whole Wheat Mix; stir dry ingredients until are just moistened. Drop by spoonfuls onto a well-greased skillet; cook over medium heat until browned on both sides. Turn over gently because pancakes are tender. Serve hot with syrup, honey or jelly. Yield about 15 (3-inch) pan cakes.

WHOLE WHEAT COFFEE CAKE

In a medium bowl, beat 1 large egg slightly with ½ cup water. Add 2¼ cups Whole Wheat Mix and ½ cup; raisins; mix just until dry ingredients are moistened. Spread evenly in greased 13x9x2-inch baking pan. Sprinkle with Crumb Topping (recipe follows); bake in preheated 400 degrees, for about 25 minutes, or until tested done. Cut in squares. If desired, serve warm.

CRUMB TOPPING

1-1/3 cups light brown sugar, packed
1 cup all-purpose flour
1 teaspoons cinnamon
¾ cup butter OR margarine

In a medium mixing bowl, combine sugar, flour and cinnamon; mix well. Add butter, mix with fork until finely mixed. Store in airtight container, in cool dry place. Yield 3½ cups topping mix.

RAISIN SAUCE FOR HAM

½ cup dark brown sugar, packed
2 tablespoons all-purpose flour
1 cup water
2/3 cup seedless raisins
¼ cup cider vinegar
Pinch of cinnamon
2 tablespoons butter OR margarine

In a medium saucepan, combine together, sugar with flour; add remaining ingredients, mix well. Over low heat, bring to a boil, cook for 1 minutes, covered, then reduce heat to simmer; cook for 5 minutes.

HOW TO COOK SUMMER SQUASH?

1. One pound zucchini (3 medium about 7 inches each) equals 3 cups sliced or 2½ cups chopped.

2. Bake whole in the oven or microwave oven, by first taking a fork and piercing squash in several places to allow steam to escape.

3. Steam, blanch or bake whole until tender. Slice in half lengthwise and scoop seeds, then scoop out pulp. Combine with cooked ingredients; bake at 375 degrees for about 10 minutes, or until heated through.

4. For deep frying, heat shortening to 375 degrees. Cut squash into strips or rounds; dredge in flour and fry until golden.

5. For stir-frying, heat oil in pan and place strips or slices in pan; cook for 2 to 3 minutes.

There is no need to pare or remove seeds, if the squash is young.

SAVORY TOMATO SAUCE

½ cup onions, chopped
¼ teaspoon garlic powder
1 tablespoon vegetable oil
2 cans (16 ozs. each) stewed tomatoes
1 can (8 ozs.) tomato sauce
1 can (6 ozs.) tomato paste
1½ cups water
1 teaspoon dried basil
2 teaspoons celery flakes
1 tablespoon dried parsley
2 teaspoons instant beef bouillon
Black pepper to taste
1 can (4 ozs) mushrooms, sliced

In a large saucepan, sauté onions and garlic powder, in hot oil, over medium heat. Mash tomatoes into small pieces with fork; add to onions. Add remaining ingredients to saucepan; reduce heat to low. Simmer, covered for 30 minutes. If serving meatballs, then pour sauce over meatballs, then simmer, covered for about 45 minutes. Stir occasionally; serve over hot spaghetti, or use in another favorite recipe.

HOW TO MAKE BAKING POWDER!

1/3 cup potassium bicarbonate
2/3 cup Cream of Tartar
2/3 cup Arrowroot

In a bowl, combine together, by sifting all ingredients. Store in a jar. Yield about 2 cups. Use like commercial kind.

CHICKEN GRAVY MIX

1½ cups nonfat dry milk
¾ cup all-purpose flour
3 tablespoons Instant Chicken
   Bouillion
¼ teaspoon ground sage
½ cup butter OR margarine

In a medium bowl, combine together, dry milk, flour, bouillon and sage. Cut in butter until mixture resembles cornmeal. Store in a tightly covered container, in the refrigerator, up to 2 months Yield about 3 cups mix, (will make 6 cups of gravy. In a saucepan, blend together, 1 cup cold water and ½ cup gravy mix. Cook over medium heat; stirring until mixture is thick and bubbly. Cook for 1 minute more. Yield 1 cup.

OLD FASHION BREAKFAST SAUSAGE

1 pound medium ground pork
1 teaspoon salt
¼ teaspoon thyme
¼ teaspoon black pepper
¼ teaspoon sage
Dash of garlic powder

In a small bowl, combine together, all ingredients EXCEPT ground pork; mix well. Sprinkle dry ingredients over the pork; mix thoroughly. Form into one large roll, or several patties or links. Refrigerate, wrapped air tight, for 2 or 3 days, to cure and to blend flavors This sausage will keep well for 3 or 4 days in the refrigerator or up to 1 month in the freezer.

VEGETABLE STOCK

2 quarts cold water
4 carrots
4 stalks celery
Salt and pepper
1 onion
2 sprigs parsley
2 tablespoons butter OR
   margarine

Wash vegetables, cut into small pieces. Put in a skillet; sauté in butter until vegetables turn yellow; add water. Simmer over low heat, for 30 minutes. Strain before using.

HOW TO MAKE CORNED BEEF! (Recipe is for 100 pounds of beef.)

Prepare meat by removing bones; cut meat into uniform sizes. Use rump, chuck or brisket. Weigh the meat; allow 8 to 10 pounds of salt to every 100 pounds of beef In a clean, water-tight container, place a layer of salt on the bottom, then a layer of meat, continue layering until container is full or meat is used up. Cover; top with a heavy amount of salt. Leave meat set for 24 hours, then cover with a solution made of 4 pounds of granulated sugar, 2 ounces baking soda and 4 gallons of water. Allow to cure 30 to 40 days at room temperature of 38 to 40 degrees. Keep meat submerged. When cured, remove meat from brine, rinse lightly, dry with paper towels and package as desired.

HOT BUTTER MAPLE SYRUP

Heat 1 cup maple syrup and ¼ cup butter OR margarine, until butter melts; mix well; serve. Yield 1¼ cups.

CRANBERRY SYRUP

1 can (12 ozs.) frozen cranberry juice
cocktail concentrate
¼ teaspoon lemon peel. grated
Dash of cinnamon
Dash of nutmeg

2 teaspoons cornstarch
1 tablespoon water

In a saucepan, combine together, cranberry juice, lemon peel and spices; bring mixture to a boil. Combine cornstarch and water together; add to mixture; boil for 1 minute. Serve warm. Yield 1½ cups.

PINEAPPLE SYRUP
1 can (20 ozs.) pineapple chunks, with juice

Place pineapple, with juice, in a blender or food processor; puree' until smooth. Pour in to a saucepan; add ¼ cup granulated sugar; mix well. Bring mixture to a boil; reduce heat to simmer; cook for 2 to 3 minutes. Remove from heat; let cool. Yield 2½ cups.

DRAWN BUTTER (serve w/lobster)

1/3 cup butter, divided
3 tablespoons all-purpose flour
½ teaspoon salt
Pinch of pepper
1½ cups hot water

In a saucepan, over low heat, melt one-half of the butter; add flour. Mix to prevent lumps, then gradually, add water, salt and pepper. Simmer for 15 minutes, then add remaining butter; mix well. Serve in individual cups with the lobster.

HOMEMADE HOPS YEAST

1 quart hop
Cover with cold water. Let
   stand for 24 to 26 hours,
   stirring occasionally, crushing
   hops with wooden spoon.
3 cups cornmeal
6 cups water

Pour cornmeal into 6 water;
cook for 30 minutes, over
medium heat, stirring
constantly. Remove from heat;
set aside; let cool. Strain hops,
pressing out all liquid. Do not
cook hops, soaking brings
out the juice. Combine hops
liquid with cooled mush, mix
thoroughly. Spread mixture
evenly in ¼ inch layer; allow
to dry thoroughly. When dry,
crack into pieces; store in a
covered container. When
needed, soften in lukewarm
water.

TO CRYSTALLIZE GINGER

1 pound ginger root
2 cups granulated sugar
1 cup water
½ teaspoon cream of tartar
*Extra-fine granulated sugar
*Put in blender to puree'
   extra-fine.

1. Soak ginger root in cold
   water over night, then drain.
   Scrape off skin; slice the
   root into ¼ inch-thick strips.

Place ginger in a saucepan;
cover with fresh water; bring
to a boil. Remove from
heat; drain, then repeat
putting back into saucepan,
cover with fresh water and
once more, bring to a boil;
remove from heat. Repeat
for a third time, then set
ginger aside.

2. Combine sugar and water;
   bring to a boil, cook for 20
   minutes, to make a syrup
   Add the ginger and cream
   of tartar to syrup mixture,
   cook over medium heat
   until the ginger root is
   translucent.

3. Remove the ginger strips
   from the syrup; spread on
   a wire rack to dry for 1 to
   2 days. When the strips
   are almost dry, roll them
   in the extra-fine sugar; let
   dry completely. Store in
   an airtight container. Yield
   about 1½ pounds.

MARASCHINO CHERRIES

5 cups *yellow cherries, pitted
5 cups granulated sugar
1 cup water
1 teaspoon almond flavoring
1 ounce red food coloring

SAUCE

1 quart hot water
2 teaspoons salt
1 teaspoon alum

* You can use other cherries, if desired. In a large mixing bowl, combine together, sauce ingredients; mix well. Then place cherries in the sauce; let stand overnight. Next day, drain cherries, put in clear water, for 1 hour. Meanwhile, make syrup by combining together, sugar, water, almond flavoring and food coloring. Over medium heat, bring to a boil; add cherries. Remove from heat; let cherries remain in syrup for 2 to 3 days or until cherries are very red; refrigerate during this time.

HOW TO MAKE PRETZELS?

2 tablespoons hot water
1 pkg. active dry yeast
1-1/3 cups warm water
1/3 cup brown sugar, packed
5 cups all-purpose flour
Extra flour
Coarse kosher salt
Baking soda

Preheat oven to 475 degrees. In a large bowl, combine together, hot water and yeast until yeast dissolves. Add warm water and brown sugar. Slowly add 5 cups flour, stirring constantly. Continue mixing until mixture is smooth and does not stick to the bowl. Place on lightly floured surface. Dip hands into the extra flour; knead dough, by pushing it down and away from you, with the palms of your hands; turn dough as you knead, until dough is elastic and smooth. Grease 2 cookie sheets. Sprinkle cookie sheets evenly, with kosher salt; set aside.

Pinch off a piece of dough about the size of a golf ball. Roll between palms of hands to a rope about 12 inches long, shape into a pretzel. Fill a large skillet with water; add 1 tablespoon baking soda. Bring to a gentle boil, use spatula to lower each pretzel into skillet; cook for about 30 seconds, then lift pretzel from skillet onto prepared cookies sheet. Sprinkle kosher salt on the top of pretzels; place in oven; bake for 8 minutes or until golden.

WHOLE WHEAT PRETZELS

1½ cups all-purpose flour
1 pkg. active dry yeast
3 tablespoons instant dry milk
2 tablespoons granulated sugar
½ teaspoon salt
1 tablespoon butter OR
  margarine
1 cup hot water
1½ cups whole wheat OR
  graham flour
1 large egg white
1 tablespoon water
Coarse salt (optional)

In a large mixing bowl, combine together, 1 cup all-purpose flour, yeast, dry milk, sugar and salt; mix to blend ingredients. Add butter and hot water; then add whole wheat flour; mix until dough forms. Gradually stir in remaining all-purpose flour to make a soft dough. Turn dough out onto floured surface; knead for 5 to 10 minutes or until dough is elastic. Cover; let rest for 15 minutes. Punch dough down, then roll into a 12-inch square. Cut into 24 strips Roll each strip into a roll 14 inches long. Shape into pretzels; place on greased cookie sheet; let stand uncovered for 20 minutes. Brush pretzels with egg white mixed with 1 tablespoon water. Sprinkle on top with coarse salt. Bake at 350 degrees, for 18 to 20 minutes or until lightly browned. Yield about 2 dozen pretzels.

LEMONADE MIX (with variations)

2 cups granulated sugar
2 cups hot tap water
Peel of 1 lemon, in ½ x2" strips
2 cups freshly squeezed lemon juice

In a uncovered microwave-safe 2 quart casserole, combine together, sugar, water and lemon peel; microwave on High (100%) 5 to 6 minutes, stirring, at half-time or until boiling, then boil for 1 minute; add lemon juice; mix well. Cool; strain; store in tightly-covered jar in the refrigerator. Yield enough for 20 glasses.

TO SERVE: shake mix well; pour ¼ cup into a 12-ounce glass; add ice, ¾ cup water OR club soda; stir well.

FOR LIMEADE MIX; prepare as directed above. using lime peel & freshly squeezed lime juice instead of lemon peel & juice. Increase sugar to 2¼ cups. Yield enough for 20 glasses

FOR ORANGEADE MIX—Prepare as directed above. but use peel of ½ orange, 2 cups fresh-squeezed orange juice and 1 cup sugar & 1 cup water. Yield enough for 14 glasses.

HOW TO MAKE INSTANT OATMEAL?

3 cups quick oats
Salt
8 plastic bags (6½ x 4")

Place ½ cup oats in blender or food processer, at a time, whirl on high until powdery. Put ¼ cup of quick oats (unpowdered), 2 tablespoons of powdered oats and ¼ teaspoon salt into plastic bags or desired container.

TO SERVE: Add ¾ cup boiling water to 1 packet; mix well.

HOW TO MAKE APPLE CIDER VINEGAR! (old recipe)

Use a wide mouth crock, with a cover. Add peelings and cores from apples, after making apple pie or sauce. Cover with cold water. Replace lid; store in warm place. Occasionally, lift lid; add more peelings and cores. Strain froth or foam as you check the vinegar. When vinegar smells and tastes as you like, then strain apple pieces; pour vinegar into sterilized bottles and cork. Label with date and contents.

JERKY SEASONING

4 green onions
1 clove garlic
1 hot chili pepper, (such as jalapeno pepper), seeded
1 tablespoon ground allspice
1 teaspoon dried thyme leaves
½ teaspoon nutmeg
½ teaspoon red pepper (optional)
2 tablespoons lime juice

Combine together, puree' in a blender or food processor. Store in a covered glass container, in the refrigerator. Yield 1/3 cup.

TO USE: Rub 2 teaspoons or more jerky seasoning over surface of meat. Let stand at least 1 hour before using. The flavor is more enhanced if meat is marinated overnight.

TIPS TO MAKE GREAT MUFFINS!

1. One of the important tips is for great muffins is to mix the batter only until all dry ingredients are moisten. DO NOT OVER MIX! Your muffins will be lighter when you mix the batter quickly, this method produces the best rising effect.

2. Always preheat the oven; do not put muffins into a cold oven.

3. Remember to mix the dry ingredients well together, in order to incorporate the baking soda and baking powder evenly throughout the batter.

4. Place water in the empty muffin cups, if your short on batter. This will save the muffin tins, plus will add moisture to the muffins.

5. Most muffins bake at 400 degrees F. but adjust recipes to your own oven. If muffins brown to quickly, then turn oven down to 375 or 350 degrees.

6. Muffins bake better when you place them on the middle shelf of your oven. On the lowest shelf muffins' bottoms brown too quickly. On the higher shelf, the muffins' tops brown too soon.

7. To know if muffins are done, test them by inserting a toothpick into the center of the muffin and it comes out clean, it is done.

8. It is best when you leave the muffins in the tin for 10 minutes, after removing them from the oven. They come out the tins more easier.

9. To store muffins, place in a covered container when they have cooled completely. You can freeze muffins up to three months.

10. You can, either microwave frozen muffin for 1 minute or less, or wrap muffins in foil and heat in the oven, at 350 degrees for 10 to 15 minutes.

NOTE: ½ teaspoon dried herbs equal 1 tablespoon fresh herbs.

WHAT ARE HERBS?
WHAT ARE SPICES?

Both herbs and spices come from plants, some time from the same plant. Herbs like basil, cilantro or tarragon are leaves of plants. Spices such as, fennel are seeds, cardamom are seed pods, saffron is of the flower. Juniper are berries, cloves are buds of plants, ginger is the rhizomes and cinnamon is the bark. Spices can be any part of the plant, except the leaves. That is the primary difference between herbs and spices.

The difference between fresh herbs and dried, is that you would use less of the dried. A fresh herb, such as basil, you should not add too early when cooking a meal, because heat robs the herb of flavor and color. It is best to add basil towards the end of cooking. Rosemary is an exception, it needs heat to soften the tough leaves. Parsley too, can be put in the pot, at the beginning.

As a general rule, 1 teaspoon of dried herbs, is equivalent in flavor, to 1 tablespoon of fresh, chopped herbs. Also it is better to add dried herbs earlier in the cooking process, so the dried herbs have ample time to release their flavor. In buying dried herbs and spices, it is best to buy them in smallest quantity for freshness. Another suggestion is, spoon, don't sprinkle herbs and spices into a simmering pot, because the rising steam can cause the rest of the contents, to lose its flavor and for the contents to clump.

Dried herbs and spices keep best, when they are stored in airtight containers, in a cool, dark place Light cause them to fade and heat reduces their flavor. The worst place to keep them is above the stove, even though its handy. Most fresh herbs will retain their freshness, from several days to a week or two in the refrigerator. Store fresh herbs wrapped loosely in paper towels, to absorb the moisture, then seal in a plastic bag. Fresh herbs should not be washed until ready to be used. To dry an abundance of fresh herbs, put herbs in a single row on a rack; leave them in a warm room until dry, about 5 days. After herbs are completely dry, then store in a airtight container

TO REMOVE CORN SILK—Rub a damp paper towel over a shucked corn.

ALCOHOL SUBSTITUTIONS

For sherry and light wines—use equal amounts of lemon juice and chicken bouillon. For desserts, use half & half, lemon juice and water OR ginger ale.

For red wines—use cranberry juice diluted with about 1/3 water.

For beer—for baking meats, especially replace with ginger ale.

Wine used in fruit desserts—replace with a lemon soft drink.

BUYING GUIDE FOR NUTMEATS!

4 ozs. walnuts, chopped equals about 1 cup.
1 lb. walnuts in shells yields about 2 cups
1 lb. pecans in shells yields about 1-1/3 cups
1 lb. pecans, chopped yields about 4 cups
1 lb. black walnuts, unshelled yields about ½ cup
1 lb. almonds in shells yields about 1 cup
1 lb. almonds, sliced yields about 3¾ cups
1 lb. filberts in shells yields about 1-1/3 cups
1 lb. Brazil nuts, sliced yields about 4 cups
1 lb. hazelnuts yields about 4 cups
1 lb. whole peanuts yields about 3 cups

QUANTITY FOODS FOR SERVING 25 PERSONS

MEAT, including fish:
Wieners—6½ pounds
Hamburger—9 pounds
Ham (with bone)—14 pounds
Turkey or chicken—13 pounds
Fish, large, whole—13 pounds

SALADS, CASSEROLES, ETC

Potato Salad—4½ quarts
Jello Salad—3 quarts
Scallop potatoes—4½ quarts
Baked Beans—3 quarts
Coffee—½ pound
Tea—½ pound
Bread—50 slices OR 3-1 pound loaves
Lettuce—1½ heads
Mixed Filling (i.e. meat, eggs, fish) 1½ quarts
Ice Cream—3¼ quarts
Cake—1-10x12 sheet cake OR 1½ x10" layer cake

VEGETABLES FOR 50 PERSONS

3 cans (Size No.10) OR 21 cans
@(16 ozs. ea.)
8 bags frozen vegetables (18
ozs. each)
15 pounds cabbage (for slaw,
@ 1/3 cup servings.
12 medium heads of lettuce
15 lbs. potatoes (mashed @ ½
cup servings)
2 bunches carrots, 2 bunches
celery
2 heads cauliflower, 2 large
green peppers

CHOCOLATE HELPFUL HINTS

CHOCOLATE "BLOOM" This is
where chocolate develops a
grey film on the surface and
is caused by cocoa butter
within the chocolate rising to
the surface. While this dulls the
color, it does not affect the
taste. As you melt or bake the
chocolate, its regular color will
reappear.

STORING CHOCOLATE—Keep
in a dry, cool place. Chocolate
can be refrigerated, but
wrap it tightly, so it does not
absorb other odors. Chocolate
becomes hard and very brittle
when cold, so allow it to come
to room temperate before using.

NOTE: 1 package (12 ozs.)
chocolate chips equals 1 cup
melted chocolate.

COOKING & BAKING SUBSTITUTIONS

For 1 cup wine, use 13
tablespoons water, 3
tablespoons lemon juice OR
vinegar and 1 tablespoon
granulated sugar

Replace ¼ cup rum with
1 tablespoon Durkee Rum
Flavoring and 3 tablespoons
water

1 tablespoon onion powder
replaces ¼ cup fresh chopped
onions.

Pinch of garlic powder replaces
1 garlic

½ teaspoon dried parsley
replaces 1 tablespoon fresh
parsley, chopped.

1 tablespoon dried mint
replaces ¼ cup fresh mint,
chopped.

¼ teaspoon ground ginger
replaces 1 teaspoon fresh
ginger, chopped.

1 teaspoon baking powder
can be replaced by using ¼
teaspoon baking soda and ¾
teaspoon Cream of Tartar.

2 large egg yolks, plus 1
tablespoon water replaces 1
whole egg in baking.

BEVERAGES FOR 50 PERSONS

1 pound ground coffee = 50 to
    60 cups
4 ounces instant coffee
1 pint cream for coffee
1 cup instant tea
9 cans (6 ozs. each) fruit juice
    concentrate
(½ cup each servings)
3 gallons wine (2 glasses @ 4
    ozs. each)

BREADS & DESSERTS FOR 50 PERSONS

5 loaves (20 ozs. each) bread,
    (about 100 slices)
4 to 6 dozen rolls or biscuits
2 sheets (15x10 inch) cake
4 layer cakes (9-inches each, 6
    to 8 slices)
8 pies (9-inches each, 6 to 8
    slices)
2 gallons ice cream
1 pint whipping cream, not
    whipped
13 quarts strawberries, (7½
    quarts crushed)

MEAT FOR DINNER FOR 50 PERSONS

35 pounds beef, standing ribs
25 pounds beef roast
13 large chickens (for salads,
    cooked & diced)
12 pounds ground meat (for
    meatloaf @ 3 oz. servings)
25 pounds ham with bone, (3
    oz. servings)
14 pounds ham, in cans (4 ozs.
    Servings)

8 pounds shrimp (medium in
    shell, 4 per serving)
18 pounds ground meat (for
    hamburgers)
10 pounds sliced meat for
    sandwiches
50 pounds whole turkey (4 ozs.
    per serving)
25 pounds turkey breast (4 ozs.
    per serving)
13 pounds wieners

MISCELLANEOUS

3 jars mustard (8 ozs. each)
1¼ pounds butter or margarine
    (50-1-inch pats)
2½ gallons potato salad
1½ gallons baked beans
25 pounds large whole fish
4 bottles ketchup (14 ozs. each)

DELI—PLATTER FOR 50 PERSONS

All meats are thinly sliced in this
recipe.
5 pounds turkey breast
5 pounds baked ham
6 pounds of pastrami
2 pounds of salami
6 pounds of assorted meat

BUFFET FOR 50 PERSONS

8 pounds cooked ham
14 pounds roast beef
2 pounds assorted cold cuts
¾ pound salami
3 pounds Cheddar cheese
3 pounds Swiss cheese
2 quarts olives, 2 quarts pickles

SUGAR SWEETENER PACKETS (Measurements)

1 packet = 2 teaspoons
1½ pakets = 1 tablespoon
6 packets = ¼ cup
8 packets = 1/3 cup
12 packets = ½ cup
18 packets = ¾ cup
24 packets = 1 cup

DIET BUTTER OR MARGARINE

(Use as a spread only, do not cook with it.)

½ teaspoon unflavored gelatin
1 tablespoon cold water
½ pound unsalted butter OR
    margarine, softened
1 cup cold skim milk
½ teaspoon butter flavor extract

In a small saucepan, soften gelatin in cold water. Cook over low heat until gelatin is dissolved OR (use glass measuring cup and heat in microwave; cool slightly). Place gelatin in a blender, gradually add butter or margarine. Very slowly add milk, scraping down sides frequently, about 10 to 15 minutes. Add butter extract. Store in covered container in refrigerator.

NOTE: EGG TIP—Beat 1 tablespoon of granulated sugar into 1 cup of whole eggs or egg yolks will allow eggs to freeze successfully.

TO WHIP EGGS EASIER—Add a pinch of salt.

HOW MUCH DO I NEED?
IF THE RECIPE CALLS FOR:

1 cup soft bread crumbs, start with—2 slices fresh bread.

1 cup egg whites, start with 6 to 7 large eggs.

1 cup egg yolks, start with 11 to 12 large eggs.

1 teaspoon grated lemon rind, start with 1 medium-sized lemon

2 tablespoons lemon juice, start with 1 medium-sized lemon.

4 tablespoons orange rind, start with 1 medium-sized orange.

4 cups sliced apples, start with 4 medium-sized apples

4 cups of sliced raw potatoes, start with 4 medium-sized potatoes.

4 cups shredded cabbage, start with 1 small cabbage (about 1 lb.)

2½ cups sliced carrots, start with 1 pound raw carrots

2 cups shredded cheese, start with ½ pound (8 ounces) cheese.

4 cups cooked noodles, start with 6 ounces dry noodles.

4 cups cooked rice, start with 1 cup raw rice.

1 cup chopped nuts, start with 4 ounces whole shelled nuts.

3 ounces dry mushrooms equals 1 pound fresh mushrooms.

½ pound fresh mushrooms equals 2½ cups sliced.

1 small garlic clove equals 1-1/8 teaspoons garlic powder,

4 cups sliced raw potatoes, equals 4 medium-size potatoes.

EMERGENCY SUBSTITUTES WHEN BAKING!

1 pkg. active dry yeast, use 1 cake compressed yeast.

1 cup granulated sugar, use 1 cup brown sugar, packed OR 2 cups sifted powder sugar.

1 cup honey, use 1¼ cup granulated sugar, plus one ¼ cup liquid.

1 cup corn syrup, use 1 cup granulated sugar, plus ¼ cup liquid.

1 square unsweetened chocolate, use 3 tablespoons unsweetened cocoa powder, plus 1 tablespoon butter OR margarine.

1 tablespoon cornstarch (for thickening), or use 2 tablespoons all-purpose flour.

VEGETABLE SEASONING MIX

8 tablespoons dried parsley
4 tablespoons dried chives
1 teaspoon dried sage
1 teaspoon oregano
1 teaspoon thyme
1 teaspoon basil
½ teaspoon celery seeds
1 teaspoon garlic powder

In a bowl, combine together, all ingredients; mix well. Store in an airtight container, away from heat and light. The garlic powder will sink to the bottom of container. Stir or shake before using. Sprinkle on vegetables, pasta, salads or soups, as desired.
Yield ¾ cup.

SPECIAL HELPS IN COOKING!

1. Blend together 1 cup soft butter and 1 cup flour Place mixture in an ice cube tray; chill well. Then cut into 16 cubes before storing in a plastic bag in the freezer. For instant medium thick white sauce. Drop 1 cube in a saucepan with 1 cup of milk. Place over low heat, stirring constantly, until mixture thickens.

2. For "No Weep Meringue"— use powdered sugar in place of regular granulated sugar.

3. To prevent soggy under crust of pie, brush with beaten egg white, before adding the filling.

4. Chop fresh parsley into ice cube trays; fill with water and freeze. As needed, drop cube into soup, stew, etc.

5. Freeze leftover vegetables, meat or soup in a covered container and when enough is accumulated, make another meal using the leftover food.

6. Use instant potatoes to thicken soup. Start out with ¼ cup, if desired, add more to make thickness wanted.

7. Keep powder sugar icing moist by adding a pinch of baking powder to it; it prevents hardening and cracking.

8. Out of powder sugar? Blend 1 cup granulated sugar with 1 tablespoon corn starch in food processor or blender on medium-high speed for 2 minutes

9. Add pinch of salt to very sour fruit while cooking and less sugar will be needed to sweeten the fruit

10. Making doughnuts—If you let doughnuts rest or set for 10 to 15 minutes before frying; the doughnuts will absorb less oil

11. Use leftover pancake batter for cutlets or thin batter with milk, then use as a dipping for bread when making French toast.

12. When making pancakes, for something different, slice a peeled apple into the batter and have apple pancakes.

MORE COOKING & BAKING SUBSTITUTIONS.

1 cup milk plus 1 tablespoon white vinegar or lemon juice equals 1 cup buttermilk in baking.

Replace cornstarch with 2 tablespoons flour.

For 1 cup honey, use 1¼ cups granulated sugar.

Need 1 cup molasses, then use ¾ cup sugar to replace it.

Need 1 cup sour cream, use 3 tablespoons butter, plus buttermilk OR yogurt.

To replace 1 teaspoon dry mustard, use 1 tablespoon prepared mustard.

Instead of 1 ounce square unsweetened chocolate, use 3 tablespoons unsweetened cocoa, plus 1 tablespoon butter OR margarine.

Beat 1 tablespoon of granulated sugar into 1 cup of whole eggs or egg yolks will allow you to freeze them successfully.

TYPES OF MARGARINE

STICK—Sold in quarter-pound sticks. Liquid oil or hydrogenated oil is first ingredient. Used for general purposes.

SOFT—Spreadable sticks and in tubs It is made with liquid oil or lightly hydrogenated oils. For general use, but if used for baking, for example, cookies will be soft.

WHIPPED—Whipped with air to increase volume 50%. Use as a spread, not advised to bake with.

LIQUID—Packaged in squeeze bottles. Similar to soft margarine. For general use.

SPREADS—Margarine is diluted with water. Use as a spread.

DIET—Same as spreads.

BLENDS—Mixtures of margarine & butter. Some resemble real margarine or butter; others are spreads. Read labels.

BUTTER MATH IN COOKING AND BAKING

Recipes may call for sticks, pounds or cups of butter (or margarine). Use this following chart to measure the amount you need.

4 sticks equal 1 pound or 2 cups

2 sticks equal ½ pound or 1 cup

1 stick equals ¼ pound or ½ cup

2/3 stick equals 2-2/3 ounces or 1/3 cup

½ stick equals 2 ounces or ¼ cup

¼ stick equals 1 ounce or 2 tablespoons

1 pat equals 1 teaspoon

WHAT ABOUT GROUND TURKEY?

It is a combination of dark and white meat or all dark meat of a turkey, depending how it is processed. Ground turkey is low in fat and high in protein. It cooks quickly, so you must be careful not to over cook it. It is a great diet food.

HONEY SUBSTITUTIONS FOR SUGAR

1. Replace sugar in recipe by using honey for up to ½ of the amount of sugar.

2. Reduce the amount of liquid by ¼ cup for each cup of honey.

3. When baking breads, etc. add ½ teaspoon baking soda for each cup of honey.

4. Reduce oven temperature by 25 degrees to prevent over browning.

FOOD STORAGE GUIDELINES

When buying dry or canned foods, make sure the date on the food item, has not expired. Also, do not purchase any can that is bulging or is swollen. <u>Stoe opened packages in air-tight containers.</u>

CUPBOARD STORAGE TIMES

Baking powder or soda—18 months
Bouillon Cubes or granules—1 year
Cake Mixes—1 year
Canned foods, commercial—1 year
Cereals—Check package date.
Chocolate, baking—1 year
Coconut—1 year
Coffee, fresh ground—2 to 3 weeks
Flour, all-purpose—1 year
Flour, Whole Wheat—6 months
Fruit, Dried—6 months
Gelatin—18 months
Herbs, Dried—1 year
Honey—1 year
Jams & Jellies 6 months
Macaroni & other dried pastas—1 year
Molasses—2 years
Nonfat milk powder—6 months
Olive oil—1 year
Peanut Butter—6 months
Pudding mixes—1 year
Rice, white—Indefinite

CUPBOARD STORAGE TIMES

Salad Dressings, commercial—6 months
Shortening—8 months
Sugar, brown—4 months
Sugar, Granulated—2 years
Syrups, corn, maple—1 year
Vanilla Extract—1 year
Vegetable Oil—1 year
Yeast, active or dry—Check pkg. date.

REFRIGERATOR AND FREEZER HINTS TO STORE MEAT
Fresh meat should be wrapped & stored in the coldest part of refrigerator. Remove meat from store wrapper, unless you plan to use it the day you buy it. It is better not to freeze processed meats because the salt in these meats become rancid very quick.

METHODS OF COOKING MEAT

One good basic rule to keep in mind is always cook meat at low or moderate temperature.

BRAISING—Brown meat on all sides in fat; season with salt and pepper. Add a small amount of liquid, if necessary. Cover pan tightly; cook at low temperature until tender.

BROILING—Many kinds of meat can be broiled, except pork and veal are seldom broiled. Steaks and chops should be at least 1-inch thick and a slice of ham should be at least 1/2-inch thick for broiling. Set oven for broiling; place meat 2 to 5 inches from heat. Broil until top of meat is brown; season with salt and pepper. Turn meat over; cook until tested done.

PANBROILING—Place meat in a skillet or on a griddle. Do not add fat or water; do not cover. Cook slowly, turning occasionally; pour fat off, as it accumulates. Brown meat on both sides; season and serve.

ROASTING—Any cut of meat can be roasted. Season with salt and pepper; place meat, fat-side up. Insert meat thermometer; do not add water, do not cover pan. Roast at 300 to 350 degrees, until tested done.

TO PAN FRY—Brown meat on both sides in a small amount of fat; season with salt and pepper. Do not cover meat; cook over moderate heat, until tested done; turning occasionally.

TO DEEP-FAT FRY—Use a deep-fryer or a large kettle; use enough fat to cover the meat completely. Heat the fat to temperature from 300 to 350 degrees. Brown meat until tested done; remove from fat; drain on paper towels.

HOMEMADE EGG SUBSTITUTE

4 egg whites
1 teaspoon vegetable oil
2 drops yellow food coloring

In a small mixing bowl, combine together, all ingredient; mix well. Yield ½ cup, equivalent to 2 whole eggs.

NOTE: Recipe calling for hard-cooked eggs can be duplicated using egg substitute prepared according to this recipe. Pour egg substitute into a 8-inch skillet. Cover tightly; cook over very low heat, for 10 minutes. Remove from heat; allow to stand, covered for 10 minutes.

OUTDOOR COOKING

One of the easiest ways to cook and have fun doing it is cooking outdoors on a grill. Fire on the grill takes about 30 to 35 minutes to reach a good bed of coals. It is a good idea to line your grill with heavy duty aluminum, for easier cleaning.

COOKING TIME will depend the kind of meat, the size and the shape of the cut. Cooking time for steaks, chops or patties varies from 10 to 12 minutes for each side and for hot dogs 15 to 20 minutes for each side. Cooking time for large cuts of meat may vary from 1 to 1½ hours for spareribs and 3½ to 5 hours for a large boneless rib roast.

WHAT ABOUT SPICES!

*Spices are used to season or flavor foods.

*Keep spices dry and away from heat to avoid deterioration.

*Spices that have been ground lose freshness more rapidly then powder spices.

*Whole spices, such as cloves, have a more stronger flavor than ground or powdered.

*For best flavor, grind whole spices just before using.

*To remove whole spices easily from soup or stew, place them in a cheesecloth bag.

EGG HINTS

ONE EGG has only 5 grams of total fat, with only 2 of those grams being saturated

WHEN REFRIGERATED and stored in their carton, eggs will keep at least 4 to 5 weeks.

DID YOU KNOW?
Half & Half is a mixture of milk and cream which the milk part contains 10.5 percent & the cream part contains 18 percent milk fat.

DID YOU KNOW?
That 2 cups corn syrup equals 1 cup granulated sugar, however do not use corn syrup to replace more than half the amount called for in a recipe. In baking you must be careful that for each 2 cups of sugar you replace that you reduce the liquid called for, excluding the corn syrup, to ¼ cup

TEMPERATURE & TEST FOR CANDY (with Candy Thermometer)

230 to 234 degrees—Thread—Syrup dropped from spoon spins 2-inch thread.

234 to 240 degrees—Soft Ball—Syrup can be shaped into a ball, but flatten when removed from water.

244 to 248 degrees—Firm Ball—Syrup can be shaped into a firm ball which does not flatten when removed from water.

250 to 266 degrees—Hard Ball—Syrup forms hard ball, but still is pliable.

270 to 290 degrees—Soft Crack—Syrup separates into threads that are not brittle.

300 to 310 degrees—Hard Crack—Syrup separates into hard brittle threads.

CARE OF CHEESE

The proper care of cheese is important because loss of natural moisture can harm the flavor. To prevent loss of moisture, stoe cheese, in the refrigerator, in a tightly covered container.

Certain type of cheese freeze very well, without damage to the flavor or texture. These are the hard and semi-hard cheeses, such American, Cheddar, Swiss, Edam, Gouda and Brick. The soft cheeses do not freeze well, because of the texture changes which can affect its use. The soft cheese include Cream, Liederkranz, Limburger and Blue cheese or Roquefort tend to become crumbly after freezing. therefore it is not recommended to freeze.

High heat tends to toughen cheese, so it is recommended to cook cheese dishes at low temperatures. Over cooking also toughens cheese.

A ½ pound of bulk cheese makes about 2 cups shredded cheese. Swiss and Cheddar that have become too dry for eating can be grated and used in cooking. Italian cheeses like Parmesan and Romana are actually made for grating.

WHAT ABOUT GARLIC!

*Garlic is used all over the world and is well-known for its pungent taste. It is suggested to buy garlic in small quantities. One bulb contains many cloves and will last quite a while. Do not store garlic in airtight container, because garlic needs air to circulate around it. It is best not to refrigerate, because garlic's odor will infiltrate the area.

*When cooking with a whole clove, stick a toothpick in the clove so that you can remove it easily, from soups or stews.

*Add a clove of garlic to a bottle of vinegar to improve the flavor.

*Add a garlic clove, minced to meat patties and meatloaf.

*Although fresh garlic is best, garlic powder, dried minced garlic or garlic salt can be substituted for the fresh.

REFRIGERATOR STORAGE TIMES

FRESH MEAT
Chops, lamb OR pork chops—3 to 5 days
Ground meats—1 to 2 days
Roasts (beef, veal)—3 to 5 days
Roasts (lamb)—3 to 5 days
Roasts (pork)—3 to 5 days

Sausage, fresh—1 to 2 days
Steaks—3 to 5 days

COOKED MEATS
Meat Dishes 3 to 4 days

PROCESSED MEATS
Bacon—1 week for opened packages
2 weeks for unopened packages
Hot dogs—Same as bacon
Ham (fully cooked) 3 to 5 days
Lunch meats—Same as bacon
Sausage, smoked—1 week

FRESH POULTRY
Whole chicken, turkey, duck OR goose 1 to 2 days
Chicken, turkey, duck OR goose pieces 1 to 2 days
Cooked casseroles—3 to 4 days

FISH—1 to 2 days

EGGS (whole)—3 weeks
Hard cheese—3 to 4 months

CHEESE
Cottage—5 days
Hard—3 to 4 months
Soft—2 weeks

BUTTER OR MARGARINE
1 month

FREEZER STORAGE TIMES

FRESH MEAT
Chops, lamb OR pork chops—4 to 6 months
Ground meats—3 to 4 months
Roasts (beef)—6 to 12 months
Roasts (lamb)—4 to 6 months
Roasts (pork, veal)—4 to 6 months
Sausage, fresh—1 to 2 months
Steaks—6 to 12 months

COOKED MEATS
Meat Dishes—2 to 3 months

PROCESSED MEATS
Bacon—1 to 2 months
Hot dogs—1 to 2 months
Ham (fully cooked)—1 to 2 months
Lunch meats—1 to 2 months
Sausage, smoked—1 to 2 months

SUNCHOKES, also known as Jerusalem Artichokes are one of the oldest vegetables. They provide a cheaper alternative to potatoes, because they can be eaten raw, baked, fried, boiled, steamed or microwaved. Sunchokes store well up to 3 weeks, loosely wrapped in the refrigerator.

USE IN SALADS—Peel and slice the raw tubers into a salad. You can combine with water cress and thinly sliced leeks. Serve with French Salad Dressing.

Jerusalem Artichokes are crisp with a nutty flavor. You can also place peeled and sliced tubers around roast beef. Let them cook in the gravy OR as a side dish, peeled and sliced, with a little oil, then roast in an oven, at 350 degrees, until tender, about 30 minutes.

PUMPKIN COOKIES (diabetic)

½ cup shortening
3 tablespoons sweetener
1 cup pumpkin, cooked
1 large egg
1 cup raisins
2 cups all-purpose flour
1 cup nuts, chopped
½ teaspoon baking powder
½ TEASPOON EACH, baking soda, salt, cinnamon, cloves, ginger and nutmeg

In a mixing bowl, cream together, shortening and sweetener; set aside. In another bowl combine together all dry ingredients; mix well. Add egg and pumpkin alternately with dry ingredients to shortening mixture. Bake at 400 degrees, for 15 minutes.

MORE SPECIAL HELPS

*When baking, 2 egg yolks, plus 1 tablespoon water replaces 1 large whole egg.

*When a recipe calls for rum, substitute 1 tablespoon rum extract, plus 3 tablespoons water, replaces ¼ cup rum.

*Chop fresh parsley; put in an ice cube tray, then fill with water and freeze. As needed, drop ice cube into boiling stew, etc.

*1 tablespoon onion powder replaces ¼ cup fresh onions, chopped OR 1 medium fresh onion.

TO CURE *HAM

1 gallon water
8 pounds salt
1 ounce saltpeter
1 ounce baking soda
2½ pounds granulated sugar
1 fresh ham, (10 to 12 pounds)

In a large saucepan, combine together, all ingredients, EXCEPT ham. Bring to a boil, skim foam from top, then cool. Place ham in a container large enough, to cover ham with cooled liquid. Allow to stand for 5 weeks, turning ham from time to time. Replace any evaporated water. Refrigerate ham in warm weather or cure hams only when the weather is cold below 40 degrees. Remove ham and hang to dry for 24 hours, by a cord.

HOMEMADE SOAP

BEFORE YOU START—A word of caution, LYE is harmful or fatal if swallowed, also causes severe burns. Keep away from your eyes and **especially keep out reach of children.**

RECIPE

1 can (12 ozs.) of lye (or 1½ cups)
5 cups <u>cold</u> water
6 pounds of clean lard

Slowly pour lye in cold water. Never use aluminum utensils to mix lye. Use enamel or iron vessel only. Mix with a wooden spoon. The chemical reaction will produce great heat, which may shatter glass, stoneware or ceramic. It will, also, melt plastic or damage aluminum. Stir lye until dissolved, then cool down portions. Melt fat until clear liquid; let cool. Grease molds with petroleum jelly or vegetable oil; set aside. Stir as you pour lye mixture into fat, about 15 to 20 minutes

SOME FREEZER TIPS

*Frozen foods lose moisture, if not adequately protected. The packaging material should be airtight, non-porous and moisture proof. Aluminum foil or freezer-safe plastic wrap are good choices to use for poultry and other unevenly shaped foods, as they mold easily to the food. Be sure to help seal the ends of plastic wrap packages with freezer tape, because the plastic wrap may not cling closed, at freezer temperatures

*Label and date all packages.

*It is important to organize freezer space into sections, for example, for meats, vegetables or desserts, etc. This will save time spent trying to locate certain items and will lower operating costs.

*When preparing meals, make double portions. With this extra portion, you can have a meal on hand, when you are rushed for time or when unexpected company appears.

*It is better to shorten cooking time by 10 to 15 minutes when you plan to freeze a meal. When you reheat a frozen meal, this will avoid overcooking the meal.

*Freezing foods causes some seasonings to lose or intensify flavor, so you may want to under-season food and when reheating, then add seasoning to taste.

*Cool hot foods to room temperature, about 30 minutes, then package, label and date, then freeze.

*Make an inventory of foods stored in freezer; keep list right in the freezer.

*It is better not to freeze too many foods at one time. Overloading causes slow freezing and result in poor food quality.

*After defrosting, it is suggested, to clean the inside of the freezer with a solution of 4 tablespoons of baking soda to 1 quart of warm water

SUGAR-FREE FUDGE

2 packages (8 ozs. each)
   cream cheese
2 squares (1 oz. each)
   unsweetened chocolate,
   melted & cooled
24 packets aspartame
   sweetener, (equivalent to ½
   cup granulated sugar
1 teaspoon vanilla extract
½ cup pecans, chopped
   (optional)

In a small mixing bowl, beat
together, cream cheese,
chocolate, sweetener and
vanilla until smooth. Fold in
pecans. Put into an 8-inch
square baking pan, lined
with foil. Cover; refrigerate
overnight. Cut into 16 squares.

WEIGHTS, MEASURES
AND EQUIVALENTS

16 ounces = 1 pound
3 teaspoons = 1 tablespoon
16 tablespoons = 1 cup
2 cups = 1 pint
4 cups = 1 quart
4 quarts = 1 gallon
8 quarts = 1 peck
A dash or a pinch = 1/8 teaspoon

SUGAR

Brown—1 pound = 3 to 2¼
   cups, firmly packed
Powder—1 pound = 3½ cups
Granulated—1 pound = 2¼ cups

CRACKERS

18 small soda, coarsely
   crumbled = 1 cup
9 graham, coarsely
   crumbled = 1 cup
About 30 vanilla wafers = 1 cup
9 slices of zwieback, finely
   chopped = 1 cup

BUTTER

1 pound = 2 cups
1 ounce = 2 tablespoons

FRUIT (Fresh)

3 medium apples, unpared = 3
   cups, pared and diced
1 quart red cherries = 2 cups,
   pitted
1 medium lemon = 3
   tablespoon juice
1 medium lemon, rind,
   grated = 1½ tablespoons
1 medium orange = ½ cup juice
1 medium orange, rind,
   grated = 2 tablespoons

FRUITS (Dried)

1 pound apricots = 4½ cups,
cooked
1 pound dates = 1¾ cups,
pitted & cooked
1 pound figs = 4½ cups cooked
1 pound prunes = 4 cups,
cooked
1 pound raisins = 4 cups,
cooked

SUGAR-FREE RECIPES FOR THE DIABETIC!

At one time, diabetics did not have very many sweet desserts they could enjoy without it becoming a health problem. Nutritionists have discovered new ways to sweeten desserts without using sugar. One way is you can substitute fruit, with its natural sugars, for regular sugar.

There are artificial sweeteners that are available. But using fruit as a sweetener is much better. Applesauce is one means to replace granulated sugar, then there are prunes, cooked and pureed. Prunes more then applesauce add a different taste. Besides applesauce and cooked prunes there are frozen, unsweetened fruit juice concentrates you can use.

PECAN QUICK BREAD (for diabetics)

2 cups all-purpose flour
4 teaspoons baking powder
1 teaspoon salt
3 tablespoons butter OR margarine
2 tablespoons vegetable oil
2 large eggs
1 cup skim milk
½ cup pecans, chopped
3 tablespoons Nutra Sweet sweetener

In a medium mixing bowl, sift together, dry ingredients. Add remaining ingredients.; mix thoroughly. Pour batter into greased loaf pan; let stand 20 minutes before baking at 350 degrees, for about 50 minutes or until tested done. Yield 1 loaf or 8 to 10 slices.

PINEAPPLE MUFFINS (sugar-free)

½ cup butter OR margarine
3 large eggs
1 cup pineapple juice
1 teaspoon lemon juice
2½ cups all-purpose flour
1 teaspoon baking soda
2 teaspoons baking powder
1 cup crushed pineapple, well drained
½ cup flaked coconut

In a large mixing bowl, combine together, butter, eggs, pineapple and lemon juice. Add dry ingredients; blend well. Fold in crushed pineapple. Spoon batter into a greased muffin tin. Bake at 350 degrees, for about 20 minutes, or until tested done. When cool you may frost muffins, if desired. Yield about 15 muffins.

APPLESAUCE COOKIES (sugar-free)

½ cup dates, diced
½ cup water
1 cup unsweetened
  applesauce
2 large eggs
3 packages sugar substitute
½ cup vegetable oil
2 cups all-purpose flour
1 teaspoon baking soda
1½ teaspoon cinnamon
½ teaspoon nutmeg
1 teaspoon vanilla extract
½ cup nuts, chopped (optional)

In a small saucepan, cook dates in water; simmer until all water is absorbed. In a medium mixing bowl, beat eggs well; add sugar substitute and oil; blend well. Add remaining ingredients; mix thoroughly Drop by teaspoon on lightly greased cookie sheet; bake at 375 degrees, for about 10 minutes or until set.

IMPOSSIBLE PUMPKIN PIE

½ cup sugar substitute
½ cup Bisquick Baking Mix
2 tablespoons butter OR
  margarine
1 can evaporated skim milk
2 large eggs
2½ teaspoons pumpkin pie
  spice
1 can (16 ozs.) pumpkin
2 teaspoons vanilla extract

In a medium mixing bowl, beat all the above ingredients until smooth. Pour into a greased 9-inch pie pan. Bake at 350 degrees, for about 50 minutes, or until set.

SUGARFREE RELISH

2 cups tomatoes, chopped
1 cup onions, diced
1 cup mixed red & green
  peppers, finely chopped
1 tablespoon white vinegar
¼ teaspoon garlic powder
2 teaspoons lemon juice

In a medium mixing bowl, combine together all above ingredients; blend well. Cover and refrigerate for 8 hours, to blend flavors. Yield 4 cups.

DIETER"S CORNBREAD

1½ cups yellow cornmeal
½ cup all-purpose flour
1 teaspoon baking powder
1 teaspoon baking soda
1 large egg, beaten
2 cups nonfat buttermilk
Vegetable cooking spray

In a medium mixing bowl, sift together, cornmeal, flour, baking powder and soda. Add beaten egg and buttermilk; mix until smooth. Pour batter into a 9-inch square baking pan, coated with vegetable spray. Bake at 400 degrees, for 35 minutes or until golden. Yield 9 servings.

SUGARLESS PINEAPPLE SLUSH

2 cans (6 ozs. ea.) orange juice
3 cans water
2 tablespoons lemon juice
6 ripe bananas, diced
1 can (20 ozs.) sugarless
   crushed pineapple,
   undrained

Combine orange juice, water
and lemon juice; set aside.
In the meantime, place
pineapple with juice into a 9x13
inch cake pan. Pour orange
juice mixture over pineapple;
add bananas; mix well. Place
covered in freezer. Remove
from freezer 1 hour before
serving. Serve slush in sherbet
dishes, if desired.

DIABETIC MACAROONS

2 cups coconut, shredded
2 tablespoons all-purpose flour
¼ teaspoon baking powder
2 large egg whites
¼ teaspoon Cream of Tartar
4 teaspoons liquid sweetener

In a medium mixing bowl,
combine together, coconut,
flour and baking powder;
set aside. In another bowl,
beat egg whites until light;
add Cream of Tartar and
sweetening. Continue beating
until peaks form. Fold egg white
mixture into coconut mixture.

Drop by rounded teaspoon
onto greased cookie sheet.
Bake at 350 degrees, for 12 to
13 minutes or until lightly brown.
Yield 2 dozen macaroons.

SUGAR-FREE PINEAPPLE MUFFINS

½ cup butter OR margarine
3 large eggs
1 cup pineapple juice
1 teaspoon lemon juice
2½ cups all-purpose flour
1 teaspoon baking soda
2 teaspoons baking powder
1 cup crushed pineapple,
   well-drained
½ cup coconut

In a large mixing bowl,
combine together, butter, eggs,
pineapple juice and lemon
juice. Add dry ingredients; mix
well. Stir in pineapple; mix well.
Spoon batter into a greased
and floured muffin tin. Bake
at 350 degrees, for about 20
minutes, or until tested done.
Yield about 15 muffins.

DIABETIC APPLESAUCE COOKIES

½ cup dates, diced
½ cup water
1 cup unsweetened
   applesauce
2 large eggs, beaten
3 pkgs. sugar substitute
½ cup vegetable oil
2 cups all-purpose flour
1 teaspoon baking soda
1½ teaspoons cinnamon
½ cup nuts, chopped
½ teaspoon nutmeg
1 teaspoon vanilla extract

In a small saucepan, cook dates in water; simmer until all water is absorbed. In a medium mixing bowl, beat eggs well, then add applesauce, sugar substitute, and oil; blend well. Add remaining ingredients; mix thoroughly. Drop by spoonfuls on greased cookie sheet. Bake at 375 degrees, for about 10 minutes, or until tested done.

IMPOSSIBLE PUMPKIN PIE FOR DIABETICS

½ cup sugar substitute
½ cup baking mix, (i.e. Bisquick)
2 tablespoons butter OR
   margarine
1 can (13 ozs.) evaporated milk
2 large eggs
2½ teaspoons pumpkin pie spice
1 can (16 ozs.) pumpkin
2 teaspoons vanilla extract

In a medium mixing bowl, combine together, all the above ingredients, beat by hand or with electric mixer, on medium speed, until smooth. Pour batter into a greased 9 or 10-inch pie pan. Bake at 350 degrees, for 55 to 60 minutes, or until tested done. Yield about 8 servings.

SUGAR-FREE BANANA QUICK BREAD

2 cups all-purpose flour
½ teaspoon baking soda
½ teaspoon salt
1 cup Splenda
¼ cup margarine, softened
2 large eggs
3 ripe bananas, mashed
1/3 cup plain yogurt
1 teaspoon vanilla extract

Preheat oven to 350 degrees. Spray loaf pan with cooking spray. In a medium mixing bowl, combine together, flour, baking soda and salt; set aside. Meanwhile, combine together, Splenda, margarine, eggs, mashed bananas, yogurt and vanilla; mix well. Add flour mixture to Splenda mixture; mix thoroughly. Put batter in lightly greased loaf pan; bake at 350 degrees, for 50 minutes or until tested done, Yield 8 to 10 slices.

SUGAR-FREE BANANA QUICK BREAD

2 cups all-purpose flour
½ teaspoon baking soda
½ teaspoon salt
1 cup Splenda
¼ cup margarine, softened
2 large eggs
3 ripe bananas, mashed
1/3 cup plain yogurt
1 teaspoon vanilla extract

Preheat oven to 350 degrees. Spray loaf pan with cooking spray. In a medium mixing bowl, combine together, flour, baking soda and salt; set aside. Meanwhile, combine together, Splenda, margarine, eggs, mashed bananas, yogurt and vanilla; mix well. Add flour mixture to Splenda mixture; mix thoroughly. Put batter in lightly greased loaf pan; bake at 350 degrees, for 50 minutes or until tested done, Yield 8 to 10 slices.

SUGAR-FREE GRAPE JELLY

4 teaspoons unflavored gelatin
½ cup water
1½ unsweetened grape juice
1 tablespoon liquid Sucaryl

Soften gelatin in water; set aside. Meanwhile, in a small saucepan, bring grape juice to a boil. Remove from heat; add softened gelatin, stirring to dissolve. Add Sucaryl and again bring to a rolling boil. Remove from heat; ladle into clean half pint jars; seal and refrigerate. Yield 2 half pint jars.

NOTE: In the directions, you will often see the amount of baking time, OR UNTIL TESTED DONE. This means, take a tooth pick and insert it in the center of the batter. If the toothpick comes out clean, then the batter is done. But, if there is still batter clinging to the toothpick, then it is not done. Check again in about 10 minutes

SUGARLESS PUMPKIN PIE

1½ cups pumpkin, cooked
2 tablespoons sugar substitute
1 teaspoon ginger
1 teaspoon cinnamon
½ teaspoon nutmeg
½ teaspoon salt
2 large egg whites, beaten to froth
1 cup sweetened condensed milk

In a mixing bowl, combine together, all ingredients (do not dilute condensed milk); mix thoroughly. Pour into a unbaked pie shell. Bake at 375 degrees, for 45 minutes, or until tested done. Yield 6 to 8 servings.

NATURAL EASTER EGG DYE

1 teaspoon white vinegar
Cold water
Eggs

In a large saucepan, place uncooked eggs in a single layer, in the bottom of pan; cover eggs with cold water; add vinegar and ingredients (below) for desired color. Bring to boiling; reduce heat to simmer; cook for 20 minutes. If a darker color is desired, then remove tops or peels from pan and let eggs stand overnight in water. Otherwise remove eggs; rinse and dry.

Red cabbage leaves = bright
    blue color.
Orange peels = light yellow
    color.
Carrot tops = yellow-green
    color.
Celery tops = light-yellow green
    color.
Red beets = red color.
Light onion skins = yellow color.
Dark onion skins = brown color.

KITCHEN SAVING TIP

IN COOKING—When meat is bland add a dash of Worcestershire Sauce, hot sauce or fried onions. When food is over salted or too spicy. for example, a soup or stew, you can add a cut raw potato, then discard potato after cooking is complete. Also, a solution is to make a second batch, omitting offensive seasoning. Combine the two batches which you can freeze half for another meal.

Chapter 12

ASSORTED VEGETABLES

WE KNOW WE ARE GROWING OLD
WHEN EVERYTHING HURTS AND
WHAT DOESN'T HURT DOESN'T WORK!

FRENCH FRIED ASPARAGUS

2 pounds fresh asparagus
1 large egg, slightly beaten
2 tablespoons water
½ cup fine bread crumbs
½ teaspoon salt
¼ teaspoon pepper
½ teaspoon paprika
½ cup Parmesan Cheese

Drain water from cooked asparagus; set aside. Combine egg and water; set aside. In a mixing bowl, combine together, bread crumbs, salt, pepper, paprika and Parmesan Cheese. Dip asparagus into bread crumb mixture, then in egg and again, dip into bread crumb mixture. Chill in refrigerator, for 1 hour, so crumbs will cling to asparagus while frying. Fry in deep-fat heated to 375 degrees, for 4 to 5 minutes. Drain on paper towels; serve hot. Yield about 6 servings.

ASPARAGUS CASSEROLE

1 can (10½ ozs.) Cream of
   Mushroom Soup
¼ cup milk
¼ cup pimento, chopped
¼ cup almonds, chopped
2 cans (16 ozs. EA.) *asparagus,
   drained
3 large eggs, hard-boiled &
   sliced
1 cup potato chips, crushed

Preheat oven to 350 degrees. Lightly grease a 6x10 inch casserole; set aside. In a saucepan, blend together, soup and milk. Add pimento and almonds; bring to a boil over medium heat. Meanwhile, arrange asparagus in the casserole; cover with hard-cooked eggs. Pour soup mixture over eggs, then top with crushed potato chips. Bake for 30 minutes. Yield 6 to 8 servings.

*NOTE:—2 cups fresh asparagus equals one pound.

EASY BAKED YAM (Oven Method)

Wash and dry medium-sized yams. Prick yams with a fork; pace in baking pan. Bake at 400 degrees, for 45 to 50 minutes, or until tender. If desired, serve yams with favorite sauce or butter, salt and pepper to taste.

YAMS (Microwave Method)

Wash and dry medium-size yams. Prick yams with a fork. Arrange yams on paper towels. in the corners of the microwave oven. (Yams placed in the center of the oven will not cook as rapidly.) Bake for 5 minutes for 1 yam, 10 minutes for 2 and 20 minutes for 4 yams or cook until tender, when pricked with a fork. Cooking time varies with the size of yam. Halfway through cooking time, turn yams over. Let stand 5 minutes before serving.

CANDIED SWEET POTATOES

4 pounds sweet potatoes,
    peeled & sliced
½ cup brown sugar, packed
4 tablespoons butter OR
    margarine
Pinch of nutmeg (optional)
1 cup marshmallows (optional)

In a large saucepan, place potatoes with water to cover; cook on medium heat until tender. Remove from heat; drain potatoes. Place potatoes in a shallow 2-quart casserole; set aside. In a skillet, combine together, sugar, butter and nutmeg. Over low heat, cook until butter has melted and sugar has dissolved, for about 3 minutes. Pour mixture over sweet potatoes; bake uncovered, 400 degrees, for about 30 minutes. Stir to turn potatoes occasionally. If desired, add marshmallows, evenly on top of sweet potatoes, during the last 10 minutes of baking time.

BOSTON BAKED BEANS

1 pound dry Navy Beans
2 quarts water
1 medium onion, chopped
¼ pound salt pork
¾ cup molasses
½ teaspoon salt
1 teaspoon dry mustard

Rinse beans in cold water; drain. Put beans in a large saucepan; add water; bring to a boil, cook for 3 minutes. Remove from heat; cover loosely; let stand for 1 hour. Return to heat; bring to a boil, then reduce heat to simmer; cover pan; cook for 1 hour or until beans are tender. Remove from heat; drain, reserving liquid. Place beans in a 2-quart casserole; add onions; mix lightly. Cut slits in pork, 1-inch deep; bury pork in beans. Combine 2 cups of reserved liquid with remaining ingredients; pour over beans; cover. Bake at 300 degrees, for 5 to 6 hours. Check casserole every hour, add more reserved liquid, if necessary. Yield about 8 servings.

RANCHER'S ZUCCHINI CASSEROLE

4 tablespoons butter OR
  margarine
6 cups zucchini, peeled &
  cubed
1/3 cup onions, chopped
1 cup carrots, shredded
1 can *Cream of Chicken Soup,
  undiluted
1 cup sour cream
1 pkg. (8 ozs.) Stuffing Mix (i.e.
  Stovetop)
1 stick butter OR margarine

In a large skillet, melt 4
tablespoons butter, over
medium heat; sauté zucchini,
onions and carrots, for about
5 minutes; set aside. In a small
bowl, combine soup and sour
cream; mix well, then fold into
vegetables. Melt 1 stick butter
in a large saucepan; add
bread crumbs with seasoned
packet; mix well. In a large
baking dish or casserole; spoon
in one-half the vegetable
mixture; then spoon in one-
half the stuffing mixture;
repeat. Bake uncovered, st
350 degrees, for about 35 to
45 minutes. Yield 4 servings.
*If desired, you can substitute
a can of Cream of Mushroom
Soup, undiluted, for the
Chicken Soup.

FRIED LETTUCE

6 to 8 lettuce leafs, (use outer
  leaves & cut into bite-size
  pieces)
1 clove garlic, minced
Salt to taste
2 slices of bacon

Prepare bacon by cutting into
small pieces, brown well in a
skillet, over medium heat; set
bacon aside. Meanwhile, chop
leftover vegetables; place
into skillet, along with minced
garlic; brown in oil. Add the
lettuce leaves; cook quickly,
stirring constantly. The lettuce is
done when transparent; season
with salt. Yield about 4 servings.

BREADED ZUCCHINI

4 to 5 medium-size zucchini
2 large eggs, beaten
1 cup bead crumbs
Salt and pepper to taste
Vegetable oil for frying
Ranch Salad Dressing (optional)

Wash; slice zucchini into ¼
inch thick slices. Pour about
¼ inch oil into a large skillet.
Place skillet over medium-high
heat. Mean while, dip zucchini
slices into beaten eggs, then
into bread crumbs. Fry on
both sides until golden brown.
Remove zucchini with a slotted
spoon; drain on paper towels.
If desired, serve with Ranch
Dressing. Yield 4 to 6 servings.

HOW TO COOK PARSNIPS?

Wash and pare parsnips, then cut into long strips. Put in a saucepan with water; bring to a boil; cook for about 20 minutes. Remove from heat; drain, add butter or margarine to taste. Can be served as a side dish.

HOW TO COOK SPAGHETTI SQUASH?

Wash and place in large saucepan; cover with water. Over medium heat, bring to a boil: cook for 30 to 40 minutes. Remove from water; cut in half length-wise; allow to cool. Remove seeds carefully; pull fibrous strands away from skin. Place on baking pan; season with butter, garlic powder and Parmesan Cheese to taste.

NOTE:—You can also, serve spaghetti squash with spaghetti sauce, as a low calorie pasta substitute.

SOYBURGERS (Meat Substitute)

2 cups soybeans, cooked
1 medium onion
1 large carrot
1 celery stalk
½ teaspoon soy sauce

Puree' cooked soybeans in blender or mash with a potato masher. Grind onion, carrot

and celery. In a medium-size bowl, combine together all ingredients; mix well. Form into patties; place on a greased baking pan. Bake at 350 degrees, for 6 to 8 minutes or until browned. Serve on a bun with cheese or as desired.

FRENCH FRIED PEPPER RINGS

Wash 3 or 4 green peppers, cut a slice at both ends; remove seeds and white membrane. Cut into thin slices; roll in flour, then dip into milk, and again in flour. Fry in hot oil, about 2 inches deep, until golden brown on both sides. Drain on paper towels and serve.

FRENCH FRIED ONION RINGS

4 large Bermuda onions, sliced
All-purpose flour
4 large eggs
2 cups milk
Cracker meal
Oil for deep frying

Peel onions, slice into ¼ inch slices separate into rings; set aside. In a small mixing bowl, beat eggs with milk. Dip onion rings in flour, then in egg mixture. Next, dip onion rings into cracker meal. Fry onion rings in deep fryer (at 360 degrees) for 2 to 3 minutes or until golden brown; drain on paper towels. Yield 4 servings.

HOW TO COOK SOYBEANS?

4 cups water
½ cup meat stock

Soak beans overnight in water, next day drain beans. In a medium saucepan, add meat stock; cover; cook over medium heat. Bring to a boil, then reduce heat to simmer; cool for 3 to 5 hours; add more liquid, if necessary. Use in recipes as desired.

LIMA BEAN CASSEROLE

1 pound large lima beans
Water
1 teaspoon salt
½ teaspoon pepper
¼ teaspoon dry mustard
½ cup vegetable oil
1 large can stewed tomatoes
    (about 3½ cups)
1 green pepper, chopped

Soak lima beans overnight in water. Next day, drain lima beans; discard water. In a large saucepan, with fresh water, bring beans to a boil over medium heat. Cook until beans are tender; drain, then add remaining ingredients; mix well. Place mixture in a covered casserole; bake at 350 degrees, for 2 hours. Yield 8 servings.

ZUCCHINI FRITTERS

2 medium zucchini, grated
1 medium carrot, grated
2 tablespoons parsley, minced
½ cup all-purpose flour
½ teaspoon salt
2 tablespoons onions, minced
1 large egg, beaten
Pinch of pepper
Vegetable oil for frying

In a bowl, mix zucchini and salt, then place in colander; let drain for 15 minutes. Squeeze out excess liquid. Combine 1 cup zucchini, carrots, onion, parsley, egg, flour and pepper; mix well. Drop by tablespoonful, in ½ inch hot oil; fry until brown on both sides; drain on paper towels. Serve hot, plain or with sauce or syrup.

A GOOD USE FOR SURPLUS ZUCCHINI

Use as a filler for hamburgers, meat loaf, soups or stuffing.

ZUCCHINI BASIC MIXTURE

1 teaspoon baking soda
1 tablespoon butter OR
  margarine
1 tablespoon vegetable oil
1 medium onion, finely chopped
1 clove garlic, minced
5 pounds zucchini, peeled &
  grated
½ teaspoon salt

In a large skillet, over medium heat, melt butter; add oil. Add onion and garlic; cook until soft. Add grated zucchini; cook for 3 to 5 minutes or until slightly tender. Season with salt, cool, then drain in colander for 5 minutes. Store in 2 or 3 cup portions, in desired containers, freeze. Mixture will last for a few days in the refrigerator and several weeks in the freezer.

NOTE: You can, also liquefy zucchini in a blender, then use 1 cup of liquefied zucchini, as a substitute, for 1 cup of milk, in baking recipes only.

SWEET POTATO FRIES

1 quart vegetable oil
4 medium sweet potatoes
Salt and pepper to taste
Ketchup (optional)

In a large saucepan. over medium-high heat, cook oil to 375 degrees, on a deep-fry thermometer. Cut potatoes length-wise, unpeeled, into 4-inch wedges; pat dry with paper towels. Carefully place half of the potatoes into hot oil. Using a slotted spoon gently stir wedges to separate; fry 4 to 5 minutes or until crisp and golden brown. Use slotted spoon to remove potatoes from oil to baking pan, lined with paper towels; keep warm in a 350 degree oven. Repeat with remaining potatoes. Season with salt and pepper; serve with ketchup, if desired. Yield 4 servings.

FRIED GREEN TOMATOES

1 medium green tomato (per
  person)
Salt and pepper to taste
White cornmeal
Bacon drippings

Slice tomatoes about ¼ inch thick, season with salt & pepper; coat with cornmeal on both sides. In a large skillet, heat enough bacon drippings to coat bottom of the pan. Fry tomatoes until lightly on both sides.

SAUERKRAUT & DUMPLINGS

6 medium potatoes
½ teaspoon salt
2 cups all-purpose flour
2 large eggs
1 can (29 ozs.) sauerkraut,
   rinsed & drained
1 onion, chopped fine
6 slices bacon, diced

Peel and grate potatoes; place in large saucepan. Add salt, flour and eggs; mix well to make a stiff dough, if needed, add more flour; set aside. Boil 6 cups water; drop dumplings by teaspoonful; cook for 10 minutes. Remove from heat; drain; set aside. Meanwhile, fry bacon and onion, cook until onion is transparent. Then add sauerkraut; mix well. Add dumplings, heat thoroughly and serve.

SAUERKRAUT HOT DOG TOPPING

1 can (15 ozs.) sauerkraut,
   rinsed & drained
¼ cup sweet pickle relish
2 tablespoons brown sugar
1 tablespoon prepared mustard
½ teaspoon caraway seeds

In a saucepan, combine together, all ingredients; cook over low heat until heated through. Serve over hot dogs. Yield 2 cups.

BROILED EGGPLANT

1 medium eggplant, (about 1
   pound)
2/3 cup Parmesan Cheese,
   grated
1/3 cup bread crumbs
1/3 cup Italian Salad Dressing

Prepare eggplant, by slicing into ¾ inch slices. Soak in cold water for 10 minutes; drain. Blot dry with paper towels. In a medium-size bowl, combine together, cheese and bread crumbs; mix well. Dip eggplant in salad dressing, then dip in crumb mixture. Coat both sides lightly. Arrange slices in a single layer in a baking pan. Broil 2 inches from heat or flame, for 7 to 10 minutes or until lightly browned. Serve immediately.

WHAT IS KOHLRABI?

Kohlrabi is a vegetable you do not see often. It resembles a potato, but actually grows above the ground. The name kohlrabi is German; kohl means cabbage and rabi means turnip. The taste is a blend of cabbage, turnip, water chestnut and artichoke.

TO PREPARE KOHLRABI—Peel outer fibrous layer; boil or steam, either whole or in halves. Boil for 15 to 20 minutes or until tender. Kohlrabi can be served uncooked. Peel; cut into sticks or slices; serve with dips or spreadable cheese.

MUSHROOM GRAVY

3 tablespoons butter OR
   margarine
1 clove garlic, minced
1 small onion, chopped
1 cup mushrooms, thinly sliced
3 tablespoons all-purpose flour
1½ cups beef stock
Pinch of nutmeg
Salt and pepper to taste

In a medium saucepan,
combine together, butter,
garlic, onions and mushrooms
Place over medium heat; sauté
until onion is tender, about 10
minutes. Gradually stir in flour,
stirring constantly, until well-
blended. Then gradually add
beef stock, stirring constantly,
until mixture has thickened,
about 5 minutes; season to
taste. Yield about 2 cups.

CRANBERRY RELISH

1 envelope unflavored gelatin
1 cup cold water
2 cups fresh OR frozen
   cranberries
1 orange, seeded & cut in
   eights
1 medium apple, peeled,
   cored & cut in eights
¾ cup granulated sugar
¼ cup walnuts, chopped

In a small saucepan, place
gelatin with water. Over low
heat, cook until gelatin is
dissolved. Place cranberries
and gelatin mixture in blender
or food processor, cover and
blend mixture until smooth.
Add orange, apple and sugar;
cover and blend until orange
peel is finely chopped. Pour
into bowl; fold in walnuts, cover
and refrigerate until well-
chilled. If desired, garnish with
orange slices. Yield about 4
servings.

TO PREPARE CORN FOR HOMINY

1 quart shelled corn
2 quarts cold water
2 tablespoons baking soda

Wash corn thoroughly; soak
overnight, combined with
baking soda. Next day, bring
to a boil, in the same water
that the corn was soaked in.
Reduce heat to simmer, 3 hours
or until the hull has loosen. If it
becomes dry during cooking
process, add more water.
Remove from heat; drain, then
wash corn in clear water, then
rub vigorously until all hulls
are removed. Bring to a boil
again, in clean water; drain.
Repeat again for a second
time, to cook until it boils, then
remove from heat; drain. Add 1
teaspoon salt for each quart of
hominy.

EASY STUFFED CABBAGE

2 pounds ground chuck
1 pkg. dry onion soup mix
1 cup rice, uncooked
2 pounds cabbage, cut up
2 cans tomato soup
2 cans water

In a large skillet, brown meat; then remove from heat; drain. Combine meat, onion soup & rice; mix well; set aside. Prepare cabbage, by cutting in pieces, then spread on the bottom of a casserole. Add meat mixture; mix thoroughly with cabbage. Mix tomato soup with water, then pour over cabbage and meat mixture. Bake at 350 degrees, for about 1½ hours, stirring occasionally. Yield 4 to 5 servings.

BROCCOLI CASSEROLE (with herb stuffing)

2 large eggs, beaten
1 medium onion, chopped
1 can (10.5 ozs.) Cream of
    Mushroom Soup
½ cup salad dressing (i.e.
    Miracle Whip)
¼ cup butter OR margarine,
    melted
2 pkgs (10 ozs. EA.) broccoli,
    cooked & drained; cut in
    pieces
1 cup Cheddar Cheese, grated
1 pkg. herb stuffing mix
    (i.e. Stovetop)

In a medium mixing bowl, combine together, eggs, onions, soup and salad dressing; mix well. Place a layer of cut broccoli, in a two-quart casserole, then a layer of cheese. Spread a layer of soup mixture evenly over the top. Repeat layers until ingredients are used up. Top with stuffing mix; sprinkle with melted butter. Bake at 350 degrees, for 30 minutes. Yield 6 to 8 servings.

MICROWAVE SPAGHETTI SQUASH

1 large spaghetti squash (about 3 lbs.)
4 strips bacon, diced
3 tablespoons butter OR margarine
1 tablespoon brown sugar
½ teaspoon salt
¼ teaspoon pepper
½ cup Swiss Cheese, shredded

Cut squash in half lengthwise; discard seeds. Place 1 squash half, cut side down, on a micro wave-safe plate. Cover; microwave on high, for 8 minutes or until easily pierced with a fork, turning once. Repeat with second squash half. When cool, scoop out squash, separating strands with a fork; set aside. In a skillet, cook bacon, over medium heat until crisp. Remove bacon from skillet to paper towels, drain, reserving bacon drippings. Add butter, brown sugar, salt and pepper to drippings. Add squash and bacon; mix well. Cook over low heat until warmed through. Remove from heat, add cheese; mix until blended. Serve immediately. Yield 4 servings.

GREEN BEAN CASSEROLE

2 pkgs, (10 ozs. EA.) of green beans
1 can (10.5 ozs.) Cream of Mushroom Soup
¼ cup almonds, slivered (optional)
2 cups dry stuffing mix
¼ cup butter OR margarine, melted

Cook green beans per package directions; drain. In a greased casserole, combine together, green beans, mushroom soup and almonds; mix well. Sprinkle stuffing mix evenly over top; spread melted butter over stuffing mix. Bake at 350 degrees, for 20 minutes. Yield 6 servings.

FRENCH FRIED OKRA

2 pounds fresh okra
2 large eggs
1 tablespoons Worcestershire Sauce
1 teaspoon garlic salt
Cornmeal

Wash and cut ends of okra; discars. Cook okra in 1-inch boiling water; cook for about 8 minutes; drain; set aside. Meanwhile, beat together, eggs, Worcestershire Sauce and garlic salt. Dip okra first into egg mixture, then dip into cornmeal to completely cover. In a deep fryer, bring about 2-inches vegetable oil to 375 degrees. Fry okra for 2 or 3 minutes or until golden. Drain on paper towels; serve immediately.

FRESH CORN PATTIES

1 cup fresh corn kernels
1 large egg, beaten
¼ cup green pepper, chopped
¼ cup al-purpose flour
Salt and pepper to taste
4 tablespoons butter OR
    margarine

In a medium mixing bowl,
combine together, corn and
beaten egg; mix well. Add
remaining ingredients EXCEPT
butter; mix thoroughly. Shape
into 3-inch patties; melt butter
in a medium-size skillet. Add
patties; fry until brown, turn
to brown the other side. Keep
warm until ready to serve. Yield
4 servings.

CREAMED PEAS

½ cup butter OR margarine,
    melted
½ cup all-purpose flour
2 cups milk
1 pound fresh peas OR 1 pkg.
    (16 ozs. frozen peas with
    pearl onions
Salt and pepper to taste

In a medium saucepan, over
medium heat, cook melted
butter and flour. Add salt and
milk, stirring constantly, until
mixture comes to a boil and
thickens. Add cooked peas to;
heat thoroughly. Yield about 4
servings.

FRENCH FRIED MUSHROOMS

½ cup all-purpose flour
¼ cup dry bread crumbs
½ teaspoon salt
¼ teaspoon pepper
¼ teaspoon thyme
¼ teaspoon rosemary
½ teaspoon oregano
1 pound fresh mushrooms
1 large egg. lightly beaten
Vegetable oil for frying

In a small mixing bowl,
combine together, flour,
bread crumbs, salt, pepper
and herbs; mix well; set aside.
Clean mushrooms, then pat dry
thoroughly, with paper towels.
Dip mushrooms in egg, then
put in flour mixture; toss to coat
well. Heat about 1-inch oil, in
medium skillet until hot. Deep-
fry mush rooms, a few at a time
until golden brown. Drain on
paper towels.

FRENCH FRIED YAMS

Wash & dry yams; peel; cut into
strips, length wise, about ½ inch
thick. In a large skillet, heat
about 1½ inches of vegetable
oil to 350 degrees. Add yams
to bottom of skillet; fry for 5
minutes or until brown & tender.
Repeat with remaining yams.
Remove from hot oil; drain on
paper towels. If desired, sprinkle
with salt. Yield 4 servings.

CORN ON THE COB

Husk corn; remove all silk. Add enough water to cover corn, then add 2 tablespoons milk & 1 tablespoon granulated sugar. Do not add salt; cover; bring to a boil. Add corn, cover; cook for 3 to 5 minutes, for young, tender corn & a little longer for older corn. Remove from heat, serve with butter.

BEER-BATTER FOR VEGETABLES

1½ cups all-purpose flour
cup *beer
½ teaspoon salt
2 tablespoons shortening
1 large egg, slightly beaten
*For accurate measure, measure beer after it becomes flat.

In a medium-size mixing bowl, combine together, flour & salt; cut in shortening until mixture resembles fine crumbs. Add egg & flat beer; beat until smooth. Use batter for assorted vegetables. Make sure vegetables are blotted dry, with paper towels or dredge in flour before dipping vegetables into prepared better. (Batter will cling better to the vegetables.) As you dip vegetables in batter, let excess drip off, then deep-fry until vegetables are golden brown.

ZUCCHINI PATTIES

4 to 5 cups zucchini, grated (5 small)
½ teaspoon salt
2 large eggs
½ cup dry breadcrumbs
½ cup fresh parsley, chopped
1 tablespoon Parmesan Cheese, grated
1 tablespoon onion, minced
Dash of pepper
Vegetable oil for frying

Prepare zucchini, by washing and trimming ends; shred zucchini with grater or food processor. Place zucchini in a sieve; sprinkle with salt; let drain for 1 hour, pressing zucchini down occasionally. In a large mixing bowl, place remaining ingredients; mix well. Fold in zucchini and refrigerate, for about 1 hour. (Mixture will thicken.) Shape into patties, using about ½ cup mixture for each patty. Place patties on wax paper until ready to fry. Sauté zucchini patties in a small amount of hot oil, on both sides until golden. Yield about 9 patties.

FRIED RADISHES

3 bunches of radishes
2 tablespoons butter OR
    margarine
1 teaspoon granulated sugar
½ teaspoon salt
Pepper to taste

Wash and slice radishes; fry in butter, for about 15 minutes or until tender, turning frequently. Season with salt and pepper. Yield 6 to 8 servings.

BRAISED FENNEL

2 pounds of fennel
½ cup butter OR margarine
1 teaspoon granulated sugar
½ teaspoon salt
Pinch of pepper
1 cup beef stock

Wash and scrape fennel; cut into 1-inch pieces. Simmer in butter until lightly browned. Add remaining ingredients, cook until tender, about 20 minutes. Yield 6 servings.

SCALLOPED POTATOES

6 medium-size potatoes
Salt and pepper to taste
2 tablespoons all-purpose flour
2 cups milk

Pare potatoes; cut into thin slices. Arrange in a layer of half of the potato slices, evenly in a greased baking dish. Sprinkle with desired amount of salt and pepper, then with 1 tablespoon of flour. Repeat with remaining ingredients, EXCEPT milk. Pour milk over the top; cover with foil; bake at 350 degrees, for 45 minutes. Remove foil; then bake for 15 minutes longer or until tested done. Yield 6 servings.

FRIED OKRA

1 pound okra
½ teaspoon salt
Pinch of pepper
1/3 cup yellow cornmeal
¼ cup bacon drippings

Wash okra; cut off ends; slice into ¼ inch rounds. In a small bowl, combine together, salt, pepper and cornmeal. Toss okra in cornmeal mixture. Heat bacon drippings in a large skillet; add okra rounds. Sauté until tender and golden.

STUFFED GREEN PEPPERS

6 green peppers
1 pound ground beef
2 stalks celery, chopped
1 medium onion, chopped
½ cup rice, uncooked
Salt and pepper to taste
Tomato sauce, spaghetti sauce
    OR tomato soup (your choice)

In a medium mixing bowl,
combine together, above
ingredients, EXCEPT green
peppers; mix well. Prepare
peppers, by removing the core
with seeds. Stuff peppers with
ground beef mixture; place in
casserole; cover with sauce or
soup diluted with a little water.
Cover casserole with foil; place
in oven, at 350 degrees, for 1
hour or until tested done.

SWEET AND SOUR CABBAGE

5 cups cabbage, shredded
1 cup water, divided
4 slices bacon, diced
2 tablespoons brown sugar
2 tablespoons all-purpose flour
1/3 cup vinegar
Salt and pepper to taste
1 small onion, sliced

In a medium-size saucepan,
cook cabbage in ½ cup
water with a pinch of salt until
tender. Remove from heat;
drain cabbage. Meanwhile,
fry diced bacon, in a small
skillet; remove all, but about 2
tablespoons of bacon grease.
Add brown sugar & flour to

skillet; stir to blend well. Add
remaining ingredients EXCEPT
cabbage and bacon; cook
until thickened, add cabbage
& bacon, heat thoroughly &
serve. Yield 4 to 6 servings.

BREADED CAULIFLOWER

1 head cauliflower (about 5
    cups) cut in florets
4 large egg yolks
1 teaspoon garlic powder
1 teaspoon onion powder
1 teaspoon fresh parsley, minced
½ teaspoon granulated sugar
½ teaspoon salt
¼ teaspoon pepper
1 cup seasoned bread crumbs
3 tablespoons Parmesan
    Cheese, grated
¼ cup butter OR margarine

In a large skillet, place
cauliflower and small amount
of water. Bring to a boil, then
reduce heat; cover; simmer
until crisp tender, about 8
minutes. Remove from heat;
drain. Place in bowl; set aside.
In a small bowl, whisk egg yolks;
add; mix well; set aside. Place
bread crumbs and Parmesan
Cheese in a large plastic bag.
Add a few cauliflower florets
at a time to egg mixture; mix
to cover with egg mixture.
Using a slotted spoon, transfer
florets to bread crumb mixture;
toss to coat. In a skillet, melt
butter over medium-high heat.
Cook cauliflower in batches,
until golden brown, about 4
minutes. Yield 4 to 6 servings.

BARBEQUE SAUERKRAUT

4 strips bacon, cooked & diced
½ onion, diced
½ cup brown sugar, packed
1 can (No. 2) tomatoes
Dash of EACH A-1 Sauce,
    Worcestershire
Sauce and Barbeque Sauce
2 cans (No.2) sauerkraut,
    chopped

Drain grease from cooked
bacon; set aside. Add onion,
brown slightly, then add brown
sugar and tomatoes; simmer
mixture for 15 minutes. Add
dashes of each sauce; mix well.
Meanwhile, drain sauerkraut,
chop, then put in a casserole;
add cooked mixture, toss lightly
to mix. Bake at 350 degrees, for
1 hour. Yield 6 servings.

Index

Zucchini (with Ginger)..........35
  "   " (with Cinnamon 35
  "   " Chocolate 51
  "   " Country 31
  "   " Pineapple...............35

BUTTERS (FLAVORED)

Blender-Made.....................477
Brandy.................................68
Butter, Drawn 502
  "   " or Margarine, Diet 512
  "   " Math 516
Cheese Roquefort...............67
Chili......................................66
Chive...................................67
Chocolate Honey.................65
Coffee..................................65
Cranberry 66
Garlic 69
Horseradish..........................67
Italian 69
Lemon..................................66
Maple..................................70
Mustard................................67
Orange 69
  "   " Honey 66
Parsley..................................67
Pecan, Honey 67
Raspberry 66
Rum 69
Tarragon 69
Steak 68

PIZZA, TACO (w/Beer Crust) ...76 & 77
PUDDING, CRACKER 150

ROLLS

Cinnamon (Made with
Cake Mix) 74
Jelly, Old Fashion...............182
No Fuss Dinner......................77
Nut (with Filling)..................173
Pecan 72
Pumpkin (w/Cream
Cheese Filling)....................235
  "   " Nut 169
Strawberry Nut 202

SHERBERT

Apple 168
Cranberry 168
Grape 166

TOAST

French...................................73
Garden 81

WAFFLES

Belgian.................................63
Pecan 83
Pumpkin................................31
Sweet Potato 46
Zucchini 83

CHAPTER 4 - NEW & OLD DESSERTS

CHAPTER 6. - MISCELLANEOUS MEATS BARBEQUE.

CHAPTER 8 - PASTA, DAIRY, CHEESE & EGG DISHES

CHAPTER 9 - NOT THE USUAL RECIPES ACORN

CHAPTER 10 - SALADS & SALAD DRESSINGS SALADS

CHAPTER 12 - ASSORTED VEGETABLES

The End